PROBABILISTIC APPROACHES TO LINGUISTIC THEORY

PROBABILISTIC APPROACHES TO LINGUISTIC THEORY

edited by

Jean-Philippe Bernardy, Rasmus Blanck, Stergios Chatzikyriakidis, Shalom Lappin, Aleksandre Maskharashvili

CSLI
PUBLICATIONS
Center for the Study of
Language and Information
Stanford, California

Center for the Study of Language and Information
Leland Stanford Junior University
Printed in the United States
26 25 24 23 22 1 2 3 4 5

Names: Bernardy, Jean-Philippe, editor. | Blanck, Rasmus, editor. | Chatzikyriakidis, Stergios, editor. | Lappin, Shalom, editor. | Maskharashvili, Aleksandre, editor.

Title: Probabilistic approaches to linguistic theory / Jean-Philippe Bernardy, Rasmus Blanck, Stergios Chatzikyriakidis, Shalom Lappin, Aleksandre Maskharashvili (eds.).

Description: Stanford : Center for the Study of Language and Information, 2022. | Includes bibliographical references. | Summary: "During the last two decades, computational linguists, in concert with other researchers in AI, have turned to machine learning and statistical techniques to capture features of natural language and aspects of the learning process that are not easily accommodated in classical algebraic frameworks. These developments are producing a revolution in linguistics in which traditional symbolic systems are giving way to probabilistic and deep learning approaches. This collection features articles that provide background to these approaches, and their application in syntax, semantics, pragmatics, morphology, psycholinguistics, neurolinguistics, and dialogue modeling. Each chapter provides a self-contained introduction to the topic that it covers, making this volume accessible to graduate students and researchers in linguistics, NLP, AI, and cognitive science"– Provided by publisher.

Identifiers: LCCN 2022033333 (print) | LCCN 2022033334 (ebook) |
ISBN 9781684000791 (trade paperback) |
ISBN 9781684000807 (ebook)

Subjects: LCSH: Computational linguistics. | Natural language processing (Computer science) | Deep learning (Machine learning)

Classification:
LCC P98 .P745 2022 (print) | LCC P98 (ebook) | DDC 410.285–dc23/eng/20220720

LC record available at https://lccn.loc.gov/2022033333
LC ebook record available at https://lccn.loc.gov/2022033334

CIP

∞ The acid-free paper used in this book meets the minimum requirements of the American National Standard for Information Sciences—Permanence of Paper for Printed Library Materials, ANSI Z39.48-1984.

CSLI Publications is located on the campus of Stanford University.

Visit our web site at
`http://cslipublications.stanford.edu/`
for comments on this and other titles, as well as for changes and corrections by the author and publisher.

Contents

Introduction

For the past sixty years symbolic algebraic methods have dominated linguistic theory. Syntax has been encoded in formal grammars, semantics in type-theoretic models, morphology and phonology in rule and constraint-based systems. During the last two decades computational linguists, in concert with other researchers in AI, have turned to machine learning and statistical techniques to capture features of natural language and aspects of the learning process that are not easily accommodated in classical algebraic frameworks. This work is producing a revolution in linguistics in which traditional symbolic systems are giving way to probabilistic and deep learning approaches.

This collection features articles that provide background to these approaches, and their application in syntax, semantics, pragmatics, morphology, psycholinguistics, neurolinguistics, and dialogue modelling.

Each chapter provides a self-contained introduction to the topic that it covers, making this volume accessible to graduate students and researchers in linguistics, NLP, AI, and cognitive science. The collection covers a broad range of methods. It features both small scale Bayesian methods with few parameters and large-scale deep neural networks with millions of parameters. Additionally, the volume provides substantial theoretical discussion of the properties of probabilistic models.

In Chapter 1 Kirov and Sproat provide an introduction to computational morphology. They describe the topic from a general perspective, and offer an overview of the typological variation exhibited across the world's languages. They then describe two kinds of system for computational morphology. First, they describe finite state methods, which have underpinned traditional models. Then they take up state-of-the-art approaches, using deep learning. They highlight the strengths and weaknesses of each approach, and they conclude with a summary of some the main open research problems in the field.

In Chapter 2, Clark discuss several strategies for probabilistic parsing with a Combinatory Categorial Grammar (CCG). He focusses on the role of a CCG supertagger, which provides the lexicalised classifications for input, that drive the parser. Clark shows that replacing the more traditional maximum entropy CCG supertagger with a BERT-based neural supertagger sharply improves the performance of the tagger on the accuracy of its structural analyses. This work illustrates a fruitful direction for future work on combining deep learning and symbolic representations in NLP.

Lexical semantics is a central area of linguistic theory. In many respects lexical content carries the bulk of semantic information. In Chapter 3 Emerson outlines the main issues in lexical semantics, focusing on a probabilistic perspective. One possibility is to represent lexical meaning as regions over an underlying space of situations, an idea adopted in Bernardy et al. in Chapter 5. Emerson proceeds to develop prior distributions over such regions: Gaussian and Bernoulli fields. He then shows how Bernoulli fields help to solve certain issues with the Rational Speech Act model for pragmatics, which is also discussed in Chapter 6.

Sutton offers, in Chapter 4, an extensive survey of probabilistic approaches to vagueness in natural language predication and classification. He explores a variety of models, indicating their strengths and weaknesses with respect to classical problems, like the sorites paradox. Sutton focuses on the connection between vagueness and semantic learning. He reports the results of several simulated learning experiments, which illuminate correlations between noise in the learning data, information theoretic pressure for a concise vocabulary (a semantic bottleneck effect), and vagueness in the acquired predicates.

In Chapter 5, Bernardy et al. develop a sentence-level semantic theory, which computes the probability conditions of sentences compositionally, through semantic functions determined by the types of their syntactic constituents. They also show how this sentence-level model expresses probabilistic inferences, with the mechanism of Bayesian updates for lexical semantics. Two alternative approaches to the priors are explored. One is based on Gaussian distributions, while other involves uniform densities in predicate spaces. Bernardy et al. evaluate their work on a custom built test suite featuring a range of syntactic and semantic constructions.

Noble et al. address pragmatics and its use in dialogue. Chapter 6 contains extensive analyses of various approaches to pragmatic reasoning, including several that rely on probabilistic accounts. While acknowledging the strengths of those approaches for a number of tasks, the authors argue that they are not meant to capture the full picture of certain kinds of dialogues which speakers regularly engage in. Instead, the authors suggest an account of pragmatic reasoning based on the notion of topoi. By combining topoi with probabilistic methods, the authors illustrate how their approach to pragmatic reasoning can explain properties of humour in dialogue.

Somashekarappa offers a wide ranging overview of recent work in neurolinguistics in Chapter 7. She examines the application of different experimental techniques to identifying the neural activity that supports cognitive functions, specifically the processing of linguistic information. An important feature of this work is that it allows us to explore the extent (if any) to which the deep neural networks current in AI and NLP actually correspond to the biological neural mechanisms of human language processing. Somashekarappa also considers the way in which human brains interpret and encode multimodal content, which combines linguistic information with input from a variety of sensory modalities. This issue is crucial to understanding the semantic grounding of natural language, and some of the core elements of human language acquisition.

In Chapter 8 Cooper et al., give a probabilistic account of first-language acquisition, focusing on the interaction between the child and the caregiver, and on modelling the communicative acts of the child. A key idea that they develop is the uncertainty involved in a child's acquisition of predicate classifiers. They argue that this uncertainty can be modelled within a probabilistic version of Type Theory with Records.

Kelleher and Dobnik, in Chapter 9, provide a summary of computational work in situated dialogue systems. This type of dialogue presents a serious challenge for distributional semantic approaches, which perform remarkably well in a variety of other NLP tasks. Kelleher and Dobnik critically discuss the problems involved in applying distributional semantics to situated dialogue. They propose a view on which both distributional and non-distributional information can be effectively combined.

In Chapter 10, Eshghi et al. address the challenges that conversational dialogue poses for both contemporary NLP and symbolic models. The latter assumes a standard separation between speaker and hearer. The authors consider a number of problems that real dialogue data pose for this view of communication. They suggest an alternative perspective according to which NL is seen as a set of skills for interaction. They describe two case studies. One is a dialogue agent learning speech acts via the use of conditional, probabilistic routines expressed in a probabilistic Dynamic Syntax-Type Theory with Records (DS-TTR) system. The second involves the acquisition of a DS-TTR grammar from child-directed utterances.

Sayeed's Chapter 11 classifies different reanalysis phenomena within a common framework. It offers a unified view in which reanalysis has three elements: a formal aspect, a probabilistic aspect, and a learning process connecting the two. Sayeed argues for the utility of this account on the basis of frequency-based and probabilistic explanations of diachronic and synchronic reanalysis from the literature. He folds these issues into a wider discussion of the relation between communicative function to a narrow faculty of language.

Taken together, these chapters provide a vivid portrait of the interaction of linguistic theory and current work in NLP. They illustrate the extent to which probabilistic methods and machine learning are transforming work in linguistics. They show that strong connections between linguistic theory and AI are now driving research in linguistic theory. This trend turns on the application of the techniques of AI to the construction of experimentally viable accounts of language acquisition and linguistic representation. This is a rich and exciting direction that will continue to shape work on natural language in the future.

1

Computational Morphology

CHRISTO KIROV AND RICHARD SPROAT

High quality morphological modeling has proven beneficial for various downstream Natural Language Processing tasks, including language modeling (Park et al., 2021), machine translation (Ataman et al., 2017), and various speech applications such as automatic speech recognition (Sak et al., 2010). This chapter presents a longitudinal review of computational approaches to morphology. We begin with a brief overview of the linguistics of morphology. We then move on to how morphological systems have traditionally been described and implemented via finite state methods[1], before moving on to a discussion of current state-of-the-art approaches to computational morphology based on deep learning.

The chapter is limited in scope primarily to systems that model *inflectional morphology in supervised settings.* The core tasks under consideration involve sequence-to-sequence mappings, and can be broadly categorized as:

- **Analysis**: Given an inflected wordform, the task is to extract its lemma, and tag it with its appropriate morphological features.
- **Generation**: The opposite of analysis. Given a lemma, and a set of morphological features, generate the wordform that corresponds to those features.

[1]There are several finite state toolkits available, e.g. (Beesley and Karttunen, 2003, Allauzen et al., 2007, Hulden, 2009, Roark et al., 2012, Beesley, 2012, Gorman and Sproat, 2021).

Probabilistic Approaches to Linguistic Theory.
Jean-Philippe Bernardy, Rasmus Blanck,
Stergios Chatzikyriakidis, Shalom Lappin,
Aleksandre Maskharashvili (eds.).

- **Regeneration**: Given an inflected form (or several inflected examples of the same or other lemmas) give the most likely form for a novel set of morphological features.

This leaves out several other tasks that naturally fall under the rubric of computational morphology. The most prominent is *segmentation*, usually defined as breaking down a word into substrings corresponding to their component morphemes. Both supervised and unsupervised approaches to segmentation have been considered, though unsupervised methods have arguably seen more research interest[2]. For a review of unsupervised methods for morphological segmentation, we refer the reader to Can and Manandhar (2014).

1.1 Introduction

Morphology deals in the problem of how a language can express in one word, what in another language must be expressed in multiple words. More specifically, it deals in how such information is encoded in pieces—conventionally called *morphemes*—that are composed into *morphologically complex* words. Consider the following examples:

(1) a. *laudabō* (= Latin 'I will praise')
   b. *gorodu* (= Russian 'to/for (the) city')
   c. *təmeyŋəlevtpəɣtərkən*
   t-ə-meyŋ-ə-levt-pəɣt-ə-rkən
   1.SG.SUBJ-great-head-hurt-PRES.1
   (= Chukchi 'I have a fierce headache.')
   d. *doghouse*
   e. *dogs*

The first example (1a) is an example of *inflectional* verbal morphology in Latin, an example wherein what English would express in three words, Latin would express in one: in addition to the stem of the verb *lauda-* 'praise', there is a component *-b* that marks the future tense in this case, and *-ō*, which marks the first person singular—as well as indicating that this is an active, as opposed to passive verb.

The second example in (b) is a case of nominal inflectional morphology: the Russian word *gorod* means 'city' and the suffix *-u* marks this as the dative case form of the word, which in English would have to be expressed as a prepositional phrase such as 'to the city'.

[2]Widely used systems include Morfessor (Virpioja et al., 2013) and Flatcat (Grönroos et al., 2014). Byte-pair-encoding (BPE) (Sennrich et al., 2016) and related methods such as Wordpiece (Schuster and Nakajima, 2012) are also used to segment data into smaller chunks for easier processing, though these aren't necessarily intended to recover morphologically meaningful segmentations.

The third example in (c) is a case of *polysynthetic* morphology in the Siberian language Chukchi. Here, several meaning-bearing units including parts meaning 'great', 'head' and 'hurt', along with various inflectional information such as that the subject is first person singular, are packed into a single morphological unit. Polysynthetic languages can convey in a single morphologically complex word, what most other languages in the world would require several words, indeed an entire sentence, to express.

Finally we turn to a couple of more prosaic examples. Example (d) is an instance of *compounding* in English. While compounding is freely available in English, in other languages the options are more restricted, and for example in Spanish the direct correspondent would be *caseta para perros* 'hut for dogs', which is a phrase rather than a single word. Finally example (e) is a case of inflectional nominal morphology in English, namely noun plural formation. One might have thought that of all of the kinds of information that a language might mark, nominal plurals are the least likely to be marked by separate words. Still, while this may be unusual, there are languages that do mark this information with a separate word. One such example is Hawaiian, as in the example *'elua a'u mau i'a* (two my PL fish) 'my two fish', where *mau* marks plurality on the following noun.[3]

A couple of questions arise at this point.

First of all, how can we say that something is a single word, as opposed to a phrase? Why is *I will go* a phrase in English, but *təmeyŋəlevtpəɣtərkən* a single word in Chukchi? This is not a completely trivial question to answer and there are a number of sometimes competing definitions of what is a word—see (Packard, 2000, chapter 2) for a comprehensive discussion of the various notions, but commonly considered criteria include:

- **Phonological criteria**: phonological rules that only apply within words can help identify when some string must be considered to be a single word. For example, in languages that have *vowel harmony* such as Hungarian (see Section 1.4.5), Finnish or Turkish, harmony only applies within words, never across words, so if one encounters a form that shows vowel harmony one can be reasonably sure that this must count as a single word.

[3]Example from https://wals.info/chapter/33.

- **Morphological criteria**: the existence of *bound* morphemes within a construction is usually an indication that one must be dealing with a single word. Thus the plural marker *-s* in English cannot stand alone and must be morphologically attached to a noun.
- **Orthographic criteria**: while not always reliable—and useless in languages where the writing system does not use spacing—spaces between words are a reflection of what the language community thinks of as a single word.

Second, the way we have posed the problem of morphology raises a couple of questions:

- Is there any kind of information that *must* be expressed morphologically—i.e. *cannot* be expressed with multiple words?
- Conversely, is there any kind of information that *cannot* be expressed morphologically—i.e. *must* be expressed with multiple words?

The answers to these questions are, as far as we know, not known.

The kind of information marked has traditionally been a taxonomic tool in morphology to distinguish in particular between *inflection* and *derivation*. Loosely put, if the kind of information being added by a morphological operation yields a different *form* of the *same* word, then the operation is inflectional. Thus, examples (a), (b), and (e) in 1 above are inflectional because, for example, *laudabō* is generally viewed as being a *form* of the Latin verb that is conventionally listed in its first person singular present indicative active form, *laudō*.

In contrast if the morphological information being marked yields a *different* word, then the operation is viewed as *derivational*, or *compounding*. There is no sense in which *doghouse* is a form of *dog* or *house*. Similarly, to take a more traditional derivational example, there is no sense in which the word *derivational* is a form of the verb *derive*. Rather it is an adjective derived from a noun derived from the verb *derive*. Evidently it would also make no sense at all to view the polysynthetic Chukchi example as being a form of any of the roots that it contains.

That said, the boundaries between inflection and derivation are not always clear and what would be considered inflectional in one language might be considered derivational in another. In Latin, verbal *aspect* is generally considered to be an inflectional property: *laudāvī* 'I have praised', the first singular active indicative *perfect* form of *laudō*, is considered to involve inflectional morphology, where the ending *-āv* marks the information that the action of the verb is completed. In contrast, in Bulgarian and many other Slavic languages, aspect is generally considered derivational: perfective *napravya'* 'to have done' is considered to be derived from (imperfective) *pravya*. In part the reason for this is that in Bulgarian, perfective verbs often carry other nuances besides just encoding perfective information. Thus imperfective *govorya* 'speak', yields a perfective form *otgovorya*, which has the meaning of 'answer'; or another perfective form of *pravya* 'do', *izpravya* has the meaning 'set upright'.

It so happens that much of the work on computational morphology and, as we shall see later on, essentially *all* of the work on machine learning of morphology has focused on inflection, and thus the problem of deriving different forms of a given word. Especially with recent neural work there has been less focus on what information is being conveyed by the morphological operation, and much more on predicting what the correct output form of a given operation is. Thus the field has been dominated by tasks of the form: "this is the dative singular form of this word, your system should tell me what the nominative plural form is."

Since this has been a major focus in the computational work on morphology, we will spend some time below reviewing some of the various ways in which languages can encode information, that is what manipulations of the base form various morphological operations may take. But one key point that is perhaps almost obvious is this: when you change a word into a different form of the same word, an *overwhelming majority of the time*, most of the word is *copied* when producing its new form. Thus *dogs* shares a substring with *dog*, and even *men* shares some material with *man*. Similarly Latin *laudabō* at least shares the root *laud* with the dictionary entry form *laudō*. Suppletive changes such as *go* ↦ *went* (or Latin examples like *ferō* 'I carry' versus *tulī* 'I have carried') are by far the exception. One would therefore expect that a major focus of neural models would be on ones where at least the copying bit comes effectively for free. But as we shall see, this is not the case, and many of the sequence-to-sequence models that people have employed for this purpose fail this basic eligibility test: without special tricks, such as prefeeding the network with many synthetic input-output pairs designed to shove into the brain of the system that it should learn to copy, many systems do rather poorly at this task.

Before turning to the discussion of neural models, however, we turn in Section 1.2 to elaborating a bit on some of the questions raised above: what kind of information does morphology encode, and how does it encode it? In Section 1.3, we give a brief discussion of *finite-state morphology*, which prior to the focus on neural machine learning, dominated the field of computational morphology.

1.2 Linguistic issues in morphology

In the introduction we loosely defined morphology as "the problem of how a language can express in one word, what in another language must be expressed in multiple words." A more formal definition would be that morphology is the analysis of the structure of words that are composed of more than one meaningful piece.

To see what is meant by this, consider the verb *mean*, which consists of exactly one meaningful piece, namely the morpheme *mean* itself: this can be broken down, of course into syllables—in this case just one, /min/; or into individual phonemes—/m/, /i/, /n/; or if one is interested in its written form into ⟨m⟩, a digraph ⟨ea⟩ and ⟨n⟩, but there is no way to break it down into other pieces that have any meaning of their own. Therefore *mean* is not, in and of itself, interesting morphologically. On the other hand, *meaningful* is interesting, because it can apparently be broken down into three pieces: *mean* followed by two *derivational* affixes, *-ing*, and *-ful*.

Broadly speaking, the field of morphology concerns itself with three basic questions:

1. What kind of information can be encoded by morphological mechanisms?
2. How is this information encoded, i.e. what *phonologically overt* mechanisms are in play in composing a complex word?
3. How do the available morphological devices interact?

In the case of *meaningful*, with respect to the first question we can say that *-ing* produces from the verb *mean* a noun *meaning*, which denotes roughly the state of what is meant by an expression, and *-ful*, which converts the noun into an adjective, meaning "having the property of meaning". With respect to the second question, these pieces of information are encoded by *suffixing* the forms *-ing* and *-ful*. Finally, by virtue of the fact that *-ing* attaches to verbs to make nouns, and *-ful* attaches to nouns to make adjectives, the components are constrained to apply in the order given, namely first attaching *-ing* to the base, followed by attaching *-ful*.

In this section we aim to give the reader a sense of the range of variation possible within each of the three topics outlined above. We state at the outset that our goal here is largely *descriptive* rather than theoretical. A great deal of the discussion of morphological theory has revolved around the question of what mechanisms should be assumed to be at play in explaining morphologically complex forms. Thus, even in a seemingly straightforward case like *meaningful*, there are disputes about whether one is combining three pieces—*mean*, *-ing*, and

-ful—more or less like "beads on a string"; or alternatively whether one starts with a piece *mean*, and then introduces the suffixes *-ing* and *-ful* by rule. So-called *Item-and-Arrangement* versus *Item-and-Process* theories—see Roark and Sproat (2007), chapter 3, for some discussion of various models of morphology with a computational interpretation—consist largely in these two respective points of view. Anticipating somewhat, most work in finite-state morphology has assumed a more or less Item-and-Arrangement view, though as we shall suggest in Section 1.3, viewed correctly as a computational problem, these theoretical distinctions largely evaporate. In any event, we will eschew these theoretical points for the time being.

1.2.1 What kind of information is encoded?

Of the three questions we just introduced, the question of what kind of information morphology encodes is in many ways the most basic. For one thing it helps to define what we mean when we talk about *words*.

English speakers would readily acquiesce to the assertion that *head* is a word, or that the morphologically complex *heads* is a word. *Headache* would also be readily considered a word, even though this consists of a *compound* of two words. Speakers may be less sure about *head scarf*, since though this seems to be a compound like *headache*, it is *written* as two words, following the normal Latin-script convention of separating words with spaces. But in general in English a word may include *inflectional* information such as number on nouns (*heads*), various kinds of *derivational* information such as deriving a stative noun from a verb or a stative adjective from a noun (*meaningful*), or one may compound two words to make a third word that somehow relates to the senses of the two base words—*headache.*

In English, a sentence like *I have a fierce headache* consists of five words given that *headache* counts as a single word, per the above discussion. But, as we have already seen above in example 1c, in Chukchi (Chukotko–Kamchatkan, Siberia), this sentence can be expressed by a single morphologically complex word (Skorik, 1961). Chukchi is a *polysynthetic* language where long words can be composed of elements that in other languages would normally be separated into separate words. Polysynthesis is common in the world's languages, and is found especially in Siberia, among a number of the Eskimo-Aleut languages of the Arctic, as well as a number of Iroquian languages of Eastern Canada and the United States.

1.2.2 How is the information encoded?

The second question introduced above is the question of how morphology encodes information, and more specifically what phonological mechanisms are used. Any speaker of English is familiar with morphological *suffixes* (such as *-ful*) and *prefixes* (such as *un-*), since these are used frequently in English to mark morphological information.

Less familiar will be *infixes*, where morphological material is added *inside* a word, though some speakers may be familiar with constructions involving so-called *expletive infixation* like *abso-bloody-lutely* (McCarthy, 1982). But infixation is common in many languages: many of the languages of the Philippines, for example, have such forms, as does the Nicaraguan language Ulwa (CODIUL, 1989, Sproat, 1992), which marks possession using infixes. Thus from *su:lu* 'dog' one can derive:[4]

su:**ki**lu	'my dog'	su:**ni**lu	'our (incl.) dog'
		su:**kina**lu	'our (excl.) dog'
su:**ma**lu	'your (sg.) dog'	su:**mana**lu	'your (pl.) dog'
su:**ka**lu	'his/her dog'	su:**kana**lu	'their dog'

Other common ways of marking morphological information include:

- Changing the vowels or consonants of a word: English exhibits a few examples of this in irregular plurals *mouse/mice* or in irregular past tense marking *sing/sang*.
- Changing the overall shape of the word: Arabic and other Semitic languages are famous for their root-and-pattern morphology whereby, for example, different derivational forms of the same verb root are produced by changing the overall shape and the vowels of the word. A root *ktb*, with the meaning 'write' shows up as *katab* in the basic verb meaning 'write', but as *kattab* in a verb meaning 'cause to write', *kātab* 'correspond', as well as in nouns derived from the same root — *kitāb* 'book', *ma-ktab* 'office', and so forth.
- Removing material — *truncation.* E.g. in Koasati (Muskogean, Louisiana) verb plurals are formed by removing material from the end of the verb root, as in ***pitáf***-*fi-n* 'slice up the middle (sg.)' versus the plural form ***pít***-*li-n*.

[4] *Inclusive* 'we' in the fourth line is the sense of 'we' that includes the listener; *exclusive* 'we' excludes the listener, and thus is logically simply the plural of 'I' (note that 'I' necessarily excludes the listener). Thus while inclusive 'we' is marked by a separate morpheme *-ni-*, exclusive 'we' is actually the plural form of 'I', using the plural infix *-na-*, which one also sees in the forms for 'your (pl.)' and 'their'.

- *Multiple exponence*, whereby an apparently single morphological function is encoded in several separate places in the word. One example is in Breton (Celtic, Brythonic, France) plurals of diminutive nouns: *bag* 'boat', *bag-où* 'boats'; but *bag-ig* 'little boat', *bagoù-igoù* 'little boats', which sports two plural suffixes *-où*.
- *Reduplication*, whereby all or part of a word is copied, possibly with changes to the copied part. *Full-word reduplication* is found in, e.g., Bahasa Indonesia/Bahasa Melayu, in noun plural formation: *orang* 'person', *orang-orang* 'people'. Partial reduplication can be prefixing, suffixing or even infixing (copying a portion of the word into an internal position in the word). Tagalog, for example, shows prefixing reduplication in future tense formation: *tulog* 'sleep', *ma**tu**tulog* 'will sleep'; *panatag* 'be at ease', *ma**pa**panatag* 'will be at ease'.

While all these devices (and others) are available to mark morphological information, they are by no means evenly distributed with regards to the *kind* of information they encode, nor are they equally common across languages. There is, for example, a *suffixing preference* across languages compared to prefixing, in that while there are many languages that have exclusively suffixing morphology, exclusively prefixing languages are rare, and more generally there is an order of magnitude more languages that are predominantly suffixing than those that are predominantly prefxing (Dryer, 2013). Processing-based explanations have been proposed for this asymmetry (Cutler et al., 1985). Grammatical case information is frequently encoded using suffixes, much less frequently using prefixes, and (as far as we know), never using infixes. The World Atlas of Language Structures (Dryer and Haspelmath, 2013), in particular Chapter 26, lists some of these morphological asymmetries in further detail.[5]

1.2.3 How do morphological devices interact?

In combining multiple morphological pieces in a word, there are usually restrictions on how these pieces must interact. In *meaningful*, as we noted above, the suffixes *-ing* and *-ful* are constrained to apply in the observed order so that, **meanfuling* is impossible as a word of English.

In this case, as also noted previously, the constraint can be understood in terms of the morphosyntactic categories that the pieces require of the base to which they attach. Again, *-ing* converts verbs like *mean* into nouns, and *-ful* converts nouns into adjectives. So this is just a case of *subcategorization*, analogous to subcategorization in

[5]https://wals.info/chapter/26

syntax. There are many cases that can be understood in terms of subcategorization. Another case in English is *derivational*, where *-ation* is a nominalizing affix that attaches to verbs (such as *derive*) and *-al* is an affix that attaches to nouns to make adjectives; this example is therefore entirely analogous to *meaningful* but involving latinate as opposed to native morphemes. Or consider *derivability*, involving the latinate affixes *-able*, which produces adjectives from verbs with the meaning of something that can undergo the process denoted by the verb; and *-ity*, which nominalizes adjectives.

But subcategorization need not involve just morphosyntactic restrictions on a base. Phonological or prosodic restrictions are also possible. Thus English comparative affixes *-er* and *-est* are famously restricted in terms of the length of the base to which they attach: *nicer*/*nicest* are fine, as are *sillier*/*silliest*, but *?compacter*/*?compactest* seem questionable and **excellenter*/**excellentest* or **humongouser*/**humongousest* are definitely impossible. Note that this is not just a matter of a closed set of adjectives allowing this formation. The novel adjective *froody* (invented by Douglas Adams in *The Hitchhiker's Guide to the Galaxy*) readily allows *froodier*/*froodiest*.

Semantic subcategorization restrictions may also obtain; on analogy with syntax, one might term these *selectional restrictions*. According to Ettinger (1974), in Italian, augmentatives ('big X') can freely attach to nouns denoting man-made objects such as *canalone* 'big canal' (from *canale*), *piazzone* 'big plaza' (from *piazza*) and *stradone* 'big street' (from *strada*). For natural objects, however there is a restriction that one cannot form augmentatives with objects that are larger than people to begin with. Thus *pietrone* 'large rock' (from *pietrà*) is fine, as are *fiorone* 'large flower' (from *fiore*) and *ciòttolone* 'large pebble' (from *ciòttolo*). However **fiumone* 'large river' (from *fiume*), **lagone* 'large lake' (from *lago*) and **pianone* 'large plain' (from *piano*) are not possible.

As one final example of restrictions on morphological combination, consider what Aronoff (1994) calls *morphomic* restrictions. One such example is the Latin *third stem* of verbs, which is the base of several participial forms, but also of a rather disparate collection of nominalizations including agentive nouns. The form of the third stem varies across verbal paradigms. In the first conjugation it is formed by adding *-āt* to the base: *laud-ō* 'I praise', third stem *laudāt-*. In the second conjugation the suffix is *-it*: *mon-eō* 'I warn', third stem *monit-*. In the third conjugation, the ending is *-t*, but with various changes to the stem, e.g. *vinc-ō* 'I defeat', third stem *vict-*. There are also various irregular and suppletive derivations such as *fer-ō* 'I bear', third stem *lāt-*.

What is regular about these is that they can all form the base of a variety of participial forms and nouns including, as noted above, agentive nouns (*victor* 'winner', *monitor* 'warner'), *-iō* nouns (*laudātiō* 'praise', *monitiō* 'warning'), the future active participle in -*ūr* (*laudātūrus* 'about to praise', *lātūrus* 'about to carry'), and several others, including some derived verb classes. As Aronoff notes (page 39), one can even find doubly-derived third stem forms as in *haesitātiō* 'indecision', which is the *-iō* noun derived from the third stem of *haesitō* 'stammer', which is itself an iterative verb derived from the third stem of *haerō* 'stick'.

What is interesting about morphomic forms is that they seem to be purely morphological in status: Aronoff notes that there is no simple phonological regularity in the derivation of the third stem across all verb classes, which on the face of it seems clear from even the small set of examples given above. More to the point, nor is there any phonological, morphosyntactic or semantic generalization that can explain the class of morphological derivations that require the third stem as the base. Rather it seems that one must assume an equivalence class whereby a set of morphological operations requires an abstract morphological category, or to put it informally: if you tell me what the third stem of this verb is, I can tell you how to form the agentive noun, the *-iō* noun, the future active participle, and so on.

In the latter characterization there is some similarity between morphomic processes and *syncretism*, whereby in morphological paradigms, two slots in a paradigm are always marked with the same form. Latin, again, offers such a case: in the nominal and adjectival paradigm, the dative plural and ablative plural forms are always identical so that no matter what the first is, the second will always have the same form. What makes this example perhaps less dramatic is that there are only two possible ways of marking the dative/ablative plural, namely *-īs* in the first two declensions and *-(i)bus* in the remaining declensions, so it is hard to know whether this syncretism is a fact that requires an explanation or is merely an accident. Assuming it is not an accident, one question is whether morphological learners can pick up on the generalization—so that to produce, say, the ablative plural form, it is sufficient to give them just the dative plural form, or vice versa. One piece of work that suggests this may be possible is (Muradoğlu et al., 2020).

1.3 Linguistics and finite-state morphology

In the previous section we gave a brief overview of morphological operations—what kind of information can be encoded, how the information is encoded, and how morphological operations interact. The main purpose of that introduction was to serve as a basis for discussion of deep learning approaches to morphology, so that one can better understand how those systems have succeeded, and failed, at covering phenomena found in the morphologies of the world's languages.

But before we turn to that topic, we would be remiss if we did not briefly discuss finite-state morphology, which has dominated computational morphology for nearly forty years. The literature on this topic has been extensive and for more details the reader is referred to previous work including (Johnson, 1972, Koskenniemi, 1983, Kay, 1987, Hankamer, 1989, Antworth, 1990, Sproat, 1992, Kaplan and Kay, 1994, Karttunen, 1995, 1996, Mohri and Sproat, 1996, Karttunen, 1998, Hetherington, 2001, Kiraz, 2001, Beesley and Karttunen, 2003, Karttunen, 2003, Yli-Jyrä and Koskenniemi, 2006, Roark and Sproat, 2007, Yli-Jyrä, 2007, Hulden, 2009, Lindén et al., 2009, Koskenniemi and Silfverberg, 2010, Beesley, 2012, Chandlee and Heinz, 2012, Drobac et al., 2012, Yli-Jyrä, 2013, Hulden, 2017, Yli-Jyrä, 2019, Beemer et al., 2020). A recent review of the area along with some practical exercises using the Pynini toolkit can be found in (Gorman and Sproat, 2021).

As we noted in Section 1.2.2, there are a number of ways in which morphological systems mark information. Classical finite-state approaches to morphology, such as Koskenniemi (1983), treated *concatenation* as the basic operation, so that a morphologically complex word was always built up by concatenating two or more pieces. Insofar as Koskenniemi's original system handled Finnish, where most morphology is indeed basically concatenative, this made sense. However it becomes difficult to treat morphological operations such as infixation, changes in the shape of the stem including Semitic root-and-pattern morphology, and truncation, where phonological material is removed as part of the operation, using concatenation.

Roark and Sproat (2007) (and Gorman and Sproat (2021)) argue that the most general operation that can capture all of these phenomena, including concatenation, is *composition*. In the most trivial case of a purely concatenative operation, say suffixation, one can treat that by composing a base $B = b_i \dots b_n$ with a suffix $s_i \dots s_m$, by representing the suffix as $S = \Sigma^* I[s_i \dots s_m]$, where Σ^* is the universal language over the alphabet from which $b_i \dots b_n$ is constructed, and $I[]$ is the insertion operation. Then one can construct the morphologically

	Incremental	Realizational
Lexical	Item-and-arrangement e.g. Lieber (1980)	"Distributed Morphology" Halle and Marantz (1993)
Inferential	"Articulated morphology" Steele (1995)	Item-and-process e.g. Matthews (1972)

TABLE 1: Four types of morphological theory, following Stump (2001), Roark and Sproat (2007).

complex form as $B \circ S$, where $\circ$ is the composition operation. A more complex 'non-concatenative' operation, such as an affix that causes a change in the form of the base, or a change in the base without an overt affix can be handled by replacing $\Sigma^* I[s_i \ldots s_m]$ with a more complex transducer that models the required changes. Thus a transducer that changes the stem vowel and introduces no other changes can be compiled (Kaplan and Kay, 1994, Mohri and Sproat, 1996) from a rewrite rule of the form $V_1 \rightarrow V_2$, where V_1 is a set of vowels in the input and V_2 are the corresponding vowels in the output. One would then apply this transducer T as before: $B \circ T$.

Viewing the basic operation in morphology as composition also allows one to cut through many of the theoretical debates that have dominated morphological discussions in theoretical linguistics. As discussed by Stump (2001), extant morphological theories can be understood as falling into one of four categories, classified along two dimensions. The first dimension relates to whether the morphological theory is *lexical* or *inferential*, i.e. whether morphemes are all listed in the lexicon and just combined, or are introduced by rule. The second dimension relates to the features themselves: on the *incremental* view, features are introduced by the morphemes when they are combined, whereas on the *realizational* view they are the triggers of morphological material being introduced. A classical *Item-and-Arrangement* view— which we alluded to previously as a "beads-on-a-string" view — is lexical and incremental; the polar opposite, namely a classical *Item-and-Process* view (Matthews, 1972) is inferential and realizational. But in fact there have been morphological theories proposed that fill all of the four logical possible slots; see Table 1.

From the point of view of computational complexity, one might initially think these different theories are also different in terms of their generative capacity. The simple concatenative operations of traditional item-and-arrangement models would seem at first blush to contrast with the apparent context-sensitive power of the rewrite rules used in item-and-process models. But this is an illusion: as C.D. Johnson showed early on (Johnson, 1972), while morphophonological rewrite rules in principle have full context-sensitive power, in their actual use in linguistics, they are much more constrained, and in fact equivalent to regular relations. Thus in a similar vein to work by Karttunen (1998, 2003) on the computational interpretation of Optimality Theory in phonology, Roark and Sproat (2007) argue that all of these theories are really equivalent when viewed computationally, and using the idea introduced above that morphological operations are in general modeled using composition; see also Gorman and Sproat (2021) for further discussion and some implemented examples. Affixation and any associated phonological implications can be modeled using composition,[6] and rewrite rules can also be modeled using composition (Johnson, 1972, Kaplan and Kay, 1994, Mohri and Sproat, 1996), so therefore the two options on the incremental-realizational dimension are equivalent. The lexical-inferential dimension concerns whether the features that are associated with morphological operations, such as the PLURAL feature associated with English nominal *-s*, are *introduced* by those operations or rather are *triggers* for those operations. But assuming that the features must be introduced somehow—the word *dog* is presumably only associated with the feature PLURAL in contexts where one wants to convey the meaning of plurality—then this difference simply comes down to whether the feature is first introduced by an operation O, and then the morphological operation M is applied; or if the two occur together as a single M'. But since regular relations are closed under composition, $M' = O \circ M$, so again there is really no difference.[7]

[6] The one problem in any finite-state model is reduplication; see (Roark and Sproat, 2007, section 2.4) for some discussion.

[7] To be sure, the equivalence just discussed refers specifically to *weak generative capacity*, the ability of two systems to generate the same output language. *Strong generative capacity*, on the other hand, is concerned whether two systems arrive at their outputs in the same way. In terms of distinguishing linguistic theories, what is frequently at issue is the structure that the different theories may assign to a given output, even if the sets of outputs of the two theories are identical. Thus, while the weak generative capacity of two systems may be equivalent, the strong generative capacity need not be so. Recent work by Dolatian et al. (2021) discusses this issue in terms of finite-state morphology. The finite-state transducers we have been assuming up until now are more formally characterized as 1-way FSTs. They are "1-way" because they are limited to reading the input in one direction only, crucially without any backtracking allowed. A more powerful mechanism is a 2-way FST, which allows for reading in two directions, controlled by a direction parameter $D = \{-1, 0, +1\}$, which allows the read head to move left, stay still, or move right relative to the input. In a conventional 1-way transducer, a move between states is defined in terms of a transition function δ that maps from input states paired with input symbols $Q \times \Sigma$ to output states paired with output symbols $Q \times \Gamma$. A

1.4 Neural approaches to morphology

As noted already, the finite-state approaches to morphology that we sketched in the previous section were the dominant approach to computational morphology for nearly forty years. One problem with these approaches, of course, is that they have traditionally required the construction of grammars by hand, which requires skill at linguistics and grammar engineering as well as knowledge of the target language. Not surprisingly, there has therefore been a lot of interest in machine learning of morphology from annotated, and in some cases unannotated, data. Early work includes (Yarowsky and Wicentowski, 2000, Schone and Jurafsky, 2001, Goldsmith, 2001). These and a few other early systems were discussed in Chapter 5 of (Roark and Sproat, 2007). There has also been work that more specifically looks at inducing morphological grammars that can be reduced to finite-state transducers. Ahlberg et al. (2014), and Durrett and DeNero (2013) propose an approach based on aligning input and output strings so as to minimize edit distance, gathering the set of edits found in the training data, and building a classifier to decide which if any edit to deploy at a given point in an input string using local phoneme context as features for the decision classification.

The above methods work well, even with limited training data, but as in much of natural language processing, neural network-based machine learning methods have become more prominent. Indeed all of the recent advances in this area have involved neural models. The core tasks in computational morphology, including inflection (lemma + features → inflected form), lemmatization (inflected form → lemma), and analysis (inflected form → morphosyntactic features) can be cast as sequence-to-sequence problems, for which modern neural network encoder/decoder architectures are particularly well suited.

These architectures typically consist of an encoder module which reads in an input string, usually in both forward and backward directions, and produces an embedded, positionwise representation of it. The decoder reads this representation using an auxiliary network called an attention mechanism, which decides what parts of the

2-way transducer augments this to map from $Q \times \Sigma$ to $Q \times \Gamma \times D$. Dolatian et al. argue that for many morphological processes, the conventional 1-way FST cannot produce a model that is *strongly* equivalent to popular linguistic theories' accounts of these phenomena, whereas a 2-way FST usually can. For example a Prosodic Readjustment theory of infixation Yu (2007), whereby an infix is really a prefix or suffix, but then gets moved into the interior of the word under certain prosodic conditions, cannot be replicated faithfully with a 1-way FST, but can be with a 2-way FST. Thus a 2-way FST is able to match this theory's strong generative capacity.

input representation are important for any given decoder decision, and produces an output sequence one symbol at a time (Bahdanau et al., 2015). This output sequence could consist either directly of output characters, or of abstract operations (e.g., edits like deletions, substitutions, and insertions) that describe a sequence of steps required to convert the input into the output (Stahlberg and Kumar, 2020, Aharoni et al., 2016). Both the encoder and decoder are typically built from either autoregressive RNN layers, such as LSTMs (Hochreiter and Schmidhuber, 1997a) or GRUs (Chung et al., 2014), or, more recently, transformer architectures which encode sequential information by attaching a position embedding to each input symbol (Vaswani et al., 2017). The attention mechanism that connects encoders and decoders can also vary. Two broad classes of attention are global, where the entire input representation is always visible to the decoder; and monotonic, where a constraint ensures the decoder only pays attention to a sliding window over the input that moves left to right (Luong et al., 2015).

While, as we will discuss below, sequence-to-sequence neural networks often achieve state-of-the-art performance in common computational morphology tasks, they also have a number of shortcomings. From a practical perspective, they tend to be useful primarily in supervised settings where ample training data is available. We will also discuss approaches to mitigate poor performance in low-resource scenarios.

More generally, neural networks have also been criticized for functioning as 'black boxes', with behavior that can be difficult to predict and interpret. Neural models, particularly recurrent networks, are very powerful—in principle capable of representing any Turning-computable function (Siegelmann and Sontag, 1995).[8] With a wide range of rules that can be learned, it is unclear if neural nets have the right inductive biases to come to the right, human-like generalizations given a finite amount of data to learn from. Through a series of case studies, we will attempt to look in the box to see whether network processing is comparable to how we believe human speakers process language. This includes their ability to pick up on linguistic cues, as well as the kinds of errors they make. This is part of a larger emerging research program, much of it in the syntax domain, that considers neural network interpretability and suitability for modeling human cognitive functions such as language (Kuncoro et al., 2017, Kim et al., 2019, Corkery et al., 2019, McCoy et al., 2020).

[8] In practice, network capacity is limited by their size, and there is no guarantee that known training methods will converge on the right function even with an unlimited amount of training data available.

orthographic			IPA			
stem	past	part.	stem	past	part.	infl. type
go	went	gone	goʊ	wɛnt	gon	suppletive
sing	sang	sung	sɪŋ	sæŋ	sʊŋ	ablaut
swim	swam	swum	swɪm	swæm	swʊm	ablaut
sack	sacked	sacked	sæk	sækt	sækt	/-t/
sag	sagged	sagged	sæg	sægd	sægd	/-d/
pat	patted	patted	pæt	pætɪd	pætɪd	/-ɪd/
pad	padded	padded	pæd	pædɪd	pædɪd	/-ɪd/

TABLE 2: Examples of inflected English verbs.

1.4.1 English past tense and the history of neural network morphology

As Pinker and Prince (1988) note, the English verb system is not notably complicated when compared to the verb systems of a great many other languages. Nonetheless, the problem of predicting the past tense of English verbs from their present tense base forms has outsized importance in the field of computational morphology due to an early neural model of the problem by Rumelhart and McClelland (1986). This work, along with its critique by Pinker and Prince (1988)—and see also (Sproat, 1992), spawned a small cottage-industry of research on learning this problem (Plunkett and Marchman, 1991, MacWhinney and Leinbach, 1991, inter alia).

For most verbs the English past test is a regular pattern, but there are islands of irregular patterns. Orthographically, the canonical regular suffix is *-ed*, which, phonologically, may be rendered as one of three phonological strings: /-ɪd/, /-d/ or /-t/. The choice is determined by the phonological properties of the previous segment. English selects /-ɪd/ where the previous phoneme is a /t/ or /d/, e.g. /pæt/↦/pætɪd/ (*pat* ↦ *patted*) and /pæd/↦/pædɪd/ (*pad* ↦ *padded*). /-d/ is used when the preceding phoneme is a voiced consonant or a vowel, maintaining voicing agreement, e.g., /sæg/↦/sægd/ (*sag* ↦ *sagged*) and /ʃoʊ/↦/ʃoʊd/ (*show* ↦ *showed*). Finally, /-t/ is used when the preceding phoneme is an unvoiced consonant, e.g., /sæk/↦/sækt/ (*sack* ↦ *sacked*). English irregular pasts are either (very rarely) suppletive, e.g., /goʊ/↦/wɛnt/ (*go* ↦ *went*), or coalesce into groups of several verbs defined by processes like ablaut (Nelson, 2010), e.g., *sing* ↦ *sang*, *ring* ↦ *rang* — see Table 2 for more examples.

The system of Rumelhart and McClelland (1986) was part of a broader research program in linguistics and cognitive science from the mid 1980's that was then referred to as *connectionism*. Their system used a fixed size perceptron network. Input words were deterministically broken down into their component phoneme trigrams, which they termed *Wickelphones*[9] after an early psycholinguistic model by Wayne Wickelgren. These structures were one-hot encoded at the input to the network. They were then passed through a single dense layer similarly connected to an array of perceptrons, activating each possible output Wickelphone. The architecture was very limited and drew harsh criticism, most notably in the work of Pinker and Prince (1988) cited above.

One key limitation was that the network, having a fixed-size feed-forward design, did not maintain any sequence information about input strings beyond what was implicitly (though ambiguously) represented by Wickelphone overlap. This was a problem both for encoding and decoding, as the output of the network was an unordered set of highly activated Wickelphones. An additional step was required to decide which actual string was being represented. Thus, several strings could be compatible with the set of activated ngrams in different arrangements: Pinker and Prince give an example from the Australian language of Oykangand which distinguishes between *algal* 'straight' and *algalgal* 'ramrod straight'; both of these strings have the identical Wickelphone set {/*#al*/, /*alg*/, /*lga*/, /*gal*/, /*al#*/}. With these caveats taken into account, the top-line accuracy of the Rumelhart-McClelland network on the English present to past mapping was only about 67%, measured on the *training* data. Furthermore, many of the network's errors were not of the sort commonly made by human English learners, such as producing *membled* for *mail*, *ated* for *eat*[10]. But many of these weaknesses were likely due not so much to Rumelhart and McClelland's design choices so much as to the limited size of the networks that one could build during the 1980's. In unpublished work by Dania Egedi and the present second author, summarized in (Sproat, 1992), a three layer feed-forward network with back propagation was trained where the inputs and outputs were not Wickelphones, but

[9] More precisely, these were further deterministically broken down into phonological feature bundles called *Wickelfeatures*. This was done to enable additional generalization below the phoneme level.

[10] Apparently, humans rarely mix regular and irregular inflections, even in error, so a child learner would be more likely to produce *eated*. Forms like *ated* do still appear in children's speech, but Pinker and Prince (1988) argue that this is a result of *ate* being misinterpreted as a present-tense stem and inflected as if it was regular.

rather standard phonemes decomposed into a flattened binary phonetic feature representation, with the inputs and outputs padded out to a fixed length. The results were quite similar to what Rumelhart and McClelland reported.

Revisiting the English past tense mapping with modern tools, Kirov and Cotterell (2018) show that nearly all of these problems evaporate when considering current sequence-to-sequence encoder/decoder architectures. They trained a network set up identically to that used in Bahdanau et al. (2015)[11], on English past tense mapping data from CELEX (Baayen et al., 1993). The raw data consisted of 4039 verb types with both present and past forms represented in IPA. Each verb was marked as regular or irregular (Albright and Hayes, 2003). The data was randomly split into 80/10/10 train/development/test portions.

The trained encoder-decoder network learned its training data with nearly 100% accuracy, including memorizing the irregular verb forms. Performance on test data was also at 100% for regular verbs. Some unseen irregulars are correctly conjugated, usually, but not exclusively, if they contain an irregular seen during training as a substring (e.g., *partake* to *partook*, where *take* was seen, but also *forsake* to *forsook*, where *sake* is, from the point of view of the model's experience, a novel bound morpheme). The *only* error the network makes in conjugating previously unseen irregular verbs is to regularize them (*throw* to *throwed*), which is what we might expect a human learner to do as well.

One place where the modern network still isn't quite human-like is in its relative judgements of nonce *wug* forms. Replicating an experiment from Albright and Hayes (2003) where humans were asked if they preferred regular or irregular exponents for novel verbs (e.g., should *rife* map to *rifed* or *rofe*), the network likelihood assigned to each of these options only correlated well with human preferences for a small percentage of random network weight initializations (Corkery et al., 2019).

1.4.2 Success on a wider range of morphological problems

Consistent with the success on the relatively simple English present to past mapping described above, neural networks have taken over the state-of-the-art across most morphological mapping tasks. Many neural

[11]Each input character had an embedding size of 300 units. The encoder consisted of a bidirectional LSTM (Hochreiter and Schmidhuber, 1997b) with two layers with a dropout value of 0.3 between them. The decoder was a unidirectional LSTM with two layers. Both the encoder and decoder had 100 hidden units. Training was done using the Adadelta procedure (Zeiler, 2012) with a learning rate of 1.0 and a minibatch size of 20. Training was done for 100 epochs. Decoding used beam search ($k = 12$).

Train		
lemma	features	word form
run	V;PST	ran
love	V;V.PTCP;PRS	loving
eat	V;PST	ate
Test		
lemma	features	word form
hate	V;V.PTCP;PRS	?
read	V;PST	?

TABLE 3: Examples of inflected English verbs as a SIGMORPHON shared task.

(and non-neural) approaches have been explored as the part of the SIGMORPHON shared tasks on morphological inflection (Vylomova et al., 2020). The core task tested in these workshops is inflection, shown in Table 3 with a hypothetical example from English. Given an input lemma and a set of morphological features, the goal is to produce the corresponding inflected form.

The latest shared tasks cover over 100 typologically diverse languages. Data for training and testing is mostly derived from UniMorph[12], which is a large multilingual database of inflected forms. For a given language, a UniMorph entry consists of a simple tuple including a lemma, inflected form, and a morphological feature vector assigned to the form by linguistically trainined annotator.[13] The task languages are deliberately arranged from very high resource (over 10,000 forms available for training) to very low resource (~100 forms available).

In general, the best-performing systems in the shared task achieve excellent performance, approaching 100% output form accuracy in the high resource scenarios, but maintaining reasonable performance (80%) even in many low resource scenarios, particularly those involving more regular morphological patterns[14]. While these models are almost always variations of the Encoder/Decoder sequence-to-sequence architecture

[12] unimorph.github.io

[13] It is important to note that UniMorph currently lacks coverage of derivational morphology. It also considers lexical properties such as animacy as inherent to the lemma, and does not mark them as features on inflected forms, except as agreement markers.

[14] (Goldman et al 2022) notes that this level of performance depends on an advantageous data split between training and testing data, where the same lemmas may appear in both, albeit with different inflections. When systems must generalize

described above (modified to allow the model to accept both a lemma and morphological features as input), special tuning is required to improve performance in low-resource cases.

1.4.3 Low-resource Strategies

In general, neural network approaches are known to require extensive training data to learn input/output mappings that generalize. In part, this is because neural models are powerful and can in principle encode a wide range of hypothetical rules for performing morphological transformations. This brings up several questions. Are the inductive biases of neural networks similar to those of human learners? If not, how can we enforce the right learning biases?

This problem is exacerbated in low resource scenarios, where the training examples do not adequately constrain the hypothesis space. Several approaches have been developed that help mitigate, though not fully resolve, the low-resource problem. One successful approach has been to prime network learning towards the right inductive biases by feeding in hallucinated training data. Since the majority of symbols are preserved by morphological operations, teaching a network that 'copying' is a useful default can be beneficial. This can be done simply by learning the identity mapping between random strings, or even strings drawn from a phonotactic model (Kann and Schütze, 2017). Of course this approach effectively trains a bias towards copying, rather than starting with a model that already has such a bias, which may be a better model of what human learners start out with.

SIGMORPHON participants have also found some limited benefits from multi-task training with related languages. This is primarily useful when the languages are close enough to share an identical symbol set and similar phonological patterns. In these scenarios (Jin and Kann, 2017), a single model is trained on mappings from multiple languages, with an independently embedded language token given to the model as input.

While these strategies are effective at equalizing neural network performance with non-neural baselines in many low-resource scenarios, there remain some languages where data is so sparse that even suitably primed networks are simply not able to generalize very well, and a fallback to a hand-tailored finite-state solution remains more effective (Vylomova et al., 2020).

---

only to unseen lemmas, performance drops by 30% on average, by as much as 90% in some low resource scenarios, and even around 10% in high-resource languages.

1.4.4 Error analysis

Gorman et al. (2019) present an analysis of the errors made by neural inflection systems across the SIGMORPHON shared tasks. They categorize errors into natural (errors that a human learner could plausibly make) and silly categories (errors that look absurd compared to human performance, such as mangled output strings that are not phonologically valid words in the language). They found very few errors in the silly category. A large percentage of the errors were caused by ambiguities that could not be resolved based on the information in the input (lexical categories like animacy and gender can affect morphological patterning, but were not consistently annotated). In other cases, the networks applied regular inflection rules to unmarked irregular inputs. As in English, while technically an error, regularization is reasonable behavior for novel inputs. Furthermore, as many as a quarter of the errors were simply the network faithfully reproducing annotation errors that were in the data. As apparent from the discussion of the English past tense above, networks have the capacity to memorize irregular mappings, so carrying forward annotation errors in this way is not unexpected.

1.4.5 Understanding Network Behavior Through Characteristic Mappings

As the discussion of the English Past tense mapping in Section 1.4.1 shows, we can learn a lot about the generalization behavior of sequence-to-sequence networks by focusing on networks trained to solve a specific mapping problem. Here, we describe additional experiments that act as further sanity checks on whether networks will generalize in linguistically sensible ways. We will look at the embedded representations induced by networks and how the attention mechanism treats these input representations as cues for making linguistic decisions.

The Hungarian Essive – Attending to Cues. Hungarian is an agglutinating language which prominently features vowel harmony. The inessive case suffix, indicating location within another object, is marked by either the *-ban* (e.g., *ház* 'house' →*házban* 'in a house') or *-ben* (e.g., *kert* 'garden' →*kertben* 'in a garden') suffix. The choice is governed by the nearest harmony-triggering vowel in the word stem. Roughly, the back vowels (/o/, /a/, etc.) trigger *-ban*, and front vowels (/e/) trigger *-ben*. A crucial wrinkle is that some vowels are considered 'transparent' to the harmony system (/i/), and do not act as a cue.

Input	a(0.0)	p(0.0)	r(0.0)	ó(0.0)	s(0.0)	**[á](1.0)**	g(0.0)		
Output	a	p	r	ó	s	á	g	b	[a]	n
Input	r(0.0)	é(0.0)	g(0.0)	**[é](1.0)**	s(0.0)	z(0.0)			
Output	r	é	g	é	s	z	b	[e]	n
Input	**[a](1.0)**	m(0.0)	c(0.0)	s(0.0)	i(0.0)				
Output	a	m	c	s	i	b	[a]	n	
Input	t(0.0)	**[ü](1.0)**	r(0.0)	r(0.0)	k(0.0)	i(0.0)	z(0.0)		
Output	t	ü	r	k	i	z	b	[e]	n

TABLE 4: Hungarian essive mapping examples. Brackets [] represent harmony triggering vowel in the input, and selected stem vowel in the input. Numbers in parentheses () represent attention weight association with each input position at the time step when the output suffix vowel is chosen by the decoder. Note the long-distance dependence in the case of *amcsiban* and *türkizben*, where harmony is triggered by the first vowel of the stem.

We trained a sequence-to-sequence network to map stems to their essive form using a dataset of 9,422 stem/essive pairs taken from the UniMorph database (split 80/20% into training/test portions). The network, using hyperparameters identical to those used for the English past tense mapping (see Section 1.4.1), achieved virtually perfect performance. Given the trained network, we can ask if the attention mechanism is acting to select relevant linguistic cues for the decoder. In particular, at the timestep that a decision must be made about whether to output /a/ or /e/ in the suffix, we expect most of the attention to be concentrated on the input representation of the harmony-triggering vowel. In fact, this is exactly what we see. 100% of the attention weight ends up where expected. See Table 4 for examples.

Romanian Plural - Learning Functional Phonological Representations. Romanian has a complex system of nominal plural marking. Unlike masculine nouns, whose plurals are deterministic, the pluralization of feminine (*fata* ↦ *fete*) and neuter (*scaun* ↦ *scaune*) nouns has eluded a simple grammatical description. The choice of plural marking (*-i*, *-e*, *-uri*, or *-ale*) appears to be a complex mixture of lexicalized stem properties, which do not generalize, and phonology-based rules of thumb which apply with some probability. See Grosu and Wilson (2016) for a review. In that work, they present a hand-tuned harmonic constraint-based grammar of the form below (referred to as a Maximum Entropy or MaxEnt grammar in phonology) to enforce the mapping.

Romanian	Network	MaxEnt
Feminine	**95.8%**	92.2%
Neuter	**86.2%**	80.3%

TABLE 5: Performance on Romanian pluralization.

This grammar assigns scores to possible output inflections according to the weighted sum of constraint violations. Let C be a family of constraints c that a suffix/stem pair can violate, where each constraint refers to a set of phonological properties (e.g., "the inflection must end in *-i* if the stem ends in /e/"). In this case, v_c is an indicator function that returns 1 only if the constraint c is violated and 0 otherwise. w_c is the weight cost associated with that violation.

$$p(\text{suffix}|\text{stem}) \propto exp(-\sum_{c \in C} w_c * v_c(\text{suffix}, \text{stem})) \qquad (1.1)$$

We use their data, consisting of 39,500 stem/plural pairs, split 80/20% into training and test sets, to build a sequence-to-sequence network instead (again, trained using the hyperparameters above). From Table 5, we see that that the network is better able to generalize than the constraint-based MaxEnt grammar.

Due to the complex morphophonological processes that govern Romanian pluralization, we would expect the embedded phoneme representations learned by the network to include the information required to break phonemes into functional clusters, so that phonemes that affect the output in a similar way obtain similar representations. This is analogous to the the concept of contrastive groups in traditional phonology theory, from which phonological features are derived (Chomsky and Halle, 1968). Figure 1 shows the Euclidean distances between the phoneme embeddings learned by the network in the Romanian pluralization task. Lightly colored cells indicate greater similarity. This allows us to visualize 'equivalence classes' of self-similar sounds. We see that most consonants form a self-similar cluster, suggesting that most consonants should behave similarly as cues. Indeed, one of the rules of thumb for pluralization discovered by linguists is that singulars that end in a consonant are pluralized by *-e*. The schwa-like *â*, and *ă*, vowels, are similar to the consonants in that they also cue for *-e*. The rest of the vowels, on the other hand, are mostly very distinct from each other—final *e*, for example, is often a cue for the *-i* affix.

	b	d	l	p	t	ţ	s	c	j	n	r	v	z	ş	a	ă	â	e	i	î	u	o
b	0																					
d	1.98	0																				
l	2.63	2.38	0																			
p	2.09	2.25	2.59	0																		
t	2.39	2.1	2.61	2.27	0																	
ţ	2.62	2.63	3.18	2.56	2.4	0																
s	2.19	1.97	2.62	2.1	2.32	2.78	0															
c	2.13	2.28	2.81	2.32	2.7	2.83	2.28	0														
j	2.08	2	2.57	2.16	2.16	2.79	2.06	2.43	0													
n	2.23	2.08	2.59	2.36	2.29	2.78	2.26	2.59	2.23	0												
r	2.42	2.25	2.63	2.51	2.43	2.69	2.49	2.68	2.51	2.35	0											
v	2.47	2.19	2.45	2.25	2.24	2.6	2.25	2.58	2.31	2.17	2.63	0										
z	2.17	1.88	2.22	2.18	2.18	2.55	2.34	2.42	2.1	2.26	2.44	1.96	0									
ş	2.66	2.57	3.11	2.51	2.74	3.16	2.58	3.03	2.36	2.91	2.77	2.84	2.57	0								
a	2.73	2.64	3.06	2.74	2.85	3.2	2.74	3.08	2.72	2.85	3.25	2.76	2.61	3.25	0							
ă	2.22	2.16	3.13	2.33	2.47	2.74	2.27	2.55	2.28	2.61	2.72	2.48	2.46	2.75	2.82	0						
â	2.39	2.43	2.68	2.19	2.41	2.73	2.42	2.78	2.16	2.24	2.81	2.19	2.26	2.85	2.44	2.6	0					
e	2.73	2.66	3.35	2.8	2.61	2.91	2.66	3.04	2.7	2.46	2.84	2.7	2.77	3.44	3.01	2.56	2.53	0				
i	2.89	2.64	2.81	2.76	2.73	3.56	2.79	3.22	2.32	2.63	3.03	2.71	2.59	2.71	2.85	2.95	2.46	3.08	0			
î	2.17	1.91	2.49	1.86	1.89	2.31	2.08	2.26	2.04	2.13	2.4	2.07	1.87	2.53	2.48	1.98	1.97	2.57	2.54	0		
u	2.56	2.49	2.98	2.55	2.82	3.16	2.47	2.91	2.3	2.54	3	2.66	2.54	3.13	2.82	2.58	2.38	2.51	2.65	2.44	0	
o	2.95	3.02	3.34	3.07	3.03	3.34	3.1	3.13	2.87	2.96	3.25	3.09	2.94	3.42	3.27	3.22	2.96	2.92	3.31	2.88	3.1	0

FIGURE 1: Euclidean distance between induced embeddings for Romanian phonemes.

If the embedded representations learned for input symbols by a network that performs a single mapping form functional clusters, we would expect a network that learns *all* possible mappings in a language to converge on representations that encompass the overall range of phonological functions served by each phoneme. Indeed, Silfverberg et al. (2018) found that, for networks trained to perform the morphological mapping tasks in the SIGMORPHON 2018 shared task, where every morphological mapping possible in the paradigm of an input lemma needed to be learned, there was a significant correlation between the pairwise cosine similarities between the embedded phoneme representations induced by the networks, and the corresponding pairwise similarities between vectors of traditional features described by phonologists, including voicing, manner, and place of articulation.

Phonotactic Generalization. Phonotactics is an aspect of phonology which governs the overall acceptability of strings within a morphophonological system. It encompasses restrictions on syllabic and prosodic structure (e.g., no /tl/ at the beginning of English syllables, and, in some languages, overall word length. Here we examine the generalization behavior of sequence-to-sequence neural networks with respect to length. In particular, can networks trained on a bounded

Train Lengths	Test Lengths	Accuracy
1-6	7-12	54%
1-12	13-18	93%

TABLE 6: Networks can generalize to longer length strings unseen in the output, but only when there is a wider variance in the length of the input strings.

set of short strings generalize to longer strings? Usually, morphological patterns apply to lemmas of any length, so failing to generalize would indicate that networks lack the appropriate inductive bias. However, one could also argue that the network is learning, what, from its perspective, is a correct phonotactic restriction.

For our case study we look at mapping Polish singular feminine nouns to their plural form in the nominative case, usually achieved with the *-y* suffix as in *kobieta*→*kobiety* [girl→girls]. As noted above, this pattern should apply to lemmas of any length. To test the ability of sequence-to-sequence neural networks to make this generalization, we examine two scenarios. First, we trained a network on 4000 mappings[15] where the output string was between length 1 and 6, but tested on 1000 mappings where the output was longer, between 7 and 12 characters. As shown in Table 6, in this case, the network fails to generalize the morphological pattern to longer strings, correctly inflecting only 54% of lemmas. The most common error is cutting off the output string prematurely.

However, when we train on 4000 samples drawn from a wider range of lengths, between 1 and 12, the network has much less trouble generalizing to lengths between 13 and 18, which is again up to six symbols longer than anything seen during training — it achieves 93% accuracy. We see then that at least one inductive bias (that morphological mapping should accept lemmas of any length) relevant to morphology doesn't come for free with sequence-to-sequence networks, or at least cannot be separated from simultaneous phonotactic learning. Networks *will* pick up on length restrictions apparent in the data, so the data itself must be prepared in such a way so as to impart the appropriate inductive bias to the model during training. In this case, it is important to present a wide range of lengths, even if not the full set of lengths that might appear at inference time.

[15] All data taken from (Woliński and Kieraś, 2016).

1.5 Open Problems

While the SIGMORPHON shared tasks show promising results for sequence-to-sequence networks across a typologically diverse range of languages, the full range of morphological systems has not been explored. Results for polysynthetic languages, such as Inuit languages, and languages that make extensive use of reduplication, such as many languages from the Austronesian family, are sparse.[16] While there are many languages that have these morphological properties, they constitute a very small percentage of the world population, and present unique challenges for computational work. On a practical level, the small number of speakers contributes to a lack of annotated (and raw) data to use for training NLP systems.[17] Furthermore, the linguistic properties of these morphologies renders them difficult to represent within the computational frameworks described throughout this chapter.

Derivation. While the UniMorph project has supplied annotated data for the bulk of SIGMORPHON shared task languages, the focus has been on annotating complete (or nearly complete) inflectional paradigms with morphosyntactic features. The limitation of this approach is that the notion of paradigm does not easily fit with all morphological operations. As we noted above, inflection morphology often can be thought of as yielding a different form of the same word. In that case one can conceive of the different forms that a given word might take in a table—a paradigm—where each slot corresponds to a certain form of the word, say the DATIVE form, or the PAST SUBJUNCTIVE THIRD PERSON SINGULAR. In the case of derivational morphology, this concept seems less natural. It is not that there are not derivational operations that can be viewed as paradigmatic; there are, and one such example is provenance adjectives like *Canadian* derived from country and city names. But in many cases derivational processes cannot really be shoehorned into paradigms. Furthermore they are often less productive than inflectional processes, and are more prone to lexical drift in that derived forms may acquire additional

[16]However, see Prickett et al. (2018) for a reduplication study using sequence-to-sequence networks with fully controlled data from an artificial language. In that scenario, networks do generalize reduplication patterns, as long as the input symbol alphabet is consistent between training and testing. See the copying problem below for discussion of why networks don't generalize when training and testing symbol alphabets differ.

[17]Frequently, data is limited to lexicons and linguistic descriptions produced by missionaries, along with translations of religious texts into the language. In the case of officially recognized minority languages, there may also be government proceedings, as in the Nanuvut-Hansard corpus of Inuktitut (Joanis et al., 2020).

meanings. Thus the adjective *derivative* is not merely an adjectival form that means that something is *derived* from something else, but has an additional connotation that implies that by being thus derived, something is therefore unoriginal: saying that an artist's work is *derivative of Picasso*, can only be interpreted as an insult.

One attempt to mitigate the lack of attention to derivation has been work of Cotterell et al. (2017) who, following progress on inflection in the SIGMORPHON shared tasks, attempted to treat derivational morphology in the same way as inflectional morphology, borrowing the concept of paradigm cells to indicate derivation processes like nominalizing a verb to expressing an agent (*walk* $\mapsto$ *walker*). The study had limited success owing to the difficulty of building consistent paradigm schemas that applied productively to all or even many lemmas.

Polysynthetic Morphology The morphological systems of polysynthetic languages, such as those in the Eskimo–Aleut family, further break the notion of morphological paradigm to the point that it becomes nonsensical, as we noted in Section 1.2. In polysynthetic languages, many morphemes are strung together to form long words, sometimes by alternating chains of derivation and inflection. Through the process of incorporation, multiple lemmas (e.g., both a verb and its direct object) can be included in the same word unit. See the example from Saint Lawrence Yupik below (Schwartz et al., 2020).

(2) *mangteghaghrugllangllaghyunghitunga*
mangteghagh-ghrugllag-ngllagh-yug-nghite-tu-nga
house-big-build-want.to-to.not-INTR.IND-1SG
('I didn't want to make a huge house.')

This level of productivity means that it is impossible to build paradigms which consist of a finite set of mappings between a single core lemma and its associated morphological variants. This precludes the use of paradigm data to train sequence-to-sequence models as in the SIGMORPHON shared tasks. Nevertheless, sequence-to-sequence models may still be relevant for mapping long words into glosses (i.e., mapping between the different representations in the Yupik example above), provided some data was available to learn the mapping. Finite state methods could be used to bootstrap such data. While single words in a polysynthetic language can pack in the information usually associated with an entire sentence, the linguistic rules by which morphemes are combined into a wordform may still be a finite state system. Prototype finite-state morphological analyzers exist for some polysynthetic languages, including Chukchi (Andriyanets and

Tyers, 2018) and Inuktitut[18], but these lack coverage and fail to parse many wordforms, or simply don't include complex grammatical features like incorporation. Very little research exists attempting to treat polysynthetic morphology as if it was actually equivalent to syntax, and deploying mechanisms used in full-sentence parsing — Homola (2011) is one of the few references.

Copying. Languages with reduplication point to a key problem with sequence-to-sequence models as they are commonly deployed, which we will refer to as the problem of copying. Many morphological operations involve copying most of an input string, attaching additional affixes, and transforming the result in order to comply with the morphophonological rules of the language. Clearly, networks can learn to copy segments they have already seen—developing this inductive bias is one of the key strategies for dealing with low resource scenarios described above. However, the standard sequence-to-sequence architecture does not independently represent the role of an input symbol from its content. In particular, there is no way to assign a meaningful embedding to a previously unseen input symbol. Typically, any such symbol would be replaced with a special [UNK] token. If such symbols are present during training, networks may learn to deal with them in a reasonable 'default' way. However, using [UNK] precludes the phonological generalization humans are capable of, treating out of vocabulary symbols according to their sound similarity with known phonemes. If phonological generalization is important, the input representation for symbols may be included to an aggregate of phonological feature embeddings, rather than a monolithic embedding representing the abstract symbol. A further mitigation is to train networks that can output instructions rather actual symbols. If the network says to copy the symbol in position 0, the output vocabulary need not contain the new symbol itself.

1.6 Conclusions

Computational morphology is an extensive topic, and we clearly cannot cover every aspect within the limits of a single chapter. However, we hope to have covered a subset of the most interesting issues. We presented a brief overview of the linguistics of morphology, giving an idea of the wide range of typological variation exhibited across the world's languages. For much of the history of computational morphology, this complexity has been described by hand-built grammars expressed as finite-state transducers. As many of the

[18]http://www.inuktitutcomputing.ca/Uqailaut/info.php

core tasks in computational morphology involve mappings between sequences (e.g., mapping an inflected form to its lemma and morphological features, or vice versa) modern sequence-to-sequence neural networks, particularly with an encoder-decoder architecture, have supplanted finite-state methods as the defacto state-of-the-art. Networks can train from data without linguist input. Furthermore, as we show across a number of case studies across Section 1.4, they often generalize in ways that line up with linguist expectations of human speakers. At the same time, networks come with several caveats. By default, they require extensive data to train effectively — a resource which simply doesn't exist for many languages. Networks lack human-like inductive biases to constrain learning, so they are 1) liable to overfit to small datasets 2) prone to generalizing from errors in poorly annotated data. Researchers have developed mitigation strategies for these problems (e.g., training networks to prefer copying by priming them with identity mappings), but there are still low-resource scenarios where finite state methods with linguistic knowledge directly injected into them remain superior.

Finally, we highlighted a number of open problems in computational morphology where simply switching to neural networks is not a solution. Derivational morphology and polysynthetic morphology are difficult to fit into the paradigm-based data schemas assumed in most of the existing research on morphological mappings. This difficulty is compounded by the fact that polysynthetic languages, along with languages that exhibit morphological features like full reduplication, tend to have few speakers. This limits the amount of data in those languages available for machine learning, and research efforts building NLP systems of any sort for these languages have been sparse. On the theoretical side, there are also fundamental challenges with machine learning morphological mappings from finite data. Aside from the incorrect inductive biases mentioned above, vanilla encoder-decoder sequence-to-sequence neural networks in particular suffer from what we deem the 'copying problem.' They cannot generalize properly over unseen symbols at inference time, as they can only represent inputs via embeddings learned during training. They also cannot 'encapsulate' an input in such a way as to separate its content from its, for example, position in a string. In other words, previously unseen input symbols cannot be stored in a generic memory register, as is possible in standard symbolic computing.

References

Aharoni, Roee, Yoav Goldberg, and Yonatan Belinkov. 2016. Improving sequence to sequence learning for morphological inflection generation: The BIU-MIT systems for the SIGMORPHON 2016 shared task for morphological reinflection. In *Proceedings of the 14th SIGMORPHON Workshop on Computational Research in Phonetics, Phonology, and Morphology*, pages 41–48. Berlin, Germany: Association for Computational Linguistics.

Ahlberg, Malin, Markus Forsberg, and Mans Hulden. 2014. Semi-supervised learning of morphological paradigms and lexicons. In *Proceedings of the 14th Conference of the European Chapter of the Association for Computational Linguistics*, pages 569–578. Gothenburg, Sweden: Association for Computational Linguistics.

Albright, Adam and Bruce Hayes. 2003. Rules vs. analogy in English past tenses: A computational/experimental study. *Cognition* 90:119–161.

Allauzen, Cyril, Michael Riley, Johan Schalkwyk, Wojciech Skut, and Mehryar Mohri. 2007. OpenFst: a general and efficient weighted finite-state transducer library. In *CIAA '07: Proceedings of the 12th International Conference on Implementation and Application of Automata*, pages 11–23. Berlin: Springer.

Andriyanets, Vasilisa and Francis Tyers. 2018. A prototype finite-state morphological analyser for Chukchi. In *Proceedings of the Workshop on Computational Modeling of Polysynthetic Languages*, pages 31–40. Santa Fe, New Mexico, USA: Association for Computational Linguistics.

Antworth, Evan L. 1990. *PC-KIMMO: A Two-Level Processor for Morphological Analysis*. Summer Institute of Linguistics.

Aronoff, Mark. 1994. *Morphology by Itself*. Cambridge, MA: MIT Press.

Ataman, Duygu, Matteo Negri, Marco Turchi, and Marcello Federico. 2017. Linguistically motivated vocabulary reduction for neural machine translation from Turkish to English. *The Prague Bulletin of Mathematical Linguistics* 108(1):331–342.

Baayen, R. Harald, Richard Piepenbrock, and Rijn van H. 1993. The CELEX lexical data base on CD-ROM .

Bahdanau, Dzmitry, Kyunghyun Cho, and Yoshua Bengio. 2015. Neural machine translation by jointly learning to align and translate. In *Internationoal Conference on Learning Representations*, vol. abs/1409.0473.

Beemer, Sarah, Zak Boston, April Bukoski, Daniel Chen, Princess Dickens, Andrew Gerlach, Torin Hopkins, Parth Anand Jawale, Chris Koski, Akanksha Malhotra, Piyush Mishra, Saliha Muradoglu, Lan Sang, Tyler Short, Sagarika Shreevastava, Elizabeth Spaulding, Testumichi Umada, Beilei Xiang, Changbing Yang, and Mans Hulden. 2020. Linguist vs. machine: rapid development of finite-state morphological grammars. In *Proceedings of the 17th SIGMORPHON Workshop on Computational Research in Phonetics, Phonology, and Morphology*, pages 162–170. Seattle.

Beesley, Kenneth R. 2012. Kleene, a free and open-source language for finite-state programming. In *Proceedings of the 10th International Workshop on Finite State Methods and Natural Language Processing*, pages 50–54. Donostia–San Sebastián.

Beesley, Kenneth R. and Lari Karttunen. 2003. *Finite State Morphology*. Stanford, CA: CSLI.

Can, Burcu and Suresh Manandhar. 2014. Methods and algorithms for unsupervised learning of morphology. In *International Conference on Intelligent Text Processing and Computational Linguistics*, pages 177–205. Springer, Kathmandu.

Chandlee, Jane and Jeffrey Heinz. 2012. Bounded copying is subsequential: implications for metathesis and reduplication. In *Proceedings of the Twelfth Meeting of the Special Interest Group on Computational Morphology and Phonology*, pages 42–51. Montréal.

Chomsky, Noam and Morris Halle. 1968. *The sound pattern of English*. Harper & Row New York.

Chung, Junyoung, Çaglar Gülçehre, Kyunghyun Cho, and Yoshua Bengio. 2014. Empirical evaluation of gated recurrent neural networks on sequence modeling. *CoRR* abs/1412.3555.

CODIUL. 1989. Diccionario elemental del Ulwa (sumu meridional). Tech. rep., CODIUL/UYUTMUBAL, Karawala Región Autónoma Atlántico Sur: Centro de Investigaciones y Documentación de la Costa Atlantica; and Center for Cognitive Science, Massachusetts Institute of Technology, Managua and Bluefields, Nicaragua.

Corkery, Maria, Yevgen Matusevych, and Sharon Goldwater. 2019. Are we there yet? Encoder-decoder neural networks as cognitive models of English past tense inflection. In *Proceedings of the 57th Annual Meeting of the Association for Computational Linguistics*, pages 3868–3877. Florence, Italy: Association for Computational Linguistics.

Cotterell, Ryan, Ekaterina Vylomova, Huda Khayrallah, Christo Kirov, and David Yarowsky. 2017. Paradigm completion for derivational morphology. In *Proceedings of the 2017 Conference on Empirical Methods in Natural Language Processing*, pages 714–720. Copenhagen, Denmark: Association for Computational Linguistics.

Cutler, Anne, John Hawkins, and Gary Gilligan. 1985. The suffixing preference: a processing explanation. *Linguistics* 23:723–758.

Dolatian, Hossep, Jonathan Rawski, and Jeffrey Heinz. 2021. Strong generative capacity of morphological processes. *Proceedings of the Society for Computation in Linguistics* 4(1):228–243.

Drobac, Senka, Miikka Silfverberg, and Anssi Yli-Jyrä. 2012. Implementation of replace rules using preference operator. In *Proceedings of the 10th International Workshop on Finite State Methods and Natural Language Processing*, pages 55–59. Donostia–San Sebastián.

Dryer, Matthew S. 2013. Prefixing vs. suffixing in inflectional morphology. In M. S. Dryer and M. Haspelmath, eds., *The World Atlas of Language Structures Online*. Leipzig: Max Planck Institute for Evolutionary Anthropology.

Dryer, Matthew S. and Martin Haspelmath, eds. 2013. *WALS Online*. Leipzig: Max Planck Institute for Evolutionary Anthropology.

Durrett, Greg and John DeNero. 2013. Supervised learning of complete morphological paradigms. In *Proceedings of the 2013 Conference of the North American Chapter of the Association for Computational Linguistics: Human Language Technologies*, pages 1185–1195. Atlanta, Georgia: Association for Computational Linguistics.

Ettinger, S. 1974. *Diminutiv- und Augmentativbilding: Regeln und Restriktionen*, vol. 54. Tübingen: Tübinger Beiträge zur Linguistik.

Goldman, Omer, David Guriel, and Reut Tsarfaty. 2022. (Un)solving morphological inflection: Lemma overlap artificially inflates models' performance. In *Proceedings of the 60th Annual Meeting of the Association for Computational Linguistics (Volume 2: Short Papers)*, pages 864–870.

Goldsmith, John. 2001. Unsupervised learning of the morphology of a natural language. *Computational Linguistics* 27(2):153–198.

Gorman, Kyle, Arya D. McCarthy, Ryan Cotterell, Ekaterina Vylomova, Miikka Silfverberg, and Magdalena Markowska. 2019. Weird inflects but OK: Making sense of morphological generation errors. In *Proceedings of the 23rd Conference on Computational Natural Language Learning (CoNLL)*, pages 140–151. Hong Kong, China: Association for Computational Linguistics.

Gorman, Kyle and Richard Sproat. 2021. *Finite-State Text Processing*. Williston, VT: Morgan Claypool.

Grönroos, Stig-Arne, Sami Virpioja, Peter Smit, and Mikko Kurimo. 2014. Morfessor FlatCat: An HMM-based method for unsupervised and semi-supervised learning of morphology. In *Proceedings of COLING 2014, the 25th International Conference on Computational Linguistics: Technical Papers*, pages 1177–1185. Dublin.

Grosu, Ioana and Colin Wilson. 2016. Experimental evidence for stem ending and size factors in Romanian plural formation. In *The 90th Annual Meeting of the Linguistic Society of America*. LSA.

Halle, Morris and Alec Marantz. 1993. Distributed morphology and the pieces of inflection. In K. Hale and S. J. Keyser, eds., *The View from Building 20*, pages 111–176. Cambridge, MA: MIT Press.

Hankamer, Jorge. 1989. Morphological parsing and the lexicon. In W. D. Marslen-Wilson, ed., *Lexical Representation and Process*, pages 392–408. MIT Press.

Hetherington, Lee. 2001. An efficient implementation of phonological rules using finite-state transducers. In *EUROSPEECH-2001*, pages 1599–1602. Aalborg.

Hochreiter, Sepp and Jürgen Schmidhuber. 1997a. Long short-term memory. *Neural Computation* 9(8):1735–1780.

Hochreiter, Sepp and Jürgen Schmidhuber. 1997b. Long short-term memory. *Neural computation* 9(8):1735–1780.

Homola, Petr. 2011. Parsing a polysynthetic language. In *Proceedings of the International Conference Recent Advances in Natural Language Processing 2011*, pages 562–567. Hissar, Bulgaria: Association for Computational Linguistics.

Hulden, Mans. 2009. Foma: a finite-state compiler and library. In *Proceedings of the Demonstrations Session at EACL 2009*, pages 29–32. Athens.

Hulden, Mans. 2017. Rewrite rule grammars with multitape automata. *Language Modelling* 5(1):107–130.

Jin, Huiming and Katharina Kann. 2017. Exploring cross-lingual transfer of morphological knowledge in sequence-to-sequence models. In *Proceedings of the First Workshop on Subword and Character Level Models in NLP*, pages 70–75.

Joanis, Eric, Rebecca Knowles, Roland Kuhn, Samuel Larkin, Patrick Littell, Chi-kiu Lo, Darlene Stewart, and Jeffrey Micher. 2020. The Nunavut Hansard Inuktitut–English parallel corpus 3.0 with preliminary machine translation results. In *Proceedings of the 12th Language Resources and Evaluation Conference*, pages 2562–2572. Marseille, France: European Language Resources Association. ISBN 979-10-95546-34-4.

Johnson, C.D. 1972. *Formal Aspects of Phonological Description*. Mouton.

Kann, Katharina and Hinrich Schütze. 2017. The LMU system for the CoNLL-SIGMORPHON 2017 shared task on universal morphological reinflection. In *Proceedings of the CoNLL SIGMORPHON 2017 Shared Task: Universal Morphological Reinflection*, pages 40–48. Vancouver: Association for Computational Linguistics.

Kaplan, Ronald M. and Martin Kay. 1994. Regular models of phonological rule systems. *Computational Linguistics* 20(3):331–378.

Karttunen, Lauri. 1995. The replace operator. In *33rd Annual Meeting of the Association for Computational Linguistics*, pages 16–23. Cambridge, MA.

Karttunen, Lauri. 1996. Directed replacement. In *34th Annual Meeting of the Association for Computational Linguistics*, page 108–115. Santa Cruz, CA.

Karttunen, Lauri. 1998. The proper treatment of optimality in computational phonology. In *Proceedings of the International Workshop on Finite State Methods in Natural Language Processing*, pages 1–12. Ankara.

Karttunen, Lauri. 2003. Computing with realizational morphology. In A. Gelbukh, ed., *Computational Linguistics and Intelligent Text Processing*, vol. 2588, pages 205–216. Springer.

Kay, Martin. 1987. Non-concatenative finite-state morphology. In *Third Conference of the European Chapter of the Association for Computational Linguistics*, pages 2–10. Copenhagen.

Kim, Najoung, Roma Patel, Adam Poliak, Patrick Xia, Alex Wang, Tom McCoy, Ian Tenney, Alexis Ross, Tal Linzen, Benjamin Van Durme, Samuel R. Bowman, and Ellie Pavlick. 2019. Probing what different NLP tasks teach machines about function word comprehension. In *Proceedings of the Eighth Joint Conference on Lexical and Computational Semantics (*SEM 2019)*, pages 235–249. Minneapolis, Minnesota: Association for Computational Linguistics.

Kiraz, George. 2001. *Computational Nonlinear Morphology: With Emphasis on Semitic Languages*. Cambridge University Press.

Kirov, Christo and Ryan Cotterell. 2018. Recurrent neural networks in linguistic theory: Revisiting Pinker and Prince (1988) and the past tense debate. *Transactions of the Association for Computational Linguistics* 6:651–665.

Koskenniemi, Kimmo. 1983. *Two-Level Morphology: A General Computational Model for Word-Form Recognition and Production*. Ph.D. thesis, University of Helsinki.

Koskenniemi, Kimmo and Miikka Silfverberg. 2010. A method for compiling two-level rules with multiple contexts. In *Proceedings of the 11th Meeting of the ACL Special Interest Group on Computational Morphology and Phonology*, pages 38–45.

Kuncoro, Adhiguna, Miguel Ballesteros, Lingpeng Kong, Chris Dyer, Graham Neubig, and Noah A. Smith. 2017. What do recurrent neural network grammars learn about syntax? In *Proceedings of the 15th Conference of the European Chapter of the Association for Computational Linguistics: Volume 1, Long Papers*, pages 1249–1258. Valencia, Spain: Association for Computational Linguistics.

Lieber, Rochelle. 1980. *On the Organization of the Lexicon*. Ph.D. thesis, Massachusetts Institute of Technology, Cambridge, MA.

Lindén, Krister, Miikka Silfverberg, and Tommi A. Pirinen. 2009. HFST tools for morphology: an efficient open-source package for construction of morphological analyzers. In *State of the Art in Computational Morphology*, pages 28–47. Springer.

Luong, Minh-Thang, Hieu Pham, and Christopher D Manning. 2015. Effective approaches to attention-based neural machine translation. *arXiv preprint arXiv:1508.04025* .

MacWhinney, Brian and Jared Leinbach. 1991. Implementations are not conceptualizations: Revising the verb learning model. *Cognition* 40(1):121–157.

Matthews, P. H. 1972. *Inflectional Morphology: A Theoretical Study Based on Aspects of Latin Conjugation*. Cambridge University Press.

McCarthy, John. 1982. Prosodic structure and expletive infixation. *Language* 58(3):574–590.

McCoy, R. Thomas, Robert Frank, and Tal Linzen. 2020. Does syntax need to grow on trees? Sources of hierarchical inductive bias in sequence-to-sequence networks. *Transactions of the Association for Computational Linguistics* 8:125–140.

Mohri, Mehryar and Richard Sproat. 1996. An efficient compiler for weighted rewrite rules. In *34th Annual Meeting of the Association for Computational Linguistics*, pages 231–238. Santa Cruz, CA.

Muradoğlu, Saliha, Nicholas Evans, and Ekaterina Vylomova. 2020. Modelling verbal morphology in Nen.

Nelson, Gerald. 2010. *English: an Essential Grammar*. Routledge.

Packard, Jerome L. 2000. *The Morphology of Chinese: A Linguistic and Cognitive Approach*. Cambridge University Press.

Park, Hyunji Hayley, Katherine J Zhang, Coleman Haley, Kenneth Steimel, Han Liu, and Lane Schwartz. 2021. Morphology matters: A multilingual language modeling analysis. *Transactions of the Association for Computational Linguistics* 9:261–276.

Pinker, Steven and Alan Prince. 1988. On language and connectionism: analysis of a parallel distributed processing model of language acquisition. In S. Pinker and J. Mehler, eds., *Connections and Symbols*. MIT Press.

Plunkett, Kim and Virginia Marchman. 1991. U-shaped learning and frequency effects in a multi-layered perception: Implications for child language acquisition. *Cognition* 38(1):43–102.

Prickett, Brandon, Aaron Traylor, and Joe Pater. 2018. Seq2Seq models with dropout can learn generalizable reduplication. In *Proceedings of the Fifteenth Workshop on Computational Research in Phonetics, Phonology, and Morphology*, pages 93–100. Brussels, Belgium: Association for Computational Linguistics.

Roark, Brian and Richard Sproat. 2007. *Computational Approaches to Morphology and Syntax*. Oxford: Oxford University Press.

Roark, Brian, Richard Sproat, Cyril Allauzen, Michael Riley, Jeffrey Sorensen, and Terry Tai. 2012. The OpenGrm open-source finite-state grammar software libraries. In *Proceedings of the ACL 2012 System Demonstrations*, pages 61–66. Jeju Island, Korea.

Rumelhart, David and Jay McClelland. 1986. On learning the past tenses of English verbs. In J. McClelland, D. Rumelhart, and the PDP Research Group, eds., *Parallel Distributed Processing: Explorations into the Microstructure of Cognition. Vol. 2: Psychological and Biological Models*, pages 216–271. Bradford Books.

Sak, Hasim, Murat Saraclar, and Tunga Gungor. 2010. Integrating morphology into automatic speech recognition. pages 354 – 358.

Schone, Patrick and Daniel Jurafsky. 2001. Knowledge-free induction of inflectional morphologies. In *Second Meeting of the North American Chapter of the Association for Computational Linguistics*.

Schuster, Mike and Kaisuke Nakajima. 2012. Japanese and Korean voice search. In *2012 IEEE International Conference on Acoustics, Speech and Signal Processing (ICASSP)*, pages 5149–5152. IEEE, Kyoto.

Schwartz, Lane, Francis M. Tyers, Lori S. Levin, Christo Kirov, Patrick Littell, Chi-kiu Lo, Emily Prud'hommeaux, Hyunji Hayley Park, Kenneth Steimel, Rebecca Knowles, Jeffrey Micher, Lonny Strunk, Han Liu, Coleman Haley, Katherine J. Zhang, Robbie Jimerson, Vasilisa Andriyanets, Aldrian Obaja Muis, Naoki Otani, Jong Hyuk Park, and Zhisong Zhang. 2020. Neural polysynthetic language modelling. *CoRR* abs/2005.05477.

Sennrich, Rico, Barry Haddow, and Alexandra Birch. 2016. Neural machine translation of rare words with subword units. In *Proceedings of the 54th Annual Meeting of the Association for Computational Linguistics (Volume 1: Long Papers)*, pages 1715–1725. Berlin, Germany: Association for Computational Linguistics.

Siegelmann, Hava T and Eduardo D Sontag. 1995. On the computational power of neural nets. *Journal of computer and system sciences* 50(1):132–150.

Silfverberg, Miikka P., Lingshuang Mao, and Mans Hulden. 2018. Sound analogies with phoneme embeddings. In *Proceedings of the Society for Computation in Linguistics (SCiL) 2018*, pages 136–144.

Skorik, P. J. 1961. *Grammatika čukotskogo jazyka: Fonetika i morfologija*. Leningrad: Nauka. In Russian.

Sproat, Richard. 1992. *Morphology and Computation*. MIT Press.

Stahlberg, Felix and Shankar Kumar. 2020. Seq2Edits: Sequence transduction using span-level edit operations. In *Proceedings of the 2020 Conference on Empirical Methods in Natural Language Processing (EMNLP)*, pages 5147–5159. Online: Association for Computational Linguistics.

Steele, Susan. 1995. Towards a theory of morphological information. *Language* 71:260–309.

Stump, Gregory T. 2001. *Inflectional Morphology: a Theory of Paradigm Structure*. Cambridge University Press.

Vaswani, Ashish, Noam Shazeer, Niki Parmar, Jakob Uszkoreit, Llion Jones, Aidan N Gomez, Łukasz Kaiser, and Illia Polosukhin. 2017. Attention is all you need. In *Advances in neural information processing systems*, pages 5998–6008.

Virpioja, Sami, Peter Smit, Stig-Arne Grönroos, Mikko Kurimo, et al. 2013. Morfessor 2.0: Python implementation and extensions for Morfessor baseline. Tech. rep., Aalto University, Helsinki.

Vylomova, Ekaterina, Jennifer White, Elizabeth Salesky, Sabrina J. Mielke, Shijie Wu, Edoardo Maria Ponti, Rowan Hall Maudslay, Ran Zmigrod, Josef Valvoda, Svetlana Toldova, Francis Tyers, Elena Klyachko, Ilya Yegorov, Natalia Krizhanovsky, Paula Czarnowska, Irene Nikkarinen, Andrew Krizhanovsky, Tiago Pimentel, Lucas Torroba Hennigen, Christo Kirov, Garrett Nicolai, Adina Williams, Antonios Anastasopoulos, Hilaria Cruz, Eleanor Chodroff, Ryan Cotterell, Miikka Silfverberg, and Mans Hulden. 2020. SIGMORPHON 2020 shared task 0: Typologically diverse morphological inflection. In *Proceedings of the 17th SIGMORPHON Workshop on Computational Research in Phonetics, Phonology, and Morphology*, pages 1–39. Online: Association for Computational Linguistics.

Woliński, Marcin and Witold Kieraś. 2016. The on-line version of Grammatical Dictionary of Polish. In *Proceedings of the International Conference on Language Resources and Evaluation (LREC)*, pages 2589–2594. Portorož.

Yarowsky, David and Richard Wicentowski. 2000. Minimally supervised morphological analysis by multimodal alignment. In *Proceedings of the 38th Annual Meeting of the Association for Computational Linguistics*, pages 207–216. Hong Kong: Association for Computational Linguistics.

Yli-Jyrä, Anssi. 2007. Transducers from parallel replace rules and modes with generalized lenient composition. In *Finite State Methods in Natural Language Processing 2007*, pages 197–212. Potsdam.

Yli-Jyrä, Anssi. 2013. On finite-state tonology with autosegmental representations. In *Proceedings of the 11th International Conference on Finite State Methods and Natural Language Processing*, pages 90–98. St Andrews, Scotland.

Yli-Jyrä, Anssi. 2019. Optimal Kornai-Karttunen codes for restricted autosegmental representations. In C. Condoravdi and T. Holloway King, eds., *Tokens of Meaning: Papers in Honor of Lauri Karttunen*. Stanford, CA: Center for the Study of Language and Information.

Yli-Jyrä, Anssi and Kimmo Koskenniemi. 2006. Compiling generalized two-level rules and grammars. In T. Salakoski, F. Ginter, S. Pyysalo, and T. Pahikkala, eds., *Advances in Natural Language Processing*, pages 174–185. Springer.

Yu, Alan CL. 2007. *A Natural History of Infixation*. No. 15 in Oxford Studies in Theoretical Linguistics. Oxford: Oxford University Press.

Zeiler, Matthew D. 2012. ADADELTA: An adaptive learning rate method. *CoRR* abs/1212.5701.

2

Something Old, Something New: Grammar-based CCG Parsing with Transformer Models

STEPHEN CLARK

2.1 Introduction

Combinatory Categorial Grammar (CCG) is a lexicalized grammar formalism in the type-driven tradition, building on historical work by Ajdukiewicz (1935) and Bar-Hillel (1953). The original formalism, often referred to as classical categorial grammar, uses the rules of forward and backward application to combine the categorial types. CCG, developed over many years by Mark Steedman (Steedman, 2000), uses a number of additional combinatory rules to deal with "movement" phenomena in natural languages – syntactic environments in which phrases are moved from their canonical argument positions, often creating an unbounded dependency between the argument and predicate. Examples in English include questions and relative clause extraction (Rimell et al., 2009). This movement phenomena is what motivated Chomsky to develop transformational grammar (Chomsky, 1965). Unlike transformational grammar, however, CCG is a "monostratal" theory in which the apparent movement of syntactic units is handled by a single level of representation. Other approaches to categorial grammar include the type-logical approach (Moortgat, 1997), in which linguistic types are the formulas of a logic and derivations are proofs, and the algebraic approach of the later work of Lambek (Lambek, 2008), in

Probabilistic Approaches to Linguistic Theory.
Jean-Philippe Bernardy, Rasmus Blanck,
Stergios Chatzikyriakidis, Shalom Lappin,
Aleksandre Maskharashvili (eds.).

which linguistic types are the partially-ordered objects of an algebra (specifically a *pregroup*), and derivations are given by the partial order.

Figure 1 gives an example CCG derivation using only the basic rules of *forward* (>) and *backward* (<) *application*. The categorial types that are assigned to words at the leaves of the derivation are referred to as *lexical categories*.[1] The internal structure of categories is built recursively from atomic categories and slashes ('\', '/') which indicate the directions of arguments. In a typical CCG grammar there are only a small number of atomic categories, such as S for sentence, N for noun, NP for noun phrase, and PP for prepositional phrase.[2] However, the recursive combination of categories and slashes can lead to a large number of categories; for example, the grammar used in the parsing experiments below has around 1,300 lexical categories. CCG is referred to as *lexicalised* because most of the grammatical information—which is language-dependent and encoded in the lexical categories—resides in the lexicon, with the remainder of the grammar being provided by a small number of combinatory rules.

One way to think of the application of these rules, or rule schema (since they apply to an unbounded set of category pairs), is that the matching parts of the combining categories effectively cancel, leading to the rules being called *cancellation laws* in some of the earlier work on categorial grammar. For example, when the lexical categories for *Exchange* and *Commission* in Figure 1 are combined, the argument N required by *Exchange* in N/N cancels with the lexical category N for *Commission*. We can also think of N/N as a function that is applied to its argument N. The *forward* in *forward application* refers to the fact that the argument is to the right. Backward (<) application—for when the argument is to the left—is used in the example when combining the subject NP *Investors* with the derived verb phrase $S[dcl]\backslash NP$.

Figure 2 shows the derivation for a noun phrase containing a relative clause, where the object has been extracted out of its canonical position to the right of the transitive verb. The bracketing structure of the lexical category of the transitive verb ($(S[dcl]\backslash NP)/NP$) means that the verb is expecting to combine with its object to the right before its subject to the left. However, in this example the object has been moved away from the verb so that is not possible. The solution provided by CCG is to use two new combinatory rules. First, the unary rule of type-raising (>**T**) turns an atomic NP category into a complex category $S/(S\backslash NP)$.

---

[1] Figure 1 follows the typical presentation for a CCG derivation with the leaves at the top.

[2] The square brackets on some S nodes in the example denote grammatical features such as [*dcl*] for declarative sentence (Hockenmaier and Steedman, 2007).

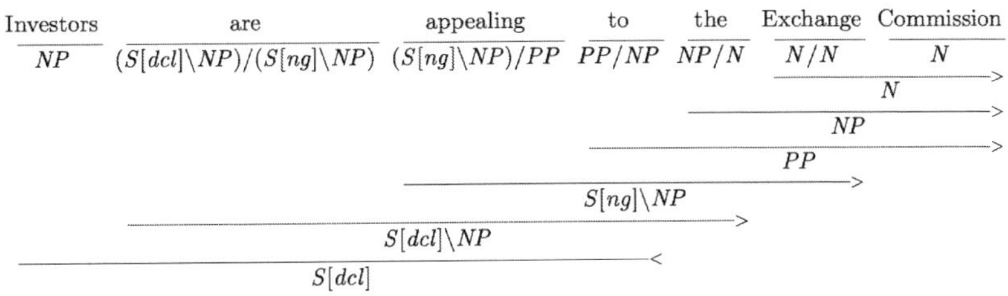

FIGURE 1: Example derivation using forward and backward application.

A useful way to think about this new category is that it's a sentence missing a verb phrase ($S\backslash NP$) to the right, which is a natural way to conceive of a subject NP as a function. Second, the rule of forward composition ($>\mathbf{B}$) enables the combination of the type-raised noun phrase ($S/(S\backslash NP)$) and the transitive verb ($(S[dcl]\backslash NP)/NP$), again with the idea that the verb-phrase categories "in the middle" effectively cancel. This results in the slightly unusual constituent $S[dcl]/NP$, which reflects the fact that the linguistic unit *the fund reached* is a sentence missing an NP to its right. Note that the lexical category for the relative pronoun in this example ($(NP\backslash NP)/(S[dcl]/NP)$) is expecting such a constituent to its right, so the relative pronoun can combine with the derived category using forward application.

There are additional combinatory rules in CCG which are designed to deal with other linguistic phenomena, including some rules in which the main slashes of the combining categories point in different directions – the so-called "non-harmonic" or crossing rules, such as backward crossed composition. These are all based on the operators of combinatory logic (Curry and Feys, 1958); hence the term *combinatory* in Combinatory Categorial Grammar. Steedman (1996), Steedman (2000) and Baldridge (2002) contain many linguistic examples which motivate the particular set of rules in the theory.

There is much work on the formal properties of CCG, including the seminal papers of Vijay-Shanker, Weir and Joshi in which it was proven that CCG is strictly more powerful than context-free grammars, but substantially less powerful than context-sensitive grammars – hence the term *mildly* context-senstive (Weir, 1992). Joshi et al. (1991) prove that CCG is weakly equivalent—i.e. generating the same string sets—to Tree Adjoining Grammar, Head Grammar, and Linear Indexed Grammar. This was a remarkable result given the apparent differences between these formalisms. Tree Adjoining Grammar (Joshi, 1987), like CCG, has become a standard grammar formalism in Computational Linguistics and has formed the basis for much experimental work in developing

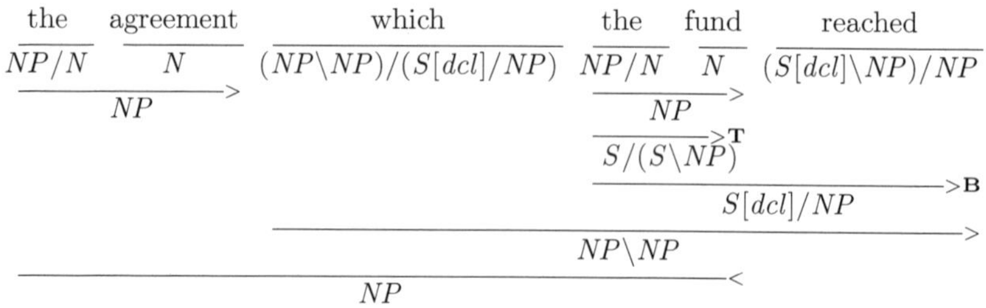

FIGURE 2: Example derivation using type-raising and forward composition.

parsers and NLP systems (Kasai et al., 2018). Kuhlmann et al. (2015) build on the earlier formal work and show that there are versions of CCG that are more powerful than CFGs, but strictly less powerful than TAG. Despite the additional power of CCG (and TAG), there are still efficient parsing algorithms for CCG (and TAG) which are polynomial in the length of the input sentence (Vijay-Shanker and Weir, 1993, Kuhlmann et al., 2018).

The mildly context-sensitive nature of CGG is much trumpeted, and rightly so given that it enables analyses of the crossing dependencies in Dutch and Swiss German (Shieber, 1985). However, it is perhaps worth pointing out that, for practical CCG parsing of English at least, the successful parsers have either used a CCG grammar which is context free by construction, being built entirely from rules instances observed in a finite CCG treebank (Hockenmaier and Steedman, 2002, Fowler and Penn, 2010), or a grammar which is context free in practice by limiting the applicability of the combinatory rules to the rule instances in the treebank (Clark and Curran, 2007b). Hence the parsing algorithms used by practical CCG parsers tend not to exploit the (somewhat complicated) structure-sharing schemes which define the more general polynomial-time parsing algorithms referenced above.

The remainder of this chapter starts out with the CCG supertagging task (Section 2.2), showing the 20-year evolution of CCG supertagging from feature-based models in which the features are defined by hand, to neural models in which the features are induced automatically by a neural network. Section 5.1 then demonstrates the gains that can be obtained by simply using a neural CCG supertagger as a front-end to an existing CCG parser, as well as additional improvements from using a neural classifier for the parsing model itself. Note that much of this chapter is a survey of existing work carried out by other researchers—or at least existing work replicated by the author—with the new material appearing in Section 2.3.2, which reports new state-of-the-art accuracy figures for the CCGbank parsing task. It also acts as something of a survey of the 20-year wide-coverage CCG parsing project that began in Edinburgh.[3] For a more detailed exposition of the linguistic theory of CCG, the reader is referred to Steedman (1996), Steedman (2000) and Baldridge (2002). For an introduction to wide-coverage CCG parsing, the reader is referred to Clark and Curran (2007b) and Hockenmaier and Steedman (2007).

2.2 CCG Supertagging

CCG supertagging is the task of assigning a single lexical category (or "supertag") to each word in an input sentence. The term *supertag* originates from the seminal work of Bangalore and Joshi (1999) for lexicalised tree-adjoining grammar (LTAG), and reflects the fact that CCG lexical categories (and elementary trees in LTAG) contain so much information. As an indication of how much information, note that the CCG grammar used in this chapter contains around 1,300 lexical categories, compared with the 50 or so part-of-speech tags in the original Penn Treebank (Marcus et al., 1993).

```
The|NP/N Trust|N ’s|(NP/N)\NP symbol|N ,|, a|NP/N sprig|N
of|(NP\NP)/NP oak|N/N leaves|N and|conj acorns|N ,|,
is|(S[dcl]\NP)/(S[pss]\NP) thought|(S[pss]\NP)/(S[to]\NP)
to|(S[to]\NP)/(S[b]\NP) have|(S[b]\NP)/(S[pt]\NP)
been|(S[pt]\NP)/(S[pss]\NP) inspired|S[pss]\NP
by|((S\NP)\(S\NP))/NP a|NP/N carving|N in|(NP\NP)/NP
the|NP/N cornice|N of|(NP\NP)/NP the|NP/N
Alfriston|(N/N)/(N/N) Clergy|N/N House|N .|.
```

FIGURE 3: A sentence from Wikipedia with the correct lexical category assigned to each word.

Figure 3 shows a sentence from Wikipedia with the correct lexical category assigned to each word (Clark et al., 2009). The words highlighted in blue demonstrate why CCG supertagging is a difficult task. The lexical category assigned to *by* takes two arguments: an NP to the right and a verb phrase ($S\backslash NP$) to the left. The lexical category assigned to *in* is similar, but takes an NP to the left. In the Penn Treebank, both of these prepositions would be assigned the part-of-speech tag *IN*. The point of the example is that, in order to assign the correct lexical category to these prepositions (or at least the second one), the supertagger has to decide whether the preposition attaches to

[3]https://groups.inf.ed.ac.uk/ccg/index.html

a noun or a verb; i.e. it effectively has to resolve a prepositional phrase attachment ambiguity, which is one of the more difficult, classical parsing ambiguities (Collins and Brooks, 1995). This led Bangalore and Joshi (1999) to describe supertagging as *almost parsing*.

The data most used for training and testing CCG supertaggers is from CCGbank (Hockenmaier and Steedman, 2007), which is a CCG version of the original Penn Treebank (Marcus et al., 1993), a corpus of newswire sentences manually annotated with syntactic parse trees. A standard split is to take Sections 2-21 (39,604 sentences) as training data, Section 00 (1,913 sentences) as development data, and Section 23 (2,407 sentences) as test data. Extracting a grammar from Sections 2-21 results in 1,286 distinct lexical category types, with 439 of those types occurring only once in the training data.

The original CCG supertagger (Clark, 2002) was a maximum entropy ("maxent") tagger (Ratnaparkhi, 1996), which was state-of-the-art for sequence labelling tasks at the time. The main difference with today's neural taggers is that the features were defined by hand, in terms of feature templates, based on linguistic intuition. For example, the NLP researcher may have decided that a good feature for deciding the correct tag for a word is the previous word in the sentence, which would then become a feature template which gets filled in for each particular word being tagged. Both types of tagger use iterative algorithms for training, typically maximising the likelihood of the (supervised) training data, with the neural models benefitting from specialised GPU hardware. Another difference is that the Transformer-based model described in Section 2.2.1 builds on a pre-trained model which has already been trained on large amounts of data to perform a fairly generic language modelling task. It turns out that this pre-training stage—which has become available since the maxent taggers because of developments in neural networks, hardware, and the availability of data—is crucial for the resulting performance of the supertagger, which is fine-tuned for the supertagging task.

The per-word accuracy for the maxent supertagger was around 92% (see Table 1), compared with over 96% for the Penn Treebank pos-tagging task (Ratnaparkhi, 1996, Curran and Clark, 2003). An accuracy of 92% may sound reasonable, given the difficulty of the task, but with an average sentence length in the treebank of around 20-25 words, this would result in approximately two errors every sentence. Given the amount of information in the lexical categories, it is crucial for the subsequent parsing stage that the supertagging is correct. Hence Clark and Curran (2004a) developed a "multitagging" approach in which the supertagger is allowed to dynamically assign more than one

SUPERTAGGER	MODEL	ACC
Clark and Curran (2007b)	Maxent	91.5
Clark and Curran (2007b) (*w/gold pos*)	Maxent	92.6
Xu et al. (2015)	RNN	93.1
Lewis et al. (2016)	BiLSTM	94.1
Lewis et al. (2016) (+tri-training)	BiLSTM	94.9
Tian et al. (2020)	Transformer	96.2

TABLE 1: Supertagger accuracy evolution on Section 00 of CCGbank. Per-word accuracy is reported.

lexical category to a word, based on how certain the supertagger is of the category for that word. Allowing more than one lexical category increases the accuracy to almost 98% with only a small increase in the average per-word lexical category ambiguity (see the end of Section 2.2.1 below).

Development of the maxent supertagger from 2007 mainly consisted of adapting it to other domains (Rimell and Clark, 2008) and using it to increase the speed of CCG parsers (Kummerfeld et al., 2010). The first paper to use neural methods for CCG supertagging was Xu et al. (2015), which applies a vanilla RNN to the sequence labelling task. This resulted in substantial accuracy improvements (Table 1), and also produced a more robust supertagger that performed better on sentences from domains other than newswire (see the paper for details). Another improvement was that the maxent supertagger relied heavily on part-of-speech (POS) tags to define effective feature templates, and the accuracy degraded significantly when using automatically assigned, as opposed to gold-standard, POS tags (see the first two rows in Table 1). The RNN supertagger was able to surpass the accuracy of the maxent supertagger relying on gold POS, but without using POS tags as input at all.

Lewis et al. (2016) improved on the performance of the vanilla RNN by using a bi-directional LSTM, and obtained additional gains by training on large amounts of automatically parsed data. More specifically, the tri-training method (row 5 in the table) uses the lexical category sequences from parsed sentences as additional training data, but only those supertagged sentences on which two different CCG parsers agree. Finally, the last row of Table 1 shows the staggering improvements that can be had—over 50% reduction in error rate compared to the original maxent model—when using a pre-trained neural language model that is fine-tuned for the supertagging task. This model is described in the next section.

Other recent neural approaches to CCG supertagging include Clark et al. (2018) and Bhargava and Penn (2020). Bhargava and Penn (2020) is noteworthy because it uses neural sequence models to model the internal structure of lexical categories, which allows the supertagger to meaningfully assign non-zero probability mass to previously unseen lexical categories, as well as model rare categories, which is important given the long tail in the lexical category distribution.

2.2.1 CCG Supertagging with a Transformer-based Model

The field of NLP has experienced a period of rapid change in the last few years, due to the success of applying large-scale neural language models to a range of NLP tasks. The new paradigm relies on taking a pre-trained neural language model, which has been trained to carry out a fairly generic language modelling task such as predicting a missing word in a sentence, and fine-tuning it through additional supervised training for the task at hand (Brown et al., 2020). Despite the generic nature of the original language modelling task, the neural model is able to acquire large amounts of linguistic (and world) knowledge which can then be exploited for the downstream task.

Another innovation which has been particularly influential is the development of the Transformer neural architecture, which consists of many self-attention layers, where every pair of words in a sentence is connected via a number of attention "heads" (Vaswani et al., 2017, Devlin et al., 2019). Each attention head calculates a similarity score between transformed representations of the respective word embeddings, where one word acts as a "query" and the other as a "key". These scores are then used by each word to derive a probabilistic mixture of all the other words in the sentence, where the mixture elements ("values") are again transformed representations of the word embeddings. This mixture acts as a powerful word-in-context representation, and stacking the attention layers a number of times, combined with some non-linear, fully-connected layers, results in a highly non-linear contextualised representation of each word in the sentence.

Tian et al. (2020) apply this method to the CCG supertagging task, with great success. Figure 4, which is an embellished version of Figure 1 from the paper, shows the neural architecture. The first component is the BERT encoder (Devlin et al., 2019), which has already been pre-trained on large amounts of text using a masked language modelling objective. The output of BERT is a word embedding for each word in the input sentence. Then, an additional neural network takes the output of BERT, and also produces an embedding for each word. This additional network has not been pre-trained, and so requires supervised

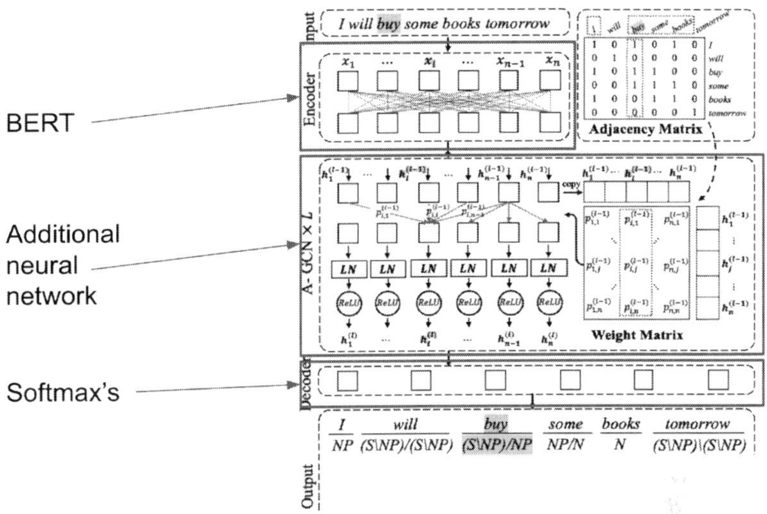

FIGURE 4: The neural architecture of the supertagger from Tian et al. (2020).

training data for its weights to be learned. In Tian et al. (2020) the additional network is a novel graph convolutional neural network (GCNN). Finally, there is an additional set of parameters which, for each output word embedding, define a softmax over the set of lexical categories. The output of the supertagger, for each input word, is the most probable lexical category according to the softmax distribution.

Training proceeds in a standard fashion, using the lexical category sequences from Sections 2-21 of CCGbank as supervised training data. The loss function is the cross-entropy loss, the minimisation of which is equivalent to putting as much probability mass as possible on each correct lexical category, relative to the incorrect lexical categories for each word (i.e. maximising the probability of the training data). A form of batch-based stochastic gradient descent is used to minimise the loss function, and dropout is used to prevent overfitting (Goodfellow et al., 2016). All of these techniques have now become standard in neural NLP. The implementation uses the neural network library PyTorch.

One feature of the neural supertagger, compared with the maxent supertagger, is that it does not model the lexical category sequence at all. One of the challenges in developing taggers using sequence modelling methods, such as HMMs (Brants, 2000), CRFs (Lafferty et al., 2001), and maxent models, is that the number of possible tag sequences grows exponentially with sentence length, so modelling them explicitly requires either heuristic methods such as beam search, or dynamic programming techniques such as Viterbi. In contrast, the probabilistic decision made by the neural supertagger of what lexical category to assign to each word is made independently of the decisions for the other words. The reason it performs so well is because of the highly contextualised nature of the output word embeddings, which already contain substantial amounts of information about the other words in the sentence.

There are a number of possibilities for the additional neural network in Figure 4. In fact, one possibility is not to add any additional layers at all, and simply fine-tune BERT, which works almost as well as the GCNN (Table 5 in Tian et al. (2020)). It is likely that adding in some additional attention layers, and training those with the supervised data, would work just as well.

If the NeST-CCG supertagger is to act as an effective front-end to a CCG parser, it would be useful for it to sometimes output more than one category for a word. In fact, NeST-CCG already has a hyperparameter which retains lexical categories based on their probabilities. Tuning this hyperparameter—let's call it γ—turns out to be highly effective for producing a multitagger. There is a trade-off between using a low γ value, which increases the chance of assigning the correct category, and a high γ which reduces the average number of categories per word. One of the motivations for supertagging is that, if the average number of categories per word can be kept low, then this greatly increases the efficiency of the parser (Clark and Curran, 2007b).

The optimal γ value depends on how "sharp" the lexical category distributions are, and this is affected by the number of training epochs for the NeST-CCG supertagger. NeST-CCG also has an additional hyperparameter—call it α—which sets a maximum number of lexical categories that can be assigned to a single word. A happy medium for these hyperparameters is $\gamma = 0.0005$, $\alpha = 10$, and 10 epochs, which results in a **multitagging accuracy of 99.3%** on the development data with **1.7 lexical categories per word** on average.[4] This compares very favourably with **97.6%** at **1.7 categories per word** from Clark and Curran (2007b). Hence the expectation is that this greatly improved multitagger will lead to improved parsing performance, which we turn to next.

[4] In order for a set of lexical categories assigned to a word to be "correct", the set needs to contain the one correct category. Hence multitagging "accuracy" increases monotonically with smaller γ values, as does the per-word ambiguity, reflecting the trade-off described above.

2.3 CCG Parsing

The job of a CCG parser is to take the output of a CCG supertagger as input, combine the categories together using the CCG combinatory rules, and return the best analysis as the output. This process requires a parsing algorithm, which determines the order in which the categories are put together; a parsing model, which scores each possible analysis; and a search algorithm, which efficiently finds the highest-scoring analysis. In addition, there are various options for what kind of analysis the parser returns as output.

The most popular form of parsing algorithms for CCG have been bottom-up, in which the lexical categories are combined first, followed by combinations of categories with increasing spans, eventually resulting in a root category spanning the whole sentence (Steedman, 2000). The first parsing algorithms to be successfully applied to wide-coverage CCG parsing were chart-based (Hockenmaier and Steedman, 2002, Clark and Curran, 2004b), followed by shift-reduce parsers (Zhang and Clark, 2011, Xu et al., 2014, Ambati et al., 2016). In this chapter we will be using a chart-based parser (described in Section 2.3.1).

The original CCG parsing models were based on lexicalised PCFGs and used relative frequency counts to estimate the model parameters, with backing-off techniques to deal with data sparsity (Hockenmaier and Steedman, 2002, Collins, 1997).[5] These were superseded by discriminative, feature-based models, essentially applying the maxent models that had worked so well for tagging to the parsing problem (Clark and Curran, 2004b, Riezler et al., 2002, Miyao and Tsujii, 2008). Alternative estimation methods based on the structured perceptron framework—which provides a particularly simple estimation technique—were also applied successfully to CCG (Clark and Curran, 2007a, Collins and Roark, 2004). The more recent neural parsing models that have been applied to CCG are mentioned in Section 2.3.2.

In terms of search, the choice is between optimal dynamic programming, heuristic beam search, or optimal A* search (Lee et al., 2016). The early CCG parsing work focused on dynamic programming algorithms (Hockenmaier and Steedman, 2002, Clark and Curran, 2004b), whereas the shift-reduce CCG parsers tended to use beam search, performing surprisingly well even with relatively small beam widths (Zhang and Clark, 2011). The CCG parser described below also uses beam search, but applied to a chart.

[5] For a number of citation lists in this section, the first citations give the relevant CCG papers, followed by the (non-CCG) work on which they were based.

Finally, the main output formats have been either the CCG derivation itself, a dependency graph where the dependency types are defined in terms of the CCG lexical categories (Clark et al., 2002, Hockenmaier and Steedman, 2002), or a dependency graph using a fairly formalism-independent representation (Clark and Curran, 2007b). It has been argued that dependency types are especially useful for parser evaluation (Carroll et al., 1998), in particular for CCG (Clark and Hockenmaier, 2002), as well as for downstream NLP tasks and applications. In this chapter the parser output will be CCG dependencies (used for evaluation), with a novel application of the derivations suggested in the Conclusion. There is also a large body of work on interpreting CCG derivations to produce semantic representations as logical forms, in particular for Discourse Representation Theory (Bos et al., 2004, 2017, Liu et al., 2021), Abstract Meaning Representation (Artzi et al., 2015), as well as for more general semantic parsing tasks (Zettlemoyer and Collins, 2005, Artzi et al., 2014).

2.3.1 CCG Parsing with a Neural Supertagger Front End

This section describes the accuracy gains that can be obtained by simply using the neural supertagger described in Section 2.2.1 as a front-end to an existing CCG parser. These experiments further demonstrate the importance of supertagging for CCG (Clark and Curran, 2004a), and further realise the original vision of Bangalore and Joshi (1999) for supertagging as almost parsing.

The CCG parser that we will use is the Java C&C parser described in Clark et al. (2015), which is essentially a Java reimplementation of the C&C parser (Clark and Curran, 2007b, Curran et al., 2007). Java C&C uses a new chart-based beam-search decoder, which removes any restrictions imposed by dynamic programming algorithms on the locality of the model features (at the cost of optimality), together with the max-violation framework of Huang et al. (2012) for training the linear model. Java C&C also has a new "skimmer" mode which enables the parser to return a dependency analysis even when there is no full spanning derivation of the input sentence in the chart.

Table 2 shows the accuracy on the development data of the original C&C parser and the Java C&C parser, the latter with both the maxent supertagger and the neural supertagger. The parser accuracy scores are the standard measures of labelled precision and recall over CCG dependencies, F-score (harmonic mean of precision and recall), and lexical category accuracy. The coverage figure is the percentage of

PARSER	S-TAGGER	P	R	F	CAT	COV.
C&C	Maxent	–	–	85.3	–	99.1
C&C †	Maxent	88.1	86.4	87.2	94.2	99.1
Java C&C †	Maxent	88.0	87.3	87.7	94.3	100.0
Java C&C	Transformer	91.9	91.5	91.7	96.3	100.0

TABLE 2: Parser accuracy of (Java) C&C on Sec. 00 with different supertaggers. Lines marked with † refer to parsers with gold POS.

sentences in Section 00 used for the evaluation. The figures for the C&C parser are taken from Clark and Curran (2007b), and those for Java C&C with the maxent supertagger from Clark et al. (2015).

Moving from row 1 to 2 in the table, we again see the reliance on POS tags as features, for both the maxent supertagger and the original C&C parsing model. Using automatically-assigned POS tags reduces the overall F-score by almost 2%. Row 3 shows the improvements that are obtained with Java C&C, both in terms of accuracy, but also in terms of coverage, since the parser now returns an analysis for all the sentences in the development data (using the "skimmer" mode mentioned above). Finally, row 4 shows the staggering improvements that can be obtained by simply replacing the maxent supertagger with the neural supertagger. The coverage is again 100% through use of the skimmer. These figures were obtained using a beam size of 32 in the parser.

2.3.2 CCG Parsing with a Transformer-based Model

The parser model used in Section 2.3.1 is a linear model based on discrete feature templates defined by hand, which raises the obvious question of whether additional gains can be obtained by using a neural model in the parser, as well as the supertagger. Some neural models for CCG parsing have already appeared in the literature (Xu et al., 2016, Xu, 2016, Lee et al., 2016, Ambati et al., 2016, Stanojević and Steedman, 2019), but none of these use the pre-trained plus fine-tuning Transformer-based paradigm that was so successful for the supertagger.

The difficulty with applying a similar technique to a parse chart is that scores need to be defined for each cell in the chart (corresponding to each span in the sentence), whereas the neural architecture only produces output embeddings for each word. Figure 5 gives the general idea (adapted from Figure 4 for the supertagger). How can the output embeddings for each word be used to produce an embedding for each span? In fact, this problem has already been solved for dependency parsing by Wang and Chang (2016), and successfully applied to the Penn Treebank constituency parsing task by Stern et al. (2017) and

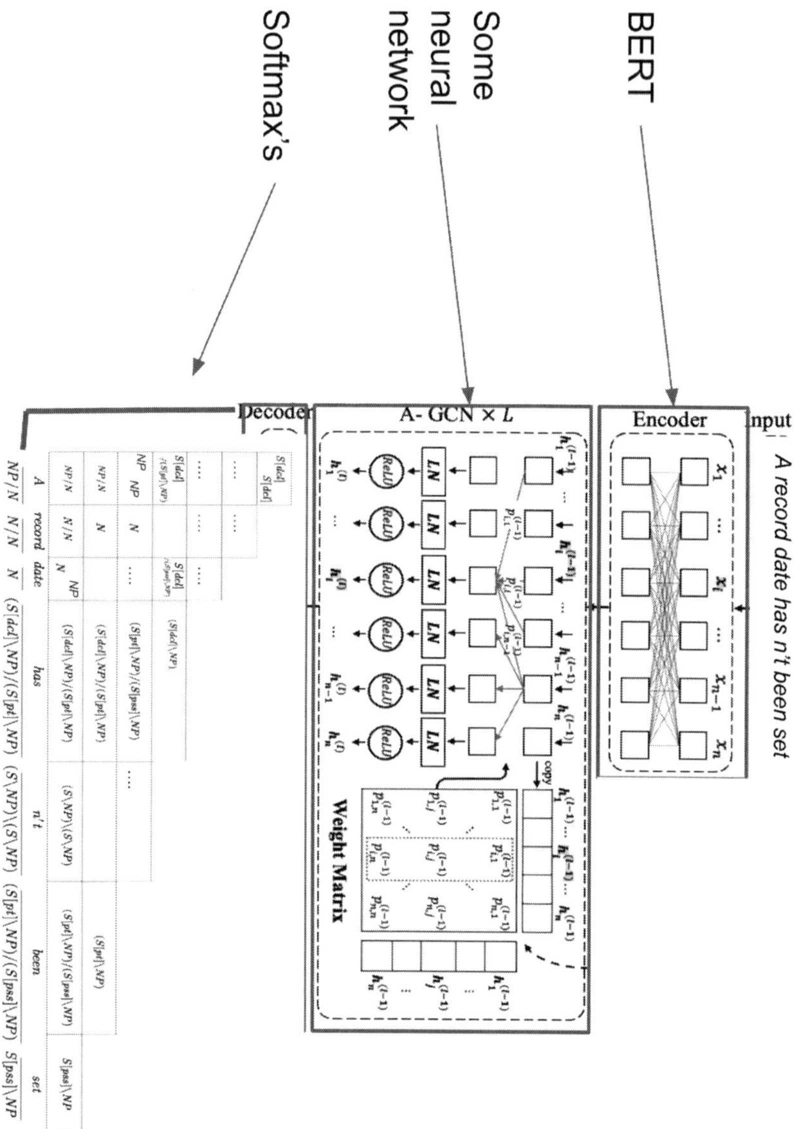

FIGURE 5: The architecture from Tian et al. (2020) adapted for chart parsing.

Kitaev and Klein (2018), in the latter case using a fine-tuned BERT encoder. The idea is to produce an embedding for a span by *subtracting* the embedding for the word at the beginning of the span from the embedding of the word at the end. This is highly intuitive for the left-to-right LSTM used by Wang and Chang (2016) (and in the bidirectional setting, the subtraction would be performed in the opposite order for the right-to-left LSTM); however, it is less intuitive for the Transformer, which has no encoding direction. Even so, Stern et al. (2017) were able to successfully adapt this method for the Transformer.

Now that we have a method of producing an embedding for each cell, an extra set of parameters can be used to define a softmax over all possible constituent labels in the chart. This softmax can then be applied to each cell, producing a list of label-score pairs, with the score for a derivation defined as the sum of the scores (log-probabilities) for each node in the derivation. Kitaev and Klein (2018) used these scores to define a Viterbi-style dynamic programming algorithm for finding the highest-scoring derivation. Note that, as for the supertagger case, the scores for each cell are calculated independently of all the other cells (i.e. there is no explicit statistical modelling of the tree structure). The reason the model is so effective, despite this very strong independence assumption, is because of the highly contextualised nature of the word embeddings used to derive the cell embeddings. However, for the CCG case (and unlike the Penn Treebank parsing problem), there is a twist: any categories that are selected by a parsing algorithm to form a derivation must conform to the combinatory rules of CCG, and the independence assumption means that the highest-scoring tree may not satisfy this constraint.

Kato and Matsubara (2021) solve this problem by defining a new representation for a CCG constituent so that the items being scored conform to the CCG grammar.[6] Here I adopt a much simpler method: only apply the score function to derivations that are produced by the grammar. That way, even if a category receives a high score for a span, it will only appear in the output if it forms part of a high-scoring, legal CCG derivation. Moreover, adapting the chart-based beam-search algorithm to use the new scores is particularly straightforward: simply replace the scores for a sub-derivation previously calculated according to the feature-based model with the scores from the neural model (where the score for a sub-derivation is the sum of the scores of the category labels on each node).

[6] A useful side-effect of the new representation is the possibility of modelling unseen categories, a feature shared with Bhargava and Penn (2020).

Parser	S-tagger/ Parser Model	P	R	F	Cat	Cov.
C&C	Maxent/Maxent	86.2	84.7	85.5	93.0	99.6
C&C (†)	Maxent/Maxent	88.3	87.0	87.6	94.3	99.6
Java C&C	T-former/Linear	92.0	91.8	91.9	96.4	100.0
Java C&C	T-former/T-former	92.8	93.0	92.9	96.5	100.0

TABLE 3: Parser accuracy of Java C&C on Sec. 23 with neural models for both supertagger and parser, compared to other supertagger-parser combinations. The symbol † indicates the use of gold POS.

Paper	S-tagger/Parser	F	Cat
Xu (2016)	LSTM/Shift-Reduce(LSTM)	87.8	94.6
Lewis et al. (2016)	LSTM/A*	88.1	–
Vaswani et al. (2016)	LSTM/Java C&C	88.3	–
Lee et al. (2016)	LSTM/A*(Tree-LSTM)	88.7	–
Yoshikawa et al. (2017)	LSTM/A*(LSTM)	88.8	–
Stanojević and Steedman (2020)	LSTM/Shift-Reduce(LSTM)	90.6	95.6
Tian et al. (2020)	T-former/EasyCCG	90.7	96.4
This chapter	T-former/Java C&C (w/T-former)	92.9	96.5

TABLE 4: Parser accuracy of Java C&C on Sec. 23 with neural models for both supertagger and parser, compared to some recent CCG parsers in the literature.

I trained a CCG parsing model by running the training code from Kitaev et al. (2019) on the derivations in Sections 2-21 of CCGbank. Following Kitaev and Klein (2018), unary chains in the CCG derivations—which arise as a result of type-raising and the unary type-changing rules in CCGbank (Hockenmaier and Steedman, 2007)—were represented as a single label. I also modified the Java C&C code so that it can take scored constituents from the neural parser as input. As before, the parser model also uses the log-probabilities from the supertagger as additional scores, but this time weighted equally with the span-based scores (so the score for a derivation is the sum of the scores on each node, including the lexical categories at the leaves).

Table 3 shows the performance of the new parser on the Section 23 test set, compared with the other C&C parsers, which use various combinations of supertagger and parser models. Replacing the linear parsing model based on hand-defined feature templates with the span-based neural model resulted in an absolute improvement of 1.0 F-score, and the improvement over the original C&C model represents a reduction in error rate of more than 50%. Moreover, the percentage of sentences that are completely correct is now 54.1 (not shown in the table), compared with 32.9% for the original C&C parser.

Table 4 shows the performance of the Java C&C parser with neural models compared with recent CCG parsing results from the literature, where all the accuracy figures are taken from the respective papers. The final F-score of 92.9 on the test set represents a new state-of-the-art for the CCGbank parsing task.

Table 5 shows the accuracy of the parser by dependency relation, with the table copied from Clark and Curran (2007b); the new figures for this work are in the final F column, and the *#deps* column gives the number of dependencies of the corresponding type in Section 00 (recalculated to reflect the 100% coverage with Java C&C). Substantial improvements over the original C&C parser can be seen across the board. Of particular note are the improvements for *np modifying prep* and *vp modifying prep*, which are dependencies potentially resulting from PP-attachment ambiguities, and the 100% accuracy scores for *object rel pronoun*, which are long-range dependencies resulting from extraction out of a relative clause and particularly difficult for parsers to recover correctly (Rimell et al., 2009).

Finally, Table 6 shows how the parser accuracy and parser speed varies with beam width. Accuracies are reported for Section 00, and the approximate speeds are calculated using the first 1,000 sentences of Section 00, running on a linux server.[7] The %-skimmed column gives the percentage of sentences that are analysed using the skimmer mode of the parser.[8] The parser is remarkably resilient to a decreasing beam width, with accuracy and coverage only being substantially affected with beam widths as low as 4. The ability of neural models to effectively utilise a large context when making decisions—thereby reducing the need for search—has been seen already for parsing, especially for shift-reduce parsing where even fully-greedy parsers can be highly accurate (Chen and Manning, 2014, Xu et al., 2016). The speeds themselves are eclipsed by the parser of Lewis et al. (2016), which can parse over 2,000 sentences a second by exploiting the efficiency of the A* parsing algorithm and running the supertagger in parallel on a GPU. However, the speeds reported in Table 6 are reasonable considering that the

[7]Model Intel Xeon W-2265 CPU @ 3.50GHz.

[8]This percentage goes up and down with beam width because there are two parameters which affect it: the beam width itself, since a smaller beam reduces the chances of the chart containing a spanning derivation; and the maximum chart size allowed by the parser, which will get hit more often—hence triggering the skimmer—with a larger beam.

Lexical category	Arg Slot		*#deps*	F(C&C)	F
N/N_{1}	1	*nominal modifier*	7 443	95.5	98.1
NP/N_{1}	1	*determiner*	4 153	96.3	98.8
$(NP\backslash NP_{1})/NP_{2}$	2	*np modifying prep*	2 390	85.4	94.3
$(NP\backslash NP_{1})/NP_{2}$	1	*np modifying prep*	2 193	83.6	93.9
$((S\backslash NP)\backslash(S_{1}\backslash NP))/NP_{2}$	2	*vp modifying prep*	1 177	72.6	85.6
$((S\backslash NP)\backslash(S_{1}\backslash NP))/NP_{2}$	1	*vp modifying prep*	1 068	71.4	84.2
$(S[dcl]\backslash NP_{1})/NP_{2}$	1	*transitive verb*	877	83.5	95.5
$(S[dcl]\backslash NP_{1})/NP_{2}$	2	*transitive verb*	923	83.9	96.0
$(S\backslash NP)\backslash(S_{1}\backslash NP)$	1	*adverbial modifier*	750	86.8	93.0
PP/NP_{1}	1	*prep complement*	885	72.5	86.4
$(S[b]\backslash NP_{1})/NP_{2}$	2	*inf transitive verb*	648	85.5	94.8
$(S[dcl]\backslash NP_{1})/(S[b]_{2}\backslash NP)$	2	*auxiliary*	480	97.8	99.2
$(S[dcl]\backslash NP_{1})/(S[b]_{2}\backslash NP)$	1	*auxiliary*	488	93.6	98.0
$(S[b]\backslash NP_{1})/NP_{2}$	1	*inf transitive verb*	529	75.8	90.5
$(NP/N_{1})\backslash NP_{2}$	1	*s genitive*	385	96.1	97.9
$(NP/N_{1})\backslash NP_{2}$	2	*s genitive*	374	98.0	99.2
$(S[dcl]\backslash NP_{1})/S[dcl]_{2}$	1	*sentential comp verb*	387	92.9	98.3
$(NP\backslash NP_{1})/(S[dcl]_{2}\backslash NP)$	1	*subject rel pronoun*	277	83.5	93.8
$(NP\backslash NP_{1})/(S[dcl]_{2}\backslash NP)$	2	*subject rel pronoun*	279	97.3	99.1
$(NP\backslash NP_{1})/(S[dcl]_{2}/NP)$	1	*object rel pronoun*	26	75.0	100.0
$(NP\backslash NP_{1})/(S[dcl]_{2}/NP)$	2	*object rel pronoun*	23	84.4	100.0
$NP/(S[dcl]_{1}/NP)$	1	*headless obj rel pron*	17	100.0	100.0

TABLE 5: Parser accuracy on Section 00 by dependency relation.

BEAM-WIDTH	F (SEC. 00)	SENTS/SEC	%-SKIMMED
64	93.0	8	0.9
32	93.0	23	0.7
16	93.0	51	0.5
8	92.9	105	0.4
4	91.7	167	2.2

TABLE 6: The speed/accuracy trade-off with different beam sizes.

implementation is in Java and has not been optimised, and the parser was run on the CPU; these speeds of around 100 sentences per second are still high enough to be used for large-scale textual data analysis.

2.4 Conclusion

This chapter has shown how a combination of Transformer-based neural models and a symbolic CCG grammar can lead to substantial gains over existing approaches to CCG parsing. The staggering improvements compared to the original C&C parser (Clark and Curran, 2004b), with overall dependency accuracies of almost 93% and complete sentence accuracies of 54%, are representative of how NLP has evolved over this time. In terms of how useful such parsers are for downstream tasks and applications, the success of large-scale language models (Brown et al., 2020) has, for now at least, largely replaced the old NLP pipeline in which parsers played a prominent role. Whether this trend will continue, and what this trend means for the nature of linguistic representation and learning, remain open questions (Lappin, 2021). However, even if this trend does continue, there may still be unforeseen roles for structural analysis in NLP; for example at Cambridge Quantum we are investigating how parsers can be used to build quantum circuits, exploiting the similarities between the compositional structures in categorial grammar and those in vector spaces, the latter of which lie at the heart of quantum computation (Coecke et al., 2010, Yeung and Kartsaklis, 2021, Lorenz et al., 2021).

Acknowledgments

Thanks to the developers of the Tian et al. (2020) and Kitaev et al. (2019) codebases for making their code freely available and so easy to use. Thanks to Mark Steedman and Julia Hockenmaier for starting the Edinburgh CCG parsing project all those years ago, and to James Curran for the great memories developing the C&C parser. Thanks to the collaborators and students down the years who have worked on the parser, including Laura Rimell, Yue Zhang, Wenduan Xu, Luana Bulat, and Darren Foong. And finally, thanks to Shalom Lappin; Ilyas Khan; Konstantinos Meichanetzidis, Dimitri Kartsaklis and the rest of the Compositional Intelligence team at Cambridge Quantum for providing feedback on this latest work.

References

Ajdukiewicz, Kazimierz. 1935. Die syntaktische konnexität. *Studia Philosophica* 1:1–27.

Ambati, Bharat Ram, Tejaswini Deoskar, and Mark Steedman. 2016. Shift-reduce CCG parsing using neural network models. In *Proceedings of the 2016 Conference of the North American Chapter of the Association for Computational Linguistics: Human Language Technologies*, pages 447–453. San Diego, California: Association for Computational Linguistics.

Artzi, Yoav, Dipanjan Das, and Slav Petrov. 2014. Learning compact lexicons for CCG semantic parsing. In *Proceedings of the 2014 Conference on Empirical Methods in Natural Language Processing (EMNLP)*, pages 1273–1283. Doha, Qatar: Association for Computational Linguistics.

Artzi, Yoav, Kenton Lee, and Luke Zettlemoyer. 2015. Broad-coverage CCG semantic parsing with AMR. In *Proceedings of the 2015 Conference on Empirical Methods in Natural Language Processing*, pages 1699–1710. Lisbon, Portugal: Association for Computational Linguistics.

Baldridge, Jason. 2002. *Lexically Specified Derivational Control in Combinatory Categorial Grammar*. Ph.D. thesis, Edinburgh University.

Bangalore, Srinivas and Aravind Joshi. 1999. Supertagging: An approach to almost parsing. *Computational Linguistics* 25(2):237–265.

Bar-Hillel, Yehoshua. 1953. A quasi-arithmetical notation for syntactic description. *Language* 29:47–58.

Bhargava, Aditya and Gerald Penn. 2020. Supertagging with CCG primitives. In *Proceedings of the 5th Workshop on Representation Learning for NLP*, pages 194–204. Online: Association for Computational Linguistics.

Bos, Johan, Valerio Basile, Kilian Evang, NJ Venhuizen, and Johannes Bjerva. 2017. The groningen meaning bank. In N. Ide and J. Pustejovsky, eds., *Handbook of Linguistic Annotation*, pages 463–496. Springer.

Bos, Johan, Stephen Clark, Mark Steedman, James R. Curran, and Julia Hockenmaier. 2004. Wide-coverage semantic representations from a CCG parser. In *Proceedings of COLING-04*, pages 1240–1246. Geneva, Switzerland.

Brants, Thorsten. 2000. TnT – a statistical part-of-speech tagger. In *Sixth Applied Natural Language Processing Conference*, pages 224–231. Seattle, Washington, USA: Association for Computational Linguistics.

Brown, Tom, Benjamin Mann, Nick Ryder, Melanie Subbiah, Jared D Kaplan, Prafulla Dhariwal, Arvind Neelakantan, Pranav Shyam, Girish Sastry, Amanda Askell, Sandhini Agarwal, Ariel Herbert-Voss, Gretchen Krueger, Tom Henighan, Rewon Child, Aditya Ramesh, Daniel Ziegler, Jeffrey Wu, Clemens Winter, Chris Hesse, Mark Chen, Eric Sigler, Mateusz Litwin, Scott Gray, Benjamin Chess, Jack Clark, Christopher Berner, Sam McCandlish, Alec Radford, Ilya Sutskever, and Dario Amodei. 2020. Language models are few-shot learners. In H. Larochelle, M. Ranzato, R. Hadsell, M. F. Balcan, and H. Lin, eds., *Advances in Neural Information Processing Systems*, vol. 33, pages 1877–1901. Curran Associates, Inc.

Carroll, John, Ted Briscoe, and Antonio Sanfilippo. 1998. Parser evaluation: a survey and a new proposal. In *Proceedings of the 1st LREC Conference*, pages 447–454. Granada, Spain.

Chen, Danqi and Christopher Manning. 2014. A fast and accurate dependency parser using neural networks. In *Proceedings of the 2014 Conference on Empirical Methods in Natural Language Processing (EMNLP)*, pages 740–750. Doha, Qatar: Association for Computational Linguistics.

Chomsky, Noam. 1965. *Aspects of the Theory of Syntax*. MIT Press.

Clark, Kevin, Minh-Thang Luong, Christopher D. Manning, and Quoc Le. 2018. Semi-supervised sequence modeling with cross-view training. In *Proceedings of the 2018 Conference on Empirical Methods in Natural Language Processing*, pages 1914–1925. Brussels, Belgium: Association for Computational Linguistics.

Clark, Stephen. 2002. A supertagger for Combinatory Categorial Grammar. In *Proceedings of the TAG+ Workshop*, pages 19–24. Venice, Italy.

Clark, Stephen, Ann Copestake, James R. Curran, Yue Zhang, Aurelie Herbelot, James Haggerty, Byung-Gyu Ahn, Curt Van Wyk, Jessika Roesner, Jonathan Kummerfeld, and Tim Dawborn. 2009. Large-scale syntactic processing: Parsing the web. Tech. rep., Center for Language and Speech Processing, Johns Hopkins University, Baltimore, MD.

Clark, Stephen and James Curran. 2007a. Perceptron training for a wide-coverage lexicalized-grammar parser. In *ACL 2007 Workshop on Deep Linguistic Processing*, pages 9–16. Prague, Czech Republic: Association for Computational Linguistics.

Clark, Stephen and James R. Curran. 2004a. The importance of supertagging for wide-coverage CCG parsing. In *Proceedings of COLING-04*, pages 282–288. Geneva, Switzerland.

Clark, Stephen and James R. Curran. 2004b. Parsing the WSJ using CCG and log-linear models. In *Proceedings of the 42nd Meeting of the ACL*, pages 104–111. Barcelona, Spain.

Clark, Stephen and James R. Curran. 2007b. Wide-coverage efficient statistical parsing with CCG and log-linear models. *Computational Linguistics* 33(4):493–552.

Clark, Stephen, Darren Foong, Luana Bulat, and Wenduan Xu. 2015. The Java version of the C&C parser: Version 0.95. Tech. rep., The University of Cambridge Computer Laboratory, Cambridge, UK.

Clark, Stephen and Julia Hockenmaier. 2002. Evaluating a wide-coverage CCG parser. In *Proceedings of the LREC Beyond Parseval Workshop*. Las Palmas, Spain.

Clark, Stephen, Julia Hockenmaier, and Mark Steedman. 2002. Building deep dependency structures with a wide-coverage CCG parser. In *Proceedings of the 40th Meeting of the ACL*, pages 327–334. Philadelphia, PA.

Coecke, Bob, Mehrnoosh Sadrzadeh, and Stephen Clark. 2010. Mathematical foundations for a compositional distributional model of meaning. In van Bentham and Moortgat, eds., *Linguistic Analysis 36 (1-4): A Festschrift for Joachim Lambek*.

Collins, Michael. 1997. Three generative, lexicalised models for statistical parsing. In *Proceedings of the 35th Meeting of the ACL*, pages 16–23. Madrid, Spain.

Collins, Michael and James Brooks. 1995. Prepositional phrase attachment through a backed-off model. In *Third Workshop on Very Large Corpora*.

Collins, Michael and Brian Roark. 2004. Incremental parsing with the perceptron algorithm. In *Proceedings of the 42nd Meeting of the ACL*, pages 111–118. Barcelona, Spain.

Curran, James, Stephen Clark, and Johan Bos. 2007. Linguistically motivated large-scale NLP with C&C and boxer. In *Proceedings of the 45th Annual Meeting of the Association for Computational Linguistics Companion Volume Proceedings of the Demo and Poster Sessions*, pages 33–36. Prague, Czech Republic: Association for Computational Linguistics.

Curran, James R. and Stephen Clark. 2003. Investigating GIS and smoothing for maximum entropy taggers. In *10th Conference of the European Chapter of the Association for Computational Linguistics*. Budapest, Hungary: Association for Computational Linguistics.

Curry, Haskell B. and Robert Feys. 1958. *Combinatory Logic: Vol. I*. North Holland: Amsterdam.

Devlin, Jacob, Ming-Wei Chang, Kenton Lee, and Kristina Toutanova. 2019. BERT: Pre-training of deep bidirectional transformers for language understanding. In *Proceedings of the 2019 Conference of the North American Chapter of the Association for Computational Linguistics: Human Language Technologies, Volume 1 (Long and Short Papers)*, pages 4171–4186. Minneapolis, Minnesota: Association for Computational Linguistics.

Fowler, Timothy A. D. and Gerald Penn. 2010. Accurate context-free parsing with Combinatory Categorial Grammar. In *Proceedings of the 48th Annual Meeting of the Association for Computational Linguistics*, pages 335–344. Uppsala, Sweden: Association for Computational Linguistics.

Goodfellow, Ian, Yoshua Bengio, and Aaron Courville. 2016. *Deep Learning*. MIT Press.

Hockenmaier, Julia and Mark Steedman. 2002. Generative models for statistical parsing with Combinatory Categorial Grammar. In *Proceedings of the 40th Meeting of the ACL*, pages 335–342. Philadelphia, PA.

Hockenmaier, Julia and Mark Steedman. 2007. CCGbank: A corpus of CCG derivations and dependency structures extracted from the Penn Treebank. *Computational Linguistics* 33(3):355–396.

Huang, Liang, Suphan Fayong, and Yang Guo. 2012. Structured perceptron with inexact search. In *Proceedings of the 2012 Conference of the North American Chapter of the Association for Computational Linguistics: Human Language Technologies*, pages 142–151. Montréal, Canada: Association for Computational Linguistics.

Joshi, A. K. 1987. An introduction to tree adjoining grammars. In A. Manaster-Ramer, ed., *Mathematics of Language*. John Benjamins.

Joshi, A. K., K. Vijay-Shanker, and D. J. Weir. 1991. The convergence of mildly context-sensitive grammar formalisms. In P. Sells, S. Shieber, and T. Wasow, eds., *Foundational Issues in Natural Language Processing*, pages 31–81. MIT Press, Cambridge MA.

Kasai, Jungo, Robert Frank, Pauli Xu, William Merrill, and Owen Rambow. 2018. End-to-end graph-based TAG parsing with neural networks. In *Proceedings of the 2018 Conference of the North American Chapter of the Association for Computational Linguistics: Human Language Technologies, Volume 1 (Long Papers)*, pages 1181–1194. New Orleans, Louisiana: Association for Computational Linguistics.

Kato, Yoshihide and Shigeki Matsubara. 2021. A new representation for span-based CCG parsing. In *Proceedings of the 2021 Conference on Empirical Methods in Natural Language Processing (EMNLP)*. Punta Cana, Dominican Republic: Association for Computational Linguistics.

Kitaev, Nikita, Steven Cao, and Dan Klein. 2019. Multilingual constituency parsing with self-attention and pre-training. In *Proceedings of the 57th Annual Meeting of the Association for Computational Linguistics*, pages 3499–3505. Florence, Italy: Association for Computational Linguistics.

Kitaev, Nikita and Dan Klein. 2018. Constituency parsing with a self-attentive encoder. In *Proceedings of the 56th Annual Meeting of the Association for Computational Linguistics (Volume 1: Long Papers)*, pages 2676–2686. Melbourne, Australia: Association for Computational Linguistics.

Kuhlmann, Marco, Alexander Koller, and Giorgio Satta. 2015. Lexicalization and generative power in CCG. *Computational Linguistics* 41(2):187–219.

Kuhlmann, Marco, Giorgio Satta, and Peter Jonsson. 2018. On the complexity of CCG parsing. *Computational Linguistics* 44(3):447–482.

Kummerfeld, Jonathan K., Jessika Roesner, Tim Dawborn, James Haggerty, James R. Curran, and Stephen Clark. 2010. Faster parsing by supertagger adaptation. In *Proceedings of the 48th Annual Meeting of the Association for Computational Linguistics*, pages 345–355. Uppsala, Sweden: Association for Computational Linguistics.

Lafferty, John D., Andrew McCallum, and Fernando C. N. Pereira. 2001. Conditional random fields: Probabilistic models for segmenting and labeling sequence data. In *Proceedings of the Eighteenth International Conference on Machine Learning*, ICML '01, pages 282–289. San Francisco, CA, USA: Morgan Kaufmann Publishers Inc. ISBN 1-55860-778-1.

Lambek, Joachim. 2008. *From Word to Sentence*. Polimetrica.

Lappin, Shalom. 2021. *Deep Learning and Linguistic Representation*. Oxford: CRC Press, Taylor and Francis.

Lee, Kenton, Mike Lewis, and Luke Zettlemoyer. 2016. Global neural CCG parsing with optimality guarantees. In *Proceedings of the 2016 Conference on Empirical Methods in Natural Language Processing*, pages 2366–2376. Austin, Texas: Association for Computational Linguistics.

Lewis, Mike, Kenton Lee, and Luke Zettlemoyer. 2016. LSTM CCG parsing. In *Proceedings of the 2016 Conference of the North American Chapter of the Association for Computational Linguistics: Human Language Technologies*, pages 221–231. San Diego, California: Association for Computational Linguistics.

Liu, Jiangming, Shay B. Cohen, Mirella Lapata, and Johan Bos. 2021. Universal Discourse Representation Structure Parsing. *Computational Linguistics* 47(2):445–476.

Lorenz, Robin, Anna Pearson, Konstantinos Meichanetzidis, Dimitri Kartsaklis, and Bob Coecke. 2021. QNLP in practice: Running compositional models of meaning on a quantum computer. Tech. Rep. arXiv 2102.12846v1, Cambridge Quantum Computing.

Marcus, Mitchell, Beatrice Santorini, and Mary Marcinkiewicz. 1993. Building a large annotated corpus of English: The Penn Treebank. *Computational Linguistics* 19(2):313–330.

Miyao, Yusuke and Jun'ichi Tsujii. 2008. Feature forest models for probabilistic HPSG parsing. *Computational Linguistics* 34(1):35–80.

Moortgat, Michael. 1997. Categorial type logics. In J. van Benthem and A. ter Meulen, eds., *Handbook of Logic and Language*, chap. 2, pages 93–177. Elsevier, Amsterdam and MIT Press, Cambridge MA.

Ratnaparkhi, Adwait. 1996. A maximum entropy model for part-of-speech tagging. In *Proceedings of the EMNLP Conference*, pages 133–142. Philadelphia, PA.

Riezler, Stefan, Tracy H. King, Ronald M. Kaplan, Richard Crouch, John T. Maxwell III, and Mark Johnson. 2002. Parsing the Wall Street Journal using a Lexical-Functional Grammar and discriminative estimation techniques. In *Proceedings of the 40th Meeting of the ACL*, pages 271–278. Philadelphia, PA.

Rimell, Laura and Stephen Clark. 2008. Adapting a lexicalized-grammar parser to contrasting domains. In *Proceedings of the 2008 Conference on Empirical Methods in Natural Language Processing*, pages 475–484. Honolulu, Hawaii: Association for Computational Linguistics.

Rimell, Laura, Stephen Clark, and Mark Steedman. 2009. Unbounded dependency recovery for parser evaluation. In *Proceedings of the 2009 Conference on Empirical Methods in Natural Language Processing*, pages 813–821. Singapore: Association for Computational Linguistics.

Shieber, Stuart. 1985. Evidence against the context-freeness of natural language. *Linguistics and Philosophy* 8:333–343.

Stanojević, Miloš and Mark Steedman. 2019. CCG parsing algorithm with incremental tree rotation. In *Proceedings of the 2019 Conference of the North American Chapter of the Association for Computational Linguistics: Human Language Technologies, Volume 1 (Long and Short Papers)*, pages 228–239. Minneapolis, Minnesota: Association for Computational Linguistics.

Stanojević, Miloš and Mark Steedman. 2020. Max-margin incremental CCG parsing. In *Proceedings of the 58th Annual Meeting of the Association for Computational Linguistics*, pages 4111–4122. Online: Association for Computational Linguistics.

Steedman, Mark. 1996. *Surface Structure and Interpretation.* Cambridge, MA: The MIT Press.

Steedman, Mark. 2000. *The Syntactic Process*. Cambridge, MA: The MIT Press.

Stern, Mitchell, Jacob Andreas, and Dan Klein. 2017. A minimal span-based neural constituency parser. In *Proceedings of the 55th Annual Meeting of the Association for Computational Linguistics (Volume 1: Long Papers)*, pages 818–827. Vancouver, Canada: Association for Computational Linguistics.

Tian, Yuanhe, Yan Song, and Fei Xia. 2020. Supertagging Combinatory Categorial Grammar with attentive graph convolutional networks. In *Proceedings of the 2020 Conference on Empirical Methods in Natural Language Processing (EMNLP)*, pages 6037–6044. Online: Association for Computational Linguistics.

Vaswani, Ashish, Yonatan Bisk, Kenji Sagae, and Ryan Musa. 2016. Supertagging with LSTMs. In *Proceedings of the 2016 Conference of the North American Chapter of the Association for Computational Linguistics: Human Language Technologies*, pages 232–237. San Diego, California: Association for Computational Linguistics.

Vaswani, Ashish, Noam Shazeer, Niki Parmar, Jakob Uszkoreit, Llion Jones, Aidan N Gomez, Łukasz Kaiser, and Illia Polosukhin. 2017. Attention is all you need. In *Advances in Neural Information Processing Systems*, pages 5998–6008.

Vijay-Shanker, K. and David Weir. 1993. Parsing some constrained grammar formalisms. *Computational Linguistics* 19:591–636.

Wang, Wenhui and Baobao Chang. 2016. Graph-based dependency parsing with bidirectional LSTM. In *Proceedings of the 54th Annual Meeting of the Association for Computational Linguistics (Volume 1: Long Papers)*, pages 2306–2315. Berlin, Germany: Association for Computational Linguistics.

Weir, David. 1992. A geometric hierarchy beyond context-free languages. *Theoretical Computer Science* 104(2):235–261.

Xu, Wenduan. 2016. LSTM shift-reduce CCG parsing. In *Proceedings of the 2016 Conference on Empirical Methods in Natural Language Processing*, pages 1754–1764. Austin, Texas: Association for Computational Linguistics.

Xu, Wenduan, Michael Auli, and Stephen Clark. 2015. CCG supertagging with a recurrent neural network. In *Proceedings of the 53rd Annual Meeting of the Association for Computational Linguistics and the 7th International Joint Conference on Natural Language Processing (Volume 2: Short Papers)*, pages 250–255. Beijing, China: Association for Computational Linguistics.

Xu, Wenduan, Michael Auli, and Stephen Clark. 2016. Expected F-measure training for shift-reduce parsing with recurrent neural networks. In *Proceedings of the 2016 Conference of the North American Chapter of the Association for Computational Linguistics: Human Language Technologies*, pages 210–220. San Diego, California: Association for Computational Linguistics.

Xu, Wenduan, Stephen Clark, and Yue Zhang. 2014. Shift-reduce CCG parsing with a dependency model. In *Proceedings of the 52nd Annual Meeting of the Association for Computational Linguistics (Volume 1: Long Papers)*, pages 218–227. Baltimore, Maryland: Association for Computational Linguistics.

Yeung, Richie and Dimitri Kartsaklis. 2021. A CCG-based version of the DisCoCat framework,. In *Proceedings of SemSpace 2021*.

Yoshikawa, Masashi, Hiroshi Noji, and Yuji Matsumoto. 2017. A* CCG parsing with a supertag and dependency factored model. In *Proceedings of the 55th Annual Meeting of the Association for Computational Linguistics (Volume 1: Long Papers)*, pages 277–287. Vancouver, Canada: Association for Computational Linguistics.

Zettlemoyer, Luke S. and Michael Collins. 2005. Learning to map sentences to logical form: Structured classification with probabilistic categorial grammars. In *Proceedings of the 21st Conference on Uncertainty in Artificial Intelligence*. Edinburgh, UK.

Zhang, Yue and Stephen Clark. 2011. Shift-reduce CCG parsing. In *Proceedings of the 49th Annual Meeting of the Association for Computational Linguistics: Human Language Technologies*, pages 683–692. Portland, Oregon, USA: Association for Computational Linguistics.

3

Probabilistic Lexical Semantics: From Gaussian Embeddings to Bernoulli Fields

GUY EMERSON

If we are to take lexical semantics seriously – that is, to have a theory that can model the meanings of words, including all their subtle connotations – then we cannot hope to write down all the details by hand. In fact, Mollica and Piantadosi (2019) estimate that the vast majority of the information required to learn a language is lexical semantics (around 96%). Data-driven techniques are necessary to move from an abstract semantic theory to a fleshed-out model of a real language. Furthermore, an explicit computational model does more than just allow us to test the theory – as we will see, using probabilistic techniques can provide new insights on old problems.

I will begin this chapter with a discussion of what we need from a theory of lexical semantics, both in terms of how meaning can be formally represented, and also in terms of how those representations can be learnt. In §3.2, I will then discuss several challenging phenomena (vagueness, polysemy, and context dependence), which probabilistic models have been developed to deal with. Tying together this discussion, in §3.3 I will spell out a view of lexical semantics in terms of probabilistic truth-conditional functions. I will then expand on this view in two ways. In §3.4, I will introduce Bernoulli Fields, which deal with some subtleties in how probabilities can be introduced to

Probabilistic Approaches to Linguistic Theory.
Jean-Philippe Bernardy, Rasmus Blanck,
Stergios Chatzikyriakidis, Shalom Lappin,
Aleksandre Maskharashvili (eds.).

a truth-conditional model, and which give a more accurate account of vagueness. Then, in §6.3.3, I will discuss pragmatic reasoning with a probabilistic truth-conditional model, giving a refinement on previous work.

3.1 Model Theory and the Lexicon

A standard approach to formal semantics is model theory (for expositions, see: Cann, 1993, Allan, 2001, Kamp and Reyle, 2013). The popularity of model theory is due to its precisely defined notion of truth, and to its compatibility with first order logic and λ-calculus. This allows us to derive the meanings of complex expressions by composing the meanings of their parts, and allows us to evaluate the truth or falsehood of sentences. Model theory was formally defined by Tarski and Vaught (1956),[1] further developed by Montague (1973), and popularised by Partee (1975) and Dowty et al. (1981).

The basic idea is that linguistic expressions acquire meaning via interpretation in a **model structure**.[2] Each model structure includes a set of **individuals** (or **entities**) – intuitively, these represent objects or people in the world. The meaning of a content word is called a **predicate**, which can be formalised as a function mapping from individuals to **truth values** – either **truth** or **falsehood** (also called **falsity**). To emphasise that there are only two possible values, truth values are also called **binary** or **Boolean**. More generally, an n-place predicate maps each n-tuple of individuals to a truth value. For example, the meaning of *dog* can be represented as a one-place predicate, that maps an individual to truth if the individual is a dog, and to falsehood otherwise. The meaning of *chase* can be represented as a two-place predicate, that maps a pair of individuals (x, y) to truth if x chases y, and to falsehood otherwise.

Alternatively, an n-place predicate can be formalised as an **extension** (or **denotation**) – the set of n-tuples of individuals for which the predicate is true. Note that for both of the above formalisations (truth-conditional functions and extensions), the interpretation of a predicate is dependent on a model structure. The difference between the two will be explored in §3.3.

At its simplest, a model-theoretic representation for a sentence includes a set of **variables** and a set of predicates taking variables as arguments. For example, we can represent the sentence *a dog chased a*

[1] For an overview, see: Hodges, 2014.

[2] I use the term "model structure" rather than just "model" or "structure", to avoid the ambiguity in both terms.

cat, with two variables and three predicates: $dog(x)$, $cat(y)$, $chase(x, y)$.[3] We also need some way to combine the truth values for each of these predicates into a single truth value for the whole sentence. In the above case, we can simply use the logical and operator, $\wedge$. Finally, we need some way to match the variables to the individuals in a model structure, which is called **quantification**. The two simplest quantifiers are the **universal quantifier** $\forall$ (we need to match the variable against every individual) and the **existential quantifier** $\exists$ (we need to find a single individual for the variable). In the above example, both x and y can be existentially quantified. We can then represent the meaning of a sentence using a logical **proposition**, where all variables are quantified – given a model structure, a proposition can be evaluated to give a truth value. The meaning of the above example could be represented by the proposition $\exists x \exists y\ dog(x) \wedge cat(y) \wedge chase(x, y)$. This is true when the model structure includes two individuals, where one is a dog, the other is a cat, and the first chases the second.

Many extensions of model theory have been proposed, and a full review would be beyond the scope of this chapter. In the rest of this section, I discuss what model theory demands from lexical semantics, and in the following section, I discuss challenges that arise.

3.1.1 Meaning and the World

As Harnad (1990) discusses, if the meanings of words are defined only in terms of other words, these definitions are circular. One goal for a semantic theory is to explain how language relates to the world, including sensory perception and motor control – this process of connecting language to the world is called **grounding**.[4] This includes connecting abstract concepts to the world, although such connections are necessarily more indirect (for further discussion, see: Blondin-Massé et al., 2008, Pecher et al., 2011, Pulvermüller, 2013, Barsalou et al., 2018).

[3]For ease of exposition, I am assuming here that each word corresponds to a single predicate. In general there may be lexical ambiguity, which will be discussed in §3.2.2. I am also using "word" in a pre-theoretic way, to avoid clunkier terms like "lexical item" or "listeme". I am not committing to a precise definition, which may be problematic (Haspelmath, 2011) and unnecessary (Emerson and Copestake, 2015). Predicates for idiomatic expressions are beyond the scope of this chapter.

[4]A stronger form of the symbol grounding problem considers how an agent could autonomously establish a connection between symbols and the world – in other words, how it could recognise that a symbol is about the world, without already knowing that it is (Steels, 2008, Taddeo and Floridi, 2005, 2007). Here, I discuss a weaker form of the problem – I assume that an agent can already recognise something as being a linguistic signal, about the world, and the challenge is knowing the details of how to match the signal to the world.

A model-theoretic approach might seem easily grounded, since each individual in a model structure could be a real-world individual. However, the details of how this should be done is not usually articulated in formal semantic accounts – to truly understand a predicate, we need to know its extension in any possible model structure, but if we are presented with a new situation containing a new set of individuals, how do we decide what the extensions are? This is not a trivial task, and should not be brushed aside. In order to generalise to new situations, we cannot represent meaning directly in terms of extensions.

To achieve this, we need to distinguish a **concept** (roughly speaking, the meaning of a word) from a **referent** (an individual in the concept's extension).[5] The importance of this distinction has been noted for some time (for example: Ogden and Richards, 1923).[6] Following Murphy (2002, pp. 4–5), I use the term "concept" without committing to a particular theory of concepts.

There is no quick fix for an extensional model theory. Some accounts contrast extensions with some notion of **intension**. For example, we might define an intension to be the set of properties common to all members of a extension (for example: Arnauld and Nicole, 1662, Jones, 1911).[7] This is sometimes called the **classical theory** of concepts (for example: Murphy, 2002, Margolis and Laurence, 2011). Representing a concept by a set of properties allows us to deal with new situations, because a new individual can be classified on the basis of its properties. However, Wittgenstein (1953, §66–71) argues against such a view of meaning, using the German word *Spiel* ("game" or "play") as an example – there is no set of necessary and sufficient conditions that characterises all types of Spiel. For example, compare chess, solitaire, tennis, and children kicking a ball against a wall. Rather than a common set of properties, we can observe a **family resemblance**

[5] In the psychological literature, the term "category" refers to a set of individuals (for example: Smith and Medin, 1981, Murphy, 2002). For a category corresponding to some concept, this is synonymous with "extension".

[6] This may remind some readers of the work of Frege (1892) or Peirce (1867), but I do not want to make the same distinction here. Frege distinguishes *Sinn* ("sense") and *Bedeutung* ("reference"). However, the Sinn of a linguistic expression is not fully formalised, and it is described as independent of any person's mind, a claim I want to avoid. Meanwhile, the Bedeutung of a sentence is taken to be a truth value, rather than a situation (see: Barwise and Perry, 1983, pp. 22–26). Peirce proposes a triadic structure of signs, and distinguishes "interpretants" and "objects". However, the interpretant is itself a sign, which leads to an infinite chain of signs, as Peirce acknowledged. This is aesthetically curious, but of little practical use.

[7] Arnauld and Nicole use the terms "compréhension" and "étendue", instead of "intension" and "extension".

between these different types of Spiel. Furthermore, Rosch (1975, 1978) experimentally demonstrated typicality effects which suggest that concepts are not structured as sets of necessary properties – some referents are seen as being more typical examples of a concept than other referents. For example, experimental participants judged oranges and apples to be more typical examples of fruit than avocados and pumpkins. So, while representing a concept as a set of properties may allow generalisation to new individuals, it is too simplistic a model.

Carnap (1947) defined an intension to be a function from possible worlds to extensions. This avoids the above problem, because for any possible world, the intension gives us the extension in that world. However, representing a concept by such a function just moves the problem further on. How do we explicitly represent such a function? Since there are infinitely many possible worlds, it would be psychologically impossible to enumerate an extension for each possible world, so we need a finite representation of the function. This unfortunately takes us back to our original problem – how do we determine an extension for each possible world?

The above definitions of "intension" do not solve the problem of how to determine extensions in new situations. However, given the philosophical and psychological arguments that the structure of concepts is complicated, perhaps it would be unreasonable to expect a purely formal solution to the problem. If concepts have too many details to write down by hand, we may need machine learning techniques to fill in the details.

A machine learning approach could embed individuals in some feature space. A natural solution is then to represent a concept, not by a point in the space, but by a **region** – a subset of the space, with a well-defined boundary. Individuals embedded inside the region are part of the extension, and individuals embedded outside the region are not. However, without any constraints on possible regions, knowing that one point is inside the region would tell us nothing about any other point being inside or outside. This would make it difficult to generalise, and hence difficult to learn such a concept. Learning will be further discussed in §4.2.3, but for now we can note that some kind of constraint is necessary.

Gärdenfors (2000, 2014) argues in favour of a specific constraint, that a concept should be modelled as a **convex** region – any straight line between two points in the region will lie entirely inside the region.

Given examples of a concept, the convexity assumption would allow us to generalise to points between the examples (the simplex spanning those examples). Building on this idea, Erk (2009a,b) gives a practical algorithm to learn convex regions, using corpus data.

Rather than representing a concept as a region, an alternative approach is to represent a concept as a **binary classifier** – a function that maps each possible input into one of two classes. In this case, the inputs represent individuals, and one class is the concept, while the other class is everything else. This approach ties in with a view of concepts as abilities, as proposed in some schools of philosophy (for example: Dummett, 1976, 1978, Kenny, 2010), and some schools of cognitive science (for example: Murphy, 2002, pp. 1–3, 134–138; Zentall et al., 2002).

Within NLP, some authors (including myself) have also suggested representing concepts as classifiers. Larsson (2013) represents the meaning of a perceptual concept as a classifier of perceptual input, in the framework of Type Theory with Records (see §3.1.3). Schlangen et al. (2016) train image classifiers using captioned images, and Zarrieß and Schlangen (2017a,b) build on this, using distributional similarity scores to help train such classifiers, by generalising one label of an image to other similar labels. Liu and Emerson (2022) train image classifiers on the Visual Genome dataset Krishna et al. (2017), and show how the logical structure of the model allows it to be used effectively for semantic tasks without images.

Both of the above approaches to representing concepts (as regions and as classifiers) allow us to model how concepts relate to individuals, including how to determine the concept's extension in a new situation. Links between the two approaches will be explored in §3.4.

3.1.2 Learning the Lexicon

I have already suggested that a fleshed out theory of meaning needs to leverage machine learning. If we take this suggestion seriously, then semantic theories are only sensible if they can be learnt effectively. We might add a further goal to make the semantic model psychologically plausible, but I will not have much to say in this chapter about how people actually learn. The focus in this section is to consider whether models expressive enough to capture semantics are also tractable enough to be implemented and used in practice. This is a necessary (but not sufficient) condition for a semantic theory.

Models can usually be analysed in terms of their **parameters** (or **weights**), independent values that must be set based on the data.[8] The parameters should be set so that the model can **generalise** to new data, rather than only describe the data it was trained on. Difficulties can come from the number of parameters, or from the computational cost of determining their values.

Work on model theory mostly focuses on formal properties, without proposing a machine learning model. One way to link model theory to machine learning is to explicitly define a model structure. For example, Young et al. (2014) use a set of images to stand for situations. Each image is annotated with a set of captions, which can be taken to be true for that image. They use rewrite rules to produce simplified captions, many of which are true for multiple images. They define the "visual denotation" of a caption to be the set of images it describes. To generalise to new images, it is necessary to train an image processing model (for example: Vinyals et al., 2015, Xu et al., 2015). However, this dataset only includes captions at the level of the whole image. Some datasets go further, and annotate individuals in an image (for example: Escalante et al., 2010, Lin et al., 2014), or even spatial relations between individuals (for example: Hürlimann and Bos, 2016). While such datasets are certainly useful, it would be difficult to annotate a dataset at the level of detail often seen in model theory. Furthermore, for abstract concepts, it is difficult to even say what kind of annotated dataset would be useful. For a model-theoretic machine learning model to scale to cover an entire language, I believe that model structures must be learnt, rather than explicitly annotated.

Distributional semantics is firmly rooted in data-driven approaches. For a survey, see: Emerson (2020b). Vector-based models are efficient to learn, and one way they have been made even more efficient is to share parameters between words, which reduces the total number of parameters. This is called **sharing statistical strength**. For example, word meaning can be represented using high-dimensional vectors defined in terms of word co-occurrences. Such a model has a large number of parameters, but this can be reduced using dimensionality reduction techniques, such as truncated SVD (Singular Value Decomposition, often called Latent Semantic Analysis when applied to co-occurrence vectors: Deerwester et al., 1990, Landauer and Dumais, 1997) – latent dimensions are shared across the vocabulary,

[8] I do not mean to ignore nonparametric models – for example, HDP (Teh et al., 2006) is a nonparametric version of LDA, where the number of topics is not fixed. However, a technical discussion of nonparametric models would be out of place here. For an introduction, see: Gershman and Blei, 2012.

and word meanings are represented in terms of a small number of latent dimensions, rather than a large number of context dimensions. Indeed, the popular Skip-gram model (Mikolov et al., 2013) can also be seen as performing dimensionality reduction (Levy and Goldberg, 2014, Cotterell et al., 2017).

However, if we move beyond vector space models, learning may become more difficult. In this chapter, I will discuss various lines of work on representing lexical meaning as a probability distribution (over various kinds of object, as I will discuss in §3.2). However, it is generally true to say that such work constrains the family of distributions, in order to reduce the number of parameters and allow efficient learning.

For example, Vilnis and McCallum (2015), Barkan (2017), and Bražinskas et al. (2018) represent meaning as a distribution over vectors. They constrain the distributions to be Gaussian distributions with diagonal covariance matrices (the diagonal constraint aligns the shape of the Gaussian with the basis vectors of the space). This means that, for an n-dimensional space, each distribution can be represented by only $2n$ parameters (n for the mean, and n for the diagonal covariances). Using a larger family of distributions allows a more expressive model, but makes learning more challenging. For example, Athiwaratkun and Wilson (2017) use a Gaussian mixture model, to capture word senses (see §3.2.2). For k senses, each with diagonal covariances, the number of parameters scales as kn, which is still manageable.

Turning to representing meaning as as a region, Dong et al. (2018) uses spherical regions, requiring $n+1$ parameters (n for the central point and 1 for the radius). Erk (2009a,b) uses regions based on distance from a central point, requiring $2n$ parameters (n for the centre, and n for the size along each basis vector). Vilnis et al. (2018) use rectangular regions aligned with the basis vectors, again requiring $2n$ parameters (one for each rectangular face).

In principle, we can push the limits of the above models by considering increasingly flexible families of distributions/regions (the contrast between the two will be discussed in §3.2.1). For example, if we drop the constraint that the shape of distributions/regions must align with the basis vectors (for example: Jameel and Schockaert, 2017), then the number of parameters scales as n^2.

Expressive probabilistic models often include **latent** variables (also called **hidden** or **unobserved** variables), whose values are not part of the observed data. For example, topic models like Latent Dirichlet Allocation (LDA: Blei et al., 2003) associate each observed word token with a latent "topic". Bražinskas et al.'s model associates each token with a latent real-valued vector (see §3.2.3). Latent variable models provide a powerful tool for defining rich probability distributions, but they make learning more challenging, since exactly calculating marginal probabilities for the observed variables requires summing over all possible values for each latent variable. In practice, approximate techniques must often be used, such as Gibbs sampling or variational inference. Nonetheless, one important benefit of such models is that they allow words to share statistical strength, because many words can use latent variables with the same value. Wang et al. (2017) show that an LDA model provides a promising approach to learning a distributional representation from a single example (**one-shot** learning).

3.1.3 Frameworks for Probabilistic Semantics

Before I turn to specific lexical phenomena, in this section I discuss existing frameworks for probabilistic semantics.

Goodman and Lassiter (2015) use probabilistic programs to represent both world knowledge (a program can generate a distribution over situations) and linguistic knowledge (a program can generate truth values for utterances in given situations). They present several hand-written programs to show how the two can interact. Each word's meaning is represented by a program, and these can be composed to produce a representation of a sentence. This is a powerful framework, given the use of latent variables (Lassiter, 2017). On the other hand, without constraints on what programs are allowed, the framework is very general, and learning such a model from data would be challenging.

In a related line of work, Bernardy et al. (2018, 2019) introduce Bayesian Inference Semantics, which again uses probabilistic programs. Predicates are represented as linear classifiers with probabilistic thresholds. Logical inference is viewed as Bayesian inference, and Markov Chain Monte Carlo methods are used to do this in practice, with the system evaluated on a textual entailment test suite.

Cooper et al. (2015) introduce a probabilistic version of Type Theory with Records (TTR) (Cooper, 2005). In this framework, the basic notions are situations and types. In classical TTR, situations are either instances of a type or not, while in probabilistic TTR, judgements of a situation being of a certain type are made probabilistically. Cooper et al. show how probabilistic types for complex expressions can be constructed compositionally, and they present a hand-written grammar. Larsson and Bernardy (2021) discuss learning in this framework, and outline a plan for implementing such a model.

In my previous work on Functional Distributional Semantics, I have proposed a probabilistic version of first-order logic (Emerson and Copestake, 2017b, Emerson, 2018, 2020c). This allows probabilistic truth-conditional functions to be composed, to give semantic representations for complex expressions. An undirected probabilistic graphical model is used for the world model (a probabilistic model structure), rather than probabilistic programs. This can be done in practice using a distributional model (Emerson and Copestake, 2016, Emerson, 2018, 2020a), with composition guided by a semantic theory such as Dependency Minimal Recursion Semantics (DMRS) (Copestake et al., 2005, Copestake, 2009).

Taking a step back from the above approaches, we can see that semantic theories often focus at the sentence level, focusing on concerns such as semantic composition, integration with syntax, and logical inference. The focus of this chapter is at the lexical level, and what I will present in §3.4 and §6.3.3 is compatible with any of the above approaches. Indeed, a point of convergence between all of the above is that semantics can be characterised in terms of probabilistic truth values. However, all of the above work (including my own) has assumed that truth values are either independently generated or generated based on a global threshold. These two options will be challenged in §3.4, before giving a more nuanced approach.

3.2 Challenges of Lexical Semantics

Every speaker of a language will have some kind of mental lexicon, containing the meaning of every word they know. In this section, I discuss challenges in representing the meanings of individual words.

Some aspects of meaning are easy to represent in model theory. For example, hyponymy can be defined straightforwardly: a predicate p is a hyponym of another predicate q, if the extension of p is a strict subset of the extension of q. This directly formalises the idea that p has a more specific meaning than q. However, other aspects of meaning are challenging for classical theories, and provide strong motivations for a probabilistic approach (for a broader discussion of the turn towards probabilistic approaches in semantics, see: Erk, 2021).

3.2.1 Vagueness

In many cases, individuals can fall along a continuum without a sharp cutoff between a predicate being true or false. For example, we can place colours (in human perception) in a three-dimensional space of hue, saturation, and brightness.[9] We can smoothly change between two colours (say, *pink* and *red*), but there is not an exact point where we switch from one term to the other. This is called **vagueness** (or **gradedness**) – predicates have borderline cases where truth values are unclear. One goal for a semantic theory is to account for this.

Vagueness is the basis of the **Sorites Paradox** (for an overview, see: Hyde and Raffman, 2018). Suppose we have one point along a continuum where a predicate is true, and another point where it is false (for example, one shade of colour that is red, and one that is not red). Suppose further, that if two points on the continuum are sufficiently close, they are indiscriminable – the difference is not perceptible, so the predicate must take the same truth values for those two points. This leads to a paradox, since we can find a sequence of points, where each is indiscriminable with the next, but the predicate is true at the start of the sequence, and false at the end. A good account of vagueness should avoid this paradox.

Vagueness has also found experimental support. For example, Labov (1973) investigated the boundaries between concepts like *cup*, *mug*, and *bowl*, asking participants to name drawings of objects in different contexts of use. For typical instances of a concept (such as a typical cup, being used to drink coffee), the term was consistently applied; meanwhile, for objects that were intermediate between two concepts (for example, an object that's wide for a cup but narrow for a bowl), terms were used inconsistently. For these borderline cases, a single person may even make different judgements at different times (McCloskey and Glucksberg, 1978).

There is a large literature on extending model theory to account for vagueness (for an overview, see: Sutton, 2013, chapter 1; Van Deemter, 2010). A direct approach is to use **fuzzy** truth values, as proposed by Zadeh (1965, 1975) – truth values are no longer binary, but rather values in the range $[0, 1]$, where 0 represents definitely being false, 1 represents definitely being true, and intermediate values represent a range of borderline cases. Fuzzy logic has not seen much use within computational linguistics. One exception is Bergmair (2010), who introduced the framework of Monte Carlo Semantics, using fuzzy truth values to allow graded inferences.

Alternatively, we can stick to binary truth values (truth and falsehood), but represent uncertainty about a truth value as a **probability**, as proposed by Edgington (1992, 1997). Sutton (2017)

[9] As argued by Saunders and Van Brakel (1997), this is a simplification of how colour terms are actually used. Nonetheless, even this simplified model of colour presents us with an interesting modelling challenge.

contrasts two places where we can put this uncertainty. One option is to say that the meaning of each lexical item is a precise predicate, but any speaker is uncertain about what this meaning is. For example, a speaker would believe that *red* corresponds to a precise range of colours, but would be uncertain about which range of colours this is. The other option is to say that predicates are inherently vague, so that they assign probabilities of truth. For example, a speaker could be certain about the meaning of *red*, but remain uncertain about whether a particular colour should be considered red – there is simply some variability in how the term is used. Lassiter (2011) and Fernández and Larsson (2014) take the former approach, while Sutton (2015, 2017) takes the latter. Both approaches can model vagueness, and avoid the Sorites Paradox. However, we will see in §6.3.3 that choosing where we place uncertainty can have a dramatic impact on the tractability of a model.

At the level of a single truth value, there is not much to decide between fuzzy and probabilistic accounts. However, in §3.4 we will see the importance of probabilistic dependence, which has no analogue in fuzzy logic.

Uncertainty has also been incorporated into distributional vector space models. Vilnis and McCallum (2015) modify Mikolov et al.'s Skip-gram model, representing words as **Gaussian embeddings** (Gaussian distributions over vectors). Barkan (2017) incorporate uncertainty into Skip-gram using Bayesian inference – rather than viewing learning as optimising word vectors, they view learning as finding the posterior distribution over word vectors, given the observed data. They approximate this posterior as a Gaussian distribution (in order to keep calculations tractable), so both of these approaches produce the same kinds of object. Balkır (2014) uses the quantum mechanical notion of a "mixed state" to naturally model uncertainty in a tensor. For example, this approach replaces vectors by matrices.

While these approaches represent uncertainty, it is challenging to use them to represent vagueness, which was defined above in terms of truth values. This basic problem is this: a distribution allows us to *generate* instances of a concept, but how can we go in the other direction, to *recognise* instances of a concept? It is tempting to classify a point using the probability density at that point – we might say that points with higher probability density are more likely to be classified as instances of the concept. However, if we compare a more general term (like *red*) with a more specific term (like *scarlet*), we run into a problem – a more general term will have its probability mass spread more thinly, and hence have a lower probability density than the more specific term, even if both terms could be considered true. I argued in §3.1.1 in favour of representing predicates as regions of space or as classifiers, and while a distribution over a space might at first sight look like a region of space, it is a different kind of object. The interplay between the two will be discussed further in §3.3, contrasting world knowledge and lexical knowledge.

3.2.2 Polysemy

The meaning of a word can often be broken up into a number of different uses, each called a **sense**. When these senses are related, they are called **polysemous**, and the phenomenon is called **polysemy**. For example, *school* can refer to a physical building, or to an institution composed of the staff and students. However, these two senses are related, since a school building is used by a school institution. This can be contrasted with **homonyms**, which are unrelated senses. For example, *school* can also refer to a group of fish, with identical spelling and pronunciation to the education sense(s). However, the fish sense and education sense(s) are not connected (and in fact have different etymologies).

All of the above senses of *school* are also **lexicalised** – they are established uses of the word, which a proficient speaker would presumably have committed to memory, rather than inferring them from the context. In contrast, suppose a speaker sees a number of planes, flying in a way that reminds them of a school of fish. If the speaker referred to the planes as a "school of planes", a listener might understand the phrase in context, even if they had never anticipated such a use of the term "school". I will discuss context-dependent meaning in §3.2.3, and in this section I will focus on lexicalised meaning. For a semantic theory that aims to capture all lexicalised meanings (which includes conventional metaphors), one goal is to model how a word can have a range of polysemous senses.

In model theory, one solution is to define a separate predicate for each sense, so that each sense has different truth conditions. However, deciding on a discrete set of senses is difficult, and practical efforts at compiling dictionaries have not provided a solution. Indeed, the lexicographer Sue Atkins bluntly stated, "I don't believe in word senses".[10]

Although the sense of a word varies across individual usages, there are many ways that we could divide usages into a discrete set of senses, a point which has been made by a number of authors (for example: Spärck-Jones, 1964, Kilgarriff, 1997, 2007, Hanks, 2000, Erk, 2010). To quantify this intuition, Erk et al. (2009, 2013) asked annotators to judge the similarity between dictionary senses, as well as the similarity

[10]Kilgarriff (1997) and Hanks (2000) both quote Atkins.

between individual usages. The similarity judgements suggest that usages cannot always be neatly clustered into discrete senses, implying that word senses do not have clear boundaries between each other. A good lexical semantic theory should therefore be able to capture variation in meaning without resorting to finite sense inventories.

Alternatively, we could represent all of the polysemous senses together as a single predicate. Indeed, Ruhl (1989) argues that even highly frequent terms with many apparent senses, such as *bear* and *hit*, can be assigned a single underspecified meaning, with the apparent diversity of senses explainable from the context. They conclude that we should initially assume that each word has a single sense, and resort to multiple senses only when we fail to identify a single sense. The challenge would then be, firstly, to accurately represent such meanings without overgeneralising to cases where they wouldn't be used, and secondly, to model how meanings become specialised in context, revealing different facets. The latter half of this challenge will be further discussed in §3.2.3 below.

In vector space models, we have a similar problem. Standard approaches to distributional semantics produce a single vector that encodes all observed occurrences of the word, which combines all senses into a single vector. An alternative is to use multiple vectors to represent different senses (for example: Schütze, 1998, Rapp, 2004), but this falls prey to the same criticism raised against model-theoretic semantics above.

However, I have already argued in the above sections that we should move away from vector space models that represent each word as a single point.

As discussed in §3.2.1 above, some previous work has instead replaced points with distributions, and these approaches have also been applied to modelling word senses. For example, Athiwaratkun and Wilson (2017) use a mixture of Gaussians, extending Vilnis and McCallum's model described in §3.2.1 above, to allow multiple senses. However, a mixture of a Gaussians ultimately models a fixed number of senses (one for each Gaussian), and so this also falls prey to the above criticism of finite sense inventories. In principle, modelling a word as a distribution could be done in a way that avoids this criticism, but this would require moving beyond finite mixture models. Piedeleu et al. (2015) use mixed quantum states, similarly to Balkır's approach mentioned in §3.2.1 above. Although they only propose using this approach for homonymy, it seems plausible that it could be extended to polysemy as well, although care would be needed to avoid finite sense inventories.

If a word is represented by a region of space, or by a classifier, we don't necessarily have the problem of finite sense inventories, since we can continuously vary between nearby points. As with parametrising a distribution, whether we can avoid finite sense inventories depends on the expressiveness of the model. For example, a classifier with a linear decision boundary can only model a single sense. However, a non-linear decision boundary could be more flexible, allowing senses (clusters of classified points) to smoothly blur into each other.

3.2.3 Context Dependence

While this chapter focuses on lexical semantics, it is important to consider how lexical representations might interact in a sentence and in a discourse.

A strength of model theory is that **compositional** mechanisms have been developed that can deal with a wide range of constructions. A traditional approach is to use λ-calculus, although alternatives exist, including a composition algebra for Minimal Recursion Semantics (Copestake et al., 2001, Copestake, 2007). Importantly, these compositional mechanisms are tightly constrained, which means that relatively simple composition rules can derive the semantics for complex sentences.

Sentences can be used to express complex thoughts, and build chains of reasoning. **Logic** formalises this, and one goal for a semantic theory is to support the logical notions of **truth**, discussed in §3.1, and **entailment**, which holds when one proposition follows from another. In model-theoretic semantics (which was the starting point of §3.1), entailment is defined in terms of truth: given that one proposition is true, we can ask whether another proposition must also be true. In contrast, **proof-theoretic** semantics takes entailment to be the primary notion (for example: Brandom, 2000): a proposition is only true relative to some set of propositions which a speaker is already committed to. Under either view, the process of deciding if an entailment holds is called **inference**.[11]

Model theory has a strong logical foundation, allowing us to evaluate the truth of a proposition in a model structure. However, the choice of logic varies between model-theoretic approaches. I argued in §3.2.1 that probabilities of truth and fuzzy truth values allow natural accounts of vagueness, and it is indeed possible to construct corresponding logics.

[11]Icard (2014) breaks this down further, separating *what* entailments hold, *how* an entailment can be inferred, and *why* an agent would infer one entailment rather than another.

In **probabilistic logic**, propositions have probabilities of being true or false, and there is a joint distribution for the truth values of all propositions (for expositions, see: Adams, 1998, Demey et al., 2013). In **fuzzy logic**, propositions have fuzzy truth values, and classical logical operators (such as: $\wedge$, $\vee$, $\neg$) are replaced with fuzzy versions (for expositions, see: Hájek, 1998, Cintula et al., 2017). Fuzzy operators act directly on truth values – for example, given the fuzzy truth values of propositions p and q, we can calculate the fuzzy truth value of the disjunction $p \vee q$. In contrast, in probabilistic logic, given probabilities of truth for p and q, we cannot calculate the probability of truth for $p \vee q$, unless we know the joint distribution.

A problem with the fuzzy approach, observed by Fine (1975), comes when we consider propositions like $p \vee \neg p$. Intuitively, this should be true regardless of what p is, but fuzzy logic can give a truth value below 1. This makes fuzzy logic less appealing (or at least, harder to interpret). On the other hand, Hájek et al. (1995) prove that fuzzy logic can provide upper and lower bounds on probabilities, providing an alternative motivation.

However, the flipside of compositionality is **context dependence**: the meaning of an expression often seems to depend on what other words it occurs with. For example, a *small elephant* is not a *small animal*, but a *large ant* is – the interpretations of *small* and *large* depend on the nouns they modify. Even the same expression can seem to have different meanings depending on the situation in which it is used. For example, the size of a *large animal* may be quite different when buying a pet and when visiting the zoo. One goal for a semantic theory is to model how meaning depends on linguistic and extralinguistic context.

Following Recanati (2012), I use **standing meaning** to refer to the context-independent meaning of a linguistic expression, and **occasion meaning** to refer to the context-dependent meaning of an expression in a particular occasion of use.[12] However, it is important to note that every usage occurs in *some* context (for discussion, see: Searle, 1980, Elman, 2009), so a standing meaning must be seen as an abstraction across usages, rather than a usage in a "null" context. A speaker who knows a word knows its standing meaning, but whenever they use or hear the word, it will have an occasion meaning.

[12]This adapts Quine (1960), who contrasts "standing sentences" and "occasion sentences". The truth of an occasion sentence depends on some preceding "stimulus" while the truth of a standing sentence supposedly does not.

In model theory, meanings are defined in terms of extensions, but we have just seen how *small* doesn't have a fixed extension (for discussion of adjectives, see: Lahav, 1989, 1993, Blutner, 1998, McNally, 2016b). One solution is to represent such terms as functions from extensions to extensions (for example: Parsons, 1970, Kamp and Partee, 1995), so that *small* maps the set of mice to the set of small mice, and so on. Another solution is to make such terms **indexical** – that is, they are functions from a context to an occasion meaning (for example: Kaplan, 1979, 1989, Recanati, 2012). Both of these approaches avoid the problem, but as with the definition of "intension" that we saw in §3.1.1, these push the problem further down the road, since they invoke more complicated objects without detailing how to represent them. As discussed in §4.2.3, it is not enough for a semantic theory to be sufficiently expressive – the semantic objects also need to be learnable. It would be implausible to represent such functions by enumerating an extension for each possible argument, and so such an approach only provides a path forward if we have a way to represent such functions efficiently. We are ultimately still left with the question of how to determine an extension given a context.

Faced with challenging real-world examples of context dependence, McNally (2016a) concludes that traditional model-theoretic approaches leave out too much of lexical semantics, and suggests that data-driven approaches might fill the gap. Probability theory is central to many context-dependent models.

Dinu and Lapata (2010) train a distributional LDA model (where each target word defines a "document"), so that a standing meaning is a distribution over latent senses ("topics", shared across all target words), which are distributions over context words. This allows occasion meanings to be calculated using Bayesian inference, conditioning on the observed context. However, by using a finite set of latent senses, this model ultimately relies on a finite sense inventory, which we want to avoid, as I discussed in §3.2.2.

Lui et al. (2012) apply LDA in a different way (in their "per-lemma" model, where each target word *token* defines a "document"): a standing meaning is a distribution over occasion meanings, which are mixtures of "topics", which are distributions over context words. Occasion meanings can vary continuously, so a finite sense inventory is avoided. However, a separate model must be trained for each target word.

Chang et al. (2014) add another generative layer to LDA, allowing them to train a single model across all target words without having a single set of senses. A standing meaning is a distribution over senses (particular to a target word), which are distributions over topics (common to all target words), which are distributions over context words. We first draw from the distribution over senses, then draw topics and words. However, in this model, a single sense chosen in each context, which again means we have a finite sense inventory. In principle, the above approaches could be combined, so that occasion meanings are topic mixtures (allowing them to vary continuously), but topics are shared (allowing words to be trained together). I am not aware if this has been tried.

Skip-gram can also be interpreted as a generative model, generating context words based on a target word. While we can see a word vector as a standing meaning, no part of the model can be seen as an occasion meaning. Bražinskas et al. (2018) add another generative layer, first generating a latent vector based on the target word, and then generating context words based on the latent vector. We can see a latent vector as an occasion meaning, and a word's distribution over latent vectors as a standing meaning.

The above discussion illustrates how probabilistic models can be defined in a modular way, with the potential for adding generative layers. Furthermore, by defining random variables for different kinds of context, we can calculate occasion meanings that simultaneously condition on all of the observed context. For example, Erk and Herbelot (2021) discuss how meaning can be dependent on both local and global context, and present a probabilistic model that incorporates both.

However, the above approaches based on LDA and Skip-gram are entirely defined in terms of generating context words, making it hard to relate them to model-theoretic semantics. Nonetheless, the common insight is that context dependence can be seen as Bayesian inference, conditioning on the observed context. If we apply this idea to model-theoretic semantics, what we get is Rational Speech Acts (RSA) (Frank and Goodman, 2012, Goodman and Frank, 2016), which has become a well-established framework for computational pragmatics.

In this framework, literal truth values are separated from pragmatic meaning. We can see standing meanings as probabilistic truth-conditional functions, and we can see occasion meanings as inferred distributions over situations. Given a standing meaning of an utterance, and a prior over situations, a **literal listener** can construct an occasion meaning for that utterance (a posterior distribution over situations), using Bayesian inference. A **pragmatic speaker** who directly observes a situation can then choose an utterance which is informative for a literal listener – in particular, they can choose the utterance which maximises a literal listener's posterior probability for the observed situation. A **pragmatic listener** performs Bayesian inference over the pragmatic speaker.

If we can express lexical semantics in terms of probabilistic truth-conditional functions, then RSA provides a natural way to derive context-dependent meanings. However, RSA doesn't tell us how to construct truth-conditional functions, and we saw in §3.2.1 and §3.2.2 that such functions may not be simple. In this chapter, I aim to provide an efficient parametrisation of such functions in higher-dimensional spaces, so that we can have a lexical semantic model that is both expressive enough to capture vagueness and polysemy, and also tractable enough to be learnt from real-world data. I will return to RSA in §6.3.3.

3.3 Truth-Conditional Functions

In the previous section, I surveyed work suggesting that we should represent lexical meanings as probabilistic truth-conditional functions. In this section, I will further analyse this approach.

To formalise the discussion in the previous section, we can consider a joint distribution over situations and truth values. To begin with, we can consider simple situations which only contain a single individual, and we can consider only a single predicate. So, we have two random variables: a variable X, representing the features of the individual, whose value is a point x in the feature space $\mathcal{X}$; and a variable T, representing the predicate's truth value for that individual, either $\top$ (truth) or $\bot$ (falsehood). Following my previous work (Emerson and Copestake, 2017a), I will use the term **pixie** to refer to a point in the feature space. Two individuals with identical features would be represented by the same pixie. A pixie is a representation of an individual, not a word, and it is useful to have a succinct term for this.

A probabilistic truth-conditional function t is a *conditional* distribution over truth values, *given a pixie*. We can write this as shown in (3.1). Note that, while the function takes values in a range, there are still only two truth values (truth and falsehood). This is in common with probabilistic logic, rather than fuzzy logic.

$$t(x) = \mathbb{P}\left(T{=}\top \mid X{=}x\right) \tag{3.1}$$

While a truth-conditional function does not represent a distribution over pixies, it can be used to define one, if we have a prior distribution $\mathbb{P}(X{=}x)$. We can then apply Bayes' Rule, as shown in (3.2). In contrast with existing work that represents lexical meaning as a probability distribution (see §3.2.1), this means that we can

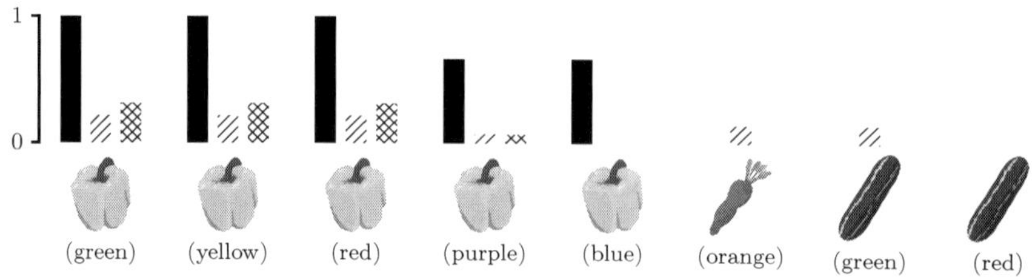

FIGURE 1: An example of Bayesian inference. We are interested in: an individual X, represented by some pixie $x \in \mathcal{X}$; and the truth value T of the *pepper* predicate for that individual.

Solid bars: the truth-conditional function $\mathbb{P}\left(T{=}\top \mid X{=}x\right)$ represents a speaker's belief about whether each pixie x can be considered a pepper.

Hashed bars: the prior $\mathbb{P}(X{=}x)$ represents the speaker's belief about an individual, based on their world knowledge. It encodes how much they expect to observe an individual with particular features.

Crosshatched bars: the posterior $\mathbb{P}\left(X{=}x \mid T{=}\top\right)$ represents their belief about an individual, if they know the *pepper* predicate is true of it. The probability mass is split between the pepper pixies, but skewed towards typical colours, and excluding colours believed impossible.

combine lexical knowledge encoded in the truth-conditional function $t(x)$ with domain knowledge or contextual knowledge encoded in the prior $\mathbb{P}(X{=}x)$. If lexical meaning is represented as a distribution, other kinds of knowledge cannot be combined in such a natural way.

$$\mathbb{P}\left(X{=}x \mid T{=}\top\right) \propto \mathbb{P}\left(T{=}\top \mid X{=}x\right)\mathbb{P}(X{=}x) \tag{3.2}$$

Fig. 1 gives a simple example of Bayesian inference. The division between $\mathbb{P}(X{=}x)$ and $\mathbb{P}\left(T{=}\top \mid X{=}x\right)$ can be seen as a division between world knowledge and conceptual knowledge. The two are not completely independent, since there is a joint distribution over the two random variables, but this can still be a useful distinction. As purple and blue are atypical colours for a pepper, a speaker might be less willing to label such a vegetable a pepper, but not completely unwilling to do so – this conceptual knowledge belongs to the truth-conditional function for the predicate. In contrast, after observing a large number of peppers, it might be reasonable to conclude that blue peppers do not exist, and purple peppers are rare, while green, yellow, and red peppers are common – this world knowledge belongs to the probability distribution over pixies.

This example also shows a clear contrast between a truth-conditional function over a space and a distribution over the space. As peppers come in many colours, the truth-conditional function $\mathbb{P}(T{=}\top \mid X{=}x)$ should take a high value for any of these colours. In contrast, to define a probability distribution $\mathbb{P}(X{=}x \mid T{=}\top)$ over pepper pixies, we must split probability mass[13] between different colours, which means we only have a small probability of each. The value of a distribution at a point depends on the size of the space, but the value of a truth-conditional function does not. The two represent different things. A distribution over a pixie space represents uncertainty about the features of an individual, for which there is a correct but unknown answer. A truth-conditional function represents an underspecified concept, where many individuals with different features could be equally regarded as instances of the concept.

Representing lexical meaning as a truth-conditional function rather than a distribution places an emphasis on classification, rather than generation. This would suggest that a speaker might be able to classify instances of a concept without being able to generate instances. Rather than speculating about blue peppers, we can also turn to empirical evidence that people learn to classify without learning to generate, being unable to draw or recall simple facts about familiar everyday objects, such as coins (Nickerson and Adams, 1979, Jones, 1990), bikes (Lawson, 2006), brand logos (Blake et al., 2015), or the printed version of the lowercase letter g, even moments after reading it (Wong et al., 2018).

3.3.1 The Usefulness of Lexical Uncertainty

It is clear that a probabilistic model requires more mathematical machinery than a classical semantic model. It is therefore natural to ask, does a semanticist really need probabilities?

From a semantic point of view, the fundamental insight of model-theoretic semantics is to separate the semantic model from the world model (the model structure). As Dummett (1976, 1978) argues, a semantic theory does not tell us truth values, but rather tells us how to calculate truth values for a given world.

[13]In fact, as colours lie in a continuous space, a distribution over pixies would be better represented with a probability density function rather than with a probability mass function. The value of a probability density function at a point would further depend on the parametrisation of the space, while the value of a truth-conditional function would not. Fig. 1 uses a finite number of pixies, rather than a continuous space, for ease of illustration.

Under this view, it doesn't matter whether the world model is probabilistic or not, because it's separate from the semantics proper. However, from a computational point of view, continuous optimisation is easier than discrete optimisation. This is essentially the reason why gradient descent is so popular in machine learning. Classical model theory usually uses discrete world models, but allowing interpolations between the discrete options can make a lot of problems easier, and probability theory gives us a natural way to do this.

So, a probabilistic world model can be useful for convenience. However, when it comes to the semantic model itself, a probabilistic model provides more than just convenience, and can also give us a more accurate model. In particular, as discussed in §3.2.1, probabilities provide a natural approach for modelling vagueness. In turn, this provides a natural basis for modelling pragmatic reasoning, which will be discussed further in §6.3.3.

3.3.2 The Unavoidability of Lexical Uncertainty

Having introduced probabilities of truth, it is natural to ask how these probabilities are supposed to be interpreted. Bayesian probability theory uses probability to represent beliefs about the world, where there is some correct but unknown answer. For example, if a physicist is uncertain about the mass of an electron, they can perform a suitable experiment, and after observing the results, they would reduce their uncertainty. However, when it comes to linguistic or conceptual knowledge, it's not clear this is the same kind of uncertainty. If a learner is uncertain about the meaning of a predicate, what experiment could they perform? Is there a correct meaning for the learner to infer?

An influential non-probabilistic account of vagueness is **supervaluationism**, which holds that a predicate does have precise truth conditions, but these truth conditions are underspecified (for example: Fine, 1975; Keefe, 2000, chapter 7).[14] A choice of precise boundary is called a **precisification** of the vague predicate. However, simply using a *set* of boundaries leads to the problem of higher-order vagueness – if a predicate specifies a set of precise boundaries, we can reasonably ask where the boundaries begin and end. The set of boundaries therefore has its own boundary, and this higher-order boundary may also need to be vague.

Intuitively, some boundaries are more plausible than others. While there might not be a fixed boundary between red and orange, as

[14] A related account is *epistemicism*, which holds that the precise truth conditions are unknown, rather than underspecified. For discussion of the difference, see: Burnett and Sutton (2020).

we go further towards orange, we would be increasingly certain that we've crossed the boundary. Following this intuition, we can replace a *set* of boundaries by a *distribution* over boundaries, which avoids the problem of higher-order vagueness, as suggested by Edgington (1992), and demonstrated by Lassiter (2011). Representing a predicate as a distribution over regions can be seen as an improvement on supervaluationism that maintains its core insight.

Given such a distribution, it would be tempting to say that a learner could ask fluent speakers for truth value judgements, and thereby reduce their uncertainty. However, for a continuous pixie space, it would require infinitely many observations to precisely determine the region in which the predicate is true. Even a finite space requires implausibly many observations, if it is high-dimensional – and the real world is certainly high-dimensional. For example, consider a pixie space with binary-valued features (the simplest possible features we could imagine). Efforts to enumerate binary features for concepts typically produce hundreds of features, even after filtering out rare ones (for example: McRae et al., 2005, Devereux et al., 2014). With just 100 binary features, we have $2^{100} \approx 10^{30}$ pixies, which is already unmanageably large. This combinatorial explosion in high dimensions is known as the **curse of dimensionality**. High dimensionality leads to data sparsity, and, as discussed by Sutton in Chapter 4, data sparsity leads to vagueness.

So if precise truth conditions are impossible to learn, what does linguistic knowledge actually consist of? Barwise and Perry (1983, pp. 16–19) suggest that linguistic meaning is a relation between utterance events and aspects of the world, determined by the way language is used by a speech community. In other words, meaning comes from a convention. It is arbitrary, in the sense of de Saussure (1916), but agreed on by the community (for further discussion of convention, see: Millikan, 1998). There can be variation between different speakers in a speech community, but even in the ideal case where speakers never contradict one another, a linguistic convention is necessarily vague, because a precise convention would not be learnable.

Motivated by these concerns of communication and learning, Sutton (2013)[15] argues that the meaning of a predicate is a probabilistic correlation between uses of the predicate and situations in the world. It expresses the probability that a speaker would classify an individual as an instance of the predicate. Vagueness is not uncertainty about the

[15]See §4.3 for a discussion of correlation, §5.2–5.4 for learning, and §6.3 for a situation-theoretic formalisation.

world (that is, the world separate from the linguistic acts themselves), but uncertainty about how to generalise a linguistic convention to a new situation.

Probabilities of truth can therefore still be seen as subjective beliefs, but rather than expressing expectations about the state of the world, they express expectations that a linguistic convention could be used in a certain way.[16] These beliefs are uncertain, firstly because of variation in the linguistic community, and secondly because of the need to generalise to new situations. While the first source of uncertainty could be removed in a hypothetical homogeneous speech community that strives to agree on a precise linguistic convention, the second source of uncertainty is inherent to learning any language that describes a world large enough to require generalisation.

3.4 Bernoulli Fields: Locally correlated truth values

For a non-probabilistic model, a truth-conditional function is equivalent to a region of space. For any region of space, we can define a truth-conditional function which classifies all pixies in the region as instances of the concept, and all pixies outside the region as not. Conversely, for any binary classifier, we can define a region of space containing all pixies that are classified as instances of the concept.

However, once we introduce uncertainty, the correspondence becomes subtler, because a distribution over regions is more general than a probabilistic binary classifier. Intuitively, knowing about regions of space is *global* information, but knowing about truth values for particular pixies is *local* information. Given a distribution over regions, knowing about truth values in one part of the space can tell us about truth values in another distant part of the space.

More precisely, given a pixie space $\mathcal{X}$ and a region-valued random variable A, we can define a truth-valued random variable T_x at each pixie $x \in \mathcal{X}$, which is true when $x \in A$ and false otherwise. This means that we can define a truth-conditional function t based on a distribution over regions, by summing (or integrating) over the distribution A. The probability that the function is true for pixie x is exactly the probability that the region A contains x.

$$t(x) = \mathbb{P}(T_x{=}\top) \tag{3.3}$$

$$= \sum_{a \ni x} \mathbb{P}(A{=}a) \tag{3.4}$$

[16] Some authors distinguish these two kinds of probability using the terms *credence* and *verity*.

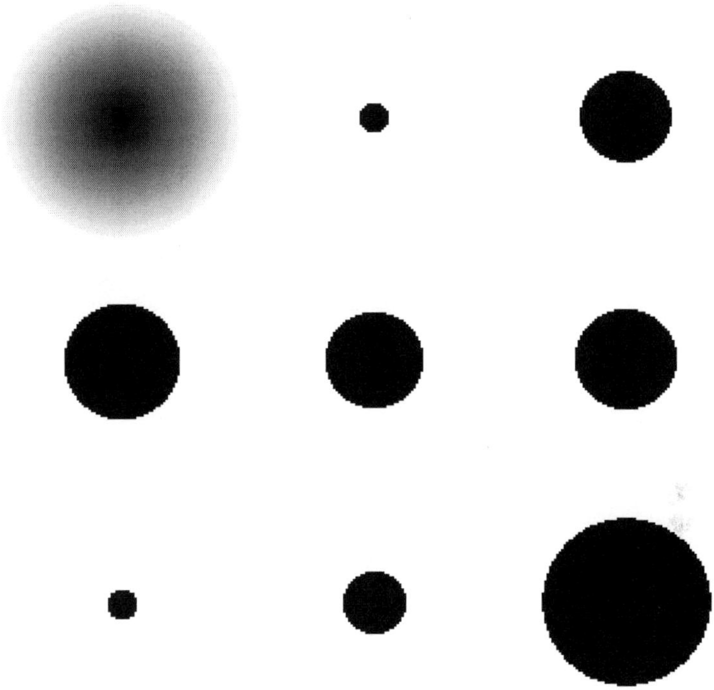

FIGURE 2: Random regions within a disc, discretised into 7860 pixies (each pixie shown as a pixel). Each pixie x has a corresponding truth-valued random variable T_x, and the top-left image shows the marginal probabilities $t(x)$ using greyscale (black is definitely true and white is definitely false). The other eight images each show a single randomly sampled region, using a global threshold. This maximises dependence: we can see that the boundary on one side of the region is perfectly correlated with the other side.

Conversely, if we have a probabilistic binary classifier t, then the marginal probability for each T_x being true is $\mathbb{P}(T_x{=}\top) = t(x)$. If there are n possible values for x, then there are n different random variables T_x. The classifier t has determined their *marginal* distributions, but it has not determined their *joint* distribution.

If we know the joint distribution, then we can define the region to be the pixies whose truth value is true: $A = \{x{\in}\mathcal{X} \mid T_x{=}\top\}$. Given only the marginal distributions, there are many ways that we could define a joint distribution, and hence a distribution over regions. One extreme would

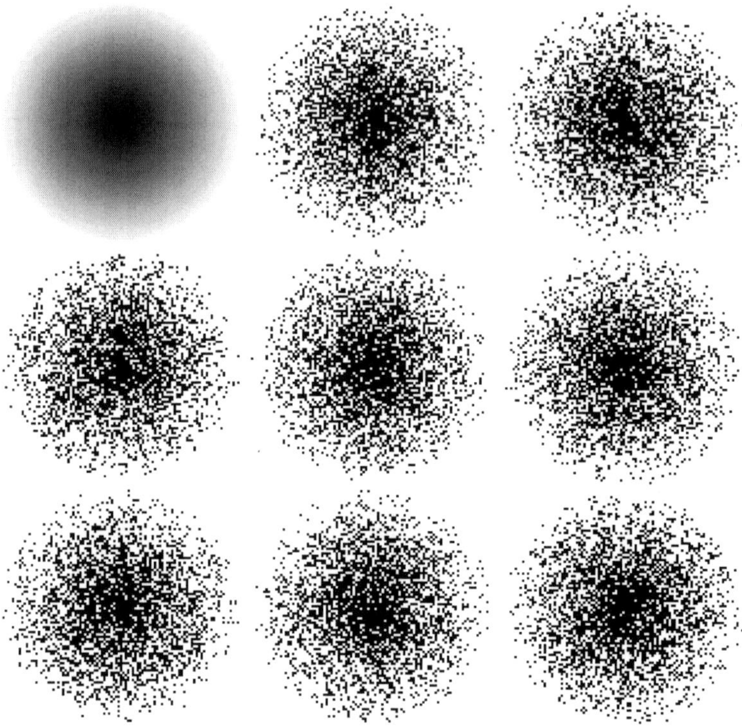

FIGURE 3: Random regions, similarly to Fig. 2, but where all truth values are independent. This minimises dependence: we can see that there is no clear boundary at all. Even if we zoomed in further (using more pixels), there would still be no clear boundary.

be to sample the truth values independently for each pixie. The other extreme would be to sample a threshold value k uniformly from $[0, 1]$, and choose truth when the classifier's value is above the threshold. This would give the region $A = \{x{\in}\mathcal{X} \mid f(x){>}k\}$. These two extremes are illustrated in Figs. 2 and 3.

These two options introduce different amounts of correlation between different truth values. Independently sampling truth values has no correlation at all – indeed, we may not even want to use the term "region", as the "boundary" is like white noise, rather than a clear line. Sampling a threshold maximises correlation – for any pair of pixies, their truth values have the maximum probability of agreement.

By allowing different levels of correlation between these two extremes, we can define different distributions over regions. In particular, it makes sense to have *local* correlations. For example, it would seem incoherent to classify one reddish-orange shade as red, but a slightly redder shade as not red. However, a classification of a reddish-orange shade would not seem to affect a classification of a reddish-purple shade. In other words, we want regions with clear boundaries, but specifying the boundary on one side of the region shouldn't specify the boundary on a different side.[17]

This gives us the goal of defining distributions over regions. However, the set of all possible regions is enormous: even for a finite n pixies, we have 2^n possible regions. Directly considering distributions over the set of all possible regions is infeasible for anything beyond the tiniest of toy models. There is therefore a tension between having a more flexible model (which can define a wider range of different distributions) and having a model with a small number of parameters (so that the model is feasible to implement in practice, and is psychologically plausible).

As an example between the extremes of flexibility and tractability, McMahan and Stone (2015) define distributions over box-shaped regions by using an independent distribution for each face of the box. Compared to using a global threshold, this gives more localised correlations: fixing the position of one face doesn't fix the other faces. However, the correlations are not completely local, either: for example, with two-dimensional boxes, fixing the position of two opposite corners also fixes the positions of the two remaining corners. Furthermore, box embeddings are also limited in flexibility, being restricted to boxes, whose boundaries are mostly flat, but with sharp corners.[18]

In the rest of this section, I will introduce **Bernoulli Fields**, which are flexible distributions over regions,[19] defined using two components: a **mean function** $t(x)$ (which specifies the marginal probability of truth for each pixie), and a **dependence function** $\theta(x, y)$ (which specifies the level of correlation of truth values, for pairs of pixies). The mean functions must take values in $[0, 1]$, but are otherwise completely

[17]There is a clear difference here compared to fuzzy logic. Rather than having a single fuzzy operator for logical "and", the operator varies according to the degree of correlation.

[18]In higher dimensions, a hypercube is increasingly "spiky", with 2^n vertices, and with distance $\sqrt{n}$ between opposite vertices compared to distance 1 between opposite faces.

[19]I aim to discuss explicit definitions of a distribution over regions. It is also possible to give an implicit definition, such as using a neural network with outputs in $[0, 1]$. Given uncertainty about the network weights, we have an implicit Bernoulli Field. To sample a region, we can sample the network weights and sample a global threshold. Explicitly calculating the distribution over regions requires marginalising out the network weights, which is generally intractable, and it may be difficult to interpret how uncertainty in network weights will affect the distribution over regions.

unconstrained, allowing Bernoulli Fields to be highly flexible. On the other hand, because we only need a mean function and a dependence function, it's possible to have a tractable parametrisation. For example, the mean function could be parametrised by a neural network, and the dependence function could be a simple function of the distance between pixies, with few or no parameters.

The technical challenge is how to combine two such functions in a way that gives a well-defined distribution over regions. My approach takes inspiration from Gaussian Processes,[20] but no previous knowledge of Gaussian Processes is assumed.[21] In §3.4.1, I first explain an important insight that can be transferred from Gaussian Processes. I build on this insight in §3.4.2 and §3.4.3, developing two different families of Bernoulli Fields, with different computational tradeoffs.

3.4.1 Finite Sets of Inputs

While we are interested in defining a distribution over *truth-valued* functions, a **Gaussian Process** defines a distribution over *real-valued* functions. This is achieved using only two components: a **mean function** $m(x)$ and a **covariance function** $k(x, y)$.

The space of all possible truth-valued functions is enormous, but the space of all possible real-valued functions is even bigger still. So how is it possible to efficiently define a distribution over this space? The important insight is that, for just about anything we would like to calculate, we don't need to consider the value of the function for all possible inputs; we can get away with only ever looking at its value for a finite set of inputs.

A Gaussian Process treats a distribution over functions as a multivariate Gaussian. When considering the entire set of inputs, this is a multivariate Gaussian with an infinite number of dimensions: for each input x, the output $F(x)$ is a single dimension of the Gaussian. Looking at the entire function F is impossible, but for any finite set of inputs $(x_1, \cdots, x_n)$, we can consider the marginal distribution for the outputs $(F(x_1), \cdots, F(x_n))$. A Gaussian Process defines this distribution as a multivariate Gaussian, using the mean function to define the mean vector $m(x_i)$, and the covariance function to define the covariance matrix $k(x_i, x_j)$. For any set of n points, we get a particular n-dimensional Gaussian, which is something we can tractably work with.

---

[20] It might therefore make sense to use the term *Bernoulli Process*, but this term already has an established meaning. I have chosen the term *field* in the sense of a function over a space (as in *random fields* and *vector fields*).

[21] For a full exposition, see: Rasmussen and Williams (2006).

Crucially, these finite-dimensional Gaussians are consistent with each other. Consider two sets of points, with one a subset of the other. Given a Gaussian Process, we have two ways to get a distribution for the subset: we can directly apply the definition to the subset; or we can apply the definition to the superset, and then marginalise out the variables that are not in the subset. For a Gaussian Process, these give exactly the same result. This means that we have a well-defined distribution for the entire function, but we can work with it in practice by only considering finite sets of inputs. For any finite set, we can directly calculate its marginal distribution.

So, to define a distribution over regions (equivalently, a distribution over truth-valued functions), we can use the above insight. We only need to define joint truth distributions for finite sets of points, as long as we can keep these distributions consistent with each other.

3.4.2 Finite Sets of Truth Values

As explained in the previous section, in order to model a predicate, we need to define distributions over finite sets of truth values. For n pixies, we have 2^n possible combinations of truth values, over which we need to define a distribution.

For one pixie x, there are two possible outcomes for T_x, and the distribution is trivial: the predicate's mean function gives us the probability $t(x)$ of truth, and $1 - t(x)$ of falsehood.

For two pixies x and y, we have four possible outcomes for the pair of truth values T_x and T_y, illustrated in the following table:

	$T_y = \bot$	$T_y = \top$
$T_x = \bot$	$p_{\bot\bot}$	$p_{\bot\top}$
$T_x = \top$	$p_{\top\bot}$	$p_{\top\top}$

The four probabilities must sum to 1, and the marginal probabilities must be correct: $p_{\top\bot} + p_{\top\top} = t(x)$ and $p_{\bot\top} + p_{\top\top} = t(y)$. This gives three linear constraints for four variables, which leaves one further degree of freedom, corresponding to the degree of dependence between the two variables. This fact is well known (for example: Teugels, 1990, Fontana and Semeraro, 2018), but what we need is a parametrisation that cleanly separates the marginal probabilities from the degree of dependence.

The difficulty of creating this clean separation can be seen by comparison with Gaussian distributions. While a univariate Gaussian can be defined by specifying the mean and variance separately, a univariate Bernoulli is fully specified by the mean. This problem unfortunately feeds into the multivariate case. Once we fix $t(x)$ and $t(y)$, there is a limit on the possible covariance of T_x and T_y.[22] This means that existing parametrisations of the multivariate Bernoulli distribution (for example: Teugels, 1990, Dai et al., 2013) are not useful for defining a Bernoulli Field.

However, in the bivariate case, there is a useful starting point. Tajar et al. (2001) and Geenens (2020) discuss how the **odds ratio**, shown in (3.5), can take any value in the range $[0, \infty]$, no matter what the marginal probabilities are. This gives us a clean separation between three degrees of freedom: the two marginal probabilities $t(x)$ and $t(y)$, and the odds ratio ω.

$$\omega = \frac{p_{\top\top} p_{\bot\bot}}{p_{\top\bot} p_{\bot\top}} \tag{3.5}$$

To avoid infinities, it can be convenient to work with either the **gamma measure** or **Yule's colligation coefficient**, as shown in (3.6) and (3.7), respectively. Both of these take values in the range $[-1, 1]$, where 1 means maximum correlation (comonotonicity), 0 means independence, and -1 means maximum anti-correlation.

$$\gamma = \frac{\omega - 1}{\omega + 1} \tag{3.6}$$

$$\Upsilon = \frac{\sqrt{\omega} - 1}{\sqrt{\omega} + 1} \tag{3.7}$$

To generalise this to the multivariate case, we can use the following **higher-order odds ratios**.[23] The third-order odds ratio ω_3 is given in (3.8), which is a ratio of the eight possible outcomes, grouped according to their **parity** (an even or odd number of variables being false). This can be further generalised to an nth-order odds ratio, given in (3.9), where β is an outcome, p_β is its probability, and $\mathrm{par}(\beta)$ is its parity, defined to be 1 when an even number of variables are false and -1 when an odd number are false.

$$\omega_3 = \frac{p_{\top\top\top} p_{\top\bot\bot} p_{\bot\top\bot} p_{\bot\bot\top}}{p_{\top\top\bot} p_{\top\bot\top} p_{\bot\top\top} p_{\bot\bot\bot}} \tag{3.8}$$

$$\omega_n = \prod_{\beta \in \{\top,\bot\}^n} p_\beta^{\mathrm{par}(\beta)} \tag{3.9}$$

[22] Taking truth and falsehood to be numerically 1 and 0, the maximum covariance is $\min\{t(x), t(y)\} - t(x)t(y)$. Similarly, the maximum correlation is $\frac{\min\{t(x),t(y)\} - t(x)t(y)}{\sqrt{t(x)(1-t(x))t(y)(1-t(y))}}$. For other measures, see: Tajar et al. (2001).

[23] For a further perspective on higher-order odds ratios, see: Rudas (2018).

For n Bernoulli random variables, there is an odds ratio for every non-empty subset. (For a singleton set, this is simply the odds $\frac{p}{1-p}$.) This gives us $2^n - 1$ parameters, which would appear to be exactly sufficient to represent any joint distribution. In fact we have the following theorem, which even applies in the edge cases where some odds ratios are undefined (both the numerator and denominator are 0) – the distribution is exactly determined by the odds ratios that exist.

Theorem 1 The n-variate Bernoulli distribution is parametrised by its odds ratios up to order n.

This parametrisation enjoys useful properties compared to previous work. Firstly, each marginal distribution is parametrised by the relevant subset of odds ratios. This stands in contrast to the parametrisation of Dai et al. (2013). Secondly, each odds ratio can take any value in the range $[0, \infty]$, regardless of the values of all lower-order odds ratios. This stands in contrast to the parametrisation of Teugels (1990). (However, fixing an odds ratio may constrain other odds ratios of the same order.)

This gives us a natural way to define a joint distribution in terms of marginal probabilities and pairwise dependences, by setting all higher-order odds ratios to 1. The naturalness of this construction is supported by the following theorem connecting odds ratios to entropy.[24] Entropy is the measure of uncertainty, and gaining information corresponds to reducing entropy. Maximising entropy subject to certain constraints means making no further assumptions beyond those constraints.[25]

Theorem 2 Of all n-variate Bernoulli distributions with given $(n-1)$-variate margins, the maximum entropy distribution has $\omega_n = 1$.

We can now define the **Maximum Entropy Bernoulli Field**, using a mean function and a dependence function: for any set of n points, the mean function determines the odds for each truth value, and the dependence function determines the odds ratio for each pair of truth values, while all higher-order odds ratios are set to 1.

Before proving the theorems, it is instructive to first see a few examples. In all cases, I write p_n for the probability that all variables are true, and p_β for the probability of an event $\beta \in \{\top, \bot, \cdot\}^n$, where $\cdot$ indicates that a variable is ignored (marginalised out).

---

[24]These two theorems also lend further support to the suggestions of Tajar et al. (2001) and Geenens (2020) that the odds ratio can be seen as a discrete copula, generalising their work to the multivariate case. Copulas are discussed in §3.4.3.

[25]This is called *the principle of maximum entropy*, which has a long history in statistical physics, and was first stated explicitly by Jaynes (1957).

Example ($n = 1$) The odds are a strictly increasing function of the probability: $\omega_1 = \frac{p_1}{1-p_1} \in [0, \infty]$. This means we can parametrise the distribution using ω_1. The maximum entropy distribution is where $\omega_1 = 1$, which means $p_1 = \frac{1}{2}$.

Example ($n = 2$) The marginal probabilities $p_{\top\cdot}$ and $p_{\cdot\top}$ are strictly increasing functions of the respective marginal odds.

By applying the inclusion-exclusion principle, we can express the probability of each outcome in terms of $p_{\top\cdot}$, $p_{\cdot\top}$, and p_2:

$$p_{\top\top} = p_2 \tag{3.10}$$

$$p_{\top\bot} = p_{\top\cdot} - p_2 \tag{3.11}$$

$$p_{\bot\top} = p_{\cdot\top} - p_2 \tag{3.12}$$

$$p_{\bot\bot} = 1 - p_{\top\cdot} - p_{\cdot\top} + p_2 \tag{3.13}$$

In the edge case that both $p_{\top\cdot}$ and $p_{\cdot\top}$ are exactly 0 or 1, the distribution is exactly determined by $p_{\top\cdot}$ and $p_{\cdot\top}$, while the odds ratio ω_2 is undefined.

In all other cases, we can see from (3.10) and (3.13) that $p_{\top\top}$ and $p_{\bot\bot}$ are increasing in p_2, and we can see from (3.11) and (3.12) that $p_{\top\bot}$ and $p_{\bot\top}$ are decreasing in p_2. These correspond to the numerator and denominator in (3.5), and hence ω_2 is increasing in p_2. This means we can parametrise the distribution using ω_2 in place of p_2. Furthermore, ω_2 has range $[0, \infty]$, taking the extreme values when one of the outcomes has zero probability.

Given fixed $p_{\top\cdot}$ and $p_{\cdot\top}$, the maximum entropy distribution is where $\omega_2 = 1$, which means the two variables are independent (this can be seen by substituting Eqs. (3.10) to (3.13) into (3.5), which reduces to $p_2 = p_{\top\cdot} p_{\cdot\top}$).

Example ($n = 3$) The inclusion-exclusion principle lets us express the joint distribution in terms of the bivariate margins and p_3:

$$p_{\top\top\top} = p_3 \tag{3.14}$$

$$p_{\top\top\bot} = p_{\top\top\cdot} - p_3 \tag{3.15}$$

$$p_{\top\bot\top} = p_{\top\cdot\top} - p_3 \tag{3.16}$$

$$p_{\bot\top\top} = p_{\cdot\top\top} - p_3 \tag{3.17}$$

$$p_{\top\bot\bot} = p_{\top\cdot\cdot} - p_{\top\top\cdot} - p_{\top\cdot\top} + p_3 \tag{3.18}$$

$$p_{\bot\top\bot} = p_{\cdot\top\cdot} - p_{\top\top\cdot} - p_{\cdot\top\top} + p_3 \tag{3.19}$$

$$p_{\bot\bot\top} = p_{\cdot\cdot\top} - p_{\top\cdot\top} - p_{\cdot\top\top} + p_3 \tag{3.20}$$

$$p_{\bot\bot\bot} = 1 - p_{\top\cdot\cdot} - p_{\cdot\top\cdot} - p_{\cdot\cdot\top} + p_{\top\top\cdot} + p_{\top\cdot\top} + p_{\cdot\top\top} - p_3 \tag{3.21}$$

In the above equations, the final term $\pm p_3$ varies in sign according to the parity of the outcome, which corresponds to the numerator and denominator in (3.8). This means that ω_3 is an increasing function of p_3. The bivariate margins are parametrised by the odds ratios up to order 2, and so the joint distribution is parametrised by the odds ratios up to order 3.

Furthermore, ω_3 has range $[0, \infty]$, taking the extreme values when one of the outcomes has zero probability. (In the edge case where both an even and an odd outcome have zero probability, ω_3 is undefined, but in this case the distribution is exactly determined by the lower-order odds ratios, which leave only one possible value for p_3.)

Given the bivariate margins, the maximum entropy distribution has $\omega_3 = 1$, which expresses a "higher-order independence". It means that the first and second variables have the same degree of dependence (expressed as their odds ratio), no matter the value of the third variable, as shown in (3.22). The same is true for other permutations of variables.

$$\frac{p_{\top\top\top}p_{\bot\bot\top}}{p_{\top\bot\top}p_{\bot\top\top}} = \frac{p_{\top\top\bot}p_{\bot\bot\bot}}{p_{\top\bot\bot}p_{\bot\top\bot}} \tag{3.22}$$

Remark 1 The definition of odds ratios in (3.9) means it is straightforward to convert from probabilities of outcomes to odds ratios. However, going in the other direction is not as simple. In the trivariate case, if we set the third-order odds ratio to 1, we can solve for p_3 in terms of the given bivariate margins. This equates the product of (3.14) and (3.18) to (3.20) with the product of Eqs. (3.15) to (3.17) and (3.21). The p_3^4 terms cancel, and so this gives a cubic in p_3, which has a closed-form solution. In the general case, this would give a polynomial of degree $2^{n-1} - 1$, which would not give a closed-form solution for $n > 3$.

Remark 2 Given the $(n-2)$-variate margins, the n-variate maxent distribution is not the same as first finding each $(n-1)$-variate maxent distribution and then finding the n-variate maxent distribution given these $(n-1)$-variate margins. Finding the probability of an outcome for n truth values in a Bernoulli Field therefore requires recursively solving for each subset, which leads to a combinatorial explosion.

This is different from the continuous case: one way to define the multivariate Gaussian distribution is as the maxent distribution given the mean and covariance. Recursively finding the maxent distribution for subsets of dimensions gives the same result as finding the maxent distribution for all dimensions at once.

Proof Sketch By the inclusion-exclusion principle, we can find the probability of any outcome in terms of p_n and the $(n-1)$-variate margins. This allows us to prove the rather more technical lemma below.[26] Induction on this lemma gives Theorem 1. Meanwhile, optimising p_n to maximise entropy gives Theorem 2, where the sign of p_n in each inclusion-exclusion formula crucially matches the parity of the outcome.

Lemma Given compatible $(n-1)$-variate margins for n Bernoulli random variables, one of the following holds:

i Exactly one joint distribution exists, and ω_n is undefined.

ii The joint distributions form a one-dimensional family, parametrised by $\omega_n \in [0, \infty]$.

Proof For any outcome $\beta \in \{\top, \bot\}^n$, we can divide the variables between those that are true and false. Let us write these sets as $I_\top$ and $I_\bot$, respectively. Now consider each subset $J \subset I_\bot$ and the corresponding event where $I_\top \cup J$ are all true (without specifying the remaining variables). By the inclusion-exclusion principle, the probability of the outcome β can be expressed in terms of the probabilities of these events. With the convention that t_I denotes the event of all variables in I being true, we have:

$$p_\beta = \mathbb{P}\left(t_{I_\top} \cap \bigcap_{i \in I_\bot} \bar{t_i}\right) = \sum_{J \subset I_\bot} (-1)^{|J|} \mathbb{P}\left(t_{I_\top \cup J}\right) \tag{3.23}$$

When $J = I_\bot$, $\mathbb{P}(t_{I_\top \cup J}) = p_n$. When $J \neq I_\bot$, $|I_\top \cup J| < n$, and so $\mathbb{P}(t_{I_\top \cup J})$ is determined by (at least one of) the $(n-1)$-variate margins. The probability of each outcome is therefore of the following form, where each k_β is determined by the $(n-1)$-variate margins:

$$p_\beta = \mathrm{par}(\beta)\,(p_n - k_\beta) \tag{3.24}$$

Hence, given the margins, the joint distribution is determined by p_n.

For the distribution to be valid, each p_β must be non-negative. Therefore, for each even outcome, k_β is a lower bound on p_n; for each odd outcome, k_β is an upper bound on p_n.

Assuming that the margins are compatible, there are two cases. In the case that the greatest lower bound is equal to the least upper bound, there is only possible value for p_n, and so only one possible joint distribution. At least one odd and one even outcome has probability 0, and so ω_n is undefined.

[26] This lemma can be seen as a special case of Theorem 10.2 given by Rudas (2018). The proof given here is more direct, and allows a direct connection to entropy for Theorem 2.

In the case that the greatest lower bound is below the least upper bound, any value of p_n between these bounds gives a valid distribution. The probability of an even outcome is strictly increasing in p_n, and the probability of an odd outcome is strictly decreasing in p_n, and so ω_n is strictly increasing in p_n. This means the distribution can be parametrised by ω_n instead of p_n. At the minimum value of p_n, an even outcome has zero probability, and so $\omega_n = 0$. At the maximum value of p_n, an odd outcome has zero probability, and so $\omega_n = \infty$.

Proof of Theorem 1 The proof is by induction. The case $n = 1$ is immediate. For $n > 1$, we can parametrise all $(n{-}1)$-variate margins by the odds ratios up to order $n{-}1$ (by inductive assumption), and therefore parametrise the joint distribution by including ω_n if it exists (by the lemma).

Proof of Theorem 2 In the degenerate case that only one joint distribution exists, it is trivially the maximum, and ω_n is undefined.

In the non-degenerate case, we can find the maximum entropy distribution by differentiating the entropy $H = -\sum p_\beta \log p_\beta$ with respect to p_n. For each outcome, we have:

$$\frac{d}{dp_n}\left(p_\beta \log p_\beta\right) = \left(\log p_\beta + 1\right)\frac{dp_\beta}{dp_n} \tag{3.25}$$

From (3.24), we can see that $\frac{dp_\beta}{dp_n}$ is either 1 (for even outcomes) or -1 (for odd outcomes). Therefore, all of the 1s cancel out, giving:

$$\frac{dH}{dp_n} = -\sum_{\beta\in\{\top,\bot\}^n} \mathrm{par}(\beta)\log p_\beta \tag{3.26}$$

The maximum must be where the gradient is equal to 0, because it cannot be located at the extreme values of p_n: at its lowest value, some even outcome has zero probability and so the gradient is infinite and positive; at its highest value, some odd outcome has zero probability and so the gradient is infinite and negative.

Setting the gradient to 0 and taking the exponential, we precisely get $\omega_n = 1$.

Summary In this section, I have presented the Maximum Entropy Bernoulli Field, which is defined in terms of probabilities of truth for single truth values and odds ratios for pairs of truth values. While this construction enjoys a number of desirable properties (underpinned by Theorems 1 and 2), it is unfortunately not tractable for a large number of truth values.

3.4.3 Local Thresholds for Truth

A major stumbling block with defining a joint distribution for truth values is that the distribution is discrete. We have already seen how the mean and covariance are intertwined, and how the maximum entropy construction leads to a combinatorial explosion. These behaviours are quite different when we consider continuous distributions such as Gaussians.

To ease the construction of a discrete distribution, we can try to go as far as possible with a continuous distribution first. More precisely, we can separate the generative process into two steps: firstly, generating a threshold for each truth value; secondly, comparing the marginal probabilities to the thresholds, to determine the truth values. If we have a way to generate correlated thresholds, we can use them to generate correlated truth values. Independent truth values correspond to independent thresholds; comonotonic truth values correspond to a shared threshold.

At first sight, this might seem to give us a bigger problem: instead of a distribution over a finite set of 2^n outcomes, we now need a distribution over an infinite set of $[0,1]^n$ outcomes. However, the continuity of this larger set is precisely what will allow us to construct a tractable distribution. Although this introduces spurious structure (a set of truth values is compatible with many sets of thresholds), we are ultimately only interested in the truth values; the thresholds simply provide a convenient mathematical scaffold.

So that each truth value's marginal distribution is correct, each threshold's marginal distribution must be uniform over $[0,1]$. However, the joint distribution can allow different levels of correlation.

In fact, a joint distribution with uniform margins[27] is known as a statistical **copula**.[28] The joint distribution for truth values can then be given in terms of the copula's cumulative distribution function C:

$$\mathbb{P}\left(T_x{=}\top, T_y{=}\top\right) = C(t(x), t(y)) \tag{3.27}$$

What we need is a way to consistently define an n-dimensional copula for any set of n points. To leverage existing work, we can do this using a Gaussian Process.

---

[27]When defining a copula, the choice of $U(0,1)$ as the standard distribution is somewhat arbitrary (for discussion: Mikosch, 2006, Klüppelberg and Resnick, 2008, Embrechts, 2009). However, it is particularly convenient for our purposes, as we are considering probability thresholds.

[28]Not to be confused with a syntactic copula. While a syntactic copula links together a subject and a predicate, a statistical copula links together two (or more) random variables.

FIGURE 4: Random regions in a unit disc, similarly to Fig. 2, but using a Gaussian Process copula with exponential covariance function $k(x, y) = \exp(-|x - y|)$. This generates regions (usually consisting of a few disconnected components) with well-defined but jagged boundaries.

The key part of a Gaussian Process is the covariance function $k(x, y)$. We are interested in encoding local correlations, and so we can restrict attention to **isotropic** covariance functions, which only depend on the distance between x and y. We can restrict further with the following two assumptions. Firstly, when the distance is zero, the (co)variance is 1. This fixes the amount of variability at each point. Secondly, as the distance increases, the covariance decreases and eventually tends to zero. This means that distant points become increasingly independent; in other words, there are only local correlations. The particular shape of the covariance function controls the kind of function the Gaussian Process generates, such as smooth or jagged functions.

FIGURE 5: Random regions in a unit disc, similarly to Fig. 2, but using a Gaussian Process copula with squared-exponential covariance function $k(x, y) = \exp\left(-|x - y|^2\right)$. This gives regions with smooth boundaries.

Given a covariance function $k(x, y)$ and n points x_i, consider the multivariate Gaussian with zero mean and covariance $k(x_i, x_j)$. This defines a **Gaussian copula**, by transforming each dimension to lie in $[0, 1]$. Each dimension has mean 0 and variance 1, so each marginal distribution is the standard Gaussian. By transforming each dimension according to the standard Gaussian's cumulative distribution function Φ, we get the uniform distribution over $[0, 1]$. This gives the cumulative distribution function for the copula as shown in (3.28), where u_i is the threshold at x_i, and $\Phi_{0,\Sigma}$ is the cumulative distribution function for a Gaussian with mean 0 and covariance matrix Σ.

$$C_{\Sigma}^{\text{Gauss}}(u_1, \cdots, u_n) = \Phi_{0,\Sigma}(\Phi^{-1}(u_1), \cdots, \Phi^{-1}(u_n)) \tag{3.28}$$

Using a *Gaussian Process copula*, we can now define a **Gaussian Process Bernoulli Field** with a mean function (taking values in $[0, 1]$), and a covariance function (defining a Gaussian Process with zero mean). For any finite set of points, we can sample from the Bernoulli Field as follows. We first use the covariance function to calculate a covariance matrix for the given points. We can then sample from the multivariate Gaussian with zero mean and this covariance matrix. Each real value is converted to a threshold, using the standard Gaussian's cumulative distribution function. The value of the mean function at each point is compared to the corresponding threshold, returning true if above and false if below.

This is illustrated in Figs. 4 and 5, for two different choices of covariance function. One choice generates regions with jagged boundaries, while the other choice generates regions with smooth boundaries.

However, there is a notable downside to using Gaussian copulas: there is no closed-form solution for the cumulative distribution function. While it's possible to take samples of truth values, as described above, it's impossible to exactly calculate the joint distribution. Even for just two truth values, calculating the joint distribution requires approximate numerical integration of a multivariate Gaussian.

Furthermore, there is no easy fix for this problem, because construction of multivariate copulas is known to be a hard problem (for example, see: Joe, 1997, §4.1). What we want is a multivariate copula which is both flexible enough in its range of dependence (i.e. each pair of thresholds has a separate dependence parameter ranging from independence to comonotonicity), and also tractable enough to be used in practice (i.e. both the cumulative distribution function and probability density function have a tractable closed-form formula).[29] We have already seen that the Gaussian copula does not have a closed form. The Frank copula has a closed form, but all pairwise correlations are the same. The Farlie-Gumbel-Morgenstern copula has a closed form, and allows each pairwise correlation to be specified separately, but restricts the size of the correlations. Discovering a sufficiently flexible and tractable copula would be a major breakthrough.

[29]A multivariate copula can also be defined as a product of bivariate copulas, but including all pairwise dependences restricts the degrees of dependence (Mazo et al., 2015). The vine pair-copula construction is more powerful, representing any multivariate copula as a product of (conditional) bivariate copulas (Aas et al., 2009). However, a vine copula requires a hierarchy for the random variables, which breaks the symmetry of our problem; it is unclear how the conditional copulas could be defined in terms of pairwise dependence parameters.

3.4.4 Summary

In this section, I have introduced the Bernoulli Field, an efficiently parametrised distribution over regions. Equivalently, it is also a distribution over binary classifiers. A Bernoulli Field is defined in terms of a mean function (e.g. a neural net) and a dependence function (e.g. exponentially decaying with distance). As the dependence function does not require learnable parameters, it can straightforwardly be added to any approach that uses probabilistic binary classifiers.

I have presented two families of Bernoulli Fields, which have different computational tradeoffs. The Maximum Entropy Bernoulli Field is mathematically elegant, underpinned by the Theorems in §3.4.2. However, it has no closed-form solution for $n > 3$, and the cost of numerically finding the solution scales exponentially. In contrast, the Gaussian Process Bernoulli Field allows tractable sampling for any number of truth values (with examples given in Figs. 4 and 5). However, it has no closed-form solution even for $n = 2$.

Bernoulli Fields provide a mathematically precise model of vagueness, which is more accurate than a threshold-based model when dealing with a multidimensional space. For many cases, the full power of a Bernoulli Field is unnecessary, because we only need to consider the mean function. For example, this is enough for comparing pairs of pixies, and is enough for demarcating a "typical" region. However, the dependence function provides additional flexibility for modelling pragmatic behaviour. This additional flexibility might seem computationally expensive, but for any given discourse, we only need to consider pixies for the discourse referents, and don't need to consider the full regions. This neatly corresponds with the computational insight discussed in §3.4.1, that in defining a distribution over regions, we only need to define distributions for finite subsets of points.

3.5 Pragmatic Reasoning with Lexical Uncertainty

As mentioned in §3.2.3, RSA provides a solid framework for pragmatic reasoning, by defining a sequence of listeners and speakers.[30] However, the original approach to vague predicates (Lassiter and Goodman, 2015, Goodman and Frank, 2016) makes two assumptions that can be relaxed. Firstly, it uses global thresholds. For a one-dimensional space (such as for length or price), using a global threshold is reasonable, as discussed by Lassiter (2011). However, a global threshold is restrictive

[30] For a tutorial on RSA, see: https://www.problang.org (Scontras et al., 2018)

in higher-dimensional spaces – even in a two-dimensional space, as can be seen in Figs. 2 to 5. As I argued in §3.4, a more accurate model would use locally correlated thresholds.

The second assumption is that literal semantics is non-probabilistic, with lexical uncertainty only introduced at the level of the pragmatic listener. In the following subsections, I will discuss problems that follow from this assumption, and then show how to introduce lexical uncertainty already at the level of the literal listener.

In the original formulation of RSA, a literal listener $L0$ aims to infer the world state s, after hearing an utterance u. Given precise truth conditions for u, and a prior $\mathbb{P}_{L0}(s)$, the literal listeners infers a posterior $\mathbb{P}_{L0}(s|u)$ by ruling out those states where u is false.

The speaker knows the true world state and aims to communicate this to the listener. An honest but lazy strategy would be to randomly choose a true utterance. The optimal strategy is to maximise the probability of the listener making the correct inference. We can then interpolate between these two extremes using an optimality parameter α. This gives us a distribution $\mathbb{P}_S(u|s)$.

Finally, a pragmatic listener performs Bayesian inference on such a speaker. Given the prior $\mathbb{P}_{L0}(s)$ and a speaker $\mathbb{P}_S(u|s)$, we can calculate a pragmatic posterior $\mathbb{P}_{L1}(s|u)$.

In this framework, previous work has modelled vague predicates using a latent variable for a global threshold (Lassiter and Goodman, 2015, Goodman and Frank, 2016). The literal listener and speaker are defined for a given threshold v, so we have distributions $\mathbb{P}_{L0}(s|u,v)$ and $\mathbb{P}_S(u|s,v)$. The pragmatic listener additionally has a prior $\mathbb{P}_{L1}(v)$ over thresholds, assumed to be independent of the world state, so that we can define $\mathbb{P}_{L1}(s,v|u)$ using Bayesian inference. The threshold is therefore pragmatically inferred, along with the world state.

To relax the first assumption mentioned above, we can replace the global threshold with a Bernoulli Field, so that v is a region, rather than a threshold. This would generalise previous versions of RSA, so that a listener can pragmatically infer regions, rather than thresholds.

However, this still leaves the second assumption mentioned above. While the pragmatic listener has a distribution over regions/thresholds, each sample from this distribution gives a literal listener and speaker with non-probabilistic semantics. In the following sections, I will first explain two downsides that follow from this assumption, and then give a more general approach which avoids these problems.

3.5.1 Problem: Intractable ambiguity

The pragmatic listener defines a joint distribution over world states, utterances, and latent variables. While the latent variables are assumed independent of the world state, they are not *conditionally independent* given an utterance. In order to calculate the pragmatic listener's posterior distribution over world states, given an observed utterance, we have to marginalise out the latent variables. However, this requires summing over all possible values for the latent variables.

If we scale up the model to include many predicates, each with its own lexical uncertainty,[31] we get a combinatorial explosion. Each predicate needs a latent variable to model its lexical uncertainty, and the pragmatic listener must consider all *combinations* of values of these latent variables. In a real world setting, the number of predicates will be vast, and each predicate will have a large number of possible precise meanings. Even if the speaker only considers 10 predicates, each of which is ambiguous between 4 possible meanings (such as a vague threshold with 4 possible values), then there are $4^{10} = 1$ million combinations. For each of these million combinations, there is a different literal listener and speaker, and exact inference for the pragmatic speaker requires summing over all of them. With 1000 predicates, each with 100 precise meanings, we get $100^{1000} = 10^{2000}$ combinations. Summing over all possibilities is neither practical nor psychologically plausible.

As we will see, this problem can be avoided by pushing vagueness down to the level of the literal listener.

3.5.2 Problem: Lack of optimality

As described above, the RSA framework includes an "optimality" parameter for the speaker. However, as the speaker and listener have a clearly defined goal (the speaker must communicate the world state to the listener), we can also find the game-theoretically optimal strategies. Ideally, as we increase the optimality parameter, we should tend towards an optimal strategy. If not, then we are forced to say that RSA models a certain class of suboptimal strategies.

In the original RSA approach to gradable predicates, optimal behaviour is not achieved, even as the optimality parameter tends to infinity. This is because the literal listener and speaker are only defined relative to a fixed value for the latent variables. As the optimality parameter is increased, the speaker tends towards optimal behaviour

[31] More generally, we would also consider other kinds of ambiguity beyond vagueness, such as syntactic ambiguity and scope ambiguity, which would further exacerbate this problem.

given the fixed values – but the pragmatic listener averages over these speakers, and the averaged behaviour will not be optimal.

To give a simple example, suppose there are three world states, where the price of a toaster is low, medium, or high. Suppose further that the prior over these world states is $(\frac{1}{4}, \frac{1}{4}, \frac{1}{2})$, and that there are only two possible utterances for the speaker. Leaving aside RSA and considering all possible game-theoretic strategies, the optimal strategy is to use one utterance for the high-price state, and the other utterance for the other two states. This maximises the amount of information conveyed (exactly 1 bit), and thereby the expected probability of the listener making the correct inference $(\frac{3}{4})$.

The RSA strategy is defined using semantics as a starting point. Suppose the speaker has to choose between uttering "expensive" and uttering nothing (which is always true). Suppose further that "expensive" is vague between two thresholds (between the low and medium prices, or between the medium and high prices). Given the higher threshold, the speaker will tend towards an optimal strategy as the optimality parameter tends to infinity (using the "expensive" utterance for the high price, and the null utterance for the medium and low prices). Given the lower threshold, the speaker will tend towards a suboptimal but still reasonable strategy (using the "expensive" utterance for the medium and high prices, and the null utterance for the low price). However, if there is an equal prior probability of each threshold, the combined strategy is worse than either of these, with a success probability of only 0.63 (compared to 0.75 and 0.67 for the two fixed-threshold strategies).

The low success probability stems from the fact that the two strategies disagree on what utterance to choose for the medium price, and combining the two strategies creates uncertainty for the listener. We will see that this problem can be avoided by pushing vagueness down to the level of the literal listener.

3.5.3 Solution: Probabilistic literal semantics

We can solve the above two problems by defining the literal listener and speaker with probabilistic semantics.[32] The literal listener has a prior over world states $\mathbb{P}_{L0}(s)$, as before. In addition, there is a prior over precise meanings $\mathbb{P}_{L0}(v)$ (a Bernoulli Field for each predicate). I will

[32]Independently of the present work, Grove and Bernardy (forthcoming) also propose pushing linguistic uncertainty down to the level of the literal listener, so that the literal and pragmatic listeners are of the same type-theoretic type. This can be seen in (3.29) and (3.35) both defining a distribution $\mathbb{P}(s, v_u \mid u)$.

write v_u for those latent variables which are relevant for utterance u (the Bernoulli Fields for the predicates appearing in u).

On observing an utterance, the literal listener rules out combinations of precise meanings and world states that are impossible. This gives a posterior distribution:

$$\mathbb{P}_{L0}(s, v_u|u) \propto \begin{cases} \mathbb{P}_{L0}(s)\mathbb{P}_{L0}(v_u) & u \text{ true of } s \text{ given } v_u \\ 0 & \text{otherwise} \end{cases} \tag{3.29}$$

Crucially, meanings are only ruled out for the predicates in the observed utterance – for all other predicates, the posterior distribution over meanings remains the same as the prior. This avoids a combinatorial explosion, as the number of predicates in an utterance is far smaller than the number of predicates in the whole vocabulary.

The speaker is defined with an optimality parameter α, as before, choosing an utterance with the aim of maximising the probability of the literal listener making the correct inference of the world state, as shown in (3.30). The speaker is not optimising for inference of the latent v_u, and so only depends on $\mathbb{P}_{L0}(s|u)$, with v_u marginalised out, which can be calculated as in (3.31).

$$\mathbb{P}_S(u|s) \propto \exp\left(\alpha \log \mathbb{P}_{L0}(s|u)\right) \tag{3.30}$$

$$\mathbb{P}_{L0}(s|u) \propto \mathbb{P}_{L0}(s) \sum_{v_u \text{ s.t. } u \text{ true of } s} \mathbb{P}_{L0}(v_u) \tag{3.31}$$

The sum in (3.31) gives the marginal probability that u is true of s, analogously to the sum in (3.4). Writing the marginal probability of truth as $t_u(s)$, we have (3.32). As discussed in §3.4.1, a Bernoulli Field is defined in terms of marginal distributions for truth values. So, if s represents a single entity and u is a single predicate, then a Bernoulli Field provides exactly what is required. If u is a complex utterance containing multiple predicates, it is possible to compositionally derive such a function t_u, as I have shown in previous work (Emerson, 2020c).

$$\mathbb{P}_{L0}(s|u) \propto \mathbb{P}_{L0}(s)t_u(s) \tag{3.32}$$

Regardless of whether Bernoulli Fields are used, and regardless of the approach to composition, (3.30) avoids a combinatorial explosion, because we only need to marginalise out one latent variable; each utterance u requires us to marginalise out its v_u, but each of these marginalisations is separate. This solves the first problem above (§3.5.1).

Furthermore, as α tends to infinity, we can observe truly optimal behaviour, solving the second problem above (§3.5.2). We can see this with the previous simple example. On observing the null utterance, the literal listener's posterior remains the same as the prior, which is $(\frac{1}{4}, \frac{1}{4}, \frac{1}{2})$. On observing "expensive", the literal listener considers the two possible thresholds, ruling out all of the prior probability mass for the low price, and ruling out half of the prior probability mass for the medium price; normalising the probability masses then gives a posterior distribution of $(0, \frac{1}{5}, \frac{4}{5})$. Comparing these two posterior distributions, we can see that the "expensive" distribution has a higher value only for the high price. Therefore, as α tends to infinity, the speaker will tend towards using "expensive" for the high price, and the null utterance otherwise, which is game-theoretically optimal.

As before, the pragmatic listener simply performs Bayesian inference for the speaker, as shown in (3.33). Once the latent variables have been marginalised out, there is no need to consider them explicitly, and so there is no further opportunity for a combinatorial explosion.

$$\mathbb{P}_{L1}(s|u) \propto \mathbb{P}_{L0}(s)\mathbb{P}_S(u|s) \tag{3.33}$$

While v_u is absent from (3.30) and (3.33), it is nonetheless possible to reason about v_u, because s, u, and v_u are jointly distributed:

$$\mathbb{P}_S(u, v_u|s) = \mathbb{P}_S(u|s)\mathbb{P}_{L0}(v_u|u, s) \tag{3.34}$$

$$\mathbb{P}_{L1}(s, v_u|u) \propto \mathbb{P}_{L0}(s)\mathbb{P}_S(u|s)\mathbb{P}_{L0}(v_u|u, s) \tag{3.35}$$

However, v_u gives the threshold for *truth*, which is not the same as the pragmatically determined threshold of *use*. We can see this in the simple example, assuming a maximally optimal speaker. On observing "expensive", the pragmatic listener infers the high price with probability 1. On observing the null utterance, the pragmatic listener infers the low and medium prices with probability $\frac{1}{2}$ each. In both cases, however, no value for v_u has been ruled out, and so the posterior distribution remains the same as the prior! In the general case, the posterior distribution over thresholds is not the same as the prior (some values might be ruled out), but we can clearly see that literal truth is distinct from pragmatic behaviour, even when both are described probabilistically. While truth-conditional semantics provides a firm basis for reasoning, pragmatic behaviour can be described without it. More precisely, pragmatic behaviour can be described with truth marginalised out.

3.5.4 Discussion: Levels of lexical uncertainty

I argued above that modelling literal semantics probabilistically avoids two problems with the original formulation of RSA, while maintaining its strengths and insights. However, we can still define the pragmatic listener to have a distribution over speakers, as in the original formulation.

This would give us two levels of lexical uncertainty, corresponding to the two distinct sources of lexical uncertainty discussed in §3.3.2.

Uncertainty in the literal semantics, discussed above, corresponds to the unavoidable uncertainty stemming from the need to generalise. Uncertainty about the speaker corresponds to variation in a speech community.

For example, suppose a pragmatic listener hears "chips" in a context containing many different kinds of fried potato. One level of uncertainty is whether the speaker means "chips" in the British sense or the American sense. A second level of uncertainty is the unavoidable vagueness of either of these senses.

We can model the latter uncertainty using a Bernoulli Field for the literal semantics of each sense. We can model the former uncertainty as a distribution over two kinds of speaker, either British or American.

We can therefore define the literal listener and speaker relative to an additional latent variable d for the dialect,[33] as $\mathbb{P}_{L0}(s, v_u|u, d)$ and $\mathbb{P}_S(u, v_u|s, d)$. The pragmatic listener then defines a distribution $\mathbb{P}_{L1}(s, v_u, d|u)$, jointly inferring the world state s, the literal semantics v_u, and the speaker dialect d.

3.6 Conclusion

In this chapter, I discussed challenges of lexical semantics, and surveyed the use of probability theory in addressing those challenges. Furthermore, I discussed not only the usefulness but also the unavoidability of probabilities, when we consider the need for language to generalise in high-dimensional spaces. I argued in favour of representing meaning as a probabilistic truth-conditional function, I explained how correlations between truth values makes this equivalent to representing meaning as a probabilistic region of space, and I presented the Bernoulli Field, which allows us to do this with an efficiently parametrised model. I gave two variants, one grounded on two novel theorems about higher-order odds ratios, and the other grounded on previous work on Gaussian Processes. Finally, I looked at how probabilistic lexical semantics can be incorporated into pragmatic reasoning, improving on previous work in the Rational Speech Acts framework.

[33] We could go further, and model many kinds of speaker, such as speakers with different levels of optimality. We could even consider speakers choosing utterances for different distributions of literal listeners, which would split the d variable into two, one for the literal listener, and one for the speaker. This would however come at a considerable computational cost, and would also be unlikely to be useful for modelling human behaviour.

References

Aas, Kjersti, Claudia Czado, Arnoldo Frigessi, and Henrik Bakken. 2009. Pair-copula constructions of multiple dependence. *Insurance: Mathematics and economics* 44(2):182–198.

Adams, Ernest W. 1998. *A Primer of Probability Logic*. No. 68 in CSLI Lecture Notes. Center for the Study of Language and Information (CSLI) Publications.

Allan, Keith. 2001. *Natural language semantics*. Blackwell.

Arnauld, Antoine and Pierre Nicole. 1662. *La logique ou l'art de penser*. Published by Jean Guignart, Charles Savreux, and Jean de Lavnay. Widely known as the *Port-Royal Logic*.

Athiwaratkun, Ben and Andrew Gordon Wilson. 2017. Multimodal word distributions. In *Proceedings of the 55th Annual Meeting of the Association for Computational Linguistics (ACL), Long Papers*, pages 1645–1656.

Balkır, Esma. 2014. *Using density matrices in a compositional distributional model of meaning*. Master's thesis, University of Oxford.

Barkan, Oren. 2017. Bayesian neural word embedding. In *Proceedings of the 31st AAAI Conference on Artificial Intelligence*, pages 3135–3143. Association for the Advancement of Artificial Intelligence.

Barsalou, Lawrence W, Léo Dutriaux, and Christoph Scheepers. 2018. Moving beyond the distinction between concrete and abstract concepts. *Philosophical Transactions of the Royal Society B* 373(1752):20170144.

Barwise, Jon and John Perry. 1983. *Situations and Attitudes*. Massachusetts Institute of Technology (MIT) Press.

Bergmair, Richard. 2010. *Monte Carlo Semantics: Robust inference and logical pattern processing with Natural Language text*. Ph.D. thesis, University of Cambridge.

Bernardy, Jean-Philippe, Rasmus Blanck, Stergios Chatzikyriakidis, and Shalom Lappin. 2018. A compositional Bayesian semantics for natural language. In *Proceedings of the 1st International Workshop on Language, Cognition and Computational Models*, pages 1–10.

Bernardy, Jean-Philippe, Rasmus Blanck, Stergios Chatzikyriakidis, Shalom Lappin, and Aleksandre Maskharashvili. 2019. Bayesian Inference Semantics: A modelling system and a test suite. In *Proceedings of the 8th Joint Conference on Lexical and Computational Semantics (*SEM)*, pages 263–272.

Blake, Adam B, Meenely Nazarian, and Alan D Castel. 2015. The Apple of the mind's eye: Everyday attention, metamemory, and reconstructive memory for the Apple logo. *The Quarterly Journal of Experimental Psychology* 68(5):858–865.

Blei, David M., Andrew Y. Ng, and Michael I. Jordan. 2003. Latent Dirichlet Allocation. *Journal of Machine Learning Research* 3(Jan):993–1022.

Blondin-Massé, Alexandre, Guillaume Chicoisne, Yassine Gargouri, Stevan Harnad, Olivier Picard, and Odile Marcotte. 2008. How is meaning grounded in dictionary definitions? In *Proceedings of the 3rd Textgraphs Workshop on Graph-Based Algorithms for Natural Language Processing*, pages 17–24. 22nd International Conference on Computational Linguistics (COLING).

Blutner, Reinhard. 1998. Lexical pragmatics. *Journal of Semantics* 15(2):115–162.

Brandom, Robert Boyce. 2000. *Articulating Reasons: An Introduction to Inferentialism*. Harvard University Press.

Bražinskas, Arthur, Serhii Havrylov, and Ivan Titov. 2018. Embedding words as distributions with a Bayesian skip-gram model. In *Proceedings of the 27th International Conference on Computational Linguistics (COLING)*, pages 1775–1789. International Committee on Computational Linguistics (ICCL).

Burnett, Heather and Peter R. Sutton. 2020. Vagueness and natural language semantics. Wiley Online Library.

Cann, Ronnie. 1993. *Formal semantics: an introduction*. Cambridge University Press.

Carnap, Rudolf. 1947. *Meaning and Necessity: A Study in Semantics and Modal Logic*. University of Chicago Press.

Chang, Baobao, Wenzhe Pei, and Miaohong Chen. 2014. Inducing word sense with automatically learned hidden concepts. In *Proceedings of the 25th International Conference on Computational Linguistics (COLING)*, pages 355–364. International Committee on Computational Linguistics (ICCL).

Cintula, Petr, Christian G. Fermüller, and Carles Noguera. 2017. Fuzzy logic. In E. N. Zalta, ed., *The Stanford Encyclopedia of Philosophy*. Metaphysics Research Lab, Stanford University, fall edn.

Cooper, Robin. 2005. Austinian truth, attitudes and type theory. *Research on Language and Computation* 3(2-3):333–362.

Cooper, Robin, Simon Dobnik, Staffan Larsson, and Shalom Lappin. 2015. Probabilistic type theory and natural language semantics. *Linguistic Issues in Language Technology (LiLT)* 10.

Copestake, Ann. 2007. Semantic composition with (Robust) Minimal Recursion Semantics. In *Proceedings of the ACL 2007 Workshop on Deep Linguistic Processing*, pages 73–80. Association for Computational Linguistics.

Copestake, Ann. 2009. Slacker semantics: Why superficiality, dependency and avoidance of commitment can be the right way to go. In *Proceedings of the 12th Conference of the European Chapter of the Association for Computational Linguistics (EACL)*, pages 1–9.

Copestake, Ann, Dan Flickinger, Carl Pollard, and Ivan A. Sag. 2005. Minimal Recursion Semantics: An introduction. *Research on Language and Computation* 3(2-3):281–332.

Copestake, Ann, Alex Lascarides, and Dan Flickinger. 2001. An algebra for semantic construction in constraint-based grammars. In *Proceedings of the 39th Annual Meeting of the Association for Computational Linguistics (ACL)*, pages 140–147.

Cotterell, Ryan, Adam Poliak, Benjamin Van Durme, and Jason Eisner. 2017. Explaining and generalizing Skip-Gram through exponential family principal component analysis. In *Proceedings of the 15th Conference of the European Chapter of the Association for Computational Linguistics (EACL), Short Papers*, pages 175–181.

Dai, Bin, Shilin Ding, and Grace Wahba. 2013. Multivariate bernoulli distribution. *Bernoulli* 19(4):1465–1483.

de Saussure, Ferdinand. 1916. *Cours de linguistique générale (Course in general linguistics)*. Edited and published by Charles Bally and Albert Sechehaye, University of Geneva.

Deerwester, Scott, Susan T. Dumais, George W. Furnas, Thomas K. Landauer, and Richard Harshman. 1990. Indexing by Latent Semantic Analysis. *Journal of the American Society for Information Science* 41(6):391–407.

Demey, Lorenz, Barteld Kooi, and Joshua Sack. 2013. Logic and probability. In E. N. Zalta, ed., *The Stanford Encyclopedia of Philosophy*. Metaphysics Research Lab, Stanford University, spring edn. The summer 2017 edition contains minor corrections.

Devereux, Barry J, Lorraine K Tyler, Jeroen Geertzen, and Billi Randall. 2014. The Centre for Speech, Language and the Brain (CSLB) concept property norms. *Behavior Research Methods* 46(4):1119–1127.

Dinu, Georgiana and Mirella Lapata. 2010. Measuring distributional similarity in context. In *Proceedings of the 15th Conference on Empirical Methods in Natural Language Processing (EMNLP)*, pages 1162–1172. Association for Computational Linguistics.

Dong, Tiansi, Chrisitan Bauckhage, Hailong Jin, Juanzi Li, Olaf Cremers, Daniel Speicher, Armin B Cremers, and Joerg Zimmermann. 2018. Imposing category trees onto word-embeddings using a geometric construction. In *Proceedings of the 6th International Conference on Learning Representations (ICLR)*.

Dowty, David R., Robert E. Wall, and Stanley Peters. 1981. *Introduction to Montague Semantics*, vol. 11 of *Studies in Linguistics and Philosophy*. Kluwer Academic Publishers.

Dummett, Michael. 1976. What is a theory of meaning? (II). In G. Evans and J. McDowell, eds., *Truth and Meaning: Essays in Semantics*, chap. 4, pages 67–137. Clarendon Press (Oxford). Reprinted in: Dummett (1993), *Seas of Language*, chapter 2, pages 34–93.

Dummett, Michael. 1978. What do I know when I know a language? Presented at the Centenary Celebrations of Stockholm University. Reprinted in: Dummett (1993), *Seas of Language*, chapter 3, pages 94–105.

Edgington, Dorothy. 1992. Validity, uncertainty and vagueness. *Analysis* 52(4):193–204.

Edgington, Dorothy. 1997. Vagueness by degrees. In R. Keefe and P. Smith, eds., *Vagueness: A Reader*, chap. 16, pages 294–316. MIT Press.

Elman, Jeffrey L. 2009. On the meaning of words and dinosaur bones: Lexical knowledge without a lexicon. *Cognitive Science* 33(4):547–582.

Embrechts, Paul. 2009. Copulas: A personal view. *Journal of Risk and Insurance* 76(3):639–650.

Emerson, Guy. 2018. *Functional Distributional Semantics: Learning Linguistically Informed Representations from a Precisely Annotated Corpus*. Ph.D. thesis, University of Cambridge.

Emerson, Guy. 2020a. Autoencoding pixies: Amortised variational inference with graph convolutions for Functional Distributional Semantics. In *Proceedings of the 58th Annual Meeting of the Association for Computational Linguistics (ACL)*.

Emerson, Guy. 2020b. What are the goals of distributional semantics? In *Proceedings of the 58th Annual Meeting of the Association for Computational Linguistics (ACL)*.

Emerson, Guy. 2020c. Linguists who use probabilistic models love them: Quantification in Functional Distributional Semantics. In *Proceedings of Probability and Meaning (PaM2020)*. Association for Computational Linguistics.

Emerson, Guy and Ann Copestake. 2015. Lacking integrity: HPSG as a morphosyntactic theory. In *Proceedings of the 22nd Annual Conference on Head-Driven Phrase Structure Grammar*, pages 75–95. Center for the Study of Language and Information (CSLI) Publications.

Emerson, Guy and Ann Copestake. 2016. Functional Distributional Semantics. In *Proceedings of the 1st Workshop on Representation Learning for NLP (RepL4NLP)*, pages 40–52. Association for Computational Linguistics.

Emerson, Guy and Ann Copestake. 2017a. Variational inference for logical inference. In *Proceedings of the Conference on Logic and Machine Learning in Natural Language (LaML)*, pages 53–62. Centre for Linguistic Theory and Studies in Probability (CLASP).

Emerson, Guy and Ann Copestake. 2017b. Semantic composition via probabilistic model theory. In *Proceedings of the 12th International Conference on Computational Semantics (IWCS)*, pages 62–77. Association for Computational Linguistics.

Erk, Katrin. 2009a. Supporting inferences in semantic space: representing words as regions. In *Proceedings of the 8th International Conference on Computational Semantics (IWCS)*, pages 104–115. Association for Computational Linguistics.

Erk, Katrin. 2009b. Representing words as regions in vector space. In *Proceedings of the 13th Conference on Computational Natural Language Learning (CoNLL)*, pages 57–65. Association for Computational Linguistics.

Erk, Katrin. 2010. What is word meaning, really? (and how can distributional models help us describe it?). In *Proceedings of the 2010 Workshop on Geometrical Models of Natural Language Semantics*, pages 17–26. Association for Computational Linguistics.

Erk, Katrin. 2021. The probabilistic turn in semantics and pragmatics. *Annual Review of Linguistics* 8.

Erk, Katrin and Aurelie Herbelot. 2021. How to marry a star: Probabilistic constraints for meaning in context. *Proceedings of the Society for Computation in Linguistics* 4(1):451–453.

Erk, Katrin, Diana McCarthy, and Nicholas Gaylord. 2009. Investigations on word senses and word usages. In *Proceedings of the Joint Conference of the 47th Annual Meeting of the ACL and the 4th International Joint Conference on Natural Language Processing of the AFNLP (IJCNLP), Long Papers*, pages 10–18.

Erk, Katrin, Diana McCarthy, and Nicholas Gaylord. 2013. Measuring word meaning in context. *Computational Linguistics* 39(3):511–554.

Escalante, Hugo Jair, Carlos A Hernández, Jesus A Gonzalez, Aurelio López-López, Manuel Montes, Eduardo F Morales, L Enrique Sucar, Luis Villaseñor, and Michael Grubinger. 2010. The segmented and annotated IAPR TC-12 benchmark. *Computer Vision and Image Understanding* 114(4):419–428.

Fernández, Raquel and Staffan Larsson. 2014. Vagueness and learning: A type-theoretic approach. In *Proceedings of the 3rd Joint Conference on Lexical and Computational Semantics (*SEM)*, pages 151–159. Association for Computational Linguistics.

Fine, Kit. 1975. Vagueness, truth and logic. *Synthese* 30(3-4):265–300.

Fontana, Roberto and Patrizia Semeraro. 2018. Representation of multivariate bernoulli distributions with a given set of specified moments. *Journal of Multivariate Analysis* 168:290–303.

Frank, Michael C. and Noah D. Goodman. 2012. Predicting pragmatic reasoning in language games. *Science* 336(6084):998–998.

Frege, Gottlob. 1892. Über Sinn und Bedeutung. *Zeitschrift für Philosophie und philosophische Kritik* 100:25–50. Usually translated into English under the title *On Sense and Reference*.

Gärdenfors, Peter. 2000. *Conceptual spaces: The geometry of thought*. Massachusetts Institute of Technology (MIT) Press.

Gärdenfors, Peter. 2014. *Geometry of meaning: Semantics based on conceptual spaces*. Massachusetts Institute of Technology (MIT) Press.

Geenens, Gery. 2020. Copula modeling for discrete random vectors. *Dependence Modeling* 8(1):417–440.

Gershman, Samuel J. and David M. Blei. 2012. A tutorial on Bayesian nonparametric models. *Journal of Mathematical Psychology* 56(1):1–12.

Goodman, Noah D. and Michael C. Frank. 2016. Pragmatic language interpretation as probabilistic inference. *Trends in cognitive sciences* 20(11):818–829.

Goodman, Noah D. and Daniel Lassiter. 2015. Probabilistic semantics and pragmatics: Uncertainty in language and thought. In S. Lappin and C. Fox, eds., *The Handbook of Contemporary Semantic Theory*, chap. 21, pages 655–686. Wiley, 2nd edn.

Grove, Julian and Jean-Philippe Bernardy. forthcoming. Probabilistic compositional semantics, purely. In *New Frontiers in Artificial Intelligence: JSAI-isAI 2021 Workshops, Revised Selected Papers*, Lecture Notes in Computer Science.

Hájek, Petr. 1998. *Metamathematics of Fuzzy Logic*. No. 4 in Trends in Logic. Kluwer Academic Publishers.

Hájek, Petr, Lluís Godo, and Francesc Esteva. 1995. Fuzzy logic and probability. In *Proceedings of the 11th Annual Conference on Uncertainty in Artificial Intelligence*, pages 237–244. Morgan Kaufmann Publishers Inc.

Hanks, Patrick. 2000. Do word meanings exist? *Computers and the Humanities* 34, Special Issue on SENSEVAL: Evaluating Word Sense Disambiguation Programs:205–215.

Harnad, Stevan. 1990. The symbol grounding problem. *Physica D: Nonlinear Phenomena* 42:335–346.

Haspelmath, Martin. 2011. The indeterminacy of word segmentation and the nature of morphology and syntax. *Folia Linguistica* 45(1):31–80.

Hodges, Wilfrid. 2014. Tarski's truth definitions. In E. N. Zalta, ed., *The Stanford Encyclopedia of Philosophy*. Metaphysics Research Lab, Stanford University, fall edn.

Hürlimann, Manuela and Johan Bos. 2016. Combining lexical and spatial knowledge to predict spatial relations between objects in images. In *Proceedings of the 5th Workshop on Vision and Language*, pages 10–18. Association for Computational Linguistics.

Hyde, Dominic and Diana Raffman. 2018. Sorites paradox. In E. N. Zalta, ed., *The Stanford Encyclopedia of Philosophy*. Metaphysics Research Lab, Stanford University, summer edn.

Icard, Thomas F. 2014. *The Algorithmic Mind: A Study of Inference in Action*. Ph.D. thesis, Stanford University. Institute for Logic, Language and Computation (ILLC) Dissertation Series, DS-2014-02.

Jameel, Shoaib and Steven Schockaert. 2017. Modeling context words as regions: An ordinal regression approach to word embedding. In *Proceedings of the 21st Conference on Computational Natural Language Learning (CoNLL)*, pages 123–133. Association for Computational Linguistics.

Jaynes, Edwin Thompson. 1957. Information theory and statistical mechanics. *Physical Review* 106(4):620–630.

Joe, Harry. 1997. *Multivariate models and multivariate dependence concepts.* CRC Press.

Jones, Emily Elizabeth Constance. 1911. *A New Law of Thought and its Logical Bearings.* Cambridge University Press.

Jones, Gregory V. 1990. Misremembering a common object: When left is not right. *Memory & Cognition* 18(2):174–182.

Kamp, Hans A. W. and Barbara Partee. 1995. Prototype theory and compositionality. *Cognition* 57(2):129–191.

Kamp, Hans A. W. and Uwe Reyle. 2013. *From Discourse to Logic: Introduction to Modeltheoretic Semantics of Natural Language, Formal Logic and Discourse Representation Theory*, vol. 42 of *Studies in Linguistics and Philosophy*. Springer.

Kaplan, David. 1979. On the logic of demonstratives. *Journal of Philosophical Logic* 8(1):81–98.

Kaplan, David. 1989. Demonstratives: An essay on the semantics, logic, metaphysics, and epistemology of demonstratives and other indexicals. In J. Almog, J. Perry, and H. Wettstein, eds., *Themes from Kaplan*, chap. 17, pages 481–563. Oxford University Press.

Keefe, Rosanna. 2000. *Theories of Vagueness.* Cambridge Studies in Philosophy. Cambridge University Press.

Kenny, Anthony. 2010. Concepts, brains, and behaviour. *Grazer Philosophische Studien* 81(1):105–113.

Kilgarriff, Adam. 1997. I don't believe in word senses. *Computers and the Humanities* 31(2):91–113.

Kilgarriff, Adam. 2007. Word senses. In E. Agirre and P. Edmonds, eds., *Word Sense Disambiguation: Algorithms and Applications*, chap. 2, pages 29–46. Springer.

Klüppelberg, Claudia and Sidney I. Resnick. 2008. The pareto copula, aggregation of risks, and the emperor's socks. *Journal of Applied Probability* 45(1):67–84.

Krishna, Ranjay, Yuke Zhu, Oliver Groth, Justin Johnson, Kenji Hata, Joshua Kravitz, Stephanie Chen, Yannis Kalantidis, Li-Jia Li, David A Shamma, et al. 2017. Visual Genome: Connecting language and vision using crowdsourced dense image annotations. *International Journal of Computer Vision* 123(1):32–73.

Labov, William. 1973. The boundaries of words and their meanings. In C.-J. Bailey and R. W. Shuy, eds., *New Ways of Analyzing Variation in English*, chap. 24, pages 340–371. Georgetown University Press. Reprinted in: Ralph W. Fasold, editor (1983), *Variation in the Form and Use of Language: A Sociolinguistics Reader*, chapter 3, pages 29–62, Georgetown University Press.

Lahav, Ran. 1989. Against compositionality: the case of adjectives. *Philosophical Studies: An International Journal for Philosophy in the Analytic Tradition* 57(3):261–279.

Lahav, Ran. 1993. The combinatorial-connectionist debate and the pragmatics of adjectives. *Pragmatics & Cognition* 1(1):71–88.

Landauer, Thomas K and Susan T Dumais. 1997. A solution to Plato's problem: The Latent Semantic Analysis theory of acquisition, induction, and representation of knowledge. *Psychological review* 104(2):211–240.

Larsson, Staffan. 2013. Formal semantics for perceptual classification. *Journal of Logic and Computation* 25(2):335–369.

Larsson, Staffan and Jean-Philippe Bernardy. 2021. Semantic classification and learning using a linear tranformation model in a probabilistic type theory with records. In *Proceedings of the Reasoning and Interaction Conference (ReInAct 2021)*, pages 14–22.

Lassiter, Daniel. 2011. Vagueness as probabilistic linguistic knowledge. In R. Nouwen, R. van Rooij, U. Sauerland, and H.-C. Schmitz, eds., *Vagueness in Communication: Revised Selected Papers from the 2009 International Workshop on Vagueness in Communication*, chap. 8, pages 127–150. Springer.

Lassiter, Daniel. 2017. Bayes nets and the dynamics of probabilistic language. In *Proceedings of Sinn and Bedeutung 21*.

Lassiter, Daniel and Noah D. Goodman. 2015. Adjectival vagueness in a Bayesian model of interpretation. *Synthese* 194(10):3801–3836.

Lawson, Rebecca. 2006. The science of cycology: Failures to understand how everyday objects work. *Memory & Cognition* 34(8):1667–1675.

Levy, Omer and Yoav Goldberg. 2014. Neural word embedding as implicit matrix factorization. In *Advances in Neural Information Processing Systems 27 (NIPS)*, pages 2177–2185.

Lin, Tsung-Yi, Michael Maire, Serge Belongie, James Hays, Pietro Perona, Deva Ramanan, Piotr Dollár, and C Lawrence Zitnick. 2014. Microsoft COCO: Common objects in context. In *Proceedings of the 13th European Conference on Computer Vision, Part V*, pages 740–755. Springer.

Liu, Yinhong and Guy Emerson. 2022. Learning functional distributional semantics with visual data. In *Proceedings of the 60th Annual Meeting of the Association for Computational Linguistics (Volume 1: Long Papers)*, pages 3976–3988. Association for Computational Linguistics.

Lui, Marco, Timothy Baldwin, and Diana McCarthy. 2012. Unsupervised estimation of word usage similarity. In *Proceedings of the 10th Australasian Language Technology Association Workshop (ALTA)*, pages 33–41.

Margolis, Eric and Stephen Laurence. 2011. Concepts. In E. N. Zalta, ed., *The Stanford Encyclopedia of Philosophy*. Metaphysics Research Lab, Stanford University, summer edn. The spring 2014 edition contains minor corrections.

Mazo, Gildas, Stéphane Girard, and Florence Forbes. 2015. A class of multivariate copulas based on products of bivariate copulas. *Journal of Multivariate Analysis* 140:363–376.

McCloskey, Michael E. and Sam Glucksberg. 1978. Natural categories: Well defined or fuzzy sets? *Memory & Cognition* 6(4):462–472.

McMahan, Brian and Matthew Stone. 2015. A Bayesian model of grounded color semantics. *Transactions of the Association for Computational Linguistics (TACL)* 3:103–115.

McNally, Louise. 2016a. Meaning at a Crossroads. [Slides]. Evening lecture at the 2016 European Summer School in Language, Logic, and Information (ESSLLI).

McNally, Louise. 2016b. Modification. In M. Aloni and P. Dekker, eds., *The Cambridge Handbook of Formal Semantics*, chap. 15, pages 442–466. Cambridge University Press.

McRae, Ken, George S. Cree, Mark S. Seidenberg, and Chris McNorgan. 2005. Semantic feature production norms for a large set of living and nonliving things. *Behavior research methods* 37(4):547–559.

Mikolov, Tomas, Kai Chen, Greg Corrado, and Jeffrey Dean. 2013. Efficient estimation of word representations in vector space. In *Proceedings of the 1st International Conference on Learning Representations (ICLR), Workshop Track*.

Mikosch, Thomas. 2006. Copulas: Tales and facts. *Extremes* 9(1):3–20.

Millikan, Ruth Garrett. 1998. Language conventions made simple. *The Journal of Philosophy* 95(4):161–180. Reprinted in: Millikan (2005), *Language: A Biological Model*, chapter 1, pages 1–23, Oxford University Press.

Mollica, Francis and Steven T. Piantadosi. 2019. Humans store about 1.5 megabytes of information during language acquisition. *Royal Society Open Science* 6(3).

Montague, Richard. 1973. The proper treatment of quantification in ordinary English. In K. J. J. Hintikka, J. M. E. Moravcsik, and P. Suppes, eds., *Approaches to Natural Language*, no. 49 in Synthese Library, chap. 10, pages 221–242. Kluwer Academic Publishers. Reprinted in: Paul Portner and Barbara H. Partee, editors (2002), *Formal semantics: The essential readings*, chapter 1, pages 17–34.

Murphy, Gregory. 2002. *The big book of concepts*. Massachusetts Institute of Technology (MIT) Press.

Nickerson, Raymond S and Marilyn Jager Adams. 1979. Long-term memory for a common object. *Cognitive Psychology* 11(3):287–307.

Ogden, Charles K. and Ivor A. Richards. 1923. *The meaning of meaning: A study of the influence of language upon thought and of the science of symbolism*. Harcourt, Brace & World, Inc.

Parsons, Terence. 1970. Some problems concerning the logic of grammatical modifiers. *Synthese* 21(3-4):320–334. Reprinted in: Donald Davidson and Gilbert Harman, editors (1972), *Semantics of Natural Language*, chapter 5, pages 127–141.

Partee, Barbara H. 1975. Montague grammar and transformational grammar. *Linguistic Inquiry* 6(2):203–300.

Pecher, Diane, Inge Boot, and Saskia Van Dantzig. 2011. Abstract concepts: Sensory-motor grounding, metaphors, and beyond. In B. Ross, ed., *The Psychology of Learning and Motivation*, vol. 54, chap. 7, pages 217–248. Academic Press.

Peirce, Charles Sanders. 1867. On a new list of categories. *Proceedings of the American Academy of Arts and Sciences* 7:287–298.

Piedeleu, Robin, Dimitri Kartsaklis, Bob Coecke, and Mehrnoosh Sadrzadeh. 2015. Open system categorical quantum semantics in natural language processing. In L. S. Moss and P. Sobocinski, eds., *Proceedings of the 6th Conference on Algebra and Coalgebra in Computer Science (CALCO)*, vol. 35 of *Leibniz International Proceedings in Informatics (LIPIcs)*, pages 270–289. Schloss Dagstuhl–Leibniz-Zentrum für Informatik.

Pulvermüller, Friedemann. 2013. How neurons make meaning: brain mechanisms for embodied and abstract-symbolic semantics. *Trends in Cognitive Sciences* 17(9):458–470.

Quine, Willard Van Orman. 1960. *Word and Object*. Massachusetts Institute of Technology (MIT) Press.

Rapp, Reinhard. 2004. A practical solution to the problem of automatic word sense induction. In *Proceedings of the 42nd Annual Meeting of the Association for Computational Linguistics (ACL), Interactive Poster and Demonstration Sessions*, pages 26–29.

Rasmussen, Carl Edward and Christopher K. I. Williams. 2006. *Gaussian Processes for Machine Learning*. Massachusetts Institute of Technology (MIT) Press.

Recanati, François. 2012. Compositionality, flexibility, and context-dependence. In W. Hinzen, E. Machery, and M. Werning, eds., *Oxford Handbook of Compositionality*, chap. 8, pages 175–191. Oxford University Press.

Rosch, Eleanor. 1975. Cognitive representations of semantic categories. *Journal of experimental psychology: General* 104(3):192.

Rosch, Eleanor. 1978. Principles of categorization. In E. Rosch and B. B. Lloyd, eds., *Cognition and categorization*, chap. 2, pages 27–48. Lawrence Erlbaum Associates. Reprinted in: Eric Margolis and Stephen Laurence, editors (1999), *Concepts: Core Readings*, chapter 8, pages 189–206.

Rudas, Tamás. 2018. *Lectures on categorical data analysis*. Springer Texts in Statistics. Springer.

Ruhl, Charles. 1989. *On monosemy: A study in linguistic semantics*. State University of New York (SUNY) Press.

Saunders, Barbara A. C. and Jaap Van Brakel. 1997. Are there nontrivial constraints on colour categorization? *Behavioral and Brain Sciences* 20(2):167–179.

Schlangen, David, Sina Zarrieß, and Casey Kennington. 2016. Resolving references to objects in photographs using the words-as-classifiers model. In *Proceedings of the 54th Annual Meeting of the Association for Computational Linguistics (ACL), Long Papers*, pages 1213–1223.

Schütze, Hinrich. 1998. Automatic word sense discrimination. *Computational Linguistics* 24(1):97–123.

Scontras, Gregory, Michael Henry Tessler, and Michael Franke. 2018. Probabilistic language understanding: An introduction to the rational speech act framework.

Searle, John R. 1980. The background of meaning. In J. R. Searle, F. Kiefer, and M. Bierwisch, eds., *Speech Act Theory and Pragmatics*, chap. 10, pages 221–232. D. Reidel Publishing Company.

Smith, Edward E. and Douglas L. Medin. 1981. *Categories and Concepts*. Harvard University Press.

Spärck-Jones, Karen. 1964. *Synonymy and Semantic Classification*. Ph.D. thesis, University of Cambridge. Reprinted in 1986 by Edinburgh University Press.

Steels, Luc. 2008. The symbol grounding problem has been solved. So what's next? In M. de Vega, A. Glenberg, and A. Graesser, eds., *Symbols and embodiment: Debates on meaning and cognition*, chap. 12, pages 223–244. Oxford University Press.

Sutton, Peter. 2022. The origins of vagueness. In J.-P. Bernardy, R. Blanck, S. Chatzikyriakidis, S. Lappin, and A. Maskharashvili, eds., *Probabilistic Approaches to Linguistic Theory*. CSLI Publications.

Sutton, Peter R. 2013. *Vagueness, Communication, and Semantic Information*. Ph.D. thesis, King's College London.

Sutton, Peter R. 2015. Towards a probabilistic semantics for vague adjectives. In H. Zeevat and H.-C. Schmitz, eds., *Bayesian Natural Language Semantics and Pragmatics*, chap. 10, pages 221–246. Springer.

Sutton, Peter R. 2017. Probabilistic approaches to vagueness and semantic competency. *Erkenntnis* .

Taddeo, Mariarosaria and Luciano Floridi. 2005. Solving the symbol grounding problem: a critical review of fifteen years of research. *Journal of Experimental & Theoretical Artificial Intelligence* 17(4):419–445.

Taddeo, Mariarosaria and Luciano Floridi. 2007. A praxical solution of the symbol grounding problem. *Minds and Machines* 17(4):369–389.

Tajar, Abdelouahid, Michel Denuit, and Philippe Lambert. 2001. Copula-type representation for random couples with Bernoulli margins. Discussion Paper 118, University Catholique de Louvain Institut De Statistique.

Tarski, Alfred and Robert L. Vaught. 1956. Arithmetical extensions of relational systems. *Compositio Mathematica* 13:81–102.

Teh, Yee Whye, Michael I. Jordan, Matthew J. Beal, and David M. Blei. 2006. Hierarchical Dirichlet Processes. *Journal of the American Statistical Association* 101(476):1566–1581.

Teugels, Jozef L. 1990. Some representations of the multivariate bernoulli and binomial distributions. *Journal of multivariate analysis* 32(2):256–268.

Van Deemter, Kees. 2010. *Not exactly: In praise of vagueness*. Oxford University Press.

Vilnis, Luke, Xiang Li, Shikhar Murty, and Andrew McCallum. 2018. Probabilistic embedding of knowledge graphs with box lattice measures. In *Proceedings of the 56th Annual Meeting of the Association for Computational Linguistics (ACL), Long Papers*, pages 263–272.

Vilnis, Luke and Andrew McCallum. 2015. Word representations via Gaussian embedding. In *Proceedings of the 3rd International Conference on Learning Representations (ICLR)*.

Vinyals, Oriol, Alexander Toshev, Samy Bengio, and Dumitru Erhan. 2015. Show and tell: A neural image caption generator. In *Proceedings of the 2015 IEEE Conference on Computer Vision and Pattern Recognition (CVPR)*, pages 3156–3164. Institute of Electrical and Electronics Engineers.

Wang, Su, Stephen Roller, and Katrin Erk. 2017. Distributional modeling on a diet: One-shot word learning from text only. In *Proceedings of the 8th International Joint Conference on Natural Language Processing (IJCNLP), Long Papers*, pages 204–213. Asian Federation of Natural Language Processing (AFNLP).

Wittgenstein, Ludwig. 1953. *Philosophical Investigations*. Blackwell. Translated by Gertrude Elizabeth Margaret Anscombe. The original German text was published in 1958 under the title *Philosophische Untersuchungen*.

Wong, Kimberly, Frempongma Wadee, Gali Ellenblum, and Michael McCloskey. 2018. The devil's in the g-tails: Deficient letter-shape knowledge and awareness despite massive visual experience. *Journal of Experimental Psychology: Human Perception and Performance* .

Xu, Kelvin, Jimmy Ba, Ryan Kiros, Kyunghyun Cho, Aaron Courville, Ruslan Salakhudinov, Rich Zemel, and Yoshua Bengio. 2015. Show, attend and tell: Neural image caption generation with visual attention. In *Proceedings of the 32nd International Conference on Machine Learning (ICML)*, vol. 37 of *Proceedings of Machine Learning Research*, pages 2048–2057.

Young, Peter, Alice Lai, Micah Hodosh, and Julia Hockenmaier. 2014. From image descriptions to visual denotations: New similarity metrics for semantic inference over event descriptions. *Transactions of the Association for Computational Linguistics (TACL)* 2:67–78.

Zadeh, Lotfi A. 1965. Fuzzy sets. *Information and Control* 8(3):338–353.

Zadeh, Lotfi A. 1975. The concept of a linguistic variable and its application to approximate reasoning—I. *Information Sciences* 8(3):199–249.

Zarrieß, Sina and David Schlangen. 2017a. Is this a child, a girl or a car? Exploring the contribution of distributional similarity to learning referential word meanings. In *Proceedings of the 15th Annual Conference of the European Chapter of the Association for Computational Linguistics (EACL), Short Papers*, pages 86–91.

Zarrieß, Sina and David Schlangen. 2017b. Obtaining referential word meanings from visual and distributional information: Experiments on object naming. In *Proceedings of the 55th Annual Meeting of the Association for Computational Linguistics (ACL), Long Papers*, pages 243–254.

Zentall, Thomas R., Mark Galizio, and Thomas S. Critchfield. 2002. Categorization, concept learning, and behavior analysis: An introduction. *Journal of the Experimental Analysis of Behavior* 78(3):237–248.

4

The origins of vagueness

PETER SUTTON

4.1 Introduction

At least one of the following two properties are usually assumed to be necessary for an expression to count as *vague*:

(1) *borderline cases*: there are things that are as much f as they are not-f);

(2) *blurred boundaries*: it is not clear where the boundary between fs and non-fs is.

On this basis, a great many natural language expressions are vague. For instance, there are examples of nouns/NPs, adjectives, VPs, PPs, and adverbial expressions that have blurred boundaries. E.g., there is no sharp cut-off between (*a*) *kitten* and (*an*) *(adult) cat*, between *tall* and *not tall/short*, between *walk* and *run*, between *under the table* and *not under the table*, or between *quickly* and *not quickly*.

A daunting amount has been written on vagueness in philosophy, linguistics, and cognitive science, and a large portion of this work has centred on (proposing solutions to) the *sorites paradox*, a logical puzzle generated by a form of slippery slope reasoning from clear cases to clear non-cases of a predicate by evoking increments so small that, so the intuition goes, they could not make a difference to whether or not one should apply that predicate. For example, if a room is (clearly) large, then a room smaller by only one square centimetre must also

Probabilistic Approaches to Linguistic Theory.
Jean-Philippe Bernardy, Rasmus Blanck,
Stergios Chatzikyriakidis, Shalom Lappin,
Aleksandre Maskharashvili (eds.).

be large, but then by repeated applications of this step, a 1 metre-square room is large, contrary to fact. The argument is troubling as it appears to show either that there is an inconsistency in how we reason about the extensions of expressions that leads us into contradiction, or that at least one of the premises of the argument is false, which, in most commonly used logics, implies that there is a sharp boundary between fs and non-fs, meaning that, contrary to our intuitions, vague predicates do not have blurred boundaries or genuine borderline cases after all.

Even setting the sorites paradox aside, there is a tension between the two main diagnostics of vagueness in (1) and (2) and classical semantic theory in the Montague-Lewis tradition. Namely, if the extensions of natural language expressions such as common nouns, adjectives and VPs are modelled in terms of classical sets (or functions from classical sets to classical sets), it is not clear how such an expression could have borderline cases or why its application conditions are blurred/non-sharp. Given the prevalence of vague expressions in natural languages, a proper treatment of the phenomenon of vagueness is therefore theoretically pressing. In this chapter, we will examine a broad family of analyses of vagueness, all of which make use of classical (Bayesian) probability theory.

Although there were some early applications of probability theory to vagueness (Borel, 1907/2014, Black, 1937), in the last eleven to twelve years, the use of this and related formal tools has seen a resurgence of interest. A core idea runs through each of these approaches – the use and/or meaning of vague expressions inherently involves uncertainty. This uncertainty has been characterised, for instance, as uncertainty about what the truth-conditions of an expression are, or, from a more agent-oriented perspective, uncertainty about whether a competent speaker would apply a vague expression in a given instance. Furthermore, some of the advocates of probabilistic approaches to vagueness have argued that probabilistic analyses of vagueness afford us more clarity on what could be termed the *origins of vagueness*, namely, why natural languages have developed vague expressions in the first place, and it is this issue that will be addressed in this chapter.

Section §4.2 provides an overview of many of the probabilistic proposals for treatments of vagueness. (For an overview of vagueness theories including non-probabilistic approaches to vagueness, see Burnett and Sutton, 2020). Although probabilistic solutions to the sorites will briefly be discussed in §4.2.5, our main area of interest here will be what, from a probabilistic standpoint, underpins why vagueness arises in the first place. Most of the work to be discussed (see §4.2.2) forms a loose consensus on this issue, namely, that some form of **noise** generates uncertainty about how to apply a predicate. In information theoretic terms, for an information channel where a message is encoded as a signal and sent to a receiver where it is decoded, noise increases uncertainty regarding the message, since it either modulates or confounds the signal, making the message harder to recover (unless the signal encodes enough redundancies (Shannon, 1948)). Although different theories propose different explanations of how noise enters the system, the unifying idea here is that this affects agents' uncertainty regarding predication and that this uncertainty, under certain other constraints, characterises vagueness. In §4.2.3, we will discuss a more minority view, namely that vagueness arises as a **byproduct of semantic learning**: an agent's learning data in some sense underspecifies how a predicate should be used in a certain situation and so the semantic representations one develops do not carve out sharply defined boundaries. Although the noise and semantic learning hypotheses are not mutually exclusive (both could contribute to vagueness in natural language), they do offer different perspectives on where the principal source of vagueness lies.

The second part of this chapter, 4.3, presents the results of a series of simulations that were run with the goal of providing a clearer picture of whether noise or a byproduct of semantic learning contributes to the evolution of vagueness. These simulations were run with a probabilistic iterated learning model (for non-probabilistic iterated learning models, see Kirby and Hurford, 2002, Kirby, 2007). In this model, for $n + 1$ generations of agents, a_0..., a_n, each agent $a_{i<n}$ provides a sample of their language as learning data for a_{i+1} and each agent $a_{j>0}$ learns on the basic of a sample of the language from a_{j-1}. Perhaps surprisingly, the results of these simulations indicate that both noise and learning data sparsity appear to contribute to the development of vagueness in a language. That is to say that, even if we assign a completely precise (non-vague) language for a_0 in the model, the introduction of noise and a restriction on the amount of learning data each agent receives generates a stable and vague language across generations.

4.2 Overview of probabilistic approaches to vagueness

4.2.1 Background

An influential philosophical proposal for the analysis of vagueness is *epistemicism*, the theory that vague predicates have sharp boundaries/thresholds that are unknowable since extension facts supervene on language usage facts, and one cannot, at least practically speaking, infer the former from the latter (Williamson, 1992, 1994).[1] From a probabilistic standpoint, some aspects of the theory are appealing, since it is a fairly natural move to recast *ignorance regarding the application conditions of a predicate* with *uncertainty regarding the application conditions of a predicate*, where this uncertainty, and reasoning in conditions of metalinguistic uncertainty can be modelled with Bayesian probability theory.

However, despite the apparent affinity with a probabilistic approach to vagueness, epistemicism has also been criticised on the basis that it is unclear how this theory can explain how meanings can be learned from instances of uses of predicates, and how agents using vague expressions can nonetheless coordinate sufficiently to communicate successfully (see, e.g., Lassiter, 2011, Sutton, 2013). Bayesian approaches assuage these concerns in one of two ways: (i) They model agents as a being uncertain regarding where the threshold for f lies, but nonetheless as approximating its location (reducing uncertainty). On this conception, probabilities are probabilities of what the truth conditions of f are (see, e.g., Fernández and Larsson, 2014, Lassiter, 2011)[2]; (ii) They interpret probabilities as reflecting an agent's estimation of how likely a competent speaker, or, alternatively, one's interlocutor, would use f, given a forced choice between a set of alternatives of say f, not-f and saying nothing (see Sutton, 2013, 2018, Lassiter and Goodman, 2017, Égré, 2017, Bernardy et al., 2018, among others). This latter perspective seems to have become more dominant in recent years. In either case, the kinds of uncertainty being assumed in these approaches will be referred to in this chapter as *metalinguistic uncertainty*.

Our focus here, however, will be on the insights Bayesian approaches can provide on the origins of vagueness (how and why vagueness arises in the first place), especially given their rootedness in theories

[1] However, for a different conception of epistemicism based on necessarily unknowable boundaries, see Sorensen (1988, 2001).

[2] A problem this gives rise to is that there are, de facto, sharp truth conditions for every vague predicate, at least relative to a context.

of learning and communication. Theories fall into two main (non-exclusive) categories: those that locate the origins of vagueness in a source of noise, and those that attribute it to a byproduct of semantic learning.

4.2.2 Noise giving rise to vagueness

This section gives a summary overview of some of the main probabilistic models that posit some form of noise as an explanation for why natural language predicates are vague.

Probabilistic linguistic knowledge. One way to assuage some of the aforementioned concerns with epistemicism is to assume a sharp boundary for vague predicates at each context such that agents imperfectly estimate where this boundary is (Frazee and Beaver, 2010, Lassiter, 2011, Fernández and Larsson, 2014, van Eijck and Lappin, 2012). Here, we will briefly outline one of these more communication-oriented views as proposed by Lassiter (2011).

Building on the dynamic logic theory in (Barker, 2002), Lassiter (2011) defines a probabilistic belief space that can be updated dynamically to model both uncertainty about the world (which possible world is actual) and metalinguistic uncertainty (what the precise meaning of an expression is in a communicative context). An agent reasons about the most likely precise interpretation of a vague expression in the context, given their beliefs about what the world is like. The basic idea here is that agents may be able to approximately converge on what the relevant threshold is for a vague expression. Although, Lassiter does not discuss noise explicitly, one way to think about this is that the inherent uncertainty we have regarding others' metalinguistic beliefs is generated by a source of noise that is seldom if ever eliminated entirely.

Approximative measurement. Égré (2017) develops a probabilistic model of vague judgement based on an idea from psychology that magnitudes, such as height, and loudness, are mentally represented only with some degree of approximation. Égré (2017) explicitly proposes that there is noise in the information channel between how the world is (sizes/height of objects etc.) relative to a unit of measurement, and the representation of these entities by agents.

Noise is represented by the value of a random variable summed over the number of units of measurement being considered, i.e., for each measurement unit (e.g., centimetres, decibels etc.), there is some chance of over- or underestimating it. These over- and under-estimations compound, so that for an entity of some size on the given scale, there is a probability distribution over the size it will be estimated to be such that the greater the variance in this distribution, the greater the amount of noise there is in the agent's estimation system. The probability of applying some predicate to an entity is derived via a context- and comparison class dependent *criterion value* which can be thought of as a kind of threshold, above which $Pr(\text{'}x\ is\ f\text{'}) > Pr(\text{'}x\ is\ not\ f\text{'})$.

Égré's (2017) proposal, furthermore, makes progress on the proposals considered above insofar as he pays closer attention to the complexities of the interactions between context and the comparison class for vague predicates and also provides an explanation of how the contextual standards of agents can diverge on the basis of *interest relativity* (See also Fara, 2000).[3]

Introducing Measurement Error. Bernardy et al. (2018, 2019) implement a compositional semantics for natural language that includes a treatment of vague gradable adjectives such as *tall.*[4] Conditional probabilities in (Bernardy et al., 2018) represent the likelihood that a competent speaker of the language would endorse an assertion, given certain evidence/assumptions/hypotheses. The predicates and individuals are represented as vectors, and the probability that a predicate applies to an individual is estimated via Markov chain Monte Carlo (MCMC) sampling over these vectors, conditioned by certain observations. Two advantages of this system are, firstly, that semantic judgements are inherently graded, which as argued by Sutton (2018) is a promising basis for modelling vagueness, and, secondly, an arbitrarily rich notion of context is built into the model via the inclusion of data (observations) upon which probabilistic judgements are conditioned (a feature which is shared by the richly-typed approaches in Fernández and Larsson 2014, see also Cooper et al. 2015 and Schuster et al. 2020).

To model vagueness, Bernardy et al. (2018, 2019) introduce a Gaussian error into probabilistic evaluation, i.e., an error due to the Gaussian distribution, which introduces additional uncertainty into a predication. The effect of this is to introduce an added amount of uncertainty into the system. As such, this approach is an explicit example of a noise-based theory of vagueness.

Game theoretic and Bayesian Pragmatics approaches. A further proposal that incorporates noise as part of the explanation of

[3]Égré (2017) also proposes further applications of his theory. For instance, how the model can be applied in the context of Égré's other work on borderline contradictions (see, e.g., Egré et al., 2013).

[4]It is beyond the scope of this chapter to go into the full details of their model (which includes a treatment of quantifiers, for instance), and so we will restrict our focus to (vague) predication.

vagueness is made within game theoretic models (Correia and Franke, 2019, Franke and Correia, 2018, Franke et al., 2011, Qing and Franke, 2014). One of the main questions that arise regarding vagueness from a game-theoretic perspective is why we should have vagueness at all, given that, on standard assumptions, vague expressions are sub-optimal communication tools compared to precise ones. A solution proposed by Correia and Franke (2019) and Franke and Correia (2018) is that vagueness can be seen as *boundedly rational* under the hypothesis that agents have an error rate in the calculation of their utilities. (See Frazee and Beaver, 2010, for an early version of a similar idea).

Relatedly, within a Rational Speech Act (RSA) model, Lassiter and Goodman (2017) propose that the interpretation of a vague adjective in context is the result of a balancing of two pressures: "the listener's preference for interpretations which are likely to be true, and the speaker's preference for interpretations that are informative" (Lassiter and Goodman, 2017, p. 3815).[5] To take their example of *tall*, hearers reason about the likely height of an individual, given a description of them as *tall* (as opposed to *not tall*, or no description), and an estimation of a contextual parameter (approximately the threshold, above which, the probability that a speaker would use *tall* instead of *not tall* is greater than 0.5). Although Lassiter and Goodman (2017) do not discuss noise explicitly, they intend their model to be an adaptation of a traditional information theoretic model of communication (Shannon, 1948), and a reasonable interpretation of their model is that part of the noise in the system generates uncertainty about what the threshold value of the adjective is in the context, given a use of that adjective to describe somebody.

To the extent that Correia and Franke (2019), Franke and Correia (2018), Franke et al. (2011), Qing and Franke (2014) have a speaker-centred approach and Lassiter and Goodman (2017) have a hearer-centred approach, the two analyses are, to some extent, different sides of the same coin. The 'error rate in the calculation of utilities' of the game-theoretic approach could, in Lassiter and Goodman's terms, be seen as attributable to the hearer's speaker model only imperfectly estimating the threshold of the relevant expression in the context, thus introducing uncertainty with respect to the point at which the use of a vague expression will successfully communicate what it is that they intend (such that this uncertainty propagates 'up' to the pragmatic hearer).[6]

[5]For further discussion of RSA models of vagueness, see Chapter 3.

[6]Correia and Franke (2019) also discuss further applications of such models such as how to simulate whether there are evolutionary advantages to vague languages

4.2.3 Vagueness and semantic learning

We now turn to the work that proposes an alternative source of vagueness, namely that it arises as a byproduct of semantic learning.

Semantic learning as a source of vagueness. van Eijck and Lappin (2012, §5.2) propose that vagueness can be seen as "the residue of probabilistic learning". Rather than noise, the idea is that the sample of a language from which a learner must establish how to properly use expressions does not necessarily fully determine their extensions because of 'gaps' in the learning data. Given a domain of entities, ordered with respect to the degree/extent that they instantiate some property (e.g., height, colour etc.), and a witnessed instance of the use of a predicate to describe one of these entities, on the plausible assumption that agents infer a higher probability of applying the same predicate to comparatively similar entities than to comparatively dissimilar entities (see Decock and Douven, 2014, for a related idea articulated in terms of conceptual spaces), vagueness can be seen as arising from the very process of learning to navigate a semantic space with a limited number of data points (as, indeed, humans must). A similar idea is echoed in (Sutton, 2013, ch. 5) in which it is argued that, given a restricted amount of learning data, a plausible means of modelling how some data points provided stronger reasons than others for forming semantic judgements regarding previously unseen cases is probabilistic reasoning.

Semantic learning and noisy approximation. Fernández and Larsson (2014) propose that expressions such as *tall* are vague as a result of two factors: (i) agents approximate a threshold value (the point at which entities transition from more probably f to more probably not-f), based on a set of witnessed situations (i.e., the learning data) in which the predicate has been used; (ii) when it comes to making judgements, agents do not perfectly track the difference between the threshold value and the relevant properties of the entity being judged (modelled by an error function, a parameter of which is a noise rate[7]). While (ii) bears similarities to some of the proposals regarding noise discussed above, (i) constitutes a different proposal for a source of metalinguistic uncertainty, namely, similar to the idea outlined by van Eijck and Lappin (2012, §5.2), an agent's learning data can underspecify what the application conditions for a predicate are. As an example of

(i.e. to different levels of imprecision employed in game-theoretic strategies), and furthermore, which levels of imprecision emerge as dominant within simulated populations.

[7] Fernández and Larsson (2014) ground this error rate based upon the empirical findings in (Schmidt et al., 2009).

how these two components work together, if noise is very high, then even if an individual's height is quite far from the threshold value, they will not be judged as being tall with a probability significantly above 0.5. If noise is very low, then even a tiny difference between an individual's height and the threshold will push the probability to 1 or 0.

4.2.4 Summary: Two sources of uncertainty

A unifying theme in all of the proposals outlined in this section is that vagueness arises as a result of some form of uncertainty being introduced into our cognitive representations. On the one hand, uncertainty can arise due to a source of noise, such as an imperfect mapping between the exact properties in the world an entity may have, and the inexact means we have for representing that property. Alternatively, uncertainty can arise due to a an insufficiency of learning data. As we have seen with Fernández and Larsson's (2014) proposal, for instance, these two sources of uncertainty could both be part of the explanation of why so many natural language expressions are vague. One of the main goals of §4.3 is to delve deeper into these potential sources of vagueness and the ways in which they interact.

4.2.5 The sorites paradox

To end this section, we turn to the sorites paradox. Rather than detailing specific probabilisitic 'solutions' to the paradox, I will outline what I take to be the commonalities between such solutions, as well as the main challenges that they face.

The structure of the paradox. The sorites paradox can be generated for any expression, such that, for some relevant dimension, we have the intuition that a small difference between two entities along that dimension cannot mark a difference in whether to apply that expression. For instance, for *tall*, the dimension is height/vertical size, for *heap*, number of entities in the heap, and for *under the table*, the relative locations of the table and the entity said to be under it. In each case, the intuition is that there are clear cases for applying these expressions, and also clear non-cases. Paradox arises if we follow the further intuition that any small change along the relevant dimension cannot take us from a clear case to a clear non-case (or even to a non-clear case), because we end up concluding that something that is a clear non-case (or a non-clear case) is a clear case, contrary to our initial assumption.

The argument has two structures, the 'short' and 'long' sorites arguments. In either case, we start with an ordering of entities $D = \langle d_0, d_1, ..., d_n \rangle$ such that for any d_i, d_{i+1} differs only slightly along some relevant dimension for a predicate f (e.g., differs in height by 1mm for *tall*). By assumption, d_0 is clearly f and d_n is clearly not-f. In the long sorites, the argument proceeds by repeated applications of modus ponens based upon *tolerance conditionals* of the form $f(d_0) \to f(d_1)$, ... $f(d_{n-1}) \to f(d_n)$. In the short sorites, the tolerance conditional premises are replaced with either a universally quantified conditional $(\forall x[f(x_i) \to f(x_{i+1})])$ or an inductive premise.

The probabilistic treatment of the paradox: With respect to both versions of the sorites, in a probabilistic setting, the categorical propositions in the argument are interpreted probabilistically. Both assumptions can have an arbitrarily high probability π. The appeal of the long sorites is explained because the probability of each tolerance conditional can be as high as $\pi - \epsilon$, for some small value ϵ. Therefore, each application of modus ponens feels like a good inference, since the drop in probability value between $f(d_i)$ and $f(d_{i+1})$ is so minute. However, over repeated applications of modus ponens, the probability of $f(d_i)$ approaches $1-\pi$ as i approaches n, therefore the conclusion has a probability of at most ϵ. This explanation of the long sorites captures the slippery slope appeal of the argument, while still diagnosing where we go wrong: inferences in which the conclusion is slightly less probable than the premises are, in general, reliable, but we can go wrong if we string too many of these inferences together.

Challenges for the probabilistic treatment of the paradox: There are at least two main challenges that probabilistic analyses of the sorites face. I take them in turn.

The short sorites: Along with other theories of vagueness such as supervaluationism (Fine, 1975, Kamp, 1975), probabilistic treatments of vagueness face a challenge when it comes to explaining the reason why the premise in the short sorites is no easier to deny than any one of the premises in the long sorites (Edgington, 1997). The basis of the problem is that, unlike any single tolerance conditional, all of which have high probabilities, the universally quantified premise in the short sorites should have a very low probability on the assumption that the probability of a universally quantified statement is the same as the probability of the conjunction of its instances. Although this problem is not trivial to explain away, one possible explanation could be attributed to a performance error or faulty heuristic in the way we evaluate multiple propositions with high probability values (see Sutton, 2013, ch. 8 for a similar point put in terms of cognitive efficiency.).

Higher-order vagueness: A version of a higher-order vagueness problem arises on a probabilistic approach to the sorites when one is forced to say something about assertion conditions. For instance, if ϕ is assertable iff $Pr(\phi) > \theta$, for some threshold θ, then there should be a sharp cut-off point in the short sorites such that $f(a_i)$ is assertable, but $f(a_{i+1})$ is not. Yet, that result seems to be antithetical to the vagueness of f. For an extensive discussion of this problem and the options probabilistic approaches have for addressing it, see (Sutton, 2018).

4.3 A probabilistic, iterated learning model

4.3.1 Overview and hypotheses

In this section, I present the results of simulations that were designed to test two of the common hypotheses that we have seen in the literature:

(H1) Vagueness arises as a result of noise – when an agent hears a vague predicate being used, due to noise, they are unsure exactly what the situation being described is like.

(H2) Vagueness arises as a result of learning based upon incomplete data – when an agent learns a predicate, they do not witness (enough) uses of that predicate. As a result, for some situations, agents are unsure whether to apply the predicate.

Both of these sources of uncertainty can, in principle, result in similar effects: the hearer's semantic representation encodes some uncertainty, and, while there may be canonical uses of the predicate in which there is little uncertainty, at the 'edges', competing predicates' extensions bleed into one another, giving rise to the borderline cases and blurred boundaries that are hallmarks of vague predicates. The goal of the simulations, which were run with a probabilistic iterated learning model for simple artificial languages, is to test whether one, both or neither of (H1) and (H2) is sufficient to derive vagueness in multiple predicates defined over a meaning space.

A further aim of this work, that distinguishes it from the approaches discussed in section 4.2, is to investigate the meaning spaces over which multiple predicates are defined. In most other approaches, at most two predicates are tested e.g., *tall* vs. *short* or *tall* vs. *not tall.* While this is understandable as a simplifying assumption, it may be beneficial to see what the effects of, e.g., noise, are when the extensions of several predicates are competing with each other for part of the domain.

In the most general terms, the simulations were as follows. We assume a series of generations of agents, one agent per generation, and an ordered set of entities. For example, these entities could be a meaning space of discrete shades of colour between red and yellow (ordered from the red shades through into the orange into the yellow).

The first agent has a completely precise, non-vague language. To take the previous example, this would mean a unique predicate for each shade, such that that predicate only applies to entities of that shade of colour. The first agent is then given a set of messages to encode in their language. These signal-message pairs, constitute a sample of the use of the first agent's language from which the second agent must learn, as best they can given the data, the extensions of each of the predicates to which they are exposed. This learned language of the second agent, which may differ from the language of the first agent, is then sampled as learning data for the third agent and so on. The purpose of this set-up is to see under what conditions a vague language arises, i.e., one in which predicates that have both clear cases, clear non-cases, and unclear cases.

The parameter that was used to test (H1) was to introduce noise into the learning data. To take the example of shades of colour, the result of noise is that if an agent is trying to refer to some particular shade of, say orange, with a predicate, f, the learner will be uncertain exactly which shade of colour that use of the predicate is being used to denote.[8] Given, however, that we are assuming an ordered meaning space (typical of that associated with vague predicates), we will assume that the closer as shade of colour is to the intended message, the more likely it is that the learner with extend the extension of f to this shade.

The parameter used to test (H2) controls the size of the *learning bottle neck* (Kirby and Hurford, 2002, Kirby, 2007). With no bottleneck, every learner witnesses at least one use of every predicate from the previous generation's language. As the bottleneck narrows, the probability of witnessing at least one use of every predicate from the previous generation's language gets lower. The effect of the bottleneck is therefore to introduce gaps in the learning data. To take our example of shades of colour once again, suppose that a learner has witnessed a predicate f_1 applied to a shade of red, and a predicate f_2 applied to a shade of orange. Based upon no further data, the agent has no direct evidence for which predicate they should use to describe the shades of reddish-orange, and so must reason whether to use f_1 or f_2, based on what shades f_1 and f_2 have been used to apply to and how close the shades of reddish-orange are to these shades. The result will be that there will be at least on shade of colour that the agent infers is neither clearly f_1 nor clearly f_2, all else being equal.

[8] This treatment of noise differs from that standardly assumed. This issue is further discussed in §4.3.2

These two parameters were modulated in order to test four conditions: 1. No noise, no bottleneck; 2. Bottleneck, no noise; 3. Noise, no bottleneck; 4. Bottleneck and noise. In all conditions, the criteria of success was whether the language of the agent in the last generation had the hallmark characteristics of vagueness, which, here, we shall assume to be predicates that have both clear cases, clear non-cases, and unclear classes. These test conditions were designed to test whether noise alone, a bottleneck alone, both noise and an bottleneck, or neither noise nor a bottleneck are sufficient to account for the emergence of a vague language, even when the starting conditions for each run were a completely precise language.

Perhaps surprisingly, these simulation runs suggest that both noise and a bottleneck are needed for vagueness to emerge.[9] In §4.3.2, I briefly discuss the differences between the iterated learning model used in these tests and others in the literature. In §4.3.4, the details of the four main test conditions are given. The results are presented in §4.3.5 and these are discussed in section §4.3.6. The formal details of the probabilistic iterated learning models are given in the appendix.

4.3.2 Comparison with other learning models

Iterated learning models. Iterated learning models (ILMs) (Kirby and Hurford, 2002, Kirby, 2007) simulate ways in which a language can evolve over generations of agents. A parameter of these models controls the size of the *semantic bottleneck* (learners may not witness every string or meaning). However, learning is neither probabilistic nor undertaken in noisy conditions: learners receive a set of string-meaning pairs and instantly learn these pairs. Kirby and Hurford's aim was to evaluate whether a language can evolve that is both *expressive* and *stable*. A language is expressive if agents, after the learning phase, are able to provide a string for any meaning that is in the meaning space. A language is stable if each learner ends up with a reasonably similar set of string-meaning pairs as the agent from whose language their training sample is provided. A major finding of these models was that compositionality is required for stable and expressive languages to emerge.

The probabilistic ILM presented here differs in three key respects from those in (Kirby and Hurford, 2002, Kirby, 2007):

[9]For a discussion of how the semantic bottleneck becomes even more acute for higher dimensional predicates, see Chapter 3.

i. **An ordering on the meaning domain** (here, the set of situations).[10] The motivation for this ordering relation is to simulate the similarity relations there are for entities in the denotations of vague expressions, e.g., entities that can be ordered from least to greatest heights, or hues that can be ordered from, say, red to yellow.

ii. **Learning is probabilistic.** If an agent is tasked with describing a situation s_i and if they have learned no predicates to describe it, then the agent infers what predicate to use on the basis of the situations close to s_i that they have witnessed being described (with at least some probability).

iii. **Noise can be introduced.** When noise is present in the simulation, agents do not receive, as their learning data, a set of predicate-situation pairs (i.e., string-meaning pairs in Kirby and Hurford's terminology). Rather, if the speaker is tasked with describing a situation s_i and chooses a predicate f_j, the learner receives only a pair of f_j and a distribution over situations with a mean centred around s_i (the standard deviation of this distribution is the noise parameter of the model).

Runs of the simulation were conducted and noise and the width of the semantic bottleneck were modulated in order to test (H1) and (H2) on the basis of whether, after some number of generations, stable, vague languages emerge. *Stability*, like in previous models will de defined in terms of whether there are significant changes between the languages of agents from one generation to another. *Vagueness* will be cast in terms of whether the resulting language has predicates that each have clear cases, clear non-cases and blurred boundaries.[11]

Modelling of Noise. As pointed out by Shalom Lappin (p.c.), this representation of noise differs from that introduced by Shannon (1948). For example, for an ordering of situations (e.g., shades of colours), s_1, s_2, s_3, and a predicate f, on a standard modelling of noise, if the original message-signal pair was $\langle s_2, f\rangle$, then, in line with some stochastic function, the learner receives either $\langle s_1, f\rangle$, $\langle s_2, f\rangle$, or $\langle s_3, f\rangle$.

[10] For brevity, I will refer to the denotations of predicates as situations, but these are, more correctly, best thought of as situations of a certain type, namely those that witness some entity with a relevant property such as a size, weight, or shade of colour etc.

[11] *Expressiveness* is not relevant for these probabilistic iterated learning models, since, unlike in non-probabilistic ILMs, agents are able to reason about likely language usage in conditions of uncertainty. Furthermore, compositionality does not factor in these models, since each data point for a learner is assumed to be a simple predication (that for some situation s_i and predicate f_j, s_i is (of type) f_j).

However, if we take seriously the idea in Égré 2017, that the relevant notion of noise is one in which the perceptual systems of humans only represent properties with some degree of approximation, then this modelling of noise does not quite fit what we want. Taking our previous example, the idea is that if an object with a shade s_2 is described as being of colour f, then, rather than assuming that a learner represents this as either $\langle s_1, f\rangle$, $\langle s_2, f\rangle$, or $\langle s_3, f\rangle$ based on some stochastic function, a more accurate model would be to assume that the learner associates f with some probability distribution over shades of colour. In other words, for any use of, say, a colour term to refer to an object, with a noisy representation system, we have evidence that it applies to some graded convex portion of the colour space centred around the actual shade of colour of that object. In future studies it would be interesting to see whether a model with a stochastic error based representation of noise would produce different results.[12]

4.3.3 The model

This section outlines the model in relatively informal terms. Please see the appendix for more details.

Languages. Languages are represented as sets of conditional probability distributions: $Pr(F|S)$ (The probability, for each predicate $f \in F$, and for each situation $s \in S$ that the agent applies f, given s). Samples of languages that provide the learning data for the next agent are probabilistic. First a random sample of situations is generated. The size of this sample is governed by a parameter data_size (see below). For each situation s_i in this sample, a predicate is chosen based upon the probability distribution for that language for s_i (from $Pr(f \in F|s_i)$).

Starting conditions. For all simulation runs, the language of the first agent (a_0) is completely precise (without vagueness). In other words, for the first agent, for each situation s_i, there is one predicate f_j such that $Pr(f_j|s_i) = 1$ (when describing a situation, there is never any uncertainty about which predicate applies to that situation), and for each predicate f_j, there is one situation s_i such that $Pr(s_i|f_j) = 1$ (for speakers of this language, when one hears a predicate being used, there is no uncertainty about what situation it describes). In other words, a_0 has enough predicates to singularly describe every type of entity in that space (e.g., a different predicate for every hue).

[12] A further possibility would be to test a combination of both error rate and probabilistic perturbation.

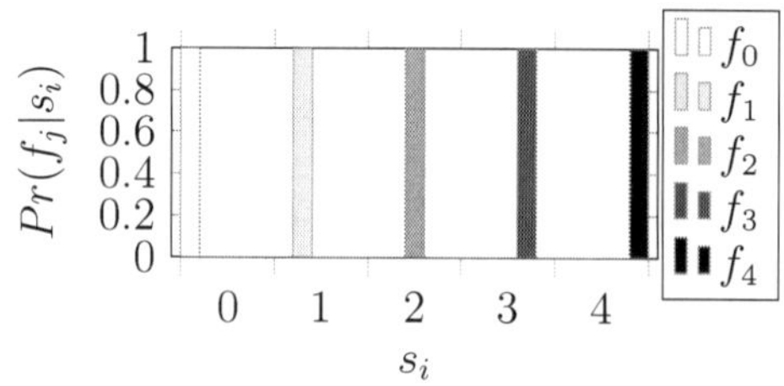

FIGURE 1: The starting condition (the language of the first agent) for a space of five situations s_0, s_1, s_2, s_3, s_4. There are also five predicates f_0, f_1, f_2, f_3, f_4.For each situation s_i there is exactly one predicate f_j such that $Pr(f_j|s_i) = 1$. In other words, the language is completely precise and predicates have non-graded extensions. This language has a vagueness score of 0.

An example of a starting condition language for a space of five situations is given in Figure 1. (Nb., in all of the simulation runs reported below, the starting number of situations and predicates was 15: $S = \{s_0, ..., s_{14}\}$ and $F = \{f_0, ..., f_{14}\}$).

Parameters. The parameters of the model that govern the four test conditions are data_size, delta, and noise:

data_size The number of situation-predicate pairs a learner witnesses. When data_size is high compared to $|S|$, there is little or no bottleneck. As data_size gets closer to the size of the situation space, the bottleneck narrows.

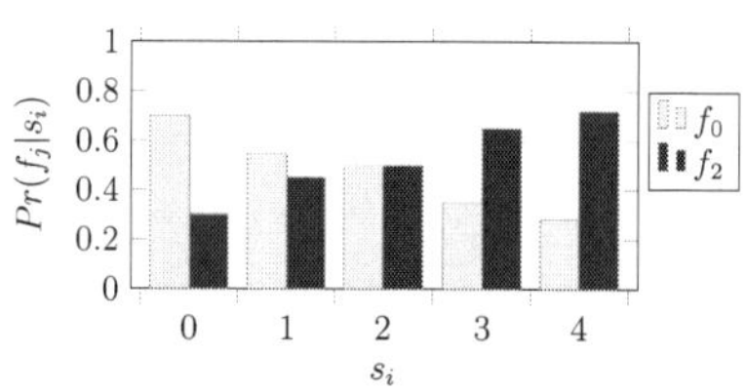

FIGURE 2: A possible ending condition for a situation space s_0-s_4. The depicted language has two predicates f_0, f_2. Both predicates fail conditions (3a) and (3c) and so the vagueness score is 0: neither predicate is vague.

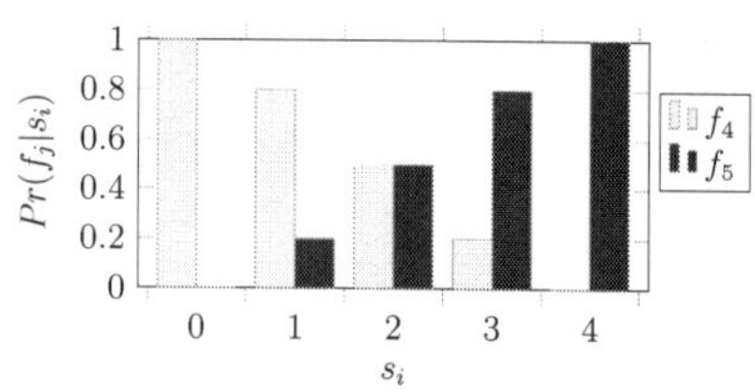

FIGURE 3: A possible ending condition for a situation space s_0-s_4. The depicted language has two predicates f_4, f_5. Both predicates meet all conditions in (3) and so the vagueness score is 1: both predicates are vague.

delta — This parameter controls reasoning about gaps in the learning data. I.e., for an extension gap G between two predicates f_i, f_j, how quickly $Pr(f_i|s \in G)$ and $Pr(f_j|s \in G)$ approach 0.5. See the appendix for details.

noise — This parameter controls the level of noise in the learning data. If the intended message is the pair of a situation s_i and a predicate f_j, then the noisy data is a normalised discrete probability distribution $Pr(s_k \in S|f_j)$ with a mean for $Pr(s_i \in S|f_j)$ and a standard deviation of noise.

Criteria of success. For each run of each test condition, the languages of the final 20 generations were checked for stability, namely, whether the number of predicates was stable. The main criterion of success was whether for each run of each test condition, the *ending condition* (the final language of this run) was vague. Vague predicates, as is defined here, are predicates that have both clear cases, clear non-cases, and non-clear classes. The criteria for this was as follows. For each run, for each predicate f_j:

(3) a. There is a clear case for f_j: $\exists s_i.Pr(f_j|s_1) > 0.8$
b. There is a non-clear case for f_j: $\exists s_i.0.2 \leq Pr(f_j|s_1) \leq 0.8$
c. There is a clear non-case for f_j: $\exists s_i.Pr(f_j|s_1) < 0.2$

The two principal ways in which predicates failed to meet these conditions were, first, they were precise and so had no non-clear cases (see, e.g., Figure 1). I.e., (3b) was false. Second, they could fail to have clear positive cases at all (i.e., (3c) was false). An example of such an outcome is given in Figure 2.

This criterion was quantified as a score in the range $[0, 1]$: the proportion of all predicates in all runs that were vague (that satisfy the conditions in (3)). This will be referred to as the *vagueness score* for a setting of the model. An example of a possible resulting language with a vagueness score of 1 is given in Figure 3).

(4) ***Vagueness score:*** For a setting of the model, the proportion of vague predicates that result on average. Where n is the sum of the number of predicates in all ending conditions, and m is the number of these predicates that satisfy the conditions in (3), the vagueness score is m/n.

4.3.4 Test conditions

The four types of simulation conditions are given in Table 1. For all conditions, the number of predicates and situations in the initial language was set to 15 ($S = \{s_0, ..., s_{14}\}$ and $F = \{f_0, ..., f_{14}\}$).

TABLE 1: The four different simulation condition types for runs of the model. For all conditions, the initial number of predicates and situations in the language of the first agent was set to 15 and simulations were run for 350 generations.

Simulation conditions	No Bottleneck	Bottleneck
No Noise	1.	2.
Noise	3.	4.

The number of generations was set to 350. A total of 258 simulation runs were conducted with 43 different parameter settings (6 runs per condition).

Condition 1. is a control condition where the expectation is that the final agent has the same precise language as the first agent. The noise parameter was set to 0.01, which, in computational terms, amounts to zero noise.[13] Runs of the simulation were tested with data_size values of 150 and 200 (both at least 10 times greater than the number of predicates and situations in the initial language, 15).

Condition 2. tests whether the bottleneck alone can yield a stable, vague language. The noise parameter was set to 0.01. The variables in Condition 2 were data_size and delta with runs for data_size values of 45, 60 and 75, each with delta-values of 0, 0.5, and 1.[14]

Condition 3. tests whether noise alone can yield a stable, vague language. Runs were conducted with data_size values of 150 and 200. delta was kept fixed at 1. The variable for these runs was the noise value. Runs were conducted for noise values 0.25, 0.275. 0.3 and 0.4.

Condition 4. combines noise and the bottleneck. Runs were conducted with data_size values of 45, 50, 60, 75, and 90. For each of these data sizes, noise values of 0.3, 0.35 and 0.4 were tested. Simulations were run with delta-values of 0.5 and 1.0.

4.3.5 Results

Condition 1: No noise, no bottleneck. All runs in the data_size = 200 and all but one in the data_size = 150 condition produced the same results, namely that the language of generation 350 was identical to the, non-vague language: 15 predicates, each of which uniquely identifies one situation. One run resulted in 14 non-vague predicates, one with

[13] For a situation distance 1 away from the situation in the initial data, the probability of the relevant predicate applying to this situation was so small, that it was treated by the computer as zero.

[14] In pre-testing, wider bottlenecks (i.e. lower data_size values) tended to lead to languages collapsing into single-predicate languages.

TABLE 2: Tables of results for the vagueness scores in Conditions 1-4: 'No bottleneck, no noise', 'Bottleneck, no noise', 'Noise, no bottleneck', and 'Noise and bottleneck'. Vagueness scores are the proportion of vague predicates to feature in the final language across all simulation runs for each setting of the model. Aside from the the 'No bottleneck, no noise' (control) condition 1, the least successful condition is 'Bottleneck, no noise' (Cond. 2), closely followed by the 'Noise, no bottleneck' Condition 3. The highest vagueness scores were produced in the 'Noise and bottleneck' Condition 4.

(a) Condition 1: No bottleneck, no noise. The effect of data_size on the vagueness score.

	delta = 1
data_size = 150	0.00
data_size = 200	0.00

(b) Condition 2: Bottleneck, no noise. The effect of data_size and delta-value on the vagueness score.

	delta = 0	delta = 0.5	delta = 1
data_size = 45	**0.62**	0.27	0.29
data_size = 60	0.38	0.09	0.19
data_size = 75	0.00	0.19	0.10

(c) Condition 3: Noise, no bottleneck. The effect of data_size and noise-value on the vagueness score.

	noise =	0.25	0.275	0.3	0.4
data_size = 150		0.28	**0.68**	0.57	0.12
data_size = 200		0.35	0.33	0.20	0.03

(d) Condition 4: Noise and bottleneck. The effect of data_size and noise-value on the emergence of vague predicates. Results given for delta = 0.5/1.0

	noise delta	0.30 0.5/1.0	0.35 0.5/1.0	0.40 0.5/1.0
data_size = 45		0.50/0.46	0.67/0.60	0.67/0.44
data_size = 50		0.43/0.50	0.73/0.75	0.80 /0.25
data_size = 60		0.31/0.40	**1.00/0.85**	0.73/0.62
data_size = 75		0.41/0.72	0.67/0.77	0.56/0.80

an extension covering two situations. The vagueness scores for these settings are given in Table 2a. (All runs scored 0.) As expected, in this control condition, no vagueness arose when there is no noise and no bottleneck.

Condition 2: Bottleneck, no noise. With these settings, a number of trends emerged (see Table 2b). First, in general, the lower the data_size, the higher the vagueness score was. Second, when data size was low (45 or 60), a low delta value increased the vagueness score. The highest result over 6 runs was for data_size = 45, delta = 0 resulting in a vagueness score of 0.62. This is not a terrible result, however, the resulting languages had only very narrow boundaries. Two typical examples of the resulting languages are given in figure 4. A further effect of the bottleneck was that the end condition language had a smaller vocabulary (2-3 predicates) than the starting condition (15 predicates).

FIGURE 4: Condition 2: Bottleneck, no noise. There were two types of typical ending conditions when data_size = 45, delta = 0 (when there was a bottleneck, but no noise).

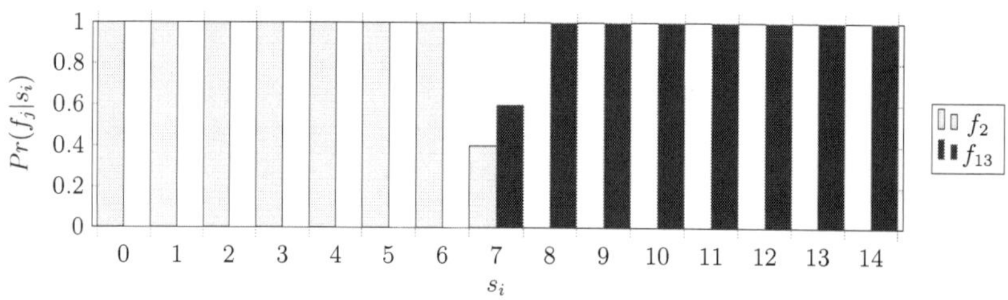

(a) First type of ending condition: A language with two predicates, in this run it was f_2 and f_{13}. Both predicates have sharply graded boundaries. In this case, only s_7 is a borderline case.

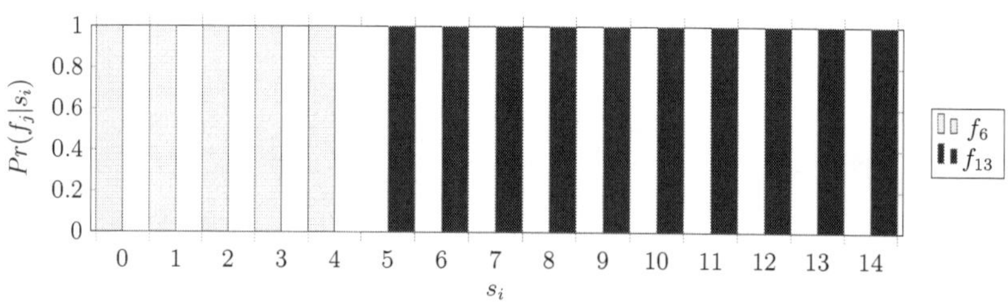

(b) Second type of ending condition: A language with two predicates, in this run it was f_6 and f_{13}. Neither predicate is vague.

Condition 3: Noise, no bottleneck. Perhaps surprisingly, the results in this condition were somewhat chaotic, even with relatively low levels of noise such as 0.25 or 0.275. Vagueness scores were not significant improvements on Condition 2, and in many runs, especially with the higher data_size of 200, other trends emerged such as partial synonymy and predicates with non-convex extensions.

FIGURE 5: Condition 3: Noise, no bottleneck. The typical end condition for runs with these settings (data_size = 150, noise = 0.275) was a language that displayed displayed some vagueness. For example, predicate f_1 below is vague. However, this model setting also resulted in non-convex predicates such as f_9 and f_{11}: f_9 has an extension gap in s_8 and s_9 and f_{11} has an extension gap in s_{10}.

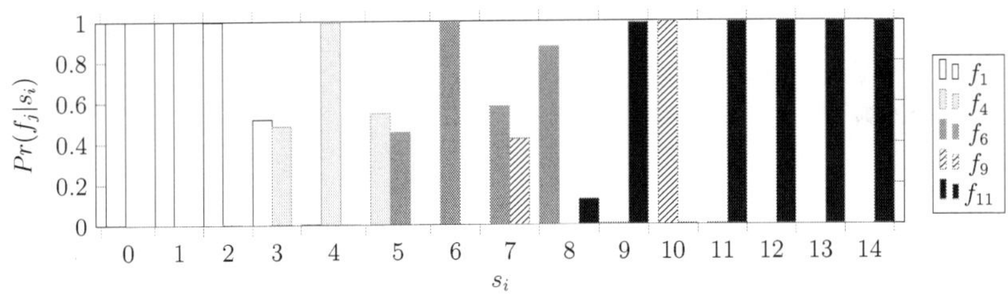

FIGURE 6: Condition 3: Noise, no bottleneck. The typical end condition for this setting of the model (data_size = 200, noise = 0.275) was a language with some vagueness. For example, predicates f_3, f_9 and f_{10} below count as vague. However, other predicates failed to be vague because they lack clear cases. For instance predicates f_0, f_2 and f_{14}. Languages also had non-convex predicates such as f_7 and f_9 below.

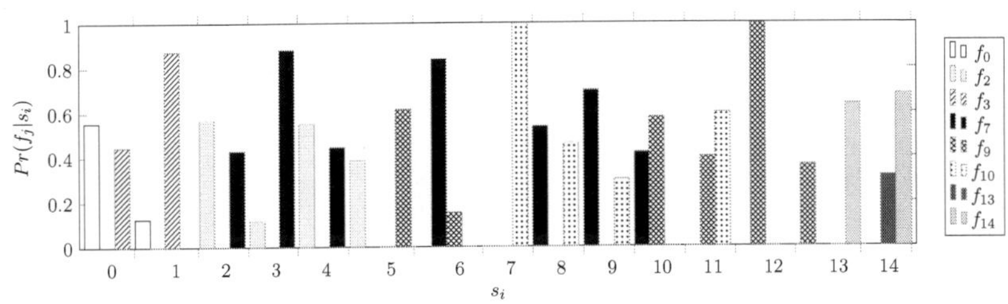

When the data_size was 150, the best vagueness score arose at the relatively low noise level of 0.275. (See Table 2c). However, at 0.68, this vagueness score is only marginally better than the best score in the bottleneck, no noise condition (0.62). In other words, like in the best settings for Condition 2., more often than not, predicates had blurred boundaries. However, in this condition, unlike in Condition 2., there were cases of non-convexity (where a predicate has an extension gap filled by another predicate), see Figure 5. In the worst runs, something evocative of partial synonymy arose, where two predicates were competing for similar parts of the situation space. Under the success criterion, these predicates were not classed as vague, since they failed to have clear cases in the meaning space.

When the data size was increased to 200, the vagueness scores decreased in all but the lowest noise level settings. The maximum score was only 0.33 (only one third of predicates met the vagueness criteria, see Table 2c). A further difference that arose with the increase of data_size to 200, was that there were typically more predicates in the final languages (an average of 7.4 predicates per run as opposed to an average of 5.7 when data_size was 150). It is possible, therefore, that the decrease in vagueness score was due, in part, to an overcrowding the situation space. In this setting, more non-convex predicates resulted as we see for f_7 and f_9 in Figure 6, for instance (f_7 has an extension gap in s_5 and s_7, and f_9 has an extension gap in s_7, s_8 and s_9). Furthermore, once again, something evocative of partial synonymy often arose, where two predicates were competing for similar parts of the situation space. Under the success criterion, these predicates were not classed as vague, since they failed to have clear cases in the meaning space. For example, f_0, f_2, f_{13}, and f_{14} in Figure 6 failed to meet this criteria, since none exceeded a probability of 0.8 in any situations. In other words, unlike the results in Condition 2 (bottleneck, no noise), lower scores resulted not from many sharp, non-vague predicates, but from many predicates that had only non-clear cases or clear non-cases.

In summary, when there was noise and no bottle neck, providing agents with too much noisy learning data seems to give rise to some vagueness, but also a lot of uncertainty where, for large swaths of the situation space no one term is inferred to apply. For noise values above 0.275, the resulting languages were chaotic, so much so that they were often hard to interpret. Interestingly, the introduction of noise decreased the vocabulary size of end condition languages (typically 5-8 predicates) compared to the starting condition (15 predicates). The decrease in vocabulary size was smaller than in Condition 2, however.

Condition 4: Bottleneck and noise. This condition yielded the most successful results. Not only was there a combination of settings that yielded resulting languages where every predicate had graded boundaries (see Table 2d), but on all settings, the average values generated were higher than in any of the other conditions. This sometimes resulted in what could be described as a prototypical image of a system of vague predicates as we see in the three-predicate language in figure 7. As in Condition 2., the vocabulary size of the ending condition of languages was smaller with a lower data_size. For instance, when data_size was 45, typically, final languages had just two predicates, see Figure 8.

FIGURE 7: Condition 4: Noise and Bottleneck. The typical end condition for this setting of the model (data_size = 60, delta = 1.0, noise = 0.35) was a language with relatively few predicates, all of which were vague. For example, the final language depicted below has three predicates f_4, f_8, and f_{10} all of which have clear cases, non clear cases and clear non-cases.

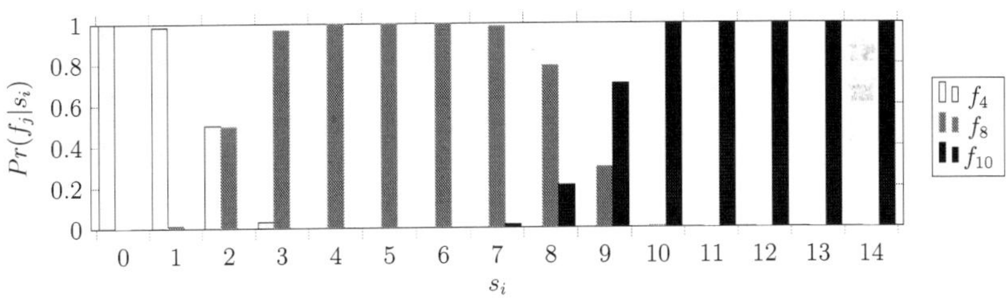

The effect of delta on the results in Condition 4 was unclear, although, in general, for higher noise values, the lower delta setting of 0.5 yielded slightly higher vagueness scores than when it was set to 1.0.

Interestingly, if we compare the results for this condition with those for noise and no bottleneck (Condition 3), we see that, not only were vagueness scores higher, but, in general, there is a greater tolerance for noise in the system when a bottle neck was also present. In Condition 3, the best results were obtained with noise set to 0.275, with results getting worse for higher noise settings such as 0.3 and 0.4. However, in Condition 4, results peaked with with a noise setting of 0.35. With a noise setting of 0.40, there was an increased tendency for languages to collapse into single predicate languages, an effect that arose to a lesser extent when noise was set to 0.35. In fact, the lower figures in Table 2d for noise = 0.35 can be attributed almost entirely to this occurrence. For the lower noise setting of 0.3, the low vagueness scores in Condition 4 arise because, although predicates have graded boundaries, the gradience of these boundaries was too sharp to fall into the definition used here.

FIGURE 8: Condition 4: Noise and bottleneck. The typical end condition for this setting of the model (data_size $\in \{45, 75\}$, noise $= 0.3$) was a language with 2-5 predicates, all of which were vague. The vocabulary size of the languages increases with data_size.

(a) When data_size = 45, delta = 1.0, the typical end condition was a language with two predicates (f_2 and f_7 below), both of which were vague.

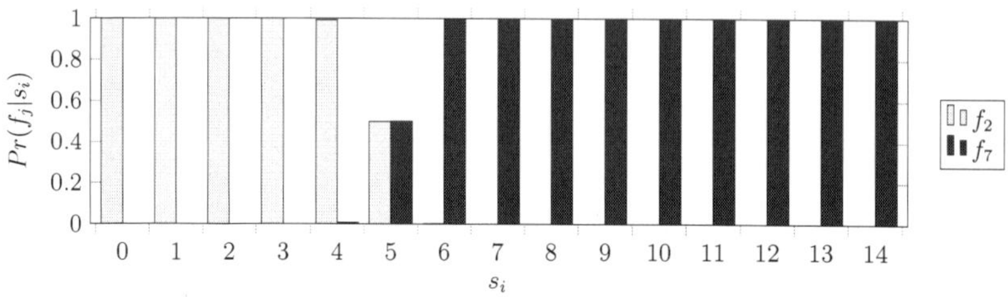

(b) When data_size = 75, delta = 1. , the typical end condition was a language with three or four predicates (the language below has four predicates f_1, f_3, f_6 and f_{11} below), all of which were vague. In the end point of the run depicted below, there is a sharp boundary between predicates f_3 and f_6. However, there is a graded boundary between predicates f_1 and f_3 and between predicates f_6 and f_{11}.

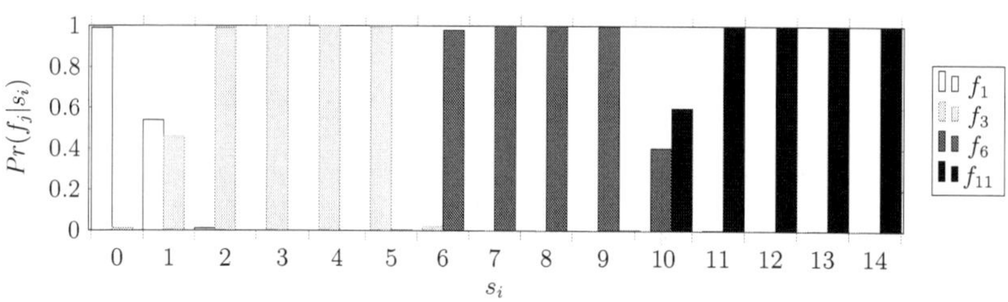

4.3.6 Discussion

The most interesting upshot of these simulations is that, although a semantic bottleneck alone or noise alone can generate some vagueness, a combination of noise and a semantic bottleneck produced the best results. In other words, a combination of (H1) and (H2) best explains the emergence of vagueness. This can be seen in the contrast between Tables 2b and 2c, on the one hand and Table 2d on the other. With both noise and a bottleneck, 50% (12/24) of the different parameter settings resulted in vagueness scores > 0.66 and the mean vagueness score across all parameter settings was 0.61. For the noise only condition only 12.5% (1/8) of the settings exceeded a vagueness score of 0.66. The mean vagueness score in this condition was 0.32. For the bottleneck only condition, no settings resulted in a vagueness score above 0.66 and the mean score was 0.24. This result does, however, raise some questions.

Why is a semantic bottleneck alone insufficient? In order to generate predicates with graded boundaries as a result of a semantic bottleneck, there need to be gaps in the learning data (of at least one situation). However, for this to occur frequently enough, the size of the learning data needs to be small. As we see in Table 2b, for the bottleneck-only condition, the highest vagueness scores occurred with a data_size parameter value of 45. Vagueness scores dropped to nearly zero when this parameter was set to 75. However, there is a lower limit on how low the data size can be. With a value lower than 45, the simulation runs collapsed into trivial one-predicate languages. Therefore, a semantic bottleneck alone can only generate some amount of vagueness, since narrowing the bottleneck further leads to learning a trivial language.

Why is a noise alone insufficient? Why do noise and a semantic bottleneck together do better? The reason why noise alone is insufficient is less clear. When the noise was set too low (at 0.25), predicates were not vague because they had sharp boundaries. When noise was increased, predicates were not vague because they did not have clear cases. One observation that may explain this, and also why a combination of noise and a bottleneck does better, is that the noise-only condition resulted in languages with significantly higher vocabulary sizes than in either the bottleneck only or noise and bottleneck conditions (2-4 predicates vs 5-9 predicates), i.e., that one effect of the semantic bottleneck is to constrain the vocabulary size of languages. This observation suggests the possibility that lower vocabulary sizes allow for more noise in the system. In other words, there seems to be an inverse relationship between how many vague predicates can be accommodated within a semantic space, on the one hand, and how much noise can give rise to this vagueness on the other: For a fixed situation space, the more predicates one has, the less noise there can be without these predicates failing to have any clear cases. Therefore, one way in which we can increase noise, and thereby the gradedness of predicate boundaries, is to constrain the size of the vocabulary independently of the noise level. As we saw from the bottleneck-alone condition, narrowing the bottleneck is one way to achieve a reduction on vocabulary size, and so it makes sense that a combination of a bottleneck and noise can allow for more vagueness.

If these conclusions are correct, then we have evidence that the introduction of the semantic bottleneck plays two roles in the emergence of stable vague languages: First, as we saw from the bottleneck-only

Condition 2, in line with Hypothesis (H2), a semantic bottleneck paired with probabilistic reasoning about data gaps can contribute to the emergence of vagueness. Second, an unexpected effect was that the bottleneck, in virtue of constraining the vocabulary size of a language, facilitates more tolerance of noise within the system, noise which, in turn, contributes to the emergence of vagueness. An obvious question this raises is whether one can separate out these two contributions of the semantic bottleneck. I address this in §4.3.7.

4.3.7 Possible criticisms of and improvements to the model

Finally, let us consider some possible objections to the model as well as ways potential ways in which the model could be refined.

An over-simplified view of communicative need. The model presented here assumes that, for each generation, the list of situations that a speaker is tasked with describing to a learner is drawn (pseudo)-randomly from a list of the situations in the situation space. However, plausibly, this assumption is an oversimplification. For example, it is not obvious that the colours and hues we encounter in the world are distributed evenly, or that, even if they were, we would be equally likely to encounter descriptions of each of them (either evolutionary or social factors might make some hues more prominent and/or likely to be described by others). Therefore, the model could be adjusted to allow for the list of situations to be described to be drawn from a non-flat distribution. It is possible, with this adjustment, that some of the more chaotic tendencies we saw in the noise-only condition and in the higher noise settings of the noise and bottleneck condition may be reduced.

An over-simplified model of communication. One way in which the probabilistic iterated learning model presented above is a refinement of non-probabilistic models is that it does not treat learning as trivial (e.g., the probabilistic model does not assume that a learner can learn an expression from one instance of a form-meaning pair). However, the model of communication in this probabilistic iterated learning model was trivial insofar as a learner received, simultaneously, all of their learning data. Arguably, one way in which the meanings of expressions can become more self-regulated is via interaction and corrective feedback loops between agents (Kempson et al., 2019). But the model presented above has no such mechanisms for coordination and interaction between interlocutors.

An over-simplified speaker (and hearer) model. The speaker and hearer models we assumed were effectively what amount to 'literal hearers' and 'literal speakers' in the Bayesian pragmatics literature (see, e.g., Lassiter and Goodman, 2017, and references therein). For example for an agent a_j with a vague language, given some situation to describe s_i, the predicate chosen by the agent was simply a sample from the distribution $Pr_{a_j}(f_j \in F|s_i)$. Arguably, however, this is too simple insofar as if the speaker is taking into account what the learner may infer from the use of one predicate over another, given the alternatives available, then, given a situation s_i, this may make the probability that a speaker will use a predicate f_j much lower than $Pr_{a_j}(f_j|s_i)$, especially if for some other predicate f_k, $Pr_{a_j}(f_k|s_i)$ is much higher than $Pr_{a_j}(f_j|s_i)$. This is because, for example, a hearer would be more likely to infer that the speaker does not intend to convey s_i, but rather a more paradigm case of f_j.

Relatedly, as pointed out by Shalom Lappin (p.c.), when learning multiple predicates, it can be advantageous to filter out inferences that have low probabilities on the basis of the learning data. A threshold-based filter plus renormalisation of likelihoods inferred from the learning data could be incorporated into future models. Plausibly, this would reduce occurrences of non-convexity in the noise, no bottleneck condition (Condition 3.), since in this condition, relatively large data sizes over many generations of agents makes the occurrence of at least some predications in the learning data based on very low conditional probabilities, quite likely.

Hard-wiring a limit on the size of the language. Since the model presented above was designed such that the language of a_0 was maximally precise, given the size of the situation space, the model was not flexible enough test a starting condition in which a large situation space is covered by relatively few precise predicates (a hard-coding of the downwards pressure on vocabulary size). It is possible that, were this to be tested, the noise-only and bottleneck-only testing conditions may have produced more concordant results.

A vague starting condition. Finally, since human languages, we may assume, never had a non-vague starting point, the model does not resolve what factors, given a vague language as a starting condition, contribute, as stable attractors, to such vagueness persisting across generations.[15] The results of these simulations do suggest that noise and a semantic bottleneck do not prevent vagueness in a language from persisting across generations in the iterated learning model, however, it would certainly be interesting, in future work, to compare the outcomes of a vague and non-vague starting condition.

[15]Thank you to Daniel Lassiter (p.c.) for raising this issue.

4.4 Conclusion

In relation to the literature discussed in section 4.2, this simulation study provides some evidence in favour of accounts that posit both some form of noise as an underlying factor in why natural language predicates are vague, and that attribute at least part of the explanation to the residue of semantic learning (see §4.3.6). In other words, the hypotheses that best account for the vagueness are a combination of (H1) and (H2). More broadly, given that both the bottleneck and noise generate conditions of uncertainty in language learning, we have evidence that vagueness arises as a result of reasoning in these conditions of uncertainty, a claim that virtually all probabilistic accounts of vagueness make in one form or another.

However, this study also uncovers something that has received less notice in the literature. As remarked in the introduction to section 4.3, a common simplifying assumption in previous approaches is to consider minimal pairs such as *tall* and *short* (possibly with the addition of a 'say nothing' alternative as in (Lassiter and Goodman, 2017)). However, when more predicates are involved, an extra crucial ingredient for stable vague languages to emerge is some kind of downwards pressure on vocabulary size (see §4.3.6). This chimes well with Zipf-inspired information theoretic analyses of the origins of ambiguity. For instance, Piantadosi et al. (2011) propose that the balancing of two pressures: *clarity* and *ease*, which can be paraphrased as pressures toward a larger vocabulary, which maps straightforwardly onto only one or a few meanings on the one hand, and a smaller vocabulary, the tokens of which are, for example, more frequent and easier to access.[16] The simulations presented here suggest that the semantic bottleneck may be one source of a pressure towards *ease* (i.e., a smaller vocabulary size), and that this pressure contributes to the emergence of vague, stable languages.

4.5 Further reading

- Early foundations of probabilistic approaches to vagueness and a discussion thereof: (Égré and Barberousse, 2014, Borel, 1907/2014, Black, 1937).
- A more philosophically oriented proposal from Edgington based on degrees of closeness to clear cases of truth that has influenced several of the papers cited above (Edgington, 1992, 1997). See also a review

[16] An important part of Piantadosi et al.'s (2011) proposal is that a prima facie decrease in clarity resulting from a smaller vocabulary can be assuaged if context reduces uncertainty about what is meant. In the context of vagueness, this idea is likely also to be highly relevant when considering the role of context in the interpretation of vague predicates.

of probabilistic approaches to vagueness from a more philosophical perspective (Sutton, 2018).

- Extension of Rational Speech Act approaches to morphological and lexical negation for expressions such as *happy* (Tessler and Franke, 2018), to probability expressions such as *likely* (Herbstritt and Franke, 2019), and to generics (Tessler and Goodman, 2019, Schuster and Degen, 2020).
- Probabilistic treatments of vague quantifiers (van Tiel et al., 2021, Emerson, 2020, Schöller and Franke, 2017).
- Collections of papers on vagueness: (Dietz and Moruzzi, 2009, Nouwen et al., 2011, Keefe and Smith, 1997)
- A handbook article that places probabilistic approaches to vagueness in the context of other theories: (Burnett and Sutton, 2020).

4.6 Acknowledgements

This research was supported by funding from the Beatriu de Pinós postdoctoral fellowships programme, funded by the Secretary of Universities and research (Government of Catalonia) and from the Horizon 2020 programme of research and innovation of the European Union under the Marie Skłodowska-Curie grant agreement no 801370. Many thanks to Gemma Boleda, Guy Emerson, Shalom Lappin, and Daniel Lassiter for their helpful comments on this version and/or earlier versions of this work.

Appendix: The probabilistic iterated learning model

This probabilistic iterative learning was coded in Python.[17] For ease of presentation, the model is represented below in mathematical and set-theoretic notation.

Preliminaries: The model assumes the following sets. F, S, and A are taken as primitives. L, I, and D, are defined further below:

$F = \{f_0, ..., f_n\}$ A set of predicates

$S = \langle s_0, ..., s_n \rangle$ An ordered set of situations

$A = \langle a_0, ..., a_n \rangle$ An ordered set of agents

$L = \{l_{a_0}, ..., l_{a_n}\}$ A set of languages, one for each agent

$I = \{i_{a_0,a_1}, ..., i_{a_{n-1},a_n}\}$ A set of intended data, one for pair of agents where $i_{a_n,a_{n+1}}$ is data a_{n+1} intends to convey to a_n

$D = \{d_{a_0,a_1}, ..., d_{a_{n-1},a_n}\}$ A set of learning data, one for pair of agents where $d_{a_n,a_{n+1}}$ is the learning data a_{n+1} receives from a_n.

[17]The code is available at https://github.com/peter-sutton/CSLIproblingbook.

Parameters: The following are parameters within the model. The parameters relevant for testing the hypotheses (H1) and (H2) are data_size, noise, and delta:

NumPredSit	the cardinality of F and S (always identical for a_0)
NumGen	the cardinality of A
data_size	the number of samples given to a_i from the language of a_{i-1}
noise	the degree to which an agent a_i can discern which situation a_{i-1} is describing with a predicate. This governs how precisely intended datasets are mapped to learning datasets.
delta	When there is a gap in the learning data set (when a learner has no direct information regarding what predicate to apply to a situation), the learner must reason about what predicate to use. This parameter affects how strongly witnessed uses of 'near-by' predicates influence this reasoning.

A language for an agent, a_k is a set of (posterior) conditional probability distributions $\{Pr_{a_k}(f_i|s_j) : f_i \in F, s_j \in S\}$. For agents $a_{i>0}$ these posterior probabilities are calculated from priors and the learning data (which provide the likelihoods) via Bayes' Rule. In cases where the learning data is 'gappy' and so provides no information about at least one situation in S, this gap is filled on the basis of reasoning about how best to extend the extensions of predicates to this/these situations.

Language for $\mathbf{a_0}$ is a set of conditional probabilities $Pr_{a_0}(f_i \in F|s_j \in S)$ (for each predicate and situation, the probability that the agent will use that predicate to describe that situation). The number of situations and predicates for a_0 is always the same. $Pr_{a_0}(f_i|s_j) = 1$ if $i = j$ and $Pr_{a_0}(f_i|s_j) = 0$ if $i \neq j$. See Figure 1.

Intended data. For each a_i, a_{i+1}, a set of tuples $\{\langle s_i, f_j\rangle : s_j \in S, f_i \in F\}$. The situations $s \in S$ are randomly generated. The size of this list is governed by the parameter data_size. The predicate in the tuple is derived from the language of a_i. The intended data is akin to what learners receive in non-probabilistic iterated learning models in which learning is trivial (i.e., the intended message is always paired with the signal). In this probabilistic model, learners do not receive the intended data, but rather the learning data which may be modulated by noise.

Learning data (likelihoods) are, for an agent a_k probability distributions $Pr_{a_k}(s_i \in S|f_j \in F, i_{a_{k-1},a_k})$, calculated from intended data with the addition of noise. Noise is governed by the noise parameter. For each member of the intended data set $t_k = \langle s_i, f_j \rangle$, we derive a distribution $Pr_{a_k}(s_i \in S|f_j, t_k)$ based on a normal distribution with a mean of s_i and a standard deviation of noise.

Example: suppose that for a space of three situations s_0, s_1, s_2, a member of the intended data set is $t_1 = \langle s_1, f_1 \rangle$. If noise= 0.5, then for a Gaussian function f, the corresponding member of the learning data set is a probability distribution:

$$\begin{aligned} Pr(s_i|f_1, t_1) &= \frac{\mathrm{f}(s_i|\mu = s_1, \sigma^2 = 0.5^2)}{\sum_{s_j \in S} \mathrm{f}(s_j|\mu = s_1, \sigma^2 = 0.5^2)} \\ Pr(s_0|f_1, t_1) &\approx 0.11 \\ Pr(s_1|f_1, t_1) &\approx 0.78 \\ Pr(s_2|f_1, t_1) &\approx 0.11 \end{aligned}$$

If a predicate, f_j is witnessed more than once in the intended dataset i then the learning data relating to that predicate is calculated as the normed average of $Pr(s_i \in S|f_j, t \in i)$, such that $t \in i$ is the set of tuples that witness f_j.

Example: Suppose following the first intended data point above, the second intended data point is $t_2 = \langle s_2, f_1 \rangle$. This gives us:

$$\begin{aligned} Pr(s_0|f_1, t_2) &\approx 0.00 \\ Pr(s_1|f_1, t_2) &\approx 0.12 \\ Pr(s_2|f_1, t_2) &\approx 0.88 \end{aligned}$$

The normed average over both of these data points is:[18]

$$\begin{aligned} Pr(s_i|f_1, t_1, t_2) &= \frac{Pr(s_i|f_1, t_1) + Pr(s_i|f_1, t_2)}{|\{t_1, t_2\}|} \\ Pr(s_0|f_1, t_1, t_2) &\approx 0.055 \\ Pr(s_1|f_1, t_1, t_2) &\approx 0.45 \\ Pr(s_2|f_1, t_1, t_2) &\approx 0.495 \end{aligned}$$

Priors for situations are calculated from the learning data:

$$Pr_a(s_i) = \frac{\sum_{f_j \in F} Pr_a(s_i|f_j, i)}{\sum_{s_k \in S, f_j \in F} Pr_a(s_k|f_j, i)}$$

Priors for predicates are also calculated from the learning data. Each item in the learning data consists of a pair of a predicate and a probability distribution over situations:

[18]The reason why s_2 gets a slight boost over s_1 is because s_2 in this toy example is at an end point in the ordering of S.

$$Pr_a(f_i) = \frac{\text{Number of instances of } f_i \text{ in the learning data for } a}{\text{data\_size}}$$

Languages for $\mathbf{a_{k>0}}$ are sets of conditional probabilities $Pr_{a_k}(f_i \in F|s_j \in S)$ (for each predicate and situation, the probability that the agent will use that predicate to describe that situation). Initial values for $Pr_{a_k}(f_i \in F|s_j \in S)$ are calculated from the learning data and priors using Bayes' theorem. If there are no situations with a prior probability of 0, these initial values are used as the language of the agent.

If there are situations with a prior probability of 0 (i.e., when some situation s_i, does not occur in the intended data set due to the semantic bottleneck), the agent reasons about which predicate to apply with what probability based on their learning datasets. This reasoning is governed by the value of the delta parameter and a distance measure between situations in the ordered tuple.

Example: Suppose we have a case where the priors for s_1 and s_2 are zero, and so we only have a partial language:

$Pr(F\|S)$	s_0	s_1	s_2	s_4
f_0	1	–	–	0
f_1	0	–	–	1

For $s_i \in \{s_1, s_2\}$, the values for $Pr(f_1|s_i)$ and $Pr(f_2|s_i)$ are calculated from the values for $Pr(f_0|s_0)$, $Pr(f_0|s_4)$, $Pr(f_1|s_0)$ and $Pr(f_1|s_4)$ along with a distance measure between situations and the delta value. Where $Dist(s_i, s_j) = abs(i - j)$,

$$Pr(f_0|s_1) \propto exp(ln(Pr(f_0|s_0) - (\text{delta} \times Dist(s_1, s_0))$$

If similar calculations are made for $Pr(f_0|s_2)$, $Pr(f_1|s_1)$ and $Pr(f_1|s_2)$, the above case yields:

delta = 1

$Pr(F\|S)$	s_0	s_1	s_2	s_4
f_0	1	0.73	0.27	0
f_1	0	0.27	0.73	1

delta = 0.5

$Pr(F\|S)$	s_0	s_1	s_2	s_4
f_0	1	0.62	0.38	0
f_1	0	0.38	0.62	1

delta = 0

$Pr(F\|S)$	s_0	s_1	s_2	s_4
f_0	1	0.50	0.50	0
f_1	0	0.50	0.50	1

References

Barker, Chris. 2002. The dynamics of vagueness. *Linguistics and Philosophy* 25(1):1–36.

Bernardy, Jean-Philippe, Rasmus Blanck, Stergios Chatzikyriakidis, and Shalom Lappin. 2018. A compositional Bayesian semantics for natural language. In M. Sinha and T. Dasgupta, eds., *Proceedings of the First International Workshop on Language Cognition and Computational Models*, pages 1–10.

Bernardy, Jean-Philippe, Rasmus Blanck, Stergios Chatzikyriakidis, Shalom Lappin, and Aleksandre Maskharashvili. 2019. Bayesian inference semantics: A modelling system and a test suite. In *Proceedings of the Eighth Joint Conference on Lexical and Computational Semantics (*SEM)*, pages 263–272.

Black, Max. 1937. Vagueness. an exercise in logical analysis. *Philosophy of Science* 4(4):427–455.

Borel, Émile. 1907/2014. An economic paradox: The sophism of the heap of wheat and statistical truths. *Erkenntnis* 79(Suppl. 5):1081–1088.

Burnett, Heather and Peter R. Sutton. 2020. *Vagueness and Natural Language Semantics*. In D. Gutzmann, L. Matthewson, C. Meier, H. Rullmann, and T.E. Zimmermann (eds.) *The Wiley Blackwell Companion to Semantics.* https://doi.org/10.1002/9781118788516.sem053, pages 1-34.

Cooper, Robin, Simon Dobnik, Staffan Larsson, and Shalom Lappin. 2015. Probabilistic type theory and natural language semantics. *LILT* 10(4).

Correia, Jose Pedro and Michael Franke. 2019. Towards an ecology of vagueness. In R. Dietz, ed., *Vagueness and Rationality*, pages 87–113. Berlin: Springer.

Decock, Lieven and Igor Douven. 2014. What is graded membership? *Noûs* 48(4):653–682.

Dietz, Richard and Sebastiano Moruzzi, eds. 2009. *Cuts and Clouds. Vaguenesss, its Nature and its Logic*. Oxford University Press.

Edgington, Dorothy. 1992. Validity, uncertainty and vagueness. *Analysis* 52(4):193–204.

Edgington, Dorothy. 1997. Vagueness by degrees. In R. Keefe and P. Smith, eds., *Vagueness: A Reader*, pages 294–316. Cambridge, MA: MIT Press.

Égré, Paul. 2017. Vague judgment: A probabilistic account. *Synthese* 194(10):3837–3865.

Égré, Paul and Anouk Barberousse. 2014. Borel on the heap. *Erkenntnis* 79(5):1043–1079.

Egré, Paul, Vincent De Gardelle, and David Ripley. 2013. Vagueness and order effects in color categorization. *Journal of Logic, Language and Information* 22(4):391–420.

Emerson, Guy. 2020. Linguists who use probabilistic models love them: Quantification in functional distributional semantics. In C. Howes,

S. Chatzikyriakidis, A. Ek, and V. Somashekarappa, eds., *Proceedings of Probability and Meaning (PaM2020)*, pages 41–52.

Emerson, Guy. 2022. Probabilistic lexical semantics: From Gaussian embeddings to bernoulli fields. In J.-P. Bernardy, R. Blanck, S. Chatzikyriakidis, S. Lappin, and A. Maskharashvili, eds., *Probabilistic Approaches to Linguistic Theory*. CSLI Publications.

Fara, Delia Graff. 2000. Shifting sands: An interest-relative theory of vagueness. *Philosophical Topics* 28.

Fernández, Raquel and Staffan Larsson. 2014. Vagueness and learning: A type-theoretic approach. In *Proceedings of the Third Joint Conference on Lexical and Computational Semantics (*SEM 2014), Dublin, Ireland, August 23-24 2014.*, pages 151–159.

Fine, Kit. 1975. Vagueness, truth, and logic. *Synthese* 30:265–300.

Franke, Michael and Jose Pedro Correia. 2018. Vagueness and imprecise imitation in signalling games. *British Journal for the Philosophy of Science* 69(4):1037–1067.

Franke, Michael, Gerhard Jäger, and Robert van Rooij. 2011. Vagueness, signaling & bounded rationality. In T. Onoda, D. Bekki, and E. McCready, eds., *JSAI-isAI 2010*, pages 45–59.

Frazee, Joey and David Beaver. 2010. Vagueness is rational under uncertainty. In M. Aloni, H. Bastiaanse, T. de Jager, and K. Schulz, eds., *Logic, Language and Meaning: 17th Amsterdam Colloquium, Amsterdam, The Netherlands, December 16-18, 2009, Revised Selected Papers, Lecture Notes in Artificial Intelligence*, pages 153–162. Springer.

Herbstritt, Michele and Michael Franke. 2019. Complex probability expressions & higher-order uncertainty: Compositional semantics, probabilistic pragmatics & experimental data. *Cognition* 186:50–71.

Kamp, Hans. 1975. Two Theories About Adjectives. In E. Keenan, ed., *Formal Semantics of Natural Languages*, pages 123–155. Cambridge: Cambridge University Press.

Keefe, R. and P. Smith, eds. 1997. *Vagueness: A Reader*. Cambridge, MA: MIT Press.

Kempson, R., E. Gregoromichelaki, and C. Howes. 2019. Language as mechanisms for interaction: Towards an evolutionary tale. In A. Silva, S. Staton, P. Sutton, and C. Umbach, eds., *Language, Logic, and Computation. TbiLLC 2018. Lecture Notes in Computer Science, vol 11456*. Springer.

Kirby, Simon. 2007. The Evolution of Meaning-Space Structure through Iterated Learning. In C. Lyon, C. Nehaniv, and A. Cangelosi, eds., *Emergence of Communication and Language*, pages 253–268. London: Springer, Verlag.

Kirby, Simon and James Hurford. 2002. The Emergence of Linguistic Structure: An overview of the Iterated Learning Model. In A. Cangelosi and D. Parisi, eds., *Simulating the Evolution of Language*, pages 121–148. London: Springer, Verlag.

Lassiter, Daniel. 2011. Vagueness as probabilistic linguistic knowledge. In R. Nouwen, U. Sauerland, H. Schmitz, and R. van Rooij, eds., *Vagueness in Communication*. Springer.

Lassiter, Daniel and Noah D. Goodman. 2017. Adjectival vagueness in a Bayesian model of interpretation. *Synthese* pages 1–36.

Nouwen, R., U. Sauerland, H.C. Schmitz, and R. van Rooij, eds. 2011. *Vagueness in Communication*. Springer.

Piantadosi, S., H. Tily, and E. Gibson. 2011. The communicative function of ambiguity in language. *PNAS* 108(9):3526–3529.

Qing, Ciyang and Michael Franke. 2014. Vagueness, and optimal language use: A speaker-oriented model. In T. Snider, S. D'Antonio, and M. Weigand, eds., *Proceedings of SALT 2014*, pages 23–41.

Schmidt, L.A., N.D. Goodman, D. Barner, and J.B. Tenenbaum. 2009. How tall is tall? compositionality, statistics, and gradable adjectives. In *Proceedings of the 31st annual conference of the cognitive science society.*, pages 3151–3156.

Schöller, Anthea and M. Franke. 2017. Semantic values as latent parameters: Testing a fixed threshold hypothesis for cardinal readings of few & many. *Linguistics Vanguard* 3.

Schuster, Annika, Corina Strößner, Peter Sutton, and Henk Zeevat. 2020. Stochastic frames. In *Proceedings of the Probability and Meaning Conference (PaM 2020)*, pages 78–85. Gothenburg: Association for Computational Linguistics.

Schuster, Sebastian and Judith Degen. 2020. I know what you're probably going to say: Listener adaptation to variable use of uncertainty expressions. *Cognition* 203:104285.

Shannon, Claude. 1948. A mathematical theory of communication. *Bell System Technical Journal* 27:379–423.

Sorensen, Roy. 1988. *Blindspots*. Oxford: Clarendon Press.

Sorensen, Roy. 2001. *Vagueness and Contradiction*. Oxford: Clarendon Press.

Sutton, Peter. R. 2013. *Vagueness, Communication, and Semantic Information*. Ph.D. thesis, King's College London.

Sutton, Peter R. 2018. Probabilistic approaches to vagueness and semantic competency. *Erkenntnis* 83(4):711–740.

Tessler, M. H. and M. Franke. 2018. Not unreasonable: Carving vague dimensions with contraries and contradictions. In *Proceedings of the 40th Annual Meeting of the Cognitive Science Society*, pages 1108–1113.

Tessler, Michael H and Noah D Goodman. 2019. Learning from generic language.

van Eijck, J. and S. Lappin. 2012. Probabilistic semantics for natural language. In Z. Christoff, P. Galeazzi, N. Gierasimszuk, A. Marcoci, and S. Smets, eds., *Logic and Interactive Rationality (LIRA) 2012, Volume 2*, pages 17–35. ILLC, University of Amsterdams.

van Tiel, Bob, Michael Franke, and Uli Sauerland. 2021. Probabilistic pragmatics explains gradience and focality in natural language quantification. *Proceedings of the National Academy of Sciences* 118(9).

Williamson, Timothy. 1992. Vagueness and ignorance. *Proceedings of the Aristotelian Society* 66:145–162.

Williamson, Timothy. 1994. *Vagueness*. London: Routledge.

5

Bayesian Inference Semantics for Natural Language

JEAN-PHILIPPE BERNARDY, RASMUS BLANCK, STERGIOS CHATZIKYRIAKIDIS, SHALOM LAPPIN AND ALEKSANDRE MASKHARASHVILI

In most classical theories of formal semantics (Montague, 1974, Barwise and Cooper, 1981, Keenan and Falz, 1985, Heim and Kratzer, 1998, Peters and Westerståhl, 2006), the meaning of a sentence is identified with its truth conditions. These are specified as functions from a domain of indices (possible worlds, contexts, situations, etc.) to the range of Boolean values {0,1}. Inference is treated as a species of logical implication, such that every valuation (or model) for which the premises of an argument are true is one for which the conclusion is true.

While truth-conditional theories of meaning have offered important insights into the semantics of natural languages, they have also missed at least two central elements of the way in which humans interpret the expressions of their language. First, these theories cannot accommodate vagueness, which is a pervasive feature of natural languages. Speakers take most sentences to be more or less true, monadic and relational predicates to apply to a greater or lesser extent to n-tuples of objects, adverbs to be approximately true of the events and situations denoted by verb phrases, etc. A common response to this issue is to treat semantic theory as a component of an idealised linguistic competence which is categorical in nature. Vagueness is then relegated

Probabilistic Approaches to Linguistic Theory.
Jean-Philippe Bernardy, Rasmus Blanck,
Stergios Chatzikyriakidis, Shalom Lappin,
Aleksandre Maskharashvili (eds.).

to performance and processing effects.[1] In order to have any substance, this response must provide a treatment of performance that permits one to predict the observed properties of vagueness when it is combined with the proposed theory of competence. To the best of our knowledge, no such account has yet been constructed. In fact, it is reasonable to suggest that vagueness and ambiguity promote information-theoretic efficiency in communication (Piantadosi et al., 2011). If this is the case, then semantic vagueness is integral to the design of natural language, and it cannot be relegated to a side effect of performance factors.

Second, updating meaning to take account of new information is an important aspect of interpretation. While dynamic semantic approaches (Heim, 1982, Groenendijk and Stokhof, 1991, Kamp and Reyle, 1993, Chierchia, 1995, Cann et al., 2009) capture certain aspects of this process, and some are even amenable to computational implementation (Itegulov et al., 2018, Bernardy and Chatzikyriakidis, 2019a,b), they are largely restricted to extending scope, binding, and co-reference across sentences in discourse. They also tend to rely on the introduction of special-purpose update mechanisms, which are added to the machinery of classical semantic theories, to express these dynamic phenomena.

In this chapter we present Bayesian Inference Semantics (BIS). This system assigns probability conditions to inferences, and it defines functions for the typed constituents of sentences that generate these conditions compositionally. This framework permits us to capture vagueness through probability distributions for predicates, and the sentential assertions that are constructed from them. Vagueness is, then, a core property of expressions in our account. This allows us to provide natural representations of scalar adjectives and vague classifier terms, while these are problematic for classical semantic theories. Using probability distributions over the definitions of predicates also permits us to handle the sorites paradox in a straightforward way. We sustain the fuzzy boundaries of classifiers through these distributions, without invoking sharp borders between objects to which classifier terms apply, and those to which they do not.

BIS is designed to handle probabilistic inferences over a wide range of syntactic constructions and semantic types. We illustrate these with an inference test suite. The role of new information in updating the interpretation of a sentence falls directly out of our Bayesian models for estimating the probability values of the sentences in the premises

[1] A similar problem arises in syntax, where the defence of classical binary accounts of grammaticality rely heavily on the competence–performance distinction. See Lau et al. (2017) for a critical discussion of this approach.

and the conclusions of an argument. We do not require special-purpose update mechanisms, and we capture the effect of new information on the interpretation of all major constituents of a sentence. The lexical content of the premises of an argument specifies the priors of the conditional probability in terms of which the posterior probability of the conclusion is estimated. As information is added through new premises, possibly modifying the lexical content of the premises, the probability value of the conclusion changes.

Many classical formal semantic theories take the indices of interpretive functions to be possible worlds of the sort used in Kripke frame semantics (Montague, 1974). If these are understood as maximal worlds in which every proposition of the language has a defined truth-value, then they raise serious problems of representational tractability (Lappin, 2015, 2018). Probability theorists also frequently talk about distributing probability over possible worlds (Halpern, 2017). In fact, they restrict these worlds to the set of situations corresponding to the outcomes for which probabilities are specified in a random variable. The other events and situations required for a complete world are marginalised out of the probability distribution. Therefore, we avoid the intractability of representing full worlds by using the non-maximal situations of probability theory.

Estimating the probability of a sentence involves reasoning under uncertainty. The obvious question is, then, what is the source of uncertainty that grounds our probabilistic semantics. Epistemicists like Williamson (1994) use probability to model vagueness as uncertainty about the boundary within which a predicate applies to the set of objects of which it is true. They posit the existence of such a boundary, but take it to be unknown in the general case. Goodman and Lassiter (2015), Lassiter and Goodman (2017) adopt a similar view in assuming a contextually determined predicate boundary which hearers estimate in interpreting the utterances of a particular speaker.

By contrast, Edgington (2001) and Lappin (2018) reject the existence of absolute boundaries for property terms, and take them to be inherently indeterminate. Lappin (2018) regards the uncertainty that generates vagueness to be the result of the language acquisition process in which speakers learn to apply the predicates and other expressions of their language to real-world situations under supervision of competent speakers. When language learners use these terms in new situations they generalise them by estimating the likelihood that a given predication holds, according to the competent speakers of the language. This underdetermination of meaning can persist into mature language use. It is an effect of semantic learning as a supervised process.

BIS is compatible with either of these accounts of vagueness. It specifies a probability distribution over the boundaries of a property for a set of objects in a property space. One could take this distribution to be accessible to further constraints to the point that the boundary becomes fully determinate. On this approach, enough information about the world may resolve the probability of a predication to 1 or 0. Alternatively, we could take the distribution to be resistant to such determination. On that assumption, the boundary over which probability is distributed becomes intrinsically unknowable, and hence it effectively disappears. As both perspectives seem viable, we do not rule out either of them here.

In a classical logic an inference is valid iff under every assignment for which the conjunction of the premisses is evaluated as 1, the conclusion also receives the value 1. By contrast, a probabilistic semantics takes the Boolean truth-values $\{0,1\}$ to be limit points in a distribution of possible values $[0,1]$. Inferences receive conditional probabilities $P(Conclusion|Premisses) = p$, where p is the the likelihood that the conclusion holds, given that the premisses do.

In designing our sampling and evaluation procedures for BIS we have sought to sustain classical validity as determined by first-order logic, as well as valid inferences that depend on standard interpretations of non-logical predicates. Our implementation is still under development, and so we have not yet succeeded in capturing all of the classical inferences in our test set.

In the work presented here we have relied on our collective judgements to determine probabilities that our models assign to non-valid inferences. These models are intended as a proof of concept for our project. We anticipate that in future work we will use crowd sourcing and systematic corpus analysis to obtain more robust data for specifying the probability values of the inferences in our test set. We will also experiment with deep learning methods to extract interpretations of predicates and other expressions, in a way that provides reliable wide coverage constraints for the models that we use to generate probabilities for inferences.

A central feature of BIS is the uniform assignment of priors to particular lexical constituents. We do not introduce any lexeme-specific knowledge.[2] Clearly, to obtain priors which incorporate real-world knowledge, properly grounded in speakers' representations of meaning, it is necessary to update these priors with suitable corpus-based

[2]As always when using Bayesian modelling, the priors have an influence on the behaviour of the system (§5.4).

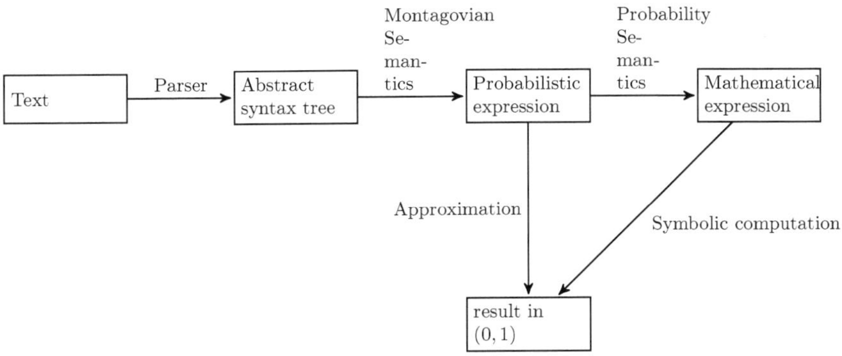

FIGURE 1: Phases in our system. Syntax is first interpreted as probabilistic expressions. Such expressions can be given a precise mathematical semantics. They can also be evaluated approximately, using Monte Carlo methods.

representations. This is possible in principle, but here we are presenting a "blank-state" system, with uniform priors, as a platform for experimenting with Bayesian semantics. Developing it into a wide-coverage framework that generates the interpretation of naturally occurring sentences by correctly predicting their probability conditions is a significant research challenge. The ultimate viability of our proposed program will depend upon meeting this challenge.

The core idea of BIS is that properties and entities are represented as spaces consisting of points (discrete or continuous). These points can be measured, and their density is computed by summation (the discrete case) or integration (the continuous case). In general, the probability of a predication is estimated by measuring the density of the relevant entities in the property space corresponding to the predicate.

Our system, BIS, consists of several subsystems, shown schematically in Fig. 1 (as labelled arrows) together with the intermediate representations that they use (in boxes). We describe and analyse each of these components in the body of the chapter. To get a sense of the intermediate representations, and how the parts of the system are articulated, we go through an example inference here, presented schematically.

Consider the following inference problem:

$$\frac{\text{Most birds fly}}{\text{A few birds fly}}$$

We wish to compute the probability

$$P(\text{A few birds fly} \mid \text{Most birds fly})$$

and test if its value is closer to 1 than 0.

The sentences are first parsed, yielding abstract syntax trees. In practice we use the Grammatical Framework (GF) tool (Ranta, 2004), but this is not essential to our account. Any parser which produces syntactic structures compatible with Montague-style categories would be suitable (see §5.1 for details). The parses that we obtain for the premise and the hypothesis, respectively, are the following.

$$P = CltoS\, Pos\, (S1\, (QNP\, most\, bird)(fly))$$
$$H = CltoS\, Pos\, (S1\, (QNP\, aFew\, bird)\, (fly))$$

The abstract syntax is then translated to a representation language which makes random variables explicit. It also makes their spaces explicit, and the measures thereof. Using these features, the probabilities of all propositions of interest can be expressed precisely. This language, and its notation is described in detail in §5.2[3]. To generate these intermediate representations, we first must express our (lack of) prior knowledge about the common nouns, verbs, etc. present in the problem. To do so we gather the lexical items and introduce them as random variables in the appropriate spaces. The premise(s) are added as extra conditions, obtained by a compositional semantics described in §5.3. These conditions effectively update the distributions of the representations of lexical items, yielding a global space of situations Ω.

$$\begin{aligned}\Omega = [&bird : Pred \\ &fly : Pred \\ &p : \mathsf{measure}([x : Ind; b : bird(x); f : fly(x)]) > \\ &\qquad \theta_m \mathsf{measure}([x : Ind; b : bird(x)])]\end{aligned}$$

We are assuming here a proportion θ_m corresponding to the meaning of "most" (see §5.3.3 for details). To make the language more concise, we unify the language of spaces and the language of propositions. Effectively, we sample p over the space of *proofs* of the given proposition. We leave the space of predicates $Pred$ unspecified here. Possible choices are spelled out in §5.3, but the reader can glance at Fig. 7 for a preview.

[3]For the impatient, the notation $x : T$ indicates that x is of type T; The dot notation $x.f$ represents accessing field f in a record x. Record types are introduced with brackets a around of a dictionary mapping fields to their types.

The truth value of the conclusion is expressed as a probability measure of a proposition over the whole space Ω that we just defined, with a suitable proportion θ_f for "few".

$$X = P_{\omega:\Omega}([x : Ind; b : \omega.bird(x); f : \omega.fly(x)]) > \theta_f \mathsf{measure}([x : Ind; b : \omega.bird(x)])$$

The expression above can be turned into a mathematical term using the semantics for spaces and probabilities (Definition 1). In our example, the expression begins with integration over the spaces of predicates:

$$\sum_{bird:Pred} \sum_{fly:Pred} \frac{\mathbf{1}(P \wedge Q)}{\mathbf{1}(P)}$$

In fact, we are using here a generalisation of summation and integration, but adopting the symbol $\sum$ for this purpose (cf. §5.2). The conditions P and Q are given by

$$P = \mathsf{measure}([x : Ind; b : bird(x); f : fly(x)]) > \theta_m \cdot \mathsf{measure}([x : Ind; b : bird(x)])$$

$$Q = \mathsf{measure}([x : Ind; b : bird(x); f : fly(x)]) > \theta_f \cdot \mathsf{measure}([x : Ind; b : bird(x)])$$

The integrations and measures are further expanded once $Pred$ is made concrete. We can see that $P \wedge Q = P$ if $\theta_m > \theta_f$, and so in this simple case, the integral evaluates to 1. Therefore, the inference is (stochastically) certain.

However, a more precise model would let θ_m or θ_f be random variables, modelling the epistemic or intrinsic uncertainty of the meaning of the quantifiers. In such a model, the inference would evaluate to a value in the [0,1] interval, depending on the exact choice of priors.

Unfortunately, for the vast majority of cases the integrals would not be computable symbolically. In this kind of situation, one typically resorts to simulated sampling, using Monte Carlo methods (see §5.2.3). We follow this approach, and it is through sampling that we evaluate integrals.[4]

Sections 5.1 to 5.3 detail the phases of our system, outlined above. In §5.1, we define and illustrate the range of constructions that BIS handles, including generalised quantifiers, scalar modifiers, and

[4]We describe an important exception in §5.3.8.

vagueness cases including the sorites cases, specifying a suitable syntax. We also describe our method of parsing sentences in Ranta's (2004) typed Grammatical Framework (GF).

In §5.2 we construct a Logic with Measurable Spaces (LMS) to make precise the notions of random variables over potentially complex spaces. To ensure the compatibility with Montague semantics, it consists of a typed logic. We support Bayesian reasoning by associating types with probability densities. We define operators for measuring spaces, and estimating the probabilities of propositions in terms of the volumes of their relevant subareas.

In §5.2.3 we describe a Markov Chain Monte Carlo (MCMC) method for sampling properties, and estimating the probability of a sentence. Such methods have been used before in linguistic applications, for example by Goodman and Stuhlmüller (2014). Even though all models sample the density of property spaces to estimate the probability of a predication, with Monte Carlo techniques certain models will converge faster than others, depending on the geometric representations of properties and objects. In fact, under certain conditions explained in §5.2.3, estimating probabilities may be computationally intractable. For this reason we discuss two different classes of representation of individuals and predicates. In particular, in §5.3.8 we consider casting properties as boxes of uniform density. This allows us to compute their density symbolically in some instances, avoiding intractability in several important cases.

In Section 5.3, we present our Bayesian semantics for natural language. A compositional semantics is specified for each GF parse structure assigned to a sentence. We describe our inference test suite in §5.4, and we assess the extent to which BIS covers it.

Section 5.5 surveys related work in probabilistic semantics. Finally, in §8.5 we offer our conclusions, and we indicate directions for future work.

5.1 Scope: Phenomena and Grammar

All,Most,Few,AFew,Every,GenericPl, Many : Quant;

Tall, Short: Adj;

ListenToOudMusic, TryHairTransplantTreatment, EnjoyTabouli : VP;

polarity items

Pos,Neg: Pol;

common nouns and relative common nouns

Linguist, BaldMan, ToupeeWearer, BasketballPlayer : CN;
Non : CN → CN;
Qual : Adj → CN → CN;
THAT : RP;
MakeRCL: RP → VP → RCl;
MakepolarRS: Pol → RCl → RS;
RelativiseCN : CN → RS → CN;

PercentOf : Card → CN → NP;
Exactly, AtLeast, MoreThan : Card → Quant;
QNP : Quant → CN → NP ;

adverbs of frequency

Never, Always, Rarely, Probably, Often, Frequently,
Occasionally, Generally, Regularly : VP → AVP;

Units of measure

Centimeter, Foot : Unit;
Measure : Card → Unit → Adj → VP;

comparatives

Equal, More, Less : CompOperator;
CanPlayChords : CompOperator → Card → VP;
ComparVP : CompOperator → Adj → NP → VP;
MoreVP : CompOperator → NP → VP;

sentences and clauses

S1 : NP → VP → Cl;
CltoS : Pol → Cl → S;
If, But, And, or : S → S → S;
Not : S → S;

FIGURE 2: Syntactic categories in our GF parses

The initial component in the sequence of semantic interpretation is the GF parsing of a natural language expression. The parse trees satisfy the homomorphism requirement of Montague (1970, 1974). They provide the domain for a compositional mapping to semantic types, which are probabilistic in our system. We identify here a subset of syntactic constructions suitable for our needs. We single out natural language phenomena that play an important role in probabilistic inference. We use GF to formulate a set of grammar rules that our parser applies in order to generate the parse trees on which our rules of semantic interpretation operate.

Our abstract grammar (Fig. 2) consists of context-free rules, while specific features of English syntax are specified in GF.

A context-free rule in the GF style is written from right to left, e.g., if X $\rightarrow$ Y Z is context-free rule, in GF it would be encoded as a constant R of type Y $\rightarrow$ Z $\rightarrow$ X, we we usually write as R : Y $\rightarrow$ Z $\rightarrow$ X. One can see this as follows: R takes two arguments of type Y and Z and returns the result of type X. That is, the rule R builds an object of type X from objects of type Y and Z. Below, we may call constants of GF, e.g. R : Y $\rightarrow$ Z $\rightarrow$ X, as rules and as constants interchangeably.

We modify standard syntactic treatments of English to achieve a more natural mapping between syntactic and semantic representations for the phenomena that we are concerned with. We are not providing a wide-coverage English grammar driven parser, but a proof of concept system for probabilistic inference. For instance, our rule IsA : CN $\rightarrow$ VP allows us to parse "is a guitarist" as a VP, where "guitarist" is a CN.

Most rules are simple and straightforward. Some of them enrich the stylistic diversity of our constructions, such as relative clauses modifying noun phrases. Also for stylistic diversity, we allow for multi-word phrases to be taken as CNs or VPs. For instance "basketball player" and "toupee wearer" are common nouns, while "enjoy tabouli" is a VP.

As Fig. 2 shows, our grammar has four kinds of constants to build clauses and sentences. Two of them are for generating/parsing sentences from sentences (discussed in §5.1.1). The rest of the rules we use to build sentences from NPs, VPs, and polarity items. In particular, we build a clause using the rule S1 : NP $\rightarrow$ VP $\rightarrow$ Cl. A sentence may have a positive or negative polarity. We model that by taking a clause and a polarity item, and build a sentence out of them, which is encoded by the rule CltoS : Pol $\rightarrow$ Cl $\rightarrow$ S.

We list below the rules which are relevant for probabilistic reasoning, and we illustrate them with examples, which form part of our test suite (§5.4).

5.1.1 Logical connectives and polarities

Our test suite contains logically complex sentences built with logical connectives, including conditionals. They are interesting mainly because of their semantic properties. On standard, logical approaches to the interpretation of such sentences, the truth-conditional meanings of connectives play the major role in defining the semantics of a complex sentence. This corresponds to the rules If, But, etc. of type S $\rightarrow$ S $\rightarrow$ S.

5.1.2 Universal quantification

Using the rule QNP : Quant $\rightarrow$ CN $\rightarrow$ NP, we produce a quantified NP from a common noun and a quantifier. An important quantifier is All, corresponding to universal quantification, which figures in the usual Aristotelian syllogisms.

The test suite example T30 (p. 214) illustrates an inference that relies on the interpretation of the universal quantifier.

(T30) P1. All intermediate logic students are Stones fans.
P2. John is an intermediate logic student.
H. John is a Stones fan.
Label:QUANTIFIER, FOL VALIDITY

In classical logic, universal statements such as "All *A*s are *B*s" are interpreted as inclusion of subsets corresponding to the predicates *A* and *B*. Because a system developed for probabilistic reasoning may interpret the universal quantifier through a probabilistic approach to set inclusion, it is useful to test chained quantifiers, as in Example T76 (p. 223).

(T76) P1. All violinists are musicians.
P2. All musicians read music.
H. All violinists read music.
Label:QUANTIFIERS, FOL VALIDITY

5.1.3 Generalised quantifiers and generics

We have a wide range of quantifiers besides the universal, including Few, and Most. We also support explicit percentages, using an *ad hoc* rule PercentOf.

Generic plurals can be expressed in several ways (see e.g. the work of Carlson (1982)), but, restricting ourselves to English, we use bare plurals (GenericPl), as in Example T11 (p. 211).

(T11) P1. Turkish coffee drinkers frequently enjoy a shot of Arak.
P2. Most people that enjoy a shot of Arak also listen to classical oud music.
H. Turkish coffee drinkers listen to classical oud music.
Label:QUANTIFIER, TEMPORAL ADVERB

We also deal with instantiations of generalised quantifiers and generics, illustrated in Example T9 (p. 211).

(T9) P1. Stones fans often prefer The Doors to The Beatles.
P2. John is a Stones fan.
H. John prefers The Doors to The Beatles.
Label:QUANTIFIER, FOL VALIDITY

5.1.4 Modal Adverbs

Modal adverbs play an important role in probabilistic inference. Adverbs of frequency such as Usually, Often, Never connect categorical judgments to probabilistic ones.

(T6) P1. All basketball players are probably tall.
H. Most basketball players are tall.
Label:QUANTIFIER, MODAL ADVERB

As an illustration, in the premise of T6 (p. 210), we have "all basketball players are probably tall", which gives rise to the hypothesis "most basketball players are tall" because of *probably.* Otherwise, one would infer the stronger hypothesis that all basketball players are tall.

Some adverbs can switch the polarity of an hypothesis when they are applied to premises, as in Example T2 (p. 210).

(T2) P1. Prolog programmers are always intermediate logic students.
P2. Intermediate logic students rarely read music.
H. Prolog programmers don't read music.
Label:QUANTIFIER, MODAL ADVERB

In general, it is necessary to study cases with frequency adverbs and quantifiers (including generics and generalised quantifiers) carefully, due to the complex interaction between the two. The semantic content of the adverb, as we model it, is the same as that of a quantifier (generalised or universal, depending on the modal adverb). Some quantifiers may not be encoded in single lexical items (like "most" and "few"), but require multi-word expressions that specify explicit numerical values. We intend our general approach to be independent of the details of the system that we build. Thus we take special care in designing our test cases to ensure that they illustrate general semantic patterns that any adequate probabilistic inference system must capture.

5.1.5 Gradation, Adjectives, and Comparatives

Many natural languages, including English, can derive comparative forms from their respective positive forms (Klein, 1980). For example, positive adjectives such as "tall" give rise to the comparative "taller". In our grammar, comparatives are supported by the rule ComparVP : CompOperator → Adj → NP → VP, where a CompOperator can be Equal, More, or Less.

(T15) P1. Mary is tall.
P2. John is taller than Mary.
H. John is tall.
Label:COMPARATIVE ADJECTIVE, TRANSITIVITY

This is relevant to probabilistic reasoning, because the presence of a gradient of probability for the predicate ("John is tall" is more probable than "Mary is tall") corresponds to the applicability of the comparative ("John is taller than Mary").

5.1.6 Units of measure

We also experiment with units of measure. We study the ability of the system to learn the relationship between observations expressed in terms of measurable quantities and qualitative judgments. In order to encode quantities, we need to add numbers to our grammar. We can parse verb phrases such as "6 feet tall".

We are interested in whether a system can *learn the meaning of an adjective* from the premises which provide information about the property corresponding to the adjective, expressed as degrees, with the help of numerical information. Our test suite contains the following example T38 (p. 216).

(T38) P1. Mary is 190 centimeters tall. Mary is tall.
P2. Molly is 184 centimeters tall. Molly is tall.
P3. Ruth is 180 centimeters tall. Ruth is tall.
P4. Helen is 178 centimeters tall. Helen is tall.
P5. Athena is 166 centimeters tall. Athena isn't tall.
P6. Artemis is 157 centimeters tall. Artemis isn't tall.
P7. Joanna is 160 centimeters tall. Joanna isn't tall.
P8. Kate is 162 centimeters tall. Kate isn't tall.
P9. Christine is 163 centimeters tall.
H. Christine isn't tall.
Label:QUANTIFIER, MODAL ADVERB

While T38 (p. 216) and T15 (p. 212) look similar, they illustrate two different aspects of our system. T15 (p. 212) tests if it captures the relation between "tall" and "taller". T38 (p. 216) requires it to correctly reflect the graded way in which the adjective "tall" applies to an object (when it is true that a person/object is tall, and when it is not).

5.2 Logic with Measurable Spaces

In this section we describe a Logic with Measurable Spaces (LMS). LMS is the representation language connecting parse structures to mathematical expressions of probabilities. We will use it to compose the meaning of inferences from the meaning of premises and hypotheses. As a first approximation, one can see LMS as a precise formalisation of informal notations used when manipulating logical expressions involving random variables. Readers familiar with these concepts can skip this section on first reading. But it will be helpful for understanding subsequent definitions.

LMS draws inspiration from several sources. Like descriptive logics, it aims at making truth computable. It features Sigma spaces (akin to Sigma types in Martin-Löf type-theory). It internalises the notion of the cardinality of spaces, expressed here as measures of spaces, as a tool for encoding the notion of event probability. Fox and Lappin (2005) use the cardinality of predicate spaces in their semantic system, for different purposes.

The syntax of LMS is comprised of two categories: spaces (ranged over by metasyntactic variables A, B, C, etc.), and expressions (ranged over by metasyntactic variables e or ϕ, ψ for Boolean expressions.)

For the purpose of this theory, we limit Boolean expressions to comparison between real-valued expressions ($e_1 \leq e_2$) and conjunctions thereof ($\phi \wedge \psi$); as well as boolean variables Real-valued expressions arise from variables, arithmetic operators (abstracted as *op*), and the measures of spaces— discussed below. Additionally we have support for pairs. We won't construct pairs, but we can extract their first or second components *via* the functions π_1 and π_2. The main objects of interest are *spaces*. Every space has two aspects: an underlying support *type* and a probability distribution over it. The types are formed by the unit type, Booleans, reals, functions, and products.

In LMS, types are used as in a programming language, to verify that nonsensical expressions are disallowed. We do not follow the tradition of intuitionistic logic, in that we ignore the inhabitants of types. Specifically, we do not consider types as propositions via the Curry-Howard isomorphism. LMS does not include quantification over

Spaces:

$A, B, \ldots$ ::=	$\mathsf{IsTrue}(\phi)$	filter space
	$\mid \Sigma(x : A)B$	sigma space
	$\mid \mathsf{Distr}(d)$	base distribution space
	$\mid \{e \mid x : A\}$	image of A under $\lambda x.e$

Expressions:

ϕ, ψ, e ::=	x	variable
	$\mid k$	constants
	$\mid \phi \wedge \psi$conjunction	
	$\mid e_1 \leq e_2$comparision	
	$\mid \pi_1(e) \mid \pi_2(e)$	projections
	$\mid op(e_i)$	arithmetic operators
	$\mid \diamond$	uninformative object
	$\mid \mathsf{measure}(A)$	internalisation of measure

Types:

$$
\begin{aligned}
\tau, \sigma ::= &\ Unit \\
\mid &\ Bool \\
\mid &\ \mathbb{R} \\
\mid &\ \tau \to \sigma \\
\mid &\ \tau \times \sigma
\end{aligned}
$$

FIGURE 3: Syntax of LMS

$$\frac{\Gamma \vdash \phi : Bool}{\Gamma \vdash \mathsf{IsTrue}(\phi) : \mathsf{Space}\, Unit}$$

$$\frac{\Gamma \vdash A : \mathsf{Space}\,\tau \qquad \Gamma, x : \tau \vdash B : \mathsf{Space}\,\sigma}{\Gamma \vdash \Sigma(x : A)B : \mathsf{Space}\,(\Sigma(x : \tau)\sigma)}$$

$$\frac{\Gamma \vdash e_i : \mathbb{R}}{\Gamma \vdash \mathsf{Distr}(d_1[e_i]) : \mathsf{Space}\,\mathbb{R}} \qquad \frac{\Gamma, x : \tau \vdash e : \sigma \qquad \Gamma \vdash A : \mathsf{Space}\,\tau}{\Gamma \vdash \{e \,|\, x : A\} : \mathsf{Space}\,\sigma}$$

$$\frac{\Gamma \vdash e_1 : \tau \qquad \Gamma \vdash e_2 : \sigma[e_1/x]}{\Gamma \vdash (e_1, e_2) : \tau \times \sigma} \qquad \frac{\Gamma \vdash e : \tau \times \sigma}{\Gamma \vdash \pi_1(e) : \tau} \qquad \frac{\Gamma \vdash e : \tau \times \sigma}{\Gamma \vdash \pi_2(e) : \sigma}$$

$$\Gamma \vdash \diamond : Unit \qquad \frac{\Gamma \vdash \phi : Bool \qquad \Gamma \vdash \psi : Bool}{\Gamma \vdash \phi \wedge \psi : Bool} \qquad \frac{\Gamma, x : \tau \vdash e : \sigma}{\Gamma \vdash \lambda x.e : \tau \to \sigma}$$

$$\frac{\Gamma \vdash e_0 : \tau \to \sigma \qquad \Gamma \vdash e_1 : \tau}{\Gamma \vdash e_0(e_1) : \sigma} \qquad \Gamma \vdash true : Bool$$

$$\Gamma \vdash false : Bool \qquad \frac{\Gamma \vdash e : Bool}{\Gamma \vdash \mathbf{1}(e) : \mathbb{R}} \qquad \Gamma \vdash k : \mathbb{R} \qquad \frac{\Gamma \vdash e_i : \mathbb{R}}{\Gamma \vdash op(e_i) : \mathbb{R}}$$

FIGURE 4: Typing rules for LMS. In the above *op* stands for an arbitrary arithmetic operator of arbitrary arity, with e_i being its operands. Similarly, we list only one logical connective ($\wedge$); others follow the same pattern.

all types, nor over all spaces. Instead, the *densities of spaces* are their logical content. Before turning to density we give a brief overview of LMS typing and its consequences. We use two judgments. First, the judgment $\Gamma \vdash e : \tau$, which is the standard typing judgment for terms in the simply typed lambda calculus. We call Boolean-valued expressions *propositions*, so if $\Gamma \vdash \phi : Bool$ holds, it means that ϕ is a proposition in context Γ. Secondly, the judgment $\Gamma \vdash A : \mathsf{Space}\,\sigma$ expresses that A is a space over the ground type σ, in a context Γ.

Because expressions are simply typed, they inherit the usual normalisation properties of typed lamdba terms (Barendregt, 1992). Any closed term of type $\mathbb{R}$ is a real number.

We now focus on spaces and distributions over them. We have four basic space constructions:

1. Given a basic with n parameters $d(x_1, ..., x_n)$, we have the space $\mathsf{Distr}(d(e_1, ..., e_n))$ (each of the parameters can be assigned any real-valued expression).
2. We can construct a space whose density is 1 when a proposition ϕ is true and 0 otherwise. It is written $\mathsf{IsTrue}(\phi)$.
3. We can construct sigma spaces. Given a space A and a space $B[x]$, we can write $\Sigma(x : A)B[x]$ for the the sigma space. The support type for this sigma space is the pair of types which support respectively A and $B[x]$. The associated distribution is a *joint* distribution. Indeed, the distribution associated with B can depend on the value x sampled from A.
4. We can take the image of a space A under a function f. This space is written $\{f(x) \mid x : A\}$. (In fact, we generalise to, and allow, any expression dependent on x instead of just $f(x)$.)

These constructions are listed in Fig. 4.

Formally, we do not manipulate densities directly, thus avoiding theoretical difficulties, in particular for $\{f(x) \mid x : A\}$. Instead, we generalise the notion of integration so that it does not just apply to distributions, but to arbitrary spaces. For this purpose we use the symbol $\sum$, as it is a natural extension of the summation operator.[5]

Definition 1 If $\Gamma \vdash A : \mathsf{Space}\,\alpha$ and $\Gamma, x : \alpha \vdash e : \mathbb{R}$, we define $\sum_{x:A} e$ (which can be read as the integral of e for x ranging over A), by induction on A:

$$\sum_{x:\mathsf{Distr}(d)} e = \int_{\mathbb{R}} \mathrm{PDF}(d, x) \cdot [\![e]\!] dx$$

$$\sum_{x:\mathsf{IsTrue}(\phi)} e = \mathbf{1}([\![\phi]\!]) \cdot [\![e[\diamond/x]]\!]$$

$$\sum_{z:\Sigma(x:A)B} e = \sum_{x:A} \sum_{y:B} e[(x,y)/z]$$

$$\sum_{y:\{e \mid x:A\}} e_2 = \sum_{x:A} e_2[e/y]$$

Definition 2 (Evaluation of expressions) The value of an expression e is written $[\![e]\!]$ and defined by induction on the structure of expressions, as is standard in the lambda calculus. We know that evaluation terminates because of our type-system. The only case that merits attention is the evaluation of $\mathsf{measure}(A)$, which is specified by the following equation:

[5] Technically, we define the integrator and the evaluation of expressions (the next two definitions) by mutual induction on the structure of space and expressions.

$$[\![\mathsf{measure}(A)]\!] = \sum_{x:A} 1$$

The expression $\sum_{x:A} 1$ integrates over the whole space the constant value 1, thus "counting" the elements of that space. Therefore it is the *measure* of the space A. Overloading the notation, we also write $\mathsf{measure}(A)$ for the measure of the space A as a meta-theoretical expression (not an LMS expression), with the same definition.

Definition 3 (Expected value) We define the *expected value* of e for a random variable x distributed in A as follows:

$$E_{x:A}(e) = \frac{\sum_{x:A} e}{\mathsf{measure}(A)}$$

Remark:

$$E_{z:(\Sigma(x:A)B)}(e) = E_{x:A}(E_{y:B}(e[(x,y)/z]))$$

Notation:

$$E_{x_0:A_0,...,x_n:A_n}(e) = E_{x_0:A_0}(\dots E_{x_n:A_n}(e))$$

Finally, we can define the *probability* of a proposition ϕ over a random variable x ranging in A as the proportion of (the measure of) the space A where ϕ holds.

Definition 4

$$P_{x:A}(\phi) = E_{x:A}(\mathbf{1}(\phi))$$

An equivalent definition is the following:

$$P_{x:A}(\phi) = \frac{\mathsf{measure}(\Sigma(x:A)\mathsf{IsTrue}(\phi))}{\mathsf{measure}(A)}$$

In general, for probabilistic inference, we define a space of possible situations Ω, and evaluate the expected truth value of some proposition ϕ over this space. The space Ω typically has a complex structure.

We now verify that $P_{x:A}(\phi)$ satisfies the expected properties of probabilities, starting with the following lemma:

Lemma 1 $\sum_{x:A}$ *is a linear operator:*

(i) $\sum_{x:A}(k \cdot t) = k \cdot \sum_{x:A} t$ *if k does not depend on x*

(ii) $\sum_{x:A}(t + u) = \sum_{x:A} t + \sum_{x:A} u$

Proof. By induction on the structure of A. □

When a space A has zero measure, the probabilities over it are undefined. Otherwise, the Kolmogorov laws of probability are respected. It is easy to verify that any probability is positive, and that the probability of *true* is 1. The last law (in its finite variant) needs a bit more work, and its proof follows.

Theorem 2 *If* $\phi \wedge \psi = false$*, then*

$$P_{x:A}(\phi \vee \psi) = P_{x:A}(\phi) + P_{x:A}(\psi)$$

Proof.

$$\begin{aligned}
E_{x:A}(\phi \vee \psi) &= \sum_{x:A} \mathbf{1}(\phi \vee \psi) && \text{by def.} \\
&= \sum_{x:A} (\mathbf{1}(\phi) + \mathbf{1}(\psi)) && \text{because } \phi \wedge \psi = false \\
&= \sum_{x:A} \mathbf{1}(\phi) + \sum_{x:A} \mathbf{1}(\psi) && \text{by linearity of } \sum_{x:A} \\
&= E_{x:A}(\phi) + E_{x:A}(\psi) && \text{by def.}
\end{aligned}$$

The result is obtained by dividing by $\mathsf{measure}(A)$. □

The property that probabilities are positive can be checked in a similar way. The assumption of unit measure ($P_{x:A}(true) = 1$) is a simple consequence of the definition.

5.2.1 Dealing with equality

In some situations it is useful to use equality of real-valued expressions (for example "John is as tall as Mary"). Perhaps the most obvious way to encode equality between x and y is by using $\mathsf{IsTrue}(x = y)$. Assuming that x and y are both taken in a space A of strictly positive measure, we can naively write the space B of equal x and y as follows.

$$B = \Sigma(x : A)\Sigma(y : A)\mathsf{IsTrue}(x = y)$$

Unfortunately, the above definition is problematic, because $x = y$ is stochastically impossible for real-valued x and y.[6] Consequently $\mathsf{measure}(B) = 0$. Therefore, when evaluating probabilities involving B, one gets division by zero, and so the probabilities are undefined using the definitions given above.

[6]Readers who are not familiar with this stochastic property can convince themselves informally that it holds by considering that getting x and y to be equal requires an impossible alignment of infinite precision. We see this formally by carrying out the computation of integrals as defined above.

A theoretical approach We need to replace $\mathsf{IsTrue}(x = y)$ with another space $x \equiv y$, such that the density of $x \equiv y$ is zero when $x \neq y$, but whose total measure is 1 (instead of 0). This can be done conceptually by increasing the density at the points where $x = y$. To do this, we must first extend the language of spaces with the $\mathsf{Factor}(e)$ construction, which acts like $\mathsf{IsTrue}(\phi)$, where but e gives directly the factor to be used in the integration (which can thus be greater than 1). That is:

$$\sum_{x:\mathsf{Factor}(e_1)} e_2 = [\![e_1]\!] \cdot [\![e_2[\diamond/x]]\!]$$

To be sure, its typing rule is as follows:

$$\frac{\Gamma \vdash e : \mathbb{R}}{\Gamma \vdash \mathsf{Factor}(e) : \mathsf{Space}\, Unit}$$

We can now come back to the problem of filtering a space by with the equality $x = y$. We know to do this with $\mathsf{Factor}()$, which multiplies the integrand by a certain factor. We need to pick a sufficiently large factor, so that integrating it over a 0-measure area produces the result 1. But we can only achieve this with an infinitely large factor.

One may think that no such space exists, but, fortunately, a space of this kind has already been extensively studied. It is known as the *Dirac δ function.* Classically, δ has a single parameter, and its density is 0 when this parameter is nonzero. Its defining property is:

$$\int_{-\infty}^{\infty} f(x)\delta(x)\,dx = f(0)$$

In terms of spaces, the same property becomes:

$$\sum_{x:\mathsf{Distr}(\delta)} t = t[0/x]$$

Hence we can define $x \equiv y$ to be for $\mathsf{Factor}(\delta(x - y))$.

We can now compute the measure of our motivating example B:

$$
\begin{aligned}
&\mathsf{measure}(\Sigma(x:A)\Sigma(y:A)x \equiv y)\\
=&\sum_{x:A}\sum_{y:A}\sum_{p:\mathsf{Factor}(\delta(y-x))} 1\\
=&\sum_{x:A}\sum_{z:\{y-x\,|\,x:A\}}\sum_{p:\mathsf{Factor}(\delta(z))} 1 && \text{by substitution}\\
=&\sum_{x:A}\sum_{z:\{y-x\,|\,x:A\}}\sum_{z:\mathsf{Distr}(\delta)} 1\\
=&\sum_{x:A}\sum_{z:\{y-x\,|\,x:A\}} 1 && \text{by } \delta \text{ property}\\
=&\sum_{x:A}\sum_{y:A} 1\\
=&\mathsf{measure}(A)^2
\end{aligned}
$$

We see that involving $x \equiv y$ does not make the measure of spaces 0, and hence probabilites remain well-defined. Computing symbolic integration involving δ is not possible in every case, but we refer the reader to Shan and Ramsey (2017) for a generic method.

A numerical approach Perhaps more disturbing than δ not being always computable, is the fact that it is not well suited to Monte Carlo methods, which we describe in §5.2.3. We are faced with the same problem that we encountered originally. If we randomly sample any x and y, and their numerical representations have a high resolution, then it will be extremely rare that $x = y$, and the Monte-Carlo approximation will not converge.

A possible solution to this problem is to increase the density in a non-zero region around the points such that $x = y$, in a smooth fashion. One way to do this is to take the density of the space $x \equiv y$ to be a Gaussian curve of a suitably small standard deviation σ[7], and which has its maximum at $x = y$:

$$\frac{1}{\sigma\sqrt{2\pi}}e^{-\frac{1}{2}(\frac{x-y}{\sigma})^2}$$

Like all probability density functions, the Gaussian has density 1, and we thereby avoid spaces of zero measure.

[7] In fact, if f_σ is a Gaussian function with mean 0 and standard deviation σ, then $\delta(x) = \lim_{\sigma\to 0} f_\sigma(x)$

While this approach is satisfying, choosing a suitable value for σ is not always straightforward. If it is too small, then we fall into the original pitfall: most of the time the density of the space will be too small to contribute significantly to the integral. Conversely, if σ is too large, then we get an excessively imprecise result. Unless otherwise stated, we have run our models with $\sigma = 1$.

5.2.2 Record notation

When dealing with complex structures involving nested Σ spaces, the expressions for projections become quickly inscrutable. For this reason we use the record notation for such spaces and the corresponding projections.

Definition 5 (Record spaces and projections) Formally, record spaces are defined by translation to Σ spaces, as follows:

$$[x_1 : A_1; \ldots ; x_n : A_n] = \Sigma(x_1 : A_1)\Sigma(x_2 : A_2) \ldots A_n$$

Additionally if $e : [x_1 : A_1; \ldots ; x_n : A_n]$, then $e.x_i$ is a shorthand for $\pi_1(\pi_2(\pi_2(\ldots e)))$ (the number of repetitions of π_2 is the index of the field in the record).

For similar reasons, we use a shorthand notation for the expected value over several variables, defined as follows:

$$E_{x_0:A_0,\ldots,x_n:A_n}(e) = E_{x_0:A_0}(\ldots(E_{x_n:A_n}(e)))$$

5.2.3 Approximation via sampling

Unfortunately, in the majority of cases (with the notable exceptions of those discussed in §5.3.8 and §5.3.4), the mathematical expressions produced by the semantics given in §5.2 contain integrals which cannot be evaluated symbolically. Hence, we are forced to resort to a numerical approximation algorithm to evaluate them. We use a variant of Gibbs sampling, which is itself an instance of a Markov Chain Monte Carlo (MCMC) method. The algorithm that we use closely follows the one described by Goodman and Stuhlmüller (2014).

All Monte Carlo methods are based on the same principle, which can be outlined as follows. To evaluate $P_{x:A}(\phi[x])$: 1. Sample a random x in A; 2. Check if $\phi[x]$ holds for a chosen value of x; 3. Repeat this process a large number of times. The ratio of the number successes to the number of tries converges to $P_{x:A}(\phi[x])$ as the number of tries tends to infinity.

In certain cases it is very hard to find any sample $x : A$. If (say) A contains an $\mathsf{IsTrue}(\psi)$ space where ψ is satisfied one time in a million, then it will be necessary to try a million samples until one try can be counted. In our application, these kind of situations will happen whenever 1. sets with many hypotheses are considered, 2. very strong hypotheses are tested. For example, "99.9 percent of men walk" requires such a precise arrangement of parameters that most samples will end up being discarded when this condition is checked.

To mitigate this problem, MCMC methods do not sample elements independently. Rather, each new sample x is based on a previous sample. Typically, only a single parameter is changed at every step. On average, the next sample is chosen to be as probable as the previous one, or more so. This way, the system is able to find many (probable) samples. But samples can form (probably) disconnected regions in the chain space, and thus certain configurations may end up being explored more thoroughly than other, equally (or more) probable ones.

Ultimately, it is up to the designer of the underlying problem to avoid the pitfalls of the approximation methods. Because the phrasing of the hypotheses are infinitely variable for any natural language, we cannot avoid these pitfalls entirely. However, certain semantic designs will be more prone to problems than others. We discuss the issues that these design questions raise in §5.4.4.

5.3 Probabilistic Compositional Semantics

Following Montague, our semantics assumes an assignment of syntactic categories to types. These assignments are standard, except that we use real numbers for adjectival phrases, as we shall see in§5.3.2.

$$\begin{aligned}
Pred &= Ind \to Prop \\
AP &= Ind \to \mathbb{R} \\
VP &= Ind \to Prop \\
NP &= VP \to Prop \\
Quant &= CN \to NP
\end{aligned}$$

Additionally, CNs are interpreted as spaces over individuals ($CN = \mathsf{Space}\,Ind$). Adjectival phrases are treated as scalars, and so they are realised as real-valued functions.

While Montague leaves all types abstract, we instead use *spaces*. That is, we give certain types a density. This is done for all categories which can be quantified over, including individuals (Ind) and predicates ($Pred$).

5.3.1 Predicates and Individuals

It is common in current work in computational linguistics to represent words by points in a vector space. As an initial implementation of this approach we define the density of this space through a Gaussian distribution. The intuition behind this model is to take a simple prior which does not assume any bias.[8] Formally, the space of individuals is taken to be a multi-variate normal distribution of dimension k, with k sufficiently large, depending on the complexity of the problem at hand.

$$Ind = Normal(0, 1)^k$$

Applying the idea that relationships between concepts can be captured by the dot product of their representations, we also represent predicates with a vector in the same distribution. An individual is said to satisfy a given predicate if the dot product of their representations is above a given bias— a bias which also is part of the representation of the predicate. An example predicate is shown in Fig. 5. Perhaps more vividly, one can represent predicates as a hyperplane— individuals falling on one side of it are deemed to satisfy it. This idea is expressed formally as follows:

$$Pred = \{\lambda x.d \cdot x + b > 0 \mid d : Normal(0, 1)^k, b : Normal(0, 1)\}$$

We sustain the property that predicates are Boolean-valued functions ($\vdash Pred : \mathsf{Space}(\mathbb{R}^k \to Bool)$ in LMS), as demanded by Montague-style semantics.

Given these basic concepts, we can specify a compositional semantics for simple phrases. In Montague semantics, the phrase "John is tall" is represented as $tall(john)$. Both the predicate $tall$ and the individual $john$ remain unspecified in that there is no information available about them beyond their types. But in our probabilistic semantics we can quantify the uncertainty attached to $john$ and $tall$ by construing them in their respective *spaces* instead of their bare *types*.

We can evaluate the expected truth value of $tall(john)$. In this case, the set of possible situations is:

$$\begin{aligned}\Omega = [&john : Ind \\ &tall : Pred]\end{aligned}$$

[8] In what follows, we will see that each orthogonal dimension of the vector space can be used to represent an indepent property of the individual. Conversely, non-orthogonal dimensions can be used to represent correlated properties.

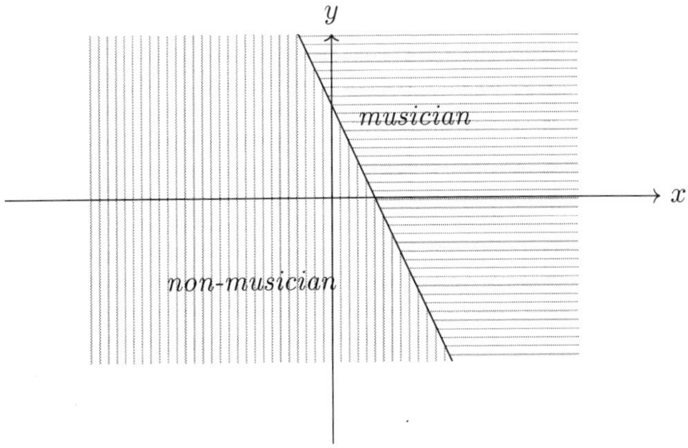

FIGURE 5: A representation of the predicate "musician" and its negation. The line patterns indicate the corresponding subspaces.

We evaluate the probability of John being tall as follows:

$$\begin{aligned} & E_{\omega:\Omega}(\omega.tall(\omega.john)) \\ = & \sum_{john:Ind} \sum_{tall:Pred} \mathbf{1}(tall(john)) \\ = & \sum_{john:Normal(0,1)^k} \sum_{b:Normal(0,1)} \sum_{d:Normal(0,1)^k} \mathbf{1}(d \cdot john + b > 0) \\ = & 0.5 \end{aligned}$$

The computation of the integrals is done by a simple symmetry argument. In the absence of further information, our semantics estimates that John has a 50% chance of being tall. This result is a direct consequence of the choice of priors that we have proposed. Other choices are possible, depending on the domain of application.

Common Nouns We express common nouns not as predicates, but as spaces. This is similar to the idea of representing nouns as types rather than predicates (Ranta, 1994, Luo, 2012, Chatzikyriakidis and Luo, 2017)). As for predicates, the space of spaces is too large to be sampled, and so we take the space of common nouns to be a restriction on the space of individuals to a random predicate:

$$CN = \{\Sigma(x : Ind)(p(x)) \mid p : Pred\}$$

5.3.2 Graded adjectives

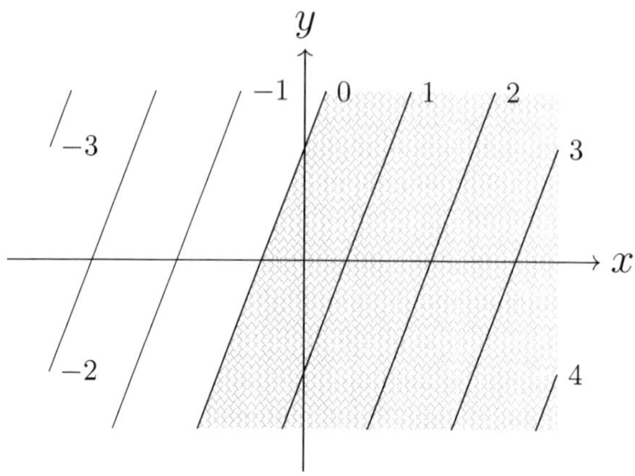

FIGURE 6: A possible representation of "tall". Because tallness is computed with a dot product, lines of equal tallness are parallel, and evenly spaced as tallness increases. Individuals are deemed "tall" if their tallness is positive, shown above as the hatched area.

Our system supports scalar predicates and comparatives. We use real-valued functions for adjectival phrases:

$$\vdash A : \mathsf{Space}\,(Ind \rightarrow \mathbb{R})$$

A graded predicate can be easily converted to a regular one with the following function, in the simply typed lambda calculus:

$$is : A \rightarrow Pred$$
$$is = \lambda g.\lambda x.g(x) > 0$$

Comparatives can be defined as the comparison of such measures:

$$more : A \rightarrow A \rightarrow Bool$$
$$more = \lambda g.\lambda x.\lambda y.g(x) > g(y)$$

So far, we have merely considered the sign of the real-valued expression $b + d \cdot x$ as the applicability of a predicate. But it can instead be interpreted as a degree to which the individual x satisfies the property characterised by (b, d). We can specify the space of adjectival phrases by

$$A = \left\{\lambda x.d \cdot x + b \,\middle|\, d : Normal(0,1)^k, b : Normal(0,1)\right\}$$

The situation is depicted graphically in Fig. 6.

With these formal instruments we can describe simple probabilistic inference problems in detail. For example, what can we infer about the tallness of John from the observation "John is taller than Mary", expressed as the following space:

$$\begin{aligned}\Omega = [&john : Ind\\ &mary : Ind\\ &tall : A\\ &p1 : \mathsf{IsTrue}(more(tall, john, mary))]\end{aligned}$$

This space is a subspace comprised of two individuals and a gradable adjective, such that one of the individual (john) is higher on the scale than the other. We can then evaluate the probability of the sentence "john is tall" if "john is taller than mary", which is, by definition:

$$E_{\omega:\Omega}(is(\omega.tall, \omega.john))$$

Using LMS semantics, it is equal to:

$$\frac{\int_{\omega:\Omega} \mathbf{1}(()is(\omega.tall, \omega.john))}{\int_{\omega:\Omega} 1}$$

Even in this relatively simple case, computing the integrals symbolically is intractable. However, with MCMC sampling, we can get the approximation 0.662.

5.3.3 Generalised quantifiers

We turn to generalised quantifiers. We need them to interpret sentences such as "most birds fly" compositionally. On a standard reading, "most" is a constraint on the ratio between the cardinality of sets:

$$most(cn, vp) = \frac{\#\{x : cn(x) \wedge vp(x)\}}{\#\{x : cn(x)\}} > \theta \tag{5.1}$$

for a suitable threshold θ. Alternatively, to avoid possible division by 0 and allow for vacuously true quantification, we have

$$most(cn, vp) = \#\{x : cn(x) \wedge vp(x)\} > \theta\ \#\{x : cn(x)\}. \tag{5.2}$$

In our framework, we replace set cardinalities with measures of spaces:

$$most(cn, vp) = \mathsf{measure}(\Sigma(x : cn)\mathsf{IsTrue}(vp(x))) > \theta\mathsf{measure}(cn) \tag{5.3}$$

The latter equality is a valid proposition in our probabilistic logic, because space measures are themselves well-formed expressions.

As a first approximation, we can let θ be a constant. For example, if “most” is meant in to designate a large portion of the population, this threshold will have a value close to one, let us say 0.9. (This is what we do when running our tests, for simplicity.) Other generalised quantifiers can be defined in the same way with a different value for θ. In our examples we define *many* with $\theta = 0.75$. However, it is possible, in fact desirable, to sample θ from a suitable distribution, so that its posterior would depend on linguistic and contextual observations.[9]

Now consider the following inference. “If many logicians are musicians, then it is likely that any given logician is a musician”. We model the relevant possible situations as follows:

$$\begin{aligned}\Omega = [&musician : Pred\\ &logician : IndSubset\\ &p1 : \mathsf{IsTrue}(many\, logician\, musician)]\end{aligned}$$

Given the premises, the estimate for the conclusion is

$$E_{\omega:\Omega,x:Ind;p2:logician(x)}(\omega.musician x) \tilde{=} 0.887$$

The model considers all possible parameter values (vectors/biases) for musicians and logicians. Then, it discards those such that

$$E_{y:Ind,p:\mathsf{IsTrue}(logician(y))}(\mathbf{1}(musician(y))) \leq \theta$$

Interestingly, because the models that we are building implement generalised quantifiers through correlation of predicates, we get ‘inverse’ correlation as well. Therefore, assuming that “many logicians are musicians", in the absence of further information, and given an individual x that is a musician, we predict a high probability for $logician(x)$.

$$E_{\omega:\Omega,x:Ind;p2:musician(x)}(\omega.logician x) \tilde{=} 0.566$$

The model’s assumptions can be augmented with the hypothesis that most individuals are not logicians. This lowers the probability of a random musician being a logician appropriately.

[9]A particularly useful prior to use for θ is the $Beta(\alpha, \beta)$ distribution, which corresponds to having made $\alpha + \beta$ observations (α negative ones and β positive ones). This way we can control the initial value of as the ratio of positive over total obervations $\beta/(\alpha + \beta)$. We can also control how much θ is sensitive to new observations: the greater the sum $\alpha + \beta$ the less the threshold will be influenced by new observations.

$$\begin{aligned}\Omega = [&musician : Pred\\ &logician : Pred\\ &p0 : most\, anything\, (not \circ logician)\\ &p1 : \mathsf{IsTrue}(many\, logician\, musician)]\end{aligned}$$

In this case

$$E_{\omega:\Omega,x:Ind;p2:musician(x)}(\omega.logician(x)) \tilde{=} 0.12$$

Now consider a more complex inference involving three predicates and four propositions. Assume that

1. Most animals do not fly.
2. Most birds fly.
3. Every bird is an animal.

Can we conclude that "most animals are not birds"? We model the possible situations as follows:

$$\begin{aligned}\Omega = [&animal : Pred\\ &bird : Pred\\ &fly : Pred\\ &p1 : (most\, animal(not \circ fly))\\ &p2 : (every\, bird\, animal)\\ &p3 : most\, bird\, fly]\end{aligned}$$

The evaluation of the conclusion that we obtain is

$$E_{\omega:\Omega}(most\, \omega.animal(not \circ \omega.bird)) \tilde{=} 0.773$$

This result holds by virtue of the fact that only models similar to the one pictured in Fig. 7 conform to the premises. One way to satisfy "Every bird is an animal" is to assume that "animal" holds for every individual, because this is compatible with all hypotheses. Then "Most animals don't fly" implies that the "fly" predicate has a large (negative) bias. Finally, "Most birds fly" can be satisfied only if "fly" is highly correlated with "bird" (the predicate vectors have similar angles), *and if the bias of "bird" is even more negative than that of "fly"*. Consequently, "bird" also has a large negative bias, and the conclusion holds.

5.3.4 Comparatives and quantifiers

Using an MCMC method to compute expected values inside the computation of an expected value (itself using MCMC) is expensive. It beneficial to consider techniques which can alleviate these costs. One such technique involves the combination of generalised quantifiers and comparatives.

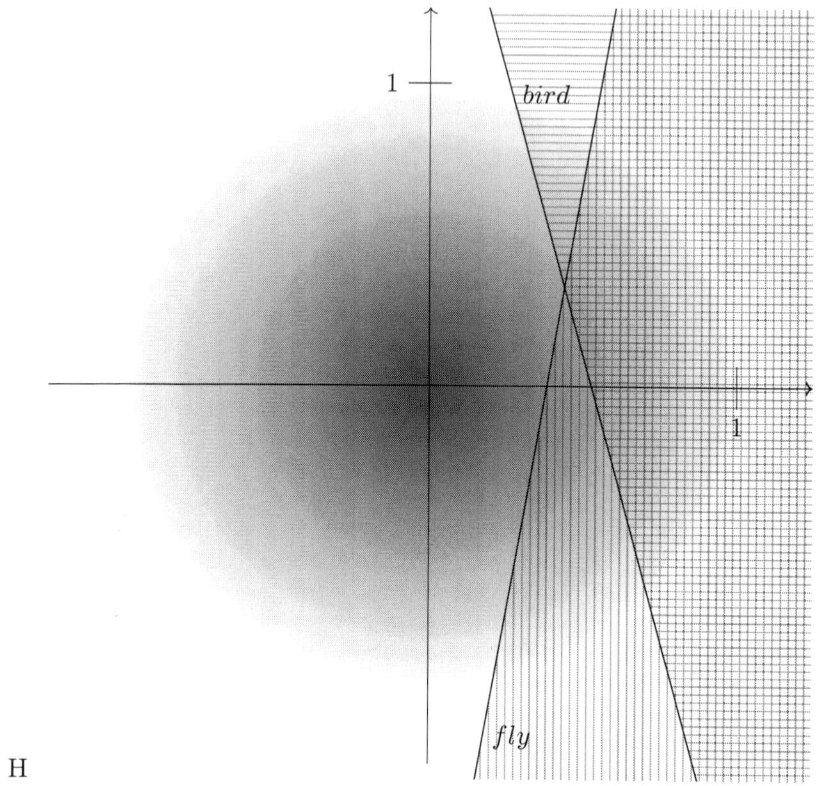

FIGURE 7: A probable configuration for the predicates in the bird example. We ignore the "animal" predicate, which can be assumed to hold for every individual. The grey area suggests the density of arbitrary individuals, a 2-dimensional Gaussian distribution in this case. Birds lie in the areas with a horizontal (and hatch) patterned areas. Flying individuals are in the vertical (and hatch) patterned areas. Note that the density of individuals in the "bird" area is small compared to that in the intersection (crosshatched area). In this model, the observations "Most individuals are not birds", "most individuals don't fly" and "Most birds fly" hold together.

Consider the phrase: "Socrates is wiser than most men". On a straightforward application of our method, as described so far, MCMC sampling proceeds to:

1. sample the predicate "man";
2. sample "wise" as a gradable predicate;
3. sample "socrates";
4. sample n men, and verify that that Socrates is wiser than θn of them, with n large

On this procedure, a step in the Markov Chain of the sampler will *always* run the expensive last step of sampling n men. Consequently, the evaluations of conclusions exemplifying this construction typically do not converge in reasonable time.

One way to speed up the computation is to use quantiles to directly evaluate comparisons with generalised quantifiers, defined as follows.

Definition 6 If $\vdash A : \mathsf{Space}\,(Ind \to \mathbb{R})$, we define

$$x = Quantile\,\theta\,A \text{ iff. } \mathsf{measure}(\Sigma(y:A)(y<x)) = \theta\,\mathsf{measure}(A)$$

Theorem 3 *If the (generalised) quantifier q is associated with a threshold θ, we can show that:*

$$q\,cn\,(\lambda y.more\,g\,x\,y) = g(y) \geq Quantile\,\theta\,\{g(x)\,|\,x:cn\}$$

This revision of the expression containing generalised quantifiers significantly improves computational cost, when running a sampler. On the left-hand-side of the equal sign in Theorem 3, one needs to do an inner evaluation of the condition every time a new y is sampled ('socrates' in our example), while, on the right-hand-side, this is not necessary. Indeed, the quantile depends only on g and cn, but not on y. With this optimisation, MCMC converges on examples such as the one above.

5.3.5 Comparatives and subsectivity

It is common to classify adjectives according to several of their inferential properties. Subsective adjectives in this classification are adjectives like *skilful*, *big*, *small* (Kamp, 2013, Partee, 2007). Subsective adjectives denote properties which are contingent on the noun class that they modify. For instance, a skilful surgeon is someone who is skilful as a surgeon, but not necessarily skilful in general. Subsectivity has interesting interactions with gradability. Gradable subsective adjectives involve a grade parameter which is class-dependent. For something to be considered a small elephant in a given context, we take a different threshold than when assessing whether an animal is small as a mouse.

The interpretations of comparative forms of these adjectives should encode these properties.

We express a gradable subsective adjectival phrase "small elephant" as "smaller than most elephants", thus reducing this phrase to the case studied in §5.3.4. We obtain

$$subsective\, g\, cn\, y = g(y) \geq Quantile\, \theta\ \{g(x) \mid x : cn\}$$

for a suitable threshold θ.

5.3.6 Semantic Learning

Bayesian models are updated to accommodate new observations. This gives rise to learning. We have seen that our framework takes account of data provided in the form of qualitative statements, including those containing generalised quantifiers. We can also accommodate information provided in sequence of observed situations. Consider the following series of statements:

- Mary is 190 centimeters tall.
- Mary is tall.
- Kate is 162 centimeters tall.
- Kate isn't tall.
- Christine is 178 centimeters tall.

The possible situations corresponding to them can be captured as follows:

$$\begin{aligned}\Omega = [\, & mary : Ind \\ & pM : tallness(mary) \equiv centimeters(190) \\ & qM : \mathsf{IsTrue}(tall(mary)) \\ & kate : Ind \\ & pK : tallness(kate) \equiv centimeters(162) \\ & qK : \mathsf{IsTrue}(not(tall(kate))) \\ & christine : Ind \\ & pC : tallness(christine) \equiv centimeters(178) \\ &]\end{aligned}$$

The definition of *centimeters* is given in §5.3.7. At this stage it is sufficient to assume that this definition correctly maps a measure in centimeters to a degree of tallness, as outlined in §5.3.2. Also, we use the equality ($\equiv$) space to deal with equality, as discussed in §5.2.1.

Given these assumptions, we can estimate the probability of Christine being tall:

$$P_{\omega:\Omega}(tall(christine))$$

Ω gives a density for the threshold of tallness which corresponds to the criterion of "tall". Hence the system learns dynamically, via a number of observations, the meaning of the adjective "tall"[10].

5.3.7 Units of measure

BIS supports reasoning with units of measure, as in "John is 6 feet tall". To interpret such sentences, we relate heights expressed as numbers to the notion of "tallness", (i.e. the grade associated with the "tall" adjective).

We treat "feet" similarly to other units of measure (as in "John is 180 cm tall"). The interpretation of measure words captures the scaling that they impose. We introduce an additional layer of meaning, which ensures that all units of measure are interpreted *a priori* in the same way. Each unit of measure u is represented by three parameters, $\alpha_u, \beta_u, \gamma_u$, each drawn from a normal distribution. The transformation from degree to numerical value is given by the expression $t_u(x) = \gamma_u x^{\alpha_u x + \beta_u}$. The numbers provided in the input ("6", "180") are then compared with the transformed measure predicates corresponding to the adjective. (In our example $t_{feet}(john \cdot v_{tall}) = 6$.) This allows BIS to simultaneously infer posterior distributions for individuals, graded predicates and units of measure.

5.3.8 Uniform boxes

As we have seen in the case of generalised quantifiers, one must often compute the measure of a subset of individuals satisfying some predicate. The form for such an expression is

$$\mathsf{measure}(\Sigma(x : Ind)(\mathsf{IsTrue}(p(x)))) = \sum_{x:Ind} \mathbf{1}(p(x))$$

Because individuals are elements in a high-dimensional space, if the density of individuals $p(x)$ is non-trivial, the above integral is often not computable symbolically. This is the case, for example, if individuals receive a Gaussian distribution. Instead the integral must be approximated numerically, typically through a Monte Carlo method.

Another option for the space of predicates is to use boxes, which are cuboids whose faces are orthogonal to the axes of the underlying Euclidean space. We take the density of individuals in this framework to be uniform.

[10]It can only learn the meaning within the bounds of this model. Here, this is not simply the threshold for tallness, as in the model of Lassiter and Goodman (2017). Rather, it find a direction in the space of individuals which corresponds to height, and a threshold along this dimension.

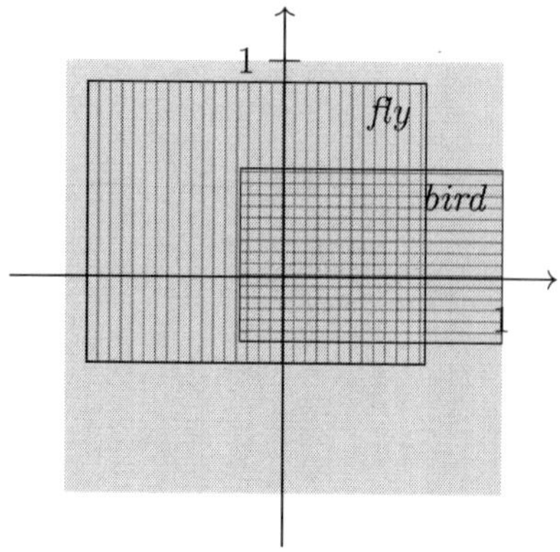

FIGURE 8: A probable configuration for the predicates in the bird example, now with box-predicates and a uniform distribution of individuals.

$$Ind = Uniform(-1,1)^k$$
$$Pred = \{\forall i.||x_i - c_i|| < d_i \mid c : Uniform(-1,1)^k, d : Beta(1,4)\}$$

Here the computation can proceed symbolically. If we assume, for simplicity, that the box fits in the (-1,1) cuboid, we can compute the volume of a common noun defined by c_i and d_i as follows:

$$\begin{aligned}
&\mathsf{measure}(\Sigma(x : Ind)(\mathsf{IsTrue}(\forall i.||x_i - c_i|| < d_i)))\\
=&\mathsf{measure}(\Sigma(x : Ind)(\bigwedge_i \mathsf{IsTrue}(||x_i - c_i|| < d_i)))\\
=&\prod_i \mathsf{measure}(\Sigma(x_i : Uniform(-1,1))(\mathsf{IsTrue}(||x_i - c_i|| < d_i)))\\
=&\prod_i d_i
\end{aligned}$$

Thanks to this symbolic estimation of predicative density the treatment of (generalised) quantifiers is computationally much cheaper with the box-based model of predicates and individuals than with the Gaussian-based technique. We show in Fig. 8 how the situation depicted in Fig. 7 is adapted to this new model.

Graded adjectives

Like the Gaussian-based model, the box-based model supports graded predicates by forming a grade g such that the corresponding non-graded predicate holds when $g(x) > 0$, *and* the area where this predicate holds

$(\Sigma(x : Ind)gx > 0)$ forms a box. We define the grade of a property defined by a center c and and width d for the individual x as $s(x, c, d)$. The space for graded adjectives A is

$$s(x, c, d) = 1 - \max\left\{ \frac{||x_i - c_i||}{d_i} \,\middle|\, i \in [1..n] \right\}$$

$$A = \left\{ \lambda x.s(x, c, d) \,\middle|\, c : Uniform(-1, 1)^k, d : Beta(1, 4) \right\}$$

This model has the additional convenient property that the space $\Sigma(x : Ind)gx > \alpha$ is a (possibly empty) box for every α. A corollary is that the predicate "more (λy. s(y,c,d)) x" is a box for every c, d and x. Consequently, generalised quantifiers over these expressions can also be computed efficiently.

We remark that the maximal degree of satisfaction with this model is 1. This property can be used in practice in models which make the absolute satisfaction grade a feature of natural language sentences.

Relative clauses

Boxes are closed under intersections. Thus if we use the expression $P \wedge Q$ to denote the intersection of the predicates P and Q, we have $(P \wedge Q)_i^l = \max(P_i^l, Q_i^l)$ and $(P \wedge Q)_i^h = \min(P_i^h, Q_i^h)$. The centre and the width of the box ($(P \wedge Q)^c$ and $(P \wedge Q)^d$ respectively) are recovered using the usual formula.

5.4 Test suite

We have constructed a test suite to illustrate BIS' coverage. We have done this, rather than adopting any of the existing test suites for inference, because none of the latter (e.g. the FraCaS test suite (Cooper et al., 1996), RTE (Dagan et al., 2006), or SNLI (Bowman et al., 2015)) are designed to assess probabilistic inference. These test suites rarely exhibit probabilistic (or quantitative) reasoning via generalised quantifiers (most, etc.), or adverbs (frequently, probably, etc.). They also do not deal with semantic learning.

Our test suite contains 84 examples, provided in §5.7. Each has one or more premises followed by a hypothesis (conclusion). Examples are annotated with respect to the semantic phenomena that occur in the inference. The phenomena were chosen because of their importance for semantic frameworks designed to handle probabilistic reasoning. While most examples in the test suite involve probabilistic reasoning, others are classically valid entailments.

Our models estimate the likelihood of an inference as the conditional probability of the conclusion, given the premises. The latter impose restrictions on the models generated to evaluate the conclusion.

The test suite is comprised of examples that are, in effect, generalised Aristotelian syllogisms. It additionally involves monotonic reasoning, probability, gradation, comparatives, and the relation of comparatives to adjectives. The latter phenomena are not taken up in traditional logical frameworks. To design examples with probabilistic inferences, we focus on semantic phenomena in natural language that introduce uncertainty into predicative judgments. For now, we limit the scope of our work to English. See §5.1 for the syntactic constructions that we associate with the examples in our test set.

Moreover, we annotate our examples with the following tags:

- FOL Validity
- Entailment
- Probable Inference
- Improbable Inference
- Contradiction
- FOL Contradiction

The first three tags fall into positive categories of entailment whereas the last three are their negative scale counterparts. Our choice of these tags is motivated by the fact that we believe that it is beneficial to test a system on classical, Aristotelian syllogisms. Since they involve quantifiers (exists and every), we want to be able to test how successful our system is in handling those, classical cases. But at the same time, we want to also consider cases of entailment where the sentences cannot adequately be accounted within FOL. For example, one may have probabilistic elements in the proposition p_1 and thus goes beyond FOL. In our test suite we want cases where we have clear entailment involving p_1, which cannot be encoded using the FOL syntax (e.g. p_1 entails p_1 cannot be encoded by FOL but it is true entailment).

Furthermore, we have Probable Inference and its negative counterpart, Improbable Inference. Many of our examples fall into these categories (due to the nature of our test suite). In particular, generalized quantifiers give rise to such inferences, which are not true entailments in logical sense, but qualify for probable inferences (or improbable ones).

There are several reasons for choosing this approach rather than labelling the examples with expected values in the range $[0, 1]$. First, the probability estimates are only numerical approximations, and so an exact value cannot be relied upon. Secondly, the output values are sensitive to the details of the chosen priors (e.g. thresholds for generalised quantifiers ("many", "most", etc.). In particular, we want to assess two different sets of priors based on different geometric configurations.

5.4.1 Principles for evaluation

There are no commonly accepted principles for evaluating the performance of a probabilistic inferencing system. For the purposes of the present chapter, we evaluate the performance of our models using the following general principles.

1. FOL validity & Entailment: An example tagged with one of these labels is counted as correctly evaluated if the model calculates the probability of the conclusion given the premises to be greater than 0.99. Symbolically, this is expressed as the condition $p(\text{conclusion}|\text{premises}) > 0.99$. Hence, the difference between FOL validity and entailment is treated as qualitative rather than quantitative.
2. Probable inference: Such an example is counted as correctly evaluated if the model calculates the probability of the conclusion given the premises to be consistently greater than the probability of the conclusion as calculated without any premises. In other words, if the premises consistently raise the probability of the conclusion. If $p(\text{conclusion}) < 1$, this can be symbolically expressed as the condition
$$p(\text{conclusion}|\text{premises}) > p(\text{conclusion}).$$
3. Improbable inference: Such an example is correctly evaluated if the premises lower the probability of the conclusion, as compared to the probability of the conclusion without any premises. If $p(\text{conclusion}) > 0$ this can be expressed by
$$p(\text{conclusion}|\text{premises}) < p(\text{conclusion}).$$
4. FOL contradiction & Contradiction: $p(\text{conclusion}|\text{premises}) < 0.01$

5.4.2 Unclear examples

Some examples in the testsuite are tagged by the special label "Unclear". These are examples where the priors are inadvertently not sufficiently specified in the premises, and the evaluation therefore only depends on the priors of the model. These priors may well differ from the real-world priors, as well as between the two models. The examples of this kind, even if they may be probable inferences in the real world, are not instances of generally acceptable argument forms since substituting one predicate for another across the premises and conclusion may yield an inference with a radically different probability. To illustrate this effect, we compare two of the unclear examples.

(T83) P1. many logicians are musicians.
P2. john is a musician.
H. john is a logician.
Label: UNCLEAR, QUANTIFIER

According to Bayes' theorem, the posterior probability $p(\text{logician}|\text{musician})$ of the conclusion can be calculated by

$$p(\text{logician}|\text{musician}) = \frac{p(\text{musician}|\text{logician})}{p(\text{logician})} p(\text{musician}).$$

The prior $p(\text{musician}|\text{logician})$ is specified by P1, but the remaining factors are entirely dependent on the model's priors. That is, the relative frequency of logicians and musicians across the domain impact the posterior probability, and also whether the posterior probability is higher or lower than the prior probability $p(\text{logician})$. To judge whether this inference should be counted as a probable inference, or as something else, we need access to the priors of the model, or to real-world knowledge about the proportion of logicians and musicians over the population.

Now consider the related example T84:

(T84) P1. many logicians are musicians.
P2. most people aren't logicians.
P3. john is a musician.
H. john is a logician.
Label: UNCLEAR, QUANTIFIERS

Here, we add an extra premise: the real-world knowledge that logicians are few. This fixes the prior $p(\text{logician})$, but $p(\text{musician})$ is still dependent on the model's priors. Indeed, we can now see the effect of the different priors of our two models. In the Gaussian model, $p(\text{musician}) \cong 0.5$, and the example evaluates to $\cong 0.1$, which is much lower than chance. By contrast, in the box model $p(\text{musician}) \cong 0.15$, and the example evaluates to $\cong 0.18$, a value somewhat greater than chance.

Since these examples depend on the priors of different predicates, it is not generally possible to assign them a tag assessing the strength of the inference. Since there then is nothing to compare the models' outputs to, the 13 unclear examples of the testsuite are excluded from the evaluation, leaving 71 examples where we have assessed the strength of the inference. The full list of unclear examples is: T4, T5, T14, T39, T40, T49–T52, T71, T79, T83, T84.

5.4.3 Evaluation of the system using the test suite

To assess the coverage and efficiency of both our Gaussian and our box models, we performed a sample run of each model across the whole test suite. The examples are run sequentially, with a 30 second timeout (triggered if no sample could be found in the space of situations described by the premises). The timeout was chosen so as to make most of the examples converge within the allotted time.[11] In overall performance the box model is superior to the Gaussian model in speed. This is illustrated by the fact that the box model yields an accurate output for example T11 (p. 211) about four times faster than the Gaussian.

Among the 71 tagged examples in the test suite, there are nine examples that current system does not cover. These are examples T7, T12, T17, T43–T46, T56, and T60. The phenomena that these examples exhibit include inherently binary predicates, and expressions like "kind of". Example T62 is also not handled, because it is designed to test three-valued probabilistic logic, which is out of scope here.

According to the principles presented above, the Gaussian model gives correct estimates for 50 of the 71 tagged examples, corresponding to an accuracy of about 70%. The box model fares somewhat better, correctly estimating 54 (76%) of the examples. We stress that, because the number of examples is small, these accuracy rates give only a rough indication of the system's performance across a wide range of phenomena. We offer error analyses in the next section.[12]

For an illustration of how our models represent vagueness, and how to evaluate examples containing vague predicates, consider example T61.

(T61) P1. Mary is 190 centimeters tall.
P2. Mary is tall.
P3. Kate is 162 centimeters tall.
P4. Kate isn't tall.
P5. Christine is 185 centimeters tall.
H. Christine is tall.

[11]Four examples (T4, T41, T48, T51) require substantially more time to converge in the box model. A factor 10 increase is rarely sufficient. Example T52 fails to converge within any reasonable timespan in the box model. The same holds for example T18 in the Gaussian model.

[12]Our code and a working version of BIS is available publicly at this URL:https://github.com/GU-CLASP/Bayesian-Inference-Semantics-for-Natural-Language . It can be run with either of the two models that we have described here. We invite interested reader to experiment with the system to get a sense of its capacity and its limitations.

Label:PROBABLE INFERENCE, POSITIVE ADJECTIVES, VAGUENESS

In the sample run, the Gaussian model returns 1. This is unexpected, because 'tall' is a vague predicate, and there is no a priori reason to regard someone with a height of 185cm as tall. In fact this result is an artefact of the sampling method. In any given run, a threshold for tallness is sampled, and in this run, that threshold is below 185cm.

In a probabilistic setting it is important to consider the average over a larger number of runs. With 100 runs (where the average starts to converge) we get results in the range 0.80–0.90. It is illuminating to compare this with a run for T70 (p. 222), where premise P5 above is replaced with "Christine is 179 centimeters tall". Averaged over 100 runs, the results are in the range 0.70–0.80. This suggests an incremental effect on the likelihood of a predication. The closer Christine's height is to that of a person who is clearly tall, the more likely is it that she is tall. A similar effect is observed with the box model, but not as sharply.

BIS generally works well on propositionally valid inferences. It also performs well with examples containing generalised quantifiers, modal adverbs, percentage determiners, and comparatives, when the number of predicates in the premises and conclusion is relatively small. The problematic examples are those with a combination of generalised quantifiers and 3 or more predicates. Also examples where the system has to relate the applicability of a gradable predicate to a particular unit of measurement can raise difficulties.

5.4.4 Error analysis

Example T57 (p. 220) shows how transitivity might fail in the Gaussian model. For that example, the Gaussian model returns a very low score, 0.11, while the box model succeeds with 0.85. The reason for this is that the generic plural in expressions like "if you ..., then you ..." is interpreted as involving a certain degree of inclusion of the predicates in question. But A and B overlapping to a certain degree, and B and C overlapping to the same degree implies little concerning the degree of overlap between A and C. A similar effect is observed in example T79 (p. 224), and this effect is also likely to cause the failure of T63 (p. 221) and T68 (p. 222). By contrast, the box model interprets inclusion of A in B by placing the box for A strictly inside the boundaries of B. This is easier to obtain, by sampling the dimensions for the box A within the box B.

Example T18 (p. 212) illustrates another kind of error. Here, the Gaussian model fails to produce an output, while the box model gives an expected high value. Indeed, the Gaussian model fails to evaluate even the second premise "Most linguists that know formal language theory dislike experimental work" on its own. This suggests that this premise is stochastically hard to satisfy in the geometry of the Gaussian model, and that sampling fails.

A third kind of error involves relating units of measurement to predicates and to other units of measurement. Both models struggle with some cases of this kind, such as T37–38, T41, and T72–T74.

(T74) P1. kate is 190 centimeters tall.
P2. kate is tall.
P3. helen is 180 centimeters tall.
P4. helen isn't tall.
P5. christine is 190 centimeters tall.
H. christine is tall.
Label: ENTAILMENT, VAGUENESS

For this example, both the Gaussian and the Box model return scores around 0.90 (averaged over 100 runs). While these are high scores, the example is tagged as an entailment, and for the evaluation to count as a success we would want a score even closer to 1. Note that the incremental effect pointed out in connection to example T61 (p. 221) remains: if we change Christine's height to 191 cm, the score increases to 0.95, and at 195 cm the score is consistently 0.99 in both models. This suggests that our model fail to correctly correlate the units of measurement to the vague predicate associated with them.

Finally, T20 (p. 213) is an outlier, exhibiting odd behaviour in both models. In the Gaussian model we consistently get a value of around 0.95. The box model, gives probability of around 0.40. Both are consistently lower than the unconditioned probability of the conclusion, but the example is tagged as a probable inference. One probable cause for this failure is that an easy way of satifying the premises is to make the first predicate (guitarist) very small and the third predicate (prefer The Doors to the Beatles) very large. Then it becomes hard to find a guitarist, and even harder to find one that doesn't prefer The Doors to the Beatles. Another reason could be that the box model is bounded by the unit box, while the Gaussian one is unbounded. This is likely to have an impact on the properties of the space covered by the different predicates.

As a conclusion, a system like BIS has many components, and it is essential to exercise it on many examples to convince oneself of its correctness. Yet, due to the sensitivity to the priors, and the imprecision of Gibbs sampling for certain models, constructing and running tests is more an art than a science. Despite these difficulties, we feel that our test suite is a success: precisely, it highlights the strengths of the system (robustness to generalised quantifiers, relation between gradable adjectives) and its weaknesses, which we have listed above.

5.5 Related work

5.5.1 Distributing Probability Over Possible Worlds

Van Eijck and Lappin (2012) propose a theory in which probability is distributed over the set of possible worlds. The probability of a sentence is the sum of the probability values of the worlds in which it is true. Our work seeks to work out some of the the ideas presented by van Eijck and Lappin (2012). Specifically, we restrict possible worlds to concrete spaces, in the form of priors. This makes it possible to model them as possible situations in the sense of the bounded sets of outcomes corresponding to the distributions of random variables. In contrast van Eijck and Lappin (2012) do not take account of priors. They assign probability to maximal worlds, leaving it unclear how these distributions are computed.

Van Eijck and Lappin also suggest an account of semantic learning which seems to require the wholistic acquisition of all the classifier predicates in a language in a correlated way.

Our system avoids these problems. Our models sample only the individuals and properties (vector dimensions) required to estimate the probability of a given set of statements. Learning is achieved by representing external inputs (Bayesian evidence) as a filter over spaces.

5.5.2 Probabilistic Type Theory

Cooper et al. (2014, 2015) propose a compositional semantics within a probabilistic type theory (ProbTTR). On their approach, the probability of a sentence is a judgment on the likelihood that a given situation is of a particular type, specified in terms of ProbTTR. They also sketch a Bayesian treatment of semantic learning.

Cooper et al.'s semantics is not implemented, and so it is not entirely clear how probabilities for sentences are computed in their system. They do not offer an explicit treatment of vagueness or probabilistic inference.

In this work, we also extend types to support a probabilistic semantics, but we do not consider the probability that a *given* object inhabits a type. In fact, because we often use continuous spaces, this value will typically be 0. Instead we assign a density to the types, which allows us to estimate the expected values of a proposition over such spaces.

5.5.3 A Philosophical Account

Sutton (2017) uses a Bayesian view of probability to support a resolution of classical philosophical problems of vagueness in degree predication. His treatment of these problems is insightful, and it seems to be generally compatible with our implemented semantics. However, it operates at a philosophical level of abstraction, and so a clear comparison is not possible.

5.5.4 Rational Speech Act Theory

Goodman and Lassiter (2015), Lassiter and Goodman (2017) implement a probabilistic semantics and pragmatics, using the WebPPL probabilistic programming language. They regard the probability of a declarative sentence as the most highly valued interpretation that a hearer assigns to the utterance of a speaker in a specified context.

On this approach, speakers express unambiguous meanings in specified contexts through their utterances, and hearers estimate the likelihood of distinct interpretations as corresponding to those that the speaker intends to convey. Their account requires the existence of a univocal, non-vague speaker meaning that hearers seek to identify by distributing probability among alternative readings.

The Goodman–Lassiter account requires the specification of considerable amounts of real-world knowledge and lexical information in order to support pragmatic inference. It appears to require the existence of a univocal, non-vague speaker's meaning that hearers estimate as the most likely one among competing readings.

On the other hand, and building on work by Sutton (2017), Cooper et al. (2015), we propose that the conditional probability of a predication expresses the likelihood that an idealised competent speaker of the language would apply the predicate to the argument, given the identified features of the object. By doing so, there is no need to assume the existence of a sharply delimited non-probabilistic reading for a predication that hearers attempt to converge on by assessing the probability of alternative readings. All predication consists in applying a classifier to new instances on the basis of supervised learning. We do not posit a contextually dependent cut-off boundary for graded predicates, but we suggest an integrated approach to graded and non-graded predication on which both types of property terms allow for vague borders.

Further advantages of our account include a probabilistic treatment of generalised quantifiers, which includes higher-order quantifiers like *most*, and a basic theory of semantic learning that is a straightforward extension of our sampling procedures for computing the marginal probability of a sentence in a model.

Goodman and Lassiter adopt a classical Montagovian treatment of generalised quantifiers, and their framework has limited coverage of syntactic and semantic structures. They also do not offer a theory of semantic learning.

Regardless, it is possible to integrate pragmatic elements in the semantics by building a rational speech act model *on top of* the models that we present here, following the method of Grove and Bernardy (2021), Grove et al. (2021).

5.5.5 Compositional Bayesian Semantics

The design of BIS is inspired by the Bayesian compositional semantic framework proposed by Bernardy et al. (2018). But BIS differs from this framework in a number of important respects. First, it has a comprehensive syntax–semantics interface through GF parsing. Secondly, it is intended to cover inference in a systematic way, including logically valid, as well as probabilistic arguments. Third, BIS has considerably wider coverage than the framework of Bernardy et al. (2018). It is constructed in such a way as to permit straightforward extension to new types of sentence structure and inference patterns.

5.5.6 Variational Inference

Emerson and Copestake (2017a,b) provide a probabilistic model in order to identify 'features' of objects in terms of the properties that apply to those objects. They develop their account as a graphical probabilistic model. They also interpret universal and existential quantifiers from a probabilistic perspective. "As are Bs" is represented as the conditional probability of B, given A, for all elements of the space, which is equal to the sum (or integral) over all elements. To compute this probability, they make use of variational inference for graphical probabilistic models.

5.5.7 Probabilistic Syllogisms

Pfeifer and colleagues (Pfeifer and Sanfilippo, 2018, Pfeifer, 2013, Gilio et al., 2015) study inference in a probabilistic setting by estimating the probability of the conclusion, given the probabilities of the premises.

They employ the notion of p-validity defined by Adams (1998). To be p-valid the uncertainty of a conclusion in an inference should not increase the cumulative uncertainties of its premises.

Their approach differs from ours in several ways. The main one is that we build a model (using Bayesian updating of priors) where the premises hold, and then we estimate the probability of the hypothesis in this model. By contrast, they provide an analytic estimation of the conclusion, given its premises. They require that certain constraints on conditional probabilities hold. Conditional probabilities are primitives for modelling an implication ("if A then B"). This allows them to avoid problems in estimating $A \rightarrow B$ when A is false. On our account we take "if...then..." statements to be cases of material implication ($A \rightarrow B = \neg A \vee B$), instead of conditional probabilities.

Pfeifer and colleagues use conditional probability as a pivot. They apply a 3-valued logical system. For two events A and B, the conditional event $A|B$ is true if $A \wedge B$ is true, false if $A \wedge \neg B$ is true, and unspecified if B is false. In future work we will explore the interpretation of the "if...then..." construction as a conditional probability, and we may incorporate Pfeifer and colleagues' insights into our semantics.

As Suppes (1966) remarks, statistical syllogisms require a specific formulation in order to be well defined as probabilistic problems. Pfeifer and colleagues (Pfeifer and Sanfilippo, 2018, Pfeifer, 2013, Gilio et al., 2015) propose to add, for certain cases, several restrictions on classical, Aristotelian syllogisms, so that they become more informative from a probabilistic perspective. We handle these cases through priors, which Pfeifer and Sanfilippo (2018), Pfeifer (2013), Gilio et al. (2015) do not make use of. The fact that we do not require additional restrictions for these examples motivates our prior driven approach. Note that in our account, this result also extends to non-classical syllogisms.

5.5.8 Probabilistic Programming Languages

Through LMS we describe types and an associated density of predicate spaces. This provides an alternative to probabilistic programming languages (Goodman et al., 2008, Borgström et al., 2013, Goodman and Stuhlmüller, 2014). These languages do not describe spaces as such. They specify functions that generate element of a certain type.

LMS offers several advantages. First, probabilistic programming languages generally do not (natively) allow the option of running an inference *within* another inference. LMS does this straightforwardly with the $\mathsf{measure}(e)$ expression. Secondly, the semantics of LMS is more straightforward than that of a probabilistic programming language. LMS does not allow sampling within expressions. Only spaces can refer to other spaces. Borgström et al. (2013) provides an instance of a probabilistic programming language equipped with a formal semantics. Third, constructing spaces is very similar to constructing types and logical formulas. We hope that LMS can be a useful tool for linguists who are familiar with the interpretation of natural language expressions through mapping of type theories (or similar logical systems).

In practice, LMS is implemented in a similar way to some probabilistic programming languages, by MCMC methods such as Gibbs sampling.

5.5.9 Modelling Predicates as Boxes

Boxes in Euclidean spaces are simple objects, and they have already been used for the geometric representation of predicates. Vilnis et al. (2018) apply boxes to encode WordNet lexical entries (unary predicates) in order to predict hypernyms. Like us, they take the distribution in the vector space to be uniform. The probability of a predicate is defined as the volume of the corresponding box. In our work, we use a Bayesian model. It is best suited to represent a small number of predicates, and to fully capture the uncertainty of the boundary for each box. Vilnis et al. (2018) opt for a neural network to learn a large number of box positions. This is appropriate, given that their data set is the complete WordNet hypernym hierarchy. Their model converges on a single mapping of predicates to precise box boundaries, rather than to a distribution over such mappings.

We have not yet tested the box representation of words proposed by Vilnis et al. (2018) for our task, but we plan to do so in future work. As our approach applies Bayesian sampling, we need to modify the sizes of certain boxes to deal with a data set of this kind. Because their representations are learned for the purpose of detecting WordNet hypernymy, they do not need to contain additional lexical information not relevant to this task.

5.6 Discussion and Conclusion

5.6.1 Test suite improvements

There are several directions in which the current test suite can be developed. First, we can extend its breadth, with a larger data set of examples. This may allow the system to learn representations for lexical items (assuming that the representation of lexical items persist throughout the test suite.) Additionally, such an expanded test suite will provide the basis for deep-learning models. We intend to use crowd-source annotation for data collection.

We will also improve the test set qualitatively. We will identify new factors driving probabilistic inference, and we will extend the test suite with examples of these factors.

We have currently tagged each example with the main factors that they exhibit. We will revise these labels to produce a more rigorous and complete system for classifying inference types. This will facilitate crowd-sourced annotation.

It will also be useful to develop a partial order over examples according to the complexity of the phenomena that they exhibit. If we have a typology and a complexity hierarchy over examples, we will be in a better position to identify the sources of peculiar behaviour in our inference system.

5.6.2 Vagueness and the sorites paradox

Our system gracefully handles vague predicates. Vagueness is introduced through random variables which can occur within such propositions. When evaluating any proposition in a random context, we integrate over this random space, and can obtain any number within the interval [0,1] for an expected truth value. This is the core of probabilistic inference.

This approach formalises the widespread intuition that sentences are, in the general case, more or less true (or false). This indeterminacy arises whenever a distribution is sampled. Clear-cut paradigm cases of predicate (non-)satisfaction are, of course, still available. The proposition $tallness_j + k > tallness_j$, will be true even though $tallness_j$ is not fixed.

Our system is robust for the sorites paradox. In our system, a set of grains becomes a heap when their number is greater than some given large (real) number. This number is given some indeterminacy by sampling it in a suitable distribution. Hence there is a "soft" transition between a small set of grains and a heap as this number increases.

5.6.3 Treatment of conditionals

Classically, conditional statements of the form "if A, then B" are interpreted as logical implication ($A \to B$) (also called material implication). Probability theory affords another possible interpretation: the probability of the event expressed by B depending on that expressed by A. If $A \to B$ is taken as an inference problem, then we adopt the natural probabilistic interpretation. In contrast, we choose the material conditional treatment of conditionals, when the conditional is embedded in one of the premises.

This choice is perhaps counterintuitive. To motivate it, consider the sentence: "if John is ill, he will not attend the meeting.".

Taking the sentence as a probabilistic inference, we compute the probability

$$P(\text{john attend the meeting}|\text{john ill})$$

The probability will depend on our prior knowledge about john and illness, specifically, the dependence between them. However, if the same sentence is found in a premise, it is understood by discarding all the situations in which *john* is simultaneously ill and attending the meeting. This is done by adding the expression john ill $\rightarrow$ john attend the meeting to the record of possible situations, effectively performing a Bayesian update on the distributional meaning of the lexical items.

We can contrast with categorical systems. There, instead of a Bayesian update, one records facts about the free variables mentioned in the conditional. When there are no such free variables, we find ourselves in a linguistic difficulty. One possibility is that the antecedent ('John is ill') is true, and it plays no role. The statement as a whole is thus wasteful, violating the Gricean maxims of quantity. The other possibility is that the antecedent is false, and then we have a counterfactual statement, which poses significant problems of its own.

In a probabilistic system the situation is more straightforward. As long as there are prior possible situations which are either compatible or incompatible with the hypothesis, the statement is informative, rather than a genuine counterfactual. In classical systems variables are either completely free or fixed, whereas probabilistic systems allow for intermediate situations.

Counterfactuals We can understand counterfactuals as locally-fictional stories. We suspend disbelief for the scope of the conditional. Classically, for example in a Montagovian system (Montague, 1970, 1974), we remove some hypothesis from the context. In probabilistic systems we are allowed the possibility of adding uncertainty to the variables mentioned in the conditional. If they were completely fixed, they could become random again. One can quantify the suspension of disbelief, rather than enforcing it categorically.

5.6.4 Mixed methods

There is a long tradition of using logic to interpret natural language. One way to see the present chapter is as departure from this tradition through the use of Bayesian models, which Goodman and Lassiter (2015) pioneered.

In contrast, we do not advocate a purely Bayesian semantics. Thanks to the symbolic evaluation of probabilities, it is possible to mix quantification over spaces, if prior/evidence is best modelled using distributions, with quantification over (non-probabilistic) types, when evidence is best modelled using traditional logical formulas (like in the case where no information about distributions is available, and we must assume that all possible cases are equally likely).

To implement these methods we need to reason about the relative measures of spaces symbolically, and this typically requires creative thought. We do not have access to a symbolic calculator that can automatically decide propositions involving non-trivial symbolic integrals.

5.6.5 Summary

In this chapter we have presented a Bayesian Inference Semantics system which captures probabilistic inferences through uniform priors for lexical items. It uses Bayesian modelling to capture informational updates. BIS is fully compositional, in the sense that the probability conditions of a sentence are calculated through functions corresponding to their syntactic constituents. We achieve probabilistic interpretations by assigning measurable spaces to both objects and properties. Estimating the probability of a predication reduces to measuring the density of the relevant objects in the space of the predicate's property. We have further experimented with two models of priors: semi-spaces of Gausian distributions, and boxes of uniform density in which density is made easier to compute by symbolic simplifications. The system supports a wide range of phenomena, which includes generalised quantifiers, modal adverbs, scalar modifiers, and vagueness. BIS captures intermediate or vague cases of predication, corresponding to the uncertain intuitions speakers have in those cases. Our account also handles the sorites paradox. BIS is evaluated on a test suite constructed for probabilistic inference. We hope that the work that we present here will stimulate discussion and further work on the role of probability in the semantics of natural language.

Acknowledgements

The research reported in this paper was supported by grant 2014-39 from the Swedish Research Council, which funds the Centre for Linguistic Theory and Studies in Probability (CLASP) in the Department of Philosophy, Linguistics, and Theory of Science at the University of Gothenburg. We are grateful to our colleagues in CLASP for helpful discussion of some of the ideas presented here.

5.7 Appendix: Test Suite

(T1) P1. every violinist is a musician.
P2. musicians generally read music.
H. if john is a violinist, then john reads music.
Label: PROBABLE INFERENCE, QUANTIFIER, MODAL ADVERB

(T2) P1. prolog programmers are always intermediate logic students.
P2. intermediate logic students rarely read music.
H. prolog programmers don't read music.
Label: PROBABLE INFERENCE, QUANTIFIER, MODAL ADVERB

(T3) P1. many bald men are toupee wearers.
P2. toupee wearers always try hair transplant treatment.
P3. john is a bald man.
H. john tries hair transplant treatment.
Label: PROBABLE INFERENCE, QUANTIFIER, MODAL ADVERB

(T4) P1. john is a basketball player.
P2. basketball players are usually taller than non basketball players.
H. john is taller than most people.
Label: UNCLEAR (WORLD KNOWLEDGE), COMPARATIVE ADJECTIVE, MODAL ADVERB

(T5) P1. john is a short basketball player.
P2. basketball players are usually less short than non basketball players.
H. john is short.
Label: UNCLEAR (WORLD KNOWLEDGE), COMPARATIVE ADJECTIVE, MODAL ADVERB, SUBSECTIVITY

(T6) P1. all basketball players are probably tall.
H. most basketball players are tall.
Label: PROBABLE INFERENCE, QUANTIFIER, MODAL ADVERB

(T7) P1. 40 percent of prolog programmers read music.
P2. violinists don't like prolog programmers that read music.
H. violinists don't like most prolog programmers.
Label: IMPROBABLE INFERENCE, PERCENTAGE DETERMINER, MODAL ADVERB, NEGATION, BINARY PREDICATE

(T8) P1. prolog programmers definitely use tail recursion.
P2. many logicians are prolog programmers.
H. logicians use tail recursion.
Label: PROBABLE INFERENCE, QUANTIFIER, MODAL ADVERB

(T9) P1. stones fans often prefer the doors to the beatles.
P2. john is a stones fan.
H. john prefers the doors to the beatles.
Label: PROBABLE INFERENCE, QUANTIFIER, TEMPORAL ADVERB

(T10) P1. if you play for the leafs, then you are probably traded from the canadiens.
P2. if you are traded from the canadiens, then you often play in the montreal forum.
P3. john plays for the leafs.
H. john plays in the montreal forum.
Label: PROBABLE INFERENCE, QUANTIFIER, MODAL ADVERB, TEMPORAL ADVERB

(T11) P1. turkish coffee drinkers frequently enjoy a shot of arak.
P2. most people that enjoy a shot of arak also listen to classical oud music.
H. turkish coffee drinkers listen to classical oud music.
Label: PROBABLE INFERENCE, QUANTIFIER, TEMPORAL ADVERB

(T12) P1. if you regularly eat humus, then you also enjoy tabouli.
P2. most people that enjoy tabouli insist on having mint tea with food.
H. if you eat humus, then you insist on having mint tea with food.
Label: PROBABLE INFERENCE, QUANTIFIER, TEMPORAL ADVERB

(T13) P1. cricket players rarely hit a home run.
P2. mary hits a home run.
H. mary isn't a cricket player.
Label: PROBABLE INFERENCE, QUANTIFIER, TEMPORAL ADVERB, NEGATION

(T14) P1. many jazz guitarists can play more than 100 chords.
P2. few violinists can play more than 10 chords.
P3. john can play more than 80 chords.
H. john is a jazz guitarist.
Label: UNCLEAR, QUANTIFIERS

(T15) P1. mary is tall.
P2. john is taller than mary.
H. john is tall.
Label: ENTAILMENT, COMPARATIVE ADJECTIVE, TRANSITIVITY

(T16) P1. mary isn't tall.
P2. mary is taller than john.
H. john isn't tall.
Label: ENTAILMENT, COMPARATIVE ADJECTIVE, TRANSITIVITY

(T17) P1. john is always as punctual as mary.
P2. sam is usually more punctual than john.
H. sam is more punctual than mary.
Label: PROBABLE INFERENCE, QUANTIFIER, MODAL/TEMPORAL ADVERB

(T18) P1. many linguists know formal language theory.
P2. most linguists that know formal language theory dislike experimental work.
H. many linguists dislike experimental work.
Label: PROBABLE INFERENCE, QUANTIFIER

(T19) P1. most conservatives don't usually support free university education.
P2. john supports free university education.
H. john isn't a conservative.
Label: PROBABLE INFERENCE, QUANTIFIER, MODAL/TEMPORAL ADVERB, NEGATION

(T20) P1. if you are a guitarist, then you are probably a stones fan.
P2. if you are a stones fan, then you generally prefer the doors to the beatles.
H. it is not the case that every person that doesn't prefer the doors to the beatles is a person that isn't a guitarist.
Label: PROBABLE INFERENCE, MODAL ADVERBS, QUANTIFIES, RELATIVE CLAUSE, NEGATION, CONDITIONAL, COMMENT: BECAUSE THE NEGATION IS IN THE RELATIVE CLAUSE, IT ACTS WITH A NARROW SCOPE, SEE ALSO 21 FOR WIDE SCOPE

(T21) P1. if you are a guitarist, then you are probably a stones fan.
P2. if you are a stones fan, then you generally prefer the doors to the beatles.
H. every person that doesn't prefer the doors to the beatles isn't a guitarist.
Label: PROBABLE INFERENCE, MODAL ADVERBS, QUANTIFIES, RELATIVE CLAUSE, NEGATION, CONDITIONAL

(T22) P1. 80 percent of basketball players are tall.
H. basketball players are probably tall.
Label: PROBABLE INFERENCE, PERCENTAGE DETERMINER, MODAL ADVERB

(T23) P1. 80 percent of basketball players are tall.
H. few basketball players aren't tall.
Label: PROBABLE INFERENCE, PERCENTAGE DETERMINER, NEGATION

(T24) P1. prolog programmers definitely use tail recursion.
P2. logicians are frequently prolog programmers.
H. logicians probably use tail recursion.
Label: PROBABLE INFERENCE, QUANTIFIER, MODAL ADVERB

(T25) P1. john is tall.
P2. all guitarists are logicians.
H. john is tall and all guitarists are logicians.
Label: FOL VALIDITY, CONJUNCTION

(T26) P1. john is tall.
P2. all guitarists are logicians.
H. john is tall.
Label: FOL VALIDITY, WEAKENING

(T27) P1. john is taller than mary.
H. john is tall.
Label: PROBABLE INFERENCE, COMPARATIVE ADJECTIVE

(T28) P1. john is taller than mary.
P2. mary is taller than sam.
H. john is taller than molly.
Label: PROBABLE INFERENCE, COMPARATIVE ADJECTIVE, TRANSITIVITY

(T29) P1. john is taller than mary.
P2. sam is taller than mary.
P3. kate is taller than christine.
H. kate is taller than john.
Label: PROBABLE INFERENCE, COMPARATIVE ADJECTIVE

(T30) P1. all intermediate logic students are stones fans.
P2. john is an intermediate logic student.
H. john is a stones fan.
Label: FOL VALIDITY, QUANTIFIER

(T31) P1. john is a guitarist.
P2. most guitarists aren't logicians.
H. john isn't a logician.
Label: PROBABLE INFERENCE, NEGATION, MODUS PONENS

(T32) P1. john is a logician.
P2. most guitarists aren't logicians.
H. john isn't a guitarist.
Label: PROBABLE INFERENCE, NEGATION, MODUS TOLLENS

(T33) H. it is not the case that john is taller than most people.
Label: PROBABLE INFERENCE, LAW OF GREAT NUMBERS (OBJECT), NEGATION

(T34) H. a few people are shorter than john.
Label: PROBABLE INFERENCE, LAW OF GREAT NUMBERS (SUBJECT)

(T35) H. it is not the case that few people are shorter than john.
Label: PROBABLE INFERENCE, LAW OF GREAT NUMBERS (SUBJECT), NEGATION

(T36) P1. john isn't a guitarist.
H. it is not the case that john is a guitarist.
Label: FOL VALIDITY, WIDE-SCOPE NEGATION

(T37) P1. mary is 190 centimeters tall.
P2. mary is tall.
P3. molly is 184 centimeters tall.
P4. molly is tall.
P5. ruth is 180 centimeters tall.
P6. ruth is tall.
P7. helen is 178 centimeters tall.
P8. helen is tall.
P9. athena is 166 centimeters tall.
P10. athena isn't tall.
P11. artemis is 157 centimeters tall.

P12. artemis isn't tall.
P13. joanna is 160 centimeters tall.
P14. joanna isn't tall.
P15. kate is 162 centimeters tall.
P16. kate isn't tall.
P17. christine is 178 centimeters tall.
H. christine is tall.
Label: ENTAILMENT, POSITIVE ADJECTIVES, VAGUENESS

(T38) P1. mary is 189 centimeters tall.
P2. mary is tall.
P3. molly is 184 centimeters tall.
P4. molly is tall.
P5. ruth is 180 centimeters tall.
P6. ruth is tall.
P7. helen is 178 centimeters tall.
P8. helen is tall.
P9. athena is 166 centimeters tall.
P10. athena isn't tall.
P11. artemis is 157 centimeters tall.
P12. artemis isn't tall.
P13. joanna is 160 centimeters tall.
P14. joanna isn't tall.
P15. kate is 162 centimeters tall.
P16. kate isn't tall.
P17. christine is 163 centimeters tall.
H. christine isn't tall.
Label: ENTAILMENT, POSITIVE ADJECTIVES, VAGUENESS

(T39) P1. many jazz guitarists can play more than 2 chords.
P2. few violinists can play more than 1 chord.
P3. john can play more than 2 chords.
H. john is a jazz guitarist.
Label: UNCLEAR, QUANTIFIERS

(T40) P1. many jazz guitarists can play more than 5 chords.
P2. few violinists can play more than 2 chords.
P3. john can play more than 4 chords.
H. john is a jazz guitarist.
Label: UNCLEAR, QUANTIFIERS

(T41) P1. john is 180 centimeters tall.
P2. john is 6 foot tall.
P3. mary is 6 foot tall.
H. mary is 180 centimeters tall.
Label: ENTAILMENT, COMPARATIVE, MEASURE

(T42) P1. mary is 190 centimeters tall.
P2. mary is tall.
P3. molly is 184 centimeters tall.
P4. molly is tall.
P5. ruth is 180 centimeters tall.
P6. ruth is tall.
P7. helen is 178 centimeters tall.
P8. helen is tall.
P9. athena is 166 centimeters tall.
P10. athena isn't tall.
P11. artemis is 157 centimeters tall.
P12. artemis isn't tall.
P13. joanna is 160 centimeters tall.
P14. joanna isn't tall.
P15. kate is 162 centimeters tall.
P16. kate isn't tall.
P17. christine is 171 centimeters tall.
H. (it is not the case that christine is tall) and (it is not the case that christine isn't tall).
Label: FOL CONTRADICTION, POSITIVE ADJECTIVES, VAGUENESS

(T43) P1. john is taller than mary.
P2. john is 185 centimeters tall.
P3. mary is 5 foot tall.
H. 185 centimeters is more than 5 foot.
Label: ENTAILMENT, COMPARATIVE, MEASURE

(T44) P1. john is taller than mary.
P2. mary is 5 foot tall.
H. john is more than 5 foot tall.
Label: ENTAILMENT, COMPARATIVE, MEASURE

(T45) P1. john is a guitarist.
P2. guitarists are kind of musicians.
H. john is a musician.
Label: PROBABLE INFERENCE, GENERALISED VAGUENESS, NOUN MODIFIER

(T46) P1. john is a guitarist.
P2. guitarists are pretty much musicians.
H. john is a musician.
Label: PROBABLE INFERENCE, GENERALISED VAGUENESS, NOUN MODIFIER

(T47) P1. john is a basketball player.
P2. basketball players are tall.
H. john is taller than 50 percent of people.
Label: PROBABLE INFERENCE, COMPARATIVE ADJECTIVE, MODAL ADVERB, PERCENTAGE DETERMINER

(T48) P1. many jazz guitarists can play more than 100 chords.
P2. few violinists can play more than 10 chords.
P3. john can play more than 80 chords.
H. john isn't a violinist.
Label: PROBABLE INFERENCE, QUANTIFIERS

(T49) P1. many jazz guitarists can play more than 100 chords.
P2. few violinists can play more than 10 chords.
P3. john can play less than 15 chords.
H. john is a violinist.
Label: UNCLEAR, QUANTIFIERS

(T50) P1. many jazz guitarists can play more than 100 chords.
P2. few violinists can play more than 10 chords.
P3. john can play more than 90 chords.
H. john is a jazz guitarist.
Label: UNCLEAR, QUANTIFIERS

(T51) P1. jazz guitarists are musicians.
P2. violinists are musicians.
P3. john is a musician.
P4. many jazz guitarists can play more than 100 chords.
P5. few violinists can play more than 10 chords.
P6. john can play more than 90 chords.
H. john is a jazz guitarist.
Label: UNCLEAR, QUANTIFIERS

(T52) P1. jazz guitarists are musicians.
P2. violinists are musicians.
P3. john is a musician.
P4. musicians can play more than 1 chord.
P5. many jazz guitarists can play more than 100 chords.
P6. few violinists can play more than 10 chords.
P7. john can play more than 90 chords.
H. john is a jazz guitarist.
Label: UNCLEAR, QUANTIFIERS

(T53) P1. john is a basketball player.
P2. basketball players are taller than most non basketball players.
H. john is taller than most non basketball players.
Label: PROBABLE INFERENCE, COMPARATIVE ADJECTIVE, MODAL ADVERB

(T54) P1. few people are basketball players.
P2. basketball players are taller than most non basketball players.
P3. john is a basketball player.
H. john is taller than most people.
Label: PROBABLE INFERENCE, COMPARATIVE ADJECTIVE, MODAL ADVERB

(T55) P1. 99 percent of people are non basketball players.
P2. basketball players are taller than most non basketball players.
P3. john is a basketball player.
H. john is taller than most people.
Label: PROBABLE INFERENCE, COMPARATIVE ADJECTIVE, MODAL ADVERB, PERCENTAGE DETERMINER

(T56) P1. if you regularly eat humus, then you also enjoy tabouli.
P2. people that enjoy tabouli insist on having mint tea with food.
H. if you regularly eat humus, then you insist on having mint tea with food.
Label: PROBABLE INFERENCE, QUANTIFIER, TEMPORAL ADVERB

(T57) P1. if you eat humus, then you also enjoy tabouli.
P2. people that enjoy tabouli insist on having mint tea with food.
H. if you eat humus, then you insist on having mint tea with food.
Label: PROBABLE INFERENCE, TRANSITIVITY OF IMPLICATION, COMMENT: DOESN'T WORK WITH PLANES, BECAUSE THE GENERIC PLURAL ISN'T TRANSITIVE EVEN COMBINED WITH OPTIMIZED UNIVERSAL

(T58) P1. if you eat humus, then you also enjoy tabouli.
P2. john eats humus.
H. john enjoys tabouli.
Label: PROBABLE INFERENCE, MODUS PONENS

(T59) P1. if you eat humus, then you also enjoy tabouli.
P2. people that enjoy tabouli insist on having mint tea with food.
H. if john eats humus, then john insists on having mint tea with food.
Label: PROBABLE INFERENCE, TRANSITIVITY OF IMPLICATION

(T60) P1. if you regularly eat humus, then you also enjoy tabouli.
P2. people that enjoy tabouli insist on having mint tea with food.
H. if john regularly eats humus, then john insists on having mint tea with food.
Label: PROBABLE INFERENCE, TRANSITIVITY OF IMPLICATION

(T61) P1. mary is 190 centimeters tall.
P2. mary is tall.
P3. kate is 162 centimeters tall.
P4. kate isn't tall.
P5. christine is 185 centimeters tall.
H. christine is tall.
Label: PROBABLE INFERENCE, POSITIVE ADJECTIVES, VAGUENESS

(T62) P1. few people are musicians.
P2. few people are non musicians.
H. (it is not the case that john is a musician) and (it is not the case that john is a non musician).
Label: FOL CONTRADICTION, COMPARATIVE ADJECTIVE, GREY AREA

(T63) P1. john is tall.
P2. few guitarists are logicians.
H. john is tall and few guitarists are logicians.
Label: FOL VALIDITY, CONJUNCTION, QUANTIFIERS

(T64) P1. john is tall.
P2. john is a musician.
H. john is tall and john is a musician.
Label: FOL VALIDITY, CONJUNCTION

(T65) P1. all guitarists are probably logicians.
H. most guitarists are logicians.
Label: PROBABLE INFERENCE, QUANTIFIERS, MODAL ADVERB

(T66) P1. all guitarists are logicians.
H. all guitarists are probably logicians.
Label: ENTAILMENT, QUANTIFIER, MODAL ADVERB

(T67) P1. few guitarists are logicians.
H. all guitarists are logicians.
Label: CONTRADICTION, QUANTIFIERS

(T68) P1. all guitarists are probably logicians.
H. all guitarists are probably logicians.
Label: FOL VALIDITY, QUANTIFIER, MODAL ADVERB

(T69) P1. all guitarists are logicians.
H. all guitarists are logicians.
Label: FOL VALIDITY, QUANTIFIER

(T70) P1. mary is 190 centimeters tall.
P2. mary is tall.
P3. kate is 162 centimeters tall.
P4. kate isn't tall.
P5. christine is 179 centimeters tall.
H. christine is tall.
Label: PROBABLE INFERENCE, POSITIVE ADJECTIVES, VAGUENESS

(T71) P1. mary is 190 centimeters tall.
P2. mary is tall.
P3. kate is 188 centimeters tall.
P4. kate isn't tall.
P5. christine is 189 centimeters tall.
H. it is not the case that christine isn't tall.
Label: UNCLEAR, NEGATIVE ADJECTIVES, VAGUENESS

(T72) P1. mary is 190 centimeters tall.
P2. mary is tall.
P3. kate is 189 centimeters tall.
P4. kate isn't tall.
P5. christine is 188 centimeters tall.
H. christine isn't tall.
Label: ENTAILMENT, POSITIVE ADJECTIVES, VAGUENESS

(T73) P1. mary is 190 centimeters tall.
P2. mary is tall.
P3. kate is 180 centimeters tall.
P4. kate is tall.
P5. helen is 170 centimeters tall.
P6. helen isn't tall.
P7. christine is 165 centimeters tall.
H. christine isn't tall.
Label: ENTAILMENT, NEGATIVE ADJECTIVES, VAGUENESS

(T74) P1. kate is 190 centimeters tall.
P2. kate is tall.
P3. helen is 180 centimeters tall.
P4. helen isn't tall.
P5. christine is 190 centimeters tall.
H. christine is tall.
Label: ENTAILMENT, VAGUENESS

(T75) P1. few people are basketball players.
P2. basketball players are taller than most non basketball players.
P3. john is a basketball player.
H. john is taller than many people.
Label: PROBABLE INFERENCE, COMPARATIVE ADJECTIVE, MODAL ADVERB

(T76) P1. all violinists are musicians.
P2. all musicians read music.
H. all violinists read music.
Label: FOL VALIDITY, QUANTIFIERS

(T77) P1. all violinists are musicians.
P2. all musicians read music.
H. 99 percent of violinists read music.
Label: ENTAILMENT, QUANTIFIERS, PERCENTAGE DETERMINER

(T78) P1. every guitarist is a logician.
P2. if every guitarist is a logician, then every musician reads music.
P3. john is a musician.
H. john reads music.
Label: FOL VALIDITY, IMPLICATION, QUANTIFIER

(T79) P1. john is a basketball player.
P2. basketball players are taller than non basketball players.
H. john is taller than 80 percent of people.
Label: UNCLEAR, COMPARATIVE ADJECTIVE, MODAL ADVERB, PERCENTAGE DETERMINER

(T80) P1. most animals don't fly.
P2. most birds fly.
P3. every bird is an animal.
H. most animals aren't birds.
Label: PROBABLE INFERENCE, QUANTIFIERS

(T81) P1. most birds fly.
H. a few birds fly.
Label: ENTAILMENT, QUANTIFIERS

(T82) P1. many logicians are musicians.
P2. john is a logician.
H. john is a musician.
Label: PROBABLE INFERENCE, QUANTIFIER

(T83) P1. many logicians are musicians.
P2. john is a musician.
H. john is a logician.
Label: UNCLEAR, QUANTIFIER

(T84) P1. many logicians are musicians.
P2. most people aren't logicians.
P3. john is a musician.
H. john is a logician.
Label: UNCLEAR, QUANTIFIERS

References

Adams, Ernest. 1998. *A Primer of Probability Logic*. Stanford: CSLI Publications.

Barendregt, Hendrik Pieter. 1992. Lambda calculi with types. *Handbook of logic in computer science* 2:117–309.

Barwise, J. and R. Cooper. 1981. Generalised quantifiers and natural language. *Linguistics and Philosophy* 4:159–219.

Bernardy, Jean-Philippe, Rasmus Blanck, Stergios Chatzikyriakidis, and Shalom Lappin. 2018. A compositional Bayesian semantics for natural language. In *Proceedings of the International Workshop on Language, Cognition and Computational Models, COLING 2018, Santa Fe, New Mexico*, pages 1–11.

Bernardy, Jean-Philippe and Stergios Chatzikyriakidis. 2019a. A computational treatment of anaphora and its algorithmic implementation. *Ms, University of Gothenburg* .

Bernardy, Jean-Philippe and Stergios Chatzikyriakidis. 2019b. A wide-coverage symbolic natural language inference system. In *Proceedings of the 22nd Nordic Conference on Computational Linguistics*. ACL.

Borgström, Johannes, Andrew D. Gordon, Michael Greenberg, James Margetson, and Jurgen Van Gael. 2013. Measure transformer semantics for Bayesian machine learning. *Logical Methods in Computer Science* 9:1–39.

Bowman, Samuel R, Gabor Angeli, Christopher Potts, and Christopher D Manning. 2015. A large annotated corpus for learning natural language inference. In *Proceedings of EMNLP*, pages 632–642.

Cann, Ronnie, Ruth Kempson, and Eleni Gregoromichelaki. 2009. *Semantics: An Introduction to Meaning in Language*. ISBN 9780521819626.

Carlson, Greg N. 1982. Generic terms and generic sentences. *Journal of Philosophical Logic* 11(2):145–181.

Chatzikyriakidis, S. and Z. Luo. 2017. On the interpretation of common nouns: Types versus predicates. In *Modern Perspectives in Type-Theoretical Semantics*, pages 43–70. Springer.

Chierchia, Gennaro. 1995. *Dynamics of Meaning: Anaphora, Presupposition, and the Theory of Grammar*. University of Chicago Press.

Cooper, R., D. Crouch, J. van Eijck, C. Fox, J. van Genabith, J. Jaspars, H. Kamp, D. Milward, M. Pinkal, M. Poesio, and S. Pulman. 1996. Using the framework. Technical report LRE 62-051r, The FraCaS consortium. ftp://ftp.cogsci.ed.ac.uk/pub/FRACAS/del16.ps.gz.

Cooper, R., S. Dobnik, S. Lappin, and S. Larsson. 2014. A probabilistic rich type theory for semantic interpretation. In *Proceedings of the EACL 2014 Workshop on Type Theory and Natural Language Semantics (TTNLS)*, pages 72–79. Gothenburg, Sweden: Association of Computational Linguistics.

Cooper, R., S. Dobnik, S. Lappin, and S. Larsson. 2015. Probabilistic type theory and natural language semantics. *Linguistic Issues in Language Technology* 10:1–43.

Dagan, Ido, Oren Glickman, and Bernardo Magnini. 2006. The PASCAL recognising textual entailment challenge. In *Machine learning challenges. Evaluating predictive uncertainty, visual object classification, and recognising tectual entailment*, pages 177–190. Springer.

Edgington, Dorothy. 2001. The philosophical problem of vagueness. *Legal Theory* 7(4):371–378.

Emerson, Guy and Ann Copestake. 2017a. Semantic composition via probabilistic model theory. In *IWCS 2017 - 12th International Conference on Computational Semantics - Long papers*.

Emerson, Guy and Ann Copestake. 2017b. Variational inference for logical inference. *CoRR* abs/1709.00224.

Fox, Chris and Shalom Lappin. 2005. *Foundations of Intensional Semantics*. Blackwell.

Gilio, Angelo, Niki Pfeifer, and Giuseppe Sanfilippo. 2015. Transitive reasoning with imprecise probabilities. In S. Destercke and T. Denoeux, eds., *Symbolic and Quantitative Approaches to Reasoning with Uncertainty*, pages 95–105. Cham: Springer International Publishing. ISBN 978-3-319-20807-7.

Goodman, Noah and Daniel Lassiter. 2015. Probabilistic semantics and pragmatics: Uncertainty in language and thought. In S. Lappin and C. Fox, eds., *The Handbook of Contemporary Semantic Theory, Second Edition*, pages 655–686. Malden, Oxford: Wiley-Blackwell.

Goodman, Noah, V. K. Mansinghka, D. Roy, K. Bonawitz, and J. Tenenbaum. 2008. Church: a language for generative models. In *Proceedings of the 24th Conference Uncertainty in Artificial Intelligence (UAI)*, pages 220–229.

Goodman, Noah and Andreas Stuhlmüller. 2014. The Design and Implementation of Probabilistic Programming Languages. http://dippl.org. Accessed: 2018-4-17.

Groenendijk, Jeroen and Martin Stokhof. 1991. Dynamic predicate logic. *Linguistics and Philosophy* 14(1):39–100.

Grove, Julian and Jean-Philippe Bernardy. 2021. Probabilistic compositional semantics, purely. In *Proceedings of LENLS18*.

Grove, Julian, Jean-Philippe Bernardy, and Stergios Chatzikyriakidis. 2021. From compositional semantics to bayesian pragmatics via logical inference. In *Proceedings of Natural Logic meets Machine Learning 2021*.

Halpern, Joseph Y. 2017. *Reasoning About Uncertainty*. Cambridge, MA, USA: MIT Press.

Heim, Irene. 1982. *The Semantics of Definite and Indefinite Noun Phrases*. Ph.D. thesis, UMass Amherst.

Heim, Irene and Angelika Kratzer. 1998. *Semantics in Generative Grammar*. Blackwell.

Itegulov, Daniyar, Ekaterina Lebedeva, and Bruno Woltzenlogel Paleo. 2018. Sensala: A dynamic semantics system for natural language processing. In *Proceedings of the 27th International Conference on Computational Linguistics: System Demonstrations*, pages 123–127.

Kamp, Hans. 2013. Two theories about adjectives. In *Meaning and the Dynamics of Interpretation*, pages 225–261. Brill.

Kamp, Hans and Uwe Reyle. 1993. *From Discourse to Logic*. Dordrecht: Kluwer Academic Publishers.

Keenan, Edward and L.M. Falz. 1985. *Boolean Semantics for Natural Language*. Berlin, New York: Springer.

Klein, Ewan. 1980. A semantics for positive and comparative adjectives. *Linguistics and Philosophy* 4(1):1–45.

Lappin, Shalom. 2015. Curry typing, polymorphism, and fine-grained intensionality. In S. Lappin and C. Fox, eds., *The Handbook of Contemporary Semantic Theory, Second Edition*, pages 408–428. Malden, MA and Oxford: Wiley-Blackwell.

Lappin, Shalom. 2018. Towards a computationally viable framework for semantic representation. In *Proceedings of the Symposium on Logic and Algorithms in Computational Linguistics 2018*, pages 47–63. Stockholm University, DiVA Portal for digital publications.

Lassiter, Daniel and Noah Goodman. 2017. Adjectival vagueness in a Bayesian model of interpretation. *Synthese* 194:3801–3836.

Lau, Jey Han, Alexander Clark, and Shalom Lappin. 2017. Grammaticality, acceptability, and probability: A probabilistic view of linguistic knowledge. *Cognitive Science* 41(5):1202–1241.

Luo, Z. 2012. Common nouns as types. In D. Bechet and A. Dikovsky, eds., *Logical Aspects of Computational Linguistics (LACL'2012). LNCS 7351*.

Montague, Richard. 1970. English as a formal language. In B. V. et al., ed., *Linguaggi nella Societa e nella Tecnica*.

Montague, Richard. 1974. The proper treatment of quantification in ordinary english. In R. Thomason, ed., *Formal Philosophy*. New Haven: Yale UP.

Partee, Barbara H. 2007. Compositionality and coercion in semantics: The dynamics of adjective meaning. *Cognitive foundations of interpretation* pages 145–161.

Peters, Stanley and Dag Westerståhl. 2006. *Quantifiers in Language and Logic*. Oxford University Press UK.

Pfeifer, Niki. 2013. The new psychology of reasoning: A mental probability logical perspective. *Thinking & Reasoning* 19(3-4):329–345.

Pfeifer, Niki and Giuseppe Sanfilippo. 2018. Probabilistic semantics for categorical syllogisms of figure II. In D. Ciucci, G. Pasi, and B. Vantaggi, eds., *Scalable Uncertainty Management*, pages 196–211. Springer International Publishing. ISBN 978-3-030-00461-3.

Piantadosi, Steven, Harry Tily, and Edward Gibson. 2011. Word lengths are optimized for efficient communication. *Proceedings of the National Academy of Sciences of the United States of America* 108:3526–9.

Ranta, Aarne. 1994. *Type-Theoretical Grammar*. Oxford University Press.

Ranta, Aarne. 2004. Grammatical framework. *Journal of Functional Programming* 14(2):145–189.

Shan, Chung-chieh and Norman Ramsey. 2017. Exact bayesian inference by symbolic disintegration. In *Proceedings of the 44th ACM SIGPLAN Symposium on Principles of Programming Languages*, POPL, pages 130–144.

Suppes, Patrick. 1966. Probabilistic inference and the concept of total evidence. In J. Hintikka and P. Suppes, eds., *Aspects of Inductive Logic*, vol. 43 of *Studies in Logic and the Foundations of Mathematics*, pages 49–65. Elsevier.

Sutton, Peter R. 2017. Probabilistic approaches to vagueness and semantic competency. *Erkenntnis* .

van Eijck, Jan and Shalom Lappin. 2012. Probabilistic semantics for natural language. In Z. Christoff, P. Galeazzi, N. Gierasimszuk, A. Marcoci, and S. Smets, eds., *Logic and Interactive Rationality (LIRA), Volume 2*. University of Amsterdam: ILLC.

Vilnis, Luke, Xiang Li, Shikhar Murty, and Andrew McCallum. 2018. Probabilistic embedding of knowledge graphs with box lattice measures. In *Proceedings of the 56th Annual Meeting of the Association for Computational Linguistics (Volume 1: Long Papers)*, pages 263–272. Association for Computational Linguistics.

Williamson, Timothy. 1994. *Vagueness*. Routledge.

6

Probabilistic pragmatics: A dialogical perspective

BILL NOBLE, VLADISLAV MARAEV, AND ELLEN BREITHOLTZ

6.1 Introduction

Much of communication relies on the implicit inferences that language users make as they interact. This is, broadly speaking, the focus of research in pragmatics. In recent years, pragmatic theories inspired by models of rational action and cooperation have extended the reach and precision of predictions that can be made about pragmatic behavior. Many conversational phenomena that are hard to account for using traditional pragmatic theories can potentially be covered by introducing a probabilistic component (Benz and van Rooij, 2007, Franke, 2009).

However, these efforts cast linguistic communication as discrete sequences of action/reaction, rather than comprehensive interaction events. They also often (though not always) assume a high degree of cooperation between actors in spite of the fact that pragmatic inference is possible in situations like argumentation where speakers have divergent objectives (Franke et al., 2012). In this paper we will argue that probabilistic approaches are relevant not only for modeling isolated instances of pragmatic reasoning, but also for highly contextualised reasoning situations which require agents to coordinate their linguistic resources, reason about previous utterances, and make use of common sense assumptions.

Probabilistic Approaches to Linguistic Theory.
Jean-Philippe Bernardy, Rasmus Blanck,
Stergios Chatzikyriakidis, Shalom Lappin,
Aleksandre Maskharashvili (eds.).

In Section 6.2 we will briefly introduce some key concepts in pragmatics before moving on to Section 6.3 in which we will summarise existing probabilistic approaches to pragmatics that have bearing on the type of examples we will consider further on. This includes work in game theoretic and Bayesian pragmatics with applications to social interaction as well as sociolinguistics. In Section 6.4 we argue that the approaches presented in the previous section are ill-equipped to explain pragmatic phenomena arising from natural dialogue. To remedy this, we suggest that pragmatic theories be integrated in a formal model of dialogue in which participants draw on shared principles of reasoning called *topoi*. Finally, in Section 6.5, we present a sketch of a probabilistic model of an instance of joke telling in which the humorous effect is related to the fact that there are several possible interpretations, which depending on context and the participants' respective take on the state of the interaction are more or less salient.

6.2 What is pragmatics?

The word "pragmatics" is derived from the Greek word for "act" or "do", and is thus intended to cover language use as opposed to linguistic meaning in the abstract. The concept traditionally covers a number of key topics, such as Deixis, Speech act theory, Presupposition, and Implicature.[1]

6.2.1 Pragmatic inference

One of the central issues in pragmatics is how implicit meaning is conveyed in speech or text. This kind of inference is usually discussed in terms of *presupposition* or *implicature*. Presupposition is often defined as an inference which survives embedding under negation (see for example Strawson, 1950).

> ... a proposition that P presupposes that Q iff Q must be true in order that P have a truth-value at all.
>
> (Stalnaker, 1974 p.48)

According to this definition, the utterance "The Queen of England is bald" presupposes that there is a Queen of England; this needs to be true for the sentence to be understood as either true or false. Another type of inference that is common in linguistic interaction is *conversational implicature*. Grice (1975) formulated a theory of implicature that attempts to systematically describe how language users can convey (and mean) more than the truth-conditional content

[1] For a thorough introduction to Pragmatics, see for example Levinson (1983), Verschueren and Verschueren (1999), Birner (2012)

of an utterance. Grice distinguishes between *what is said* and *what is implicated.* The former corresponds to the truth-conditional meaning of an utterance and the latter to what a speaker conveys by uttering a certain string of words in a certain context. In this theory, implicature relies on agents who assume (though perhaps are unaware of) the *cooperative principle* elaborated as four *maxims* of rational and efficient communication. According to the maxims contributions should be truthful, as specific as necessary but not too specific, relevant, and presented in an orderly manner. In the exchange below, from Grice (1975), **B**'s reply that there is a garage around the corner would not be very helpful if **B** knew the garage to be closed, not to sell petrol, etc..

(A) 1. **A**: I am out of petrol
    2. **B**: There is a garage around the corner

A expects **B**'s utterance to be a relevant, truthful and complete reply, based on background knowledge and an assumption that **B** is being cooperative.

By adhering to, or blatantly ignoring (*flouting*) the maxims and the cooperative principle, a speaker may express a lot more than the truth-conditional content of his/her utterance. Grice's theory has been extended and developed in a number of different ways, see for example Horn (1984), Levinson (2000) (Neo-Gricean) and Sperber and Wilson (1995), Carston and Hall (2012) (Relevance theory).

Pragmatic theories of inference explain how assumptions are added to the discourse context without being explicitly mentioned. This phenomenon was discussed by Stalnaker (1974) and Karttunen (1974) in the context of presupposition, but the term *accommodation* was coined by Lewis (1979) to describe a particular kind of inference. A simple example of presupposition accommodation can be found in the sentence "The Queen of England is bald", mentioned above, where the definite noun phrase "The Queen of England" presupposes the existence of a Queen of England. If a language user were to hear the sentence uttered, and not already be aware that England has a Queen, they would accommodate this presupposition and the fact that there is a Queen of England would be integrated into their information state.

This instance of accommodation is very straightforward. However, there are many cases where inferences involving a much higher degree of uncertainty are accommodated. Lewis considers accommodation as a general process not necessarily limited to presuppositions. Other types of accommodation are discussed for example in Cooper and Larsson (2010) (questions) and Breitholtz (2020) (topoi). We will return to these in Section 6.4.1.

6.3 Probabilistic approaches to pragmatics

Since pragmatics deals with what is implicit in linguistic communication, it is naturally tied up with uncertainty and especially *inference under uncertainty.*[2]

Recall the exchange in (A), in which **A** infers from **B**'s statement that there is a garage around the corner at which one can get petrol. If **A** had reason to think **B** might be lying, unknowledgable, or otherwise untrustworthy, or if they were unsure of the surface-level meaning of **B**'s utterance (for example, because of a dialectal difference in the meaning of the word *garage*), then **A** would have to take their uncertainty into account in the inference that petrol is available around the corner. Mathematically, it is natural to formalize uncertainty with probabilistic notions — probability distributions, random variables (and dependencies between them), priors, posteriors and so on.

While all of the formal pragmatic models we'll consider in this chapter deal with probability in some way, they differ in the *theoretical* role that probability plays. When uncertainty is modeled as a probability distribution over alternatives, what claim does the theorist make about the relationship between the mathematical model and the phenomena being modelled? There are at least a few different possible answers, which we characterize as follows:

- **Strong probabilistic cognitivism:** Some aspect of the linguistic agent's cognitive state effectively *is* (or is isometric to) a probability distribution. For example, the agent consciously or unconsciously assigns numerical probabilities to certain events, interpretations, etc.
- **Weak probabilistic cognitivism:** The behavior of individual agents conforms to the predictions made by a probabilistic model, whether or not there are cognitive causal factors that themselves correspond to mathematical structures from probability theory.
- **Aggregate probabilistic modeling:** Such models don't claim to capture individual cognition or behavior but rather, probability distributions models the *data* (which may be aggregated over many utterances and/or dialogues and/or speakers).

[2]Aside from uncertainty, another aspect of linguistic meaning for which probabilistic modeling is naturally suited is *vagueness*, however our focus in this chapter is on pragmatic phenomena that specifically arise from the interaction between speakers and the uncertainty that entails. For more on vagueness, see Chapter 4 of this volume.

It isn't always explicit which of these modeling goals probabilistic models of pragmatics seek to achieve. Naturally, this can make results difficult to interpret from a psycholinguistic perspective—readers should be wary, for example, of taking model fit on data aggregated over multiple speakers and utterances as evidence for hypotheses stated in terms of probabilistic cognitivism. Even when the modeling goal is not explicit, it can be helpful to have these different possible goals in mind.

In the remainder of this section, we give an overview of several different research traditions in probabilistic pragmatics. Each of these strains of research are interconnected and influence each other, so there is no one natural starting place, but we begin with referring expression generation because it is the longest-running of the fields we will mention.

6.3.1 Referring expression generation

A *referring expression* is any linguistic expression that is intended to pick out a particular entity in a given context. Referring expression generation (REG) is the task of automatically generating successful referring expressions, given a perceptual scene (e.g., an image) and a target entity.

Referring expressions may use names, adjectival and noun phrases, pronouns, determiners, and various other constructions to achieve the goal of uniquely identifying the target entity. Although language users tend to be very good at coming up with successful referring expression in a given context, the procedure is far from trivial since it depends heavily on context. Suppose a speaker wanted to refer to entity *a* in the following scene:

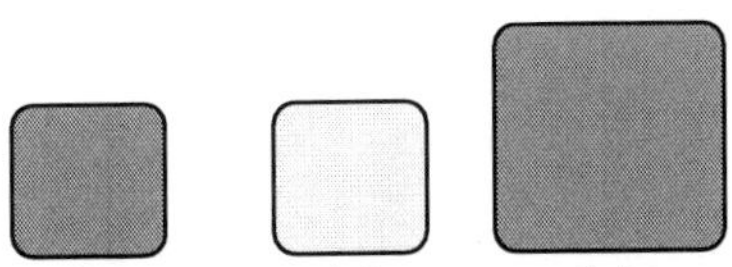

(a) (b) (c)

They might produce the referring expression *the small dark square*. This uniquely picks out (a) since (b) is lightly shaded and (c) is larger than (a). Already we see that there is some context dependence, since the descriminativity of *small* is afforded by comparison with the other entities in the scene.

Reference also depends on dialogue context (Clark, 1996). Suppose that the same speaker-listener pair is subsequently confronted with another scene:

(a) (d) (c)

The small dark square would probably no longer successfully refer to (a) since there is another square which more emphatically fits that description. The speaker might now refer to (a) as *the small medium-shaded square*, but what if they wanted to refer to (d)? Without the previous dialogue context, *the small dark square* might work, but if this same expression had previously been used to refer to (a), confusion may arise. So it is that referring expressions can depend on both visual *and* discourse context. A strong dependence on context and the ability to manipulate which kinds of context are important make REG a popular test case for computational pragmatics.

Indeed, the relationship between REG and Gricean maxims was recognized from the very earliest work on REG (Appelt, 1985, Dale and Reiter, 1995), where it is noted that expressions that over-specify the target entity may, as a result of violating the maxim of quantity, generate a conversational implicature that confuses the listener.[3] Strictly following Gricean maxims, however, would not produce the most human-like expressions—on the contrary, experimental evidence suggests that humans routinely violate the maxim of quantity by over-describing referants, and that listeners have no problem with these descriptions (Engelhardt et al., 2006). In the example above, it would not be unusual for a human speaker to refer to (b) as "the small light square" even though "the light one" would fully disambiguate it.

However, most work in REG is not explicitly concerned with the linguistic processes by which humans generate referring expressions, but rather has the goal of automatically generating expressions similar to those that humans produce under similar circumstances, or that maximize some other goal such as discriminativity. Nevertheless, REG algorithms are often inspired by pragmatic principles. Indeed, some studies have explicitly set out to use REG as a way of testing pragmatic hypotheses (see 6.3.3 for some examples).

6.3.2 Game theoretic pragmatics

Game theory is the study of a certain kind of idealized model of strategic interaction between agents. From a game theoretic perspective, interesting situations are those in which the outcome of

[3]See Krahmer and van Deemter (2012) for a survey of REG that includes some of the earliest work on the subject.

a given action depends on the actions of the other agents involved. In such situations, agents may take into account what they believe about the likely actions of other agents, as well as their preferences among the possible outcomes. Game theory seeks to give an account of the *strategies* available to agents; that is, the principles by which they select an action. In linguistic applications, the actions available to game theoretic agents represent possible utterances (for speakers) and responses to those utterances (for listeners). Listener actions are typically reducible to the semantic interpretation of the speaker's utterance, but are presented in terms of subsequent actions that depend on the listener's interpretation. These subsequent actions account for the utility received by speaker and listener as a result of the exchange.

In what follows, we will briefly introduce some concepts of game theory before moving on to discuss how they have been applied in pragmatics, paying particularly close attention to tho probabilistic aspects of those models.[4]

A key assumption in game theory is that agents are *rational*; that is, that their actions intend to bring about outcomes they prefer while minimizing costs associated with acting. As is common practice in economics, the cost of an action and the value (positive or negative) that agents derive from an outcome are measured in terms of *utility*, which is given a real number value in some abstract unit, often called *utils*. Rationality, then, is operationalized as *utility maximization* — rational agents are those who act in such a way that seeks to maximize the utility they receive from the outcome of their actions. In other words, given an agent with a set of possible actions $\mathcal{A}$, and utility function $U : \mathcal{A} \to \mathbb{R}$, the agent is assumed to select an action satisfying:[5]

$$U(a) = \max\{U(b) \mid b \in \mathcal{A}\}$$

The utility derived from a given action is not always certain. Epistemic uncertainty is uncertainty about the situation in which the action takes place, as in a poker game where the player doesn't know what cards their opponent holds. There may also be stochastic uncertainty about the outcome of an action, as in the uncertainty involved in drawing a card or rolling a die. Due to uncertainty, actions are, in general, not associated with a unitary outcome and its utility, but with a probability distribution over *possible* outcomes and their

[4]For more complete introductions to game theory with a focus on its applications to linguistics, see Benz and van Rooij (2007), Franke (2009, 2013).

[5]In cases where more than one action satisfies this criterion, either is considered rational.

associated utilities. Thus maximization of an action's *expected utility*, $E[U(a)]$ operationalizes rationality where uncertainty is involved.

The rationality assumption rules out actions whose expected utility is strictly lower than another action, regardless of the actions of other agents. Such an action is referred to as *strictly dominated* by the alternative action.

This is exemplified by the well-known *prisioner's dilemma*, which is usually introduced with a story that goes something like this: Two people are suspected of a crime. They are detained by police and questioned separately with no way to communicate. The police have offered each of the suspects a deal, which leaves them with a choice: they can *betray* the other and talk to the police, or *stay silent*. If one of the suspects chooses betrayal while the other stays silent, the one who talks to the police will be set free without spending any more time in jail, but the other suspect will spend three years in prison. If both suspects decide to betray the other, they will each be locked up for two years, but if they both stay silent, there is still enough evidence to send them each away for one year. We assume that while they can't communicate, each suspect understands the options available to everyone, and the results of each of the four possible outcomes, making it a game of *complete information*.[6]

The exact story isn't important in game theoretic terms, since what makes one game different from another is the structure of the actions available to the players and the relative utility of the different possible outcomes. This structure can be represented in so-called *normal form* as follows:

	b_1	b_2
a_1	$(-1,-1)$	$(-3,0)$
a_2	$(0,-3)$	$(-2,-2)$

In this table, $A_a = \{a_1, a_2\}$ are the actions available to agent a (*stay quiet* and *betray*, respectively) and likewise for agent b. Each cell of the table gives the utility for a and b if agent a performs action a_i and agent b performs b_j; that is, $(U_a(a_i, b_j), U_b(a_i, b_j))$.

By looking at this table, we can easily see that for agent a, (sometimes referred to as the *row player*, since their action chooses between rows in the normal form table) action a_2 strictly dominates a_1 since $U_a(a_2, b_j) > U_a(a_1, b_j)$ for both $j = 1$ and $j = 2$. Since the game is symmetric, this same reasoning applies to b: each suspect derives

[6]Not to be confused with a game of *perfect information*, which it is not, since neither player knows what the other will do.

more utility from reporting on the other, regardless of which action the other one takes. This leaves a_2/b_2 as the only *Nash equilibrium*; that is, it is the only outcome in which neither player could increase their utility by unilaterally changing their strategy.[7]

The apparent paradox presented by the prisoner's dilemma is that if both players follow that course of action (which the rationality assumption implies they should), it will result in a longer cumulative prison sentence than if both players had remained silent.

The prisoner's dilemma is a classic introduction to game theory and the concept of strict domination, but since there is no communication involved, it is not particularly interesting to linguists. For modeling communication, a specific kind of game known as *sequential games* are particularly useful. In sequential games, each player acts with knowledge of the previous player's action. While it is possible to represent sequential games in normal form, the normal form representation is more naturally suited to games with one round of actions that all players perform simultaneously. For sequential games, *extensive form* representation is more common. For the sake of explication, the extensive form representation of the prisoner's dilemma is as follows:

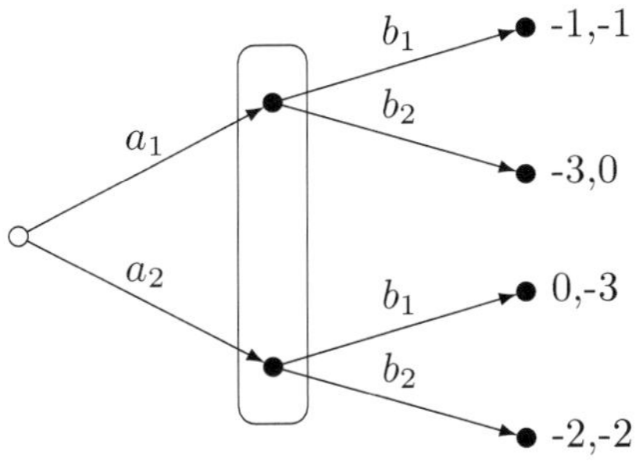

The nodes of the tree represent possible game states, and the arrows between them are actions. Thus, if player a performs a_1, b still has a choice between actions b_1 and b_2. The simultaneous play of the prisoners dilemma setup is represented here by an *information set* in the second round of play; the box drawn around the nodes indicates that those two game states are indistinguishable by b. In game theoretic terms,

[7]The Nash equilibrium is what is known in game theory as a *solution concept*. In general, a solution concept may not necessarily result in a single solution to a given game, but stronger solution concepts eliminate more outcomes. As we will see, different solution concepts have been applied in game theoretic accounts of pragmatics.

this is equivalent to both players choosing their action simultaneously, but as we will see later, the possibility of multiple information sets is important for modeling communication.

A final concept we will introduce in this section is the distinction between *cooperative* versus *competitive* games. In a cooperative game, also known as a *coordination game*, the agent's incentives are aligned, meaning that they would like to coordinate their actions to bring about an outcome that is beneficial for both players. In a *pure coordination game*, the player's payoffs are identical in each outcome. On the other end of the spectrum, a *purely competitive* game, or *zero-sum game*, is one in which the payoffs sum to zero (or equivalently to another constant) in every outcome, meaning that the players are essentially competing for the same pool of utility. Naturally, there are many games that lie somewhere on the spectrum between cooperative and competitive. Which kind of game is most suited to modeling linguistic communication depends on how one thinks of communication more generally and the particularities of the situation being modeled.

Signalling games

Lewis (1969) introduced a class of game theoretic models called *signalling games* as a way of justifying convention as the basis for linguistic meaning. Signalling games (as they were first introduced) are collaborative sequential games of two players: a *sender*, s, and a *receiver*, r. The sender starts out with some (randomly selected) private information, $t \in T$, conventionally referred to as the sender's *type*. Intuitively, the type is the information or propositional content that the sender wants to communicate. The sender also has a set M of messages they can send, and the receiver has a set A of actions they can perform. The actions could be a set of interpretations, in which case it may make sense to assume that $A = T$, though in the more general case the action space could be different from the set of sender types.

Since the game is sequential, the message the sender selects can depend on their t and the action the receiver chooses may depend on the message, m. Signalling games is collaborative because, at least in the original description, $U_s(t, a) = U_r(t, a)$ for all $t \in T$ and $a \in A$.

While signalling games were developed as a model of linguistic communication, the Lewisian formulas have actually been more influential in economics, to explain the role that signalling has in certain economic behaviors, such as the advertising of credentials by job-seekers (Spence, 1973), and the public actions of business owners ahead of their company's initial public offering (Brealey et al., 1977).

Evolutionary game theory

Evolutionary game theory relaxes some of the rationality assumptions imposed by the premise of traditional game theory. Instead of computing the maximum expected utility for every action, players act according to rules that are gradually updated over many rounds of play. Sometimes, as in their application to evolutionary biology, the rounds are conceived of as generations in some population of agents. In other cases, the rounds can be thought of as iterated play by a single agent, for example to model an agent learning. It is not always made explicit in linguistic applications which of these two interpretations is intended.

The first works to apply evolutionary game theory to the linguistic setting (Young, 1993, Blume et al., 1993) can be seen as an extension of Lewis (1969)'s work on convention. They sought to show how evolutionary pressures can encourage the development of systematic communication, even without (initially) conventional word meanings.

Later, this class of models received some empirical support when Jäger (2007) showed that the case marking systems in various languages correspond to different evolutionarily stable solutions in a game where communicative effort is shared by a speaker with costly utterances and a hearer, who must disambiguate between possible interpretations. Expanding on this work, Jäger (2008) characterize the class of evolutionary games that will lead to stable solutions.

Game-theoretic explanations of pragmatic inferences are not necessairily incompatible with Grice's (1975) own treatment of such phenomena, since he maintains that the proposed maxims should be derivable from principles of rational communication. For example, van Rooij (2004) used evolutionary game theory to explain why "(un)marked expressions typically get an (un)marked interpretation", a phenomenon discussed by Horn (1984). Traditional Gricean accounts for such inferences rely on the *maxim of manner*. In the game theoretic model, the inference can be derived from conventions that result from repeated playing of a certain signalling game by rational agents.

Benz and van Rooij (2007) similarly use signalling games to develop a general theory of conversational implicature: By assuming that connective tissue, the receiver can work backwards to extract information that is not part of the literal content of a message.

As van Rooij and de Jager (2012) point out, the evolutionary game theoretic solution concept is strictly stronger than that of the Nash equilibrium in signaling games — many of the signalling games interpretations of Gricean pragmatic phenomena also have interpretations in evolutionary game theory.

Games of partial information

Another line of work uses *games of partial information.* These games are similar to signalling games, but situation regarding the receiver's ignorance of the speaker's type can be more complex. Parikh (2006) argues that games of partial information are strictly stronger than signalling games because the signals available to the speaker depend on the speaker's intention. The following is an example of a game of partial information game (reproduced from (Parikh, 1992); also analysed in (Parikh, 2006)).

> Assume that **A**, dressed in business attire with briefcase in hand, on a street crowded with pedestrians rushing to work in midtown Manhattan at 8.30 a.m. on a Tuesday, meets a good friend, **B**, who asks him where he is headed. **A** responds with the sentence below:

(B) φ: I'm going to the bank.

This utterance, φ, is contrasted two other possible utterances:

(C) μ: I'm going to the financial bank.
μ': I'm going to the river bank.

The situation can be represented as follows:

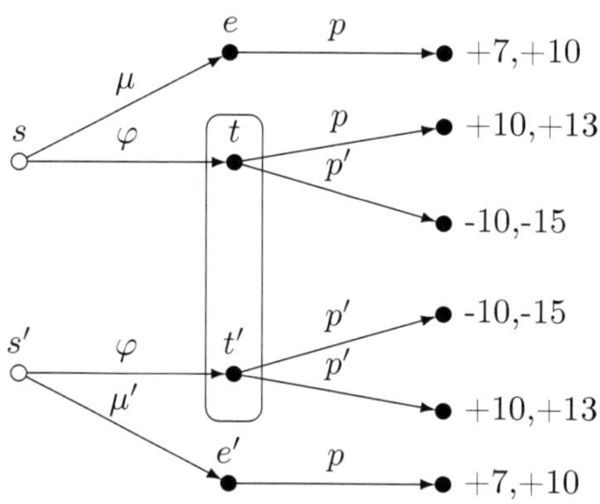

Here, s is the situation where **A** is going to the financial bank, and p is the corresponding proposition (or more precisely, the act of **B** believing that proposition to be true). Likewise s' the situation where he is going to the river bank and p' is the corresponding belief by **B**.

Another difference with Lewisian signalling games is that different utterances are presumed to have different costs, which is why the outcomes of the μ and μ' branches give less utility for **A**: The more specific utterances are considered for some reason to be more costly.[8]

In the game above, the Nash equilibrium solution concept gives

$$\{(s, \varphi), (s', \mu'); (\{t, t'\}, p)\}$$

as the solution, meaning that unless **A** is actually going to the riverbank, they will utter the simpler but literally ambiguous φ, and B will interpret φ (correctly) as p.

In addition to conversational implicature, games of partial information have been used to analyse utterance (as opposed to sentence) meaning (Parikh, 1991), illocutionary force, miscommunication, and other pragmatic phenomena (Parikh, 2001).

Game theory for sociolinguistics

Although pragmatics and sociolingusitics are considered different disciplines, their subject matter often overlaps — both pragmatics and sociolinguistics are concerned with how interactive dynamics affect interpretation in a real-world setting. For that reason, sociolinguistics is also naturally suited to game theoretic analysis. Burnett (2017, 2019) develops *social meaning games*, which seek to explain how an utterance can carry both a literal meaning and a social meaning, which conveys something about the speaker in relation to the social context.

6.3.3 Rational speech act models

In this section, we likewise attempt to provide an introduction to RSA for readers unfamiliar with the framework, but we also tread new territory by trying to systematically lay out the modeling choices RSA permits and assumptions it makes, thereby characterizing the space of pragmatic theories that RSA models well, and those that it excludes.[9]

The motivation behind rational speech acts (RSA) (Frank and Goodman, 2012) begins in the same place as Austin (1962)'s speech act theory, namely, with the observation that speech *is* action.[10] Whereas Austin's next move is to consider the different *kinds* of action that can be taken in the form of speech, RSA takes speech-as-action as a

---

[8]This could be, for example, because they are longer, though equating message cost to utterance length is a controversial assumption.

[9]For more extensive introductions to RSA we refer the reader to Yuan et al. (2018), Scontras et al. (2018, 2021).

[10]In this chapter, we shall distinguish between the modeling framework, which we call RSA and the original RSA model presented by Frank and Goodman (2012), which we refer to as the pragmatic listener/pragmatic speaker model.

reason to apply a *rational actor* model in explaining the behavior of speakers. This move makes it possible to bring game theoretic modeling (traditionally more common in fields like behavioral economics) to bear in the analysis of linguistic behavior (and ultimately, pragmatic meaning).

While the RSA framework can be used to model a wide array of situations in which speakers decide what to say and how to interpret their interlocutor's utterances, it is nevertheless not theory neutral. RSA makes the assumption that the source of pragmatic meaning is rational agents who reason about each other's linguistic behavior in order to communicate, and that those rational agents possess introspective transparency with respect to their own intentions. By way of exception, we note that White et al. (2020) considers the possibility of a more distant relationship between social reasoning and pragmatic behavior, developing a model in which the pragmatic behavior is first reasoned about and later routinized. The model does not strictly fit into the RSA framework, however, as it includes a neural network (the routinized part) that learns from a Bayesian model (the RSA part).

In the next section, we will try to give a general description of the RSA framework by noting where the RSA framework permits choices that may reflect different linguistic and behavioral theories. First, however, we present the original RSA model by Frank and Goodman (2012) as a place to start, from which we can consider various deviations.[11]

Vanilla RSA

The model imagines a reference game scenario, in which a speaker attempts to communicate some world state, s, with an utterance, u.[12]

The model stipulates a *literal listener*, who assigns a probability over a set of interpretations (states), given an utterance as follows:

$$P_{L_0}(s \mid u) \propto [\![u]\!](s) \cdot P(s) \tag{6.1}$$

Here, $[\![u]\!]$ is understood to be the literal meaning of u. In a classical truth theoretic semantics, this would be a function from states to truth values — indeed, this is how Frank and Goodman (2012) uses it, letting $[\![u]\!](s) = 1$ just in case u is true of s. In general, however, other interpretations are possible—Grove et al. (2021), for example, interprets $[\![u]\!]$ as a probabibility distribution over propositions as a way of accounting for ambiguity in the literal meaning of u. In either

[11]See Scontras et al. (2021) for a recent review of applications of RSA.

[12]We use the framing of *states* and *utterances* as in Scontras et al. (2021)'s excellent introduction to RSA, since it is more general than the original framing of *referents* and *words* employed by Frank and Goodman (2012).

case, (6.1) says that the literal listener assigns probability to a given interpretation, s, in proportion to its inclusion in the meaning of u, as well as the prior probability of s.

Next, the *pragmatic speaker* chooses an utterance based on its utility:

$$P_{S_1}(u \mid s) \propto exp(\alpha \cdot U_{S_1}(s; u)) \tag{6.2}$$

Here, U_{S_1} is the utility that the speaker derives from a literal listener's interpretation of having utterance u interpreted as s, where $C(u)$ gives the cost of utterance u:

$$U_{S_1} = log P_{L_0}(s \mid u) - C(u) \tag{6.3}$$

Unlike the literal listener, the pragmatic speaker takes their interlocutor into account when choosing an action—the utility assigned to a given utterance depends on the likelihood that they estimate the literal listener will assign to the intended meaning.

Finally, the pragmatic listener imagines that their interlocutor chose an utterance as a pragmatic speaker and assigns probability to interpretations based on yet another Bayesian inference:

$$P_{L_1}(s \mid u) \propto P_{S_1}(u \mid s) \cdot P(s) \tag{6.4}$$

Like the pragmatic speaker, the pragmatic listener takes their interlocutor's decision process into account, choosing an interpretation s in proportion to the likelihood their interlocutor would have uttered u if they intended s. Unlike the pragmatic speaker, the pragmatic listener assumes that their interlocutor is also pragmatic.

RSA variants

Deviating from the vanilla RSA presented above, there are many modeling choices that the RSA framework presents, including:

The depth of social recursion This can include choosing different depths of social recursion for the actual speaker and listener versus the mental model used by their interlocutor. In vanilla RSA, for example, the rational speaker uses the depth 1 rational listener as their mental model, which is also the model used for the *actual* listener. But it could be that the actual listener is instead modeled as a depth 2 listener.

The α parameter The α parameter is sometimes characterised as the *degree of rationality*, but it might be more accurately described as modeling an *aspect* of rationality, namely the extent to which an agent's choices are probabilistically proportional to—versus determined by—their relative utility.

The utility function The predictions of the RSA model may differ depending on the goals of the speaker.[13] Goodman and Stuhlmüller (2013) takes speaker uncertainty into account, using expected utility, as the objective. Potts et al. (2016) uses a cost function that depends on lexical frequency and/or the presence of alternative formulations. Finally, Qing and Franke (2015) systematically explores different utility functions.

There is some vagueness in what distinguishes RSA from other game theoretic approaches to pragmatics, but in general, the RSA tradition tends to combine game theoretic modeling with experimental pragmatics. In contrast to the theoretical work in game theoretic pragmatics (Section 6.3.2), RSA has placed less focus on identifying the appropriate solution concept for communication games, and has restricted its attention to quite simple toy scenarios in which a referring expression is selected from a limited set of alternatives. One criticism of the RSA paradigm is that the laboratory games typically used in RSA experimental work may tend to elicit rational puzzle-solving strategies in the subjects of experiments, rather than the kind of reasoning that is typical for natural dialogue. Going beyond these simple answer-response scenarios to consider situations that are more genuinely dialogical may reveal different patterns of reasoning and pragmatic inference on the part of the interacting agents.

6.3.4 Challenges for probabilistic pragmatics

As described in Section 6.2, Grice (1975) proposed a set of conversational maxims as a basis for explaining pragmatic implicature. These maxims are derived from the assumption that linguistic communication takes place between agents who are perfectly rational and cooperative. Pragmatic theories in the Gricean tradition appeal to particular maxims to explain why an implicature does or does not arise in a given situation. Such explanations are *ad hoc* in the sense that there is often no meta-level theory for why a maxim should apply in one situation but not another, or what to expect when maxims are in conflict.

The approaches discussed in this section aspire to make the intuitions captured in Gricean pragmatics precise by connecting instances of linguistic behaviour more directly to the assumptions behind the maxims. In doing so, game theoretic models have demonstrated that many implicatures are preserved under conditions of imperfect cooperativity (see e.g., Franke et al., 2012). With regard to rationality, RSA and game theoretic models have ways of tweaking how rationality

[13]See Goodman and Frank (2016, box 1) for more examples of work that manipulates the speaker's utility function.

is expressed, by use of different game theoretic solution concepts (van Rooij, 2004, Parikh, 2001) and through the α parameter and depth of recursion in the case of RSA (Zaslavsky et al., 2021). However, these models still fundamentally rely on the assumption that agents act in their own self-interest and that these interests are transparent to the agents themselves.

If the goal of pragmatic theory is to explain the behaviour of actual speakers (and not that of *homo economicus*), theories that relax or do away with the rationality assumption are necessary.[14] Game theoretic and RSA models can, however, be instrumental as *normative* models of linguistic behavior; that is, a model that predicts what an agent *should* do if they *were* acting rationally (according to a particular definition of rationality). These models may be used to represent a causal factor that is predictive (though not determinate of) the behaviour of actual speakers, and their fit to aggregate data (aggregated over time or populations) can be taken as evidence for that causal factor. Such considerations motivate the use of evolutionary game theory in pragmatics, as well as some work on RSA (White et al., 2020).[15]

The models discussed in this section are successful at doing away with Gricean maxims, instead deriving implicatures from the assumptions that underlie those maxims. However, they fall short of providing a unified meta-level theory. Instead, both game theory and RSA can be seen as frameworks through which a researcher can express a very specific linguistic situation — often restricted to a single utterance or very short exchange with limited options. It is out of scope for these frameworks to explain how the agents' incentives and potential actions arise or what effect an utterance has on the incentives and potential actions available in the *next* exchange.

Without this connective tissue, probabilistic models of pragmatics remain every bit as *ad hoc* as the Gricean approaches that preceded them.

6.4 A Dialogical approach to pragmatics

Many pragmatic phenomena, such a Gricean implicatures and speech acts, have often been studied without considering a wider notion of dialogue context. The context of dialogue brings on additional

[14] *Homo economicus* is a tongue-in-cheek moniker for the artificial subject of economic study—humans in contrast are not perfectly self-interested, introspective, or rational. Some branches of encomomics such as behavioral economics seek to study the consequences of relaxing rationality assumptions.

[15] The authors would like to thank Julian Grove for insightful conversations on the role of normative modeling in linguistic theory.

constraints and considerations. For instance ones related to the goals of a particular conversational genre, such as negotiation or quarrel. In such cases cooperativeness can be violated even on the basic level (Castelfranchi, 1992). Other examples of absence of cooperativeness may include dialogues with artificial agents or neuroatypical people: even though the conversation assumes the absence of cooperation and mind-reading skills, the other participant can still interpret what has been said, or, if needed, take action to clarify it.

Gricean accounts of pragmatics assume that to understand a speaker's utterance, the hearer should recognise the *intention* that the speaker expressed by producing that utterance. One counterexample to this requirement is garden-path humour, e.g. "Should a person stir his coffee with his right hand or his left hand? Neither. He should use a spoon."[16], where the initial question posed is clearly not uttered with its bona fide intention, and if the sneaky intention is recognised correctly by the hearer, the humorous clash would not take place.

6.4.1 Reasoning in dialogue

One common problem for approaches to pragmatic reasoning in the context of dialogue modeling is that they don't pay enough attention to context. One reason for this, as suggested by Breitholtz et al. (2017), is that they are extensions of models developed to account for the truth value of sentences in terms of possible worlds rather than the meaning of utterances in interaction. Exceptions to this are for example Ginzburg (2012), Cooper (Fourthc.), Breitholtz (2020), Larsson and Traum (2000) who employ information state models of language that make it possible to account for how coordination of the dialogue progresses with successive utterances, and provides a structured characterisation of the information available to dialogue participants and offers a principled way in which asymmetries in shared knowledge can be represented.

Reasoning in dialogue often involves non-logical common-sense inferences, often referred to as *enthymematic*. An enthymeme is an argument which appeals to what is in the listener's mind. This means that unlike a syllogism, the inference presented as the conclusion of such argument is negotiable, cancellable. In (D), **A** presents an argument that she cannot make it to a party because she is going to a wedding, but since the bride is pregnant she might be able to come later on.

[16]From Esar (1952)

(D) 1. **A**: Oh! I'm invited to a wedding that night.
2. **A**: But the bride is pregnant,
3. **A**: so I might drop by in the wee hours.

(Breitholtz, 2014a, p1)

Thus, A communicates that the bride being pregnant is a *reason* for her being able to come to the party after all. To be efficient, or even understandable, this argument requires some underpinning notion or rule which sanctions it.

Such underpinning principles of reasoning have been discussed at length in the literature on rhetoric and argumentation (e.g. Toulmin, 2003, a.o.). However, the idea of rules of thumb available to language users, which justify statements, suggestions or other types of utterances goes back to early classical times. The Sophists taught their students to argue based on *topoi* — principles that had proved successful in similar types of arguments in the past (Jarratt, 1998). In modern times, the concept of topoi was introduced in linguistics as a theory of linguistic meaning with parts of discourse being connected by topoi (Ducrot, 1988). On this view the set of topoi accessible to an individual do not constitute a monolithic logical system, but represents a set of resources at the disposal of a dialogue participant for producing and interpreting arguments.

In the philosophy of language the type of reasoning involved in enthymematic arguments has been discussed in terms of implicatures (Grice, 1975, Sperber and Wilson, 1995), which are reached via assumptions of rationality and relevance. The necessity of background knowledge or common ground is not denied, but its role in a theory of pragmatic inference is often not described in a precise way. In the literature on non-monotonic logic the principles warranting conclusions are called *default rules*; that is, rules that are true if there is nothing to contradict them.

One of the advantages of using topoi as the underpinning for arguments, rather than default rules, is that the set of topoi of one agent does not need to be consistent or lead to consistent conclusions even within one model or domain (Breitholtz, 2020). This ability to follow various strains of reasoning — including inconsistent ones — seems to be a prerequisite for the complex type of interactive language understanding and problem solving that humans master so well.

6.4.2 Formal theories of dialogue

There are several approaches which aim at formal analyses of pragmatic inferences in a dialogical context.

KoS (Ginzburg, 2012) provides among the most detailed theoretical treatments of domain-general conversational relevance, especially for query responses — see Purver (2006) on Clarification Requests, Łupkowski and Ginzburg (2017) for a general account — which ties into the KoS treatment of non-sentential utterances. These utterances, which are often treated as performance data in standard syntactic and semantic theory, are crucial for modeling naturalistic dialogue. In this domain KoS has among the most detailed analyses (Fernández et al., 2007, Ginzburg, 2012).

Like in Lewis (1979) KoS likens language to a game, containing players (interlocutors), goals and rules. KoS represents language interaction in terms of the dynamically changing context. The meaning of an utterance is how it changes the context. In contrast to most approaches (e.g. Roberts, 2012), which represent a single context for both dialogue participants, KoS keeps a separate representation for each participant. The information state comprises a private part and a public part. The latter is called *Dialogue Game Board* (DGB) and it represents information that has been publicised in the current interaction. It tracks things that are assumed to be shared, such as visual space, moves (utterances, their form, content and illocutionary force), and questions under discussion.

KoS is based on the information-state update (ISU) approach, following several authors, including Larsson (2002) and Ginzburg (2012). In this view we present the information available to each participant of the dialogue (either a human or an artificial agent) in a rich information state. Being rich entails that the information state contains a hierarchy of facts, including the ones that are thought to be shared and the ones that have not been yet publicised.

The formal framework used in KoS is TTR, a Type Theory with Records (Cooper, 2005b, Cooper and Ginzburg, 2015). There has been a wide range of work in this formalism including the modeling of intentionality and mental attitudes (Cooper, 2005a), generalised quantifiers (Cooper, 2013), co-predication and dot types in lexical innovation, frame semantics for temporal reasoning, reasoning in hypothetical contexts (Cooper, 2011), spatial reasoning (Dobnik and Cooper, 2017), enthymematic reasoning (Breitholtz, 2014b), clarification requests (Purver, 2006, Ginzburg, 2012), negation (Cooper and Ginzburg, 2012), non-sentential utterance resolution (Fernández et al., 2007, Ginzburg, 2012) and iconic gesture (Lücking, 2016). In the case study of joke interpretation in Section 6.5 we will use a version of KoS formalised in TTR.

A brief introduction to TTR TTR is based on the notion that agents perceive an individual object that exists in the world in terms of being *of a particular type.* Such basic judgements performed by agents can be denoted as "a : Ind", meaning that a is an individual, in other words a is a *witness* of (the type) Ind (ividual). This is an example of a *basic* type in TTR, namely types that are not constructed from other types. An example of a more complex type in TTR is a *ptype* which is constructed from predicates, e.g. $fresher\_than(a, b)$, "a is fresher than b". A witness of such a type can be a situation, a state or an event. To represent a more general event, such as "one individual item is fresher than another individual item" *record types* are used. Record types consist of a set of fields, which are pairs of unique labels and types. The record type which will correspond to the aforementioned sentence is the following:

$$\begin{bmatrix} \mathrm{x} & : & Ind \\ \mathrm{y} & : & Ind \\ \mathrm{c_{fresh}} & : & fresher\_than(\mathrm{x}, \mathrm{y}) \end{bmatrix} \tag{6.5}$$

The witnesses of record types are *records*, consisting of a set of fields which are pairs of unique labels and values. In order to be of a certain record type, a record must contain at least the same set of labels as the record type, and the values must be of a type mentioned in the corresponding field of the record type. The record may contain additional fields with labels not mentioned in the record type. For example, the record (6.6) is of a type in (6.5) iff $a : Ind$, $b : Ind$, $s : fresher\_than(a, b)$ and q is of an arbitrary type.

$$\begin{bmatrix} \mathrm{x} & = & a \\ \mathrm{y} & = & b \\ \mathrm{c_{fresh}} & = & s \\ \mathrm{c_{price}} & = & q \end{bmatrix} \tag{6.6}$$

TTR also defines a number of type construction operations. Here we mention only the ones that are used in this chapter.

1. *List types*: if T is a type, then $[T]$ is also a type — the type of lists each of whose members is of type T. The list $[a_1, \ldots, a_n] : [T]$ iff for all i, $a_i : T$. Additionally, we use a type of non-empty lists, written as $_{ne}[T]$, which is a subtype of $[T]$ where $1 \leq i \leq n$. We assume the following operations on lists: constructing a new list from an element and a list (cons), taking the first element of list (head), and taking the rest of the list (tail).

2. *Function types*: if T_1 and T_2 are types, then so is $(\lambda r : T_1.T_2)$, the type of functions from records of type T_1 to record type T_2. Additionally, T_2 may *depend* on the parameter (the witness of type T_1 passed to the function).

We model pragmatic arguments (enthymemes) and principles of reasoning (topoi) as function types from a situation of one type to another type of situation. For example, the function below has an antecedent type (the domain of the function) representing a type of situation where there are two objects and one of them is fresher than the other, and a result type (the co-domain of the function) representing a type of situation where the fresher object is better.

$$\lambda r : \begin{bmatrix} \text{x} & : \textit{Ind} \\ \text{y} & : \textit{Ind} \\ \text{c}_{\text{fresher}} & : \textit{fresher\_than}(\text{x}, \text{y}) \end{bmatrix} . \begin{bmatrix} \text{c}_{\text{better}} : \textit{better\_than}(r.\text{x}, r.\text{y}) \end{bmatrix} \tag{6.7}$$

Following Ginzburg (2012) and Larsson (2002) we will model the progress of dialogues in terms of the *information states* of the dialogue participants. In our analysis we will focus on the part of a dialogue participant's information state that is shared. That is, what has in some way been referred to in the dialogue, or what is necessary to integrate in the information state for a dialogue contribution to be interpreted in a relevant way. We will refer to this shared part of an interlocutor's information state as the DGB of that participant. We are particularly interested in how individual agents draw on individual (and sometimes distinct) resources. We will therefore use separate DGBs for each agent, rather than letting the DGB represent a God's eye view notion of context. For example, although a topos may be of central relevance in the dialogue, it does not appear on the DGB until it has been made explicit, or until something has been said which has caused it to be accommodated. However, we also assume that a dialogue participant has access to a set of *rhetorical resources* which are not necessarily assumed to be shared. These are topoi that the speaker whose information state we model has access to, but that cannot be expected to be shared yet based on what has been said in the dialogue. This means of course that many topoi related to common knowledge and common sense are not considered shared in the dialogue, i.e., part of the DGB, until they have been introduced explicitly or by means of accommodation. We model the information state of an agent as a record type where the label DGB is associated with a record type of features that are assumed to be shared (these could be "latest utterance", "question under discussion" etc. — here we will only spell out the features that are focused in our analysis). The label "rhet_resources" represents the private part of an agent's information state where the agent can find topoi to invent arguments and warrant inferences.

$$\begin{bmatrix} \text{rhet\_resources} : & \begin{bmatrix} \text{topoi} : [\mathit{Topos}] \end{bmatrix} \\ \text{dgb} & : \begin{bmatrix} \text{eud} & : [\mathit{Enthymeme}] \\ \text{topoi} : [\mathit{Topoi}] \end{bmatrix} \end{bmatrix} \tag{6.8}$$

6.5 Case study: Humour

In Section 6.3 we discussed the main lines of research that apply probabilistic models to pragmatic phenomena. These theories focus on accounting for isolated instances of reasoning that are not embedded in dialogical context. This is also true of probabilistic models of sociolinguistic phenomena. Such models look to statistically account for particular linguistic choices made by an agent in the context of a language user at a specific point in time (Burnett, 2019). In Section 6.4, we argued that probabilistic models of pragmatic reasoning must be situated in a dialogical framework to incorporate a richer account of context — one that includes the interactive situation and background of the participants, and which is incrementally refined over the course of an interaction. In this section we will consider examples of reasoning in interaction where one speaker is engaging the other in a joke. Humour is a linguistic activity that relies on both dialogicity and reasoning under uncertainty. In humour, different aspects of context and reasoning are highly integrated, and the context changes incrementally as a result of the interaction. Moreover, it is an activity where the participants' priors affect how likely they are to "get the joke", and where each addition of new information to the discourse model adjust these priors.

6.5.1 Humour and inference

There is a long tradition of analysing humour from a linguistic perspective, most notably in the Semantic-Script Theory of Verbal Humour, SSTH (Raskin, 1985). Interpreting humour requires inherent dialogicity and multiple perspective taking, which has been described using the notion of different "story worlds" available to the interlocutors (Ritchie, 2018) and formally addressed using enthymematic reasoning drawing on topoi (Breitholtz and Maraev, 2019, Maraev et al., 2021). A humorous effect is often created when one inference gives way to an inference arising from an alternate interpretation. The shift in interpretations can be explained by accommodating different topoi. Let us consider an example:

(E) "Is the doctor at home?" the patient asked in his bronchial whisper. "No," the doctor's young and pretty wife whispered in reply. "Come right in!" (Raskin, 1985, p. 109)

This joke (which is widely discussed in the literature on humour) takes advantage of the fact that there are two different topoi that are evoked at different stages of its progression. After the first part we are told that there is a man who is speaking with a whispering voice who is looking for a doctor. A reasonable explanation for this would be that the man is in need of a doctor, which is invoked by the use of "bronchial" which has disease associations, like "bronchitis". An underpinning topos at this stage would be something like "if the doctor is at home, he will help the patient". However, when we learn that the doctor is not at home and that his wife asks the guy at the door to come in, a more applicable topos might be something along the lines of "if the husband is not at home his wife may carry on an affair". This interpretation of the situation might become more likely when the listener learns that the person who answers the door is the doctor's wife and that she is young and pretty. However, the real shift happens when we learn that the doctor *not* being at home is presented as a reason for the man to come inside. We argue that in order for a joke like this to work there must be at least two ways of interpreting the situation, and one of them needs to be more likely to the person who is presented with the joke in order for them to be somewhat surprised by the eventual shift to the other interpretation.

The relevance of probabilities for the interpretation of jokes has been noted by Kao et al. (2013), who present probabilistic model of sentence comprehension accounting for the interpretation of jokes.[17] Crucially, a probabilistic model for this explanation of humor cannot rely on a population-level statistics, since the humorous effect is achieved in the individual speakers.

6.5.2 Probabilistic rhetorical resources

In the previous section we showed how competing available topoi which invite very different inferences in a particular situation contribute to humour. We will now move on to consider how uncertainty is relevant to these inferences and how the humorous effect is in fact often reached by adding information that makes one topos more likely to be accommodated, rendering other acceptable topoi less likely and making the punchline more effective.

[17] However, their study is restricted to homophone puns, and does not assume an interactive perspective.

The humour arising from (E) can be explained by a shift from accommodating one topos to accommodating an entirely different topos. However, other jokes rely on some lingering uncertainty in the respective inferences.

Imagine a conversation such as the one below where **A** is telling **B** a joke. This joke elicits a humorous effect in **B** in two places — once after turn 3, where **B** produces a light chuckle and once (presumably) after turn 7, which might be considered to be the joke's ultimate punchline.

(F) 1 **A** How do you put an elephant into a fridge?
2 **B** Hmm, I don't know?
3 **A** Open the door, put the elephant inside, close the door.
4 **B** Haha okay
5 **A** How do you put a giraffe into the fridge?
6 **B** Open the door, put the giraffe inside, close the door?
7 **A** Wrong! Open the door, get the elephant out, put the giraffe inside, close the door.

Breitholtz and Maraev (2019) analyse this joke in terms of salient and non-salient topoi. However, this analysis considers topoi as either applicable or non-applicable, whereas in fact the priors associated with the topoi are not likely to be 1 or 0 but somewhere in between. An account that considers this kind of gradience is more realistic and can also explain why some people may respond in a way that ruins the joke — it is because their priors are not the ones expected in the set up of the joke.

The success of the joke relies not only on **A**'s utterances but also on **B** participating in and contributing to the interaction. For this reason there are ways in which the joke might fail to have a humorous effect. For example, the joke relies on **B** making certain inferences rather than others based on different principles of reasoning, or topoi, which are all available to **B**. The success of the joke depends on the salience of these topoi. Furthermore, the humorous effect of turn 7 relies on the setup given by the rest of the dialogue. We want to explain how this setup affects which principles of reasoning are most salient and how they are subverted by turn 7 — in other words, we want to explain why **A** expects **B** to find the punchline funny.

The topic of the first question "how do you put an elephant into a fridge?" evokes a set of topoi in the mind of the listener (in the information state of our model these appear in the field "rhet_resources"). These are basic principles based on spatial relations such as "if you open a container and put an object in, the object will be in the container", "in order to fit an object in a container there must be enough space" and also topoi concerning fridges and elephants such as "a fridge is smaller than an elephant". We represent these principles of reasoning merged in one topos τ_c encompassing all of them. They act as constraints represented as *ptypes*. For instance, in the field c_{space} of (6.9). However, all of the constraints introduced by the relevant topoi will not be regarded as equally important. To capture this we assign weights to the constraints in the topos.

$$\tau_c = \lambda r : \begin{bmatrix} x & : \mathit{Ind} \\ y & : \mathit{Ind} \\ z & : \mathit{Ind} \\ p_1 & : \mathit{Float} \\ p_2 & : \mathit{Float} \\ \mathrm{c_{obj}} & : \mathit{object}(z) \\ \mathrm{c_{space}} & : \mathit{has\_enough\_space\_for}(x, z, p_1, p_2) \\ \mathrm{c_{fridge}} & : \mathit{fridge}(\mathrm{x}) \\ \mathrm{c_{agent}} & : \mathit{agent}(\mathrm{y}) \\ \mathrm{c_{open}} & : \mathit{open}(\mathrm{y}, \mathrm{x}) \\ \mathrm{c_{put}} & : \mathit{put\_in}(\mathrm{y}, \mathrm{z}, \mathrm{x}) \end{bmatrix} . \quad \begin{bmatrix} \mathrm{s} : \mathit{in}(r.\mathrm{z}, r.\mathrm{x}) \end{bmatrix} \tag{6.9}$$

We can assign additional parameters p_1 and p_2 to a constraint which determine probabilities, correspondingly, that the constraint holds and that it is relevant for the situation. For current purposes we treat these probabilities as independent. Given the context of the question "How do you put an elephant into a fridge?" we can say that the issue whether the container (a fridge) has enough space for fitting an object (an elephant) is important for answering it and that in most cases fridges will not have enough space for elephants. An aspect of this imaginary situation would look as follows:

$$\begin{bmatrix} \mathrm{s_{space}} & = & \mathit{has\_enough\_space\_for}(f, e, 0.001, 0.988) \end{bmatrix},$$

where f and e are imaginary instances of a fridge and an elephant.

The applicability of a topos to a situation can be derived from the probabilities assigned to its constraints. For instance, one can characterise a topos as applicable if probabilities for its constraints are above a certain threshold (say, 0.5 for this example). Therefore, τ_c is not applicable.

In contrast, in some other context, either a narrative context of a fiction or a different cultural context, the priors for the c_{space} constraint can be different. For instance, if the joke is told in a context of a fairy tale where things can shrink in their size all the time, the likelihood of this constraint to hold would be much higher, e.g.

$$\left[\ s_{\text{space}} \ = \ \textit{has\_enough\_space\_for}(f, e, 0.643, 0.988)\ \right].$$

In this case the topos τ_c can be applied and the listener can just answer something along the lines of "Well, just put the elephant inside", which would ruin the joke. Similarly if the doctor's wife joke (E) is told in the context where affairs and lovers were just recently discussed, it might raise the probability of the lover topos from the beginning and diminish the surprise effect of the punchline, hence making the joke less funny.

6.6 Conclusion

In this paper we have considered the use of probabilistic methods in pragmatics, particularly with respect to the pragmatics of dialogue. First, we gave a brief account of the type of problems treated in pragmatics, focusing on inference. We then moved on to consider probabilistic approaches to pragmatics, focusing on RSA models and game theoretic models. Models in these traditions give a more rigorous account of pragmatic phenomena than traditional Gricean analyses. By taking seriously the idea that speech is action (Austin, 1962), they are able to apply mathematical tools that have been developed to model human behavior in disciplines such as economics. However, these models still fundamentally rely on the assumption that agents act in their own self-interest and that these interests are transparent to the agents themselves. On the contrary, much of human linguistic interaction is not particularly goal-directed.

Structurally, RSA and game-theoretic models don't resemble dialogue, which is the most basic and ubiquitous of all linguistic activity — in particular, they are non-incremental, only considering linguistic inferences that happen between discrete utterances selected from a finite action space. They also typically don't consider interactions beyond a single speaker-listener exchange and while extensions to multiple utterances are possible, they quickly become intractable, rendering them unsuitable for the analysis of a full dialogue. While RSA and game-theoretic models have a lot of explanatory power as a tool for analysing data collected in controlled experimental settings where parameters are reduced to a minimum, they do not handle natural dialogue very well.

When dialogue participants reason, their inferences tend to be based on common sense assumptions that are not universally rational. However, the assumptions, or topoi, could be more or less rational and thus more or less probable in the context of a particular situation involving a particular agent. This may lead her to assume one salient topos rather than another when drawing inferences. One type of dialogue which relies on the perceived probabilities of salient topoi is dialogue involving humour, such as dialogical jokes. In the final section of the paper we sketched a model of how probabilities can be introduced in a model of dialogue with a rich representation of context. In our sketch we focused on how the priors of a topos change during the course of the interaction, accounting for how a topos that was highly salient at the outset of a joke ends up having a very low probability towards its end. Although our model is merely a sketch, we believe it suggests that probabilistic approaches are indeed useful also in accounting for natural "messy" dialogue. However, more work — empirical as well as formal — is required to develop this model to integrate more aspects of natural dialogue while retaining the coverage of well-studied pragmatic phenomena.

6.7 Acknowledgments

Ellen Breitholtz, Vladislav Maraev and Bill Noble were supported by grant 2014-39 from the Swedish Research Council (VR) for the establishment of the Centre for Linguistic Theory and Studies in Probability (CLASP) at the University of Gothenburg. Additionally, Ellen Breitzholtz was supported by VR grant 2016-0116 – Incremental Reasoning in Dialogue (IncReD).

References

Appelt, Douglas E. 1985. *Planning English Sentences*. Studies in Natural Language Processing. Cambridge: Cambridge University Press. ISBN 978-0-521-43803-2.

Austin, J. L. 1962. *How to Do Things with Words*. Cambridge: Harvard University Press.

Benz, Anton and Robert van Rooij. 2007. Optimal assertions, and what they implicate. A uniform game theoretic approach. *Topoi* 26(1):63–78.

Birner, Betty J. 2012. *Introduction to pragmatics*, vol. 38. John Wiley & Sons.

Blume, Andreas, Yong-Gwan Kim, and Joel Sobel. 1993. Evolutionary Stability in Games of Communication. *Games and Economic Behavior* 5(4):547–575.

Brealey, Richard, Hayne E. Leland, and David H. Pyle. 1977. Informational Asymmetries, Financial Structure, and Financial Intermediation. *The Journal of Finance* 32(2):371–387.

Breitholtz, Ellen. 2014a. *Enthymemes in Dialogue: A micro-rhetorical approach*. Ph.D. thesis, University of Gothenburg.

Breitholtz, Ellen. 2014b. Reasoning with topoi–towards a rhetorical approach to non-monotonicity. In *Proceedings of the 50th anniversary convention of the AISB, 1st–4th April 2014, Goldsmiths, University of London*.

Breitholtz, Ellen. 2020. *Enthymemes and topoi in dialogue: The use of common sense reasoning in conversation*, vol. 41 of *Current Research in the Semantics/Pragmatics*. Brill.

Breitholtz, Ellen, Christine Howes, and Robin Cooper. 2017. Incrementality all the way up. In *Computing Natural Language Inference Workshop at the International Conference on Computational Semantics (IWCS)*.

Breitholtz, Ellen and Vladislav Maraev. 2019. How to put an elephant in the title: Modeling humorous incongruity with topoi. In *Proceedings of the 23rd Workshop on the Semantics and Pragmatics of Dialogue - Full Papers*. London, United Kingdom: SEMDIAL.

Burnett, Heather. 2017. Sociolinguistic interaction and identity construction: The view from game-theoretic pragmatics. *Journal of Sociolinguistics* 21(2):238–271.

Burnett, Heather. 2019. Signalling games, sociolinguistic variation and the construction of style. *Linguistics and Philosophy* .

Carston, Robyn and Alison Hall. 2012. Implicature and explicature. In H.-J. Schmid, ed., *Cognitive Pragmatics*, chap. 3, pages 47–84. Berlin/Boston: de Gruyter.

Castelfranchi, Cristiano. 1992. No more cooperation, please! In search of the social structure of verbal interaction. In *Communication from an artificial intelligence perspective*, pages 205–227. Springer.

Clark, Herbert H. 1996. *Using Language*. Cambridge University Press.

Cooper, Robin. 2005a. Austinian truth, attitudes and type theory. *Research on Language and Computation* 3(4):333–362.

Cooper, Robin. 2005b. Records and record types in semantic theory. *Journal of Logic and Computation* 15(2):99–112.

Cooper, Robin. 2011. Copredication, quantification and frames. In S. Pogodalla and J.-P. Prost, eds., *Logical Aspects of Computational Linguistics (LACL 2011)*. Springer.

Cooper, Robin. 2013. Clarification and generalized quantifiers. *Dialogue and Discourse* 4:1–25.

Cooper, Robin. Fourthc. From perception to communication: An analysis of meaning and action using a theory of types with records (TTR). https://sites.google.com/site/typetheorywithrecords/drafts.

Cooper, Robin and Jonathan Ginzburg. 2012. Negative inquisitiveness and alternatives-based negation. In *Logic, Language and Meaning*, pages 32–41. Springer.

Cooper, Robin and Jonathan Ginzburg. 2015. Type theory with records for natural language semantics. *Handbook of Contemporary Semantic Theory, The* pages 375–407.

Cooper, Robin and Staffan Larsson. 2010. Accommodation and reaccommodation in dialogue. *R. Bäuerle, U. Reyle, & TE Zimmermann (Hg.): Presuppositions and discourse. Essays offered to Hans Kamp. Bingley, UK: Emerald Group Publishing. S* pages 101–124.

Dale, Robert and Ehud Reiter. 1995. Computational Interpretations of the Gricean Maxims in the Generation of Referring Expressions. *Cognitive Science* 19(2):233–263.

Dobnik, Simon and Robin Cooper. 2017. Interfacing language, spatial perception and cognition in type theory with records. *Journal of Language Modelling* 5(2):273–301.

Ducrot, Oswald. 1988. Topoï et formes topique. *Bulletin d'études de la linguistique française* 22:1–14.

Engelhardt, Paul E, Karl GD Bailey, and Fernanda Ferreira. 2006. Do speakers and listeners observe the gricean maxim of quantity? *Journal of memory and language* 54(4):554–573.

Esar, Evan. 1952. *The treasury of humorous quotations*. Phoenix House.

Fernández, Raquel, Jonathan Ginzburg, and Shalom Lappin. 2007. Classifying ellipsis in dialogue: A machine learning approach. *Computational Linguistics* 33(3):397–427.

Frank, Michael C. and Noah D. Goodman. 2012. Predicting pragmatic reasoning in language games. *Science (New York, N.Y.)* 336(6084):998.

Franke, M. 2009. *Signal to Act: Game Theory in Pragmatics*. AmsterdamInstitute for Logic, Language and Computation. ISBN 978-90-5776-202-4.

Franke, Michael. 2013. Game Theoretic Pragmatics. *Philosophy Compass* 8(3):269–284.

Franke, Michael, Tikitu De Jager, and Robert Van Rooij. 2012. Relevance in cooperation and conflict. *Journal of Logic and Computation* 22(1):23–54.

Ginzburg, Jonathan. 2012. *The interactive stance*. Oxford University Press.

Goodman, Noah D. and Michael C. Frank. 2016. Pragmatic Language Interpretation as Probabilistic Inference. *Trends in Cognitive Sciences* 20(11):818–829.

Goodman, Noah D. and Andreas Stuhlmüller. 2013. Knowledge and Implicature: Modeling Language Understanding as Social Cognition. *Topics in Cognitive Science* 5(1):173–184.

Grice, H. P. 1975. Logic and Conversation. In P. Cole, ed., *Speech Acts*, no. 3 in Syntax and Semantics, pages 44–55. New York: Acad. Pr, 5th edn. ISBN 978-0-12-785423-6.

Grove, Julian, Jean-Philippe Bernardy, and Stergios Chatzikyriakidis. 2021. From compositional semantics to Bayesian pragmatics via logical inference. In *Proceedings of the 1st and 2nd Workshops on Natural Logic Meets Machine Learning (NALOMA)*, pages 60–70. Groningen, the Netherlands (online): Association for Computational Linguistics.

Horn, Laurence. 1984. Toward a new taxonomy for pragmatic inference: Q-based and r-based implicature. *Meaning, form, and use in context* 42.

Jäger, Gerhard. 2007. Evolutionary Game Theory and Typology: A Case Study. *Language* 83(1):74–109.

Jäger, Gerhard. 2008. Evolutionary stability conditions for signaling games with costly signals. *Journal of Theoretical Biology* 253(1):131–141.

Jarratt, Susan C. 1998. *Rereading the sophists: Classical rhetoric refigured*. SIU Press.

Kao, Justine T, Roger Levy, and Noah D Goodman. 2013. The funny thing about incongruity: A computational model of humor in puns. In *Proceedings of the Annual Meeting of the Cognitive Science Society*, vol. 35.

Karttunen, Lauri. 1974. Presupposition and linguistic context. *Theoretical linguistics* 1(1):181–194.

Krahmer, Emiel and Kees van Deemter. 2012. Computational Generation of Referring Expressions: A Survey. *Computational Linguistics* 38(1):173–218.

Larsson, Staffan. 2002. *Issue-based dialogue management*. Ph.D. thesis, University of Gothenburg.

Larsson, Staffan and David R Traum. 2000. Information state and dialogue management in the trindi dialogue move engine toolkit. *Natural language engineering* 6(3-4):323–340.

Levinson, Stephen C. 1983. *Pragmatics*. Cambridge University Press.

Levinson, Stephen C. 2000. *Presumptive meanings: The theory of generalized conversational implicature*. MIT Press.

Lewis, David. 1979. Scorekeeping in a language game. *Journal of Philosophical Logic* 8(1):339–359.

Lewis, David K. 1969. *Convention: A Philosophical Study*. Wiley-Blackwell.

Lücking, Andy. 2016. Modeling co-verbal gesture perception in type theory with records. In *Proceedings of the 2016 Federated Conference on Computer Science and Information Systems*, pages 383–392.

Łupkowski, Paweł and Jonathan Ginzburg. 2017. Query responses. *Journal of Language Modelling* 4(2):245–292.

Maraev, Vladislav, Ellen Breitholtz, Christine Howes, Staffan Larsson, and Robin Cooper. 2021. Something old, something new, something borrowed, something taboo: Interaction and creativity in humour. *Frontiers in Psychology* 12:1443.

Parikh, Prashant. 1991. Communication and strategic inference. *Linguistics and Philosophy* 14(5):473–514.

Parikh, Prashant. 1992. A game-theoretical account of implicature. In Y. Vardi, ed., *Proceedings of the 4th Conference on Theoretical Aspects of Rationality and Knowledge*, pages 85–94. Monterey, California.

Parikh, Prashant. 2001. *The Use of Language*. CSLI Lecture Notes. Stanford, Calif: CSLI Publications. ISBN 978-1-57586-354-2 978-1-57586-355-9.

Parikh, Prashant. 2006. Pragmatics and Games of Partial Information. In A. Benz, G. Jäger, and R. van Rooij, eds., *Game Theory and Pragmatics*, Palgrave Studies in Pragmatics, Language and Cognition, pages 101–122. London: Palgrave Macmillan UK. ISBN 978-0-230-28589-7.

Potts, Christopher, Daniel Lassiter, Roger Levy, and Michael C. Frank. 2016. Embedded Implicatures as Pragmatic Inferences under Compositional Lexical Uncertainty. *Journal of Semantics* 33(4):755–802.

Purver, M. 2006. CLARIE: Handling clarification requests in a dialogue system. *Research on Language & Computation* 4(2):259–288.

Qing, Ciyang and Michael Franke. 2015. Variations on a Bayesian Theme: Comparing Bayesian Models of Referential Reasoning. In H. Zeevat and H.-C. Schmitz, eds., *Bayesian Natural Language Semantics and Pragmatics*, Language, Cognition, and Mind, pages 201–220. Cham: Springer International Publishing. ISBN 978-3-319-17064-0.

Raskin, Victor. 1985. *Semantic mechanisms of humor*. Synthese language library, 24. Dordrecht: Reidel. ISBN 9027718210.

Ritchie, Graeme. 2018. *The Comprehension of Jokes: A Cognitive Science Framework*. Routledge.

Roberts, Craige. 2012. Information structure: Towards an integrated formal theory of pragmatics. *Semantics and Pragmatics* 5:6–1.

Scontras, Gregory, Tessler Michael Henry, and Michael Franke. 2018. Probabilistic language understanding: An Introduction to the Rational Speech Act Framework. https://www.problang.org/.

Scontras, Gregory, Michael Henry Tessler, and Michael Franke. 2021. A practical introduction to the Rational Speech Act modeling framework. *arXiv:2105.09867 [cs]* .

Spence, Michael. 1973. Job Market Signaling. *The Quarterly Journal of Economics* 87(3):355–374.

Sperber, D. and D. Wilson. 1995. *Relevance: Communication and cognition*. Blackwell, 2nd edn.

Stalnaker. 1974. Pragmatic presuppositions. In M. K. Munitz and P. Unger, eds., *Semantics and Philosophy*. New York University Press.

Strawson, Peter F. 1950. On referring. *Mind* 59(235):320–344.

Sutton, Peter. 2022. The origins of vagueness. In J.-P. Bernardy, R. Blanck, S. Chatzikyriakidis, S. Lappin, and A. Maskharashvili, eds., *Probabilistic Approaches to Linguistic Theory*. CSLI Publications.

Toulmin, Stephen E. 2003. *The uses of argument*. Cambridge University Press.

van Rooij, Robert. 2004. Signalling Games Select Horn Strategies. *Linguistics and Philosophy* 27(4):493–527.

van Rooij, Robert and Tikitu de Jager. 2012. Explaining Quantity Implicatures. *Journal of Logic, Language and Information* 21(4):461–477.

Verschueren, Jef and Jan Verschueren. 1999. *Understanding pragmatics*. Oxford University Press.

White, Julia, Jesse Mu, and Noah D. Goodman. 2020. Learning to refer informatively by amortizing pragmatic reasoning. *CogSci* .

Young, H. Peyton. 1993. The Evolution of Conventions. *Econometrica* 61(1):57.

Yuan, Arianna, Will Monroe, Yu Bai, and Nate Kushman. 2018. Understanding the Rational Speech Act model. *CogSci* pages 2759–2764.

Zaslavsky, Noga, Jennifer Hu, and Roger Levy. 2021. A Rate–Distortion view of human pragmatic reasoning. *Proceedings of the Society for Computation in Linguistics* 4(1):347–348.

7

Neuro-computation for Language processing

VIDYA SOMASHEKARAPPA

Computational neuroscience uses mathematical models, brain abstractions, and theoretical analysis to understand the principles that are responsible for the development of cognitive abilities, structure, and physiology of the nervous system. Neurolinguistics is the relationship between language, the structure, and function of the nervous system, for instance explaining the link between the brain's language processing systems concerning eye movements. It differentiates the link and the information processing modes that allow us to function and demonstrate our preferences in the way information is processed. The principal modes of processing this information are through auditory, visual, and kinesthetic systems (Gordon and Fleisher, 2011). In this chapter, we examine the experimental analyses of novel data and synthesize new models of biological phenomena.

Biological neural models also known as the *spiking neural models* are mathematical descriptions of the properties of certain cells in the nervous system that generate the electrical potential across their cell membranes, approximately one millisecond in duration called the action potentials or spikes. They were recorded in 1952 for which a Nobel Prize was awarded in 1963 paving the way for early neural modeling. The major information processing units of the nervous system are these spikes that are transmitted along the axon and synapses from the sending neuron to other neurons. Simple mathematical models such as

Probabilistic Approaches to Linguistic Theory.
Jean-Philippe Bernardy, Rasmus Blanck,
Stergios Chatzikyriakidis, Shalom Lappin,
Aleksandre Maskharashvili (eds.).

Hodgkin-Huxley models describe the membrane voltage as a function of the input current and the activation of the ions. It mostly consists of nonlinear differential equations describing the behavior of ion channels that permeate the cell membrane of the squid giant axon (Hodgkin and Huxley, 1952). They are integrate-and-fire models that describe the membrane voltage as a function of the input current and predict spike times without a description of the biophysical processes that shape the time course of an action potential.

The immense complexity of language and its connections with other systems have been studied for over 60 years. Computational representation theories mainly constitute grammar and aspects of language use (Chomsky, 2000). Implementation research, the study of the structure and the function of the brain, comes from neurobiology, on how brain structures and different forms of brain activity develop perception and cognition. In terms of employed methodologies to study the brain i.e., different types of invasive/non-invasive imagining with various dependent variables, the size of the object concatenated where small represents neuron channels, large implies population and areas.

One of the approaches to studying the linguistic link between the brain and language is by analyzing the principles of the language structure of brain-damage-induced language impairments. Based on the approaches used for aphasia therapy, language has an internal organization that can be described by a system of rules. Language representation in the brain is traditionally considered to be in the two centers: anterior and posterior regions (Basso et al., 2013). Decoding and encoding, the two complementary processes, are most commonly used to analyze the representation of information in the human brain. Decoding uses neural activity to predict the stimuli, while encoding uses the stimuli to predict the brain activity.

The neural language models have been a growing trend in computational neuroscience research, most often, using the neural data from individuals, for example, vector representations predicting brain activity during reading, (Bingel et al., 2016) where recorded subjects were reading fiction material: “Harry Potter and the Sorcerer’s Stone” were based within the sentence context for the same purpose. Within context, listening using contextualized word representation (ELMo) contributed to composing of supra-word meaning to capture the compositional meaning of multi-word event/argument structure and expressions (Toneva et al., 2020).

Syntactic surprisal mapped across various languages follows the left lateralization technique of language processing and comprehension consisting of the inferior parietal lobule, middle temporal gyrus, and

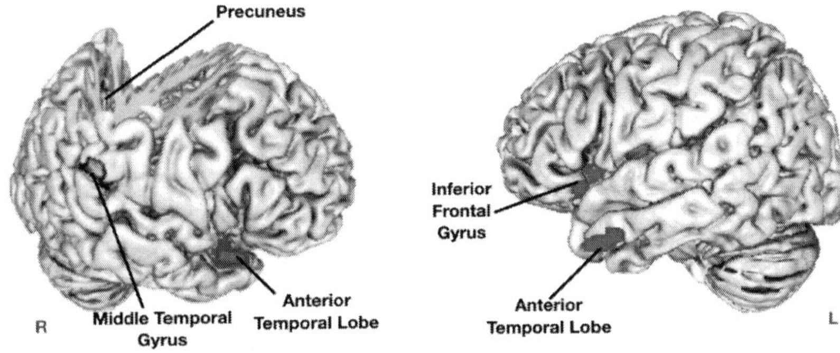

FIGURE 1: Representations of brain regions

inferior frontal gyrus alongside bilateral processing of the anterior temporal lobe (Henderson et al., 2016). Lexical surprisal also left the lateralized network, predominantly consists of the inferior frontal gyrus, Posterior temporal gyrus, interior temporal sulcus, middle frontal gyrus and partly extends to the bilateral regions of the anterior temporal lobe and superior temporal gyrus (see figure 1)(Brennan et al., 2016, Willems et al., 2015, Lopopolo et al., 2018, Shain et al., 2020).

The major amount of brain lateralization research comes from the aphasia clinical investigations that explain anterior regions forming basic syntactic constructions, phonological planning, and organizing word output. While the posterior regions link lexical semantics to world knowledge and deal with lexical access and word meaning. By testing the brain localization hypothesis in normal individuals, evoked response potential experiments have allowed us to bridge the gap to some extent (Watters et al., 1999).

In that case, the neurobiological structures that are part of language could perform operations equivalent in power to finite-state machines; it is plausible for sharp computational restrictions in the neural computation of language. The Turing machine's computational power is required for the computations executed by the brains of simple organisms like ants, in which case even the comparatively 'simple' neural circuitry is capable of computational operations which are as powerful as a Turing machine (Gallistel and King, 2009).

7.1 Cognitive Models

In this section, we enumerate different theories and their relationship to neural language learning. An array of different language and speech phenomena support various models of lexical retrieval. Usually, it is

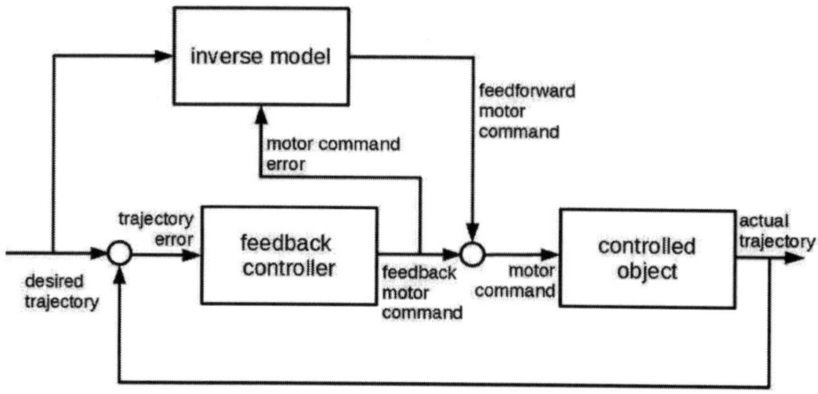

FIGURE 2: A box-and-arrow model of motor control (adapted from Wolpert et al. (1998))

speech errors: although they indicate short malfunctions of the language system, at the same time they provide valuable insight into how this system should function normally. There are numerous types of such errors. Phoneme-level errors can result in a word or non-word form (e.g. "look → cook" vs. "look → mook"), and they give a few insights. For example, we plan things. Morpheme and word errors, word movements, and environmental intrusions do something different. Other phenomena provide insight into how we access lexical knowledge: hesitations, self-monitoring, and pause analysis; the "tip of the tongue" effect (TOT), and the data from reaction time studies (Martin, Laine, 2004).

A boom in cognitive sciences in the 1990s strongly influenced linguists, who concentrated on the cognitive aspects of language models. First advanced models of lexical-retrieval (Martin et al., 1994), use an information-processing framework to describe the language components involved. They are mostly based on two assumptions. Firstly, by equalling the human brain to the computer with 18 processors, storage units, and pathways. Hence, the "box and arrow" view on language organization, where boxes symbolize storage units for phonological, morphological, or semantic word representations and arrows stay for processes between these representations (see figure 2). Secondly, viewing semantical and phonological word components as strictly independent and assuming that processing and retrieval of these two components occur independently. "Box and arrow" models concentrate on language mental representations and processes of encoding and decoding the messages' components.

The basic and important notion was that word meaning and word form is retrieved independently. Fromkin (1971) was the first to develop a functional model, by studying error corpus data and describing several sequential stages of producing a single word. The data from the corpus of naturally occurring speech errors in healthy adults allows the suggestion that a set of linguistic representations have a strong psychological basis.

However, these models with their initial emphasis on the independence of semantic and phonological word form retrieval were challenged by the data. They were based on error word substitution that resulted in real words occurring more often than resulting in non-words. Consequently, word substitutions where the replacement is both phonologically and semantically related to the intended word occurred more frequently. A model with an editor was proposed; this editor is sensitive to either phonetics or semantics and hence is more likely to miss the word which is both semantically and phonologically related to the target one. Box and arrow models' explanatory power weakened with time.

In the work of Vigliocco et al. (2011), an elegant overview of the psychological organization of grammatical categories was given, in line with the described three cognitive models of lexical retrieval. They define three main approaches to verb versus noun categorization depending on when this occurs during processing, whether the knowledge of the grammatical category is required and whether it can be defined for each word independently.

The lexicalist approach suggests that grammatical class information is always available, retrievable, and is specified early at the lexical level of processing. This view is supported by EEG data, which indicates that grammatical categorization occurs very early in sentence comprehension, and by some error corpus data when the grammatical class is almost always preserved in mistakes.

In the next approach, the combinatorial views, it is assumed that grammatical class is not lexically specified but rather retrieved during sentence processing. These theories assume that grammatical class is only relevant for integration processes, so there is no need to store it separately at the word level; grammatical class is prescribed based on the position of the word and the quality of the inflectional and derivational affixation they take. Thus, grammatical class is a result of procedural knowledge.

Finally, the emergentist views assume that grammatical class is not prescribed during lexical or syntactical processing, but rather is derived from a combination of constraints, like known semantic limitations or statistical information on the co-occurrence of various languages units. These psychological models of verb versus noun categorization find some evidence in various neural models of grammatical category organization, which will be described later.

7.2 Neural Models

The classical Wernicke-Lichtheim model includes several regions (wernicke's area, broca's area, parietal-temporal area, auditory cortex) and connections between them and was based on patients' post-mortem data. These regions, according to the model, are responsible for word production. However, further studies as well as the emergence of neuroimaging technologies specified the knowledge on the matter.

Lesion studies provided the first insight into areas associated with naming. If the patient with brain damage in a given area shows a naming deficit, it is implied that the brain has developed some specialization and that the area is somehow involved in the process. These lesion studies report naming being affected. In imaging studies, object and action naming was revealed to be related to vast cortical networks as well as the left inferior frontal gyrus, left dorsal premotor, and bilateral occipitotemporal and parietal areas. In addition, action naming seems to be more demanding on the level of neural processing than object naming: not only cortical sites, traditionally associated with language processing, are involved in the action naming, but motor areas as well.

In the review by Vigliocco and colleagues (Vigliocco et al., 2011), they followed the evolution of neural illustration on words from different grammatical classes. These approaches bear some correspondence to the three cognitive architectures defined in the previous section. The first hypothesis was driven by neuropsychological studies and suggests that verbs and nouns are presented in somewhat separable brain networks. Left temporal areas process nouns, while left inferior frontal areas engage with verbs. That implies that the networks engaging processing words from dissimilar conceptual domains (objects and actions) would further be fractionated to extract the grammatical class of words. This hypothesis follows the lexicalist approach to verb versus noun mental representation.

A second possibility is that it is not nouns and verbs in isolation but rather the morpho-syntactic processes that relate to nouns and verbs that are computed in partially distinct neural networks. For example, it is recommended that left temporal areas are engaged by processes that integrate nouns into phrases, and left inferior and especially middle frontal areas are specifically engaged by processes that integrate verbs into phrases. That means that morpho-syntactic processes that apply to words from these different grammatical classes would be computed by brain networks in near physical proximity to the networks engaged by the semantic content of words. Such a neural model is well-suited with weak lexicalist views and with some of the combinatorial views - those that distinguish syntactic processes related to nouns and verbs, given that we can observe differences between noun and verb processing (and in the corresponding neural systems) only when sentences are produced/comprehended, once semantic correlates and processing demands are controlled.

The final hypothesis assumes no separate networks for neural distinct for verbs and nouns; rather neural distinct is assumed for words denoting actions versus words referring to objects, irrespective of their grammatical class. All the shared networks will be engaged in sentence processing, and the extent to which such a network would be engaged would depend upon the processing complexity and demands of the task or the types of morpho-syntactic processes. This final hypothesis is attained with those combinatorial views that do not assume specialized processes for words from altered grammatical classes and emergentist cognitive architectures.

7.3 Connectionist models

Neurolinguistics has had a considerable account in computational modeling where static and symbolic data structures have been used by the conventional models on which the functions take action to produce linguistic output. The connectionist approach, on the other hand, uses graded-dynamic representations that are refined by a simple structure providing an adequate exposition of higher-order behaviors utilizing distributional networks of simple processing units and they have been used to model primary motor and sensory systems. Hence, through a single framework, they have provided substantial insight into how functional cognitive capacities may arise from neural hardware, even though these models have had success there are significant problems in understanding the link between cognition and the brain. The "neuron-like" element units are still abstract connectionist entities that only approximate real neurons.

Whilst the average firing rate is represented by the activation levels of a small collection of neurons, it is possible that the temporal characteristics of the neuronal spike, encode information and would make a single real activation value insufficient to a model real representation of neurons. Furthermore, the models still show inadequacy in moving incrementally to the computational capacities of symbolic models, specifically, problems in productivity, systematicity and generativity are rather awkwardly handled by connectionist models (Fodor and Pylyshyn, 1988), nevertheless, a binding problem overcome these shortcomings (Mozer et al., 1992, Shastri and Ajjanagadde, 2000).

Local connectionist models, such as LINK (Hendler, 1989; Kruschke, 1992), were developed as the answer to these challenges. Four stages of word processing, similar to Levelt's were conceptual representation, semantic features, lexical, phonological. But rather than being a semi-independent entity, the lexical level here served as a buffer between semantic and phonological features, and one can observe feedforward and feedback connections between these two processes. Access to lexical form is constantly re-evaluated by two-way pathways from phonological and semantical levels of processing. Thus, the word in its lexical form is derived from the context. However, all lexical knowledge about the word is stored on this level of word processing.

Distributed connectionist models (Chen and Peng, 1999) elaborated on how this formation occurred. Interestingly, if the lexical level is lower, it is supposed that all relevant information in this domain is gathered not by access to the lexical representation but rather by the strong influence of semantic context and phonological constraints. Word features and the relations between the semantics, the phonetics, and the final form are rather learned through experience than pre-set. Lexical knowledge about words is determined by the context, and this determination process is flexible with time - the system can learn how to detect the lexical meaning in various surroundings.

7.4 Electrophysiology and Imaging

Electrophysiology recordings report neural activity directly with high temporal precision but are less accurate for neurons with lower activity. Imaging on the other hand can sample neural activity of hundreds of neurons in a local area and can be targeted to specific cell-types. In this section we explore various ways of how the data obtained can be used to improve neural language models.

7.4.1 fMRI

fMRI is a neuroimaging technique that measures the changes in the oxygen level of the blood during brain activity, relying on the coupled cerebral blood flow and neuronal activation that is blood flow increases when the brain area is in activation. It provides 3D scans of the brain with high spacial resolution, and for statistical analysis, the brain scans can be fragmented into voxels (cubes of constant size), and these voxels vary based on the size and shape of the brain along with the precision of the scanner and are usually processed as flattened vectors even though the location can be identified with three-dimensional dimensional coordinates by ignoring the spatial relationship between the voxels. The data requires some statistical filtering, where preprocessing accounts for timing of the scan slices, corrects the motion of the participant's head, and adjusts linear trends in the signal. Aligning is required to group voxels into brain regions of individual scans of various sizes and shape for comparisons across subjects.

Bhattasali and Resnik (2021), identified distinct patterns in neuronal activity for topical surprisal and lexical surprisal by detecting patterns differing neuro-anatomical correlates. These suggest that broad and local contextual cues during sentence processing, recruit different brain areas, and these functionally contribute to the processing of various dimensions of informational contexts during comprehension. These methods have contributed to operationalizing and testing the hypothesis of sentence processing in neurocognitive mechanisms.

The performance of NLP models can increase by leveraging the brain activity, the fMRI data over state-of-the-art unsupervised parts of speech tagging (PoS) enables 4% error reduction (Bingel et al., 2016), besides using the fMRI signals to better understand and evaluate the structure of the computational models of the language. Recently, it's been used for performing pronoun resolution and classifying move annotations (Li et al., 2018, Vodrahalli et al., 2017). The language model BERT performs has been fine-tuned to align with the brain recordings and it performs better at syntactic tasks (subject-verb agreements) and these show a knowledge transfer from human language processing to NLP tasks. Although the improvements are of a smaller magnitude and require verification on other datasets (Mahowald et al., 2022).

7.4.2 EEG and Eye-tracking

The electrical neuronal activity produces currents in the brain spreading through the head. These reach the scalp and as a result, the voltage fluctuations can be recorded as the electroencephalogram (EEG), which reflects electrical brain activity with millisecond temporal resolution.

The eye movements can be tracked non-intrusively using infrared light and a camera using an eye-tracking device. Based on the sampling rate it provides temporal fine-grained recordings of one or both eyes. Based on first-word fixations, the eye gaze can capture lexical access

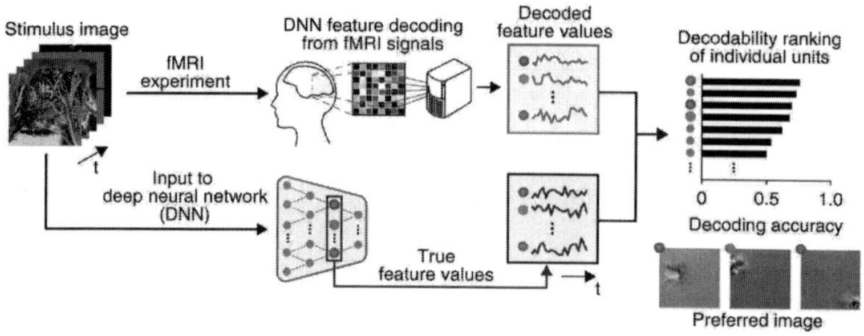

FIGURE 3: Brain Decoding

and early syntactic processing. Later fixations measure the syntactic reprocessing and general disambiguation and these features reflect in words that are fixated multiple times. Rayner (1998), provides a survey of fixation duration as a proxy for cognitive processing established by various eye movement features enabling the study of early and late cognitive textual processing.

EEG and eye-tracking data have been leveraged to improve performance and yield significant results over baseline in sentiment analysis, named entity recognition and relation classification (Hollenstein et al., 2020). Incorporating the eye-tracking data, in NLP, into models by using scan paths can denote the fixation trajectory over a text span, revealing syntactic reanalysis, comprehension problems, and text difficulty

7.4.3 MEG

The neuronal currents also produce magnetic fields that can be measured using a magnetoencephalogram (MEG), capturing better spatial resolution of the electrical brain activity and more informative for semantic categorization. Participants were presented with picture-to-word sequence pairs where the two elements were matching pairs or not. For example, high predictability included a picture of an apple which was followed by the word apple and in the low predictability scenario, a picture of a banana was followed by the word apple. The task was to match the picture to the word described. It was found that the noun prediction modulated the MEG response in the brain especially correlated to the frontotemporal areas which are associated with the lexical categories. They are also in the lower level sensory areas such as the visual cortex (Dikker and Pylkkänen, 2012).

It has been possible to align embeddings from recurrent neural network language model with word by word MEG activity (Wehbe et al., 2014), to compare and interpret word and sequence embeddings.

There are dissociable patterns with phone-level and morphosyntactic predictions related to earlier responses between 100- 400 ms mostly in temporal areas while the lexical-semantic predictions have later responses i.e., greater than 400 ms across a large set of cortical areas (Lopopolo et al).

For predictions regarding word meaning, the neural responses at the level of speech sounds are modulated in a top-down fashion. This states that the predictions not only take place at multiple abstract levels but module each other at the same time. In Heilbron et al. (2021), an EEG and a MEG study, decomposed word predictions from a transformer neural network (GPT-2) to a different level of analysis linguistically. All the above-discussed results, the different linguistic levels, that modulate or co-constrain each other are in accord with the interactive sentence processing (Marslen-Wilson, 1975).

7.5 Semantics

The distinct spatial pattern of the neural activity correlated to pictures viewed of certain semantic categories presented the first computational model that made testable predictions using functional magnetic resonance imaging (fMRI) from concrete nouns (Mitchell et al., 2008). The participants were instructed to think about a concept while measuring the brain signal.

The signal is then averaged for each of the participants for 60 concepts over multiple trials. Imaging data collected during word presentation was then trained using a linear model to predict activity from the word vector, theorizing that the distributional properties of nouns are related to the neural semantic representations in the human brain. Following, subsequent theories explain the prediction tasks from concrete to abstract nouns, text fragmentation, and sentences (Wang et al., 2013, Wehbe et al., 2014, Huth et al., 2016, Sun et al., 2021)

Extensively, word vectors have been used to predict patterns in neuronal activity and evaluate the performance accordingly (Murphy, 2012, Anderson et al., 2017, Abnar et al., 2019, Wang et al., 2020). Recently deep learning models and natural language processing provides an opportunity for distributional representation of words or sentences to encode richer semantic information. Pretrained language models and human language mechanisms explore to capture more information semantics, syntax, and common sense knowledge (Shah et al., 2019, Toneva and Wehbe, 2019, Minnema and Herbelot, 2019).

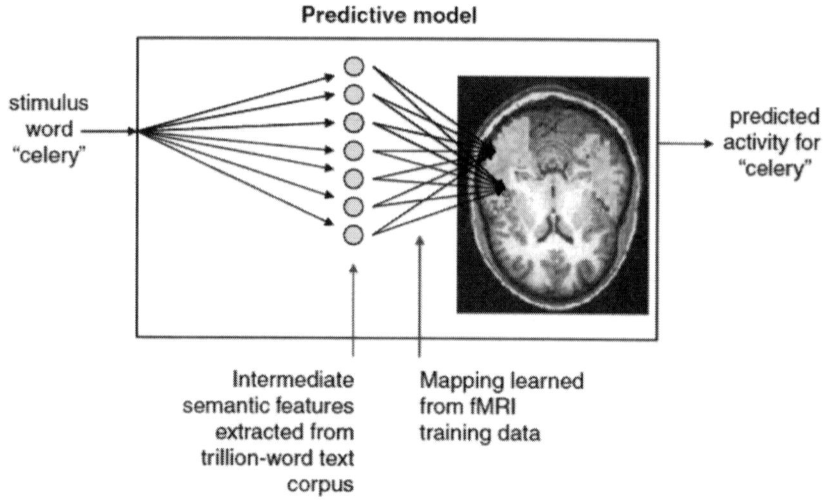

FIGURE 4: Word Stimuli predicting fMRI (Mitchell et al., 2008)

7.6 Mirror Neurons

Embodying neurolinguistics requires brain embedding of multiple mirror systems. Modeling has shown how to analyze the basic macaque-like mechanisms for grasping, and analyze initializing attempts to project this capability to the imitation of single actions (Oztop et al., 2006). By developing models of complex imitation and addressing how complex actions can be structured by the recognition of the sub-goals they serve to achieve, neuroscientists suggest the mirror neuron system as a possible explanation behind the dynamics of emotional contagion (Decety and Ickes, 2011). Investigating whether the hierarchical structures from this process are comparable to those used in language formation, as well as, the transition from praxic imitation to pantomime.

Human-robot interactions similar to human-human interactions congregate information from the facial features, gaze, and gestures during communication. Advanced artificial intelligence and machine learning technologies have changed the nature of consumer interactions by allowing robots to assist with services. Connie, a service robot, was hired as a concierge by Hilton Worldwide, for example, (Gursoy et al., 2019). The Japanese hot spring resort Kinosaki Onsen has adopted an interactive approach. A humanoid robot will speak with tourists in the information center (Krüger et al., 2015). A company situated in Hong Kong has lately made the news, Sophia, the world's first humanoid robot capable of displaying emotions, with nearly 60 different emotions to choose from (Chuah and Yu, 2021). Furthermore, the COVID-19 epidemic is a motivating force behind workplace robotics. Robots have been envisioned by businesses as a way to improve general service and assist in the smooth operation of activities throughout this new period of "normalcy" (Wu et al., 2021).

Customers' negative emotions (such as fear, sadness) during human-robot interactions should not be ignored (Christou and Chatzigeorgiou, 2020), since they may result in unpleasant reactions. However, whether emotional contagion can be exploited in human-robot contact is still an ongoing question. The relevance of expressing emotion in human-robot communication is highlighted by the fact that revealing emotions promote human resemblance and strengthens emotional ties between people and robots (Lopez-Rincon, 2019, Prasad et al., 2020). Customer emotions can help with satisfaction (Yu and Ngan, 2019), value co-creation (Neuhofer et al., 2020), and adoption of new technologies in the context of human-robot services (Fuentes-Moraleda et al., 2020).

There is an issue of action sequencing and, in some situations, encapsulating complex actions. Ferrari et al. (2005) presented data on parietal mirror neurons for grasping that was sorted according to the overall objective (e.g., a mirror neuron for grasping may fire only when the grasp precedes bring-food-to-mouth, not putting-food-in-container, and vice versa), related to the robotic actions discussed earlier. Such discoveries must be integrated, to further, establish neurological mechanisms that promote parallelism between "motor constructions" and linguistic constructs. How do the basal ganglia interact with cortical regions in hierarchical language processing; and to what extent can developmental mechanisms be modeled in sufficient detail to help us better understand what innate mechanisms are required for a brain to be language-ready.

7.7 Multimodal and Multilingual Brain

Multi-modal data are obtained from the real world by humans and conceptual representations are formed within the brain. During the collection of data, subjects can be given text, image, and auditory stimuli at the same time and are also required to think of the properties of these stimuli. In this way, in addition to text-based information, some researchers use multi-modal features of vision and audio to foresee brain activity (Ruan et al., 2016, Bulat et al., 2017).

To build the visual features the common approach is to utilize the deep neural networks such as VGG (Jaderberg et al., 2015) and ResNet (Huth et al., 2016), to extract features from ImageNet that belong to the same class. These features extracted are then averaged across the class of images so that the salient features are retained and the resulting class can be used to correlate with the specific brain activity, similarly the auditory and acoustic features are extracted from real sounds, such as the jingle of bells. Each of these features can be used to predict the specific brain activity, and image/multimodal features provide much better performance.

The majority of NLP research, as well as the majority of available cognitive data sources, is conducted in English. However, it is generally recognized that language processing changes in active brain regions between native and foreign-language speakers (Perani et al., 1996). Furthermore, second language learners read differently than native speakers (Dussias and Piñar, 2010). Although the same general structures are active for both languages, eye-tracking and fMRI research on bilingualism reveal that variances within these generic structures exist between languages and levels of processing (Marian and Spivey, 2003, Dehghani et al., 2017). Cop et al. (2017) propose an English-Dutch eye-tracking corpus suited to examine the multilingual reading process to boost bilingual eye-tracking research.

There are also discrepancies in how dialects and standard variants are processed, according to Lundquist and Vangsnes (2018) for Norwegian dialects and Stocker and Hartmann (2019) for German variations. As a result, not only is it critical to account for these differences in human language processing using NLP methods, but it is also critical to account for language-specific characteristics in NLP approaches. There is still a lack of research on how many of the findings would translate to other languages.

7.8 Challenges and Limitations

The most commonly used brain activity data are from fMRI, EEG, MEG, and eye-tracking, while each has its advantages and disadvantages. We face various issues concerning modeling decisions to use cognitive inputs to improve computational models. In this section, we discuss the benefits and drawbacks of each type of brain signal recording, the factors to consider when selecting a dataset, and the features that may be derived from the data. Finally, how they could be incorporated into machine learning models and their assessments in choosing the type of signal and dataset accordingly. The linguistic level based on which the signals are considered when selecting a form of the cognitive signal varies from word level to phrase or sentence to the discourse level. A proper preprocessing is essential while using multiple datasets recordings from a similar modality. To extract word-level signals in a continuous stimulus, MEG or eye-tracking data is appropriate compared to hemodynamic lag and low temporal resolution in fMRI.

Humans create conceptual representations based on their own experiences. As a result, different people's brains respond to the same concept in various ways (igloos may never have existed in the tropics, for example, an Indonesian person living in java). These disparities in experiences have resulted in significant differences across participants in the same trial. The wide variation in performance among subjects can be seen (Gauthier and Levy, 2019, Hilgard et al., 2021).

Eye-tracking has numerous advantages as an indirect metric for reducing cognitive workload at different stages of reading and comprehension processing. It gives extensive temporal information ranging from millisecond-accurate eye movements and has been a great tool to leverage various NLP tasks at different processing levels. While the precision and recall are trivial, are consistent across tasks. Eye-tracking for NLP has a large corpus of psycholinguistic research, a variety of recognized metrics, and the intuitive link from features to words.

Another recording technology with a high temporal resolution is electroencephalography (i.e. multiple samples per second). However, because the electrodes record electrical activity at the brain's surface - through the bone – it's impossible to pinpoint exactly where the signal is coming from. EEG signals are routinely used in brain-computer interfaces for classification, for example, classifying text difficulty for voice recognition (Chen et al., 2019), but they are infrequently used to improve NLP tasks (Hollenstein et al., 2019). Furthermore, there are many unanswered concerns about EEG yet which features are most appropriate, but there aren't enough EEG data from naturalistic reading accessible. MEG, on the other hand, provides superior temporal and spatial resolution, making it ideal for NLP. Unfortunately, there are limited MEG datasets from naturalistic investigations available.

Despite this, there are certain similarities in the way subjects represent concepts. In some research (Gu et al., 2021), data from numerous subjects are used to train the model, which is subsequently applied to fresh subjects. The findings revealed that the model might decode the brain activity of an unknown individual to a degree. However, as the number of training subjects grows, performance will not always improve. Learning the universality of brain activity across subjects is unavoidable, and future research can go in two ways to find breakthroughs. To begin, employing adversarial training to learn the commonalities between distinct distributions, assuming that the brain activity of subjects is represented by distinct distributions. Secondly, taking into consideration the idea of pre-training in NLP and computer vision and applying it to situations. Using data from numerous subjects to train a model, then using new subject data to fine-tune the pre-trained model. In this sense, the model preserves the similarity of most themes while also reflecting their differences.

A pure linear transformation is used in the majority of brain activity decoding investigations. "It is conceivable that some grammatical information — among other aspects of the input — is maintained in the fMRI signal but not legible by a linear decoder," Gauthier and Levy (2019) quoted. To decode concrete nouns, Cao and Zhang (2019) employed a three-layer neural network, which performed better than linear regression. However, this could be because neural networks in general can fit data better. This cannot be explained as a result of the nonlinear nature of human notion representation.

The most fundamental issue is that the existing studies do not fully reveal the neurological mechanism of human language processing. As an example, consider computer vision, the neurological mechanics of human visual pathways are currently being investigated, and we can duplicate visual pathways to develop visual networks. The convolution region of the most traditional neural network CNN, for example, mimics the human visual systems' receptive field. However, because we know so little about the neurological mechanisms involved in language processing, it's challenging to employ neural networks to model human brain language processing directly. The most extensively used NLP neural networks RNN (Hochreiter and Schmidhuber, 1997), and Transformers (Vaswani et al., 2017) replicate human behavior that is, eye movement rather than neural activity in reading phrases. In general, the network in computer vision is closer to the human visual system, whereas the model in natural language processing (NLP) is temporarily focused on emulating human reading behavior. This could explain why the field of computer vision research is progressing so quickly.

7.9 Ethics

Ethical issues that occur when using human language processing signals in NLP are crucial for discussion. As researchers in the field, largely rely on existing datasets compiled by psychologists, first and foremost, it requires an emphasis on the importance of thinking about the high-level ramifications of the research work. Examining the ramifications of the interplay between humans and computers, between what can be recorded from a human brain and what can be retrieved from those signals, is exceedingly important. What potential do the generated results have? What is the ultimate goal of the application? What effect does this have on people and society?

Secondly, it is critical to remember that researchers have a responsibility to protect individuals (Šuster et al., 2017) and all of the data gathered from people who were willing to volunteer their brain activity for scientific purposes. As a result, both the participants and their data should be handled with respect, even if we are using provided data rather than recording it ourselves as NLP practitioners. Although the data is anonymized after recording, it is necessary to avoid the possibility of inferring individual participants from the models.

Finally, the data's origins and any biases within them should be taken into account. The majority of psychological studies rely on research participants who are western, educated, industrialized, wealthy, and democratic (so-called WEIRD)(Henrich et al., 2010). Because it was assumed that human nature is universal, that conclusions from this group would apply to all other populations, psychological data were highly skewed. Exclusion or demographic misrepresentation can have serious implications, which cannot be overlooked (Hovy and Spruit, 2016). Caliskan et al. (2017) went a step further, demonstrating that text corpora include recoverable and accurate traces of our historical biases and have found that these biases may be retrieved from text and are also reflected in eye movements and brain activity recordings (Herlitz and Lovén, 2013, Fabi and Leuthold, 2018).

As a result, it's critical to note that these biases – participant sampling as well as experimental biases – are spread throughout multiple trials as a result of extensive reuse of the same corpora, and researchers should be cautious in their interpretation of the results.

References

Abnar, Samira, Lisa Beinborn, Rochelle Choenni, and Willem Zuidema. 2019. Blackbox meets blackbox: Representational similarity and stability analysis of neural language models and brains. *arXiv preprint arXiv:1906.01539* .

Anderson, Andrew James, Jeffrey R Binder, Leonardo Fernandino, Colin J Humphries, Lisa L Conant, Mario Aguilar, Xixi Wang, Donias Doko, and Rajeev DS Raizada. 2017. Predicting neural activity patterns associated with sentences using a neurobiologically motivated model of semantic representation. *Cerebral Cortex* 27(9):4379–4395.

Basso, Anna, Margaret Forbes, and François Boller. 2013. Rehabilitation of aphasia. *Handbook of clinical neurology / edited by P.J. Vinken and G.W. Bruyn* 110:325–34.

Bhattasali, Shohini and Ps Resnik. 2021. Using surprisal and fmri to map the neural bases of broad and local contextual prediction during natural language comprehension. In *Findings of the Association for Computational Linguistics: ACL/IJCNLP 2021, Online Event, August 1-6, 2021*, pages 3786–3798.

Bingel, Joachim, Maria Barrett, and Anders Søgaard. 2016. Extracting token-level signals of syntactic processing from fmri - with an application to pos induction. In *Proceedings of the 54th Annual Meeting of the Association for Computational Linguistics, ACL 2016, August 7-12, 2016, Berlin, Germany, Volume 1: Long Papers*, pages 747–755.

Brennan, Nicole, Kyung Peck, and Andrei Holodny. 2016. Language mapping using fmri and direct cortical stimulation for brain tumor surgery: The good, the bad, and the questionable. *Topics in magnetic resonance imaging : TMRI* 25:1–10.

Bulat, Luana, Stephen Clark, and Ekaterina Shutova. 2017. Speaking, seeing, understanding: Correlating semantic models with conceptual representation in the brain. In *Proceedings of the 2017 Conference on Empirical Methods in Natural Language Processing*, pages 1081–1091.

Caliskan, Aylin, Joanna J Bryson, and Arvind Narayanan. 2017. Semantics derived automatically from language corpora contain human-like biases. *Science* 356(6334):183–186.

Cao, Lu and Yue Zhang. 2019. Investigating lexical and semantic cognition by using neural network to encode and decode brain imaging. In *International Workshop on Human Brain and Artificial Intelligence*, pages 84–100. Springer.

Chen, Chyi-Tsong and Shih-Tein Peng. 1999. Intelligent process control using neural fuzzy techniques. *Journal of Process Control* 9:493–503.

Chen, Xiaogang, Bing Zhao, Yijun Wang, and Xiaorong Gao. 2019. Combination of high-frequency ssvep-based bci and computer vision for controlling a robotic arm. *Journal of neural engineering* 16(2):026012.

Chomsky, Noam. 2000. New horizons in the study of language and mind. *New Horizons in the Study of Language and Mind.* .

Christou, Evangelos and Chryssoula Chatzigeorgiou. 2020. Adoption of social media as distribution channels in tourism marketing: A qualitative analysis of consumers' experiences. *Journal of Tourism, Heritage & Services Marketing (JTHSM)* 6(1):25–32.

Chuah, Stephanie Hui-Wen and Joanne Yu. 2021. The future of service: The power of emotion in human-robot interaction. *Journal of Retailing and Consumer Services* 61:102551.

Cop, Uschi, Nicolas Dirix, Denis Drieghe, and Wouter Duyck. 2017. Presenting geco: An eyetracking corpus of monolingual and bilingual sentence reading. *Behavior research methods* 49(2):602–615.

Decety, Jean and William Ickes. 2011. *The social neuroscience of empathy.* Mit press.

Dehghani, Mostafa, Hamed Zamani, Aliaksei Severyn, Jaap Kamps, and W Bruce Croft. 2017. Neural ranking models with weak supervision. In *Proceedings of the 40th International ACM SIGIR Conference on Research and Development in Information Retrieval*, pages 65–74.

Dikker, Suzanne and Liina Pylkkänen. 2012. Predicting language: Meg evidence for lexical preactivation. *Brain and language* 127.

Dussias, Paola and Pilar Piñar. 2010. Effects of reading span and plausibility in the reanalysis of wh-gaps by chinese-english l2 speakers. *Second Language Research* 26.

Fabi, Sarah and Hartmut Leuthold. 2018. Racial bias in empathy: Do we process dark-and fair-colored hands in pain differently? an eeg study. *Neuropsychologia* 114:143–157.

Ferrari, Pier Francesco, Stefano Rozzi, and Leonardo Fogassi. 2005. Mirror neurons responding to observation of actions made with tools in monkey ventral premotor cortex. *Journal of cognitive neuroscience* 17(2):212–226.

Fodor, Jerry and Zenon Pylyshyn. 1988. Connectionism and cognitive architecture: A critical analysis. *Cognition* 28:3–71.

Fromkin, Victoria A. 1971. The non-anomalous nature of anomalous utterances. *Language* pages 27–52.

Fuentes-Moraleda, Laura, Patricia Diaz-Perez, Alicia Orea-Giner, Ana Munoz-Mazon, and Teresa Villace-Molinero. 2020. Interaction between hotel service robots and humans: A hotel-specific service robot acceptance model (sram). *Tourism Management Perspectives* 36:100751.

Gallistel, Charles and Adam King. 2009. *Memory and the Computational Brain: Why Cognitive Science Will Transform Neuroscience.* ISBN 9781405122870.

Gauthier, Jon and Roger Levy. 2019. Linking artificial and human neural representations of language. *arXiv preprint arXiv:1910.01244* .

Gordon, Nathan and William Fleisher. 2011. *Effective Interviewing and Interrogation Techniques*. Academic Press. ISBN 0123819865.

Gu, Xiaotong, Zehong Cao, Alireza Jolfaei, Peng Xu, Dongrui Wu, Tzyy-Ping Jung, and Chin-Teng Lin. 2021. Eeg-based brain-computer interfaces (bcis): A survey of recent studies on signal sensing technologies and computational intelligence approaches and their applications. *IEEE/ACM transactions on computational biology and bioinformatics* .

Gursoy, Dogan, Oscar Hengxuan Chi, Lu Lu, and Robin Nunkoo. 2019. Consumers acceptance of artificially intelligent (ai) device use in service delivery. *International Journal of Information Management* 49:157–169.

Heilbron, Micha, Kristijan Armeni, Jan-Mathijs Schoffelen, Peter Hagoort, and Floris P de Lange. 2021. A hierarchy of linguistic predictions during natural language comprehension. *bioRxiv* pages 2020–12.

Henderson, John, Wonil Choi, Matthew Lowder, and Fernanda Ferreira. 2016. Language structure in the brain: A fixation-related fmri study of syntactic surprisal in reading. *NeuroImage* 132.

Henrich, Joseph, Steven J Heine, and Ara Norenzayan. 2010. Most people are not weird. *Nature* 466(7302):29–29.

Herlitz, Agneta and Johanna Lovén. 2013. Sex differences and the own-gender bias in face recognition: A meta-analytic review. *Visual Cognition* 21(9-10):1306–1336.

Hilgard, Sophie, Nir Rosenfeld, Mahzarin R Banaji, Jack Cao, and David Parkes. 2021. Learning representations by humans, for humans. In *International Conference on Machine Learning*, pages 4227–4238. PMLR.

Hochreiter, Sepp and Jürgen Schmidhuber. 1997. Long short-term memory. *Neural computation* 9(8):1735–1780.

Hodgkin, A.L. and A.F. Huxley. 1952. A quantitative description of membrane current and its application to conduction and excitation in nerve. *The Journal of physiology* 117:500–44.

Hollenstein, Nora, Maria Barrett, and Lisa Beinborn. 2020. Towards best practices for leveraging human language processing signals for natural language processing. In *Proceedings of the Second Workshop on Linguistic and Neurocognitive Resources*, pages 15–27. Marseille, France: European Language Resources Association. ISBN 979-10-95546-52-8.

Hollenstein, Nora, Antonio de la Torre, Nicolas Langer, and Ce Zhang. 2019. Cognival: A framework for cognitive word embedding evaluation. *arXiv preprint arXiv:1909.09001* .

Horikawa, Tomoyasu, Shuntaro C Aoki, Mitsuaki Tsukamoto, and Yukiyasu Kamitani. 2019. Characterization of deep neural network features by decodability from human brain activity. In *Scientific data*, 6(1): 1–12.

Hovy, Dirk and Shannon L Spruit. 2016. The social impact of natural language processing. In *Proceedings of the 54th Annual Meeting of the Association for Computational Linguistics (Volume 2: Short Papers)*, pages 591–598.

Huth, Alexander G, Wendy A De Heer, Thomas L Griffiths, Frédéric E Theunissen, and Jack L Gallant. 2016. Natural speech reveals the semantic maps that tile human cerebral cortex. *Nature* 532(7600):453–458.

Jaderberg, Max, Karen Simonyan, Andrew Zisserman, et al. 2015. Spatial transformer networks. *Advances in neural information processing systems* 28:2017–2025.

Krüger, Julia, Mathias Wahl, and Jörg Frommer. 2015. Making the system a relational partner: users' ascriptions in individualization-focused interactions with companion-systems. *interaction* 5:6.

Li, Jixing, Murielle Fabre, Wen-Ming Luh, and John Hale. 2018. The role of syntax during pronoun resolution: Evidence from fmri. In *Proceedings of the Eight Workshop on Cognitive Aspects of Computational Language Learning and Processing*, pages 56–64.

Lopez-Rincon, Alejandro. 2019. Emotion recognition using facial expressions in children using the nao robot. In *2019 International Conference on Electronics, Communications and Computers (CONIELECOMP)*, pages 146–153. IEEE.

Lopopolo, Alessandro, Stefan Frank, Antal Van den Bosch, Annabel Nijhof, and Roel Willems. 2018. The narrative brain dataset (nbd), an fmri dataset for the study of natural language processing in the brain. In *Proceedings of LREC 2018*.

Lundquist, Björn and Øystein A Vangsnes. 2018. Language separation in bidialectal speakers: Evidence from eye tracking. *Frontiers in psychology* 9:1394.

Mahowald, Kyle, Evgeniia Diachek, Edward Gibson, Evelina Fedorenko, and Richard Futrell. 2022. Grammatical cues are largely, but not completely, redundant with word meanings in natural language. *CoRR* .

Marian, Viorica and Michael Spivey. 2003. Competing activation in bilingual language processing: Within-and between-language competition. *Bilingualism: Language and cognition* 6(2):97–115.

Marslen-Wilson, William D. 1975. Sentence perception as an interactive parallel process. *Science* 189(4198):226–228.

Martin, Nadine, G.S. Dell, E.M. Saffran, and Myrna Schwartz. 1994. Origins of paraphasias in deep dysphasia: Testing the consequences of a decay impairment to an interactive spreading activation model of lexical retrieval. *Brain and language* 47:609–60.

Minnema, Gosse and Aurélie Herbelot. 2019. From brain space to distributional space: The perilous journeys of fMRI decoding. In *Proceedings of the 57th Annual Meeting of the Association for Computational Linguistics: Student Research Workshop*, pages 155–161. Florence, Italy: Association for Computational Linguistics.

Mitchell, Tom M, Svetlana V Shinkareva, Andrew Carlson, Kai-Min Chang, Vicente L Malave, Robert A Mason, and Marcel Adam Just. 2008. Predicting human brain activity associated with the meanings of nouns. *science* 320(5880):1191–1195.

Mozer, Michael C., Richard S. Zemel, Marlene Behrmann, and Christopher K. I. Williams. 1992. Learning to segment images using dynamic feature binding. *Neural Computation* 4(5):650–665.

Murphy, Kevin P. 2012. *Machine learning: a probabilistic perspective*. MIT press.

Neuhofer, Barbara, Bianca Magnus, and Krzysztof Celuch. 2020. The impact of artificial intelligence on event experiences: a scenario technique approach. *Electronic Markets* pages 1–17.

Oztop, Erhan, Mitsuo Kawato, and Michael Arbib. 2006. Mirror neurons and imitation: A computationally guided review. *Neural networks* 19(3):254–271.

Perani, Daniela, Stanislas Dehaene, Franco Grassi, Laurent Cohen, Stefano F Cappa, Emmanuel Dupoux, Ferruccio Fazio, and Jacques Mehler. 1996. Brain processing of native and foreign languages. *NeuroReport-International Journal for Rapid Communications of Research in Neuroscience* 7(15):2439–2444.

Prasad, Vignesh, Ruth Stock-Homburg, and Jan Peters. 2020. Advances in human-robot handshaking. In *International Conference on Social Robotics*, pages 478–489. Springer.

Rayner, Keith. 1998. Eye movements in reading and information processing: 20 years of research. *Psychological bulletin* 124:372–422.

Ruan, Qingwei, Grazia D'Onofrio, Daniele Sancarlo, Zhijun Bao, Antonio Greco, and Zhuowei Yu. 2016. Potential neuroimaging biomarkers of pathologic brain changes in mild cognitive impairment and alzheimer's disease: a systematic review. *BMC geriatrics* 16(1):1–9.

Shah, Deven, H Andrew Schwartz, and Dirk Hovy. 2019. Predictive biases in natural language processing models: A conceptual framework and overview. *arXiv preprint arXiv:1912.11078* .

Shain, Cory, Idan Blank, Marten Schijndel, William Schuler, and Evelina Fedorenko. 2020. fmri reveals language-specific predictive coding during naturalistic sentence comprehension. *Neuropsychologia* 138.

Shastri, Lokendra and Venkat Ajjanagadde. 2000. From simple associations to systemic reasoning: A connectionist representation of rules, variables and dynamic bindings. *Behavioral and Brain Sciences* 16.

Stocker, Kurt and Matthias Hartmann. 2019. "next wednesday's meeting has been moved forward two days": The time-perspective question is ambiguous in swiss german, but not in standard german. *Swiss journal of psychology* 78(1-2):61.

Sun, Jianwei, Zhiyuan Tang, Hengxin Yin, Wei Wang, Xi Zhao, Shuaijiang Zhao, Xiaoning Lei, Wei Zou, and Xiangang Li. 2021. Semantic data augmentation for end-to-end mandarin speech recognition. *arXiv preprint arXiv:2104.12521* .

Šuster, Simon, Stéphan Tulkens, and Walter Daelemans. 2017. A short review of ethical challenges in clinical natural language processing. *arXiv preprint arXiv:1703.10090* .

Toneva, Mariya, Tom Mitchell, and Leila Wehbe. 2020. Combining computational controls with natural text reveals new aspects of meaning composition.

Toneva, Mariya and Leila Wehbe. 2019. Interpreting and improving natural-language processing (in machines) with natural language-processing (in the brain). *arXiv preprint arXiv:1905.11833* .

Vaswani, Ashish, Noam Shazeer, Niki Parmar, Jakob Uszkoreit, Llion Jones, Aidan N Gomez, Łukasz Kaiser, and Illia Polosukhin. 2017. Attention is all you need. In *Advances in neural information processing systems*, pages 5998–6008.

Vigliocco, Gabriella, David P Vinson, Judit Druks, Horacio Barber, and Stefano F Cappa. 2011. Nouns and verbs in the brain: a review of behavioural, electrophysiological, neuropsychological and imaging studies. *Neuroscience & Biobehavioral Reviews* 35(3):407–426.

Vodrahalli, Kiran, Po Hsuan Chen, Yingyu Liang, Christopher Baldassano, Janice Chen, Esther Yong, Christopher Honey, Uri Hasson, Peter Ramadge, Kenneth Norman, and Sanjeev Arora. 2017. Mapping between fmri responses to movies and their natural language annotations. *NeuroImage* 180.

Wang, Lin, Zude Zhu, Marcel Bastiaansen, Peter Hagoort, and Yufang Yang. 2013. Recognizing the emotional valence of names: An erp study. *Brain and Language* 125(1):118–127.

Wang, Zhonghao, Mo Yu, Yunchao Wei, Rogerio Feris, Jinjun Xiong, Wen-mei Hwu, Thomas S Huang, and Honghui Shi. 2020. Differential treatment for stuff and things: A simple unsupervised domain adaptation method for semantic segmentation. In *Proceedings of the IEEE/CVF Conference on Computer Vision and Pattern Recognition*, pages 12635–12644.

Watters, Paul, Brigitte Stemmer, and Harry Whitaker. 1999. Handbook of neurolinguistics. *Language* 75:621.

Wehbe, Leila, Brian Murphy, Partha Talukdar, Alona Fyshe, Aaditya Ramdas, and Tom Mitchell. 2014. Simultaneously uncovering the patterns of brain regions involved in different story reading subprocesses. *PloS one* 9:e112575.

Willems, Roel, Stefan Frank, Annabel Nijhof, Peter Hagoort, and Antal Van den Bosch. 2015. Prediction during natural language comprehension. *Cerebral cortex (New York, N.Y. : 1991)* 26.

Wolpert, Daniel, R Christopher Miall, and Mitsuo Kawato. 1998. Internal models in the cerebellum. *Trends in cognitive sciences* 2:338–47.

Wu, Laurie, Alei Fan, Yang Yang, and Zeya He. 2021. Robotic involvement in the service encounter: a value-centric experience framework and empirical validation. *Journal of Service Management* .

Yu, Chung-En and Henrique F Boyol Ngan. 2019. The power of head tilts: gender and cultural differences of perceived human vs human-like robot smile in service. *Tourism Review* .

8

Learning Language Games Probabilistically: From Crying to Compositionality

ROBIN COOPER, JONATHAN GINZBURG AND STAFFAN LARSSON

8.1 Introduction

There's a picture of Cassandra, ten days old, interacting with her older brother, Dominic. Elisabet thought she was smiling at him, but Anna, Cassandra's mother, who was there at the time, thinks that she was aiming for Dominic's nose, thinking that it would be a source of nourishment. You cannot be sure, of course, and you can only interpret such events with a certain probability. In this chapter we argue that probability estimation is not only important for the interpretation of young children's actions but also that context dependence and probability estimation is central for the child herself during the emergence of communicative ability.

A theory of language acquisition aims at explaining how children come to speak a natural language, typically the one spoken by their caregivers (with interesting exceptions to this e.g., when deaf children have non–signing caregivers as documented by Rowe and Goldin-Meadow, 2009.) The focus of such efforts is on the period when the child starts producing or comprehending adult-like utterances, with success correlated with reaching the correct final state ('adult grammar')

Probabilistic Approaches to Linguistic Theory.
Jean-Philippe Bernardy, Rasmus Blanck,
Stergios Chatzikyriakidis, Shalom Lappin,
Aleksandre Maskharashvili (eds.).

and mirroring word and construction learning trajectories. Different paradigms with much insightful work have emerged: pure grammar induction work such as Clark and Eyraud (2006) has refuted *poverty of stimulus* arguments by showing that the syntax of constructions such as polar interrogatives can be learned entirely based on distributional evidence, without biases. Much attention has been provided to word learning using cross-situational word learning (Siskind, 1996, Yu and Siskind, 2013) and Bayesian approaches (Bohn et al., 2021). Abend et al. (2017) offer an interesting recent development—simultaneous learning of words and syntax using just statistical learning on strings paired with logical forms.

The perspective we provide here is different in several key ways: first, in contrast to the lion's share of formal work on acquisition, we focus on the fact that interaction between child and caregiver is a key component of the process. The learning mechanism we appeal to incorporates interaction in an intrinsic way.[1] Second, we aim at modelling the child's communicative *acts* from its earliest stages including productions that do not resemble adult utterance types through to the two word stage. Abend et al. (2017) argue correctly that generalizing beyond the input is a key requirement for accounts of language acquisition. In some of the phenomena we deal with here the child's output is significantly different from the input; we argue that the account we offer extends to later stages in acquisition.

Our perspective will also be different with respect to the type of model we offer. We will provide snapshots of stages in the emergence of the adult linguistic sign system. Each stage will be described (and partially formalized) in terms of language games, i.e., recurring patterns in linguistic interaction. We suggest that the gradual development of the ability to participate in increasingly complex language games encompasses development along three different tiers – from signals to signs, from simple emotional states to information states, and from reflex actions to information state updates.

Firstly, going from signals to signs. The infant is able to perceive its surroundings, and also to produce verbal signals, e.g. crying. Later, they might start keeping track of different speakers; at some point,

[1] The importance of interaction is sometimes downplayed by noting that there are societies in which children are rarely addressed directly until they are about four years old, for instance in Samoa (Ochs, 1982). In fact, according to Ochs, Samoan children do acquire their language via interaction, though typically in a multi–party environment where older siblings play an important role and mothers a less direct role than in Anglo–American middle class settings. As Lieven (1994) notes, the developmental trajectory in such cases involving multi-party, decreased maternal interaction is quite different.

they start associating (verbal) sounds with specific referents; at later stages still, they might associate certain utterance forms with questions, etc.. Secondly, we model a development from simple internal states (such as joy or discomfort), via simple judgements and expectations, to increasingly complex structures resembling information states. Thirdly, we describe a development from reflex actions, via action rules that license actions (including verbal action) on internal states or shared dialogue states, to action rules that begin to resemble information state updates that can be used to model practical and abstract reasoning and dialogue management.

Our proposed model will sometimes have a slightly speculative character, possibly under-determined by (but as far as we can tell consistent with) current empirical evidence. The model we put forward here is thus a tentative, though relatively broad proposal concerning how the adult linguistic sign system might emerge. Also, insofar as specific parts of our model were to be empirically disproved, we nevertheless hope that the *type* of model we offer could generate competing proposals formulated in the same broad framework encompassing probabilistic reasoning, interaction, language games, action rules and information states.

This chapter is structured as follows: In Section 8.2 we provide a very brief overview of the state of the art of research on children's prelinguistic and early linguistic actions as well as type theory based approaches to the perception and interpretation of action. In Section 8.3 we will discuss the nature of the uncertainties involved in adult communication with children in the early stages of language acquisition and indicate how this can be modelled using a type-theoretic apparatus. In Section 8.4 we show how this apparatus can be employed in the development of action rules that explain how children can progress from non-linguistic to linguistic interaction. Finally, in Section 8.5 we draw some conclusions.

8.2 Overview of the state of the art

In this section we will give an overview of previous work on early communicative ability in children (8.2.1) and the use of type theory to analyze the perception and interpretation of action (including linguistic action) (in 8.2.2)

8.2.1 Early communicative ability

We distinguish the following key stages in the development of interaction.

1. **Crying Stage**: from birth children use crying as a signal understood by adults to communicate anguish, anger, and care-seeking (Cecchini et al., 2010).
2. **Smiling/laughing Stage**: at 6-8 weeks, infants begin exchanging smiles with their caregivers; frequently these smiles are Duchenne smiles, assumed to encode genuine pleasure and affiliation (Fogel et al., 1997). At 10-17 weeks infants begin to laugh; a majority of these laughs are isolated (i.e., initiated by the child); some can be viewed as an expression of increased arousal of pleasure or amusement (Nwokah et al., 1994), and the latter indicates that the infant already has a notion of incongruity (Ginzburg et al., 2020).
3. **Pointing Stage**: from around 8 months, the child begins to show shared attention of objects, manifested by pointing (Tomasello, 2003, Rowe and Goldin-Meadow, 2009).
4. **Vocal communication**: by six months, there is evidence that children associate words with appropriate situations at above chance level and associate closely related words (Bergelson and Aslin, 2017). From about 9 months, a child begins to possess a phonologically stable repertory of vocalisations with consistent meanings (Halliday, 1975).
5. **One word stage**: from around 11 months, the child begins to make utterances of adult spoken language words whose median length is about one (the 'one word stage'); These can communicate answers to questions, labels for objects in the visual field, and requests. (Dore, 1975, Ninio, 1992, Moradlou, 2019).
6. **Two word stage**: from around 15 months, the length of the child's utterance crosses the 2 word threshold; (Berk and Lillo-Martin, 2012, Bloom, 1968). Utterances can now involve entities that are not in the immediate context and questions begin to be posed (Stritzinger, 2021).

8.2.2 Types and the interpretation of action

A central notion of type theories which follow in the footsteps of Martin-Löf type theory (Martin-Löf, 1984, Nordström et al., 1990) is that of a judgement that an object a is of type T, in symbols, $a : T$. In TTR, a Type Theory with Records (Cooper, 2012, Cooper and Ginzburg, 2015, Cooper, forthc) it is made explicit that such judgements can be related to perception. The perception of a situation involves classifying it as being of a certain type. One kind of situation type in TTR is known as a *ptype*, that is, a type constructed from a predicate and appropriate arguments. For example, if s is a situation where individual

a hugs another individual b, then we say that s is of the type 'hug(a,b)', that is, s : hug(a, b). Thus an agent who perceives s as a situation in which a hugs b makes this type judgement. We think of these types as corresponding to what Gibson (1979) would call *invariants.* This means that the type 'hug(a,b)' corresponds to whatever it is that situations where a hugs b have in common. Thus types are part of the world in whatever sense commonalities (invariants) between different situations are part of the world. Is there a sense in which types are in the heads of agents which perceive a situation to be of a certain type? If an agent is *attuned* (using Gibson's terminology) to a type there must be some pattern of neural activation corresponding to the type which takes place in the agent's brain since it is presumably not by magic that an agent is able to distinguish different types of situations. Thus there is a sense in which a type to which an agent has access as a cognitive resource (that is, is attuned to) is present (or at least represented) in the agent's brain. When we say that an agent makes a judgement that a situation is of a certain type we mean to leave it open whether this is a conscious judgement or not. We mean only that the perception of the situation involves the brain activation corresponding to the type. There may, or may not, be an additional conscious experience of having made an inference that the observed situation is of that type. We think that both cases occur but we do not distinguish between them.

Ptypes give us types of situations involving particular individuals. Thus, given two individuals a and b, the type 'hug(a,b)' is the type of situations in which a hugs b. In addition we need more general types than this, for example, the type of situations where somebody hugs somebody, that is the type of situations in which hugging is going on between some individuals. In TTR we use *record types* for this purpose. A record type is a finite set of fields each consisting of a label and a type or a label and a pair of a *dependent type* and a sequence of paths in the record type where the values required by the dependent type are to be found in the record being checked against the type. The set of fields must be a function in the sense that any label may occur only once as the first member of an ordered pair which is a field. Consider the representation of a record type in (1).

$$(1) \quad \begin{bmatrix} \mathrm{x} & : & \mathit{Ind} \\ \mathrm{y} & : & \mathit{Ind} \\ \mathrm{e} & : & \mathrm{hug(x,y)} \end{bmatrix}$$

A *record* of the type in (0) is also a set of ordered pairs, this time of labels and objects again with the requirement that any label occur only once as the first element of one of the fields. For a record, r, to be of this type it must contain fields with the same labels as in the type (it may contain more fields with other labels) and each of the objects in the fields with matching labels must be of the type given in the corresponding field of the record type. This means that any record of the type (0) would be of the form in (1).

$$(2) \quad \begin{bmatrix} \text{x} & = & a \\ \text{y} & = & b \\ \text{e} & = & s \\ \ldots & & \end{bmatrix}$$

$$\text{where} \quad \begin{array}{l} a : \mathit{Ind} \\ b : \mathit{Ind} \\ s : \text{hug}(a,b) \end{array}$$

Note that 'hug(x,y)' in (1) is not strictly a ptype since 'x' and 'y' are not individuals, as required for the arguments of the predicate 'hug', but labels. We use 'hug(x,y)' as a convenient readable notation for the pair (1).

(3) $\langle \lambda v_1{:}\mathit{Ind}\ .\ \lambda v_2{:}\mathit{Ind}\ .\ \text{hug}(v_1,v_2), \langle \text{x},\text{y} \rangle \rangle$

(0) is a pair consisting of a dependent type, that is, a function (in this case of two arguments) which returns a type, and a sequence of paths in the record potentially of this type where arguments can be found for the dependent type so that we determine a type. We call a field with such a pair a *dependent field.*

Sometimes we need to partially specify a general type like (1) by tying down one or more of the fields to a specific value. For this we use a *manifest field* as in (1).

$$(4) \quad \begin{bmatrix} \text{x} & : & \mathit{Ind} \\ \text{y=fido} & : & \mathit{Ind} \\ \text{e} & : & \text{hug(x,y)} \end{bmatrix}$$

This is the type of situation where some individual hugs the individual 'fido'. Any record of this type would be one meeting the conditions in (1).

$$(5) \quad \begin{bmatrix} \text{x} & = & a \\ \text{y} & = & b \\ \text{e} & = & s \\ \ldots & & \end{bmatrix}$$

$$\text{where} \quad \begin{array}{l} a : \mathit{Ind} \\ b : \mathit{Ind} \text{ and } b \text{ is 'fido'} \\ s : \text{hug}(a,b) \end{array}$$

For any two types, T_1 and T_2 there is a corresponding meet type, $(T_1 \wedge T_2)$. $a : (T_1 \wedge T_2)$ iff $a : T_1$ and $a : T_2$. Alternative names for meet types are conjunctive types or intersection types. If T_1 and T_2 are record types then there will always be a record type which is equivalent to the meet type in the sense that it has exactly the same witnesses. We will call this record type the *merge* of T_1 and T_2, $T_1 \dot{\wedge} T_2$, with a dot under "$\wedge$". Merge in TTR corresponds to unification in feature logics, although it is a little more complicated given the nature of types and in particular the use of dependent fields in record types. We will not go into the details of the definition here but refer the reader to Cooper (forthc, Chap. 2). However, in (1) we give some illustrative examples.

(6) a. $\begin{bmatrix}\text{x} : T_1\end{bmatrix} \dot{\wedge} \begin{bmatrix}\text{y} : T_2\end{bmatrix} = \begin{bmatrix}\text{x} : T_1 \\ \text{y} : T_2\end{bmatrix}$

b. $\begin{bmatrix}\text{x} : T_1\end{bmatrix} \dot{\wedge} \begin{bmatrix}\text{x} : T_2\end{bmatrix} = \begin{bmatrix}\text{x} : T_1 \dot{\wedge} T_2\end{bmatrix}$

c. $\begin{bmatrix}\text{x} : T_1 \\ \text{y} : T_2\end{bmatrix} \dot{\wedge} \begin{bmatrix}\text{x}{=}a{:}T_1\end{bmatrix} = \begin{bmatrix}\text{x}{=}a{:}T_1 \\ \text{y} : T_2\end{bmatrix}$

The merge operation is symmetric, that is, you can take the arguments in either order and the same result will be obtained. In addition we have an operation of *asymmetric merge*, $T_1 \boxed{\dot{\wedge}} T_2$, where the second argument takes priority over the first. (This corresponds to priority unification in typed feature structures.) We give some illustrative examples in (1).

(7) a. $\begin{bmatrix}\text{x} : T_1\end{bmatrix} \boxed{\dot{\wedge}} \begin{bmatrix}\text{y} : T_2\end{bmatrix} = \begin{bmatrix}\text{x} : T_1 \\ \text{y} : T_2\end{bmatrix}$

b. If it is *not* the case that both T_1 and T_2 are record types, then $\begin{bmatrix}\text{x} : T_1\end{bmatrix} \boxed{\dot{\wedge}} \begin{bmatrix}\text{x} : T_2\end{bmatrix} = \begin{bmatrix}\text{x} : T_2\end{bmatrix}$
If it *is* the case that both T_1 and T_2 are record types, then $\begin{bmatrix}\text{x} : T_1\end{bmatrix} \boxed{\dot{\wedge}} \begin{bmatrix}\text{x} : T_2\end{bmatrix} = \begin{bmatrix}\text{x} : T_1 \boxed{\dot{\wedge}} T_2\end{bmatrix}$

c. $\begin{bmatrix}\text{x} : T_1 \\ \text{y} : T_2\end{bmatrix} \boxed{\dot{\wedge}} \begin{bmatrix}\text{x}{=}a{:}T_1\end{bmatrix} = \begin{bmatrix}\text{x}{=}a{:}T_1 \\ \text{y} : T_2\end{bmatrix}$

d. $\begin{bmatrix}\text{x}{=}a{:}T_1 \\ \text{y} : T_2\end{bmatrix} \boxed{\dot{\wedge}} \begin{bmatrix}\text{x}{=}b{:}T_1\end{bmatrix} = \begin{bmatrix}\text{x}{=}b{:}T_1 \\ \text{y} : T_2\end{bmatrix}$

Situations often involve change and we can account for this by thinking of situations as strings of component situations. Thus if s_1 and s_2 are situations we can form the string $s_1 s_2$. Situations can be thought of as records or strings of records. If $s_1 : T_1$ and $s_2 : T_2$ then $s_1 s_2 : T_1 \frown T_2$. For any two types T_1 and T_2, there is a concatenation type $T_1 \frown T_2$ whose witnesses are strings of a witness of T_1 followed by a witness of T_2. This is a slight simplification of what is needed to deal with string types. For details see Cooper (forthc, Chap. 2).

We think of types as being resources that are available to an agent. There are a number of actions that an agent can perform using a type. These actions are called *type acts* (Cooper, 2014, forthc, Chap. 2). Central among the type acts are the kinds of judgements that are available in a Martin-Löf type theory. Where in a Martin-Löf type theory we represent a judgement such as $s : T$ (s is of type T), in our theory of action we represent the fact that agent A judges s to be of type T as (1).

(8) $s :_A T$

In a Martin-Löf type theory there is also a non-specific form of judgement, the judgement that there is something of type T. This is often written in Martin-Löf type theory as T true. In our action theory we represent that an agent, A, makes a non-specific judgement that there is something of type T as (1).

(9) $:_A T$

In addition to judgement acts, we add other kinds of acts. One of these is creation acts. Especially when we are reasoning about situations, it is important to be able to talk about the act of creating a situation of a type. We use (1) to represent that agent, A creates something of type T.

(10) $:_A T!$

Note that there is no specific version of creation acts ($s :_A T!$). Once something has been created (or come into existence), you cannot create that very same thing again, only something else of the same type.

Type acts can be licensed or, in the sense of Gibson (1979), *afforded* by certain conditions holding, where the conditions may be a previous type act. For Gibson affordances represent possibilities or opportunities for action which are presented by the world to an agent. We use *action rules* of the form (1) to express these affordances. As with types, we think of the action rules as being regularities (invariants) in the world to which an agent may be attuned. As such, we figure that the affordances correspond to patterns of neural activity, but we leave open the degree to which this corresponds to conscious reasoning, assuming that some cases are conscious but that many are not.

(11) $$\frac{\varphi_0 \quad \varphi_1 \quad \cdots \quad \varphi_n}{\psi}$$

where $\varphi_0, \varphi_1, \ldots, \varphi_n$ are the conditions and ψ is the afforded type act. We use the wavy line to indicate that such rules are somewhat similar to inference rules in a standard logic, though with the important difference that ψ does not follow from $\varphi_0, \varphi_1, \ldots, \varphi_n$ but is afforded by them. The fact that type act ψ is afforded does not mean that it is necessarily carried out. There may be a complication which prevents the act or perhaps the agent simply chooses not to perform the act which is afforded to her. Thus we cannot conclude from the conditions being met that the afforded act is performed.

In reasoning about such affordances we often want to refer to strings of situations, that is, situations occurring in a temporal order. To deal with this we use *string types* (Cooper, forthc, Chap. 2). Here we simplify some of the details of string types. If T_1 and T_2 are types, then there is also a type $T_1{}^\frown T_2$. $s : T_1{}^\frown T_2$ just in case $s = s_1 s_2$ (that is, the concatenation of s_1 and s_2) and $s_1 : T_1$ and $s_2 : T_2$.

In probabilistic TTR (Cooper et al., 2015) we introduce the probability that an object a is of type T, $p(a : T)$, and also the probability that there is something of type T, which we represent as $p(T)$. These can be combined as expected for conditional probabilities as in (1).

(12) $p(a : T_1 | b : T_2)$ the probability that $a : T_1$ given that $b : T_2$

$p(a : T_1 | T_2)$ the probability that $a : T_1$ given that there is something of type T_2

$p(T_1 | a : T_2)$ the probability that there is something of type T_1 given that $a : T_2$

$p(T_1 | T_2)$ the probability there is something of type T_1 given that there is something of type T_2

In addition we introduce the notation in (1).

(13) $p(T_1 || T_2)$ the probability that something is of type T_1 given that it is also of type T_2

We also introduce probabilities of events of a certain type following another event using the notation in (1).

(14) $p(T_2 \langle | T_1)$ the probability that there is a string $s_1 s_2$ of type $T_1{}^\frown T_2$ given that $s_1 : T_1$

8.3 Uncertainty in early communication

One of the most dramatic cases of uncertain communication is the kind of situation that arises between adults and children in the early stages of language acquisition.

...

(15) Mother: what is it?
Child: that door.
Mother:hmm?
Mother:what is it?
Child: duck.
Mother:do you want to look at the duck?
Mother:hmm?
Child: door.
Mother:well open the door then.
(Aran01, Manchester Corpus, (Rowland et al., 2003))

There is a great deal of uncertainty involved in trying to understand what children say. There seems to be a good deal of evidence that at least some of the time children, even at the one-word stage, are using single word utterances to express something like a proposition or a request (or command) rather than simply referring to what is expressed by the word. See, for example, McNeill (1970, p. 20) for some early references in the literature. Clark and Casillas (2016, p. 322) give a striking example of how a child (18 months) uses one word to refer to a situation where a bird had landed on his head, reproduced in (1).

(16) Mother: Did you see Philip's bird? Can you tell Herb?
Child: head, head, head.
Mother: What landed on your head?
Child: bird.

While adult speakers of the language clearly also use single word utterances to indicate complete propositions (for example, in short answers to questions, Ginzburg, 2012), they would not normally do so in this type of context unless they were experiencing difficulty in speaking. Discussing such holophrastic utterances, Tomasello (2003) claims that they often have the same communicative intention as that of the adult expressions from which they were learned, meaning they are often used to express complete sentences. We do not know whether the child in (0) had heard a sentence such as *The bird landed on your head*. What seems more important is that the child is able to classify a situation in which the bird lands on his head and that the word *head* can be used to refer to heads. Thus he can use a single word to express a significant part of the situation he wishes to talk about.

Cooper (1990) discussed this from the perspective of situation theory. Paraphrasing what he says in terms of TTR, we can imagine a situation, s, in which Anna hugs Andrew, that is,

(17) s : hug(Anna, Andrew)

A child appears to be able describe this situation by a number of different kinds of utterances. At the one word state we might get approximations of *Anna, Andrew* or *hug.* At the two word stage we might get combinations of these words such as *hug Andrew* or *Anna hug.* We cannot be sure, however, that the child is describing the situation as being a witness of the type in (0). Thus if Anna, on meeting her friend Andrew, gives him a hug and then turns to her father and says *Andrew,* it is not clear whether she is reporting the fact that she hugged Andrew or saying something like *That's Andrew* or *It's nice to see Andrew.* Having witnessed the situation and heard Anna's utterance the father might entertain any of the three types in (1), among many others, as possible contents of Anna's utterance.

(18) a. $\left[\ \text{e} \ : \ \text{hug(Anna,Andrew)}\ \right]$
b. $\left[\ \text{x=Andrew} \ : \ \textit{Ind}\ \right]$
c. $\left[\ \text{e} \ : \ \text{think(Anna, } [\text{e : nice(}[\text{e : see(Anna,Andrew)}])])\ \right]$

If these are the three types that the father is considering, the best he can do is come up with a probability distribution over the three types. There can be several factors which contribute to the construction of this distribution. Suppose that he judges that each of the types is definitely witnessed, that is, for each of the types, T, $p(T) = 1$. What we are representing here is the estimation of the real world possibility by Anna's father. Using F to represent the father, we might represent this explicitly as $p_F(T) = 1$. We may also, in a more detailed analysis, want to make the types (0a and c) more specific, relating them to the particular situation, s, that he observed. That can be achieved by using corresponding types with a manifest field indicating the particular situation, s, as in (1).

(19) a. $\left[\ \text{e=}s \ : \ \text{hug(Anna,Andrew)}\ \right]$
b. $\left[\ \text{e=}s \ : \ \text{think(Anna, } [\text{e : nice(}[\text{e : see(Anna,Andrew)}])])\ \right]$

Whichever types we choose, the probability which the father ascribes to their being realized will influence the probability distribution which he associates with the content of her utterance of the word *Andrew.*

If these probabilities were the only factor involved, the distribution that the father would assign to the content of the utterance would be one in which each of the three types has equal probability, that is they each have probability .333.... The probability of one of the types, T, in the distribution is the probability of the type divided by sum of the probabilities for all the types. We could spell this out in the following way. Suppose that u is the utterance event that he observes where Anna utters the word *Andrew*. We could say that u is of the type (1) (simplifying the treatment of speech events in Cooper, forthc).

(20) $\begin{bmatrix} \text{sp=Anna} & : & \textit{Ind} \\ \text{phon} & : & \text{“Andrew”} \\ \text{cont} & : & \textit{Type} \end{bmatrix}$

If u is of this type, then u's speaker, u.sp, is Anna, u's phonology, u.phon, is of the phonological type "Andrew" (that is, the type of speech event where the word *Andrew* is uttered) and its content, u.cont, is some type (that is, a witness for the type of types, *Type*). Let us call the type in (0), $T_{(0)}$. The father can be sure that u is of type $T_{(0)}$ on the basis of his observation. He can assign the probability as indicated in (1). Of course, the utterance may have been indistinct or he may not have been paying full attention, so in practice this could also involve a distribution over different types.

(21) $p_F(u : T_{(20)}) = 1$

Let us suppose that the father, F, is considering a set of alternative types, *Alt*, as possible contents for Anna's utterance, u, then according to the view that he considers the alternatives as likely interpretations to the extent that he considers them to be likely to be true, we would have for any $T_{\text{alt}} \in \textit{Alt}$,

(22) $p_F(u : (T_{(20)} \wedge\!\!\!\!\cdot\;\, [\text{cont}{=}T_{\text{alt}}{:}\,\textit{Type}])) = \dfrac{p_F(T_{\text{alt}})}{\sum\limits_{T \in \textit{Alt}} p_F(T)}$

If he is slightly less sure that Anna is happy to see Andrew, that is the probability of there being a witness for 18c (or the more specific type 19b, if you prefer) is, say, .95, then the probabilities for the three types in the distribution would be 1/2.95, 1/2.95 and .95/2.95 (approximately, 0.339, 0.339 and 0.322). Of course, there may be other factors that go into determining this distribution, such as his previous experience with Anna's utterances and what they seem to mean. A large part in determining what types to consider in the first place depends on his judgements about the situation he witnessed which he believes gives rise to her utterance. The hypotheses would be different if Anna were arriving home from a trip out with her mother and announced *Andrew*. Then, without help from the mother, it might be more difficult to come up with the hugging type though perhaps (18b and c)would still be candidates.

There are two things that an adequate theory of this kind of communication must explain:

1. how a child can use one word to express something that would seem to require a phrase or a sentence in the adult language
2. how an adult on hearing a one word expression from a child can interpret it as something that would seem to require a phrase or a sentence in the adult language, *even if the child only meant to refer to what is represented by the word.*

We shall address both of these below.

8.4 From the prelinguistic to the multi-word stage

8.4.1 Prelinguistic abilities

Learning to participate in dialogue can be cast as learning to produce appropriate utterances (and actions) in relation to utterances (and actions) by the caregiver – that is, to learn to participate in language games, including the production of minimal (i.e. two-turn) language games (P_1, P_2) (consisting of linguistic and non-linguistic actions P_1 and P_2) from more or less innate capabilities. The first of these is the attunement to some prelinguistic types, including event types. The second is *reflex behaviours* such as crying when something is unpleasant. The third is the ability to generate *expectations* based on previously observed sequences of events.

From prelinguistic to linguistic information states

An essential part of our approach to analyzing the kind of communication we are discussing is to think first in terms of non-linguistic information states and allow linguistic information states to be supervenient on them. When a child is born it is confronted with a stream of experiences of the world mediated through its sensory apparatus. Within hours the child learns to distinguish feeding from non-feeding situations and the association between an unpleasant feeling of hunger and a subsequent feeding event. The baby learns to classify different kinds of situations. In terms of TTR we say that the child becomes attuned to different types of situations, *Feeding*[2], *NonFeeding*, *PersonWithMilkPresent*, *PersonWithoutMilkPresent*,.... There is nothing linguistic about this basic perception and categorization of situations in the world. It is an essential ability which is necessary to be able to interact with and

[2]Although we here give these types mnemonic names for purposes of illustration, this does of course not mean that the child assigns any linguistic structure or form to the types.

survive in the world. For example, the ability to classify situations in this way is important for the baby to be able to suck at the right time and then swallow. Some babies take a little longer to master this coordination than others but all babies must manage it if they are to survive. In TTR we think of types as being invariants across situations in something like the sense of Gibson (1979), that is whatever it is about different situations which enables us to classify them as being similar. Particularly important kinds of invariants across situations are those we categorize as individuals. Babies learn to classify pretty well all situations in which their mother or caregiver is present as well as other individuals which show up regularly in their environment. All this is done without language. Indeed it is not exclusive to humans. Non-linguistic animals can also make these kinds of distinctions. They are attuned to types in a similar way, though perhaps not the same types, that is, not the same invariants across situations, due in part to their different perceptual apparatus.

This means that Anna can, in a prelinguistic state, be able to recognize situations in which she is involved, distinguish Andrew from other individuals and recognize situations in which one individual hugs another. Therefore it is not particularly surprising that for a given situation, *s* that she has observed prelinguistic Anna can make the classification represented in (17).[3] Note that although this is a complex type, constructed from a predicate and its arguments, this does not of itself mean that it has to correspond to a complex neural event, although if we were to follow something like the compositional neural interpretation of types suggested by Cooper (2019), the neural representation of this type would involve at the very least six neurons—not much by neurological standards.

Given that the child has already become attuned to this type it is not surprising that they should indicate that type by using language to refer to one of the components of the type or at least be interpreted by adults as so doing. The child has limited linguistic resources (only being able to utter one word at a time in the one word stage) and we are used to interpreting short utterances produced by adult speakers of the language. For example, if I am standing near the buttons in a lift and somebody else gets in and says *Six* I am likely to interpret this as a request that I press button six as that is where the other person wants to get off (Ginzburg, 1994). Similarly, if I meet somebody crawling on the ground in the desert who is obviously in a bad way and this person

[3]We are ignoring here the fact that Anna also recognizes that she, herself, is Anna. For some discussion of the treatment of *de se* phenomena in this framework see Cooper (forthc).

says *Water* I am likely to interpret this as a request for water to drink rather than, say, a description of a flood. We are very good at making these kinds of guesses based on context, even if we do not always get it right.

How do children move from the prelinguistic stage to the linguistic stage? More specifically, how do they move from being attuned to prelinguistic types to being attuned to types reflecting linguistic meanings? We explore the idea that that this happens to a large extent as a result of situated interaction between the child and its caregivers, where non-linguistic types gradually are replaced by increasingly sophisticated linguistic types (including complex types). Learning to participate in situated linguistic interaction involves at least two things: learning to produce appropriate followup utterances (and actions) to utterances by the caregiver, and connecting linguistic items to the perceptually available situation. In the rest of this section, we will see how probabilistic mechanisms can explain how innate reflex behaviours, together with some other fundamental capabilities, can provide a scaffolding for moving from the protolinguistic to the linguistic stage.

In the following, we assume that some types are pre-linguistic (and even to some extent innate), such as types related to face recognition, object detection, associating stimuli with expectations, recognising and identifying basic "biological" activities (eating etc.), recognising biological signals (hunger), and producing non-verbal signals (crying etc).

Reflex behaviours

We also assume that infants can produce certain behaviours (or actions) such as crying. Using action rules (as described in Section 8.2.2), we can express associations that agents, including infants and first language learners, make. For example, the existence of something unpleasant (perceived by proprioception) licences crying:

$$(23)\quad \frac{:_A \mathit{Unpleasant}}{:_A \mathit{Cry}!}$$

This action rule is intended to model a more or less innate reflex behaviour present in infants. The rule says that for agent A the presence of unpleasantness licenses crying, or more specifically, creating a situation where there is crying. This licensing need not be thought of as a deliberative or conscious process, but simply expresses an association between two things - unpleasantness and the action of crying. It thus captures a reflex behaviour of crying in the face of unpleasantness.

Generating expectations

We assume that infants can observe sequences of events (including actions), that we encode as TTR *string types* $E_1{}^\frown E_2{}^\frown \ldots {}^\frown E_t$. Based on this, they generate expectations concerning future events. Repeated exposure to a string type such as $E_1{}^\frown E_2$ results in an observation of E_1 giving rise to an expectation of E_2. One way to explain the generation of such expectations is to assume that infants somehow keep track of conditional probabilities $p(E_2\langle|E1)$ of event types following other event types as introduced in (14). Extending the account of probabilistic learning in Larsson et al. (2021) to string types, we can compute $p(E_2\langle|E_1)$ from a history of probabilistic judgements J as follows:[4]

(24)

$$p(E_2\langle|E_1) = \frac{\sum_{s\in \mathrm{J}} p(s : E_1{}^\frown E_2)}{\sum_{s\in \mathrm{J}} p(s : E_1)}$$

Based on such likelihoods, the probability of a situation s_t being of an event type can be computed provided the probability of a preceding string of situations s_{t-1} is of the appropriate string type:[5]

(25)

$$p(s_t : E_2) = p(E_2\langle|E_1)p(s_{t-1} : E_1)$$

To use this for modelling expectations, we take it that expectations are modelled as probabilities, so that a more probable event is more expected than a less probable event. For example, if crying frequently

[4] $s \in \mathrm{J}$ is simplified notation for $s = s_1\ s_2$, $\langle j_1, j_2\rangle \in \mathrm{J}$, j_1.sit $= s_1$, j_2.sit $= s_2$. The items in J are *probabilistic Austinian proposition*, i.e., objects (records) that correspond to, or encode, probabilistic judgements. Probabilistic Austinian propositions are records of this type:

$$\begin{bmatrix} \text{sit} & : & \textit{Sit} \\ \text{sit-type} & : & \textit{Type} \\ \text{prob} & : & [0,1] \end{bmatrix}$$

A probabilistic Austinian proposition φ of this type corresponds to the judgement that φ.sit is of type φ.sit-type with probability φ.prob. We assume that $\langle j_1, j_2\rangle \in \mathrm{J}$ whenever j_2 follows j_1 and the agent in question treats them as a sequence of related events rather than as two unrelated events. (Obviously we are sweeping a lot under the rug here; we are simply assuming that J is structured to reflect perceived associated sequences of event, no matter how this is done and on what grounds.)

[5] See Cooper (forthc, Chap. 2) for discussion of an example.

results in the caregiver taking some action such as feeding, the child will repeatedly observe $Cry^\frown Feed$, which will increase $p(Feed_{t+1}\langle|Cry_t)$ and hence generate an expectation of feeding after crying.

The output from expectation generation can be a probability distribution over a set of alternative event types E to follow an observed event of type E_1. Alternatively, one could apply an argmax function over the event types in E to find the most likely one, and regard this as the predicted type of event to follow an observed event, $s : E_1$. That is, the predicted type of the next event is:

(26)

$$\underset{E' \in \mathrm{E}}{\operatorname{argmax}}\ p(E'\langle|E_1)p(s_1 : E_1)$$

Note that we are not claiming that children explicitly calculate probabilities of string types as detailed above. The equations provided here are intended as a model of cognitive processes.

8.4.2 From crying to (minimal) language games

Given the three capabilities described above, we can sketch an account of how the child learns to use verbal (but still non-linguistic) signals that result in some desired action from the caregiver. This involves a feedback loop where the adult caregiver interprets crying in context and tries to do something that stops the child from crying. Apart from crying caused by hunger or other bodily discomfort, a child may, for example, experience a displeasure from missing its toy bird, which might lead to crying (possibly a slightly different kind of crying than that caused by hunger (Cecchini et al., 2010)):[6]

(27) $$\frac{s^* :_A \mathit{MissingBird}}{:_A \mathit{CryBird}!}$$

This crying is a verbal signal, but it is not (at least initially) a linguistic signal in the sense of being at least to some extent conventionally determined.[7] Provided that the caregiver reliably interprets this crying as a sign of the child missing its toy bird, and consequently providing the bird to the child, this provides the child with several occasions to observe strings of events of this type:

(28) $\mathit{CryBird}^\frown \mathit{GetBird}$

For each such observation, the likelihood

[6] We use s^* to denote the current situation attended to.

[7] This distinction is more difficult to maintain for sign language, where up to 50% of signs encode iconicity (Goldin-Meadow and Brentari, 2017).

(29) $p(GetBird\langle|CryBird)$

of a *GetBird* to follow a *CryBird* event increases.[8] In this way, over time the particular noise made by the child may become associated with the action (by the adult) of providing the child with the toy bird. This means that the child has now learned a minimal language game - making a certain noise and getting the toy bird as a result.

Extrapolating from this in a somewhat speculative manner, we can perhaps here find an explanation of the existence of non-public language of infants (Halliday, 1975) at a certain stage of development, where they produce non-standard words that are nevertheless associated with fairly clear meanings. Thus, in Halliday's diary study of his son, the initial stable phase Halliday describes (Halliday, 1975, p. 148) involves 12 forms: 4 imperative ('give me that/my bird', 'do that/do that right now') 3 express affiliation ('nice to see you', 'nice to see you at last', 'it's me'), 2 involve predication on an entity in visual focus ('that's moving/nice') 2 involve evaluations ('that's interesting/tastes nice), and one signals sleepiness. These initial communications, then, involve in a significant way expectations of actions from the caregiver, expressions of affiliation with the caregiver, and of positive valence:

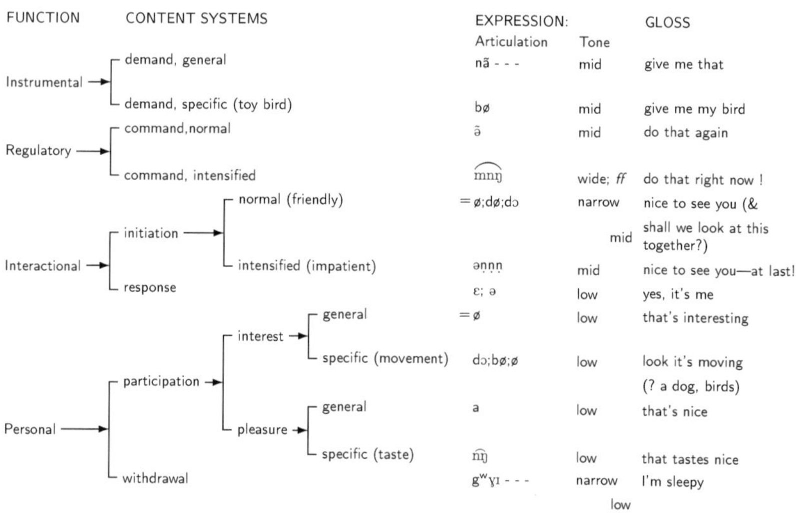

FIGURE 1: Halliday's description of the first stable phase of his son, Nigel, (Halliday, 1975, page 148)

[8]Provided no other event is a more frequent followup to *CryBird*.

According to this explanation, at least some non-standard words have their origin in reflex verbalisations by the child that gradually become differentiated and associated with specific actions and related items in the kind of minimal language games exemplified above.

The expectation of an action from the caregiver (in this case, giving the toy bird to the child), we hypothesize, at some point becomes part of a behaviour from the child that can be regarded as more goal-directed: crying *in order to* get the toy bird. However, notice that the initial behaviour is entirely reflex-based. It is only the adult's behaviour, paired with the infant's ability to generate expectations on future action, that provides the scaffolding for goal-directed behaviour. Note also that the goal-directed behaviour (crying in order to get the toy bird) is, from the caregiver's perspective, initially indistinguishable from the reflex behaviour (crying because of missing the toy bird). It is only later, when the goal directed behaviour becomes too complex to be accountable for in terms of reflexes, that the existence of goal-directed behaviour in the child becomes clearly visible. Putting it differently, this is when it becomes useful to apply an intentional stance (Dennett, 1987) to the child's behaviour.

8.4.3 The smiling stage: understanding communicative feedback

To model goal-directed behaviour, we need more than just probabilies of actions given other actions. We also need a concept of *reward*, so that attaining a goal gives a reward to the agent. Reinforcement learning provides a simple computational model of reward-driven learning in the form of *Q-learning*, where an agent tries select actions that maximize the expected reward over time. The probabilistic account of learning sketched above can be extended more or less straightforwardly to a Markov Decision Process (MDP) (see Figure 2[9]) of the kind that Q-learning assumes. An MDP[10] is characterized by (1) a set of states S an agent can be in, (2) a set of actions A the agent can take, (3) a reward $r(a, s), a \in A, s \in S$, that the agent receives for taking an action in a state, and (4) probabilities $p(s' \mid s, a)$ of a state s' given action $a \in A$ in state $s \in S$.

The MDP model assumes that state transitions are Markovian:

(30) $P(s_{t+1} \mid s_t, s_{t-1}, \ldots, s_0, a_t, a_{t-1}, \ldots, a_0) = P(s_{t+1} \mid s_t, a_t)$

---

[9]Picture by waldoalvarez - Own work, CC BY-SA 4.0, https://commons.wikimedia.org/w/index.php?curid=59364518

[10]This explanation is based on http://courses.washington.edu/ling575/SPR2017/slides/ling575_class5_statdm_flat.pdf

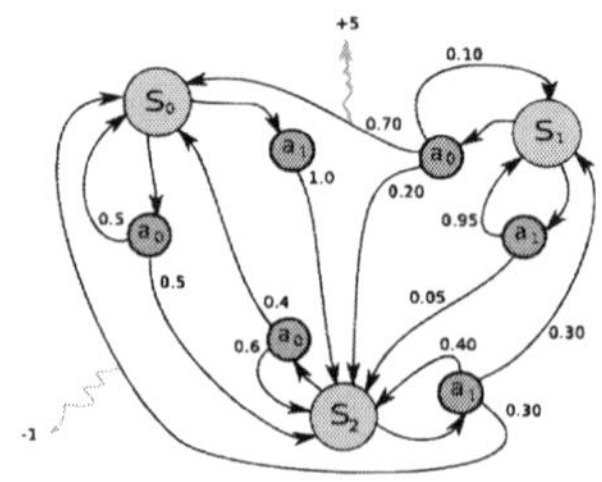

FIGURE 2: An example MDP. Nodes are states S_i, arcs are actions a_j associated with probabilities $p(S_i, a_j)$ of taking an action in a state. Integers (+5, -1) are rewards associated with actions in certain states.

i.e., the probability of a state s_{t+1} given a trajectory in state space depends only on the most recent state s_t and action a_t. To briefly describe reinforcement learning (Q-learning), we note that the cumulative reward Q of a sequence is the reward $R(s_0, a_0)$ of the first step in the sequence plus the discounted sum of utilities of individual future states[11]:

(31) $Q([s_0, a_0, s_1, a_1, s_2, a_2, \ldots]) = R(s_0, a_0) + \gamma Q([s_1, a_1, s_2, a_2, \ldots])$

The expected cumulative reward $Q(s, a)$ for taking a particular action from a particular state can be computed by the Bellman equation:

(32) $Q(s, a) = R(s, a) + \gamma \sum_{s'} P(s' \mid s, a) \max_{a'} Q(s', a')$

What this says is that the expected cumulative reward for a given state/action pair is immediate reward for current state plus the expected discounted utility of all possible next states s', weighted by probability of moving to that state s' and assuming once there we take optimal action a'.

For now, we will assume that children can recognize rewards and we formalize this as classifying rewarding situations as being of type *Reward*. We leave the formal integration of MDPs into ProbTTR for future work, but we note here some potential uses of MDPs, and Q-learning. The most obvious benefit is the ability to model goal-driven behaviour where the infant takes actions to maximise some reward, such as getting the toy bird in our previous example. We can also use rewards to model more immediate emotional rewards to the infant based on parental feedback, including affiliation. Based on such short-term emotional reward and the slightly more long-term reward of attaining

[11] The term *discounted* here refers to a weight factor γ that makes rewards have less impact the further into the future they are.

a (non-communicative) goal, the Q-learning model might be able to account for how rewards are fed backward and forward to become associated also with successful communication, i.e. the attainment of communicative goals, and hence with positive communication-related feedback from the caregiver such as nodding and repetition to show successful perception, understanding and acceptance of the infant's utterance. In this way, the child would become endowed with the ability to monitor communicative success based on caregiver feedback.

8.4.4 From pointing to the one word stage

Most work on the one word stage until now has focussed on describing it in functional terms, ignoring that it involves utterance types where content arises by combining material from the word uttered and the context. An initial grammar that tries to do just this is given in (Moradlou, 2019). The grammar can be presented in terms of the type hierarchy in Figure 3. The types are partitioned into assertoric and non-assertoric utterances, grouped under the label *interj-utt* in Figure 3. The latter involve three subtypes: calls, requests, and *repetition acknowledgement*(ack), utterances which involve repeating a word from a previous parental utterance. The assertoric utterances include visually-based predications, grouped under the label *vis-utt*, whose subject is the entity in focal attention. They also include *short answers* to *wh*-questions, here given the label *Decl-frag(ment)-cl(ause)* (Ginzburg and Sag, 2000), where the predicate is the question posed by the parent.

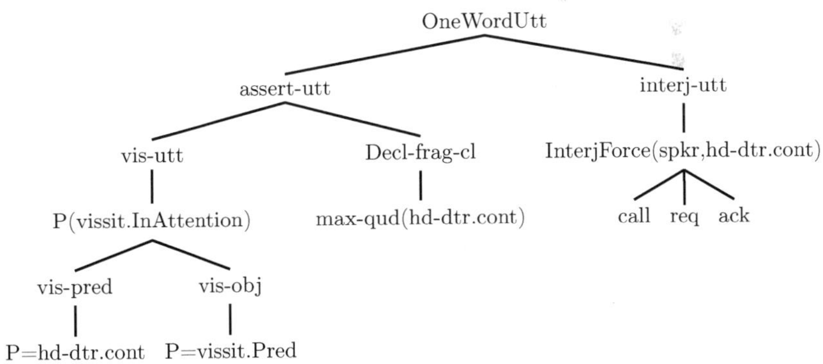

FIGURE 3: Type Hierarchy for one word stage based on data from the Providence corpus.

In what follows we offer accounts of how the types for *VisUtt, Decl-frag-cl*, and *ack* might be learnt.

In the one word stage, children go beyond pre-linguistic types and learn, for example, to recognize and identify non-biological activities (e.g. looking at pictures in a picture book, henceforth *the picture book activity* represented by the type *PictureBookActivity* or *PBA* for short), recognize phonemes, associate perceptual and phonological stimuli (thus acquiring perceptual meaning), make attempts at phonological generation (imitation) and naming perceived objects (as in the picture book activity). To manage these activities, the essential aspect of meaning seems to be the one relating perceptual input to phonological representations (linguistic expressions), but of course other aspects of meaning, such as ontological meaning, may be present already at this stage. (One reason to think that ontological meaning may play a role already at the one word stage is that ontological meaning gives important clues as to which kind of classifier should be associated with a word; for example, a colour word should be associated with a colour classifier.)

Imitation

To account for types such as *Repetition Acknowledgement* in the one word stage, we will need to assume a capability of imitation, i.e. the reproduction (more or less faithful) of an observed caregiver behaviour. Imitation is presumably achieved by a combination of innate mechanisms and trained behaviour, where successful imitation is reinforced based on positive adult feedback. Using action rules, we can encode the communicative ability to repeat the utterances of others (as perceived by the learner). A very simple model just involves repeating any observed sound recognised as linguistic in nature (here we use *Phon* to represent the type "Phonology", that is, the type of vocalizations obeying the sound rules of a language[12]):

(33) $$\frac{s^* :_A T \qquad T \sqsubseteq Phon}{:_A T!}$$

While such mechanisms may indeed be present in infants, at later stages they may associate linguistic sounds with protolinguistic signs (objects of type *Sign*, formalised as records contining (at least) a field 'phon' (for phonology) and a field 'speaker').

[12]The type *Phon* would be a different type for different languages. Thus properly we should distinguish $Phon_{English}$, $Phon_{Swedish}$ and so on

(34)
$$\frac{e :_A \mathit{Sign} \qquad e.\text{phon} :_A T \qquad e.\text{speaker} \neq A}{:_A \left[\begin{array}{lll} \text{phon} & : & T \\ \text{speaker}{=}A & : & \mathit{Ind} \end{array}\right]!}$$

The latter rule also keeps track of the speaker (distinguishing self from other), which can be useful to explain why children do not repeat their own utterances endlessly (although sometimes they seem to) but only those of their dialogue partners.

The pointing stage: establishing a shared focus and classifying objects

In first language acquisition, training of perceptual classifiers typically takes place in situations where the referent is in the shared focus of attention and thus perceivable to the dialogue participants. For our current purposes, we assume that our DPs (Dialogue Participants) are able to establish a shared focus of attention.

In Larsson (2015), a formal semantics for low-level perceptual aspects of meaning is presented. The key idea is to model *perceptual meanings as classifiers of perceptual input*. Here, we will assume that infants have some basic capabilities of classifying objects and situations based on perceptual data. We also assume that they are able to learn to classify new types of objects and situations. Larsson (2015) shows how perceptual classification can be modelled in TTR, and Larsson (2020) reformulates and extends this formalisation to probabilistic classification. For our current purposes, we can define a classifier κ as a function which takes as input a situation where (1) some object (labelled foo, for "focused object") is in the shared focus of attention and (2) when attending to this object the agent perceives visual information labelled img (for image). The output of the classifier is a type.

(35)
$$\kappa : \left[\begin{array}{lll} \text{foo} & : & \mathit{Ind} \\ \text{img} & : & \mathit{Image} \end{array}\right] \to \mathit{Type}$$

Given this, we can say that an agent A judges a situation s to be of a type T iff the classifier κ, when applied to s, yields T:

(36)
$$s :_A T \text{ iff } \kappa(s) = T$$

For example, for the case of perceiving and classifying a situation s as one where there is a dog (i.e. a situation of type *DogPerc*) using a classifier κ_{animal}, we have

(37)

$$s :_A \mathit{DogPerc} \text{ iff } \kappa_{\text{animal}}(s) = \mathit{DogPerc}$$

Salient Object Identification Games

A basic kind of language game for learning perceptual meanings consists of a caregiver, B, making sure a shared focus of attention has been established, and then saying the word for the object in the shared focus of attention (Moradlou et al., 2020):

(38)

$$\mathit{DogPerc}^\frown \begin{bmatrix} \text{phon} & : & \text{“dog”} \\ \text{speaker}{=}B & : & \mathit{Ind} \end{bmatrix}$$

When observing such strings of events, the child can train a classifier that takes perceptual input from a shared focus of attention and which has the type *DogPerc* as one of its possible outputs.[13] To make things simple, we can assume that the child when exposed to this kind of input will have (or if needed, create) a classifier *WPerc* corresponding to each word W it can differentiate, and then train this classifier on each exposure to W in the manner described in Larsson (2015) and related publications. This will gradually increase the conditional probability of an utterance of “dog” following the perception of a dog:

(39)

$$p(\begin{bmatrix} \text{phon} & : & \text{“dog”} \\ \text{speaker} & : & \mathit{Ind} \end{bmatrix} \langle | \mathit{DogPerc})$$

We hypothesize that at some point, the child combines the imitation game with the observation of object naming, and takes the step to imitate the expected caregiver utterance, i.e. to utter the expected word rather than to wait for the adult to do it. On our way of expressing things, this amounts to adopting the following action rule:

(40)

$$\frac{s^* :_A \mathit{DogPerc}}{:_A \begin{bmatrix} \text{phon} & : & \text{“dog”} \\ \text{speaker}{=}A & : & \mathit{Ind} \end{bmatrix}!}$$

The caregiver may of course encourage this behaviour by clearly giving the turn to the child and eyeing it encouragingly, and also by providing positive feedback when the child attempts to name the object. (Below, we will see how questions from the caregiver can come to act as a cue for the child to name the object in the shared focus of attention.)

[13] This can either be a binary classifier for dogs vs. not-dogs, or something more like an animal classifier.

In general, the step of going from expecting an event to producing it oneself can be described in terms of a general action rule linking prediction and licensing. According to this rule, an agent is licensed to produce the expected event following a previous event (where E is a set of alternative event types to follow an observed event of type E)[14]

$$\text{(41)}\quad \frac{s^* :_A E}{:_A \operatorname*{argmax}_{E' \in \mathrm{E}} p(E'\langle|E)p(s^* : E) \boxed{\dot{\wedge}} \,[\text{speaker}{=}A{:}\mathit{Ind}]!}$$

where

$$\text{(42)}\quad \operatorname*{argmax}_{E' \in \mathrm{E}} p(E'\langle|E_1)p(s_1 : E_1)$$

is the event E expected to follow E_1 based on A's previous experience, and

$$\text{(43)}\quad E \boxed{\dot{\wedge}} [\text{speaker}{=}A{:}\mathit{Ind}]$$

is like E except that the speaker field now specifies self as the speaker.

Learning perceptual meanings

Assuming that the child gets an emotional reward in reaction to making the appropriate utterance in a language game, either an emotional reward or a reward based on perceived communicative success, we assume that this results in training the relevant classifier. For example, perceiving and classifying a situation s as a situation where there is a dog (formally, judging $s :_A \mathit{DogPerc}$ since $\kappa_{\text{animal}}(s) = \mathit{DogPerc}$), saying "dog" and receiving positive feedback from the caregiver (formalized below as s being of type *Reward*) could result in training the classifier κ_{animal} with s as a positive example of type *DogPerc* (where $s^*[0]$ is the first element in the string s^*):

$$\text{(44)}\quad \frac{s^* :_A \mathit{DogPerc}^\frown \begin{bmatrix}\text{phon} : \text{“dog”} \\ \text{speaker}{=}A{:}\mathit{Ind}\end{bmatrix}^\frown \mathit{Reward}}{:_A \text{train}(\kappa_{\text{animal}}, s^*[0], \mathit{DogPerc})!}$$

Salient Object Identification Games with Questions

Moradlou and Ginzburg (2014) investigated children's answering behaviour for *wh*-questions, in a study using the Rollins corpus, (Rollins, 2003). They classify question–answer interactions in three semantic/pragmatic classes of increasing complexity; with a view

[14]In this action rule, the premise is stated as discrete even though it is a judgement with a certain probability $p(s^* :_A E)$. We can interpret this as stating that s^* is more likely to be of type E than to be of another type in a set of alternatives to E.

towards how these classes of interactive behaviors facilitate learning of question meanings, they call them *games*. These games are hierarchical in that each more complex class generalizes the less complex game class.

We will here deal only with the first class, so-called Salient Object Identification games, where a question is asked prompting for an appropriate descriptor of an object presented to the child:

(45) a. [Mother turns page to reveal page with mirror on it.]: who's that? who's that? huh? can you see? rabbit.

b. [Mother walks Big Bird up] who's that? who's that? is that Big_Bird?

We can account for the type of behaviour exemplified above in (0), again using action rules but now embellishing these with an utterance from the caregiver as well as explicitly delimiting the coverage of this rule to a specific activity (here, *PictureBookActivity*). The caregiver utterance need not necessarily be recognized by the child as such, just as long as it is recognized as a cue for naming the object in the shared focus of attention. Following the same pattern as hypothesized for simple salient object identification games, we assume the child repeatedly observes a sequence of action where the caregiver, B, first utters "What is that?" (or some variant thereof) in a situation of the type *PictureBookActivity* which is also classified as being of type *DogPerc*, i.e. a situation where a dog is in the shared focus of attention, and then utters "dog":

(46)
$$\mathit{PictureBookActivity} \wedge \mathit{DogPerc} \wedge \begin{bmatrix}\text{phon : “What is that?”}\\ \text{speaker}{=}B{:}\mathit{Ind}\end{bmatrix} ^\frown \begin{bmatrix}\text{phon : “dog”}\\ \text{speaker}{=}B{:}\mathit{Ind}\end{bmatrix}$$

Taking the step from prediction to licensing as above, this yields an action rule licensing the child to utter "dog":

(47)
$$\frac{s^* :_A \mathit{PictureBookActivity} \qquad s^* :_A \mathit{DogPerc} \qquad u^* :_A \begin{bmatrix}\text{phon : “What is that?”}\\ \text{speaker}{=}B{:}\mathit{Ind}\end{bmatrix}}{:_A \begin{bmatrix}\text{phon : “dog”}\\ \text{speaker}{=}A{:}\mathit{Ind}\end{bmatrix}\ !}$$

Learning ontological semantics

In Cooper and Larsson (2009), work towards a formal account of how children can learn ontological semantics from adult feedback is presented. In general, adult utterances can provide hints regarding what kind of thing something is. For example, a child can learn that "purple" is a colour from hearing the utterance "Bring me the purple cup, not the red one!", provided they already know "red" refers to a colour (cf Carey and Bartlett, 1978). We can describe this by saying that the child learns that *Purple* is a subtype of *Colour*.

We believe that learning ontological semantics can have consequences for perceptual semantics, since it may give hints about which classifier is relevant. For example, if purple is a colour, then a colour classifier (rather than e.g. a shape classifier) should be trained with examples of purple things.

Similarly, having learned that cats are animals, a child may also train their animal classifier on exampes of cats, and can use it to classify situations involving cats. Formally $s :_A \mathit{CatPerc}$ iff $\kappa_{\text{animal}}(s) = \mathit{CatPerc}$, and we can add an action rule licensing utterances of "cat":

$$(48)\quad \frac{s^* :_A \mathit{PictureBookActivity} \qquad s^* :_A \mathit{CatPerc} \qquad u^* :_A \begin{bmatrix}\text{phon} : \text{“What is that?”}\\ \text{speaker}{=}B{:}\mathit{Ind}\end{bmatrix}}{:_A \begin{bmatrix}\text{phon} : \text{“cat”}\\ \text{speaker}{=}A{:}\mathit{Ind}\end{bmatrix}\ !}$$

Here we assume that A has understood that *CatPerc* and *DogPerc* are mutually exclusive types and also subtypes of a common supertype *AnimalPerc*. In general, of course, this is not the only way that things can go. For example, at one stage A might have different and unrelated classifiers for cats and dogs, and not know that these are mutually exclusive types. Alternatively, the child can have cats and dogs subsumed under a wider class such as *StuffInPictureBooks*.

8.4.5 From simple language games to lexical entries

In our examples above of looking at a picture book, when the caregiver says "What is that?", the child classifies the object in the shared focus of attention and utters the name of the (type of) animal. However, the link between *DogPerc* and the word "dog" is at this stage only encoded in an action rule which can be used in a specific language game. Over time, the child will encounter similar situations where the perception of a dog is associated with the word "dog" (that is, a type of phonological situation), and at some point it becomes useful to generalise and keep track of the connection between referent and word independently of specific language games. We call the entities that make these connections *lexical entries*. The generalisation to lexical entries allows us to reformulate action rules involved in language games in a way that generalizes over several different types of objects (in general, types of situations) that might be found in the picture book.

Following Larsson (2020) (and adding a field for phonology), we represent a lexical entry encoding the (perceptual) meaning of predicates as records containing four fields:

- Phonology (phon): a phonological event.
- Classifier parameters (params): a (possibly empty) record containing classifier parameters.
- Background meaning (bg): a record type representing assumptions about the context of utterance (presuppositions); for our current purposes, we are assuming a situation where a single object (labelled foo for focused object) is in the shared focus of attention and is being perceived.
- Interpretation function (interp), taking a situation of type bg and providing a ptype encoding a contextual interpretation of an utterance in the context of that situation
- Classification function (clfr) that can be used to make a judgement as to whether an (interpreted) utterance correctly describes a situation.

An example of a generalized action rule for the picture book activity, together with a lexical entry (for "dog"), is shown below. We assume that in lexical entries, meanings are associated with predicates such as dog, which are used in ptypes. Below, *Lex* is the type of lexical entries (and suppressing the condition $s^* :_A PictureBookActivity$ for readability):

(49) $$\frac{L :_A Lex \quad s^* :_A L.\text{bg} \quad L.\text{clfr}(s^*) = L.\text{intrp}(s^*) \quad u^*.\text{phon} :_A \text{“What is that?”}}{:_A \begin{bmatrix} \text{phon} : L.\text{phon} \\ \text{cont}{=}L.\text{intrp}(s^*) : Type \end{bmatrix}!}$$

where

$$Lex = \begin{bmatrix} \text{phon} & : & Phon \\ \text{params} & : & Rec \\ \text{bg} & : & RecType \\ \text{intrp} & : & \text{bg} \rightarrow Type \\ \text{clfr} & : & \text{bg} \rightarrow Type \end{bmatrix}$$

$$\mathbf{L}_{dog} = \begin{bmatrix} \text{phon} & = & \text{“dog”} \\ \text{params} & = & AnimalParams \\ \text{bg} & = & \begin{bmatrix} \text{foo} & : & Ind \\ \text{perc} & : & Perc \end{bmatrix} \\ \text{intrp} & = & \lambda r{:}\text{bg} \,.\, \text{dog}(r.\text{foo}) \\ \text{clfr} & = & \lambda r{:}\text{bg} \,.\, \kappa_{animal}(r.\text{foo}, \text{params}) \end{bmatrix}$$

$$\mathbf{L}_{cat}=\begin{bmatrix} \text{phon} & = & \text{“cat”} \\ \text{params} & = & \mathit{AnimalParams} \\ \text{bg} & = & \begin{bmatrix} \text{foo} & : & \mathit{Ind} \\ \text{perc} & : & \mathit{Perc} \end{bmatrix} \\ \text{intrp} & = & \lambda r{:}\text{bg} \;.\; \text{cat}(r.\text{foo}) \\ \text{clfr} & = & \lambda r{:}\text{bg}{\cdot}\kappa_{animal}(r, \text{params}) \end{bmatrix}$$

$\mathbf{L}_{dog}$:*Lex*, $\mathbf{L}_{cat}$:*Lex*

For example, for $L = \mathbf{L}_{dog}$ (leaving out $s^* :_A$ *PictureBookActivity* and $\mathbf{L}_{dog} :_A$ *Lex* and also abbreviating *AnimalParams* as *AP*):

(50) $$\frac{s^* :_A \begin{bmatrix}\text{foo} :\mathit{Ind} \\ \text{perc}{:}\,\mathit{Perc}\end{bmatrix} \quad \kappa_{animal}(s^*, AP) = \text{dog}(s^*.\text{foo}) \quad u^*.\text{phon} :_A \text{“What is that?”}}{:_A \begin{bmatrix}\text{phon} : \text{“dog”} \\ \text{cont}{=}\text{dog}(s^*.\text{foo}){:}\,\mathit{Type}\end{bmatrix}!}$$

8.4.6 Compositionality and the multi-word stage

As we discussed above, there is already compositionality in the one word stage, involving a combination of semantic material from a word and from context. In multi-word stages, compositionality and hence compositional meaning becomes essential, as the child learns to compose (perceptual) meanings (classifiers) to enable them to, for example, judge whether a sentence or phrase correctly describes a visual scene, or to answer questions about a visual scene.

We sketch an account of how multi-word stages emerge, using the approach we have developed earlier. More specifically we sketch how simple predication emerges from visual predication.

Our account involves the parent and child playing the *Advanced Salient Object Identification game* (see section 8.4.4 for SOI games.). By the time the one word stage is established, the child can participate by answering the question posed by the adult in an SOI game with a one word answer. In the advanced SOI-game, the parent responds to this with a synonymous utterance, involving an overt subject that refers to the object in focal attention.

Again following the same pattern as hypothesized above, we assume the child repeatedly observes a sequence of actions where the caregiver, B, first utters “What is that?” (or some variant thereof) in a situation of the type *PictureBookActivity* which is also classified as being of type *DogPerc*, i.e. a situation where a dog is in the shared focus of attention, and then utters a multi-word construction such as “That is a dog”:

(51) $$\mathit{PBA} \wedge \mathit{DogPerc} \wedge \begin{bmatrix}\text{phon} : \text{“What is that?”} \\ \text{speaker}{=}B{:}\mathit{Ind}\end{bmatrix} {}^\frown \begin{bmatrix}\text{phon} : \text{“That is a dog”} \\ \text{speaker}{=}B{:}\mathit{Ind}\end{bmatrix}$$

Again taking the step from prediction to licensing as above, this yields an action rule licensing the child to utter "That is a dog":

$$(52)\quad \frac{s^* :_A \textit{PictureBookActivity} \qquad s^* :_A \textit{DogPerc} \qquad u^* :_A \begin{bmatrix}\text{phon : "What is that?"}\\ \text{speaker}{=}B{:}\textit{Ind}\end{bmatrix}}{:_A \begin{bmatrix}\text{phon : "That is a dog"}\\ \text{speaker}{=}A{:}\textit{Ind}\end{bmatrix}\ !}$$

While in this example the child learns to utter what we would consider a syntactically complete sentence, this does not necessarily add anything in terms of semantics; the child need not understand "that", "is" or "a", or even the construction "that is a _". However, in later stages of linguistic development, more (semantically) complex questions and answers may be introduced. For example, when looking at a picture of a dog under a tree, the adult may ask "Where is the dog?" and follow up with "The dog is under the tree!".

If the picture book also contains, say, a picture of a dog on a table, then the same question might be asked by the adult but this time followed up by "The dog is on the table!". Here, it is clear that several words (not just one) carry semantic weight – in addition to recognizing dogs, the game introduces trees and tables, as well as geometrical relations.

To respond correctly to the adult's question, the child needs minimally to distinguish the two pictures and the two sentences, and to associate each utterance with the appropriate picture:

$$(53)\quad \frac{s^* :_A \textit{PBA} \qquad s^* :_A \textit{DogUnderTree} \qquad u^* :_A \begin{bmatrix}\text{phon : "Where is the dog?"}\\ \text{speaker}{=}B{:}\textit{Ind}\end{bmatrix}}{:_A \begin{bmatrix}\text{phon : "The dog is under the tree"}\\ \text{speaker}{=}A{:}\textit{Ind}\end{bmatrix}\ !}$$

$$(54)\quad \frac{s^* :_A \textit{PBA} \qquad s^* :_A \textit{DogOnTable} \qquad u^* :_A \begin{bmatrix}\text{phon : "Where is the dog?"}\\ \text{speaker}{=}B{:}\textit{Ind}\end{bmatrix}}{:_A \begin{bmatrix}\text{phon : "The dog is on the table"}\\ \text{speaker}{=}A{:}\textit{Ind}\end{bmatrix}\ !}$$

It might be argued that it is unlikely that a child would go immediately from one word utterances to complete sentences involving subject, predicate and object. From this viewpoint, it would be pedagogically wise to first introduce tables (a dog under a table) before moving on to other geometrical relations (a dog on a table). In fact, it may well be that gradual increments, even if not preconceived by the caregiver, happen quite naturally. In reaction to a question "Where is the dog?", a likely answer from the child is "Tree" (rather than "The dog is under the tree" or even "Under the table"). That is, the child may not yet understand "under", but still get that the tree is involved.

$$(55)\quad \frac{s^* :_A PBA \qquad s^* :_A \mathit{DogAndTreePerc} \qquad u^* :_A \begin{bmatrix}\text{phon} : \text{“Where is the dog?”} \\ \text{speaker}{=}B{:}\mathit{Ind}\end{bmatrix}}{:_A \begin{bmatrix}\text{phon} : \text{“Tree”} \\ \text{speaker}{=}A{:}\mathit{Ind}\end{bmatrix} \; !}$$

When the child utters "Tree", it would be quite natural for the caregiver to echo back the full answer: "Yes, the dog is under the tree!". Eventually, the child may catch on and produce incrementally more faithful renderings of the adult's answer, as they learn more of the words and meanings involved. Crucially, this process involves the caregiver interpreting the child's extremely elliptical utterance. We propose that this unpacking which adults do of childrens' one word utterances, echoing back complete sentences which the child may then repeat parts of, gradually moving to the multi-word stage, is an important part of the interactive process of language acquisition.

While it may in principle be possible for the child to merely memorize these utterance pairs and associate them with the right pictures, it can be assumed that this will get increasingly intractable. As more questions of this sort are introduced, the child may eventually generalize across multiple instances and learn to assign appropriate (perceptual) meanings "tree", "table", "under" and "on", and to compose these together. Exactly how this happens is of course a very interesting question, but one that we leave aside for now. However, we may note that the type *DogAndTreePerc* used in (55) can be analysed as the combination (formally, a meet type) of the perceptual meanings associated with "dog" and "tree", *DogPerc* and *TreePerc*:

$$(56)\quad \mathit{DogAndTreePerc} = \mathit{DogPerc} \wedge \mathit{TreePerc}$$

This can be seen as a step on the way to decomposing a complete utterance into parts that each contribute their individual meaning to the meaning of the whole utterance. This process eventually enables the child to go beyond merely classifying a situation with respect to the presence or absence of a certain type of object (e.g. a dog) to putting together a complex classifier for situations where certain relations hold between objects (e.g. where a dog is under a tree). We can express this as making a judgement

$$(57)\quad s^* :_A \begin{bmatrix}\text{obj} & : & \mathit{DogPerc} \\ \text{lmk} & : & \mathit{TreePerc} \\ \text{c} & : & \text{under(obj,lmk)}\end{bmatrix}$$

where s^* is judged to be a situation where an object (labelled obj) classified as a dog and a landmark (labelled lmk) classified as a tree stand in the 'under' relation[15].

$$\text{(58)}\quad \frac{s^* :_A PBA \qquad s^* :_A \begin{bmatrix} \text{obj} : \textit{DogPerc} \\ \text{lmk} : \textit{TreePerc} \\ \text{c} \quad :\text{under(obj,lmk)} \end{bmatrix} \qquad u^* :_A \begin{bmatrix} \text{phon : ``Where is the dog?''} \\ \text{speaker}{=}B{:}\textit{Ind} \end{bmatrix}}{:_A \begin{bmatrix} \text{phon : ``The dog is under the tree''} \\ \text{speaker}{=}A{:}\textit{Ind} \\ \text{cont}{=} \begin{bmatrix} \text{obj} : \textit{DogPerc} \\ \text{lmk} : \textit{TreePerc} \\ \text{c} \quad :\text{under(obj,lmk)} \end{bmatrix} : \textit{RecType} \end{bmatrix} !}$$

$$\text{(59)}\quad \frac{s^* :_A PBA \qquad s^* :_A \begin{bmatrix} \text{obj} : \textit{DogPerc} \\ \text{lmk} : \textit{TablePerc} \\ \text{c} \quad :\text{on(obj,lmk)} \end{bmatrix} \qquad u^* :_A \begin{bmatrix} \text{phon : ``Where is the dog?''} \\ \text{speaker}{=}B{:}\textit{Ind} \end{bmatrix}}{:_A \begin{bmatrix} \text{phon : ``The dog is on the table''} \\ \text{speaker}{=}A{:}\textit{Ind} \\ \text{cont}{=} \begin{bmatrix} \text{obj} : \textit{DogPerc} \\ \text{lmk} : \textit{TablePerc} \\ \text{c} \quad :\text{on(obj,lmk)} \end{bmatrix} : \textit{RecType} \end{bmatrix} !}$$

We follow Moradlou et al. (2020) in assuming that children's actions are often driven by curiosity about how a question gets resolved. Learning the meaning of interrogative utterances involves in the initial stages learning to associate questions the child is curious about with situationally appropriate corresponding utterances made by an adult. It is only at a later stage that the understanding proceeds via combinatory processes that compose word meanings (e.g., those of *wh*-words) into complex meanings. Hence, we are not here attempting to describe how the child assigns meaning to the adult's interrogative utterance. Instead, we are merely assuming that the child can use the question to focus on the relevant visual aspects of s^* and put together a set of relevant complex classifiers[16] , each corresponding to (the perceptual meaning of) a possible answer to the question.

Of course, in the long run keeping track of action rules for each answer to a question becomes impractical, and further abstraction is required. Given that the learner is able to figure out which answers resolve a question, a rule generalising over questions and answers may

[15]The classifier for the predicate 'under' can, for example, be one that extracts the position of the object relative to the landmark in s^* and checks that it is within a specified area that counts as 'under' the landmark. Acquiring such a classifier (or a similar one) is, we assume, part of learning the meaning of 'under'.

[16]We do not provide the precise formulation of the compositional semantics here, but merely note that "dog" contributes [obj:*DogPerc*], "tree" contributes [lmk:*TreePerc*] and "under" contributes [c:under(obj,lmk)], and correspondingly for "table" and "on". These can be composed using the merge operator $\dot{\wedge}$, with some relabelling required.

be formulated. The rule states that if B asks a question Q which is resolved by an answer P, which is also the type of the perceived situation, then A may make an utterance with content P.

(60)
$$\frac{s^* :_A PBA \quad s^* :_A \mathrm{P} \quad u^* :_A \begin{bmatrix}\text{speaker}{=}B{:}\mathit{Ind}\\ \text{cont}{=}Q{:}\mathit{RecType}\end{bmatrix} \quad :_A \text{resolves}(P,Q)}{:_A \begin{bmatrix}\text{speaker}{=}A{:}\mathit{Ind}\\ \text{cont}{=}P{:}\mathit{RecType}\end{bmatrix}\,!}$$

This rule resembles rules proposed to govern adult dialogue interaction (Ginzburg, 2012). We have thus followed a progression from rules expressing a reflex-like licensing of crying based on an unpleasant feeling to a general rule guiding linguistic interaction, in this case a rule for providing compositional answers to questions in dialogue.

8.5 Conclusion

In this chapter we show how parents might use the tools of probability in understanding the very early utterances of their children. Our main focus, however, has been on providing an initial sketch of how communicative activity emerges in children from the earliest days, where it involves primarily crying, through a vocal stage where non-adult vocal signals become stable temporarily, from which emerges the one word stage, where adult words are used as entire utterances. We concluded with a brief sketch of how our approach also leads to the first stage where word meanings compose—the two word stage. In the interaction between adults and children in these early stages it is essential that the adults can interpret the earlies utterances of children in the way that we characterize early in the paper.

There is also recent work that we see as being broadly in line with the current proposal, for example the work by Yang et al. (2022) on the interplay between syntax, semantics and pragmatics in the interactive acquisition of questions. Also, Breitholtz and Howes (2020) investigate (in part by formalisation in TTR) how children's acquisition of language requires their learning of not just words/concepts and linguistic structure, but how these interact in dialogue with knowledge about the world, our interlocutors, the shared environment and social norms.

Our account has been formulated using probabilistic TTR, a probabilistic version of the rich theory of types, TTR. We have used probabilistic TTR to offer a formal account of the emergence of *expectations* concerning sequences of actions in situated interaction. This allows us to offer an account of simple language games parents play with their children, which on our account, building on much earlier work, underlie the emergence of linguistic and non-linguistic communicative competence. It also enables us to offer an account for the emergence of lexical entries and the grammar rules of the one word and two word stages.

In so doing, we offer what we believe to be one of the first formal sketches of acquisition that spans the earliest days of life up to the emergence of multi-word compositionality.

8.6 Acknowledgements

Many thanks to Rasmus Blanck for comments on an earlier version and to Andy Lücking for his help with Figure 1. We also acknowledge support from a grant from the Swedish Research Council (VR project 2014-39) for the establishment of the Centre for Linguistic Theory and Studies in Probability (CLASP) at the University of Gothenburg, from the French National Research Agency (ANR) as part of the program "Investissements d'Avenir" (reference: ANR-10-LABX-0083)—it contributes to the IdEx Université de Paris – ANR-18-IDEX-0001, and from a senior fellowship from the Institut Universitaire de France to Jonathan Ginzburg. Cooper's work on this paper was supported in part by the project Incremental Reasoning in Dialogue (IncReD), VR project 2016-01162.

References

Abend, Omri, Tom Kwiatkowski, Nathaniel J Smith, Sharon Goldwater, and Mark Steedman. 2017. Bootstrapping language acquisition. *Cognition* 164:116–143.

Bergelson, Elika and Richard N Aslin. 2017. Nature and origins of the lexicon in 6-mo-olds. *Proceedings of the National Academy of Sciences* 114(49):12916–12921.

Berk, Stephanie and Diane Lillo-Martin. 2012. The two-word stage: Motivated by linguistic or cognitive constraints? *Cognitive psychology* 65(1):118–140.

Bloom, Lois Masket. 1968. *Language development: Form and function in emerging grammars*. ERIC.

Bohn, Manuel, Michael Henry Tessler, Megan Merrick, and Michael C Frank. 2021. How young children integrate information sources to infer the meaning of words. *Nature human behaviour* 5(8):1046–1054.

Breitholtz, Ellen and Christine Howes. 2020. Communicable reasons: How children learn topoi through dialogue. In *Proceedings of the 24th Workshop on the Semantics and Pragmatics of Dialogue - Full Papers*. Virtually at Brandeis, Waltham, New Jersey: SEMDIAL.

Carey, Susan and Elsa Bartlett. 1978. Acquiring a single new word. *Papers and Reports on Child Language Development* 15:17–29.

Cecchini, Marco, Carlo Lai, and Viviana Langher. 2010. Dysphonic newborn cries allow prediction of their perceived meaning. *Infant Behavior and Development* 33(3):314–320.

Clark, Alexander and Rémi Eyraud. 2006. Learning auxiliary fronting with grammatical inference. In *Proceedings of the Tenth Conference on Computational Natural Language Learning (CoNLL-X)*, pages 125–132.

Clark, Eve V. and Marisa Casillas. 2016. First language acquisition. In K. Allan, ed., *The Routledge Handbook of Linguistics*, chap. 20, pages 311–328. London New York, NY: Routledge. ISBN 9781315718453.

Cooper, Robin. 1990. Information in the early stages of language acquisition. In R. Cooper, K. Mukai, and J. Perry, eds., *Situation Theory and its Applications*, vol. 1, pages 343–354. CSLI Publications.

Cooper, Robin. 2012. Type Theory and Semantics in Flux. In R. Kempson, N. Asher, and T. Fernando, eds., *Handbook of the Philosophy of Science*, vol. 14: Philosophy of Linguistics, pages 271–323. Elsevier BV. General editors: Dov M. Gabbay, Paul Thagard and John Woods.

Cooper, Robin. 2014. How to do things with types. In V. de Paiva, W. Neuper, P. Quaresma, C. Retoré, L. S. Moss, and J. Saludes, eds., *Joint Proceedings of the Second Workshop on Natural Language and Computer Science (NLCS 2014) & 1st International Workshop on Natural Language Services for Reasoners (NLSR 2014) July 17-18, 2014 Vienna, Austria*, pages 149–158. Center for Informatics and Systems of the University of Coimbra.

Cooper, Robin. 2019. Representing Types as Neural Events. *Journal of Logic, Language and Information* 28(2):131–155.

Cooper, Robin. forthc. *From Perception to Communication: a Theory of Types for Action and Meaning*. Oxford University Press.

Cooper, Robin, Simon Dobnik, Shalom Lappin, and Staffan Larsson. 2015. Probabilistic Type Theory and Natural Language Semantics. *Linguistic Issues in Language Technology* 10(4):1–45.

Cooper, Robin and Jonathan Ginzburg. 2015. Type theory with records for natural language semantics. In S. Lappin and C. Fox, eds., *The Handbook of Contemporary Semantic Theory*, pages 375–407. Wiley-Blackwell, 2nd edn.

Cooper, Robin and Staffan Larsson. 2009. Compositional and ontological semantics in learning from corrective feedback and explicit definition. In J. Edlund, J. Gustafson, A. Hjalmarsson, and G. Skantze, eds., *Proceedings of DiaHolmia: 2009 Workshop on the Semantics and Pragmatics of Dialogue*, pages 59–66. Department of Speech, Music and Hearing, KTH.

Dennett, Daniel Clement. 1987. *The intentional stance*. MIT press.

Dore, John. 1975. Holophrases, speech acts and language universals. *Journal of Child Language* 2(01).

Fogel, Alan, K Laurie Dickson, Hui-Chin Hsu, Daniel Messinger, G Christina Nelson-Goens, and Eva Nwokah. 1997. Communication of smiling and laughter in mother-infant play: Research on emotion from a dynamic systems perspective. *New directions for child development* pages 5–24.

Gibson, James J. 1979. *The Ecological Approach to Visual Perception*. Houghton, Mifflin and Company. Also available in a Classic Edition published by Psychology Press, 2015.

Ginzburg, Jonathan. 1994. An update semantics for dialogue. In H. Bunt, ed., *Proceedings of the 1st International Workshop on Computational Semantics*. Tilburg: ITK, Tilburg University.

Ginzburg, Jonathan. 2012. *The Interactive Stance: Meaning for Conversation*. Oxford: Oxford University Press.

Ginzburg, Jonathan, Chiara Mazzocconi, and Ye Tian. 2020. Laughter as language. *Glossa* .

Ginzburg, Jonathan and Ivan A. Sag. 2000. *Interrogative Investigations: the form, meaning and use of English Interrogatives*. No. 123 in CSLI Lecture Notes. Stanford: California: CSLI Publications.

Goldin-Meadow, Susan and Diane Brentari. 2017. Gesture, sign, and language: The coming of age of sign language and gesture studies. *Behavioral and Brain Sciences* 40.

Halliday, Michael Alexander Kirkwood. 1975. *Learning How to Mean–Explorations in the Development of Language.*. London: Edward Arnold.

Larsson, Staffan. 2015. Formal semantics for perceptual classification. *Journal of Logic and Computation* 25(2):335–369. Published online 2013-12-18.

Larsson, Staffan. 2020. Discrete and probabilistic classifier-based semantics. In *Proceedings of the Probability and Meaning Conference (PaM 2020)*, pages 62–68. Gothenburg: Association for Computational Linguistics.

Larsson, Staffan, Jean-Philippe Bernardy, and Robin Cooper. 2021. Semantic learning in a probabilistic type theory with records. In *Proceedings of Workshop on Computing Semantics with Types, Frames and Related Structures 2021*.

Lieven, Elena. 1994. Crosslinguistic and crosscultural aspects of language addressed to children. In *Input and Interaction in Language Acquisition*. Cambridge: Cambridge University Press.

Martin-Löf, Per. 1984. *Intuitionistic Type Theory*. Naples: Bibliopolis.

McNeill, David. 1970. *The Acquisition of Language: The Study of Developmental Psycholinguistics*. New York: Harper & Row.

Moradlou, Sara. 2019. *Early Child Grammars*. Ph.D. thesis, Université de Paris.

Moradlou, Sara and Jonathan Ginzburg. 2014. Learning to understand questions. In P. Muller and V. Rieser, eds., *Proceedings of SemDial 2014 (DialWatt)*. Heriot Watt University.

Moradlou, Sara, Xiaobei Zheng, Ye Tian, and Jonathan Ginzburg. 2020. Wh-questions are understood before polar-questions: Evidence from english, german, and chinese. *Journal of Child Language* pages 1–27.

Ninio, A. 1992. The Relation of Children's Single Word Utterances to Single Word Utterances in the Input*. *Journal of Child Language* .

Nordström, Bengt, Kent Petersson, and Jan M. Smith. 1990. *Programming in Martin-Löf's Type Theory*, vol. 7 of *International Series of Monographs on Computer Science*. Oxford: Clarendon Press.

Nwokah, E. E., H. C Hsu, O. Dobrowolska, and A. Fogel. 1994. The development of laughter in mother- infant communication: Timing parameters and temporal sequences. *Infant Behavior and Development* 17(1):23–35.

Ochs, Elinor. 1982. Talking to children in western samoa. *Language in society* 11(1):77–104.

Rollins, Pamela Rosenthal. 2003. Caregivers' contingent comments to 9-month-old infants: Relationships with later language. *Applied Psycholinguistics* 24(2):221–234.

Rowe, M. and Susan Goldin-Meadow. 2009. Early gesture selectively predicts later language learning. *Developmental Science* .

Rowland, Caroline, Julian Pine, Elena Lieven, and Anna Theakston. 2003. Determinants of acquisition order in wh-questions : re-evaluating the role of caregiver speech. *Journal of Child Language* 30:609–635.

Siskind, Jeffrey Mark. 1996. A computational study of cross-situational techniques for learning word-to-meaning mappings. *Cognition* 61(1-2):39–91.

Stritzinger, Joshua. 2021. *Stage II Grammar*. Master's thesis, Université de Paris.

Tomasello, Michael. 2003. *Constructing a Language : a Usage-Based Theory of Language Acquisition*. Cambridge, Mass: Harvard University Press. ISBN 0674010302.

Yang, Yu'an, Daniel Goodhue, Valentine Hacquard, and Jeffrey Lidz. 2022. Are you asking me or telling me? learning to identify questions in early speech to children. In *In Proceedings of Linguistics Society of America 2022*.

Yu, Haonan and Jeffrey Mark Siskind. 2013. Grounded language learning from video described with sentences. In *Proceedings of the 51st Annual Meeting of the Association for Computational Linguistics (Volume 1: Long Papers)*, pages 53–63.

9

Distributional Semantics for Situated Spatial Language? Functional, Geometric and Perceptual Perspectives

JOHN D. KELLEHER AND SIMON DOBNIK[1]

9.1 Introduction

Distributed (continuous dense vector based) representations have a number of semantic and computational advantages for Natural Language Processing (NLP). For example, a distinctive and pervasive characteristic of natural language is the vagueness of many semantic concepts (van Deemter, 2010). Continuous vector based representations, combined with distance based measures of similarity, provide an intuitive semantic space (where the meaning of a concept is understood as a general region rather than as a point) for encoding vagueness (Karlgren and Kanerva, 2021). Furthermore, understood in this way vector based representations also provide a natural basis for automatic generalisation from terms to concepts (Hinton et al., 1986). At the same time, from a computational perspective vector based representations provide both convenient intra-modal interfaces in multi-modal NLP systems and intra-lingual representations in machine translation systems (Kelleher, 2019).

[1]Both authors contributed equally.

Probabilistic Approaches to Linguistic Theory.
Jean-Philippe Bernardy, Rasmus Blanck,
Stergios Chatzikyriakidis, Shalom Lappin,
Aleksandre Maskharashvili (eds.).

Notwithstanding the fact that the advantages of distributed representations have been known for some time, for many years symbolic (local) representations–either based on logical formalisms or knowledge engineering–were dominant within NLP. However, systems built using these symbolic formalisms often struggle to adequately manage the ambiguity inherent in natural language, and the brittleness of rules based analysis (Gazdar, 1996). Throughout the 1990s the ground work was laid for the adoption of distributed representations within mainstream NLP. Examples of early work in this direction include (Schütze, 1993) and (Lund and Burgess, 1996). A commonality across both of these works is that the vector representation is learned from data through an analysis of lexical co-occurrence within a large-corpus. Today this focus on lexical co-occurrence is often framed as implementing the *distributional hypothesis* (Harris, 1954), popularised by Firth (1957) as the meaning of "a word is characterised by the company it keeps". These early works on inducing vector based representations through lexical co-occurrence can be seen as the progenitors of more recent work such as *word2vec* (Mikolov et al., 2013) and the Sesame Street models of ELMo (Peters et al., 2018) and BERT (Devlin et al., 2019).

The combination of distributional semantics with distributed representations, in tandem with modern methods for training of large neural language models, is now the dominant approach in NLP. Indeed, the dominance of this distributional+distributed+neural paradigm has begun to invite criticism, in particular with respect to claims attributing "understanding" to these models. For example, Bender and Koller (2020) propose a distinction between form and meaning—defining "(linguistic) meaning to be the relation between linguistic form and communicative intent"—and build on this distinction to argue that "the language modelling task, because it only uses form as training data, cannot in principle lead to learning of meaning". In a similar vein, Bisk et al. (2020) argue that "meaning does not arise from the statistical distribution of words" and argue that NLP as a field must move beyond solely training on massive internet based corpora, to consider aspects of meaning arising from perception, embodiment and social/interpersonal communication.

Sahlgren and Carlsson (2021) provide a counter voice to these criticisms. Although (Sahlgren and Carlsson, 2021) share a scepticism of claims that current language models achieve natural language understanding, they also argue that criticisms of distributional semantics as a basis for ultimately achieving language "understanding" are founded on the erroneous assumption that language meaning is a single and uniform phenomenon, and error that they name "the singleton fallacy". Furthermore, Sahlgren and Carlsson (2021) argue that criticisms of distributional approaches to semantics that are based on a distinction between form and meaning are fundamentally "dualist" and "defeatist": requiring the creation of an "entire human in silico" before allowing the attribution of natural language understanding to a computational system. By contrast, they propose that even if a distinction between form and meaning holds then there must be a linguistic correlate between form and meaning, and distributionalist approaches access this linguistic correlate enabling a system to access meaning: "in the sense that intentions (meanings) have the effects on linguistic signal (form) it will be possible to learn these effects by simply observing the signal" (Sahlgren and Carlsson, 2021, pg.5).

One thing that Bender and Koller (2020), Bisk et al. (2020) and Sahlgren and Carlsson (2021) do agree on is the importance of multimodality as a future research direction for natural language understanding. On this they also agree that in testing the extent to which a distributional approach can attain understanding of language it is a unnecessary restriction to only consider distributions across textual data, with all three pointing to the success of research on image captioning (e.g. Xu et al. (2015), Lindh et al. (2018), Herdade et al. (2019), Lindh et al. (2020)). Indeed, Sahlgren and Carlsson (2021) go so far as to argue that these systems can claim a "visual understanding" of language, and pose the question of whether there is anything about language that cannot be learned from a distributional analysis of a large (potentially multimodal) corpus?

In our view, an important omission from the current discussion on the extent to which language meaning is learnable via a distributional analysis of multimodal data is the question of situated spatial language. Visually situated dialogue is spoken from a particular point of view within a physical or simulated context, and from a computational semantics perspective provides a useful test-bed for grounding language meaning in vision (Kelleher, 2003, Dobnik, 2009). From a practical perspective a natural domain of application for situated dialogue systems is human-robot interaction (Kelleher and Kruijff, 2005a, Kruijff et al., 2006a, Dobnik and de Graaf, 2017). From a theoretical semantics perspective the resolution of linguistic references to referent's in the visual domain is interesting for a range of reasons. First, it requires intra-modal fusion (identifying that different occurrence of an object within a modality concern the same object, such as different views of the same object) and inter-modal fusion (Kruijff et al., 2006b). Second, is requires the system to have a perceptual memory both to enable intra-modal fusion (see (Kelleher, 2006) on co-reference classes), but also to enable the system to ground references to entities that were previously seen (Kelleher et al., 2005, Kelleher and Dobnik, 2019, Dobnik and Silfversparre, 2021). An inherent part of situated dialogue is spatial language, including references that refer to entities through their location (i.e., locative expressions) such as *the person near the table* (Kelleher and Costello, 2009), or references to contextually defined spatial regions, such as *the front of the room* in the robot command *go to the front of the room* (Hawes et al., 2012).

An error made by many researchers new to the field of situated spatial language is to equate spatial semantics with Euclidean geometry. However, a deeper analysis of the meaning of spatial descriptions reveals that the extent of the spatial regions linguistically described as *near the table* or *front of the room* are not definable via geometry alone. The definition of these regions are also sensitive to functional use, the perspective of the speaker and hearer, and the distribution of objects and the configuration of the enclosing region. Indeed, we believe that it is the oversimplification, by many researchers, of spatial semantics as equating to geometry, that is part of the reason why the challenge of spatial language is so often overlooked in discussions on linguistic meaning. This is most clearly seen in discussions relating to the ability of image captioning systems to ground language in vision. For example, as noted above, Sahlgren and Carlsson (2021) posit that these systems can claim to have a "visual understanding" of language despite that fact that, as Kelleher and Dobnik (2017) highlight, the "visual understanding" of spatial language attained by many of these systems is fundamentally limited by the fact that CNN visual encoders focus on *what* is in an image, and (deliberately) discard information relating to *where* an object is. Furthermore, although there are recent image captioning systems that explicitly address the challenge of spatial language (see for example (Yang et al., 2019, Yao et al., 2018, Herdade et al., 2019)) all of these approaches are founded on geometric features extracted from an object detector, and essentially reduce spatial semantics to geometry between bounding boxes.

Motivated by Sahlgren and Carlsson (2021) question of *what cannot be learned from a distributional analysis of a large (potentially multimodal) corpus*, and by a desire to highlight situated spatial language as a challenge for natural language understanding that requires more than geometry, in this chapter we examine aspects of the meaning of situated spatial language that might or might not be learnable via a distributional approach. The chapter begins by reviewing previous work on distribution semantics (Section 9.2), and this if followed by a review of previous work on situated spatial language (Section 9.3) that is structured around three themes of research: geometric approaches (Section 9.3.1), perception (Section 9.3.2), and functional aspects (Section 9.3.3). Following this review we discuss experimental work on identifying spatial knowledge from distributions of words over contexts (Section 9.4) and finally how distributional information interacts with representations of other modalities of probabilistic grounded language models (Section 9.5).

9.2 Distributional hypothesis

The history of distributional semantics can be traced at least as far back as (Harris, 1954). However, for this work we will limit our review to the most recent generation of computational work within the distributional tradition, beginning with the models of *word2vec* (Mikolov et al., 2013) and *GloVe* (Pennington et al., 2014).

A fundamental distinction on approaches to distributional semantics induced from corpora can be drawn based on the conceptualisation of the context used in the analysis. For example, some approaches, such as Latent Semantic Analysis (LAS) (Deerwester et al., 1990), use the documents in the corpus to define context and base the analysis on a "term-document" matrix. The focus of these approaches on the occurrences of terms within a document means that they are most naturally applied to document/information retrieval tasks.

By contrast, both word2vec and GloVe define context in terms of a window of words either side of a word. In these approaches each instance of a term in a corpus is taken to define an instance of a context, with the width of the contexts being hyper-parameter of a model and often being truncated by sentence boundaries. Given these instance+window based contexts, word2vec proceeds by training a neural network to make predictions of term co-occurrences within these contexts, either by predicting what terms co-occur with a given term (i.e., the continuous bag-of-words task) or what term co-occurs with a given context (i.e, the skip-gram task). This neural network model is trained by randomly initialising the distributed representation (embedding) for each term and then using the back-propagated errors of the network on the task to learn the term embeddings. GloVe, on the other hand, begins its analysis by constructing a "term-term" matrix where an entry in the matrix records the number of times that the column term occurred within the context window of an instance of the row term. This matrix is constructed by first identifying for each term in the vocabulary all instances of the term in the corpus, applying the context window onto each instances, and then for each term in the vocabulary recording the number of total number of occurrences of these terms across these contexts. A neural network model is then trained to predict the log of the co-occurrence count of two terms given the embeddings of the two terms as input.

Both of these distributional based models of semantics, GloVe and word2vec, are widely used within natural language processing research. However, as is natural with any successful and widely adopted research approach there has been an array of subsequent research that have critically assessed and extended these approaches in different ways. For example, Kacmajor and Kelleher (2020) highlight the distinction between thematic and taxonomic semantic relatedness, and their experiments indicate that although these models are good at capturing thematic relatedness they are limited in their ability to capture taxonomic relatedness. Interestingly, this limitation, however, provides an example of how the potential limitations of a distributional analysis can be addressed through the design of the corpus the analysis is performed on. For example, a number of researchers have explored combining a random walk process over a lexical taxonomy (such as WordNet) to generate a synthetic corpus so that proximity in the corpus reflects proximity within the taxonomy, and then applying a distributional analysis to the resulting corpus as a method for injecting taxonomic semantics into embeddings (Maldonado et al., 2019, Klubička et al., 2019, Kacmajor et al., 2020).

Another, perhaps better known, critique of the word2vec and GloVe methods is that they generate a single semantic representation (embedding) for a term, the implication being that this single semantic representation cannot do justice to the variety of meanings a term can have across difference contexts of uses. The best-known solutions developed for this drawback (e.g., ELMo (Peters et al., 2018) and BERT (Devlin et al., 2019)) have retained the core concept of a distributional semantics but coupled this with the contextual dynamism offered by language models, in order to generate contextualised embeddings that represent the meaning of a term in the given context.

Finally, the fact that these distributional based semantic models typically use distributed representations has meant that another critique of these methods is that it is difficult to understand what information they are capturing and encoding through the distributional analysis. This has resulted in a growing body of work focused on developing methods for *probing* these representations—e.g., (Salton et al., 2016, Conneau et al., 2018, Forbes et al., 2019, Ettinger, 2020, Nedumpozhimana and Kelleher, 2021, Ilinykh and Dobnik, 2021a,b,

2022, Nedumpozhimana et al., 2022)—in order to understand what information is encoded within them. This body of analytical work has revealed that these distributional based methods can capture and encode information relating to syntactic information (such as parts of speech, chunks, and subject-predicate agreements), semantic information (relating to semantic roles, entity types and relations), and of particular interest for the focus of this chapter although these methods can struggle with task requiring world knowledge, such as pragmatic inference, they are competitive on knowledge induction tasks (e.g., filling in blanks "cats like to chase __"), and they also have some ability with respect to capturing affordances and properties of objects (Rogers et al., 2020).

The abilities of these methods to capture and encode world knowledge, such as the properties of objects and their affordances, suggest that these distributional methods may be suitable for capturing aspects of spatial linguistic meaning that traditional approaches have struggled with. In the next section we will review the literature of spatial language, and following that we will present our analysis of the suitability of distributional methods to progress research on the spatial language semantics.

9.3 Situated spatial language

Physical sciences have developed ways in which space can be described with a high degree of accuracy, for example by measuring distances and angles. Furthermore, such measures can be represented on a continuous scale of real numbers. However, humans refer to space quite differently: descriptions such as "the chair is to the left of the table" or "turn right at the next crossroad" refer to discrete units such as points, regions and volumes and require knowledge about how the objects related interact with each other. We can also take different spatial perspectives which are frequently not explicitly described. For example, the same object can be to the left or to the right of another object depending on the viewpoint taken. Human spatial descriptions bridge perceptual and conceptual domains and are notoriously vague. Consequently, they need to be evaluated relative to each other and relative to the perceptual (visual salience, cf. (Kelleher et al., 2005)) and linguistic (discourse salience, cf. (Brennan and Clark, 1996)) contexts in which they occur and which changes as the interaction unfolds.

Spatial descriptions have been studied extensively in linguistics, computational linguistics, psychology, computer science and geo-information science. Classical surveys of their semantics can be found in

Herskovits (1986), Miller and Johnson-Laird (1976) and Talmy (2000). There are different categories of spatial descriptions which have slightly different properties. *Locative descriptions* describe locations of objects and individuals in scenes, for example "the chair is to the left of the table" or "the chair is between the table and the sofa". The object whose locations is being described is normally described as *target* while the other object whose location must be previously known is called the *landmark*. The spatial (locating) relationship between the target object and the landmark is frequently described using spatial terms that involve prepositions (e.g., 'X on Y', 'X in front of Y'). In English there are approximately 80 spatial prepositional descriptions in common use (Landau, 1996), and a distinction is made between those that primarily indicate a topological (i.e., contact, support, and so on) or proximal relationship (e.g., *at*, *on*, *in*, *near*, and so on), and those that indicate a directional or projective relationship (e.g., *behind*, *above*, *in front of*, and so on) (Kelleher and Kruijff, 2006). Spatial descriptions can also be describing actions in which case the relations involve verbs, for example "a skater is jumping over a fire hydrant". In this case the verb is further describing the nature of relation between the objects. Hence, the previous description of action is parallel to "a skater over a fire hydrant". *Route descriptions* and *route instructions* such as "follow this road until the next crossroad and then turn left" are another class of spatial descriptions where there is no explicit landmark object, since this is implicitly assumed to be the agent following the instruction.

Although the challenges for their modelling are well defined descriptively, to date there has been no unified computational model to represent their meaning. Early attempts in this direction were based on first order logic representations, see for example (Winograd, 1976) and (Miller and Johnson-Laird, 1976). However, these only represent the conceptual knowledge and ignore how this knowledge maps to the environment. Since these early works there has been a significant amount of work on spatial semantics that draw on the environmental context (often modelled through geometric models), perceptual factors and cues (such as visual occlusion and perspective), and world knowledge (capturing functional roles and affordances).

9.3.1 The geometry of the environment

From a computational semantics perspective the contextual environment of a spatial reference is often represented through a two-dimensional or three-dimensional coordinate frame in which we can represent objects and angles and distances between them. Psycho-linguistic research has found that people decide whether a spatial relation between a target object and an landmark object applies by anchoring a *spatial template* on the landmark that defines regions of differing degrees acceptability around the landmark where a given relation holds, see e.g. (Gapp, 1994, Logan and Sadler, 1996). Often these experiments were deliberately designed to exclude confounding factors, such as object roles and affordances and so forth. For example, in the experiments reported in Logan and Sadler (1996) the visual stimuli were 7-by-7 grid marked white regions with an O in the centre cell of the grid and an X in one of the other grid cells, and the accompanying linguistic descriptions of the form *The X is near to the O*. Given paired visual and linguistic stimuli subjects were asked to rate the acceptability of the description relative to the visual ground. Using this experimental setup, Logan and Sadler (1996) studied the semantics of the following prepositions: *above*, *below*, *over*, *under*, *left of*, *right of*, *next to*, *away from*, *near to*, and *far from*. The analysis of their results revealed that patterns of acceptability varied across these prepositions (i.e., each preposition has its own spatial template), but that there was similarity between groups of prepositions (for example, *next to* and *near to* have similar meanings). Table 1 lists the spatial template for *near to* as reported in Logan and Sadler (1996). The analysis of these spatial templates revealed a number of parameters relating to the extent of different regions of acceptability for given prepositions, such as the 90° maximum angle of deviation from the canonical direction vector for the acceptability of a projective prepositions (such as above *above*). Later experimental work explored how the shape and extent of spatial templates are affected by other contextual factors. For example, Costello and Kelleher (2006) explored how the presence and location of other (*distractor*) objects affected on the semantics of proximity (see Figure 1); Kelleher et al. (2009) investigated how topological distinctions, such as contact or overlap, affected acceptability judgements and distinctions between *at*, *on*, *in*, and *near*. Building on these experimental results a number of geometrically defined models of spatial semantics have been proposed, including (Regier and Carlson, 2001, Kelleher and Kruijff, 2005b, Kelleher et al., 2006, Kelleher and van Genabith, 2006). Several of these models have been implemented in robotic systems and have been used to ground the robot's interpretation of spatial commands in its sensor data, e.g. Gorniak and Roy (2004), Brenner et al. (2007), Schütte et al. (2017), Dobnik (2009).

1.74	1.90	2.84	3.16	2.34	1.81	2.13
2.61	3.84	4.66	4.97	4.90	3.56	3.26
4.06	5.56	7.55	7.97	7.29	4.80	3.91
4.47	5.91	8.52	**O**	7.90	6.13	4.46
3.47	4.81	6.94	7.56	7.31	5.59	3.63
3.25	4.03	4.50	4.78	4.41	3.47	3.10
1.84	2.23	2.03	3.06	2.53	2.13	2.00

TABLE 1: 7-by-7 cell grid with mean goodness ratings for the relation *the X is near to the O* as a function of the position occupied by X as reported in Logan and Sadler (1996).

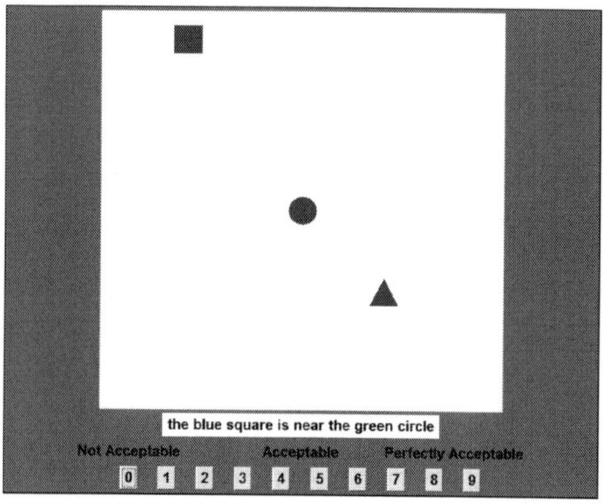

FIGURE 1: A example trial stimulus from the experiment reported in (Costello and Kelleher, 2006)

9.3.2 Perception, cognition, and perspective

Moving beyond the geometric relationships between entities in an environment, spatial semantics is also dependent on a range of factors that arise through embodiment, cognition, perception and perspective. Ullman (1980, 1984) argues against a 'direct perception' basis of visual perception and cognition, and instead proposes that the base representation provided by the visual perception module likely does not contain information about spatial relations but rather this derived through *visual routines*. This view is supported by psycho-linguistic evidence that suggests that spatial relations are not pre-attentively available, (Treisman and Gormican, 1988), and that their perception requires attention (Logan, 1994, 1995).

It is certainly the case that perception, and cognitive processes relating to perception (e.g., perceptual phenomena such as visual occlusion, visual attention, perceptual memory), affect the processing of spatial language. For example, eye-tracking research has found that visual context influences spoken word recognition and syntactic processing, even during the earliest stages of language processing (Tanenhaus et al., 1995). Also, neuro-physiological studies have suggested two distinct visual neural pathways: the *ventral* pathway processes extract information relating to *what* is in a scene, whereas the *dorsal* pathway—the *where/how*—extracts the information necessary to inform the grasping and manipulation of objects, such as size, orientation and location (Mishkin et al., 1983). Landau and Jackendoff (1993) use this neuro-physiological distinction to build an explanation of why language only distinguishes a relatively small number of distinct spatial relations as compared with the human capacity to encode and differentiate a very large number of faces and object types, and further suggest that *dorsal*, or *where*, pathway is the basis for the processing of spatial semantics (the reasoning being here that this pathway only provides a limited information about the detailed geometry of a visual scene and this limited information basis restricts the number of spatial distinctions encoded by language). Extending perceptual processing to include attentional mechanisms and constraints, the *attention vector sum model* proposed by Regier and Carlson (2001) can be understood as extending the *spatial template* paradigm to accommodate the role of visual attention in the processing of spatial templates. Furthermore, the interaction between visual and linguistic attention and perceptual memory has also been studied and modelled (Kelleher and van Genabith, 2004, Kelleher, 2006, Kelleher et al., 2005, Kelleher and Dobnik, 2019).

Another important cognitive factor that impinges on the semantics of spatial description is the perspective that the speaker and hearer assume is relevant for the spatial description. This is most obvious in the interpretation of directional (or projective) descriptions, such as "to the left of". These require a model of perspective which includes a viewpoint parameter (Maillat, 2003). In literature on spatial semantics, this model of perspective is often termed the *frame of reference*, and computationally modelled as consisting of six half-line axes with their origin at the landmark. In English these half-line axes are usually labelled *front*, *back*, *right*, *left*, *above*, *below*. Three different frames of reference are distinguished in most European languages (Levinson, 1996):

- *intrinsic/object centred*: the orientation of the co-ordinate system is aligned with the landmark object; e.g., the front direction is aligned with the direction the front of the landmark object is pointing towards.
- *relative/viewer centred/deictic*: assumes an ego-centric (observer's) perspective on the scene (typically that of the speaker)—distinct from the orientation of the objects being described—and the orientation of the co-ordinate system is aligned with the observer's view (i.e., front being defined as 'in front of' the speaker)
- *absolute/environment centred/allocentric*: the orientation of the co-ordinate system is aligned with salient properties of the environment; e.g., the above-below axes is aligned with gravity.

The viewpoint may be defined linguistically "from your view" or "from there" but it is frequently left out. This can be either inferred from the perceptual context (if only one interpretation is possible), object affordances ("a person behind the counter") or dynamics of perceptual and linguistic interaction in which case it is negotiated and aligned between conversational partners (Dobnik et al., 2014, 2015, 2020). There is a significant body of experimental work that has examined how ambiguity in relation to intended frame of reference affects cognitive processing and interpretation of a spatial description (Carlson-Radvansky and Irwin, 1993, 1994, Carlson-Radvansky and Logan, 1997, Kelleher and Costello, 2005, Li et al., 2011, Schultheis and Carlson, 2017). One of the findings from this work being that ambiguity with respect to the intended perspective (reference frame) of the speaker can result in multiple spatial templates being activated during the interpretation and competing and interacting to form a new context specific spatial template (Schultheis and Carlson, 2018).

The examples of directional/projective prepositions is also useful in terms of motivating work on the effect of perceptual phenomena, such as visual occlusion, on spatial semantics. For example, Jackendoff and Landau (1991) argue that visual occlusion likely impacts on the semantics of projective prepositions. Similarly the analysis of Vandeloise (1991) on the semantic distinctions between the French prepositions "devant/derriere" (approximately "before" and "behind") states that in many instances the distinction is based on the presence of absence of object occlusion. Furthermore, Kelleher et al. (2011) report psycho-linguistic experiments that demonstrate the effect of perceptual occlusion on the semantics of *in front of*, and that the predictive performance of the attention vector sum model of Regier and Carlson (2001) can be improved by integrating occlusion as a factor into the model.

The fact that on the one hand spatial relations are not pre-attentively available (i.e., the extracting and processing of these relations are triggered by language), and on the other that there is a variety of perceptual and cognitive factors that affect spatial semantics, raises the question of whether the identification and processing of spatial relationships is primarily driven by outputs of the visual system or by language. To paraphrase Talmy (1983): does language structure the perception of space, or does perception of space structure the processing of language? Allowing some stretching and tolerance in the discussion, this question of the primacy of language or perception for linguistic spatial semantics echoes the discussion we made in the introduction relating the proposition from Sahlgren and Carlsson (2021) that even if a distinction holds between form and meaning there must be a linguistic correlate between them, and distributionalist approaches can access this correlate. Broadly in this vein, Jackendoff (1985) has argued that grammatical structure offers an important source of evidence for understanding cognition, and uses the semantics of spatial expressions as a core exemplar in his analysis. By contrast, Lakoff and Johnson (1980) put space and spatial perception as a core building block of conceptual structure, and hence the extensive use of *spatial metaphor* in language. However, in more recent years there has been a growing awareness of the role of embodiment, the grounding of semantics in action, and the related concepts of object function and affordances. We will review work on these concepts in relation to spatial language in the following section.

9.3.3 Embodiment, world knowledge, object function and affordances

Noë (2004) argues that perception depends on the capacity for action: "Perceptual experience acquires content thanks to our possession of bodily skills. What we perceive is determined by what we do (or what we know how to do)." Although spatial linguistic semantics is not a central concern for Noë, his *enactive* approach to meaning aligns with a range of work on embodiment and spatial meaning. For example, Barsalou et al. (1999) sets out a perceptual theory of knowledge where the brain captures patterns of sensory-motor activations during perceptual experience, then through selective attention schematic representations of these sensory-motor patterns are stored in memory to form perceptual symbols. These perceptual symbols then become organised into *simulators*. Words then acquire meaning through associations with the simulators for the entities and events to which they refer. Of particular relevance to this discussion, Barsalou argues that spatial relations (and spatial terms) can be understood as simulators:

> "During the perception of a balloon above a cloud, for example, selective attention focuses on the occupied regions of space, filtering out the entities in them. As a result, a schematic representation of above develops that contains two schematic regions of space within one of several possible reference frames .... Following the similar extraction of information on other occasions, a simulator develops that can render many different *above* relations." (Barsalou et al., 1999, p.593)

Roy (2005) adopts a similar perspective to Barsalou and Noë, and proposes *semiotic schemas* as a framework for grounding language in action and perception. In this framework a schema is a structured network of belief that is grounded in an agent's environment through a causal-predictive cycle of action and perception. Furthermore, the basis of language production and comprehension involves operations on schemas. The form of schema most relevant to spatial descriptions, such as "the ball is in the cup", are *situation schemas* which might encode beliefs that the ball and cup are in *contact* and that the cup *contains* the ball. These beliefs are connected to perception and action by, for example if the ball and cup are in contact then the agent can predict that if they look at the cup they will likely see the ball in the vicinity, similarly the belief relating to cup containing the ball can be linked to action and perception by the fact that if the cup (the container) is moved the ball should also be perceived to move.

Building on the theoretical and empirical work relating spatial semantics to embodiment, action and perception, Coventry and Garrod (2004) propose a *functional geometric framework* for treatment of the semantics of spatial prepositions. A core element of the framework is a recognition and foregrounding of the affect of an object's functional role or affordances in the processing of some spatial prepositions. For example, Coventry and Garrod (2004) report experiments that examined differences in how functional roles and geometry affected the interpretation of the prepositions *over*, *under*, *above*, and *below*. In one of these experiment one object (an umbrella) had the function of protecting another object (a person) from falling rain. In this experiment the visual stimuli used in a trial consisted of drawing of a man holding an open umbrella and in some images rain is falling and in others there is no rain. The geometric relationship between the man and the umbrella varied across the images. In one set of images the umbrella was in the normal position of use (aligned with the gravitational plane and above the man); in a second set of images the umbrella was rotated 45° of vertical so that it was diagonally in front of and above the man; and, in a third set of images the umbrella was rotated 90° of vertical so that is was pointing along the horizontal axis in front of the man. Across these three sets of images there was no rain falling, or rain was falling and either falling onto the umbrella or the man. Each trial consisted of presenting one of the images to the subject along with a statement of the form *The umbrella is over the man* or *The umbrella is above the man*, and asking the subjects to score the appropriateness of the description. The analysis revealed that the variation in the geometric relationship between the man and the umbrella has the expected affect: rotating the umbrella away from the gravitational plane reduced the appropriateness of both *over* and *above*. The analysis also revealed, however, that the umbrella's functional role of protection also affected the appropriateness ratings. Scenes where the umbrella blocked the rain received higher scores than the corresponding umbrella and man configuration scenes where the umbrella did not block the rain. These studies also found that *over* and *under* were more influenced by functional roles as compared with *above* and *below*, and conversely that *above* and *below* were more sensitive to geometric factors. Overall the functional geometric framework can be understood as calling for a multi-factorial approach to spatial semantics, as Coventry and Garrod argue the "functional geometric framework, therefore, requires geometric routines, extra-geometric routines that capture dynamic-kinematic relations between objects, and stored representations that reflect stereotypical functional relations between objects" (Coventry and Garrod, 2004, p.127). The breadth of the factors considered in the functional-geometric framework together with the perceptual, cognitive, and embodied perspective reviewed above demonstrates the complexity and richness of situated spatial language as a test case for linguistic semantics.

9.4 What can a distributional analysis reveal about spatial language?

Our review of the literature on spatial language highlighted three major sources of information that inform spatial language use: the geometry of the environment; perception, cognition and perspective; and embodiment, world knowledge, object function and affordances. It is relatively easy to programme a computer to implement geometric models. Consequently, the majority of previous computational work on modelling spatial language has focused on creating geometric models of the environment based on sensor readings and implementing semantic models for spatial terms based on functions that define spatial templates within these geometric models. By contrast relatively little computational work has been done on modelling functional factors affecting spatial language use. This is primarily because, compared with geometric considerations, it is not obvious how to capture and integrate functional knowledge into computational models. However, here we argue that distributional analysis may be a useful approach to capture this functional relationships between objects. As we noted in the introduction, probing research on distributed representations learned through distributional analysis of text reveals that these embeddings do encode information with respect to affordances and properties of objects. In this section we explore the potential for distributional analysis to capture these functional based relationships between objects.

9.4.1 Distributional analysis of image captions reveals the functional and geometric bias of spatial prepositions

(Dobnik and Kelleher, 2013) describes two experiments where the *functional* and *geometric* bias of spatial relations is identified automatically from word distributions in the corpus text and the results are compared with the results of the psycholinguistics studies Coventry and Garrod (2004). The approach uses the textual parts of the IAPR TC-12 Benchmark corpus (Grubinger et al., 2006) and the 8K Image Flickr dataset (Rashtchian et al., 2010). It is important for the study that the descriptions are extracted from vision and language corpora so that the descriptions are constrained by the visual scene. A preliminary study was done on relations extracted from the British National Corpus (BNC) where the results were not clear cut since there were also frequent non-spatial metaphorical uses of the same relations, for example "in/over three days". The descriptions from both corpora are parsed for dependencies and then rules are manually constructed to normalise words and extract semantic representations of the form Relation(Target, Landmark). The reported results depend on the quality of the dependency parsing and the coverage of the extraction patterns.

The first experiment examines whether the strength of association between the target and landmark objects as captured in a language model corresponds to how strongly the objects are functionally related. The intuition underpinning the first experiment was that functional constraints are stronger than geometric ones, because they are focusing on particular dynamic kinematic routines between objects that are otherwise geometrically relatable. To measure the strength of the association between objects and relations Dobnik and Kelleher (2013) use Log Likelihood Ratio (Dunning, 1993),

$$log\lambda = log\frac{L(H_1)}{L(H2)} \tag{9.1}$$

which is a log ratio of the likelihood of the hypothesis H_1 over the hypothesis H_2 where H_1 is that the words in a bigram w_1w_2 are independent and H_2 that they are dependent. It therefore tells us how many times more likely H_2 is compared to H_1 and $-2log\lambda$ approximates the χ^2 distribution. The results indicate that the most likely relation for a target and landmark pair "boy-shirt" is "in" and then "with". The most likely relations for the landmark "umbrella" and some other target (e.g. people, boy, table, child, sculpture...) are either "with" and "under".

The second experiment reported in Dobnik and Kelleher (2013) was motivated by the observation that different relations have different selectional properties that can be related and this should be reflected in an information theoretic measure such as *entropy.* If some relations are functionally biased towards particular target-landmark pairs then this should be reflected in a lower entropy over the target-landmark pairs that occur with that relation in the corpus. Note that entropy measures uncertainty, via the distribution across possibilities, and so an entropy based analysis of a corpus naturally aligns with a distributional perspective on language. For example, in the experimental studies such as (Coventry and Garrod, 2004) "in", "on" and "over" have been identified as being influenced by the functional component and these relations are predicted by the corpus study to have a low entropy of target-landmark pairs compared to their corresponding geometrically biased variants such as "above". (Dobnik and Kelleher, 2013) did find that functionally influenced prepositions, such as "over", do tend to have lower entropy over their target-landmark pairs as compared with non-functionally sensitive counterpart, such as "above".

Dobnik and Kelleher (2014) present two additional experiments based on the same datasets. First, the target and landmark objects that occur with a particular relation are clustered in conceptual categories. The conceptual categories of targets and landmarks occurring with each relation are determined using the synsets of WordNet and the *class-labelling algorithm* (Widdows, 2003) which given a list of words finds a hypernym that subsumes as many words in the list as possible and is applied recursively until all the words are exhausted. The extracted conceptual categories represent semantic classes of target and landmark objects that occur with each relation. Then, based on these clusters, patterns of relations relating different conceptual categories are automatically extracted. Following the previous intuition that functional relations constrain more specific objects it is expected that functional relations will give rise to more patterns as well as these patterns containing more specific classes of objects, and hence more conceptual categories. Tuples ⟨target, relation, landmark⟩ are rewritten as ⟨target-class, relation, landmark⟩ such as (i) travel.v.01 over object.n.01 (9/713), bridge.n.01 over object.n.01 (23/713), bridge.n.01 over body of water.n.01 (42/713) and (ii) person.n.01 under tree.n.01 (7/213), shirt.n.01 under sweater.n.01 (8/213), person.n.01 under body of water.n.01 (11/213), person.n.01 under artifact.n.01 (13/213). The numbers in the brackets indicate the number of times an example following that pattern occurs in the dataset out of the total number of times a relation is found. The automatically extracted patterns reveal different situations of objects being related reflecting human conceptualisation of objects and space which require quite distinct geometric arrangements. In fact, they are similar to examples of spatial relations reported in linguistic literature such as (Herskovits, 1986, Levinson, 2003).

Returning to the question of assessing the functional sensitivity of different spatial relations, the question of how general and specific are the relational patterns for a given preposition arises: recall the intuition that the more functionally sensitive the semantics of a spatial preposition the more specific the objects it encodes relationships between? To estimate the specificity of the extracted patterns, and hence the specificity (functional sensitivity) of the preposition that occurs within the patterns, Dobnik and Kelleher (2014) calculated the following measures: (i) the average depth of the target and landmark synset hypernyms, (ii) the number of patterns created, and (iii) the entropy of examples of these patterns in the dataset. Their results were that the ranking of spatial prepositions across these three measures in terms of specificity of the patterns the prepositions occur within had high agreement. Furthermore, in these rankings spatial preposition that are known to be functionally sensitive—based on experimental work such as (Coventry and Garrod, 2004)—were found to be more specific in terms of the patterns they occurred in.

What the experiments in (Dobnik and Kelleher, 2013) and (Dobnik and Kelleher, 2014) demonstrate is that distributional analysis of corpora can reveal information relating to the functional semantics of spatial prepositions.

9.4.2 Neural language models attain different perplexity when generating functional and geometric relations

The previous method extracts targets and landmarks for a given relation independently to form patterns of relations between them. However, during interaction a describer chooses one of the objects they would like to refer to and then a particular landmark conditioned on the target: this has to be functionally associated with the target and visually and linguistically salient in the interaction. The interpreter exploits this salience of the landmark to locate a suitable target which means that the conditioning is reversed here: potential targets are identified by being conditioned on the landmark. Since a relation describes a particular functional and geometric interaction between target and landmark it is conditioned by both. (Dobnik et al., 2018) examines how such relations are captured in a *neural language model* (Bengio et al., 2003, Mikolov et al., 2010, Salton et al., 2017) and also attempts to identify their functional geometric bias by examining language model *perplexity*.

A neural language model estimates the probabilities of a sequence of words by optimising the parameters of the neural architecture based on *cross-entropy loss*. The loss of a neural language model comparing the predicted words with the ground truth is the average *surprisal* over that batch of data. From the loss a measure of *perplexity* can be defined for a particular sequence of words T as follows:

$$Perplexity(S, P) = 2^{E_S[-log_2(P(w_{1:T}))]} \tag{9.2}$$

Perplexity therefore indicates a measure of fit of the language model with a sample sequence. Returning to spatial relations, if descriptions involving functional spatial relations are more selective in choice of their vocabulary (target, landmark and relation) then such sequences are more predictable in the dataset which means that this will result in lower perplexity of the language model.

Dobnik et al. (2018) use the Visual Genome corpus (Krishna et al., 2017) for their experiments. The Visual Genome corpus is a crowd-source annotated corpus of 108K images including *relationships* between objects identified in bounding boxes, for example "cup on table", "girl holding on to bear" and "woman standing on snow". The data is split into 10-folds and a neural language model is trained and validated over these sequences and average results are reported. Dobnik et al. (2018) extracted static spatial relations from these patterns using a dictionary of terms reported in (Landau, 1996, Herskovits, 1986). Other pre-processing steps include re-writing composite spatial relations as single tokens ("jumping_over" and "to the left of", "to left of" → "left") and some additional text normalisation and selection was performed to reduce unwanted variation in the text. The descriptions were then structured into sequences following the pattern <s> target relation landmark </s>. Once the pre-processing was completed the data was split into 10-folds and a neural language model was trained and validated over these sequences and average results calculated.

Figure 2 shows the average perplexities of descriptions containing particular spatial relations. Dark grey and black identify relations that are known to have a functional or geometric bias respectively. Descriptions of the same bias cluster together. Furthermore, descriptions containing relations with a functional bias are more predictable by a language model than those that have a geometric bias. It therefore follows that in the latter relations a geometric grounding plays a stronger role in order for them to be interpretable. Overall, these experiments demonstrate that language models learn specific contexts for both functionally and geometrically-biased spatial relations.

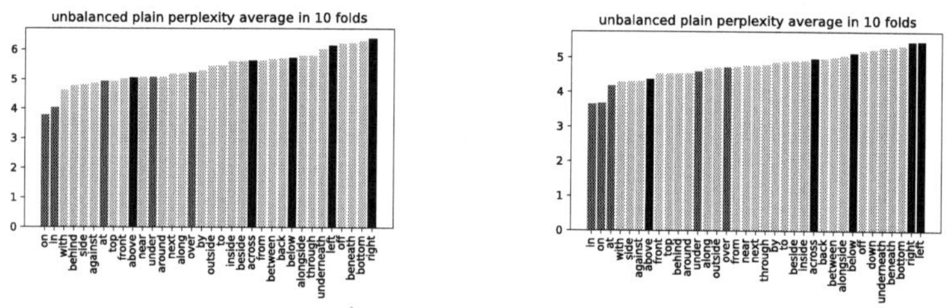

(a) test-set

(b) training set

FIGURE 2: Mean perplexities of spatial descriptions of LM1 (dark grey: functionally biased, black: geometrically biased relations).

In a follow up experiment Ghanimifard and Dobnik (2019a) evaluate these contexts more closely using the same method. We have seen that spatial relations are similar or dissimilar depending on what kind of context target and landmark objects they occur with. If two relations occur with similar targets and landmarks, then projecting a relation in the context of the second relation will lead to a low average surprisal of the language model measured by its perplexity. This way all relations can be compared with each other: descriptions containing a particular relation are first collected and then the relation is swapped by another relation and an average perplexity of the language model over this collection of descriptions is calculated. This is repeated for all relations. The average perplexity values over the relations can then be represented

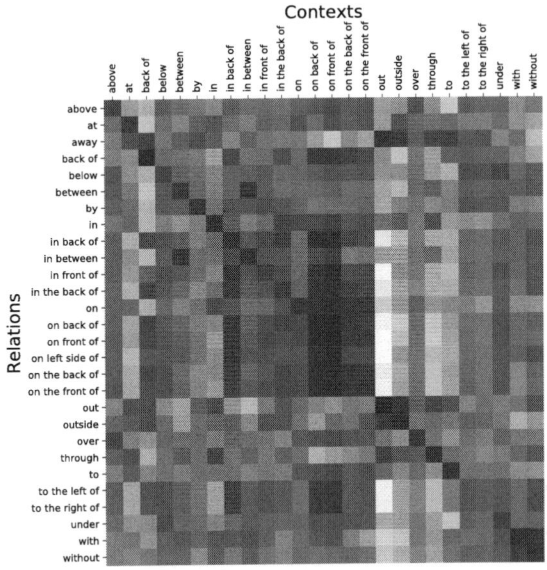

FIGURE 3: A matrix of perplexity vectors for 28 spatial relations and 26 contexts.

as values of a vector defined by the contexts. Using this methodology Ghanimifard and Dobnik (2019a) analysed the swapability of relations, in terms of the relative increase of perplexity when a relation is swapped. Figure 3 shows the perplexity vectors for 28 relations over 26 contexts. K-means clustering of these contextual vectors identifies clusters of similar vectors and relations that have similar selectional biases.

These perplexity vectors for spatial relations appear to be so strongly discriminative of the relation so that they can be used in several common semantic reasoning tasks. For example, they were tested in the odd-one-out task where relations are grouped on the basis of the geometric criteria, e.g. axes "left" and "right", containment "in" and "out" and proximity "near". To these pairs an odd word is added from another pair that the model must identify. The results indicate that the perplexity vector of a language model trained on textual information can discriminate words by the geometric criteria without ever seeing the scenes that descriptions are referring to. This is because functional and geometric knowledge are complementary and bias to one particular knowledge means less bias to the other. Overall, the work demonstrates that although spatial relations have different selectional requirements there are similarities between their functional and geometric bias. Furthermore, knowing the functional bias one is able to predict also the geometric bias since they are in complementary distribution. This way language models might be capturing some grounding information about the world without ever experiencing the world.

If functional and geometric bias are complementary then differences for different spatial relations should also be observable in the geometric domain. The literature on spatial cognition gives a plenty of examples of situations where particular relation would be chosen by a speaker but where objects are displaced from the typical location where we would expected them to be based on the geometric considerations alone. For example, "the umbrella is over a man" still holds when this is held horizontally providing that it is protecting the person from the rain and "apples are in a bowl" is acceptable where the volumes of some apples are not contained in the volume of the bowl as long as the bowl is constraining the movement of the apples so that they do not fall of the heap of the apples that are geometrically contained in the bowl. This suggest that due to the effect of the functional interactions between objects their locations represented as bounding boxes are expected to be more variable and diverging from the geometric axes, thus *where* they are. However, such relations are more restrictive in terms of *what* objects they relate to as shown in the previous discussion. The opposite is expected for geometrically biased relations.

(Dobnik and Ghanimifard, 2020) tests this hypothesis on the Visual Genome corpus (Krishna et al., 2017) using a similar extracting and pre-processing method to the one described earlier, this time also including descriptions of actions that refer to dynamic relations between objects. To calculate the relation between bounding boxes of target and landmark for a particular relation *dense vectors* with dimensions $[x, y, d]$ are created, where x and y represent directions between two points p_1 representing the target and p_2 representing the landmark in a 2-dimensional space and d is the Euclidean distance between these two points. The distance is assigned a negative prefix if p_2 from the target is also a point in the landmark. Otherwise, the distance is a positive value. The vectors are inspired by the Attentional Vector Sum (AVS) model (Regier and Carlson, 2001) in terms of capturing directions and by the spatial template model (Logan and Sadler, 1996) in terms of capturing distances. The two kinds of representations are also motivated by the difference between *projective* ("to the left of") and *topological relations* ("near"). While the former are sensitive to distance and direction, the latter are only sensitive to distance. An image is segmented into a grid of 7×7 locations and for each location representing target and landmark

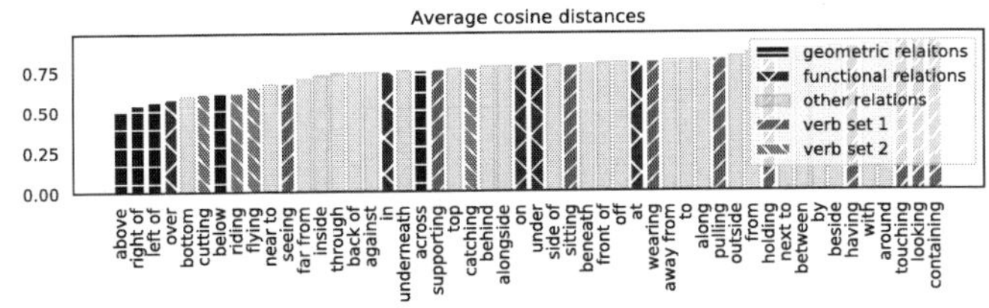

FIGURE 4: The average cosine distance of dense vectors $[x, y, d]$ from the average dense vector per spatial relation.

such a vector is calculated. Vectors are then collected across images for each instance of that relation between objects and finally averaged into a single vector. Using a similar method spatial templates from (Logan and Sadler, 1996) are also converted to single comparable vectors. A cosine similarity between these vectors indicates that vectors extracted from the Visual Genome are similar to those vectors from the spatial template experiments which validates the approach.

In order to estimate the variation of target and landmark objects that is indicative of functional and geometric bias a deviation of individual vectors from the average vector for a particular relation is determined using cosine distance as shown in Figure 4. An average cosine distance close to 0 indicates a stronger central tendency and therefore a geometric bias. Functionally and geometrically biased relations reported in the literature are indicated in brown and blue respectively. Verb set 1 are those verbs reported in (Collell et al., 2018) where the location of the landmark is predicted the least from the y dimension (e.g. "see") and Verb set 2 are those where the location of the target is most strongly predicted from the y dimension (e.g. "flying"). Figure 4 demonstrates that the dense vectors for the geometrically-biased relations tend to deviate from the mean dense vectors less than those for functionally-biased relations and the same trend is observed with the two groups of verbs. The clustering of cosine similarities for individual relations reveals different contexts of object interactions resembling different conceptualisations of (Herskovits, 1986) and that there may be an overlap of vectors between geometric and functional locations where both of these constraints are satisfied.

The preceding discussion demonstrates that an important part of semantics of spatial relations which also include verbs is captured by distributed representations that are estimated from word contexts. The semantics that distributed representations capture are those that refer to functional interactions between objects, the dynamic kinematic routines that reflect human take on the world and are therefore part of the common-sense semantic knowledge about *what* objects are interacting. Since objects and events are taking place in physical space different relations also refer to *where* these objects are, how they are grounded in the geometric representation of space. Different relations are biased to function or geometry differently and so the bias can be evaluated on a scale rather than being fixed for two classes of relations. Importantly, since the two dimensions of meaning are complementary to each other, a bias to one is also reflected in the other and therefore predictions of one also has implications on the prediction of the other. Furthermore, the experimental study in (Dobnik and Åstbom, 2017) suggests that this bias is not fixed even for individual relations and that contextual factors might affect it.

9.5 Grounded language models

In the previous section we have examined the contribution of semantic information for different kind of linguistic descriptions but how is this information captured as representations of probabilistic neural language models? We call language models that contain semantic information from word and perceptual contexts *probabilistic grounded language models.* Descriptions contain sequences of words that might be grounded in different modalities to a different degree as well as there are dependencies between words or structures in these descriptions which define the *compositionality* of natural language. (Ghanimifard and Dobnik, 2017) examines to what degree a neural language model is able to learn compositionality of complex spatial descriptions that contain one or more spatial relations, connectives such as "and", "either" and "or", the modifier "not" and other (distractor) words such as functional words which are expected to have no perceptual but only linguistic grounding in the word contexts. If meaning of linguistic representations is compositional as suggested by formal semantics (Montague, 1974, Blackburn and Bos, 2005) which requires that every composed semantic representation has an interpretation relative to a model, then in the case of grounded language models we should observe that the predictions of sequences of words will map to the underlying perceptual representations.

Ghanimifard and Dobnik (2017) generate an artificial dataset of descriptions over locations from the acceptability judgements reported in (Logan and Sadler, 1996), for the prepositions *above*, *below*, *over*, *under*, *left of*, *right of*, *next to*, *away from*, *near to* and *far from*, and the connectives described above. Locations are the 48 locations the target object can occupy in the 7×7 grid used in the experiment, see Table 1 (the 49th location is the centre where the landmark is located).

Examples are created for individual expressions. For the grounded language model an LSTM is used as encoder and decoder. The input is an embedding vector learned from the one-hot encoded words which is concatenated with the location of the target and the output is a prediction of the following word. For example, assuming the target object is located in the top left quadrant of the grid, if the model is provided the input embedding for the sequence *left of and* then the correct next word prediction would be *above*. The model is evaluated on held-out sequences of composed descriptions where individual word tokens have been seen during training but their compositions are novel to the model. The next word probabilities over the vocabulary returned by a model can be thought of as acceptability judgements of words for that particular input location and can be aggregated to create spatial templates. The spatial templates generated from the data of a grounded neural language model on new composed phrases can then be compared with the original spatial templates from which the training data has been generated. Correlation with Spearman's ρ indicates that overall there is a high correlation between the predicated and the ground truth spatial templates when evaluated on the same dataset as the training one. Similarly the model is also able to predict simple descriptions containing a single relation while only seeing composed phrases during training. Effectively, the model has learned how to decompose phrases in terms of perceptual grounding.

These results indicate that grounded neural language models can capture very well semantic information from word and perceptual contexts in the form of *grounded dense word embeddings*. However, it is important to note that not all language models ground the meanings of spatial relations, indeed during generation (for example in an image captioning scenario) language models often generate ungrounded relations which are also known as *hallucinations* of language models.

For example, Ghanimifard and Dobnik (2018) examine the adaptive attention in a pre-trained model of (Lu et al., 2017). They start by extracting spatial descriptions and their corresponding images from the MS-COCO test corpus and investigating where the model directed its attention to when processing an image and a spatial description. Note that in this model the attention is explicitly modelled as complementary between the attention on the image features and attention from the language model. A comparison of the POS-tags of words that receive visual attention reveals that this is primarily focused on those tags that make up noun-phrases, e.g. NUM, NOUN, ADJ, DET, while VERB receives moderate attention and ADV(erbs) and ADP(ositions) are among the least attend POS-tags, only above PRON and PRT.

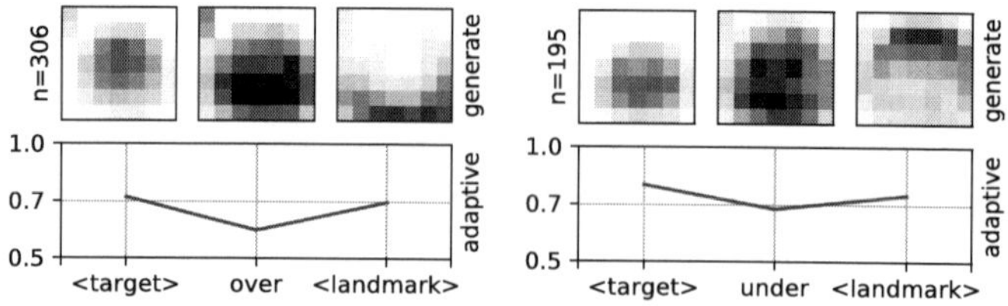

FIGURE 5: Average visual and language attention over a grid of 7×7 locations in images. Darker values indicate stronger visual attention and weaker language attention. The shades are relative to each other only within a box.

Average adaptive attention on words referring to targets, relations and landmarks is also estimated. As shown in Figure 5 this analysis reveals that spatial relations overall receive less visual attention than targets and landmarks. It is also interesting that landmarks receive slightly less visual attention than targets, perhaps because they can be predicted from the sequential language model. The visual attention for relations is not only weaker but also more dispersed which indicates that it is not capturing geometric arrangements between target and landmark that we observe in spatial templates but is driven by some other factors, possibly related to the representations of targets and landmarks.

Visual features from pre-trained object classifiers are therefore useful for identifying objects but not relations between objects which are not directly identified by visual features. What happens in the same model when geometric features about the objects are explicitly added and a grounded language model is allowed to attend over them as well? What is the optimal representation of geometry between targets and landmarks? Ghanimifard and Dobnik (2019b) extend the previous model of adaptive attention to a model that can attend different representations of the scene: (a) visual features from bounding boxes of annotated objects, (b) ordered visual features of the target and landmark bounding boxes, (c) ordered features representing geometric relations between the target and landmark objects. The models are compared to two baseline models: (i) model without attention and (ii) a model with adaptive attention over the visual features of the entire scene. For training and evaluation again Visual Genome is used (Krishna et al., 2017). The descriptions generated from these annotations are therefore simple descriptions containing <s> target relation landmark </s>. A comparison of cross-entropy loss of different models indicates that top-down infused knowledge about objects and their geometric arrangement has a positive effect compared to using

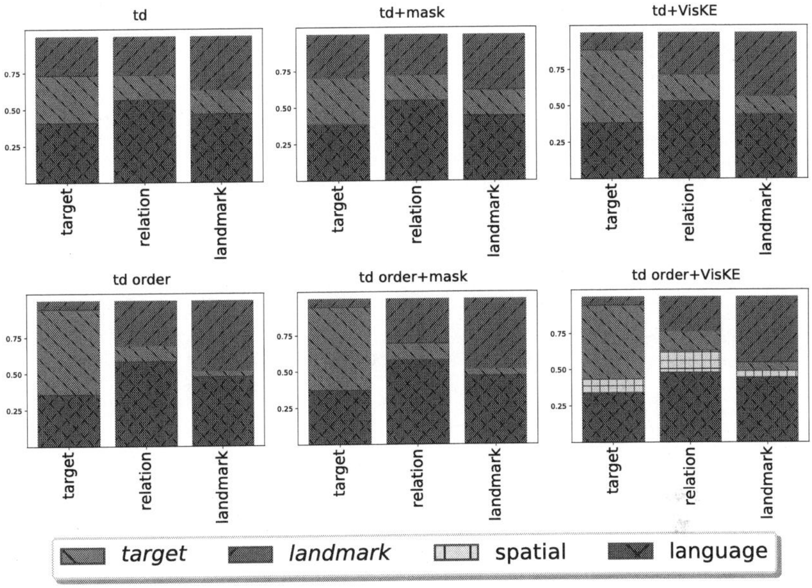

FIGURE 6: The average adaptive attention β on targets, relations and landmarks for different models. td: visual features within object bounding boxes, td order: ordered visual features of target and landmark objects, +mask: added masks of object bounding boxes as geometric features, +VisKE: added geometric relations between bounding boxes from VisKE (Sadeghi et al., 2015)

purely bottom-up knowledge. Overall, (b) identification of visual features of targets and landmarks leads to the largest improvement, greater than (c) geometric relations between targets and landmarks. When (b) and (c) are used together this leads to a further but small improvement over (b). Difference between relations are observed which suggests that not all features are equally relevant for all relations.

Figure 6 shows adaptive attention for individual parts of a description in respect of different features. The results indicate that only in the second case (td order), where the visual features of a target and a landmark are explicitly identified, geometric spatial features are used and that VisKE features (Sadeghi et al., 2015) which represent geometric properties and relations between target and landmark bounding boxes are more effective than masked representations of object bounding boxes. Identification of the visual features of targets and landmarks (td order) is better than only providing visual features of objects (td) as this family of models is able to attend better the target and landmark descriptions. Overall, the investigation shows that integration of top-down features has a positive effect on the performance of grounded language models but different features have different effect on different classes of relations. The results indicate that the question of feature representation and optimal information fusion is still very much open for the current and future research on grounded vision and language models.

9.6 Conclusion

The background to this article is the ongoing debate relating to the level of language "understanding" large language models, that encode a distributional analysis of text corpora, can claim. We have proposed that situated spatial language is a useful use-case for this debate to consider. This proposal is based on the observation that the variety of information types that spatial language draws upon make it a challenging research topic for computational systems. In particular, successfully understanding and generating situated spatial language requires the ability to blend geometric, perceptual, and functional/world knowledge. A key argument put forward in this article is that distributional semantics may provide an approach that is particularly suited to learning and encoding the functional/world knowledge information necessary to process spatial language. In support of this argument, in the later half of this article we have showcased a number of works that have demonstrated how distributional analysis (be it via an entropy based analysis of image captions, or the behaviour of language models) can reveal aspects of spatial semantics related to function. Much more work is necessary to understand precisely how distributional analysis can be best integrated with geometric and perceptual models to fully do justice to the richness of situated spatial semantics. However, we believe that recognising that distributional analysis provides basis to learning functional relationships between objects provides a useful direction for future work on spatial language.

Acknowledgements

The research of Kelleher was supported by the ADAPT Centre for Digital Content Technology which is funded under the SFI Research Centres Programme (Grant 13/RC/2106_P2) and is co-funded under the European Regional Development Fund. The research of Dobnik was supported by a grant from the Swedish Research Council (VR project 2014–39) for the establishment of the Centre for Linguistic Theory and Studies in Probability (CLASP) at the University of Gothenburg.

References

Barsalou, Lawrence W et al. 1999. Perceptual symbol systems. *Behavioral and brain sciences* 22(4):577–660.

Bender, Emily M. and Alexander Koller. 2020. Climbing towards NLU: On meaning, form, and understanding in the age of data. In *Proceedings of the 58th Annual Meeting of the Association for Computational Linguistics*, pages 5185–5198. Online: Association for Computational Linguistics.

Bengio, Yoshua, Réjean Ducharme, Pascal Vincent, and Christian Janvin. 2003. A neural probabilistic language model. *Journal of Machine Learning Research* 3(6):1137–1155.

Bisk, Yonatan, Ari Holtzman, Jesse Thomason, Jacob Andreas, Yoshua Bengio, Joyce Chai, Mirella Lapata, Angeliki Lazaridou, Jonathan May, Aleksandr Nisnevich, et al. 2020. Experience grounds language. In *Proceedings of the 2020 Conference on Empirical Methods in Natural Language Processing (EMNLP)*, pages 8718–8735.

Blackburn, Patrick and Johan Bos. 2005. *Representation and inference for natural language. A first course in computational semantics*. CSLI Publications.

Brennan, Susan E and Herbert H Clark. 1996. Conceptual pacts and lexical choice in conversation. *Journal of Experimental Psychology: Learning, Memory, and Cognition* 22(6):1482–1493.

Brenner, Michael, Nick Hawes, John D Kelleher, and Jeremy L Wyatt. 2007. Mediating between qualitative and quantitative representations for task-orientated human-robot interaction. In *Proceedings of the International Joint Conference on Artificial Intelligence*, pages 2072–2077.

Carlson-Radvansky, Laura A and David E Irwin. 1993. Frames of reference in vision and language: Where is above? *Cognition* 46(3):223–244.

Carlson-Radvansky, Laura A and David E Irwin. 1994. Reference frame activation during spatial term assignment. *Journal of memory and language* 33(5):646–671.

Carlson-Radvansky, Laura A and Gordon D Logan. 1997. The influence of reference frame selection on spatial template construction. *Journal of memory and language* 37(3):411–437.

Collell, Guillem, Luc Van Gool, and Marie-Francine Moens. 2018. Acquiring common sense spatial knowledge through implicit spatial templates. *Proceedings of the AAAI Conference on Artificial Intelligence* 32(1).

Conneau, Alexis, German Kruszewski, Guillaume Lample, Loïc Barrault, and Marco Baroni. 2018. What you can cram into a single $&!#* vector: Probing sentence embeddings for linguistic properties. In *ACL 2018-56th Annual Meeting of the Association for Computational Linguistics*, vol. 1, pages 2126–2136. Association for Computational Linguistics.

Costello, Fintan J and John Kelleher. 2006. Spatial prepositions in context: The semantics of near in the presence of distractor objects. In *Proceedings of the Third ACL-SIGSEM Workshop on Prepositions*.

Coventry, Kenny R and Simon C Garrod. 2004. *Saying, seeing and acting: The psychological semantics of spatial prepositions*. Psychology Press.

Deerwester, Scott, Susan T Dumais, George W Furnas, Thomas K Landauer, and Richard Harshman. 1990. Indexing by latent semantic analysis. *Journal of the American society for information science* 41(6):391–407.

Devlin, Jacob, Ming-Wei Chang, Kenton Lee, and Kristina Toutanova. 2019. Bert: Pre-training of deep bidirectional transformers for language understanding. In *Proceedings of the 2019 Conference of the North American Chapter of the Association for Computational Linguistics: Human Language Technologies (NAACL-HLT)*, pages 4171–4186.

Dobnik, Simon. 2009. *Teaching mobile robots to use spatial words*. Ph.D. thesis, University of Oxford: Faculty of Linguistics, Philology and Phonetics and The Queen's College, Oxford, United Kingdom.

Dobnik, Simon and Amelie Åstbom. 2017. (Perceptual) grounding as interaction. In V. Petukhova and Y. Tian, eds., *Proceedings of Saardial – Semdial 2017: The 21st Workshop on the Semantics and Pragmatics of Dialogue*, pages 17–26. Saarbrücken, Germany.

Dobnik, Simon and Erik de Graaf. 2017. KILLE: a framework for situated agents for learning language through interaction. In J. Tiedemann and N. Tahmasebi, eds., *Proceedings of the 21st Nordic Conference on Computational Linguistics (NoDaLiDa)*, pages 162–171. Northern European Association for Language Technology (NEALT), Gothenburg, Sweden: Association for Computational Linguistics.

Dobnik, Simon and Mehdi Ghanimifard. 2020. Spatial descriptions on a functional-geometric spectrum: the location of objects. In J. Šķilters, N. S. Newcombe, and D. Uttal, eds., *Spatial Cognition XII: Proceedings of the 12th International Conference, Spatial Cognition 2020, Riga, Latvia*, pages 219–234. Cham, Switzerland: Springer International Publishing.

Dobnik, Simon, Mehdi Ghanimifard, and John D. Kelleher. 2018. Exploring the functional and geometric bias of spatial relations using neural language models. In *Proceedings of the First International Workshop on Spatial Language Understanding (SpLU 2018) at NAACL-HLT 2018*, pages 1–11. Association for Computational Linguistics, New Orleans, Louisiana, USA.

Dobnik, Simon, Christine Howes, and John D. Kelleher. 2015. Changing perspective: Local alignment of reference frames in dialogue. In C. Howes and S. Larsson, eds., *Proceedings of goDIAL – Semdial 2015: The 19th Workshop on the Semantics and Pragmatics of Dialogue*, pages 24–32. Gothenburg, Sweden.

Dobnik, Simon and John D. Kelleher. 2013. Towards an automatic identification of functional and geometric spatial prepositions. In *Proceedings of PRE-CogSci 2013 Production of referring expressions – bridging the gap between cognitive and computational approaches to reference at CogSci*, pages 1–6. Berlin, Germany.

Dobnik, Simon and John D. Kelleher. 2014. Exploration of functional semantics of prepositions from corpora of descriptions of visual scenes. In *Proceedings of the Third V&L Net Workshop on Vision and Language at COLING*, pages 33–37. Dublin, Ireland: Dublin City University and the Association for Computational Linguistics.

Dobnik, Simon, John D. Kelleher, and Christine Howes. 2020. Local alignment of frame of reference assignment in English and Swedish dialogue. In J. Šķilters, N. S. Newcombe, and D. Uttal, eds., *Spatial Cognition XII: Proceedings of the 12th International Conference, Spatial Cognition 2020, Riga, Latvia*, pages 251–267. Cham, Switzerland: Springer International Publishing.

Dobnik, Simon, John D. Kelleher, and Christos Koniaris. 2014. Priming and alignment of frame of reference in situated conversation. In V. Rieser and P. Muller, eds., *Proceedings of DialWatt – Semdial 2014: The 18th Workshop on the Semantics and Pragmatics of Dialogue*, pages 43–52. Edinburgh.

Dobnik, Simon and Vera Silfversparre. 2021. The red cup on the left: Reference, coreference and attention in visual dialogue. In E. Breitholtz, K. Georgila, and D. Schlangen, eds., *Proceedings of PotsDial - Semdial 2021: The 25th Workshop on the Semantics and Pragmatics of Dialogue*, Proceedings (SemDial), pages 50–60. Potsdam, Germany.

Dunning, Ted. 1993. Accurate methods for the statistics of surprise and coincidence. *Computational Linguistics* 19(1):61–74.

Ettinger, Allyson. 2020. What BERT is not: Lessons from a new suite of psycholinguistic diagnostics for language models. *Transactions of the Association for Computational Linguistics* 8:34–48.

Firth, John R. 1957. A synopsis of linguistic theory, 1930–1955. *Studies in linguistic analysis* Special volume of the Philological Society:1–32.

Forbes, Maxwell, Ari Holtzman, and Yejin Choi. 2019. Do neural language representations learn physical commonsense? *arXiv preprint arXiv:1908.02899* .

Gapp, Klaus-Peter. 1994. Basic meanings of spatial relations: Computation and evaluation in 3d space. In B. Hayes-Roth and R. E. Korf, eds., *AAAI*, pages 1393–1398. AAAI Press/The MIT Press. ISBN 0-262-61102-3.

Gazdar, Gerald. 1996. Paradigm merger in natural language processing. In I. Wand and R. Milner, eds., *Computing tomorrow: future research directions in computer science*, pages 88–109. Cambridge University Press.

Ghanimifard, Mehdi and Simon Dobnik. 2017. Learning to compose spatial relations with grounded neural language models. In C. Gardent and C. Retoré, eds., *Proceedings of IWCS 2017: 12th International Conference on Computational Semantics*, pages 1–12. Montpellier, France: Association for Computational Linguistics.

Ghanimifard, Mehdi and Simon Dobnik. 2018. Knowing when to look for what and where: Evaluating generation of spatial descriptions with adaptive attention. In L. Leal-Taixé and S. Roth, eds., *Computer Vision – ECCV 2018 Workshops. ECCV 2018*, vol. 11132 of *Lecture Notes in Computer Science (LNCS)*, pages 1–9. Proceedings of the Workshop on Shortcomings in Vision and Language (SiVL), ECCV 2018, Munich, Germany: Springer, Cham.

Ghanimifard, Mehdi and Simon Dobnik. 2019a. What a neural language model tells us about spatial relations. In A. Bhatia, Y. Bisk, P. Kordjamshidi, and J. Thomason, eds., *Proceedings of the Combined Workshop on Spatial Language Understanding (SpLU) and Grounded Communication for Robotics (RoboNLP)*, pages 71–81. North American Chapter of the Association for Computational Linguistics: Human Language Technologies (NAACL-HLT 2019), Minneapolis, Minnesota, USA: Association for Computational Linguistics.

Ghanimifard, Mehdi and Simon Dobnik. 2019b. What goes into a word: generating image descriptions with top-down spatial knowledge. In K. van Deemter, C. Lin, and H. Takamura, eds., *Proceedings of the 12th International Conference on Natural Language Generation (INLG-2019)*, pages 1–15. Association for Computational Linguistics, Tokyo, Japan.

Gorniak, Peter and Deb Roy. 2004. Grounded semantic composition for visual scenes. *Journal of Artificial Intelligence Research* 21:429–470.

Grubinger, Michael, Paul D. Clough, Henning Müller, and Thomas Deselaers. 2006. The IAPR benchmark: A new evaluation resource for visual information systems. In *Proceedings of OntoImage 2006: Workshop on language resources for content-based mage retrieval during LREC 2006*. Genoa, Italy: European Language Resources Association.

Harris, Zellig S. 1954. Distributional structure. *Word* 10(2-3):146–162.

Hawes, Nick, Matthew Klenk, Kate Lockwood, Graham Horn, and John Kelleher. 2012. Towards a cognitive system that can recognize spatial regions based on context. In *Proceedings of the AAAI Conference on Artificial Intelligence*, vol. 26.

Herdade, Simao, Armin Kappeler, Kofi Boakye, and Joao Soares. 2019. Image captioning: Transforming objects into words. *Advances in Neural Information Processing Systems* 32:11137–11147.

Herskovits, Annette. 1986. *Language and spatial cognition: an interdisciplinary study of the prepositions in English*. Cambridge: Cambridge University Press.

Hinton, Geoffrey E., James L. McClelland, and David E. Rumelhart. 1986. Distributed representations. In D. E. Rumelhart, J. L. McClelland, and the PDP Research Group, eds., *Parallel Distributed Processing*, vol. 1, chap. 3, pages 77–109. MIT Press.

Ilinykh, Nikolai and Simon Dobnik. 2021a. How vision affects language: Comparing masked self-attention in uni-modal and multi-modal transformer. In L. Donatelli, N. Krishnaswamy, K. Lai, and J. Pustejovsky, eds., *Proceedings of the 1st Workshop on Multimodal Semantic Representations (MMSR) at IWCS 2021*, pages 45–55. Groningen, Netherlands (Online): Association for Computational Linguistics.

Ilinykh, Nikolai and Simon Dobnik. 2021b. What does a language-and-vision transformer see: The impact of semantic information on visual representations. *Frontiers in Artificial Intelligence: Identifying, Analyzing, and Overcoming Challenges in Vision and Language Research* 4(767971):182–203.

Ilinykh, Nikolai and Simon Dobnik. 2022. Attention as grounding: Exploring textual and cross-modal attention on entities and relations in language-and-vision transformer. In *Findings of the Association for Computational Linguistics: ACL 2022*, pages 4062–4073. Association for Computational Linguistics, Dublin, Ireland.

Jackendoff, Ray and Barbara Landau. 1991. Spatial language and spatial cognition. In *Bridges between psychology and linguistics*, pages 157–182. Psychology Press.

Jackendoff, Ray S. 1985. *Semantics and cognition*, vol. 8. MIT press.

Kacmajor, Magdalena and John D Kelleher. 2020. Capturing and measuring thematic relatedness. *Language Resources and Evaluation* 54(3):645–682.

Kacmajor, Magdalena, John D Kelleher, Filip Klubicka, and Alfredo Maldonado. 2020. Semantic relatedness and taxonomic word embeddings. *arXiv preprint arXiv:2002.06235* .

Karlgren, Jussi and Pentti Kanerva. 2021. Semantics in high-dimensional space. *Frontiers in Artificial Intelligence* 4:123.

Kelleher, John and Fintan J Costello. 2005. Cognitive representations of projective prepositions. In *Proceedings of the Second ACL-Sigsem Workshop of The Linguistic Dimensions of Prepositions and their Use in Computational Linguistic Formalisms and Applications*.

Kelleher, John and Geert-Jan M Kruijff. 2005a. A context-dependent algorithm for generating locative expressions in physically situated environments. In *Proceedings of the Tenth European Workshop on Natural Language Generation (ENLG-05)*.

Kelleher, John and Geert-Jan M Kruijff. 2006. Incremental generation of spatial referring expressions in situated dialog. In *Proceedings of the 21st international conference on computational linguistics and 44th annual meeting of the association for computational linguistics*, pages 1041–1048.

Kelleher, John, Geert-Jan M Kruijff, and Fintan J Costello. 2006. Proximity in context: an empirically grounded computational model of proximity for processing topological spatial expressions. In *Proceedings of the 21st International Conference on Computational Linguistics and 44th Annual Meeting of the Association for Computational Linguistics*, pages 745–752.

Kelleher, John, Colm Sloan, and Brian Namee. 2009. An investigation into the semantics of English topological prepositions. *Cognitive Processing* 2(10):233–236.

Kelleher, John and Josef van Genabith. 2004. Visual salience and reference resolution in simulated 3-d environments. *Artificial Intelligence Review* 21(3):253–267.

Kelleher, John and Josef van Genabith. 2006. A computational model of the referential semantics of projective prepositions. In *Syntax and Semantics of Prepositions*, pages 211–228. Springer.

Kelleher, John D. 2003. *A perceptually based computational framework for the interpretation of spatial language*. Ph.D. thesis, Dublin City University.

Kelleher, John D. 2006. Attention driven reference resolution in multimodal contexts. *Artificial Intelligence Review* 25(1):21–35.

Kelleher, John D. 2019. *Deep learning*. MIT press.

Kelleher, John D and Fintan J Costello. 2009. Applying computational models of spatial prepositions to visually situated dialog. *Computational Linguistics* 35(2):271–306.

Kelleher, John D., Fintan J. Costello, and Josef van Genabith. 2005. Dynamically structuring updating and interrelating representations of visual and linguistic discourse. *Artificial Intelligence* 167(1):62–102.

Kelleher, John D. and Simon Dobnik. 2017. What is not where: the challenge of integrating spatial representations into deep learning architectures. In *Conference on Logic and Machine Learning in Natural Language (LaML 2017)*, vol. 1 of *CLASP Papers in Computational Linguistics*, pages 41–52.

Kelleher, John D and Simon Dobnik. 2019. Referring to the recently seen: reference and perceptual memory in situated dialogue. In *Extended papers from the Conference on Dialog and Perception*, vol. 2 of *CLASP Papers in Computational Linguistics*, pages 41–50.

Kelleher, John D and Geert-Jan M Kruijff. 2005b. A context-dependent model of proximity in physically situated environments. In *Proceedings of the 2nd ACL-SIGSEM Workshop on The Linguistic Dimensions of Prepositions and their Use in Computational*.

Kelleher, John D, Robert J Ross, Colm Sloan, and Brian Mac Namee. 2011. The effect of occlusion on the semantics of projective spatial terms: a case study in grounding language in perception. *Cognitive Processing* 12(1):95–108.

Klubička, Filip, Alfredo Maldonado, Abhijit Mahalunkar, and John Kelleher. 2019. Synthetic, yet natural: Properties of wordnet random walk corpora and the impact of rare words on embedding performance. In *Proceedings of the 10th Global Wordnet Conference*, pages 140–150.

Krishna, Ranjay, Yuke Zhu, Oliver Groth, Justin Johnson, Kenji Hata, Joshua Kravitz, Stephanie Chen, Yannis Kalantidis, Li-Jia Li, David A Shamma, Michael Bernstein, and Li Fei-Fei. 2017. Visual Genome: Connecting language and vision using crowdsourced dense image annotations. *International Journal of Computer Vision* 123(1):32–73.

Kruijff, Geert-Jan M, John D Kelleher, Gregor Berginc, and Aleš Leonardis. 2006a. Structural descriptions in human-assisted robot visual learning. In *Proceedings of the 1st ACM SIGCHI/SIGART conference on Human-robot interaction*, pages 343–344.

Kruijff, Geert-Jan M, John D Kelleher, and Nick Hawes. 2006b. Information fusion for visual reference resolution in dynamic situated dialogue. In *International Tutorial and Research Workshop on Perception and Interactive Technologies for Speech-Based Systems*, pages 117–128. Springer.

Lakoff, George and Mark Johnson. 1980. *Metaphors We Live By*. Chicago and London: The University of Chicago Press.

Landau, Barbara. 1996. Multiple geometric representations of objects in languages and language learners. In P. Bloom, M. A. Peterson, L. Nadel, and M. F. Garrett, eds., *Language and space*, A Bradford Book, chap. 8, pages 317–363. Cambridge, Massachusetts and London, England: The MIT Press.

Landau, Barbara and Ray Jackendoff. 1993. "What" and "where" in spatial language and spatial cognition. *Behavioral and Brain Sciences* 16(2):217–238.

Levinson, Stephen C. 1996. Frames of reference and Molyneux's question: Crosslinguistic evidence. *Language and space* 109:169.

Levinson, Stephen C. 2003. *Space in language and cognition: explorations in cognitive diversity*, vol. 5. Cambridge: Cambridge University Press. ISBN 0521812623 (hb).

Li, Xiaoou, Laura A Carlson, Weimin Mou, Mark R Williams, and Jared E Miller. 2011. Describing spatial locations from perception and memory: The influence of intrinsic axes on reference object selection. *Journal of Memory and Language* 65(2):222–236.

Lindh, Annika, Robert Ross, and John Kelleher. 2020. Language-driven region pointer advancement for controllable image captioning. In *Proceedings of the 28th International Conference on Computational Linguistics*, pages 1922–1935.

Lindh, Annika, Robert J Ross, Abhijit Mahalunkar, Giancarlo Salton, and John D Kelleher. 2018. Generating diverse and meaningful captions. In *International Conference on Artificial Neural Networks*, pages 176–187. Springer.

Logan, Gordon D. 1994. Spatial attention and the apprehension of spatial relations. *Journal of Experimental Psychology: Human Perception and Performance* 20(5):1015.

Logan, Gordon D. 1995. Linguistic and conceptual control of visual spatial attention. *Cognitive psychology* 28(2):103–174.

Logan, Gordon D. and Daniel D. Sadler. 1996. A computational analysis of the apprehension of spatial relations. In P. Bloom, M. A. Peterson, L. Nadel, and M. F. Garrett, eds., *Language and Space*, pages 493–530. Cambridge, MA: MIT Press.

Lu, Jiasen, Caiming Xiong, Devi Parikh, and Richard Socher. 2017. Knowing when to look: Adaptive attention via a visual sentinel for image captioning. In *Proceedings of the IEEE Conference on Computer Vision and Pattern Recognition (CVPR)*.

Lund, Kevin and Curt Burgess. 1996. Producing high-dimensional semantic spaces from lexical co-occurrence. *Behavior research methods, instruments, & computers* 28(2):203–208.

Maillat, Didier. 2003. *The semantics and pragmatics of directionals: a case study in English and French*. Ph.D. thesis, University of Oxford: Committee for Comparative Philology and General Linguistics, Oxford, United Kingdom.

Maldonado, Alfredo, Filip Klubička, and John Kelleher. 2019. Size matters: The impact of training size in taxonomically-enriched word embeddings. *Open Computer Science* 9(1):252–267.

Mikolov, Tomas, Kai Chen, Greg Corrado, and Jeffrey Dean. 2013. Efficient estimation of word representations in vector space.

Mikolov, Tomáš, Martin Karafiát, Lukáš Burget, Jan Černockỳ, and Sanjeev Khudanpur. 2010. Recurrent neural network based language model. In *Eleventh Annual Conference of the International Speech Communication Association*.

Miller, George A. and Philip N. Johnson-Laird. 1976. *Language and perception*. Cambridge: Cambridge University Press.

Mishkin, Mortimer, Leslie G Ungerleider, and Kathleen A Macko. 1983. Object vision and spatial vision: two cortical pathways. *Trends in neurosciences* 6:414–417.

Montague, Richard. 1974. *Formal Philosophy: Selected Papers of Richard Montague*. New Haven: Yale University Press. ed. and with an introduction by Richmond H. Thomason.

Nedumpozhimana, Vasudevan and John Kelleher. 2021. Finding BERT's idiomatic key. In *Proceedings of the 17th Workshop on Multiword Expressions (MWE 2021)*, pages 57–62.

Nedumpozhimana, Vasudevan, Filip Klubicka, and John D. Kelleher. 2022. Shapley idioms: Analysing BERT sentence embeddings for general idiom token identification. *Frontiers in Artificial Intelligence* 5.

Noë, Alva. 2004. *Action in perception*. The MIT Press.

Pennington, Jeffrey, Richard Socher, and Christopher Manning. 2014. Glove: Global vectors for word representation. In *Proceedings of the 2014 conference on empirical methods in natural language processing (EMNLP)*, pages 1532–1543.

Peters, Matthew E., Mark Neumann, Mohit Iyyer, Matt Gardner, Christopher Clark, Kenton Lee, and Luke Zettlemoyer. 2018. Deep contextualized word representations. In *Proceedings of the 2018 Conference of the North American Chapter of the Association for Computational*

Linguistics: Human Language Technologies, Volume 1 (Long Papers), pages 2227–2237. New Orleans, Louisiana: Association for Computational Linguistics.

Rashtchian, Cyrus, Peter Young, Micah Hodosh, and Julia Hockenmaier. 2010. Collecting image annotations using Amazon's Mechanical Turk. In *Proceedings of the NAACL HLT 2010 Workshop on creating speech and language data with Amazon's Mechanical Turk*. Los Angeles, CA: North American Chapter of the Association for Computational Linguistics (NAACL).

Regier, Terry and Laura A. Carlson. 2001. Grounding spatial language in perception: an empirical and computational investigation. *Journal of Experimental Psychology: General* 130(2):273–298.

Rogers, Anna, Olga Kovaleva, and Anna Rumshisky. 2020. A primer in bertology: What we know about how BERT works. *Transactions of the Association for Computational Linguistics* 8:842–866.

Roy, Deb. 2005. Semiotic schemas: A framework for grounding language in action and perception. *Artificial Intelligence* 167(1-2):170–205.

Sadeghi, Fereshteh, Santosh K Kumar Divvala, and Ali Farhadi. 2015. Viske: Visual knowledge extraction and question answering by visual verification of relation phrases. In *Proceedings of the IEEE conference on computer vision and pattern recognition*, pages 1456–1464.

Sahlgren, Magnus and Fredrik Carlsson. 2021. The singleton fallacy: Why current critiques of language models miss the point. *Frontiers in Artificial Intelligence* 4:131.

Salton, Giancarlo, Robert Ross, and John Kelleher. 2016. Idiom token classification using sentential distributed semantics. In *Proceedings of the 54th Annual Meeting of the Association for Computational Linguistics (Volume 1: Long Papers)*, pages 194–204.

Salton, Giancarlo, Robert Ross, and John Kelleher. 2017. Attentive language models. In *Proceedings of the Eighth International Joint Conference on Natural Language Processing (Volume 1: Long Papers)*, pages 441–450.

Schultheis, Holger and Laura A Carlson. 2017. Mechanisms of reference frame selection in spatial term use: computational and empirical studies. *Cognitive science* 41(2):276–325.

Schultheis, Holger and Laura A. Carlson. 2018. Inter-process relations in spatial language: Feedback and graded compatibility. *Cognition* 176:140–158.

Schütte, Niels, Brian Mac Namee, and John Kelleher. 2017. Robot perception errors and human resolution strategies in situated human–robot dialogue. *Advanced Robotics* 31(5):243–257.

Schütze, Hinrich. 1993. Word space. In *Advances in neural information processing systems*, pages 895–902.

Talmy, Leonard. 1983. How language structures space. In *Spatial orientation*, pages 225–282. Springer.

Talmy, Leonard. 2000. *Toward a cognitive semantics: concept structuring systems*, vol. 1 and 2. Cambridge, Massachusetts: MIT Press.

Tanenhaus, Michael K, Michael J Spivey-Knowlton, Kathleen M Eberhard, and Julie C Sedivy. 1995. Integration of visual and linguistic information in spoken language comprehension. *Science* 268(5217):1632–1634.

Treisman, Anne and Stephen Gormican. 1988. Feature analysis in early vision: evidence from search asymmetries. *Psychological review* 95(1):15.

Ullman, Shimon. 1980. Against direct perception. *Behavioral and Brain Sciences* 3(3):373–381.

Ullman, Shimon. 1984. Visual routines. *Cognition* 18(1-3):97–159.

van Deemter, Kees. 2010. *Not Exactly: In Praise of Vagueness*. Oxford University Press.

Vandeloise, Claude. 1991. *Spatial prepositions: A case study from French*. University of Chicago Press.

Widdows, Dominic. 2003. Unsupervised methods for developing taxonomies by combining syntactic and statistical information. In *Proceedings of the 2003 Conference of the North American Chapter of the Association for Computational Linguistics on Human Language Technology*, vol. 1, pages 197–204. Association for Computational Linguistics.

Winograd, Terry. 1976. *Understanding Natural Language*. Edinburgh University Press.

Xu, Kelvin, Jimmy Ba, Ryan Kiros, Kyunghyun Cho, Aaron Courville, Ruslan Salakhudinov, Rich Zemel, and Yoshua Bengio. 2015. Show, attend and tell: Neural image caption generation with visual attention. In *International conference on machine learning*, pages 2048–2057. PMLR.

Yang, Xu, Kaihua Tang, Hanwang Zhang, and Jianfei Cai. 2019. Auto-encoding scene graphs for image captioning. In *Proceedings of the IEEE/CVF Conference on Computer Vision and Pattern Recognition*, pages 10685–10694.

Yao, Ting, Yingwei Pan, Yehao Li, and Tao Mei. 2018. Exploring visual relationship for image captioning. In *Proceedings of the European conference on computer vision (ECCV)*, pages 684–699.

10

Action coordination and learning in dialogue

ARASH ESHGHI, CHRISTINE HOWES, AND ELENI GREGOROMICHELAKI

10.1 Introduction: The challenge of conversational AI

Conversational Artificial Intelligence (AI) systems (such as Amazon Alexa, Microsoft Cortana, Apple Siri) have recently become ubiquitous and are now an integral part of our everyday lives. There have been huge advancements recently in the achievement of conversational AI with many claims regarding the closeness of attaining the goal of artificial general intelligence (AGI) based on these successes (see e.g. Bommasani et al., 2021). Nevertheless, in practice, the scope of this success has been limited. End-users of such systems often treat them in the same way they would another human in that they have expectations of naturalness, intelligence, flexibility, and smooth interaction, leading regularly to disappointment and frustration (Moore, 2017, Clark et al., 2019, Chaves and Gerosa, 2021, Park et al., 2017, Luger and Sellen, 2016, Fischer et al., 2019) because these systems do not offer this expected potential.

The reason for this is that natural language (NL) use in general, but especially in conversation, presents numerous challenges that have been traditionally distinguished and isolated from each other as pertaining to various encapsulated modules. For example, autonomous domains of competence such as syntax, semantics, and pragmatics

Probabilistic Approaches to Linguistic Theory.
Jean-Philippe Bernardy, Rasmus Blanck,
Stergios Chatzikyriakidis, Shalom Lappin,
Aleksandre Maskharashvili (eds.).

are distinguished while non-verbal aspects of NL processing like facial expressions, eye gaze, manual gestures are ignored, as are the effects of the physical and cultural environment. This standard strategy of separating phenomena and treating them as encapsulated modules with idiosyncratic vocabularies led rule-based approaches to an inability to integrate seamlessly the various assumptions that are required for the resolution of various challenging aspects of processing in dialogue. As a result, open-ended and multi-domain artificial conversational systems, in particular, have been found to be unmanageably complex, brittle, and unreliable.

The advent of end-to-end neural architectures suggested that the challenge of successful meshing of all aspects of multimodal processing in dialogue could be overcome (see Vinyals and Le, 2015, Serban et al., 2016, Li et al., 2017, Lowe et al., 2017, Wolf et al., 2019, a.o.). End-to-end dialogue systems are trained directly on large amounts of conversational data, learning a mapping from dialogue history to a system response, either in a supervised or unsupervised fashion, without modularisation of conversational knowledge. Such systems are robust and general with respect to the domains they are designed to deal with. Nevertheless, it seems that progress has stagnated and that the provision of even larger amounts of data will not improve the situation (see e.g. Lowe et al., 2017, Zadrozny, 2021), even when using large-scale, state of the art, Transformer-based models (Vaswani et al., 2017, Devlin et al., 2019) pretrained on dialogue data (see e.g. Bao et al., 2020, Noble and Maraev, 2021, Caldarini et al., 2022).

Recent large-scale end-to-end neural systems (e.g. Wolf et al., 2019), while displaying impressive capacities with regard to producing fluent surface structures, do not adequately capture human capacities in learning *appropriately adaptive* conversational behaviours. Often the responses of such systems are generic, uninformative, and neglectful of the overall coherence of a dialogue in that they take into account only the immediately previous turn(s) thus lacking consistency with respect to the longer history of the dialogue and its future prospects with respect to achieving some goal (see e.g. Li et al., 2020, Vinyals and Le, 2015, Shang et al., 2015, Sordoni et al., 2015). As a result, they can also be unreliable with respect to trustworthy responses because, as they predict single utterances at a time, they ignore the purposeful nature of action in dialogue in the service of achievement of local and global goals. On the whole, today's conversational AI systems are *static* in that they are unable to adjust to the dynamic environment of the dialogue history and evolving goals and do not come equipped with strategic skills to enable them to negotiate the ambiguity, vagueness, and nuances of human-to-human conversation, and thus adapt to new people, tasks, and situations.

We argue below that what is needed is a radical reconceptualisation of linguistic models away from conceptions of NL as a shared code (Sec. 10.2). Instead, we suggest viewing NLs as sets of skills for goal-driven (inter)action and coordination in order to exploit *affordances* in the socio-material environment of an agent (Sec. 10.3). Efforts should thus focus on linguistically implemented feedback mechanisms such as *repair* that allow interacting agents to coordinate their actions (Sec. 10.4). In terms of models, neural or otherwise, such a move should enable designs that are able to *actively adapt* to previously unseen situations. In terms of artificial agents, it should enable their using the immediate local feedback from their environment including their interlocutor. Thus this approach goes well towards the direction of freeing conversational interfaces from the shackles of the data on which they were trained. Crucially, this move should involve dynamic, predictive models that are able to actively engage with the world, observe the effects of what they do/say and not just in how the conversation moves forward. In addition, they need to be checking the effects brought about in their *multimodal*, physical situation of utterance. In the face of prediction error, model architectures would, on this view, allow real-time, focused and local updates to their parameters. Doing this using just underlying large-scale neural language models seems very promising but remains an open problem in terms of the requisite neural architectures, attention mechanisms, training objectives as well as the nature of the data. In Sec. 10.5, we present a low-level, dynamic model of NL interaction and coordination. The model, DS-TTR, is a combination of Dynamic Syntax (Kempson et al., 2016, 2001) and Type Theory with Records (Cooper, 2005, Cooper and Ginzburg, 2015), that we argue satisfies the desiderata listed above. In Sec. 10.6 we present a couple of case studies showing how such a model can be implemented and used in practice to bootstrap interaction.

10.2 The inadequacy of code models

On the one hand, what artificial conversational architectures show is that the complexity of NL behaviour is underappreciated due to the apparent ease with which people handle their everyday interactions. As a result, human communication is often modelled under the 'code model', namely, as one agent coding and transmitting a message (the 'sender') with reception and decoding at another agent (the 'receiver'). This approach has failed spectacularly to account for the complexity and subtlety of sense-making in human interaction (see, e.g., Fowler and Hodges, 2016). Models of communication which assume idealised perfect speakers and listeners sharing mental representations of interpretations of meaning – dating back to Shannon and Weaver (1949), but still underlying much research today, can only ever be an abstraction, and one that we argue is detrimental to understanding successful communication (see also Rączaszek-Leonardi et al., 2014).

On the other hand, the backlash against this simple-minded approach led to models of high modularity, domain specificity, and complexity. This was due to fact that it was deemed necessary to enhance the code model with individualistic recursive reasoning about others' mental states, as in Gricean, Neo-Gricean, and Post-Gricean accounts of NL, and accompanying plan-based and belief desires and intention (BDI) dialogue models (e.g. Grosz and Sidner, 1986, Matheson et al., 2000). Recent responses to the ineffectiveness of end-to-end conversational AI include pleas to return to such highly complex intentionalist approaches (e.g. Kopp and Krämer, 2021). But these approaches were in fact the reason of failure of rule-based/symbolic dialogue systems with explicit hand-crafted, but in the end intractable, 'mind-reading' components (see e.g. Gregoromichelaki et al., 2011, Mirski and Bickhard, 2021).

We believe that progress in dialogue modelling is impeded due to such standard assumptions that still underlie much research in linguistics, cognitive science, and AI. These assumptions are shown to be unsustainable, when we consider dialogue and interaction both for traditional rule-based approaches and modern neural architectures. Standard theories of communication rely on a separation between speaker and hearer, with the speaker encoding and transmitting a message, and the hearer decoding it. Even in intention-based accounts, speaker and hearer share the linguistic 'code' (the language, some NL) and the only possibility for accommodating the function of errors is to characterise them as "noise" to be eliminated. Successful communication is characterised as the hearer correctly discovering the message which the speaker intended to convey, and this is assumed to be the norm of what actually happens. This basic assumption underlies most psychological and pragmatic theories of interaction including the Interactive Alignment Model (Pickering and Garrod, 2004, see below), Gricean pragmatics (Grice, 1975) and Relevance Theory (Sperber and Wilson, 1995) which assume an underlying literal meaning enhanced by context-specific pragmatic inferences to uncover the *speaker*'s intention.

However, the actions of participants in dialogue form a system of coupled components (see, e.g., De Jaegher and Di Paolo, 2007) with the result that *feedback mechanisms*, like constant error indication and adjustment, are crucial for the stability, maintenance, and self-organisation of the system. Given the moment-by-moment need for action coordination, participants do not need explicit representations of others' or their own mental states, as correctly assumed in deep learning models, and neither do they need to converge on a shared 'code' or shared criteria of success. Instead, their conceptions and contributions need to be complementary to sustain a social practice whose normative character is defined externally to their own private or explicit rationalisations of their behaviour.

Rethinking our conception of successful communication away from shared codes or sufficiently similar mental representations puts the flexibility and dynamism of NL at the heart of communication. As Healey et al. (2018a) state "[i]nstead of thinking of effective communication as formulating a "perfect" message, it becomes about finding optimal ways to uncover and address misunderstandings". We go further and do not characterise these practices as uncovering 'misunderstanding' or 'miscommunication', terms suggesting that they are somehow in opposition to some common understanding and common ground. Instead, we characterise successful coordination (rather than "communication") as the local, incremental resolution of inevitable perturbations in the self-organisation of a complex dynamical system enabling people to contribute to larger social organisations that constitute their ecological niche ('form of life'). From a psychological perspective, the rapidity and highly incremental nature of turn-taking exchanges in dialogue (Levinson and Torreira, 2015, Sacks et al., 1974) shows that intractable exhaustive reasoning about some optimal local outcome is not what participants aim for (cf. Frank and Goodman, 2012). Instead, practices of navigating through, and local adjustment to, an incrementally evolving landscape of affordances provided by the ecological niche and participants' own actions enable the forms of distributed cognition observed in dialogue (e.g. Dingemanse, 2020). Transferring this insight to the domain of language technology, this assumption partially explains the limited success of language models in mimicking many aspects of human performance. We attribute the substantial current shortcomings of such models to the limited variety of data they are exposed to, i.e., lack of multimodal data (see e.g. Hanjie et al., 2021, Hill et al., 2020, Ruis et al., 2020, Röder et al., 2021, Lappin, 2021), lack of ability to actively interact with the data (cf. Li et al., 2017, Lewis et al., 2017) so lack of feedback, and their lack of physical embodiment (see e.g. Pustejovsky and Krishnaswamy, 2021). From this perspective, we suggest that progress in modelling human dialogue and conversational AI requires a radical reconception of NLs as mechanisms for (inter)action.

10.2.1 Human-human dialogue

The simplifications of characterising communication as attempts to adjust the replication of mental states are shown to be inadequate when we consider dialogue as shown in example (61), taken from the British National Corpus (BNC: Burnard, 2000). Units of meaning are co-created incrementally (Kempson et al., 2016, Hough et al., 2015) by multiple interlocutors using incomplete utterances (e.g. line 7 – Purver et al., 2011), with phenomena such as cross-person compound contributions (where one person continues another's utterance, as in lines 7 and 8 – Lerner, 1991, Howes, 2012), repairs (e.g. the clarification requests in lines 4 and 6 – Sacks et al., 1974, Purver, 2004), and disfluencies (e.g. the pause and restart in line 9 – Hough, 2015) – seen as 'performance errors' in traditional linguistics – becoming crucial in the sense-making activities of the participants.

(61) a. **J:** Can you think of any catalysts?
b. **A:** Er is it potassium permanganate?
c. **J:** <unclear>
d. **A:** What
e. **J:** Pla <pause> a duck billed
f. **A:** Pardon?
g. **J:** A duck billed
h. **A:** Platypus.
i. **J:** And it's not platypus it's <pause> sounds like a type of pen.
j. **A:** Platinum.
k. **J:** Right, platinum. (BNC; file FMR 728-737)

This short extract in which a chemistry tutor (J) prompts a student (A) to answer the question posed in line 1, neatly illustrates the characteristic divergence and convergence that is key to driving dialogue forwards. From a standard individualistic perspective, one can characterise the exchange as indicating that, from J's perspective, A's response in line 2 is not the expected answer – it is divergent with it. A finally produces the expected answer (thus demonstrating convergence with J's expectations) in line 10. This is a valid way of describing the process and it might be the way that a single participant might rationalise or abstract the dialogue process into a narrative that they construct post hoc.

However, from a realistic modelling perspective, it neglects the fact that both participants operate in a context (a 'teaching context') that imposes normative constraints in what their actions should be aiming at as they perform the roles assigned to them by that sociocultural convention that constitutes the practice they are enacting. There are no 'teacher' or 'student' roles outside this socially-afforded context. The practice the participants engage in thus constitutes their (temporary) identities and action possibilities afforded to them. So, both participants' actions are now subsumed under the overall normative perspective that their actions should be relevant to the elicitation of some particular answer to a question posed by J, with both of them operating as a coherent system performing complementary actions towards that goal and compensating for each other's failings to contribute appropriately.

This normativity is imposed to the participants because there is a joint goal, not only between the participants but including a goal-driven process of the societal 'form of life' in general pervading the interaction. On the other hand, none of the two participants on their own has an overview of exactly what this overall goal consists in and how it can be achieved even though they become aware of their obligations and opportunities as they are enacting their roles. In effect, the cognition required for achieving this goal is distributed (Hutchins, 1995) not only across the participants' individual capacities but, crucially, the sociocultural environment that provides the state space and the normativity, correctness or incorrectness, of their joint action trajectory.

This distributed and systems perspective shows that the ecological sociocultural environment in which the interaction takes place directs the participants' unreflective but, nevertheless, fluent navigation towards the goal. The to and fro where A's indications of how far they can reach with respect to contributing to the goal is explicitly conveyed not only by assertions but also by clarification requests and completable utterances (Gregoromichelaki et al., 2020b), elsewhere characterised as "fragments". As is shown here, this is not a case of communication 'breaking down' but of opportunities to engage in further enactment of exactly the 'teaching' practice they are engaged in. J compensates by revealing affordances that might be obscured from A's perception by making manifest more local, perhaps in another context seemingly irrelevant, "incorrect", affordances, which are functional in this particular environment to allow both of them to reach a point of sufficient satisfaction of their mission: after a cue in line 5 fails to elicit the required convergence, J exploits the predictability of the compound noun phrase 'duck-billed platypus' to get A to produce the first syllables of the answer to the original question. This is an illustration in miniature of the learning and developmental process that Gibson (1966) calls the 'education of attention'.

This management of the divergent and convergent contexts with respect to the normative imperatives of the sociocultural environment is incrementally and locally managed, with a hierarchy of joint goals and subgoals emerging in an unplanned and opportunistic fashion as each participant makes contributions that create opportunities for the other to make timely and appropriate responses and compensatory moves when such goals seem to be threatened (Howes and Eshghi, 2021). Such uncertainty with respect to what the activity exactly consists in, what concepts are relevant, how the practice is going to develop, in general, what the affordances are, is built-in in our awareness and visible in the talk's surface: teacher and student can only have probabilistic expectations as to what they are required to do moment-by-moment and this is the most effective strategy they should adopt given the usual uncertainty of the environment (otherwise, their behavioural adjustments will be threatened by "overfitting"). But they can trust the process unreflectively because they have available strategies, built into NL practices, that will correct and adjust their performance based on the feedback received.

In this dialogue, there is an asymmetry between the speakers, as J, the tutor, is both the expert, and more socially powerful than A, the student. But, in fact, this asymmetry is endemic, diagnostic of not just all child/adult (Duveen and Psaltis, 2013, Kunert et al., 2011) or expert/non-expert exchanges (such as tutoring dialogues or doctor/patient consultations, Lu et al., 2007, Pilnick and Dingwall, 2011), but all interactions. Differences in experiences, cultural background, individual physiology, and social communities all contribute to differences in our NL use, meaning that we never share the "same" language as anybody we nevertheless successfully interact with (Clark, 1998). This raises an important practical question: How can we communicate successfully when individual differences in language use are not the exception but the norm?

10.3 Language as action

We argue that the answer to this question relies on reconceptualising NL as a set of skills for interaction (Kempson et al., 2016, Gregoromichelaki et al., 2019, 2020b). This recasts language use in *actionist* terms, in parallel with recent actionist theories of perception (Nöe, 2004, Bickhard, 2009). Actionism holds that perception is not a series of snapshots of scenes in the world leading to their inferential manipulation as representations in the brain (Marr, 1982). Rather, perception is engagement with the world – an embodied agent activity and achievement.

The motivation for this perspective starts with the assumption that, in order to survive, organisms have to play an active part in controlling their environment and keeping it within desirable states (thus embodying systemic principles like self-maintenance, self-organisation, autopoiesis, see, e.g. Di Paolo, 2008, Di Paolo and De Jaegher, 2012). For an organism to exert such control, its adaptation to its environment equips it with abilities to perceive predictable relationships between its actions and ensuing perceptual stimulations (*sensorimotor contingencies*) since the purpose of perception/action is to ensure agent effective adaptability.

Under this view, adaptive exploration and exploitation of environmental resources makes use of the agent's practical and embodied know-how of such sensorimotor contingencies, i.e., direct perception-action links (see, e.g, Buhrmann et al., 2013, Maye and Engel, 2011) rather than brain-internal cognitive inferential or representational resources. Sensorimotor contingencies are lawful regularities in the dynamic relation between the agent and the environment, the ecological niche, patterns of dependence of changes in the sensory input as a function of an agent's movements (Gibson, 2014). Consequently, the information agents perceive about entities and their potential for interaction outcomes is expressed in terms of *predictions* and it is perspectival in the sense that it is agent-relative. It is also mediated through the invocation of complex regular patterns, *constraints* (Barwise and Perry, 1983, Rączaszek-Leonardi and Kelso, 2008), originating from social as well as natural learning experiences but not via internal skull-bound world models. Various such learned expectations (hierarchically-organised sequences of predictions) based on memorised holistic patterns of experience (*policies*) are built up through reiterated interactions with the environment and are then deployed in subsequent encounters (see also Bickhard, 2009). For human agents, in addition, learning to perceive refers to what is offered through their direct time-extended interactions with the sociocultural environment, which is a significant constitutive part of the human ecological niche. Therefore "perception" of an entity will then be primarily constituted by the set of expectations it invokes concerning the possible interactions enabled through it (its *affordances*), not some objective individuation or categorisation as a type of entity. Agents are not passive perceivers but act to realise the predictions (anticipations) they expect to receive as feedback from the environment, thus predictions can also serve as goals (see e.g. Gregoromichelaki et al., 2020c, Friston et al., 2012a). Such predictions can be confirmed or disconfirmed through the feedback so that they are the basic source of learning This view is intended to replace the static, internalist-inferential view of "perception" as the association of stimuli with mental symbols stored and recovered as propositional knowledge.

Analogously, competence with NLs does not require an abstract representational level or language of thought (Fodor, 1975), but can be viewed in terms of the linguistic and non-linguistic actions (utterances and, e.g., gestures) that can be performed in particular situations. In any type of engagement with others or the environment, an agent acts via NL means in order to perceive the predicted consequences of their interactions, instead of constructing and refining representations of these interactions to serve as guidance for its action. Such predictions are generated by means of the agent's embodied sensorimotor knowledge of the relevant sociocultural niche, i.e., by routinised anticipations (the 'grammar' in a Wittgensteinian sense, e.g., Forster, 2009), of how its various actions will change features of the sociomaterial world. For individual agents, such predictions are shaped and constrained by what is licensed within the current sociomaterial context, i.e., within the *normativity* of the socially-distributed nature of the grammar.

This means that no individual agent can be solipsistically aware of the significance of its own action: by observing its consequences (*feedback*), the very act of speaking (or writing) in a particular context reveals to participants (potentially abstractions over) the normatively constrained triggers of actions for the words used as well as generating structured anticipations of further possible developments, the latter thereby becoming further affordances within that conversational exchange. Thus a concrete action has both backward effects, in that it shapes the dialogue history under a particular conceptualisation, and forward effects, i.e., it opens up new trajectories in the current landscape of affordances. This is a more radical version of the empirically derived notion of the three-position "architecture" of conversation in Conversational Analysis (CA) or the retroactive and proactive effects of utterances (see e.g. Arundale, 2008, 2020). Since any action interpretation in dialogue has provisional status, only a probabilistic distribution over effects is ever possible. Hence, so-called 'repair' processes (i.e. feedback) are not confined to the highly noticeable explicit attempts, like asking for clarifications or correction, but it is a constant feature of interaction.

10.3.1 Exploiting probabilistic uncertainty in interactions

It is now becoming widely accepted that certainty either over interpretations or action outcomes is neither a feasible goal nor a criterion of success for human interaction. Both uncertainty and the variety of multiple affordances in the human ecological niche introduce complexity due to the fact that agents do not perceive only one affordance at a time. Agents always perceive a continuously restructured dynamic landscape of affordances that consists of various possibilities for action soliciting their attention. Cisek & Kalaska (2010) propose that 'affordance competition' is resolved by humans and animals through active moment-to-moment exploration of the field of available affordances without realising an overall plan of action but by being drawn towards the most rewarding predicted outcomes.

Regarding the contribution of individual agents, the Skilled Intentionality Framework (Rietveld et al., 2018) reconstructs Friston's framework that is underpinned by the Free-energy Principle and active inference (Friston, 2010, 2011, Mathys et al., 2011) in non-representational, ecological, and action-oriented terms. Based on Bayesian statistics and machine learning approximate Bayesian inference, the free-energy principle is a proposal for modelling living self-organising systems like humans and other animals. The framework built around this principle assumes that living organisms are equipped with generative models generating top-down predictions about causes of received perceptual input from their environment. In order for such organisms to maintain themselves successfully in their environment, they constantly seek to reduce the prediction error that ensues due to discrepancies between their predicted sensory input and the actual ("bottom up") input they receive from the environment. Long-term reduction of prediction error ('minimisation of free energy') can be achieved by either changing the generative model (*perceptual inference*) or acting in the world to change the sensory input received (*active inference*). In the domain of human cognition, Friston's framework has received entirely solipsistic interpretations conceiving of the generative model as inducing brain-internal representations encoding information about an inaccessible external environment (Hohwy, 2013) in the same way that a neural network or distributional language model can be construed as a system performing learning and inference in isolation of its environment and hence facing the 'symbol grounding problem' (Harnad, 1990, Gao et al., 2018, Kottur et al., 2016).

However, a more plausible non-cognitivist interpretation is that an agent's generative model reflects the attunement of the agent's embodiment to its physical environment, for example, by establishing the regulation of its metabolic needs ('homeostasis'). For a more complex social agent, the generative model, in addition, incorporates embodied assumptions of normativity, i.e., the regular, expected ways of acting in the practices the agent participates in (e.g. Kirchhoff and Froese, 2017, Bruineberg et al., 2018a,b). From this perspective, rather than encoding information about an inaccessible environment, neural states contribute to the embodied capacities of changing the environment through action. The goal of active inference is to steer an agent's interactions with the ecological niche in such a way that the agent's actions harmonise with the affordances of the sociomaterial environment. Perceptual inference under this interpretation affects the agent's internal (endogenous) dynamics and can be conceptualised in terms of inducing patterns of action-readiness. Since, at any moment, a whole landscape of affordances confronts complex agents, there needs to be a way for the agent to select the relevant set of affordances that is predicted to yield the most rewarding outcome. In the Ecological Psychology literature, such relevant affordances are termed 'solicitations' to distinguish them and emphasise the agent's perspective and contribution to the determination of affordances, which are environment-agent relations. The Skilled Intentionality Framework proposes that the solicitation of multiple complex affordances towards humans can be modelled as triggering states of 'action readiness' (Frijda et al., 2014) within individual organisms. These are affective states, rather than the explicit formation of 'goals', 'intentions' and the like. Thus perceptual inference regulates action readiness as the agent is motivated to act based on its disattunement with the environment (its prediction error) which has an emotional effect on the agent's awareness.

Perceiving (i.e. predicting) complex nested structures of potential affordances constitutes, in our terms, *conceptualisations* of the situation as offered by the grammar and perceived by an agent at a particular time. Developing competence with the grammar, in the sense of an agent being solicited by appropriate action-inducing potential, requires training and developing skills. For human agents, this is accomplished through participation in 'practices', i.e., coordinated patterns of behaviour of multiple individuals, within which NL interactivity is arguably the canonical case. Individuals or groups of individuals can then respond selectively to relevant (sets of) affordances since they have become attuned to the normativity of each particular situation. As a result, they act under the guidance of resolving 'affective tensions', i.e., emotional responses like feelings of discontent or dissatisfaction, rather than "rational" deliberations through propositional beliefs/intentions. Such feelings of tension are aroused by the discrepancies (overwhelming prediction failure, i.e., prediction error) between a concrete situation and the embodied skills of perceiving the norms of the situation type that the agent(s) have acquired by training. Agents resolve such tensions by resorting to their expertise and acting accordingly. Their familiarity with the interactive environment allows them to intervene and restore perception of the expected affordances of the situation type.

10.4 Action coordination in dialogue

On the view proposed here, NL behaviours are understood as practices, with their normativity underpinned by a set of conditional actions (the 'grammar') inducing ongoing emergent flows that can be approximated in more individualistic, abstract, and detached terms as the often-studied notions of context, content, intentions, speech acts and the like. On the present view, NLs, both in terms of syntactic structure and conceptualisation potential, are first and foremost coordinative action-control devices both with respect to the environment and other individuals; and a grammar formalism is duly determined directly in terms of defining the normative constraints (i.e. setting out and traversing the landscape of predicted affordances) that operate top-down to guide such action (see also Trafford, 2017, Zadrozny, 2020).

Affordances which, under our interpretation are publicly available resources, trigger motivations for action within agents (*solicitations*, e.g. Dreyfus, 2013). However, affordances are not, as standard, simply properties of the environment. Instead they are relations between agent abilities and what the current sociomaterial environment reliably makes available. This means that the shifting set of affordances in dialogue concerns the collective potential of the interactants, rather than individual perspectives whose meshing needs to be explicitly negotiated/represented. Interlocutors thus acquire a joint perspective as long as they operate as a system with its own self-organisation underpinned by prediction error minimisation (as modelled within the Free Energy Principle framework in its ecological/enactive interpretation, e.g., Bruineberg et al., 2018a). So the local and shifting landscape of affordances and the state and abilities of the agents involved determine at each moment a demarcated 'field of affordances', i.e. a subset of the landscape of affordances that are perceived as relevant by the agents. This provides for a joint conceptualisation of the current action potential with minute adjustments at each subsentential stage resulting in the appearance of planned rational action at the macro-level and as strategically introduced repair of intention recognition failures as in (62) and (63).

(62) (a) A: so ... umm this afternoon ...
(b) B: let's go watch a film
(c) A: yeah

(63) (a) A: I'm pretty sure that **the**
(b) B: **programmed visits**?
(c) A: programmed visits, yes, I think they'll have been debt inspections. [BNC KS1 789-791]

However, the function of what have been characterised as overt repairs is not some extraordinary feature of just some dialogue exchanges. The function and maintenance of a complex dynamic system requires constant interaction with the environment and adjustment of the participants' action/perception by reducing their independent potential while non-summatively maximising their joint capacities, otherwise it will just be the juxtaposition of two independent agents acting on their own.

10.4.1 Repair

The function of feedback in a coupled system is a primary regulatory factor in subsuming the individual components under a system architecture. Independently, the components will have available a multitude of degrees of freedom. In order to interact successfully and tractably, degrees of freedom need to be mutually constrained and this is achieved by the agents performing complementary and compensatory actions in the service of joint action (De Jaegher and Di Paolo, 2007, Paolo et al., 2018). So balancing and counterbalancing a complex but unified process can only be achieved by continuous work that ensures the self-organisation of the system. Most research on dialogue considers repair – specifically clarification requests such as the "what?" and "pardon?" in (61) – to index misunderstandings between individuals (mismatches between people's takes on the dialogue). In our view, however, repair as a separate category of constructions (Clark, 1996), turns out to be an artefact of assuming that interlocutors aim for the establishment of shared common world "representations", with speech acts contributing propositional contents (Poesio and Rieser, 2010, Ginzburg, 2012) in the service of reasoning and planning. These assumptions, which we argue are fallacious when interaction is properly characterised as skilled action use, also underpin the currently popular Rational Speech Acts model (RSA; Frank and Goodman, 2012, Goodman and Frank, 2016), which assumes that speakers reason over others' (presumed) intentions. A global RSA model does not seem to be computationally tractable (e.g. Cohn-Gordon et al., 2018), while the general availability of local repair mechanisms have been demonstrated to remove the need for such higher-order modelling in agent simulations (Van Arkel et al., 2020). This is not to deny that people can reason over others beliefs, desires and intentions (BDI). Rather, we claim that this is a higher-order skill not a necessary foundation for successful interaction (Gregoromichelaki et al., 2011).

This stance also inverts the usual assumptions about *backchannels*, which are considered to be "positive" feedback, signalling understanding (Fujimoto, 2007). On our view, a backchannel passes up an opportunity for so-called "repair" (Schegloff, 1993) or, in our terms, transforms the field of affordances in a monotonic manner. Such signals therefore acquire their myriad functions as a direct consequence, depending on the action in progress when the backchannel is produced. For example, if the speaker is telling a story, a backchannel may function as a *continuer*; if giving directions, it may *acknowledge* identification of a landmark; and if offering an opinion, it may indicate *agreement*. This position – supported by experimental evidence (Howes et al., 2012, Healey et al., 2018b, Mills, 2007, Mills and Healey, 2006) – means that rather than treating backchannels as multiply ambiguous, and completely opposite to clarification requests, we can unify them as *procedural* mechanisms for managing the types of transformations induced moment-by-moment in the field of affordances (Howes and Eshghi, 2021).

We turn now to a formalism that, we argue, captures such a notion of repair as a natural consequence of the incremental and domain-general architecture in terms of affordances that is assumed to underlie NL grammar.

10.5 Dynamic Syntax and Type Theory with Records (DS-TTR)

Dynamic Syntax (DS; Cann et al., 2005, Kempson et al., 2001, 2016) is a constraint-based (or model-theoretic, Pullum and Scholz, 2001) grammar architecture that models the dynamic, real-time, incremental interpretation of word-sequences (comprehension) or linearisation of contents (production) relative to a fine-grained concept of dialogue context (see Sec. 10.5.4 below). The DS syntactic engine, including the lexicon, is underpinned by a specialised version of Propositional

Dynamic Logic (PDL), which is a multimodal logic able to express probabilistically licensed transition events (*actions*) among the states of a dynamic system (Sato, 2011; see Fig. 1 where outgoing edges/actions from each node form a learnable (Eshghi et al., 2013b) probability distribution conditioned on the current state or DS tree). As a result, DS is articulated in terms of conditional and goal-driven actions whose accomplishment either gives rise to expectations of further actions, tests the environment for further contextual input, or leads to abandonment of the current strategy due to its being unviable in view of more competitive alternatives (see Fig. 1). In current versions of DS, words, morphology, and syntax are all modelled as *affordances*, i.e., indicators of opportunities for (inter-)action (Gregoromichelaki, 2018, Gregoromichelaki et al., 2019, 2020b,a). Both participants' opportunities for action, as well as their perspectives, are modelled in a unified model of the whole system, rather than assuming that the grammar is an individualistic mechanism inside one person's head. Participants' interactions are modelled as incrementally opening up a range of options so that selected alternatives can be pursued either successfully or unsuccessfully: even though a processing path might look highly favoured initially, due to the changing conditions downstream, it might lead to an impasse so that processing is aborted and backtracking to an earlier state is required (Sato, 2011).

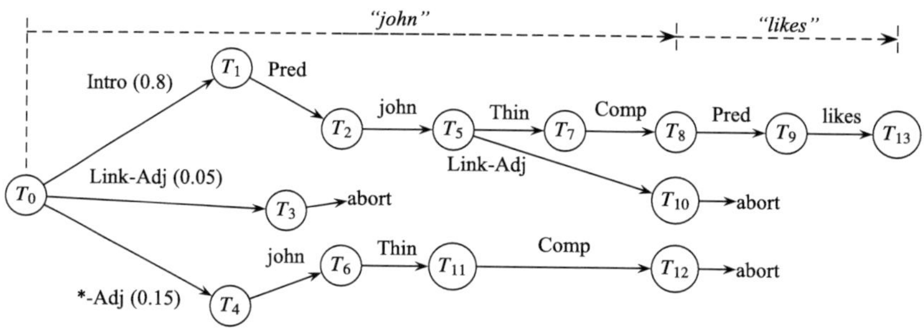

FIGURE 1: DS-TTR parsing as a Directed Acyclic Graph (DAG): actions (edges) are probabilistic transitions between partial trees (nodes).

Given these inherent properties, DS has lent itself particularly well to dialogue modelling and analysis in the past decade or so (see Purver et al., 2006, Gargett et al., 2009, Gregoromichelaki et al., 2011, Howes, 2012, Eshghi et al., 2015, Kempson et al., 2016, Howes and Eshghi, 2021, among others). Dialogue is modelled as the incremental and interactive composition of action sequences triggered by words either from oneself (in production) or an interloculor (in comprehension) in an incrementally evolving context, enabling unitary explanations of ellipsis (Kempson et al., 2015), self-repair (Hough and Purver, 2012), split utterances (Howes et al., 2011, Howes, 2012, Kempson et al., 2016), clarification requests (Gargett et al., 2009, Eshghi et al., 2015) and other feedback (Howes and Eshghi, 2021).

10.5.1 Type Theory with Records (TTR)

Recent efforts (e.g., Eshghi et al., 2012, Purver et al., 2011, 2010) have incorporated TTR (Cooper, 2012, 2005) and probabilistic versions of TTR (e.g., Hough, 2015, Hough and Purver, 2014a, 2017, Hough et al., 2018) as the conceptualisation formalism assumed by DS. Here we assume a version with types ('concepts') reinterpreted in DS dynamic terms as types of PDL actions (programs) (Gregoromichelaki et al., 2020b,a) – it is within this so-called DS-TTR fusion that we express our models below.

TTR is an extension of standard type theory, and has been shown to be useful in contextual and semantic modelling in dialogue (see e.g. Ginzburg, 2012, Fernández, 2006, Purver et al., 2010, among many others), as well as the integration of perceptual and linguistic semantics (Larsson, 2015, Dobnik et al., 2012, Yu et al., 2016). With its rich notions of underspecification and subtyping, TTR has proved crucial for DS research in strongly incremental semantic specification (Purver et al., 2011, Hough, 2015), as well as specification of richer concepts of dialogue context (Purver et al., 2010, Hough, 2015). Furthermore, Hough and Purver (2014b, 2017) use a probabilistic variant of TTR (Cooper et al., 2015) in combination with DS to flesh out a model of probabilistic inference for incremental reference processing and it has been shown, on this basis, how robotic design can benefit from modelling the perception of affordances of objects in the environment (Hough et al., 2018, 2020). But DS-TTR is in principle compatible with any version of probabilistic versions of TTR and other such frameworks (e.g. Cooper et al., 2014)

TTR: a quick formal introduction

In TTR, conceptual structures are specified as *record types*, which are sequences of *fields* of the form $[\ l : T\ ]$ containing a label l and a type T. Record types can be witnessed (i.e. having an instantiation, hence 'true') by *records* of that type, where a record is a sequence of label-value pairs $[\ l = v\ ]$. We say that $[\ l = v\ ]$ is of type $[\ l : T\ ]$ just in case v is of type T.

$$R_1 : \begin{bmatrix} l_1 & : T_1 \\ l_{2=a} & : T_2 \\ l_{3=p(l_2)} & : T_3 \end{bmatrix} \quad R_2 : \begin{bmatrix} l_1 & : T_1 \\ l_2 & : T_{2'} \end{bmatrix} \quad R_3 : []$$

FIGURE 2: Example TTR record types

Fields can be *manifest*, i.e. defined in terms of a singleton type e.g. $[\ l : T_a\ ]$ where T_a is the type of which only a is a member; here, we write this as $[\ l_{=a} : T\ ]$. Fields can also be *dependent* on fields preceding them (i.e. higher) in the record type (see Fig. 2).

The standard subtype relation $\sqsubseteq$ can be defined for record types: $R_1 \sqsubseteq R_2$ if for all fields $[\ l : T_2\ ]$ in R_2, R_1 contains $[\ l : T_1\ ]$ where $T_1 \sqsubseteq T_2$. In Fig. 2, $R_1 \sqsubseteq R_2$ if $T_2 \sqsubseteq T_{2'}$, and both R_1 and R_2 are subtypes of R_3. This subtyping relation allows semantic information to be incrementally specified, i.e. record types can be indefinitely extended with more constraints: this inherent property has been the central reason for turning towards TTR for a formalism in which unfolding conceptual structures are represented in incremental parsing and generation.

Record Types as interaction potentials In this chapter, we follow Gregoromichelaki et al. (2020b), and argue that under the actionist perspective on successful communication as coordinative action – see earlier Sec. 10.3 – linguistically-relevant RTs should not be identified with Austinian propositions (i.e., a situation being of a particular type), as in Cooper (2005), Cooper and Ginzburg (2015) following tradition in NL Semantics. Instead, with the aid of Dynamic Syntax, we propose their reformulation as dynamically constructed ad hoc conceptualisations of situations inducing further actions (predictions) capturing, and enabling, the formation of fields of affordances (see Sec. 10.6 for an operationalisation of this idea). On this view, RTs are not taken to classify perceptual input or sensory information (cf. Larsson, 2011, Dobnik et al., 2012, Yu et al., 2016), but instead trigger action policies inducing predictions for further interaction. What they classify are therefore (inter)action potentials, thus allowing agents to predict and causally associate what they do or say with the outcomes that these actions are likely to have in their environment, with this crucially including how an interlocutor may or may not respond. As we will see below in Sec. 10.6, the DS-TTR hybrid also allows agents to use exploration through trial-and-error to *learn* the probabilistic associations between what they say and what is likely to happen afterwards (*reinforcement learning*), leading to particular action/word sequences becoming routinised as ways of bringing about particular perlocutionary effects.

10.5.2 Parsing and generation of linguistic actions

In DS-TTR, parsing or generating a string of words or non-verbal tokens, induces some organisation of a state space of activity possibilities (a 'field of affordances') in combination with top-down actions ensuing from preexisting skills and dispositions of the participants involved (the 'grammar') (cf. Zadrozny, 2020). This either transforms the existing state space, adds new structures to it, or removes existing paths through it. Locally, the immediate path trajectory moves through a tree-shaped state space with nodes as states traversed by means of constraints expressed by the modal operators (e.g. $\langle\downarrow\rangle$, $\langle\uparrow\rangle$, $\langle\uparrow_*\rangle$) of a modal tree logic (the Logic of Finite Trees; LOFT: Blackburn and Meyer-Viol, 1994) expressing topological relations among current or future anticipated nodes. The tree-shaped organisation reflects the conceptualisation structure induced by the unfolding utterance in terms of function-argument articulations. More globally, the state space is presented as a directed acyclic graph (ICS-DAG, Interaction Control States DAG) that records possible paths of actions in a landscape defined by what the grammar, acting as a controller of the normativity pertaining to linguistic actions, allows as predictions of future interaction possibilities.

DS-TTR trees are always binary-branching when they have reached a stable organisation because they underpin the dynamic and incremental computation implemented as a combination of functors with their argument. However, as information becomes gradually available, intermediate stages will involve 'structural uncertainty', where so-called 'unfixed nodes' will be constructed triggering predictions and search for their appropriate accommodation in the binary tree organisation. Tree nodes thus correspond to terms in the lambda calculus and function application actions are conventionally indicated with argument nodes appearing on the right and functor nodes to the left. Node states can also host constraints on what input/output is predicted to occur indicated as labels. For example, an argument node might be one of the lowest types in the hierarchy of types ($Ty(e)$), standing for a generic type of entity) and then its sister might be of type ($Ty(e \rightarrow t)$) that receives that type as input and returns a type t ($Ty(t)$) as output (the label component t should not be taken as indicating a truth-evaluable proposition as in formal semantics frameworks since, for example, questions, imperatives, non-finites etc.

can all be characterised as $Ty(t)$). Functor-argument structures can be built recursively on that basis (e.g. $Ty(e \rightarrow (e \rightarrow t))$). These type labels thus indicate what is possible for the node type to be expanded into or act as constraints as to what further actions can be taken when the pointer appears on such a node. For example, lexical entries are introduced with IF-THEN conditional actions that make reference to expectations regarding these type labels. So these types are indicators of the structural function-argument organisation of the complex conceptual structure that is being built. On the other hand, record types of Type Theory with Records (Fig. 4) expand such types to a more fine-grained articulation of content and appear also on tree nodes. But, since such types can also be defined as graph structures, we assume here that they can be introduced and built incrementally by means of the PDL apparatus of DS, so that what appears on the node is an abbreviation of an embedded subgraph of the higher level tree graph (see also Kempson et al., 2001, ch.9). Both trees and labels can be *partial* in every respect, introduced initially by prediction, in the form of unsatisfied (indicated with a ?) so-called *requirements* for any element defined within the formalism (e.g. $?Ty(e)$, is a requirement for future development to $Ty(e)$). The satisfaction of predictions can only be launched by proceeding from a specific point on the tree and this is indicated by a *pointer*, $\diamondsuit$, labelling the node currently under development and relative to which any input/output can be defined. The potentially variable position of the pointer relative to a local tree accounts for variable licensed word-order possibilities in each language. The purpose of the grammar is both to induce and satisfy these predictions by licensing (consuming or producing) linguistic actions thus providing a normative perspective in the parsing/generation process. Thus knowledge of the grammar is literally knowledge of "how to go on" (Wittgenstein, 1953, para. 154) in an interaction. Since the possibilities that the grammar makes available are probabilistically ranked, the notion of grammaticality is very local (i.e., non-sentential, word-by-word transition probabilities) and gradient (see e.g. Lappin, 2021) and potentially defined for any combination of lexical actions, with higher 'surprisal' values assigned to unusual, i.e., not yet routinised, combinations (cf. Lau et al., 2017, 2020).

The dynamics of what constitutes 'syntax' in DS-TTR, is defined in terms of conditional packages of *actions*: procedural specifications for updates of the state space. Action sequences can be retrievable as uninterruptable chunks (*macros*). So-called *computational macros* are invoked without any linguistic input triggering their execution and only the pointer's presence at a node satisfying the conditional constraints included in the macro is necessary; and *lexical macros* are language-specific action policies corresponding to and triggered by specific lexical tokens. All action macros are presented in an IF...THEN...ELSE format and correspond to transition edges (formalised as action PDL operators) along states of the tree or the ICS DAG (see e.g. Figs. 7 and 8). Formally, macros are composed sequences of PDL atomic actions (formalised as (multi)modal operators) such as make, put and go, which reflect state space updating operations. For example, make creates a new node, go moves the pointer there, and put decorates the pointed node with a prediction regarding some node label.

Computational macros form a small, fixed set. Some enforce the overarching constraints imposed by the lambda calculus and the modal logic tree formalism (LOFT: Blackburn and Meyer-Viol, 1994): for example, ELIMINATION, performs beta-reduction of a node's daughters, and annotates the mother node with the result, while THINNING removes satisfied requirements. Other computational actions enable the fundamental predictivity and dynamics of DS-TTR, e.g. COMPLETION, which moves the pointer up and out of a sub-tree once all requirements therein are satisfied; and ANTICIPATION which moves the pointer from a mother node to a daughter node with any unfulfilled requirements thus expecting the resolution of a prediction in the immediate next step. While the former set of actions are *inferential*, thus not adding any new information to the trees, the latter set introduce alternative parse paths, thus capturing structural ambiguity: COMPLETION for example, precludes any further development of the current sub-tree because it moves the pointer up and out of it. The successful parse or generation of a word w_1 thus amounts to finding a sequence of computational actions (possibly empty) leading to a tree that satisfies the preconditions of the lexical action for w_1. The search process through predicted future actions and the history of both taken and abandoned action possibilities is recorded in the ICS DAG, with (partial) trees as nodes, and actions as edges.

Lexical actions are associated with word forms in a DS-TTR lexicon. Like computational actions, these are state space update macros composed of sequences of atomic actions. Fig. 3 shows an example for a proper noun, *John*. The action checks whether the pointed node (marked as $\Diamond$) has a prediction (in DS-TTR terms, *requirement*) for the occurrence of type e; if so, it satisfies this prediction with providing type e, introduces the conceptual potential associated with *John* (see section 10.5.1 for details) and the bottom restriction

$\langle\downarrow\rangle\bot$ (meaning that the node cannot have any daughters). Otherwise (if there is no prediction of $?Ty(e)$), the action aborts, meaning that the word *John* cannot be parsed in the context of the current tree.

Action

John	**IF**	$?Ty(e)$
	THEN	put($Ty(e)$)
		put($\left[\ x_{=john} : e\ \right]$)
	ELSE	ABORT

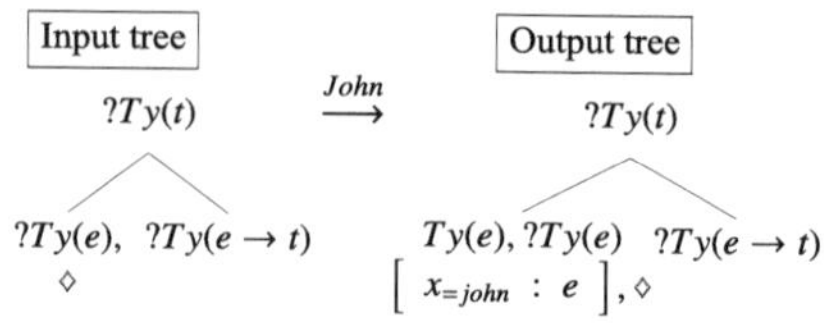

FIGURE 3: Lexical action for the word 'John'

Fig. 4 shows "John arrives", parsed incrementally, starting with an empty tree, with only the root node's daughters predictively introduced without any lexical grounding, and ending with a complete tree. The intermediate steps show the effects of Completion, which moves the pointer up and out of a complete node, and of Anticipation, which moves the pointer down from the root to its functor daughter.

The DS-TTR framework integrates various forms of uncertainty as an explanatory factor for syntactic/semantic phenomena. As an illustration of syntactic uncertainty, we display in Fig 5 the (condensed) steps involved in beginning the parsing of a standard long-distance dependency, *Who hugged Mary?*. The basic idea implemented in the DS-TTR modelling of such dependencies is that the sentence-initial phrase is introduced with recorded constrained uncertainty as to which role it will eventually play downstream in the tree-construction process. While the process continues, the so-called 'unfixed node' hosting the underderspecified *wh*-content (formalised as a metavariable in need of substitution) needs to be kept in memory awaiting its resolution. The resolution of the structural uncertainty regarding the position of the unfixed node as subject will be provided in the next steps (see Fig. 6 for one path in the DAG traversal) but the content resolution of the metavariable will normally needs to be provided by the interlocutor. This structural and content uncertainty is an example of how to resolve a number of other syntactic/semantic puzzles regarding the processing of pronouns, anaphors, *wh*-elements, clitics, and various so-called "movement" operations[1]. Here the task starts with a set of probabilistically-weighted predicted *Interaction Control States* (ICSs) represented in the ICS DAG. At this stage, which might be, let's assume, the first utterance in a dialogue, the DAG landscape displays

[1]The detailed justification of DS-TTR as a grammar formalism is given elsewhere (Kempson et al., 2001, 2011, 2016, 2017, Eshghi et al., 2011, a.o.).

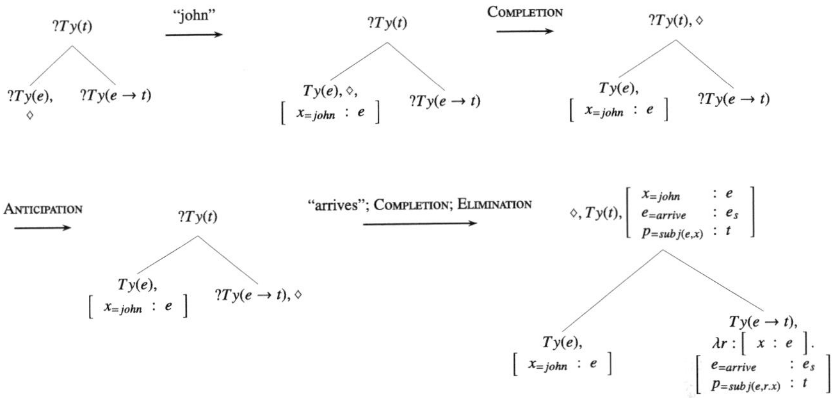

FIGURE 4: Incremental parsing in DS-TTR: *"John arrives"*

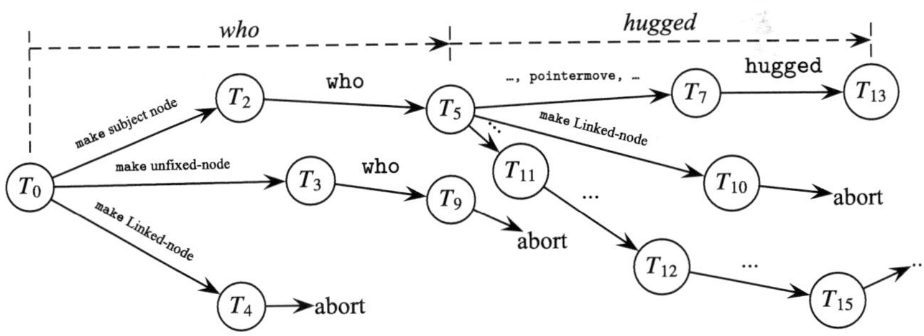

FIGURE 5: Processing *Who hugged*

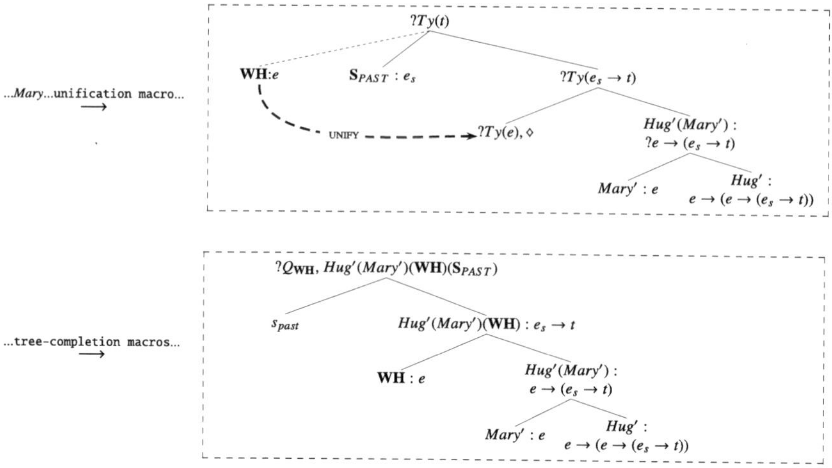

FIGURE 6: Structural uncertainty in DS-TTR: last steps of processing *Who hugged Mary?*

all the potential opportunities for parsing or producing verbal actions, prompting lexical actions as licensed by the grammar of English. These potential actions are assumed to be "virtually present" for the participants even though they are not all eventually actualised.[2] Either participant might then take the initiative to begin the articulation of an utterance while the other is in a state of preparedness checking whether the path pursued by the other interlocutor conforms to their expectations or whether they need to take over and compensate for their lack of coordination (Eshghi et al., 2015). Many alternative processing paths unfold at each step as affordances of the sociomaterial environment are taken up or are gradually abandoned (see also Sato, 2011, Eshghi et al., 2013b, Hough, 2015).[3]

[2]For relevant notions of "virtual presence", see Noë (2012), DeLanda (2013)

[3]A more realistic graph would also include the possibilities of non-verbal actions, not only gestures, but also physical voluntary actions like, for example, the physical response to a command or request. It is our claim that any "speech act" can be performed non-verbally (see, e.g., Clark, 2012, Gregoromichelaki and Kempson, 2015 and (64)-(65)). Accordingly, physical and grammatical NL actions readily compose with each other exactly because they perform meshing contributions in human interaction (Gregoromichelaki, 2018):

(64) She played [PLAYING TUNE ON THE PIANO] not [PLAYING ANOTHER TUNE ON THE PIANO]

(65) OK, let's do it together. So we have [ARM MOVEMENT DEMONSTRATION] and then we go [LEG MOVEMENT DEMONSTRATION]

10.5.3 Conceptualisation as state transitions

The conceptual structure being built here is indefinitely extendible (see Cooper, 2012) and "non-reconstructive" in the sense that it is not meant as a passive inner model of the world (see also Clark, 2017a,b) but as a means of interaction, that is contact, with the world via the predictions generated regarding subsequent processing. Accordingly, the affordances that constitute the conceptual structure are viewed as relational (see also Chemero, 2009, Bruineberg et al., 2018a): a pairing of (aspects of) the world with a (joint) perspective, namely, those affordances of the sociomaterial world that are accessible relative to the agent(s)' relevant sensorimotor skills shaped by prior experiences and the ecological niche.[4] Here we assume a perspectival construal of types as accessible affordances to an agent or group of agents. Following standard assumptions in ecological psychology and phenomenology, it is part of the force of an affordance that the perceiving/acting agent becomes aware that they are manipulating the world from a particular point of view. This awareness is enabled as part of the agent's sensorimotor knowledge of regularities and lawful variations regarding the changes in the environment that are caused by the agent's own actions as opposed to actions/events affecting the agent. When multiple agents are coupled as a temporarily assembled agentive system, but also in cases where experts use tools or patients use prostheses, the collective perception/action possibilities that emerge for the newly-formed systemic unit are not the result of simple summation of what is possible for the individual components but a new perspective for each individual which incorporates their function as a component of the overarching system (Di Paolo and De Jaegher (2012)). Thus the joint landscape of affordances can be much more or much less affordances depending on "enabling" or "disabling" couplings. In both cases, agents are able to perceive this new regime and generally capable to adjust their contributions in complementary ways (Mills and Gregoromichelaki, 2010, Mills, 2014).

The relativisation of the structure of human conceptual types against practice-based abilities has normative implications, in that the agent(s) might fail to achieve what is genuinely afforded to them by the socio-material environment, or the agent(s) might fail to take up the multitude of affordances that have been perceived as potential ("virtual") paths of action. Moreover, given that they engage with real properties of the sociomaterial context (see also Pickering and Garrod, 2021), the

[4]In this actionist and externalist perspective, we diverge from standard construals of TTR as in Ginzburg (2012), Cooper, forthcoming.

consequences of misapplying their abilities will be detectable by the agents themselves as 'error signals' when their predictions are falsified. Such failure is inevitable and constant and it is, in fact, the source that leads to further finer-grain differentiations in the agents' sociomaterial environment so that local adjustment and long-term learning and adaptation are the outcomes (Bickhard (2009); cf. Friston (2010, 2011)).

Given this requisite dynamicity and world grounding, type (concept) labels, like Hug' or $Arrive'$ here stand for abbreviations of triggers for complex sets of action potentials embedded under the DAG ICS nodes as nested affordances. Such labels then constitute additional ICS choice points in the generation of further potential paths within the DAG. Given this view of concepts, what individuates each such label is its distinguished provision of sets of available actions realisable in the next steps within the field of affordances (the DAG). To take a "syntactic" type as an example, type t is differentiated from type $(e_s \rightarrow t)$ in that the former (minimally) leads to the prediction of a left daughter of type e_s and a right daughter of type $(e_s \rightarrow t)$ whereas the latter leads to the prediction of e and $(e \rightarrow (e_s \rightarrow t))$. This is what differentiates these types, not their distinct labels. Within the grammar, such types either contribute tests in the conditional procedures that implement the operation of grammatical and extra-linguistic actions or trigger searches for appropriate words, or expand the current structure and annotations with the anticipation of further developments. But, even more pertinently here, such types do not have any model-theoretic content beyond the transitions they allow or curtail in the traversal of the states of the PDL model that underpins DS-TTR. Similarly, we take concept labels such as Hug' or $john'$[5] as triggering access to nested structures of potential actions regarding aspects of (mental or physical) interaction with an event of hugging or interacting with John, some of which will be taken up and others abandoned. As such, the types induced by the grammar (aka 'concepts') are mainly constituted by subpersonal mechanisms, however, the results of their operation can be brought to consciousness by processes of reification for purposes of, e.g., linguistic negotiation, explicit planning, theory construction, or teaching.

The actionism foundation of DS-TTR suggests that the sensorimotor knowledge-as-action underpinning to cognition implicates conceptual understanding from the earliest stages of perceptual access (unlike, e.g., existential phenomenology – Dreyfus, 2013 – and related views).

[5] For the view that such entity concepts are tracking abilities allowing the accumulation of knowledge about individuals, see Millikan (2000).

However, conceptual abilities do not, as in standard models, proceed via an intermediate cognitive stage before initiating the control of action, for cognition is not seen as separate from the sensorimotor grounding of agent performance. Under this view, concepts are not the rich internal representational structures of standard views – they are skills. For our purposes, we argue that in perceiving some entity and identifying it as a dog, it is not a static retinal image that becomes associated with the application of the 'Dog' type. Instead, memorised patterns of current and past interactions are invoked to construct ad hoc a pattern of predicted interactions that differentiates the particular entity in the current context through its particular set of affordances as, e.g., a threat or a rewarding experience with incrementally adjustable behaviour of approach or avoidance (Gregoromichelaki et al., 2019, Bickhard and Richie, 1983). On this view, conceptual understanding cannot be taken as static pattern-matching but is, instead, an achievement: it is time-extended, incremental, and based on trial-and-error rather than an automatic mapping of experience to internal categories or propositional knowledge.

Moreover, due to their basis in action, concepts are necessarily always fragile and incomplete, amenable to modification by prediction-error minimisation: in general, the specification of action guidance must allow flexibility to fit different situations and changing conditions and, therefore, successful situated action execution depends on leaving some degrees of freedom unbound (Suchman, 1987). This is notably echoed in NL phenomena like the so-called "polysemy" or "coercion" phenomena where word meanings are notoriously shiftable even within a single context. It is also indicated by the now established assumption of gradient grammaticality or well-formedness (e.g. Lappin, 2021). The latter, in our terms, is reduced to the effects of social normativity on complex, ad hoc conceptualisation sense-making activities, as DS-TTR rejects the notion of a distinct level of syntactic representations. Such phenomena clearly reflect the fact that NL use involves learning and adjustment as an interactional system self-organises around the needs and goals of the interlocutors. As Mills (2011, 2014) and Mills and Gregoromichelaki (2010) argue, interlocutors encountering a novel situation, interactively and incrementally organise their joint and complementary predictions to establish via trial-and-error ad hoc routines for coordinating with each other. This is shown in experiments (e.g. Healey and Mills, 2006) where dyads of participants playing "the maze game", gradually develop group-specific procedural interdependence employing NL structures with highly ad hoc sequential-position-dependent meanings.

Given affordance competition, agents select their next actions based on possibilities (probabilistically) grounded on these types which function as 'outcome indicators' (Bickhard and Richie, 1983) so that the predictions yielded by these types might be reinforced (verified) or abandoned (fail) in the next steps. As long as they remain as live possibilities, the operations induced by the types will keep triggering flows of predictions for further (mental or physical) action even if particular paths of sequences of nested predictions are not taken up. Maintaining even abandoned options is required for the explicit modelling of conversational phenomena like clarification, self/other-corrections (66), etc. but also, quotation, code-switching, humorous effects and puns (Hough, 2015, Gregoromichelaki, 2018) (see, e.g., (67)).

(66) John went swimming with Mary, um. . . , or rather, surfing, yesterday.
['John went surfing with Mary yesterday']

(67) The restaurant said it served meals any time so I ordered breakfast during the Renaissance.
[Stephen Wright joke]

10.5.4 Overt feedback as pruning of action sequences

However, these live but unactualised predictions, in the case of dialogue, reach the limits of their (virtual) existence when it is no longer possible for either participant to backtrack successfully in order to extend or "repair" ICS node elements due to the fact that the relevant paths have decayed in the DAG history. Memory mechanisms are implicated in how far the currently active DAG records go. This decay and elimination can also be facilitated and induced by the explicit verbal efforts (aka "overt feedback") on the part of the interlocutors, which can be seen as an efficiency strategy to intervene to reduce DAG complexity and lessen the burden on memory requirements.

In DS-TTR, *context*, required for processing various forms of context-dependency – including pronouns, VP-ellipsis, self-repair and short answers – is considered the global state space ICS DAG, which encompasses the virtual field of affordances for the conversational participants (or a dynamically developing 'situation convention', Bickhard (2009)). Edges here correspond to DS-TTR actions – both computational and lexical macros – and nodes correspond to tree subspaces updated after the application of each action (Sato, 2011, Eshghi et al., 2012, Kempson et al., 2015) – see Fig. 1. Here, we take a coarser-grained view of the DAG with edges corresponding to words (sequences of computational actions followed by a single lexical action) rather than single actions, and dropping abandoned parse paths (see Hough, 2015, for details) – Fig. 7 shows an example.

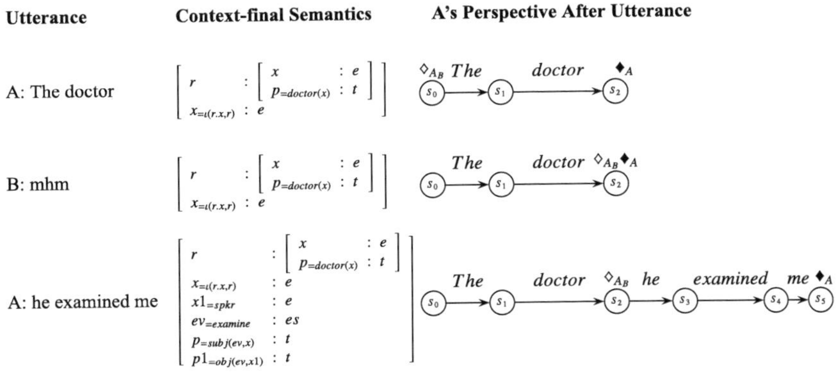

FIGURE 7: Backchannels as movement of coordination pointers on Interaction Control States (ICS); from A's perspective.

As Eshghi et al. (2015), Howes and Eshghi (2017, 2021) show, the processing and integration of utterances that have been characterised as explicit feedback in dialogue can be captured using the ICS DAG, enhanced with the perspectival conception of affordances we discussed earlier (Sec. 10.5.3), in this case, implemented as two *coordination pointers*: the *self-pointer*, ♦; and the *other-pointer*, ♢. These pointers indicate the points up to which the dialogue participants have each marked the material as "grounded", i.e., liable to decay from memory storage.

Any action causes ICS pointer movement, and, as we said earlier, any action possibility includes the interlocutors' own perspective of the effect on the ICS. Such perspectives, which are crucial for demarcating self- and other-action may, as we will see below, provide divergent ICS trajectories for each participant with convergence as a result of clarification interaction and repair processes more generally. The self-pointer, $♦_A$, on participant A's ICS view tracks the point to which A has given evidence for reaching. The other-pointer, $♢_{AB}$, tracks where the other participant, B, has given evidence for reaching. For example, an utterance produced by A will move A's self-pointer to the rightmost node of the ICS; on B's ICS perspective, it is the other-pointer that moves to the same location. On this model, the intersection of the path back to the ICS root from the self- and other-pointers is taken to be grounded, with the effect that parse or production search within this grounded pathway is precluded, thus removing the computational cost associated with finding alternative interpretation pathways, as well as formally explaining how conversations move forward.

This model has been shown to account for backchannels (Howes and Eshghi, 2017, 2021), clarificational exchanges and other corrections Eshghi et al. (2015). Clarification Requests (CR) cause branching on the ICS, where the current path is abandoned and another branch constructed – a subsequent response to the CR plus the acknowledgement of this response eventually realigns the two coordination pointers, and the interlocutors' individual ICS perspectives as a consequence.

Backchannels Fig. 7 is a step-by-step illustration of how the ICS with only A's perspective develops as the dialogue proceeds, and as B's backchannel, 'mhm' is processed. After producing the first utterance, A's self-pointer, $\blacklozenge_A$, is on s_2, the right-most node of her ICS so far. B's backchannel "passes the opportunity to repair" (Schegloff, 1982), thus moving A's other-pointer, $\lozenge_{A_B}$, to the same node and so grounding "the doctor". A's subsequent continuation creates new edges, and moves her self-pointer to the new right-most node. At this point, A's new utterance needs further feedback from B to be grounded: divergence of pointer positions thus represents 'forward momentum' in conversation (elsewhere called *discursive potential*; Ginzburg, 2012).

Overt repair Fig. 8 shows an example of a clarificational exchange, as in (68):

(68) (a) A: The doctor examined me...
(b) B: Chorlton?
(c) A: no, Fitzgerald

It shows the incremental updates arising in the clarifier's perspective (B) in example ((68)), a case of a non-local CR which requires backtracking.[6] Initially, B successfully parses A's utterance, thus moving the other-pointer ($\lozenge_{B_A}$) to the right-most node of his DAG. Not having secured a referent for "the doctor" with enough certainty, he then aims to produce the CR, *Chorlton?*, which involves backtracking to "the doctor" node in order to produce it. At this juncture A's and B's perspectives have diverged: A's self-pointer ($\blacklozenge_A$) appears at the rightmost DAG edge, which B knows (hence $\lozenge_{B_A}$), while B has not grounded that edge. B's production of the CR causes A to have to parse it. This serves to re-align pointer positions for A and B, the result of which is both of them focussing on "the doctor"-subtree as the source of the misalignment.

[6]For space reasons we do not here include the clarification recipient's (A) point of view.

Utterance	Context-final semantics	B's Perspective after utterance
(a) A: The doctor examined me	$\left[\begin{array}{ll} r & : \left[\begin{array}{ll} x & : e \\ p_{=doctor(x)} & : t \end{array}\right] \\ x_{=\iota(r.x,r)} & : e \\ x1_{=spkr} & : e \\ ev_{=examine} & : es \\ p_{=subj(ev,x)} & : t \\ p1_{=obj(ev,x1)} & : t \end{array}\right]$	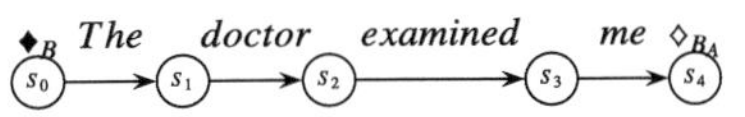
(b) B: Chorlton?	$\left[\begin{array}{ll} r & : \left[\begin{array}{ll} x & : e \\ p_{=doctor(x)} & : t \\ p1_{=Chorlton(x)} & : t \end{array}\right] \\ x_{=\iota(r.x,r)} & : e \\ x1_{=spkr} & : e \\ ev_{=examine} & : es \\ p_{=subj(ev,x)} & : t \\ p1_{=obj(ev,x1)} & : t \end{array}\right]$	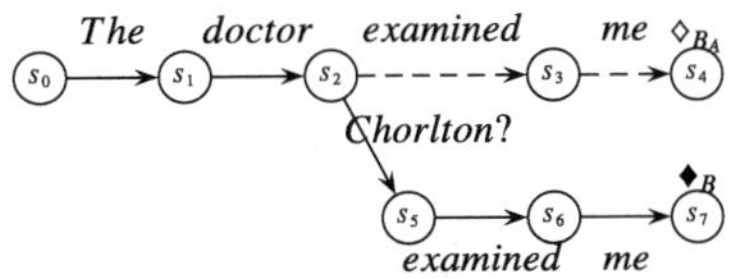
(c) A: (no,) Fitzgerald	$\left[\begin{array}{ll} r & : \left[\begin{array}{ll} x & : e \\ p_{=doctor(x)} & : t \\ p1_{=Fitzgerald(x)} & : t \end{array}\right] \\ x_{=\iota(r.x,r)} & : e \\ x1_{=spkr} & : e \\ ev_{=examine} & : es \\ p_{=subj(ev,x)} & : t \\ p1_{=obj(ev,x1)} & : t \end{array}\right]$	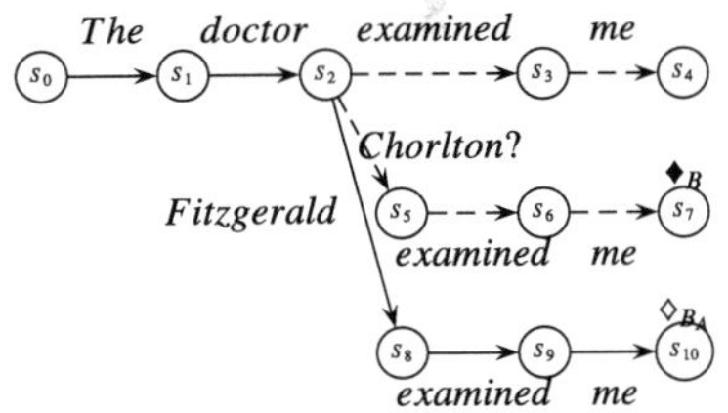
(d) B: uh-huh	$\left[\begin{array}{ll} r & : \left[\begin{array}{ll} x & : e \\ p_{=doctor(x)} & : t \\ p1_{=Fitzgerald(x)} & : t \end{array}\right] \\ x_{=\iota(r.x,r)} & : e \\ x1_{=spkr} & : e \\ ev_{=examine} & : es \\ p_{=subj(ev,x)} & : t \\ p1_{=obj(ev,x1)} & : t \end{array}\right]$	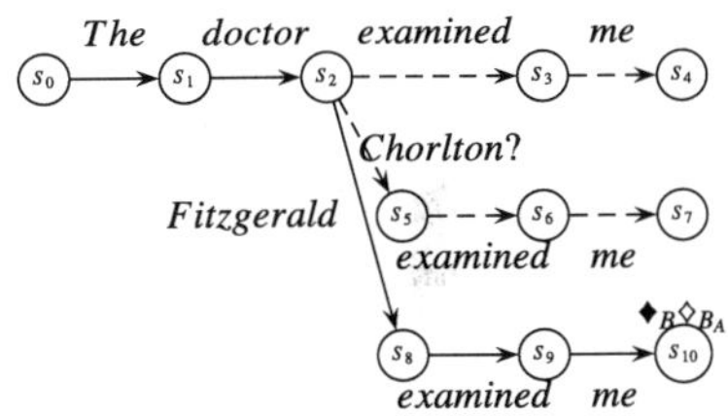
(e) A (accept): yes/mhm	$\left[\begin{array}{ll} r & : \left[\begin{array}{ll} x & : e \\ p_{=doctor(x)} & : t \\ p1_{=Chorlton(x)} & : t \end{array}\right] \\ x_{=\iota(r.x,r)} & : e \\ x1_{=spkr} & : e \\ ev_{=examine} & : es \\ p_{=subj(ev,x)} & : t \\ p1_{=obj(ev,x1)} & : t \end{array}\right]$	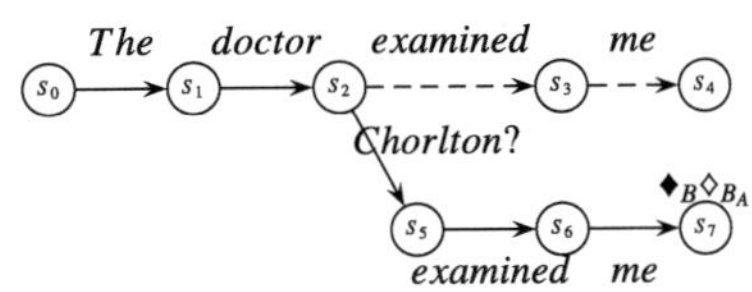

FIGURE 8: Overt Repair as editing action sequences - from B's perspective; turn (e) comes after (b)

A can now offer a confirmatory or a negative response to the CR. (c), in Figure 8 illustrates the latter case, with the utterance of *no* reflecting the abandonment of the "Chorlton?" branch, rather than the denial or rejection of a propositional content. This is followed by a correction of B's CR, thus forcing B's other-pointer ($\diamondsuit_{B_A}$) out of the "Chorlton?" branch, and inducing the construction of the new, "Fitzgerald" branch. At this juncture, B's self- ($\blacklozenge_B$) and other-pointers ($\diamondsuit_{B_A}$) are on different branches. This can be taken as representing the requirement for further action to be taken in order to realign pointer positions. Especially for B, whose pointer is now on an abandoned branch, this can constitute an obligation to ground the new information provided by A's repair *Fitzgerald*, thus accounting for the forward momentum created by the negative response. B's final backchannel, in 7(d), then serves to realign his two pointers, signalling acceptance to A, who, having processed the backchannel moves her other-pointer ($\diamondsuit_{A_B}$) to the same node, $s10$, thus ending the clarification sequence with the achievement of a realignment of A's and B's perspectives.

An alternative parsing path is illustrated in (e) of Figure 8. It represents the case where A, after the clarification in 7(b), confirms that the doctor is in fact Chorlton. This simply involves, for B, moving his other-pointer ($\diamondsuit_{B_A}$) to the end of the "Chorlton?" branch, thus confirming the referent of *the doctor* as Chorlton. This, unlike the negative response in 7(c) which necessitated rejecting already established branches and pointer divergence, ends the clarification sequence.

Both alternatives end up with A's and B's perspectives aligned as the result of repair and backchannelling and set for the continuation of the dialogue.

The account above puts structural, surface forms of context-dependency at the centre of the explanation of participant coordination and feedback in dialogue: various forms of context-dependent expression, from the weakest – backchannels, which have little or no semantic content, to the strongest – utterance continuations, all serve to narrow down the otherwise mushrooming space of interpretation pathways. Their pervasiveness is therefore not coincidental, but strategic, and serves to make dialogue computationally tractable.

This account gives formal rigour to the view expressed above under which language provides a set of interactional mechanisms – such as ellipsis, repair and backchannels – for dealing with the persistent potential for miscommunication (Healey et al., 2018b, Kempson et al., 2016).

10.6 Learning through affordance exploration

We said earlier (Sec. 10.1) that one of the main problems with rule-based models of dialogue, and NL in general, was that a rigid set of hand-crafted rules is applied to the processing and production of behaviour in interactions with the users. As a result, such systems lack flexibility to adjust their responses to various particular tasks by modifying their action policies under the receipt of feedback by the user or the environment. This brittleness is due to the fact that domain-specific and separate knowledge structures are assumed in their architectures lacking the ability to dynamically adapt to open-domain tasks. Low-level, e.g. syntactic and semantic NLU and NLG components, cannot interact and be influenced by the task at hand or the discourse context. Rigid categories of, e.g., intent detection or slot-filling, along with separated modules of dialogue state tracking and policy learning only allow for very task-specific behaviours, often erroneous when faced with ambiguity, noisy input, and less frequent user needs. DS-TTR characteristically does not distinguish between different modular capacities for embodied non-linguistic and linguistic action (Gregoromichelaki, 2013, 2018); neither does it postulate separate knowledge bases for theoretically demarcated linguistic areas like syntax, semantics, pragmatics (Gregoromichelaki et al., 2013). This is under the assumption that all the phenomena identified as separate and indicative of autonomy in these domains have been shown to be influenced by interactions across all presumed levels. It is shown that any update that is performed to adjust processing in the current context might need to take into account all aspects of that context, for example, even the notion of well-formedness has to be defined as context-sensitive and incremental (see e.g. (62)-(63) earlier). Therefore, given the uncertainty and rapid shifting of the sociomaterial environment, for agent behaviours to be adaptable so that they can intervene and avail themselves of opportunities, all such previously considered modularisations are cashed out uniformly in action terms as affordances underpinned by adjustable sensorimotor knowledge on the part of individual agents.

On the other hand, data-driven, end-to-end dialogue systems based on deep learning methods require large amounts of data and often fail to converge and generalise to best overall dialogue policies online, offering generic, uninteresting responses instead. This can be due to learning only simple local associations of input/output with lack of long-term goal-directed processing, ability to act jointly with other agents, and the high-frequency of uninformative responses in the training data. What is not usually implemented is the human tendency for forward-looking policies to exploit and explore the environment, including the conversational environment, for affordances, opportunities for action to receive rewards or avoid dangers. For this human characteristic to be implemented, agents have to be modelled as 'continual learners' (Roller et al., 2020). Exploring via trial-and-error the shifting landscape of affordances is crucial for the adaptability of agent systems (either sole embodied agents or groups of agents, Adolph, 2020, Veissière et al., 2020). Human conceptualisations of situations at hand, in the form of the solicitations perceived as states of action-readiness (see section 10.3.1 earlier), depends on building skills that arise from the accumulation of multimodal experiences and acquiring skill within practices ('language games') available in the particular 'form of life' inhabited by the agent. Language use according to these assumptions is no different since its function is to guide the perception and creation of such social conceptualisations via the establishment of grammar models, i.e., in our view, sets of actions (*macros*) that have been proved rewarding in previous interactions.

It is for these reasons that words, morphology, and syntax are all modelled as affordances in DS-TTR, i.e., indicators of opportunities for (inter)action and the source of normativity (notions of 'correctness/incorrectness' embodied in a grammar). As we saw earlier, such interactions incrementally open up a range of options for the interlocutors so that selected alternatives can be pursued either successfully or unsuccessfully: even though a processing path might look highly favoured initially, due to the changing conditions downstream, it might lead to failure so that processing is aborted and backtracking to an earlier state is required. The potential for failure or success relative to goals imbues the activities of the system, even though mainly subpersonal and perceived as affective states of 'action readiness', with a notion of normativity arising from the routinisation of action sequences retrievable as chunks (macros). Such macros impose licensed expectations (predictions) that can in turn operate as triggers resulting in nested structures of affordances constraining potential interactions. This normative field of nested anticipations of further interactions built on the basis of prior trial-and-error efforts comes to constitute an instantiation of the *grammar* in particular concrete occasions. Such ad hoc grammars are what prompts or constrains the actions of the individuals participating in a dialogue. The grammar in this sense can be seen as an embodied generative model (e.g. Kirchhoff and Froese, 2017) allowing interlocutors to perform step-by-step a coordinated mapping from perceivable stimuli (phonological strings) to conceptual and physical actions or vice-versa.

In the following sections, we will consider two case studies of how the above ideas can work in practice. Firstly, we show how DS-TTR action policies can be learned through exploring environmental contingencies and acquiring skills in predicting suitable trajectories within the evolving landscape of affordances via Reinforcement Learning methods. Reinforcement Learning mechanisms can be subsumed under the more general framework of self-organisation via the Free Energy Principle and active inference (see e.g. Friston et al., 2012b, Tschantz et al., 2020) which we take here in its enactive interpretation as concerning states of action readiness. Secondly, we show how the 'education of attention' assumption about learning how to perceive affordances (Gibson, 1966) can be cashed out in DS-TTR terms. We focus on summarising the following areas of current research:

a. the so-called BABBLE method in Eshghi and Lemon (2014), Kalatzis et al. (2016), Eshghi et al. (2017) for bootstrapping interaction. This work combines DS-TTR with Reinforcement Learning, implementing and evaluating a method that allows fully incremental dialogue systems to be learned from small amounts of raw, unannotated dialogue data.
b. the work on grammar learning in Eshghi et al. (2013a,c) who present and evaluate a method for learning an incremental DS-TTR grammars from data in which utterances are paired with conceptualisation structures standing for the sense-making activities available to an agent.

10.6.1 Bootstrapping interaction: Learning how to do things with words

Eshghi and Lemon (2014), Kalatzis et al. (2016) and Eshghi et al. (2017) combine DS-TTR with Reinforcement Learning, implementing and evaluating a method that allows fully incremental dialogue systems to be learned from small amounts of raw, unannotated dialogue data. This work shows how a dialogue agent can learn to perform dialogue acts (or speech acts) together with their attendant, interactional structures within a particular domain of language use (i.e. a *language game*) without any of this being provided in advance in the form of supervision. The model relies on what the authors call 'babbling': the dynamic and local trial-and-error generation and composition of action sequences (macros) *in a particular context*, and in interaction with a simulated interlocutor, using a DS-TTR grammar. This babbling mechanism amounts to what Gregoromichelaki et al. (2020b) call the 'exploration of the field of affordances' in the agent's environment which includes the interlocutor. This leads to establishing conditional, probabilistic expectations about the outcomes of such low-level action sequences, for example, a question answered, a request fulfilled, some information given, a promise accepted etc. What is learned is thus probabilistic routines (macros) for producing desired *perlocutionary effects* in the agent's environment.

The BABBLE method

In this section we describe the BABBLE method for combining DS-TTR with Reinforcement Learning for learning Dialogue Management (DM) and Natural Language Generation (NLG) policies for a particular dialogue domain, and where these two problems are treated as a joint decision/optimisation problem.

The BABBLE method starts with two resources: a) a DS-TTR parser DS_{TTR} (either learned from data, as in Eshghi et al., 2013a, or constructed by hand), for incremental language processing, but also, more generally, for tracking the context of the dialogue using the DS_{TTR} model of feedback (Eshghi et al., 2015, Howes and Eshghi, 2017, 2021); b) a set D of transcribed successful dialogues in the target domain.

We perform the following steps overall to induce a fully incremental dialogue system from D:

a. Automatically induce the Markov Decision Process (MDP) state space, S, and the dialogue goal, G_D, from D;
b. Automatically define the state encoding function $F : C \rightarrow S$; where $s \in S$ is a (binary) state vector, designed to extract from the current context of the dialogue, the semantic features observed in the example dialogues D; and $c \in C$ is a DS-TTR context, viz. a pair of TTR Record Types: $\langle c_p, c_g \rangle$, where c_p is the content of the current, *PENDING* clause as it is being constructed, but not necessarily fully grounded yet; and c_g is the content already jointly built and *GROUNDED* by the interlocutors (loosely following the DGB model of Ginzburg, 2012).
c. Define the MDP action set as the DS_{TTR} lexicon L (i.e. actions are words);
d. Define the reward function R as reaching G_D, while minimising dialogue length.

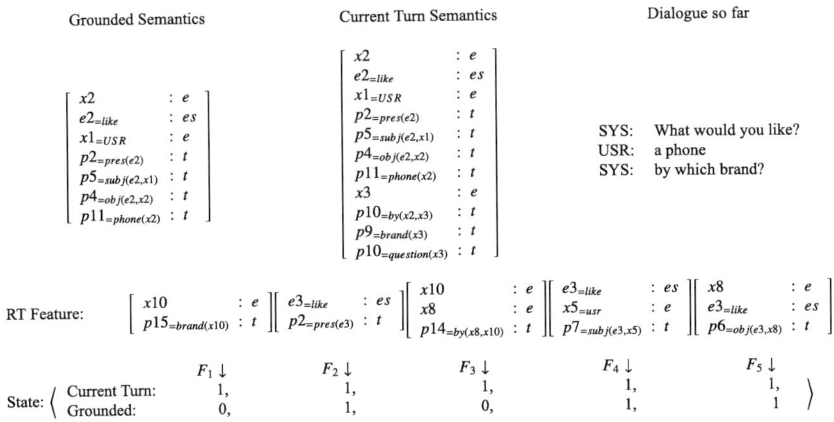

FIGURE 9: Semantics to MDP state encoding with RT features

We then solve the generated MDP using Reinforcement Learning, with a standard Q-learning method: train a policy $\pi : S \rightarrow L$, where L is the DS_{TTR} Lexicon, and S the state space induced using F. The system is trained in interaction with a (semantic) simulated user, also automatically built from the dialogue data and described in the next section.

The state encoding function, F As shown in Fig. 9 the MDP state is a binary vector of size $2 \times |\Phi|$, i.e. twice the number of the RT features. The first half of the state vector contains the grounded features (i.e. agreed by the participants) ϕ_i, while the second half contains the current semantics being incrementally built in the current dialogue utterance. Formally: $s = \langle F_1(c_p), \ldots, F_m(c_p), F_1(c_g), \ldots, F_m(c_g)\rangle$; where $F_i(c) = 1$ if $c \sqsubseteq \phi_i$, and 0 otherwise. (Recall that $\sqsubseteq$ is the RT subtype relation).

Simulating the interlocutor

The user simulation is in charge of two key tasks during training: (1) generating user turns given the domain-specific action triggers or contexts; and (2) word-by-word monitoring of the utterance so far generated by the system during exploration (i.e. babbling grammatical word sequences) by the system. Both (1) and (2) use the full machinery of the DS_{TTR} parser, as well the state encoding function F, described above. They are thus performed based on the *context* of the dialogue so far, as generated by DS_{TTR}, the result of parsing or generation of word sequences (rather than, e.g. being based on string or template matching).

The rules required for (1) and (2) are extracted *automatically* from the raw dialogue data, D, using DS_{TTR} and F. The dialogues in D are parsed and encoded using F incrementally. For (1), all the user action triggers that trigger the user to generate a turn, $s_i = F(c)$ – where c is a DS-TTR context – immediately prior to any user turn is recorded, and mapped to what the user ends up saying in those contexts - for more than one training dialogue there may be more than one candidate (in the same context/state). The rules thus extracted will be of the form: $s_{trig} \rightarrow \{u_1, \ldots, u_n\}$, where u_i are user turns.

Now note that the s_i's prior to the user turns also immediately follow system turns. And thus to perform (2), i.e. to monitor the system's behaviour during training, we only need to check further that the current state resulting from processing a word generated by the system, subsumes – is extendible to – one of the s_i. We perform this through a simple bitmask operation (recall that the states are binary). The simulation can thus semantically identify erroneous/out-of-domain actions (words) by the system. It would then terminate the learning episode and penalise the system immediately, aiding speed of training significantly.

Discussion

What is learned Using the method above, what is learned through RL exploration of lexical action pathways – trial and error generation or 'babbling' – is a policy mapping Record Types of TTR (dialogue contexts) to individual lexical actions or words, thus incrementally specifying what the agent should say/do in each of the contexts encountered enough times during training. Taken together with the ICS DAG (see above, Sec. 10.5.4), these contexts thus encode potentials for interaction to achieve some goal, that is, affordances in the agent's immediate environment.

Generalisation/bias The method described above has enabled prototype incremental dialogue systems to be bootstrapped automatically from small amounts of raw, unannotated dialogue data. For example, Eshghi et al. (2017) show that their resulting model can process 74% of the Facebook AI bAbI dataset even when trained on only 0.13% of the data (only 5 dialogues); and that it can in addition process 65% of bAbI+, a corpus they created by systematically adding self-corrections, restarts and hesitations to the bAbI dataset.

We argue that this generalisation capacity results from: (1) the predictive power of the underlying Dynamic Syntax incremental processing engine which provides constraints on how lexical actions can dynamically compose to form larger structures that simultaneously encode expectations about future possibilities; and (2) the inference power inherent within the Type Theory with Records (TTR) conceptualisation framework whose record types were used as action triggers. This allows equivalence classes to be formed during learning over different interaction potentials whereby alternative action pathways are captured as 'synonymous' viz. as having the same perlocutionary effect. This generalisation power thus results from the combined power the Dynamic Syntax syntactic engine on the one hand, and the TTR inference engine on the other.

Multi-modality As noted, the DS-TTR framework has already been used to integrate perceptual and linguistic semantics (see Yu et al. (2016), Hough et al. (2018, 2020)). Given the non-modularity assumption underpinning DS-TTR, and its attendant continuity between linguistic and non-linguistic actions (see above and Gregoromichelaki (2013, 2018)), it is only natural that learning through affordance exploration, or the BABBLE method outlined above, should also extend seamlessly to cross-modally grounded situations of utterance, or language games (e.g. manipulating objects together, cooking together, and the like). In what we presented above, the interactive exploration of dialogue trajectories is used to learn the causal associations between what the agent might say, and how the dialogue would continue (e.g. the interlocutor providing a specific piece of information). But this discovered/learned perlocutionary effect need not be purely linguistic, but can equally be an effect observed in the non-linguistic (e.g. visual), physical or simulated environment of the dialogue (e.g. the interlocutor moving an object, going from one place to another or taking other actions in the world).

Future work will therefore explore integration of the BABBLE method with state of the art computer vision models (e.g. LXMERT (Tan and Bansal, 2019), Resnet-based models, or scene graph prediction models (Xu et al., 2017, Chen et al., 2019)), which can be used to infer high level representations of the visual scene. These observations will then constitute the non-linguistic context of the dialogue, and will form components of the reward function for RL. This in turn allows learning of dialogue trajectories that lead to particular task outcomes in the visual environment of the agent.

10.6.2 Grammar induction

As a second case study of how *affordance exploration* underpins learning, we turn to work on incremental grammar induction where essentially the same mechanism of trial-and-error composition of macros is used to learn DS-TTR grammars from data in a weakly supervised setting.

Eshghi et al. (2013a) describe a method for inducing probabilistic DS-TTR lexicons from sentences paired with DS-TTR trees (see below) representing the function-argument structure of conceptualisation potentials organising sense-making activities discriminated in a fine-grained manner with assignments of typing information. Here we follow the general logic of the enactive version of the Free Energy Principle and active inference in that we assume that perception (sense-making) consists in predicting the sensory outcomes of agents' own actions interacting with environmental affordances and using prediction errors to either amend the predictions accordingly or take further action to improve predictive accuracy. Eshghi et al. (2013b) then go on to extend this work to induce DS-TTR lexicons (a set of word forms associated with action macros) from the CHILDES corpus (MacWhinney, 2000). This work takes real child-directed utterances and pairs them with sense-making activity indicators (conceptualisations) in the form of TTR Record Types (see above, but also Cooper, 2005, Cooper and Ginzburg, 2015), thus providing weaker supervision. By assuming only the availability of a small set of general action sequence composition operations, reflecting the properties of the lambda calculus and the Logic of Finite Trees (LOFT, Blackburn and Meyer-Viol, 1994) that underpins DS-TTR, they ensure that the lexical actions learnt include the grammatical constraints and corresponding compositional structure of the language.

Their method exhibits incrementality in two senses: *incremental learning*, with the grammar being extended and refined as each new data point becomes available; an ensuing inherently *incremental, probabilistic grammar* for parsing and production, suitable for use in incremental dialogue systems (Purver et al., 2011) and for modelling human-human dialogue.

Problem statement

Our induction procedure now assumes as input:

- a known set of DS_{TTR} computational macros.
- a set of training examples of the form $\langle S_i, R_{T_i} \rangle$, where $S_i = \langle w_1 \ldots w_n \rangle$ is an utterance in the language and R_{T_i} – henceforth referred to as the *target RT* – is the record type representing a situation conceptualisation, a set of available affordances, induced by S_i.

The output is a grammar specifying the possible lexical macros for each word form in the corpus. Given our data-driven approach, we take a probabilistic view: we take this grammar as associating each word form w with a probability distribution θ_w over lexical actions. For use in parsing, this distribution should specify the posterior probability $p(a|w, T)$ of using a particular action a to parse/generate a word form w in the context of a particular partial tree T.

Hypothesis construction by affordance exploration

The DS procedural framework is *monotonic*: actions can only *extend* the current (partial) tree T_{cur}, deleting nothing except satisfied requirements. Thus, lexical actions can be hypothesised by incrementally exploring the space of all monotonic, well-formed extensions T of T_{cur}, whose maximal conceptualisation affordances collected under R is a supertype of (extendible to / subsumes) the target R_T (i.e. $R_T \sqsubseteq R$). This gives a bounded space described by a DAG equivalent to that of section 10.5.4 - see Fig. 1: nodes are trees; edges are possible tree-building actions; pathways start from T_{cur} and end at any tree that can instantiate R_T. Edges may be either known computational actions or new *lexical hypotheses*. The space is further constrained by the properties of the lambda-calculus and the state transitions imposed by the constraints expressed in the modal tree logic LoFT (not all possible trees and extensions are well-formed).

General tree-building actions The lexical hypotheses comprising these DAG paths are divided into two general classes: (1) *tree-building* hypotheses, which hypothesise appropriately typed daughters to compose a given node; and (2) *content* hypotheses, which decorate leaf nodes with appropriate supertypes of R_T (non-leaf nodes then receive their content via beta-reduction/extension of daughters).

Tree-building actions can be divided into two general options: functional decomposition (corresponding to the addition of daughter nodes with appropriate types and formulae which will form a suitable mother node by beta-reduction); and type extension. We do not go into any details on the latter here, but note that possible type extensions constitute their own search space modelled using Record Type lattices (see Eshghi et al., 2013b, Hough and Purver, 2014b).

Figure 10 shows example *tree-building* action hypotheses which extend a mother node with a type requirement to have two daughter nodes which would (once themselves developed) combine to satisfy that requirement. On the left, a general rule in which a currently pointed node of some type X can be hypothesised to be formed of types e and $e \rightarrow X$ (e.g. if $X = e \rightarrow t$, the daughters will have types e and

$?Ty(X), \diamond$	**IF**	$?Ty(X)$
		$X \neq e$
	THEN	$make(\langle\downarrow_0\rangle); go(\langle\downarrow_0\rangle)$
		$put(?Ty(e)); go(\langle\uparrow\rangle)$
		$make(\langle\downarrow_1\rangle); go(\langle\downarrow_1\rangle)$
$?Ty(e)$ $?Ty(e \rightarrow X)$		$put(?Ty(e \rightarrow X)); go(\uparrow)$
	ELSE	ABORT

$?Ty(e), \diamond$	**IF**	$?Ty(e)$
	THEN	$make(\langle\downarrow_0\rangle); go(\langle\downarrow_0\rangle)$
		$put(?Ty(cn)); go(\langle\uparrow\rangle)$
		$make(\langle\downarrow_1\rangle); go(\langle\downarrow_1\rangle)$
$?Ty(cn)$ $?Ty(cn \rightarrow e)$		$put(?Ty(cn \rightarrow e)); go(\uparrow)$
	ELSE	ABORT

FIGURE 10: Target-independent tree-building hypotheses

$e \rightarrow (e \rightarrow t))$. This reflects only the fact that DS-TTR trees correspond to lambda calculus terms, with e being a possible type. The other is more specific, suitable only for a type e node, allowing it to be composed of nodes of type cn and $cn \rightarrow e$ (where $cn \rightarrow e$ turns out to be the type of determiners), but again reflects only general semantic properties which would apply in any language.

Hypothesis splitting

Hypothesis construction therefore produces, for each training sentence $\langle w_1 \ldots w_n \rangle$, all possible sequences of actions that lead from the axiom tree T_0 to the target tree T_t (henceforth, the *complete* sequences); where these sequences contain both lexical hypotheses and general computational macros. To form discrete lexical entries, we must split each such sequence into n sub-sequences, $\langle cs_1 \ldots cs_n \rangle$, with each *candidate subsequence* cs_i, corresponding to a word w_i, by hypothesising a set of word boundaries.

Eshghi et al. (2013a,b) go on to describe how this splitting process can work and lead to distinct word hypotheses, w_i, and how the probability distribution $p(a|w, T)$ can be estimated using an incremental version of the Expectation Maximisation (or EM) algorithm.[7]

Discussion

Using the method outlined above, Eshghi et al. (2013b) show how grammars (normative action policies) can be learned from child-directed dialogue utterances annotated with conceptualisation potential here assumed to be provided by the multimodal environment surrounding the learner. The grammars learned are shown to have wide parsing coverage (92%), as well as good semantic accuracy (F-Score of 0.85).

The process described above of exploring the space of possible tree-building action sequences that extend some tree to another tree whose maximal conceptualisation potential subsumes the target set of affordances R_T is essentially the same as the 'babbling', or *affordance exploration* mechanism discussed above in Sec.10.6.1. While the mechanism is the same, there are at least two key differences here:

[7] We do not go into more detail here, but refer the interested reader to the original papers.

(i) In the problem above, of bootstrapping interaction, actions corresponded to words, and the underlying grammar was input to the learning. Here, action hypotheses are abstract: they merely specify very general procedures for extending the tree, albeit constrained by the properties of the lambda calculus and the modal tree logic, LoFT.

(ii) The trial-and-error generation or babbling mechanism of 10.6.1 was constrained by *interaction potentials*, i.e. possible responses in specific cases from the interlocutor. Here, the search space is constrained by R_T, under current assumptions, the conceptualisation trajectories opened up by reaching the goal: local action pathways that do not subsume further R_T trajectories (i.e. are not extendible to it: when $R_T \not\sqsubseteq R$) are abandoned.

As we said earlier (section 10.5.3), we don't take RTs as monolithic structures with symbols standing for entities in the world. Instead, following the enactive logic of the Free Energy Principle and active inference we construe such types in the same way as DS syntactic types, in the sense that they are individuated by means of the actions that they make available. So, for example, a type like Dog' expands into a set of sensorimotor contingencies (Nöe, 2004, Bickhard, 2009) arising from the agents' experience with dogs. These are expressed as nested structures introduced with associated requirements as standard in DS-TTR and constitute anticipations of potential interactions with the individual entity so characterised (Bickhard and Richie, 1983). In addition, as affordances, they also include the perspectival effects of the agent's action in proposing to conceptualise this entity by use of the particular word form associated with the Dog' type.

Limitations

Computational complexity As Eshghi et al. (2013b) themselves note, the overall time complexity of the algorithm outlined above of hypothesising all action sequences that subsume the goal R_T is exponential in the number of fields in the goal R_T. This is because the algorithm relies on the construction of incremental conceptualisation pathways that explore all trajectories leading from the empty type, R_ϵ, to the goal R_T; thus traversing all the super-types of R_T (all R_S such that $R_T \sqsubseteq R_S$) in all possible orders along the way. Since the number of super-types of R_T is exponential in the number of fields in R_T, this algorithm has an exponential time complexity.

To evaluate their algorithm, Eshghi et al. (2013b) thus had to limit their training data to shorter sentences which also had smaller conceptual structures, with fewer fields in the goal R_T.

Curriculum Learning Nevertheless, it is not reasonable to assume that acquisition of grammars in children starts from long, complex sentences or interactions with complex embedded structures. Instead, children start learning words as part of short and simple dialogue exchanges, within simple language games (e.g. getting something to eat, asking for an object, getting the other to attend to an object, giving and taking, etc.), with the process of language acquisition often viewed as correlated with the length of child-produced utterances (Ginzburg and Kolliakou, 2009, Brown, 1973). Over time, they then use this knowledge in learning more complex syntactic and conceptual manipulations.

This *curriculum learning* strategy (Bengio et al., 2009) is compatible with the incremental hypothesis construction algorithm above: while Eshghi et al. (2013b) learn from each training example individually, starting from scratch each time, this does not have to be the case: action sequences learned from shorter utterances and simpler conceptual structures can be *reused* later in the context of more complex examples, thus exponentially reducing the search space and the complexity of learning from these more complex examples.

Future work will therefore explore a curriculum learning strategy to overcome the computational complexity of Eshghi et al.'s 2013b algorithm.

Learning from feedback In the formal and computational literature, the complexity of the grammar induction problem has currently been only assessed on the basis of the assumption of an independent syntactic and/or semantic structure that has to be learned on the basis of discovering rules and representations (although cf. Steedman, 2002, for a view of grammar as affordances in the BDI tradition). This formulation of the problem is ill-posed from the DS-TTR perspective, which seeks to formulate a more holistic model of grammar that includes both the generator and parser, their interactions, as well as the sociomaterial environment (see also Pickering and Garrod, 2021). This perspective allows the DS-TTR system to invoke learning regimes that embed learning of verbal actions within domain-general systems of action policy learning like RL. Here the assumption is that the added complexity of dependencies between synergistically organised components will prove to be not a liability but an advantage: this is the intuition pursued in the development of end-to-end architectures and their current successes as well as argued for in the psycholinguistic literature on language learning (e.g. Rączaszek-Leonardi et al., 2013, 2018). Additionally, as Lappin (2021) also notes, general RL methods are now being used by simulated agents to display generalising behaviours and one-shot learning of linguistic actions integrated into policies that respond to multimodal signals (see e.g. Hill et al., 2021)

These insights open new avenues for how to improve current computational architectures and NL theoretical frameworks by including features of human interactivity in the proposed models. It has been a traditional assumption in formal linguistics that human language acquisition cannot involve so-called "negative evidence", i.e., explicit corrections are neither provided to the child learning the language neither can they be processed as corrections given the child's capacities. However, these claims have been disputed and shown to be untenable. Saxton (1997), Saxton et al. (1998, 2005), Chouinard and Clark (2003), Clark and Lappin (2011) among others argue that negative feedback in the form of reformulations and corrections constitutes useful reliable input for inducing a grammar especially when the discourse context, i.e., the surrounding sociomaterial affordances, is simultaneously taken into account, which is what the uniform non-modular formulation of a DS-TTR grammar is trying to capture. Formal models of dialogue as well as grammar learning and induction methods now advocate taking into account feedback from an interlocutor or teaching partner (see, e.g., Ginzburg, 2012, Angluin and Becerra-Bonache, 2017, Liu et al., 2018). In future work with simulated agents, we plan to incorporate through further work with RL the impact of feedback, both corrective and confirming, in the induction of a full DS-TTR grammar from the types of sparse data and one-shot learning observable in human language acquisition.

10.7 Concluding discussion

In this chapter, we suggested that despite considerable recent advancements in deep learning methods for Natural Language Processing, progress in the area of dialogue modelling and Conversational AI has plateaued. We argued that this is because of the very wide predominance of the code model of communication under which agents are supposed to manipulate and transmit mental representations via NL to then be recovered and duplicated in the mind of the interlocutor. This construal of communication leads to passive agents and models of agents that do not learn interactional feedback mechanisms, instead of fixed representations, with the result that they remain *static* during interaction or at prediction time. We further argued that this view should be replaced by a strongly enactive perspective on NLs, agent communication, and coordination in conversation. Research in robotics, psychology, and neuroscience, but also machine learning, currently converge on the perspective that prediction error minimisation is the mechanism under which agent performance is adjusted and developed dynamically to deal with the uncertainty and contingent nature of outcomes in everyday interactions with the environment and other agents. This perspective presupposes that agents do not carry around within their skulls explicit models of the world but, instead, they possess and gradually refine bodily skills (which includes mental skills) for dealing with the constantly changing circumstances of the surrounding sociomaterial environment. The affordances of the environment are revealed in real-time to interacting agents based on constant 'education of attention' processes that, crucially for humans, include NL-induced sociocultural conceptualisations of the material environment. This means that artificial agents should primarily be provided with embodiment (even if in simulation forms) and opportunities for interaction, along with learning and adjustment as is currently possible with deep learning methods.

We presented two case studies using Dynamic Syntax and Type Theory with Records (DS-TTR), an inherently action-based grammar formalism, showing how exploration of affordances and environmental communication contingencies using the grammar as a generative model enabling prediction induces learning. In one case, we showed how a dialogue agent can *learn to perform dialogue acts (or speech acts)* together with their attendant interactional structures without any of this being provided in advance in the form of supervision. What is learned in this case are conditional, probabilistic routines for producing desired *perlocutionary effects* in the agent's environment. In the second case study, we saw how the same trial-and-error generation mechanism for affordance exploration enables DS-TTR grammars to be learned from child-directed utterances.

Future DS-TTR work will explore lexical learning from live, multi-modal interaction whereby lexical entries for simple, proto-grammars can be induced from real-time feedback.It will also integrate the BABBLE framework with Deep Reinforcement Learning and state of the art computer vision techniques in a visually grounded setup whereby a conversational agent can learn to interact with and produce goal-directed effects in its physical (or simulated) environment.

Acknowledgements

We would like to thank Stergios Chatzikyriakidis and Jean-Philippe Bernardy for constructive comments on an earlier draft of this chapter, infinite patience, and ensuing discussion. The content of this contribution has emerged from our collaborations over many years with our friends: thank you Ruth Kempson, Greg Mills, Pat Healey, Julian Hough, Matthew Purver, Oliver Lemon, Robin Cooper, Staffan Larsson, Mehrnoosh Sadrzadeh, Simon Dobnik, Ellen Breitholtz, Asad Sayeed, Graham White, Jonathan Ginzburg among others. Arash Eshghi's research is supported by Alana AI Ltd. Chris Howes was supported by two grants from the Swedish Research Council (VR); 2016-0116 – Incremental Reasoning in Dialogue (IncReD), and VR grant 2014-39 for the establishment of the Centre for Linguistic Theory and Studies in Probability (CLASP) at the University of Gothenburg.

References

Adolph, Karen E. 2020. An Ecological Approach To Learning In (Not And) Development. *Human development* 63(Suppl 3-4):180–201.

Angluin, Dana and Leonor Becerra-Bonache. 2017. A model of language learning with semantics and meaning-preserving corrections. *Artificial Intelligence* 242:23–51.

Arundale, R.B. 2008. Against (gricean) intentions at the heart of human interaction. *Intercultural Pragmatics* 5(2):229–258.

Arundale, Robert B. 2020. *Communicating & Relating: Constituting Face in Everyday Interacting*. Oxford University Press. ISBN 978-0-19-093363-0.

Bao, Siqi, Huang He, Fan Wang, Hua Wu, and Haifeng Wang. 2020. PLATO: Pre-trained dialogue generation model with discrete latent variable. In *Proceedings of the 58th Annual Meeting of the Association for Computational Linguistics*, pages 85–96. Online: Association for Computational Linguistics.

Barwise, J. and J. Perry. 1983. *Situations and Attitudes*. Cambridge, MA: MIT Press.

Bengio, Y., R. Louradour, R. Collobert, and J. Weston. 2009. Curriculum learning. In *Proceedings of ICML*, pages 41–48.

Bickhard, Mark H. 2009. The interactivist model. *Synthese* 166(3):547–591.

Bickhard, Mark H. and D. Michael Richie. 1983. *On The Nature Of Representation: A Case Study Of James Gibson's Theory Of Perception*. New York: Praeger.

Blackburn, Patrick and Wilfried Meyer-Viol. 1994. Linguistics, logic and finite trees. *Logic Journal of the Interest Group of Pure and Applied Logics* 2(1):3–29.

Bommasani, Rishi, Drew A. Hudson, Ehsan Adeli, Russ Altman, Simran Arora, Sydney von Arx, Michael S. Bernstein, Jeannette Bohg, Antoine Bosselut, Emma Brunskill, Erik Brynjolfsson, Shyamal Buch, Dallas Card, Rodrigo Castellon, Niladri Chatterji, Annie Chen, Kathleen Creel, Jared Quincy Davis, Dora Demszky, Chris Donahue, Moussa Doumbouya, Esin Durmus, Stefano Ermon, John Etchemendy, Kawin Ethayarajh, Li Fei-Fei, Chelsea Finn, Trevor Gale, Lauren Gillespie, Karan Goel, Noah Goodman, Shelby Grossman, Neel Guha, Tatsunori Hashimoto, Peter Henderson, John Hewitt, Daniel E. Ho, Jenny Hong, Kyle Hsu, Jing Huang, Thomas Icard, Saahil Jain, Dan Jurafsky, Pratyusha Kalluri, Siddharth Karamcheti, Geoff Keeling, Fereshte Khani, Omar Khattab, Pang Wei Koh, Mark Krass, Ranjay Krishna, Rohith Kuditipudi, Ananya Kumar, Faisal Ladhak, Mina Lee, Tony Lee, Jure Leskovec, Isabelle Levent, Xiang Lisa Li, Xuechen Li, Tengyu Ma, Ali Malik, Christopher D. Manning, Suvir Mirchandani, Eric Mitchell, Zanele Munyikwa, Suraj Nair, Avanika Narayan, Deepak Narayanan, Ben Newman, Allen Nie, Juan Carlos Niebles, Hamed Nilforoshan, Julian Nyarko, Giray Ogut, Laurel Orr, Isabel Papadimitriou, Joon Sung Park, Chris Piech, Eva Portelance, Christopher Potts, Aditi Raghunathan, Rob Reich, Hongyu Ren, Frieda Rong, Yusuf Roohani, Camilo Ruiz, Jack Ryan, Christopher Ré, Dorsa Sadigh, Shiori Sagawa, Keshav Santhanam, Andy Shih, Krishnan Srinivasan, Alex Tamkin, Rohan Taori, Armin W. Thomas, Florian Tramèr, Rose E. Wang, William Wang, Bohan Wu, Jiajun Wu, Yuhuai Wu, Sang Michael Xie, Michihiro Yasunaga, Jiaxuan You, Matei Zaharia, Michael Zhang, Tianyi Zhang, Xikun Zhang, Yuhui Zhang, Lucia Zheng, Kaitlyn Zhou, and Percy Liang. 2021. On the Opportunities and Risks of Foundation Models. *arXiv:2108.07258 [cs]* .

Brown, Roger. 1973. *A first language: The early stages*. Harvard University Press.

Bruineberg, Jelle, Anthony Chemero, and Erik Rietveld. 2018a. General ecological information supports engagement with affordances for 'higher' cognition. *Synthese* 196(12):5231–5251.

Bruineberg, Jelle, Erik Rietveld, Thomas Parr, Leendert van Maanen, and Karl J Friston. 2018b. Free-energy minimization in joint agent-environment systems: A niche construction perspective. *Journal of Theoretical Biology* 455:161–178.

Buhrmann, Thomas, Ezequiel Alejandro Di Paolo, and Xabier Barandiaran. 2013. A Dynamical Systems Account of Sensorimotor Contingencies. *Frontiers in Psychology* 4.

Burnard, Lou. 2000. *Reference Guide for the British National Corpus (World Edition)*. Oxford University Computing Services.

Caldarini, Guendalina, Sardar Jaf, and Kenneth McGarry. 2022. A Literature Survey of Recent Advances in Chatbots. *Information* 13(1):41.

Cann, Ronnie, Ruth Kempson, and Lutz Marten. 2005. *The Dynamics of Language*. Oxford: Elsevier.

Chaves, Ana Paula and Marco Aurelio Gerosa. 2021. How Should My Chatbot Interact? a Survey on Social Characteristics in Human–Chatbot Interaction Design. *International Journal of Human–Computer Interaction* 37(8):729–758.

Chemero, Anthony. 2009. *Radical Embodied Cognitive Science*. Cambridge, MA: MIT Press.

Chen, Vincent, Paroma Varma, Ranjay Krishna, Michael Bernstein, Christopher Re, and Li Fei-Fei. 2019. Scene graph prediction with limited labels. In *International Conference on Computer Vision*.

Chouinard, Michelle M and Eve V Clark. 2003. Adult reformulations of child errors as negative evidence. *Journal of child language* 30(3):637–669.

Cisek, Paul and John F. Kalaska. 2010. Neural Mechanisms for Interacting with a World Full of Action Choices. *Annual Review of Neuroscience* 33(1):269–298.

Clark, Andy. 2017a. Busting out: Predictive brains, embodied minds, and the puzzle of the evidentiary veil. *Noûs* 51(4):727–753.

Clark, Andy. 2017b. How to knit your own Markov blanket: Resisting the second law with metamorphic minds. In T. M. . W. Wiese, ed., *Philosophy and Predictive Processing: 3. Frankfurt Am Main: MIND Group.*. Johannes Gutenberg-Universität Mainz.

Clark, Alexander and Shalom Lappin. 2011. *Linguistic Nativism and the Poverty of the Stimulus*. Wiley-Blackwell.

Clark, Herbert H. 1996. *Using Language*. Cambridge: Cambridge University Press.

Clark, Herbert H. 1998. Communal lexicons. In K. Malmkjær and J. Williams, eds., *Context in Language Learning and Language Understanding*, chap. 4, pages 63–87. Cambridge: Cambridge University Press.

Clark, Herbert H. 2012. Wordless questions, wordless answers. In De Ruiter, Jan P, ed., *Questions: Formal, Functional and Interactional Perspectives*, pages 81–100. Cambridge: Cambridge University Press.

Clark, Leigh, Nadia Pantidi, Orla Cooney, Philip Doyle, Diego Garaialde, Justin Edwards, Brendan Spillane, Emer Gilmartin, Christine Murad, Cosmin Munteanu, Vincent Wade, and Benjamin R. Cowan. 2019. What Makes a Good Conversation? challenges in Designing Truly Conversational Agents. In *Proceedings of the 2019 CHI Conference on Human Factors in Computing Systems*, pages 1–12. New York, NY, USA: Association for Computing Machinery. ISBN 978-1-4503-5970-2.

Cohn-Gordon, Reuben, Noah D. Goodman, and Christopher Potts. 2018. An Incremental Iterated Response Model of Pragmatics. *arXiv:1810.00367 [cs]* .

Cooper, Robin. 2005. Records and record types in semantic theory. *Journal of Logic and Computation* 15(2):99–112.

Cooper, Robin. 2012. Type theory and semantics in flux. In R. Kempson, N. Asher, and T. Fernando, eds., *Philosophy of Linguistics*, vol. 14 of *Handbook of the Philosophy of Science*, pages 271–323. Amsterdam: North Holland (Elsevier).

Cooper, Robin, Simon Dobnik, Shalom Lappin, and Staffan Larsson. 2014. A probabilistic rich type theory for semantic interpretation. In *Proceedings of the EACL Workshop on Type Theory and Natural Language Semantics (TTNLS)*. Gothenburg, Sweden: Association for Computational Linguistics.

Cooper, Robin, Simon Dobnik, Shalom Lappin, and Staffan Larsson. 2015. Probabilistic type theory and natural language semantics. In *Linguistic Issues in Language Technology, Volume 10, 2015*.

Cooper, Robin and Jonathan Ginzburg. 2015. *Type Theory with Records for Natural Language Semantics**, chap. 12, pages 375–407. John Wiley & Sons, Ltd. ISBN 9781118882139.

De Jaegher, Hanne and Ezequiel Di Paolo. 2007. Participatory sense-making. *Phenomenology and the Cognitive Sciences* 6(4):485–507.

DeLanda, Manuel. 2013. *Intensive Science and Virtual Philosophy*. London: Bloomsbury.

Devlin, Jacob, Ming-Wei Chang, Kenton Lee, and Kristina Toutanova. 2019. BERT: Pre-training of deep bidirectional transformers for language understanding. In *Proceedings of the 2019 Conference of the North American Chapter of the Association for Computational Linguistics: Human Language Technologies, Volume 1 (Long and Short Papers)*, pages 4171–4186. Minneapolis, Minnesota: Association for Computational Linguistics.

Di Paolo, Ezequiel. 2008. Extended Life. *Topoi* 28(1):9.

Di Paolo, Ezequiel and Hanne De Jaegher. 2012. The interactive brain hypothesis. *Frontiers in Human Neuroscience* 6:163.

Dingemanse, Mark. 2020. Resource-rationality beyond individual minds: the case of interactive language use. *Behavioral and Brain Sciences* 43:e9.

Dobnik, Simon, Robin Cooper, and Staffan Larsson. 2012. Modelling language, action, and perception in Type Theory with Records. In *Proceedings of the 7th International Workshop on Constraint Solving and Language Processing*, pages 51–63.

Dreyfus, Hubert L. 2013. The myth of the pervasiveness of the mental. In J. K. Schear, ed., *Mind, Reason, and Being-in-the-World*. London: Routledge.

Duveen, Gerard and Charis Psaltis. 2013. The constructive role of asymmetry in social interaction. In S. Moscovici, S. Jovchelovitch, and B. Wagoner, eds., *Development as a Social Process: Contributions of Gerard Duveen*, pages 133–154. Abingdon, UK: Routledge.

Eshghi, Arash, Julian Hough, and Matthew Purver. 2013a. Incremental grammar induction from child-directed dialogue utterances. In *Proceedings of the 4th Annual Workshop on Cognitive Modeling and Computational Linguistics (CMCL)*, pages 94–103. Sofia, Bulgaria: Association for Computational Linguistics.

Eshghi, Arash, Julian Hough, Matthew Purver, Ruth Kempson, and Eleni Gregoromichelaki. 2012. Conversational interactions: Capturing dialogue dynamics. In S. Larsson and L. Borin, eds., *From Quantification to Conversation: Festschrift for Robin Cooper on the occasion of his 65th birthday*, vol. 19 of *Tributes*, pages 325–349. London: College Publications. ISBN 978-1-904987-91-2.

Eshghi, Arash, Christine Howes, Eleni Gregoromichelaki, Julian Hough, and Matt Purver. 2015. Feedback in conversation as incremental semantic update. In *Proceedings of the 11th International Conference on Computational Semantics (IWCS)*, pages 261–271. London, UK: ACL.

Eshghi, Arash and Oliver Lemon. 2014. How domain-general can we be? Learning incremental dialogue systems without dialogue acts. In *Proceedings of the 18th SemDial Workshop on the Semantics and Pragmatics of Dialogue (DialWatt)*, pages 53–61.

Eshghi, Arash, Matthew Purver, and Julian Hough. 2011. DyLan: Parser for Dynamic Syntax. Tech. rep., Queen Mary University of London. EECSRR-11-05.

Eshghi, Arash, Matthew Purver, and Julian Hough. 2013b. Probabilistic induction for an incremental semantic grammar. In *Proceedings of the 10th International Conference on Computational Semantics (IWCS 2013) – Long Papers*, pages 107–118. Potsdam, Germany: Association for Computational Linguistics.

Eshghi, Arash, Matthew Purver, Julian Hough, and Yo Sato. 2013c. Probabilistic grammar induction in an incremental semantic framework. In D. D. and P. Y., eds., *CSLP, Lecture Notes in Computer Science*, vol. 8114 of *Lecture Notes in Computer Science*, pages 92–107. Berlin, Heidelberg: Springer.

Eshghi, Arash, Igor Shalyminov, and Oliver Lemon. 2017. Bootstrapping incremental dialogue systems from minimal data: Linguistic knowledge or machine learning? In *Proceedings of the 2017 Conference on Empirical Methods in Natural Language Processing (EMNLP)*, pages 2220–2230.

Fernández, Raquel. 2006. *Non-Sentential Utterances in Dialogue: Classification, Resolution and Use*. Ph.D. thesis, King's College London, University of London.

Fischer, Joel E., Stuart Reeves, Martin Porcheron, and Rein Ove Sikveland. 2019. Progressivity for voice interface design. In *Proceedings of the 1st International Conference on Conversational User Interfaces*, CUI '19. New York, NY, USA: Association for Computing Machinery. ISBN 9781450371872.

Fodor, Jerry A. 1975. *The Language of Thought*, vol. 5. Cambridge, MA: Harvard University Press.

Forster, Michael N. 2009. *Wittgenstein on the Arbitrariness of Grammar*. Princeton University Press. ISBN 978-1-4008-2604-9.

Fowler, Carol A. and Bert Hodges. 2016. Finding common ground: Alternatives to code models for language use. *New Ideas in Psychology* 42:1–6.

Frank, Michael C. and Noah D. Goodman. 2012. Predicting pragmatic reasoning in language games. *Science* 336(6084):998–998.

Frijda, Nico H, K Richard Ridderinkhof, and Erik Rietveld. 2014. Impulsive action: Emotional impulses and their control. *Frontiers in Psychology* 5:518.

Friston, Karl. 2010. The free-energy principle: A unified brain theory? *Nature Reviews Neuroscience* 11(2):127–138.

Friston, Karl. 2011. Embodied inference: Or "I think therefore I am, if I am what I think". In *The Implications of Embodiment: Cognition and Communication*, pages 89–125. Charlottesville, VA: Imprint Academic. ISBN 978-1-84540-240-2.

Friston, Karl, Spyridon Samothrakis, and Read Montague. 2012a. Active inference and agency: Optimal control without cost functions. *Biological Cybernetics* 106(8):523–541.

Friston, Karl, Spyridon Samothrakis, and Read Montague. 2012b. Active inference and agency: Optimal control without cost functions. *Biological Cybernetics* 106(8):523–541.

Fujimoto, Donna T. 2007. Listener responses in interaction: A case for abandoning the term, backchannel. *Journal of Osaka Jogakuin College* 37:35–54.

Gao, Jianfeng, Michel Galley, and Lihong Li. 2018. Neural Approaches to Conversational AI. In *The 41st International ACM SIGIR Conference on Research & Development in Information Retrieval*, SIGIR '18, pages 1371–1374. New York, NY, USA: Association for Computing Machinery. ISBN 978-1-4503-5657-2.

Gargett, Andrew, Eleni Gregóromichelaki, Ruth Kempson, Matthew Purver, and Yo Sato. 2009. Grammar resources for modelling dialogue dynamically. *Cognitive Neurodynamics* 3(4):347–363.

Gibson, James J. 1966. *The Senses Considered as Perceptual Systems*. The Senses Considered as Perceptual Systems. Oxford, England: Houghton Mifflin.

Gibson, James J. 2014. *The Ecological Approach to Visual Perception: Classic Edition*. New York: Psychology Press.

Ginzburg, Jonathan. 2012. *The Interactive Stance: Meaning for Conversation*. Oxford: Oxford University Press.

Ginzburg, Jonathan and Dimitra Kolliakou. 2009. Answers without questions: The emergence of fragments in child language. *Journal of Linguistics* 45(3):641–673.

Goodman, Noah D. and Michael C. Frank. 2016. Pragmatic language interpretation as probabilistic inference. *Trends in Cognitive Sciences* 20(11):818–829.

Gregoromichelaki, Eleni. 2013. Grammar as action in language and music. In M. Orwin, R. Kempson, and C. Howes, eds., *Language, music and interaction*, pages 93–134. College Publications.

Gregoromichelaki, Eleni. 2018. Quotation in Dialogue. In P. Saka and M. Johnson, eds., *The Semantics and Pragmatics of Quotation*, Perspectives in Pragmatics, Philosophy & Psychology, pages 195–255. Cham: Springer International Publishing. ISBN 978-3-319-68747-6.

Gregoromichelaki, Eleni, Stergios Chatzikyriakidis, Arash Eshghi, Julian Hough, Christine Howes, Ruth Kempson, Jieun Kiaer, Matthew Purver, Mehrnoosh Sadrzadeh, and Graham White. 2020a. Affordance competition in dialogue: the case of syntactic universals. In *Proceedings of the 24th Workshop on the Semantics and Pragmatics of Dialogue*.

Gregoromichelaki, Eleni, Christine Howes, Arash Eshghi, Ruth Kempson, Julian Hough, Mehrnoosh Sadrzadeh, Matthew Purver, and Gijs Wijnholds. 2019. Normativity, meaning plasticity, and the significance of Vector Space Semantics. In *Proceedings of the 23rd Workshop on the Semantics and Pragmatics of Dialogue*. London, United Kingdom: SEMDIAL.

Gregoromichelaki, Eleni, Christine Howes, and Ruth Kempson. 2020b. Actionism in syntax and semantics. In *Dialogue and Perception - Extended Papers from DaP2018*, vol. 2 of *CLASP Papers in Computational Linguistics*, pages 12–27. Gothenburg: GUPEA.

Gregoromichelaki, Eleni and Ruth Kempson. 2015. Joint Utterances and the (Split-) Turn-Taking Puzzle. In *Interdisciplinary Studies in Pragmatics, Culture and Society*, pages 703–743. Springer.

Gregoromichelaki, Eleni, Ruth Kempson, Christine Howes, and Arash Eshghi. 2013. On making syntax dynamic:. In I. Wachsmuth, J. d. Ruiter, P. Jaecks, and S. Kopp, eds., *Alignment in Communication: Towards a New Theory of Communication*, pages 57–85. John Benjamin.

Gregoromichelaki, Eleni, Ruth Kempson, Matthew Purver, Gregory J. Mills, Ronnie Cann, Wilfried Meyer-Viol, and Patrick G. T. Healey. 2011. Incrementality and intention-recognition in utterance processing. *Dialogue and Discourse* 2(1):199–233.

Gregoromichelaki, Eleni, Gregory James Mills, Christine Howes, Arash Eshghi, Stergios Chatzikyriakidis, Matthew Purver, Ruth Kempson, Ronnie Cann, and Patrick G. T. Healey. 2020c. Completability vs (In)completeness. *Acta Linguistica Hafniensia* 52(2):260–284.

Grice, H. Paul. 1975. Logic and conversation. *Syntax and Semantics* 3(S 41):58.

Grosz, Barbara J. and Candace L. Sidner. 1986. Attention, intentions, and the structure of discourse. *Computational Linguistics* 12(3):175–204.

Hanjie, Austin W., Victor Zhong, and Karthik Narasimhan. 2021. Grounding Language to Entities and Dynamics for Generalization in Reinforcement Learning. *arXiv:2101.07393 [cs]* .

Harnad, Stevan. 1990. The symbol grounding problem. *Physica D: Nonlinear Phenomena* 42(1):335–346.

Healey, Patrick G. T., Jan Peter de Ruiter, and Gregory J. Mills. 2018a. Editors' introduction: Miscommunication. *Topics in Cognitive Science* 10(2):264–278.

Healey, Patrick G. T. and Gregory J. Mills. 2006. Participation, precedence and co-ordination in dialogue. In *Proceedings of the 28th Annual Conference of the Cognitive Science Society*, pages 1470–1475.

Healey, Patrick G. T., Gregory J. Mills, Arash Eshghi, and Christine Howes. 2018b. Running repairs: Co-ordinating meaning in dialogue. *Topics in Cognitive Science* 10(2):367–388.

Hill, Felix, Olivier Tieleman, Tamara von Glehn, Nathaniel Wong, Hamza Merzic, and Stephen Clark. 2020. Grounded Language Learning Fast and Slow. *arXiv:2009.01719 [cs]* .

Hill, Felix, Olivier Tieleman, Tamara von Glehn, Nathaniel Wong, Hamza Merzic, and Stephen Clark. 2021. Grounded language learning fast and slow. In *International Conference on Learning Representations (ICLR)*.

Hohwy, Jakob. 2013. *The Predictive Mind*. Oxford University Press. ISBN 978-0-19-968273-7.

Hough, Julian. 2015. *Modelling Incremental Self-Repair Processing in Dialogue*. Ph.D. thesis, Queen Mary University of London.

Hough, Julian, Lorenzo Jamone, David Schlangen, Guillaume Walck, and Robert Haschke. 2020. *Dialogue and Perception - CLASP Papers in Computational Linguistics*, vol. 2, chap. A Types-As-Classifiers Approach to Human-Robot Interaction for Continuous Structured State Classification, pages 28–40. Centre for Linguistic Theory and Studies in Probability (CLASP), Department of Philosophy, Linguistics and Theory of Science (FLOV), University of Gothenburg.

Hough, Julian, Lorenzo Jamone, David Schlangen, Guillaume Walck, Robert Haschke, et al. 2018. Towards a Types-as-Classifiers Approach to Dialogue Processing in Human-Robot Interaction. In *Proceedings of the Workshop on Dialogue and Perception (DaP 2018), Gothenburg*.

Hough, Julian, Casey Kennington, David Schlangen, and Jonathan Ginzburg. 2015. Incremental semantics for dialogue processing: Requirements, and a comparison of two approaches. In *Proceedings of the 11th International Conference on Computartional Semantics (IWCS)*. London, UK.

Hough, Julian and Matthew Purver. 2012. Processing self-repairs in an incremental type-theoretic dialogue system. In *Proceedings of the 16th Workshop on the Semantics and Pragmatics of Dialogue (SeineDial)*, pages 136–144. Paris, France.

Hough, Julian and Matthew Purver. 2014a. Lattice theoretic relevance in incremental reference processing. In *Proceedings of the RefNet Workshop on Psychological and Computational Models of Reference Comprehension and Production*. Edinburgh.

Hough, Julian and Matthew Purver. 2014b. Probabilistic type theory for incremental dialogue processing. In *Proceedings of the EACL 2014 Workshop on Type Theory and Natural Language Semantics (TTNLS)*, pages 80–88. Gothenburg, Sweden: Association for Computational Linguistics. ISBN 978-1-937284-74-9.

Hough, Julian and Matthew Purver. 2017. Probabilistic record type lattices for incremental reference processing. In S. Chatzikyriakidis and Z. Luo, eds., *Modern Perspectives in Type-theoretical Semantics*, pages 189–222. Springer.

Howes, Christine. 2012. *Coordination in Dialogue: Using Compound Contributions to Join a Party*. Ph.D. thesis, Queen Mary University of London.

Howes, Christine and Arash Eshghi. 2017. Feedback relevance spaces: The organisation of increments in conversation. In *Proceedings of the 12th International Conference on Computational Semantics (IWCS)*. ACL.

Howes, Christine and Arash Eshghi. 2021. Feedback relevance spaces: Interactional constraints on processing contexts in Dynamic Syntax. *Journal of Logic, Language and Information* Accepted for publication.

Howes, Christine, Patrick G. T. Healey, Matthew Purver, and Arash Eshghi. 2012. Finishing each other's ... responding to incomplete contributions in dialogue. In *Proceedings of the 34th Annual Meeting of the Cognitive Science Society*, pages 479–484. Sapporo, Japan. ISBN 978-0-9768318-8-4.

Howes, Christine, Matthew Purver, Patrick G. T. Healey, Gregory J. Mills, and Eleni Gregoromichelaki. 2011. On incrementality in dialogue: Evidence from compound contributions. *Dialogue and Discourse* 2(1):279–311.

Hutchins, Edwin. 1995. *Cognition in the Wild*. MIT Press. ISBN 978-0-262-58146-2.

Kalatzis, Dimitrios, Arash Eshghi, and Oliver Lemon. 2016. Bootstrapping incremental dialogue systems: Using linguistic knowledge to learn from minimal data. In *Proceedings of the NIPS 2016 Workshop on Learning Methods for Dialogue*. Barcelona.

Kempson, Ruth, Ronnie Cann, Arash Eshghi, Eleni Gregoromichelaki, and Matthew Purver. 2015. Ellipsis. In S. Lappin and C. Fox, eds., *The Handbook of Contemporary Semantic Theory*. Oxford: Wiley-Blackwell.

Kempson, Ruth, Ronnie Cann, Eleni Gregoromichelaki, and Stergios Chatzikiriakidis. 2016. Language as mechanisms for interaction. *Theoretical Linguistics* 42(3-4):203–275.

Kempson, Ruth, Ronnie Cann, Eleni Gregoromichelaki, and Stergios Chatzikyriakidis. 2017. Action-Based Grammar. *Theoretical Linguistics* 43(1-2):141–167.

Kempson, Ruth, Eleni Gregoromichelaki, and Christine Howes(eds.). 2011. *The Dynamics of Lexical Interfaces*. Studies in Constraint Based Lexicalism. Stanford, CA: CSLI.

Kempson, Ruth, Wilfried Meyer-Viol, and Dov Gabbay. 2001. *Dynamic Syntax: The Flow of Language Understanding*. Oxford: Wiley-Blackwell.

Kirchhoff, Michael D. and Tom Froese. 2017. Where There is Life There is Mind: In Support of a Strong Life-Mind Continuity Thesis. *Entropy* 19(4):169.

Kopp, Stefan and Nicole Krämer. 2021. Revisiting human-agent communication: The importance of joint co-construction and understanding mental states. *Frontiers in Psychology* 12:597.

Kottur, Satwik, Ramakrishna Vedantam, Jose M. F. Moura, and Devi Parikh. 2016. Visual Word2Vec (vis-w2v): Learning Visually Grounded Word Embeddings Using Abstract Scenes. In *Proceedings of the IEEE Conference on Computer Vision and Pattern Recognition*, pages 4985–4994.

Kunert, Richard, Raquel Fernández, and Willem Zuidema. 2011. Adaptation in child directed speech: Evidence from corpora. *Proceedings of the 15th Workshop on the Semantics and Pragmatics of Dialogue (LosAngelogue)* .

Lappin, Shalom. 2021. *Deep Learning and Linguistic Representation*. CRC Press. ISBN 978-1-00-038032-3.

Larsson, Staffan. 2011. The TTR perceptron: Dynamic perceptual meanings and semantic coordination. In *Proceedings of the 15th Workshop on the Semantics and Pragmatics of Dialogue (SemDial 2011 - Los Angelogue)*, pages 140–148.

Larsson, Staffan. 2015. Formal semantics for perceptual classification. *Journal of Logic and Computation* 25(2):335–369.

Lau, Jey Han, Carlos Armendariz, Shalom Lappin, Matthew Purver, and Chang Shu. 2020. How Furiously Can Colorless Green Ideas Sleep? sentence Acceptability in Context. *Transactions of the Association for Computational Linguistics* 8:296–310.

Lau, Jey Han, Alexander Clark, and Shalom Lappin. 2017. Grammaticality, Acceptability, and Probability: A Probabilistic View of Linguistic Knowledge. *Cognitive Science* 41(5):1202–1241.

Lerner, Gene H. 1991. On the syntax of sentences-in-progress. *Language in Society* pages 441–458.

Levinson, Stephen C. and Francisco Torreira. 2015. Timing in turn-taking and its implications for processing models of language. *Frontiers in Psychology* 6:731.

Lewis, Mike, Denis Yarats, Yann Dauphin, Devi Parikh, and Dhruv Batra. 2017. Deal or no deal? end-to-end learning of negotiation dialogues. In *Proceedings of the 2017 Conference on Empirical Methods in Natural Language Processing*, pages 2443–2453. Copenhagen, Denmark: Association for Computational Linguistics.

Li, Margaret, Stephen Roller, Ilia Kulikov, Sean Welleck, Y-Lan Boureau, Kyunghyun Cho, and Jason Weston. 2020. Don't say that! making inconsistent dialogue unlikely with unlikelihood training. In *Proceedings of the 58th Annual Meeting of the Association for Computational Linguistics*, pages 4715–4728. Online: Association for Computational Linguistics.

Li, Xiujun, Yun-Nung Chen, Lihong Li, Jianfeng Gao, and Asli Celikyilmaz. 2017. End-to-end task-completion neural dialogue systems. In *Proceedings of the Eighth International Joint Conference on Natural Language Processing (Volume 1: Long Papers)*, pages 733–743. Taipei, Taiwan: Asian Federation of Natural Language Processing.

Liu, Bing, Gokhan Tür, Dilek Hakkani-Tür, Pararth Shah, and Larry Heck. 2018. Dialogue Learning with Human Teaching and Feedback in End-to-End Trainable Task-Oriented Dialogue Systems. In *Proceedings of the 2018 Conference of the North American Chapter of the Association for Computational Linguistics: Human Language Technologies, Volume 1 (Long Papers)*, pages 2060–2069. New Orleans, Louisiana: Association for Computational Linguistics.

Lowe, Ryan Thomas, Nissan Pow, Iulian Serban, Laurent Charlin, Chiao-Wei Liu, and Joelle Pineau. 2017. Training end-to-end dialogue systems with the ubuntu dialogue corpus. *Dialogue Discourse* 8:31–65.

Lu, Xin, Barbara Di Eugenio, Trina C Kershaw, Stellan Ohlsson, and Andrew Corrigan-Halpern. 2007. Expert vs. non-expert tutoring: Dialogue moves, interaction patterns and multi-utterance turns. In *International Conference on Intelligent Text Processing and Computational Linguistics*, pages 456–467.

Luger, Ewa and Abigail Sellen. 2016. "like having a really bad pa": The gulf between user expectation and experience of conversational agents. In *Proceedings of the 2016 CHI Conference on Human Factors in Computing Systems*, CHI '16, page 5286–5297. New York, NY, USA: Association for Computing Machinery. ISBN 9781450333627.

MacWhinney, Brian. 2000. *The CHILDES Project: Tools for Analyzing Talk*. Mahwah, New Jersey: Lawrence Erlbaum Associates, 3rd edn.

Marr, David. 1982. *Vision: A Computational Investigation into the Human Representation and Processing of Visual Information*. San Francisco: WH Freeman and Company.

Matheson, Colin, Massimo Poesio, and David Traum. 2000. Modeling grounding and discourse obligations using update rules. In *Proceedings of the 1st Meeting of the North American Chapter of the Association for Computational Linguistics (NAACL)*. Seattle, Washington.

Mathys, Christoph, Jean Daunizeau, Karl Friston, and Klaas Stephan. 2011. A Bayesian Foundation for Individual Learning Under Uncertainty. *Frontiers in Human Neuroscience* 5:39.

Maye, A. and A. K. Engel. 2011. A discrete computational model of sensorimotor contingencies for object perception and control of behavior. In *2011 IEEE International Conference on Robotics and Automation*, pages 3810–3815.

Millikan, Ruth Garrett. 2000. *On clear and confused ideas: An essay about substance concepts*. Cambridge: Cambridge University Press.

Mills, Gregory J. 2007. *Semantic co-ordination in dialogue: The role of direct interaction.*. Ph.D. thesis, Queen Mary University of London.

Mills, Gregory J. 2011. The emergence of procedural conventions in dialogue. In *IProceedings of the 33rd Annual Conference of the Cognitive Science Society*.

Mills, Gregory J. 2014. Dialogue in joint activity: Complementarity, convergence and conventionalization. *New Ideas in Psychology* 32:158–173.

Mills, Gregory J. and Eleni Gregoromichelaki. 2010. Establishing coherence in dialogue: Sequentiality, intentions and negotiation. In *Proceedings of the 14th Workshop on the Semantics and Pragmatics of Dialogue*.

Mills, Gregory J. and Patrick G. T. Healey. 2006. Clarifying spatial descriptions: Local and global effects on semantic co-ordination. In *Proceedings of the 10th Workshop on the Semantics and Pragmatics of Dialogue (SEMDIAL)*. Potsdam, Germany.

Mirski, Robert and Mark H. Bickhard. 2021. Conventional minds: An interactivist perspective on social cognition and its enculturation. *New Ideas in Psychology* 62:100856.

Moore, Roger K. 2017. Is Spoken Language All-or-Nothing? implications for Future Speech-Based Human-Machine Interaction. In K. Jokinen and G. Wilcock, eds., *Dialogues with Social Robots: Enablements, Analyses, and Evaluation*, Lecture Notes in Electrical Engineering, pages 281–291. Singapore: Springer. ISBN 978-981-10-2585-3.

Noble, Bill and Vladislav Maraev. 2021. Large-scale text pre-training helps with dialogue act recognition, but not without fine-tuning. In *Proceedings of the 14th International Conference on Computational Semantics (IWCS)*. Association for Computational Linguistics.

Nöe, Alva. 2004. *Action in Perception*. MIT Press, 1st edn.

Noë, Alva. 2012. *Varieties of presence*. Harvard University Press Cambridge, MA.

Paolo, Ezequiel A. Di, Elena Clare Cuffari, and Hanne De Jaegher. 2018. *Linguistic Bodies: The Continuity between Life and Language*. MIT Press. ISBN 978-0-262-03816-4.

Park, Hae Won, Mirko Gelsomini, Jin Joo Lee, and Cynthia Breazeal. 2017. Telling stories to robots: The effect of backchanneling on a child's storytelling. In *Proceedings of the ACM/IEEE International Conference on Human-Robot Interaction*, pages 100–108. ACM.

Pickering, Martin and Simon Garrod. 2004. Toward a mechanistic psychology of dialogue. *Behavioral and Brain Sciences* 27:169–226.

Pickering, Martin J and Simon Garrod. 2021. *Understanding Dialogue: Language Use and Social Interaction*. Cambridge: Cambridge University Press.

Pilnick, Alison and Robert Dingwall. 2011. On the remarkable persistence of asymmetry in doctor/patient interaction: A critical review. *Social science & medicine* 72(8):1374–1382.

Poesio, Massimo and Hannes Rieser. 2010. Completions, coordination, and alignment in dialogue. *Dialogue and Discourse* 1:1–89.

Pullum, Geoffrey and Barbara Scholz. 2001. On the distinction between model-theoretic and generative-enumerative syntactic frameworks. In G. Morrill, P. Le Groote, and C. Retore, eds., *Proceedings of the 4th International Conference on Logical Aspects of Computational Linguistics (LACL)*, pages 17–43. Springer.

Purver, Matthew. 2004. *The Theory and Use of Clarification Requests in Dialogue*. Ph.D. thesis, University of London.

Purver, Matthew, Ronnie Cann, and Ruth Kempson. 2006. Grammars as parsers: Meeting the dialogue challenge. *Research on Language and Computation* 4(2-3):289–326.

Purver, Matthew, Arash Eshghi, and Julian Hough. 2011. Incremental semantic construction in a dialogue system. In *Proceedings of the 9th International Conference on Computational Semantics (IWCS)*, pages 365–369. Oxford, UK.

Purver, Matthew, Eleni Gregoromichelaki, Wilfried Meyer-Viol, and Ronnie Cann. 2010. Splitting the 'I's and crossing the 'you's: Context, speech acts and grammar. In P. Łupkowski and M. Purver, eds., *Proceedings of the 14th Workshop on the Semantics and Pragmatics of Dialogue*, pages 43–50. Poznań: Polish Society for Cognitive Science.

Pustejovsky, James and Nikhil Krishnaswamy. 2021. Embodied Human Computer Interaction. *KI - Künstliche Intelligenz* 35(3):307–327.

Rietveld, Erik, Damiaan Denys, and Maarten Van Westen. 2018. Ecological-enactive cognition as engaging with a field of relevant affordances. *The Oxford handbook of 4E cognition* page 41.

Rączaszek-Leonardi, Joanna, Agnieszka Dębska, and Adam Sochanowicz. 2014. Pooling the ground: Understanding and coordination in collective sense making. *Frontiers in Psychology* 5:1233.

Rączaszek-Leonardi, Joanna, Iris Nomikou, and Katharina J. Rohlfing. 2013. Young Children's Dialogical Actions: The Beginnings of Purposeful Intersubjectivity. *IEEE Transactions on Autonomous Mental Development* 5(3):210–221.

Rączaszek-Leonardi, Joanna, Iris Nomikou, Katharina J. Rohlfing, and Terrence W. Deacon. 2018. Language Development From an Ecological Perspective: Ecologically Valid Ways to Abstract Symbols. *Ecological Psychology* 30(1):39–73.

Rączaszek-Leonardi, Joanna and Kelso, Scott J. A. 2008. Reconciling symbolic and dynamic aspects of language: Toward a dynamic psycholinguistics. *New Ideas in Psychology* 26(2):193–207.

Röder, Frank, Ozan Özdemir, Phuong D. H. Nguyen, Stefan Wermter, and Manfred Eppe. 2021. The Embodied Crossmodal Self Forms Language and Interaction: A Computational Cognitive Review. *Frontiers in Psychology* 12:3374.

Roller, Stephen, Y.-Lan Boureau, Jason Weston, Antoine Bordes, Emily Dinan, Angela Fan, David Gunning, Da Ju, Margaret Li, Spencer Poff, Pratik Ringshia, Kurt Shuster, Eric Michael Smith, Arthur Szlam, Jack Urbanek, and Mary Williamson. 2020. Open-Domain Conversational Agents: Current Progress, Open Problems, and Future Directions. *arXiv:2006.12442 [cs]* .

Ruis, Laura, Jacob Andreas, Marco Baroni, Diane Bouchacourt, and Brenden M. Lake. 2020. A Benchmark for Systematic Generalization in Grounded Language Understanding. *arXiv:2003.05161 [cs]* .

Sacks, Harvey, Emmanuel A. Schegloff, and Gail Jefferson. 1974. A simplest systematics for the organization of turn-taking for conversation. *Language* 50(4):696–735.

Sato, Yo. 2011. Local ambiguity, search strategies and parsing in Dynamic Syntax. In E. Gregoromichelaki, R. Kempson, and C. Howes, eds., *The Dynamics of Lexical Interfaces*. Stanford, CA: CSLI Publications.

Saxton, Matthew. 1997. The contrast theory of negative input. *Journal of Child Language* 24(1):139–161.

Saxton, Matthew, Carmel Houston–Price, and Natasha Dawson. 2005. The prompt hypothesis: Clarification requests as corrective input for grammatical errors. *Applied Psycholinguistics* 26(3):393–414.

Saxton, Matthew, Bela Kulcsar, Greer Marshall, and Mandeep Rupra. 1998. Longer-term effects of corrective input: An experimental approach. *Journal of Child Language* 25(3):701–721.

Schegloff, Emanuel A. 1982. Discourse as an interactional achievement: Some uses of 'uh huh' and other things that come between sentences. *Analyzing discourse: Text and talk* 71:93.

Schegloff, Emmanuel A. 1993. Reflections on quantification in the study of conversation. *Research on Language and Social Interaction* 26:99–128.

Serban, Iulian, Alessandro Sordoni, Yoshua Bengio, Aaron Courville, and Joelle Pineau. 2016. Building end-to-end dialogue systems using generative hierarchical neural network models. *Proceedings of the AAAI Conference on Artificial Intelligence* 30(1).

Shang, Lifeng, Zhengdong Lu, and Hang Li. 2015. Neural Responding Machine for Short-Text Conversation. *arXiv:1503.02364 [cs]* .

Shannon, Claude E. and Warren Weaver. 1949. *A Mathematical Model of Communication*. Champaign, IL: University of Illinois Press.

Sordoni, Alessandro, Michel Galley, Michael Auli, Chris Brockett, Yangfeng Ji, Margaret Mitchell, Jian-Yun Nie, Jianfeng Gao, and Bill Dolan. 2015. A Neural Network Approach to Context-Sensitive Generation of Conversational Responses. In *Proceedings of the 2015 Conference of the North American Chapter of the Association for Computational Linguistics: Human Language Technologies*, pages 196–205. Denver, Colorado: Association for Computational Linguistics.

Sperber, Dan and Deirdre Wilson. 1995. *Relevance: Communication and Cognition*. Oxford: Blackwell, 2nd edn.

Steedman, Mark. 2002. Plans, affordances, and combinatory grammar. *Linguistics and Philosophy* 25(5):723–753.

Suchman, Lucy A. 1987. *Plans and situated actions: The problem of human-machine communication*. Cambridge, UK: Cambridge University Press.

Tan, Hao and Mohit Bansal. 2019. LXMERT: Learning cross-modality encoder representations from transformers. In *Proceedings of the 2019 Conference on Empirical Methods in Natural Language Processing and the 9th International Joint Conference on Natural Language Processing (EMNLP-IJCNLP)*, pages 5100–5111. Hong Kong, China: Association for Computational Linguistics.

Trafford, James. 2017. Reconstructing intersubjective norms. *Phenomenology and Mind* 13:176–182.

Tschantz, Alexander, Beren Millidge, Anil K. Seth, and Christopher L. Buckley. 2020. Reinforcement Learning through Active Inference. *arXiv:2002.12636 [cs, eess, math, stat]* .

Van Arkel, Jacqueline, Marieke Woensdregt, Mark Dingemanse, and Mark Blokpoel. 2020. A simple repair mechanism can alleviate computational demands of pragmatic reasoning: Simulations and complexity analysis. In *the 24th (Virtual) Conference on Computational Natural Language Learning (CoNLL 2020)*, pages 177–194. ACL.

Vaswani, Ashish, Noam Shazeer, Niki Parmar, Jakob Uszkoreit, Llion Jones, Aidan N. Gomez, undefinedukasz Kaiser, and Illia Polosukhin. 2017. Attention is all you need. In *Proceedings of the 31st International Conference on Neural Information Processing Systems*, NIPS'17, page 6000–6010. Red Hook, NY, USA: Curran Associates Inc. ISBN 9781510860964.

Veissière, Samuel P. L., Axel Constant, Maxwell J. D. Ramstead, Karl J. Friston, and Laurence J. Kirmayer. 2020. Thinking through other minds: A variational approach to cognition and culture. *Behavioral and Brain Sciences* 43.

Vinyals, Oriol and Quoc Le. 2015. A Neural Conversational Model. *arXiv:1506.05869 [cs]* .

Wittgenstein, L. 1953. *Philosophical Investigations, Trans. G.E.M. Anscombe*. Oxford: Blackwell.

Wolf, Thomas, Victor Sanh, Julien Chaumond, and Clement Delangue. 2019. Transfertransfo: A transfer learning approach for neural network based conversational agents. *ArXiv* abs/1901.08149.

Xu, Danfei, Yuke Zhu, Christopher B. Choy, and Li Fei-Fei. 2017. Scene graph generation by iterative message passing. In *Proceedings of the IEEE Conference on Computer Vision and Pattern Recognition (CVPR)*.

Yu, Yanchao, Arash Eshghi, and Oliver Lemon. 2016. Training an adaptive dialogue policy for interactive learning of visually grounded word meanings. In *Proceedings of the 17th Annual Meeting of the Special Interest Group on Discourse and Dialogue (SIGDIAL)*, pages 339–349. Los Angeles.

Zadrozny, Wlodek W. 2020. Towards Coinductive Models for Natural Language Understanding. Bringing together Deep Learning and Deep Semantics. *arXiv:2012.05715 [cs]* .

Zadrozny, Wlodek W. 2021. Abstraction, Reasoning and Deep Learning: A Study of the "Look and Say" Sequence. *arXiv:2109.12755 [cs]* .

11

Reanalysis, probability, and the faculty of language

Asad B. Sayeed

11.1 Introduction

"Reanalysis" is a term that is widespread in the linguistics literature, but it covers a whole range of phenomena at all of the traditional levels of representation. On the surface, some of these combinations of phenomena and representation level are so different, it is easy to think that the word "reanalysis" is referring to a collection of separate phenomena. However, there are potential elements in common that may cause us to reconsider reanalysis as a single generalized umbrella phenomenon. In this chapter, I intend to illustrate that both the synchronic and the diachronic aspects of reanalysis have three elements: a formal or structural aspect, a probabilistic aspect, and a learning process or adjustment algorithm that connects the two. The formal or structural aspect may differ by level of representation, but at least from a syntactic, semantic, and possibly even pragmatic perspective, these may just be language-specific capacities of human cognition that allow for highly structured formal representation. Without this characterization, it becomes very difficult to conceive of what a probabilistic framework is operating *on*, in order to make the structural reassignment observed in reanalysis phenomena. At the same time, it works the other way: even a principles-and-parameters-style

Probabilistic Approaches to Linguistic Theory.
Jean-Philippe Bernardy, Rasmus Blanck,
Stergios Chatzikyriakidis, Shalom Lappin,
Aleksandre Maskharashvili (eds.).

framework, with a strong commitment to cognitively-ingrained formal representation, is typically still dependent on frequency-based indirect accounts of reanalysis influencing language change.

Furthermore, I will discuss reanalysis in sentence processing as one of the points at which the formal considerations of the syntax/semantics interface meet communicative need, mediated by processes that can be characterized in probabilistic terms. Reanalysis refers to the revision of the "already-built" parts of the representation of an utterance, be it syntactic, semantic, or both. It is a broad concept that accommodates the restructuring considered to occur when, for instance, "garden path" sentences are resolved, or when context disambiguates an attachment or scope ambiguity. Linguists of a more formal bent have focused on the "what" of reanalysis—what structures change and how to update them—while psycholinguists have focused more on the "when" of reanalysis, at what point in processing does it really "happen" to an utterance that its structure must be updated.

This issue bears upon a central controversy in linguistics: what is the "division of labour" in the linguistic sciences? What the proper object of linguistic investigation (de Saussure, 1916/1983) is, continues to be a fraught matter between the different subfields and approaches of linguistics. Linguistics should be the study of language, but that is a tightly circular statement. Does it mean the study of communication? Does it mean the study of a stream of structured sequential output from human articulatory systems, such as sound and movement? Perhaps the question can be partly resolved by attempting to separate the linguistic from the non-linguistic, that is, what specifically pertains to the behaviour we call language, and what may be behaviours associated with language but are also present in other domains of cognition.

For example, humans use language for communication, but they can use other modalities for communication—Picasso's Guernica, despite being highly abstract, is rich with structure and meaning. Few would refer to it as "language" in the same sense as a sentence in Arabic or Tagalog, unless they were specifically committed to the idea that language has no difference from any other medium of communication. Those things that are *sine qua non* in language, but not necessarily in the human uses of language, are referred to in some quarters as the "Narrow Faculty of Language" (Wacewicz, 2012, Hauser et al., 2002, Fitch et al., 2005).

Then there are the aspects of communication that have a specific influence on the observed forms of linguistic expression, an influence that may be separate from the conditions of communication in general. I will refer to this as "linguistic communication" to avoid the specific claims that underpin ideas such as the "broad faculty of language" and so-called "interface conditions". Hauser et al. (2002) suggest that there may not be very much in the narrow faculty of language itself: merely the recursion required to represent the structures observed in language.

While some have argued (Taraban and Bandara, 2017) that this is too small a set of characteristics for the narrow faculty of language, others have argued that recursion should not be considered a *sine qua non* of human language and that language typology is too diverse to identify a core "narrow" characteristic (Evans and Levinson, 2009). Still others have argued that recursion is a shared characteristic over other domains of cognition (Jackendoff and Pinker, 2005) in a way that makes it difficult to identify a "language-specific" form of recursion, or further, that is it futile to try to identify any such characteristics specific to language outside of a holistic "ecological" perspective (Steffensen and Fill, 2014) or at least a perspective that starts from the assumption that recursion develops from communicative need (Thibault, 2005).

Given the above, at least these three questions are a significant matter of debate: (1) what are the *sine qua non* of language, (2) what aspect of language *use* can be accounted for simply as an aspect of communication, and (3) what are the communicative factors that affect observed linguistic forms?

If we improve our handle on answering (3), we eliminate aspects of linguistic science that fully belong in (1) and (2), thereby implicitly affording us an answer. "Linguistic communication" sits "between" language and communication, relating relevant aspects of both. It could, for example, be the case that there is *nothing* in the "Narrow Faculty of Language" that is not somehow conditioned on environmental and communicative need—this cannot be decided *a priori*, and indeed, the sheer quantity of language-specific behaviour that has been catalogued by linguists suggests this is the unlikelier hypothesis. Nevertheless, it remains a possibility that at some point in the distant future, some, e.g., of the more exotic island constraints may well support a viable analysis in terms of social/cultural/environmental need.

Reanalysis is a term that appears in several subfields of linguistics. For example, it appears in historical linguistics as the tendency over time to impose a new morphological partitioning over a word with an origin in a different set of morphemes assembled by speakers of, e.g., a previous generation. From a synchronic perspective, at the syntactic and semantic levels, it refers to an occurrence in the derivation of an utterance where already-built structure must be "unmade" and "remade" using a process outside the assumed rules of inference for structure-building—or, if reanalysis rules are explicitly included in the formal system, the invocation of rules that appear to make structure-building "non-monotonic" in some sense relative to the details of the formalism in question.

In the remainder of the chapter, I will discuss the "what" of reanalysis—the contexts in which the concept is invoked in contemporary linguistic analysis—and then refer to existing work on how the "when" of reanalysis can be partly accounted for by probabilistic reasoning. First, I will discuss why it is worth it to specifically reconsider reanalysis in this context. Then I will cast the concept of reanalysis in two contrasting senses, synchronic and diachronic, with the intention of arguing that both represent different aspects of the same family of phenomena in relation to human language processing. I will then proceed to discuss reanalysis in the diachronic sense, illustrating the capacity of reanalysis to act on linguistic structures in even in an interactive and multi-speaker setting.

Next, I will discuss reanalysis from a synchronic perspective; that is, the occurrences at the level of individual interactions and processing where language-users reassign structure as they receive the input. Finally, I will conclude by discussing reanalysis as a phenomenon and its place in mediating the division of labour between formal, recursive structure and probabilistically-driven variation in a contemporary linguistic research programme.

11.2 Why reanalysis specifically?

There are many linguistic phenomena for which production or processing can be characterized in probabilistic terms, and many of these represent points at which formal representations specific to the faculty of language could plausibly interact probabilistically with communication via language. Lexical choice in production can be characterized in exactly these terms—a probabilistic process that is often represented as though it were constrained by formal semantic and syntactic considerations. For example, when the human processor encounters *the criminal arrested ...*, it is likely to interpret it as a reduced relative clause and predict that the next structure will be a prepositional phrase and the next word will be *by (the police)*. On the other hand, if it were to encounter *the police arrested*, the parser may produce a distribution that predicts *the* as the next word heralding a noun phrase.

With some caveats (Alabdulkarim et al., 2021, Zellers et al., 2019), large, attention-based language models have been successful in producing highly coherent-seeming texts using very little explicit formal structure, appearing to replicate aspects of the behaviour of the human language user. This suggests that a non-trivial formulation of the narrow faculty of language would *not* be necessary in the context of the straightforward generation of sentences by humans. Reanalysis, in contrast, operates by definition via a major revision of structure that presupposes the existence of such a formal structure.

The status of reanalysis as a linguistic phenomenon impinges on the "division of labour" question: what, if anything, belongs in the narrow faculty of language? Visual illusions also require reprocessing of some kind. But is that reprocessing at its root the same mechanism as the reanalysis of utterances? Or does it affect objects and structures in a manner different from potentially analogous processes in the other domains of cognition, such that a "domain-general", "connectionist" viewpoint would not be adequate?

Reanalysis phenomena can be identified in different expressions of the language faculty, such as at the syntactic and the semantic level, over input structures that seem, at first glance, to be specific to language. Thus, to propose that there is no relevant role of a narrow faculty of language as apart from communication would be to propose either that reanalysis in language is a scientific illusion or that other elements of cognition that may exhibit structure do so in a manner fundamentally indistinguishable from language. The burden of this claim is much higher than merely claiming that contemporary neural language modeling obviates the need for formal representations to be a core element of the study of human language.

11.3 Diachronic vs. synchronic reanalysis

Reanalysis was originally invoked as a mechanism of language change at a lexical and morphological level (Poultney, 1958, Cowan, 1960), and then later applied via syntactic theory to account for grammatical change. Reanalysis in this sense is, on the surface, an effect of language learning processes similar to other linguistic change processes. In this case, the change does not immediately involve an alteration to the interpretation of a surface form in a single language user (Langacker, 1977, Timberlake, 2021), but rather, a discrepancy arising over time between groups of speakers as to how the same structure is understood.

Examples of this process operating in semantics can be found in several studies by Eckardt (2006). One such example is the development of French negation, particularly split negations such as *ne ... pas* and *ne ... rien*. These originally developed from the Latin negation *non*, but with an additional post-verbal modifier that came, in the case of *pas*, from the Old and modern French word for "step" in English. Eckardt recounts how the use of these and other words in Old French as attested by medieval writings eventually became grammaticalized into the French complex negation. In Eckardt's theory, these words became idiomatic, emphatic focus constructions in Medieval French and then transitioned to becoming negative-polarity items. A further step was for them to have emphatic and stylistic weight. Finally, that weight is lost, as the focusing alternatives cease to be salient to the speaker and listener. At that point, they become grammaticalized negation words.

This is a story that takes place over several steps, and requires the semantic relationships between particular lexical items to shift in understanding despite the same construction being used. Once the shift in semantics takes place, the shift in the syntactic requirements of the French negation structure follows. This process requires that at some point, a French speaker intends words like *pas, goutte, rien* to have negative-polarity item interpretations, but a later language user interprets it differently, with a different semantic and syntactic structure.

By contrast, reanalysis in a synchronic sense involves a single listener, but there are at least two mechanisms involved. I will refer to one of these as *intra-sentential* reanalysis, where the parser cannot assign a structure to the whole utterance without reanalyzing a previous part, and *contextually-driven* reanalysis, where an utterance can at first be assigned a full structural interpretation, but later utterances or other pragmatic context force a reassessment of that structure.

The "classic" case of intra-sentential reanalysis is the garden-path sentence of the well-known variety, *the horse raced past the barn fell.* At *fell*, an assignment of structure to *the horse raced past the barn* must be revised to give *fell* its main verb status. This reanalysis is quite drastic from a syntactic standpoint, as *the horse raced past the barn* must be reinterpreted as a reduced relative clause.

A contextually-driven case of reanalysis is scope ambiguity resolution. This reanalysis takes place at the level of semantic structure and involves a sentence with the structure already assigned. The utterance *every student climbed a tree* has at least two interpretations with two corresponding semantic structures—that every student climbed a single tree, or there were multiple trees for the students, and students climbed corresponding trees. The latter option is generally held to be the "standard" interpretation of English-speakers, because it matches conventional intuitions about trees and climbing students.

However, if the subsequent sentence is *the tree was large enough to hold them all*, then the conventional intuition is false; thus, there is a single tree that all the students climbed. This requires the radical revision of a structure already formed, depending on how we represent the formal structure.

11.4 The diachronic perspective: syntactic reanalysis and language change

Language change is rife with reanalysis of the form described in Eckardt's French negation study. Lightfoot (2003) discusses syntactic change in terms of a principles-and-parameters framework-based notion of parameter-setting via cues. He illustrates this via the loss of V-to-I raising in English, namely the unwillingness of English-speakers to accept sentences like **Went John to the grocery store?* rather than the sentence with do-support, *Did John go to the grocery store?* By contrast, most closely-related Germanic languages permit full inverted-order yes/no questions without do-support as do earlier dialects of English.

What produced this change? In Lightfoot's view, this stemmed from a reanalysis of the structure of the corresponding declarative sentences to exclude the I-position as a target of V-movement. That is, previous dialects of English permitted sentences with multiple auxiliaries like *John can shall go to the grocery store* in the manner that V-to-I languages like German and French still permit. Lightfoot hypothesizes that disappearance of this structure can be predicted by a reduction in frequency of the post-V adverbial, as in *John shall buy frequently cheese at the grocery store*, where the verb is marked as being at a higher position and part of the I complex headed by the auxiliary.

Lightfoot cites empirical work from Ellegård (1953) to show that exactly this correlation—the reduction in frequency in post-V adverbials versus the reduction in frequency of question inversion—took place in the seventeenth century. Lightfoot suggests that the post-V adverbial is a parameter cue for I as a target of V-movement, and its decline meant the eventual necessity of do-support for yes/no questions.

Lightfoot's cueing approach to the loss of question inversion in English is based on a frequency-based approach to structural change in language. The proposed mechanism presupposes that there is a learning machine in human cognition that is capable of formal analysis and representation and is also capable of counting in order to determine whether the parametric tipping point has been crossed. This can be considered in terms of a crude probabilistic function: that is, the probability of seeing V-to-I movement in a learner's utterances is dependent on the probability of a cue threshold being passed in the input, where the cue is the count of positive evidence that I is a target for V-movement, such as post-V adverbial placement.

Nevertheless, the principles-and-parameters framework has its critics, not least the critique by its own creators (Chomsky, 1995). If language change cannot easily be traced to the setting of a small number of parameters—even if highly influenced by frequency effects—how do we characterize the evidentiary basis for language change? Zuraw (2003) situates syntactic change in the context of language change frameworks that aggregate parametric change in terms of large sets of parameters. Zuraw cites the Constant Rate Hypothesis of Kroch (1989), which holds that grammatical parameters change in the aggregate at a constant rate, even if individual parameters differ in change rate in a given community. Kroch hypothesizes that language change at the syntactic level takes place in an "S-shaped curve" that can be characterized by the logistic function, where a low-frequency variant makes a rapid transition to a high-frequency variant at some ceiling frequency. *Inter alia*, Kroch is able to fit the do-support data of Ellegård (1953) to the Constant Rate Hypothesis.

Zuraw suggests that the connectionist approach proposed by Tabor (1994) could be a way to understand and quantify how a non-surface phenomenon such as reanalysis could be affected by changes in the frequency distributions of surface forms by treating syntactic phenomena as dimensions of word representations in a neural network. Zuraw speculates that the hidden layers of such a network may represent the abstract properties affected by reanalysis. This viewpoint prefigures the extensive contemporary work on language modeling where the dimensions are instead conceived of in abstract terms (Mikolov et al., 2013), work that extends to investigation of lexical meaning change (Noble et al., 2021a, Del Tredici et al., 2019, Kim et al., 2014).

11.5 Reanalysis from a synchronic perspective

11.5.1 Formal underpinnings of reanalysis

While aspects of language change may be driven by reanalysis processes, the evidence for this is largely confined to surface-level changes, driven indirectly by individual-level reanalysis occurring in the generational "handover" of language learning. Where the collective intuitions are not available, we must instead rely on speaker intuitions or psycholinguistic tests.

The outwardly observed form of a case of reanalysis given an individual language user is that the language user, upon processing something that does not match expectations, is forced either to reject the utterance or attempt to find a new representation. This leads to the question of what it means to fail an expectation, insofar as we can quantify expectations of future events in probabilistic terms, but also insofar as we need to define the "shape" of such expectations, such that they can be failed.

A large and partially successful research program has been developed around the notion of surprisal, the negative log-probability of future events given a history (Hale, 2001), as a model for the effort of processing linguistic input. Roark et al. (2009) developed a parser that reports surprisal values for a constituency parse on an incremental basis, with anticipated expectations mismatches incurring a higher surprisal value, and they showed that their model surprisal predicted English reading times. Demberg et al. (2012) found that the surprisal values from the Roark et al. parser also correlated with speech production rate, and later investigations found that a trigram-based vector-space semantic model had the same effect (Sayeed et al., 2015).

Quantifying high processing load in terms of mismatched expectations leaves a final question of the structure to which the expectation applies and the mechanics of resolving it. From a formal perspective, a number of different approaches have been proposed for syntactic and semantic reanalysis. These fall roughly into repair, reparsing, and reranking approaches (Grodner et al., 2003, Lewis, 1998). Repair approaches involve backtracking and rewriting strategies that require the sophisticated unwinding of a parsing process in the manner of a depth-first search for a derivation that converges with expectations, or at minimum a sophisticated derivation editor that can cut out the incorrect structure and paste in a corrected one. Reparsing and reranking strategies can be seen together as reprocessing approaches. In the former, a derivation is simply expunged up to a certain point in its history and the same input reprocessed from memory. In the latter, the parser keeps track in some form of multiple derivations ranked by probability and promotes a formerly lower-probability derivation to higher probability once the best derivation fails.

A further type for formal mechanics for allowing reanalysis is to incorporate significant underspecification in the underlying parsing formalism. Such approaches, e.g., Demberg and Keller (2008), avoid retracting or rewriting already-built structure but instead use structures with placeholders that represent possible future structure.

Parallel derivations fill those placeholders with alternatives given the same surface form, eliminating derivations that are not compatible with the incrementally-processed utterance.

11.5.2 Costs and processing effort

All of these approaches have in common the idea of some operation taking place when the mismatch is encountered, and they differ in how they predict the "costs" of a failed expectation will be realized. The question of processing cost is made complicated by the different potential sources of cost. A first answer may be to say that the "processing cost" of reanalysis is somehow related to the cost of unmaking and remaking structure. There was some early evidence for this (Sturt et al., 1999, 2001) but it leads to a methodological question of the degree to which the measurement of "effort" are artifacts of the basic formalism employed.

At a semantic level, the reanalysis process implied in the late re-resolution of scope-ambiguity can be very drastic in a logical formalism for the semantics that requires very fine-grained compositionality (Champollion, 2010), whereas a formalism that implies fewer changes to the semantic formalism may be less drastic (Sayeed and Demberg, 2012, Sayeed, 2016). Since there are very many design choices and motivations that go into the building of a general syntactic formalism or parser, it is a very complex task to decide what precisely should go into such a theory—especially when it appears that predictability seem already to account for much of the experimental data in reading times (Roark et al., 2009).

At the other end, a viewpoint that holds that probabilistic models (with or without a high degree of latent structure) ultimately allow for reanalysis phenomena to be "explained away" in terms of lexical representation and predictability (Frank and Hoeks, 2019) may not be entirely empirically viable (Van Schijndel and Linzen, 2018, van Schijndel and Linzen, 2021). Even if hierarchical structure is implicitly discovered inside the model, it does not mean that revision of structure is absent from human processing but rather that sophisticated neural models are capable of representing an unknown underlying formal structure.

Von der Malsburg and Vasishth (2011) show that human experimental participants in eye-tracking experiments actually employ multiple types of strategies in processing syntactic garden path sentences accommodating different degrees of formal processing. They are even able to trace the probability of deploying these strategies to individual differences between experiment participants. At the semantic level, Dwivedi (2013) and Sayeed et al. (2019) also show that there is strategic variation in how the reanalysis of quantifier scope ambiguity is accomplished by human language users—that the human processor uses both strategies that are based on contextual cues and communicative needs while having a formal apparatus available to it.

Just as in the diachronic case—where reanalysis drives intergenerational change in the structural analyses of utterances—the case of "synchronic" reanalysis taking place at an individual-speaker level still requires theoretical frameworks that connect a probabilistic characterization of language learning and processing to a capacity for formalism-driven cognition that is stubbornly difficult to eliminate empirically.

11.6 Reanalysis in a probabilistic scientific programme for language

Nevertheless, although reanalysis in its different guises has a very large literature across the different linguistic sub-fields, treatments of reanalysis as an umbrella for a set of very analogous phenomena, if not a cognitively unitary phenomenon, are comparably few, even confined to the more abstract levels of representation; I discuss some of them in this chapter as illustration. But if we are to find a basis to investigate and "reanalyze reanalysis" as some kind of single category of language use occurrences, we will subsequently need to at least find a theoretical basis for the probabilistic connection between the "formal" linguistic cognition (or narrow faculty of language) as well as a methodological basis for investigating it.

One strategy I propose in this is to "double down" on recent existing work on language change for lexical meaning. From a synchronic perspective, probability-based estimation of processing difficulty for structures at the more abstract levels of representation (Demberg and Keller, 2009, Levy, 2011), particularly when the difficulty leads to reanalysis, is difficult to accomplish, since the evidence is not apparent in the surface form—we can only know that trained language models actually encode the variant representation if they provide the right implicatures (Liu et al., 2019). An alternative is to take into account the idea of indirectly-related surface cues as Lightfoot and Zuraw both employ the concept.

There is, by contrast, an example already of language change analysis being applied to explain changes in a property with only abstract representation. Lexical meaning is also an abstract, "non-surface" property of phonological words or morpheme groups the change in which can nevertheless be identified by distributional characteristics and expressed as probabilities. Similarly, the reanalyses that are at least sometimes involved in driving syntactic and semantic change often have very abstract and distributional connections to the actual observed change, as we see in the case of English V-to-I movement. Approaches that make use of a large-scale corpus-based analysis of lexical-semantic change also appear to require the involvement of social network analysis and dialogic factors in linguistic interaction for a realistic picture of the triggers of change and opportunities to detect it (Noble et al., 2021b,a).

Syntactic language change in particular is known to be surprisingly fast when it happens—for example, the full shift from SVO to VSO order in Modern Welsh is believed to have taken place mostly in the 18th century (Willis, 1998), in keeping with the implications of the Constant Rate Hypothesis and the sigmoid characteristic of parametric language change. Stochastic approaches involving larger quantities of texts to detect the triggers of reanalysis-driven language change become therefore feasible.

Since diachronic reanalysis is partly driven by producer/processor analysis mismatch, the implied reanalysis on the part of the processor means that by integrating the synchronic and diachronic approaches, we can get a better picture of how probability mediates between external, communicative forces and the narrowly formal aspects of linguistic representation in the faculty of language. If reanalysis is best characterized in terms of formal representations at the level of the individual processor, then what are the triggers that instigate the type of reanalysis that leads to longer-term language change? If there are common patterns in these triggers, and the scope of variation is not unlimited, then we would go some way to reconciling the formal architecture of the language faculty with observed linguistic diversity.

Finally, I return to my original, larger-picture question about what truly belongs inside the concept of the "narrow faculty of language". A crucial piece of evidence for whether there even *is* a non-trivial faculty of language apart from mere rewards from communicative needs would be whether there really is abstract structure involved in the way in which humans interact with language and whether there are constraints on how this structure is learned and manipulated by the processor that are not explainable directly in terms of environmentally-situated individual communication outcomes. Unifying theories of reanalysis that come from different domains of linguistics provides an opportunity to find precisely where formal processing apart from lexical predictability is truly necessary for human language to exist in its observed form.

References

Alabdulkarim, Amal, Siyan Li, and Xiangyu Peng. 2021. Automatic story generation: Challenges and attempts. *NAACL HLT 2021* page 72.

Champollion, Lucas. 2010. Quantification and negation in event semantics. *The Baltic International Yearbook of Cognition, Logic and Communication* 6(1).

Chomsky, Noam. 1995. *The Minimalist Program*. Cambridge, MA: MIT Press.

Cowan, William. 1960. Review of The Structure of Maltese: A Study in Mixed Grammar and Vocabulary, by J. Aquilina. *Language* 36(1):179–184.

de Saussure, Ferdinand. 1916/1983. *Course in General Linguistics*. London: Duckworth. (trans. Roy Harris).

Del Tredici, Marco, Raquel Fernández, and Gemma Boleda. 2019. Short-term meaning shift: A distributional exploration. In *Proceedings of the 2019 Conference of the North American Chapter of the Association for Computational Linguistics: Human Language Technologies, Volume 1 (Long and Short Papers)*, pages 2069–2075.

Demberg, Vera and Frank Keller. 2008. A psycholinguistically motivated version of TAG. In *Proceedings of the Ninth International Workshop on Tree Adjoining Grammar and Related Frameworks (TAG+9)*, pages 25–32. Tübingen, Germany: Association for Computational Linguistics.

Demberg, Vera and Frank Keller. 2009. A computational model of prediction in human parsing: Unifying locality and surprisal effects. In *Proceedings of the Annual Meeting of the Cognitive Science Society*, vol. 31.

Demberg, Vera, Asad Sayeed, Philip Gorinski, and Nikolaos Engonopoulos. 2012. Syntactic surprisal affects spoken word duration in conversational contexts. In *Proceedings of the 2012 joint conference on empirical methods in natural language processing and computational natural language learning*, pages 356–367.

Dwivedi, Veena D. 2013. Interpreting quantifier scope ambiguity: Evidence of heuristic first, algorithmic second processing. *PloS one* 8(11):e81461.

Eckardt, Regine. 2006. *Meaning change in grammaticalization: An enquiry into semantic reanalysis*. Oxford University Press.

Ellegård, Alvar. 1953. *The auxiliary do: The establishment and regulation of its use in English*. Gothenburg studies in English. University of Gothenburg.

Evans, Nicholas and Stephen C. Levinson. 2009. The myth of language universals: Language diversity and its importance for cognitive science. *Behavioral and Brain Sciences* 32(5):429–448.

Fitch, W Tecumseh, Marc D Hauser, and Noam Chomsky. 2005. The evolution of the language faculty: clarifications and implications. *Cognition* 97(2):179–210.

Frank, SL and JCJ Hoeks. 2019. The interaction between structure and meaning in sentence comprehension. recurrent neural networks and reading times. In *Proceedings of the 41st Annual Conference of the Cognitive Science Society*, pages 337–343. [Sl: sn].

Grodner, Daniel, Edward Gibson, Vered Argaman, and Maria Babyonyshev. 2003. Against repair-based reanalysis in sentence comprehension. *Journal of Psycholinguistic Research* 32(2):141–166.

Hale, John. 2001. A probabilistic Earley parser as a psycholinguistic model. In *Second Meeting of the North American Chapter of the Association for Computational Linguistics*.

Hauser, Marc D., Noam Chomsky, and W. Tecumseh Fitch. 2002. The faculty of language: what is it, who has it, and how did it evolve? *Science* 298(5598):1569–1579.

Jackendoff, Ray and Steven Pinker. 2005. The nature of the language faculty and its implications for evolution of language (reply to Fitch, Hauser, and Chomsky). *Cognition* 97(2):211–225.

Kim, Yoon, Yi-I Chiu, Kentaro Hanaki, Darshan Hegde, and Slav Petrov. 2014. Temporal analysis of language through neural language models. In *Proceedings of the ACL 2014 Workshop on Language Technologies and Computational Social Science*, pages 61–65.

Kroch, Anthony S. 1989. Reflexes of grammar in patterns of language change. *Language Variation and Change* 1(3):199–244.

Langacker, Ronald W. 1977. Syntactic reanalysis. In C. Li, ed., *Mechanisms of syntactic change*, pages 57–139. Austin: University of Texas Press.

Levy, Roger. 2011. Integrating surprisal and uncertain-input models in online sentence comprehension: formal techniques and empirical results. In *Proceedings of the 49th annual meeting of the Association for Computational Linguistics: Human Language Technologies*, pages 1055–1065.

Lewis, Richard L. 1998. Reanalysis and limited repair parsing: Leaping off the garden path. In *Reanalysis in sentence processing*, pages 247–285. Springer.

Lightfoot, David. 2003. Grammatical approaches to syntactic change. *The Handbook of Historical Linguistics* page 495.

Liu, Xiaodong, Pengcheng He, Weizhu Chen, and Jianfeng Gao. 2019. Multi-task deep neural networks for natural language understanding. In *Proceedings of the 57th Annual Meeting of the Association for Computational Linguistics*, pages 4487–4496.

Mikolov, Tomas, Ilya Sutskever, Kai Chen, Greg S Corrado, and Jeff Dean. 2013. Distributed representations of words and phrases and their compositionality. In *Advances in neural information processing systems*, pages 3111–3119.

Noble, Bill, Asad Sayeed, Raquel Fernández, and Staffan Larsson. 2021a. Semantic shift in social networks. In *Proceedings of *SEM 2021: The Tenth Joint Conference on Lexical and Computational Semantics*, pages 26–37.

Noble, Bill, Kate Viloria, Staffan Larsson, and Asad Sayeed. 2021b. What do you mean by negotiation? annotating social media discussions about word meaning. In *Proceedings of the Workshop on the Semantics and Pragmatics of Dialogue (SemDial 2021)*.

Poultney, James W. 1958. Observations on the Italic dialects and Latin. *The Classical World* 52(2):33–37.

Roark, Brian, Asaf Bachrach, Carlos Cardenas, and Christophe Pallier. 2009. Deriving lexical and syntactic expectation-based measures for psycholinguistic modeling via incremental top-down parsing. In *Proceedings of the 2009 Conference on Empirical Methods in Natural Language Processing: Volume 1 - Volume 1*, EMNLP '09, page 324–333. USA: Association for Computational Linguistics. ISBN 9781932432596.

Sayeed, Asad. 2016. Representing the effort in resolving ambiguous scope. In *Proceedings of Sinn und Bedeutung*, vol. 20, pages 604–621.

Sayeed, Asad and Vera Demberg. 2012. Incremental neo-davidsonian semantic construction for TAG. In *Proceedings of the 11th International Workshop on Tree Adjoining Grammars and Related Formalisms (TAG+11)*, pages 64–72.

Sayeed, Asad, Stefan Fischer, and Vera Demberg. 2015. Vector-space calculation of semantic surprisal for predicting word pronunciation duration. In *Proceedings of the 53rd Annual Meeting of the Association for Computational Linguistics and the 7th International Joint Conference on Natural Language Processing (Volume 1: Long Papers)*, pages 763–773. Beijing, China: Association for Computational Linguistics.

Sayeed, Asad, Matthias Lindemann, and Vera Demberg. 2019. Verb-second effect on quantifier scope interpretation. In *Proceedings of the Workshop on Cognitive Modeling and Computational Linguistics*, pages 134–139.

Steffensen, Sune Vork and Alwin Fill. 2014. Ecolinguistics: the state of the art and future horizons. *Language Sciences* 41:6–25. Ecolinguistics: the Ecology of Language and the Ecology of Science.

Sturt, Patrick, Martin J. Pickering, and Matthew W. Crocker. 1999. Structural change and reanalysis difficulty in language comprehension. *Journal of Memory and Language* 40(1):136–150.

Sturt, Patrick, Martin J Pickering, Christoph Scheepers, and Matthew W Crocker. 2001. The preservation of structure in language comprehension: Is reanalysis the last resort? *Journal of Memory and Language* 45(2):283–307.

Tabor, Whitney. 1994. *Syntactic innovation: A connectionist model*. Ph.D. thesis, Stanford University.

Taraban, Roman and Achintha Bandara. 2017. Beyond recursion: Critique of hauser, chomsky, and fitch. *East European Journal of Psycholinguistics* 4(2):58–66.

Thibault, Paul J. 2005. Brains, bodies, contextualising activity and language: do humans (and bonobos) have a language faculty and can they do without one? *Linguistics and the Human Sciences* 1(1):99–125.

Timberlake, Alan. 2021. 3. reanalysis and actualization in syntactic change. In C. N. Li, ed., *Mechanisms of Syntactic Change*, pages 141–178. University of Texas Press.

Van Schijndel, Marten and Tal Linzen. 2018. Modeling garden path effects without explicit hierarchical syntax. In *CogSci*.

van Schijndel, Marten and Tal Linzen. 2021. Single-stage prediction models do not explain the magnitude of syntactic disambiguation difficulty. *Cognitive Science* 45(6).

Von der Malsburg, Titus and Shravan Vasishth. 2011. What is the scanpath signature of syntactic reanalysis? *Journal of Memory and Language* 65(2):109–127.

Wacewicz, Slawomir. 2012. The narrow faculty of language: What is it, who has it, and how is it defined? *Theoria et Historia Scientiarum* 9:217–229.

Willis, David WE. 1998. *Syntactic Change in Welsh: A Study of the Loss of the Verb-second*. Oxford university press.

Zellers, Rowan, Ari Holtzman, Hannah Rashkin, Yonatan Bisk, Ali Farhadi, Franziska Roesner, and Yejin Choi. 2019. Defending against neural fake news. In H. Wallach, H. Larochelle, A. Beygelzimer, F. d'Alché-Buc, E. Fox, and R. Garnett, eds., *Advances in Neural Information Processing Systems 32*, pages 9054–9065. Curran Associates, Inc.

Zuraw, Kie. 2003. Probability in language change. *Probabilistic linguistics* pages 139–176.

Contributors

Jean-Philippe Bernardy is a researcher at the University of Gothenburg. His main research interest is in interpretable linguistic models, in particular those built from first principles of algebra, probability, and geometry.

Rasmus Blanck is a Senior lecturer in Logic and Theoretical Philosophy at the University of Gothenburg. His research interests lie close to the intersection of linguistics, logic, and philosophy.

Ellen Breitholtz is a Senior Lecturer in Linguistics at the Centre for Linguistic Theory and Studies in Probability (CLASP), in the Department of Philosophy, Linguistics, and Theory of Science, University of Gothenburg. Her research interests are the semantics and pragmatics of dialogue, specifically reasoning in dialogue, and ways of modelling such reasoning using computational methods.

Stergios Chatzikyriakidis is Professor of Computational Linguistics at the University of Crete. He has previously held posts at the University of Gothenburg, CNRS, University of London, and the Open University of Cyprus. His research interests are in computational semantics and formal syntax/semantics.

Stephen Clark is Head of Artificial Intelligence at Quantinuum. Previously he was a Research Scientist at DeepMind, and before that spent 14 years as a Member of Faculty at the Departments of Computer Science of the Universities of Oxford and Cambridge. He holds a BA in Philosophy from the University of Cambridge, and a PhD in Computer Science and Artificial Intelligence from the University of Sussex.

Robin Cooper is Professor Emeritus and Senior Researcher at the Centre for Linguistic Theory and the Study of Probability (CLASP), Department of Philosophy, Linguistics and Theory of

Science, University of Gothenburg. In recent years his research has been mainly involved with the development of TTR (a theory of types with records) and his book on the topic is forthcoming with Oxford University Press.

Simon Dobnik is a Professor of Computational Linguistics at University of Gothenburg. He is a member of the Centre for Linguistic Theory and Studies in Probability (CLASP), where he leads a research group on situated language, perception and cognitive systems. His research interests include computational models of language and perception (e.g. vision), situated dialogue systems used in human-robot interaction, computational representations of meaning (semantics) in language models, and learning semantic representations in under-resourced scenarios.

Guy Emerson is a Departmental Early-Career Academic Fellow and an Affiliated Lecturer at the Department of Computer Science, University of Cambridge, a Research Fellow at Gonville & Caius College, Cambridge, and an Executive Director of Cambridge Language Sciences. His core research interests are in computational semantics.

Arash Eshghi is Assistant Professor of Computer Science at Heriot-Watt University, and Co-founder and Head of Linguistics at Alana AI Ltd. His research is situated at the interface between Natural Language Processing, Theoretical Linguistics, and Cognitive Science. It focuses on real-time, dynamic language processing in dialogue, grammar learning from interaction, and the development of natural and adaptive Conversational AI.

Jonathan Ginzburg is Professor of Linguistics at Université Paris Cité (formerly Paris 7). He has held appointments at the Hebrew University of Jerusalem and King's College, London. He is one of the founders and currently associate editor of the journal *Dialogue and Discourse*. His research interests include semantics, dialogue, language acquisition, and musical meaning.

Eleni Gregoromichelaki is a Professor of Linguistics at the University of Gothenburg. Her research interests include situating human interaction processes of any form within more general theories of information, and the formal/computational modelling of linguistic phenomena within psycholinguistically-informed dynamic models.

Christine Howes is a Senior Lecturer in Computational Linguistics at the Centre for Linguistic Theory and the Study of Probability (CLASP), Department of Philosophy, Linguistics, and Theory of

Science, University of Gothenburg. Her research focuses on linguistic interaction, specifically on how people use available resources to coordinate their understanding in conversation.

John D. Kelleher is a Professor of Computer Science at Technological University Dublin. He is a Principal Investigator and TU Dublin lead in the Science Foundation Ireland ADAPT Research Centre in Digital Content Technology, and the SFI Centre for Research Training in Digitally Enhanced Reality (D-REAL). His research is focused on situated dialog systems, in particular the roles of memory and attention in the interface between language and vision. He works on machine learning for natural language processing and precision medicine.

Christo Kirov is a research-focused software engineer at Google Research NYC, working on NLP in multilingual settings. His background is in Computational Linguistics, having earned his PhD from the Cognitive Science department at Johns Hopkins University. Before joining Google, he held postdoctoral positions at the Georgetown Linguistics department, and the Center for Language and Speech processing at JHU.

Shalom Lappin is Professor of Computational Linguistics at the University of Gothenburg, Professor of Natural Language Processing at Queen Mary University of London, and Emeritus Professor of Computational Linguistics at King's College London. His research focuses on the application of machine learning and probabilistic models to the representation and the acquisition of linguistic knowledge.

Staffan Larsson is Professor of Computational Linguistics in the Department of Philosophy, Linguistics, and Theory of Science at the University of Gothenburg. He is a member of the Centre for Linguistic Theory and Studies in Probability (CLASP), as well as Chief Science Officer and co-founder of Talkamatic AB. He is member of the Editorial Board of the *Journal of Logic and Computation.* His areas of interest include dialogue, dialogue systems, language and cognition, pragmatics, formal semantics, semantic coordination, and philosophy of language.

Vladislav Maraev is a PhD candidate in the Centre for Linguistic Theory and Studies in Probability (CLASP) in the Department of Philosophy, Linguistics, and Theory of Science, University of Gothenburg. He has a background in network engineering, cognitive science, and natural language processing. His PhD project is focussed on laughter in interaction and ways of enhancing spoken dialogue systems.

Aleksandre Maskharashvili is a postdoctoral scholar at The Ohio State University. His research concerns logical, probabilistic, and machine learning approaches to natural language, with a focus on discourse, dialogue, and inference.

Bill Noble is a PhD student in the Centre for Linguistic Theory and Studies in Probability (CLASP) in the Department of Philosophy, Linguistics, and Theory of Science, University of Gothenburg. His work investigates the dynamics of lexical meaning in dialogue and in speech communities, using a variety of formal, computational, and statistical modelling methods.

Asad B. Sayeed is an associate professor of computational linguistics at the University of Gothenburg, and a member of the Centre for Linguistic Theory and Studies in Probability (CLASP) in the Department of Philosophy, Linguistics, and Theory of Science. Prior to that, he was a researcher at Saarland University. He obtained his Ph.D. in computer science from the University of Maryland at College Park. He works at the borders between linguistic theory, machine learning, cognitive modelling, and computational social science.

Vidya Somashekarappa is a PhD candidate in Computational Linguistics at CLASP, University of Gothenburg. Her research interests are in AI, Human-Robot Interaction, Computer Vision and Dialogue. She has a background in Cognitive Neuroscience and has conducted research using fMRI, TMS, t-DCS, EEG, BCI and Eye-tracking.

Richard Sproat is a research scientist at Google, Japan, where he works on applications of deep learning to text processing and speech. His research interests include computational morphology, finite-state methods, text normalization, speech technology and the computational analysis of writing systems and symbol systems.

Peter R. Sutton is a Beatriu de Pinós postdoctoral researcher in semantics at Universitat Pompeu Fabra in Barcelona. His main areas of interest are countability, polysemy and vagueness. He is currently undertaking a three-year project *Abstract nouns: polysemy and countability* that is funded by the Secretary of Universities and research (Government of Catalonia), and the European Union under the Marie Skłodowska-Curie grant agreement no 801370.

Glossary

Accommodation: One explanation for how listeners incorporate implicatures is that the content of the implicature is that which it is necessary to assume in order to interpret (to accommodate) the surface meaning of an utterance.

Action coordination: During interaction, people interleave their individual actions in such a way as to smoothly achieve the performance of a joint action together.

Actionism (Noë, 2014): Perception is an activity rather than, as standardly, a series of snapshots of scenes in the world with their subsequent inferential manipulation as representations in the brain

Attention-based language model: Recent technique in the statistical modelling of linguistic sequences involving weighted probabilities for the relative "importance" of elements of a sequence

Action potential: Sudden, fast, transitory, and propagating change of the resting membrane potential

AGI – artificial general intelligence: The ability of Artificial Intelligence systems to act intelligently, as humans do, across a variety of tasks, situations, and contexts, including the use of human language to communicate

Attunement to a type: The ability of an agent to recognise objects of that type

Bernoulli distribution: A probability distribution defined over two outcomes (heads/tails, success/failure, truth/falsehood), characterised by a single parameter (probability of heads/success/truth)

Code model of communication: According to this model, a speaker selects a message from a predefined set of messages, encodes this message into a signal in natural language, and transmits it to a listener through a channel of communication.

Computer vision: Field of artificial intelligence (AI) that enables computers and systems to derive meaningful information from digital images, videos and other visual inputs

Connectionist: Approach in cognitive science that focuses on analysing behaviour from the point of view of connections in a neural network

Constant rate hypothesis: Idea that grammatical parameters change overall at a constant rate, even if individual parameters differ in rate of change (Kroch, 1989)

Contextually-driven: Affected by factors exterior to the internal semantic or syntactic structure of a sentence

CNN - convolutional neural network: A specific type of artificial neural network that uses perceptrons, a machine learning unit algorithm, for supervised learning, to analyse data

Conversational AI: Dialogue systems, chatbots, or sometimes conversational interfaces

Cooperative principle: An assumption that speakers act cooperatively to communicate with their interlocutors, and assume that their interlocutors do the same. The cooperative principle is further elaborated by Grice's (1975) four maxims of cooperative conversation (quantity, quality, relation, and manner).

CRF - conditional random field: A standard conditional model from structured machine learning for the statistical modeling of labeled sequences, such as sequences of words and part-of-speech tags

Cross-entropy loss: A standard loss function in machine learning for training a probability distribution over a set of labels. In general, loss is the average surprisal of a language model over a batch of data comparing the predicted sequence with the ground truth.

Curry-Howard isomorphism: The Curry-Howard isomorphism connects systems of formal logic (intuitionistic logic) and models of computation

***De se* phenomena:** Phenomena pertaining to first-person reasoning

DGB - dialogue game board: A model of the information state that comprises a public part and a private part

Diachronic: View of language that focuses on changes in speaker-population behaviour over time

Dirac δ function: A generalised function or distribution over the reals with the following properties: a) its value is zero at any point except zero, and b) its integral over the real line equals one

Distributed cognition: Cognitive processes are considered as distributed over sociocultural systems and the material environment so that cognition can include artifacts and tools, teams of people, and culture-specific interpretations of reality (see e.g. Hutchins, 1995).

***Do*-support:** Questions in English sometimes have *do*-support, since the verb does not invert, as in "Do you know what I said?".

Dynamic Syntax: A purely action-based grammar formalism which models language processing as the word-by-word process of constructing conceptual structures with no independent level of syntactic structure over words.

Ecological psychology: A situated and non-representationalist approach to cognition

EEG - electroencephalogram: A test to monitor the electric sensitivity of the brain and thereby detect disorders if any, using electrodes

Electrical potential: The amount of work needed to move a unit charge from a reference point to a specific point against an electric field

Embedding: In machine learning, a learned representation in a continuous space. Embeddings are most typically vectors, but some machine learning models learn other kinds of embedding

Embodiment: The theory of embodied cognition emphasises that many aspects of cognition are shaped and dependent upon the body. Cognitive process are both directly affected through the perceptual abilities and types of actions a body enables, and more broadly through the contexts (social, cultural, and so on) that emerge due to the shared embodiment of the individuals that create and inhabit a society

Enactivism The core idea is that cognition is an embodied process, based on self-organising and recurrent sensorimotor patterns (Varela et al., 1993).

End-to-end neural systems: Systems that implement end-to-end learning by training and deploying a single neural model representing a complex target system. The model realises the complete target system, without the intermediate modules usually present in traditional pipeline designs.

Enthymeme: An argument that appeals to something that is not explicit in the argument, but that resides in the mind of the listener

Entropy: An information-theoretic measure that indicates a degree of uncertainty in data, in particular the randomness versus predictability

Epistemicism: A theory of vagueness according to which vagueness is a form of ignorance about the precise semantic values of expressions. For instance, *tall* has a precise meaning, but we do not, and in some versions of the theory, cannot know what it is.

Eye tracking: The process of measuring either the point of gaze (where one is looking), or the motion of an eye relative to the head

fMRI - functional magnetic resonance imaging: Measures brain activity by detecting changes associated with blood flow

Gaussian Process: A generalisation of the multivariate Gaussian distribution to distributions over real-valued functions. Real-valued functions over the reals form an infinite-dimensional space, so a Gaussian Process can be seen as an infinite-dimensional Gaussian

Game theory: The formal representation of strategies and moves in human interaction

- **Complete information game:** A game in which the options available to all agents are known by all other agents
- **Information set - game theory:** A set of game states that are indistinguishable by a certain agent, given their knowledge of the game
- **Partial information game:** A generalisation of signalling games (Parikh, 2006) in which the signals available to an agent depend on their intention (which is unknown or partially known to the other player)

Sequential game: A game in which turns are taken in sequence, where each player has knowledge of the previous player's action

Signalling game: A type of game introduced by David Lewis (1969) to model collaborative sequential communication between two agents

GCNN - graph convolutional neural network: a type of neural network which applies convolutional operations over the nodes in a graph.

Gibbs sampling: An MCMC algorithm. It samples variables iteratively from their conditional distributions

Grounding language in action and perception: Relating linguistic references or descriptions to corresponding entities and events in the physical state of an agent or its perceptual environment

Humanoid robot: Robot resembling the human body in shape

Implicature: Information that is not explicit in the literal meaning of a utterance, but that is nevertheless conveyed by it. The sentence "The queen of England is bald" implies that there is a queen of England.

ILM - iterated learning model: A type of learning model in which each generation of learners becomes the data source for the subsequent generation

Intentional stance: A strategy, so dubbed by the philosopher Daniel Dennett, of construing the behavior of an entity as if this entity were a rational agent able to make choices among courses of action based on its current beliefs and goals

Interest relativity: Arguably a variety of content sensitivity. A term is interest relative if its semantic value varies with the interests (e.g., goals) of the agents using or evaluating the expression.

Inter-modal fusion: Identifying that a perceptual view or reference to an entity within one modality corresponds to an entity within another modality. For example, resolving a linguistic reference to a perceived object

Intra-modal fusion: Identifying that different occurrence of an object within a modality concern the same object, such as different views of the same object

Linear regression: Linear approach for modelling the relationship between a scalar response and one or more explanatory variables (also known as dependent and independent variables)

LMS – logic with measurable spaces: A representation language used to connect parse structures with mathematical expressions of probabilities

Locative expression: A referring expression that describes the location of one object (the target) in terms of its position relative to another object (the landmark)

Log-likelihood ration: A log ratio of the likelihood of the hypothesis H1 over the hypothesis H2 where H1 is that the words in a bigram w_1w_2 are independent, and H2 that they are dependent

LSTM - long short-term memory network: a type of RNN with a specially designed memory cell to deal with long-range dependencies in sequential data

Bi-directional LSTM: an LSTM which processes sequential data in both directions, concatenating the representations at each time step

MEG - magnetoencephalography: Non-invasive technique for investigating human brain activity that allows the measurement of ongoing brain activity on a millisecond-by-millisecond basis, and it shows where in the brain activity is produced

Markov chain: A stochastic model representing a sequence of possible events, where the probability of each event relies only on the state associated with the previous event

HMM - Hidden Markov Model: a standard generative model from structured machine learning for the statistical modeling of labeled sequences, such as sequences of words and part-of-speech tags

MCMC – Markov chain monte carlo methods: A class of algorithms/methods that are used to sample from a probability distribution

Martin-Löf type theory: A form of type theory that was created to support the development of constructive mathematics. One of its main features is the use of dependent types

Metalinguistic uncertainty: Uncertainty about the semantic value of an expression (as opposed to uncertainty about some fact about the world)

Mirror neurons: Brain cells that react both when a particular action is performed and when they are only observed

Monte carlo methods: A family of algorithms that use random sampling in order to produce numerical results

Multivariate Gaussian distribution: A generalisation of the normal (Gaussian) distribution to multiple dimensions

Nash equilibrium: A pairing of agents and strategies (in a game) in which no player could increase their utility by unilaterally changing their strategy

negative-polarity item: Words and expressions like "any" and "at all" that can only be used in certain "negative" contexts

Noise: A technical term from information theory. When noise is present in the system, this may impede recovering the message from the signal

Object affordances: The actions that the physical properties of an object enable. For example, a chair affords the action of sitting

PDL – propositional dynamic logic: A logic that models how action effects a change of the world.

Perplexity: A measure of fit of a language model with a sample sequence based on the loss of a neural language model

Pixie: A representation of an entity in terms of its features

PLM - pretrained language models: Pretrained with unlabelled text data, and can be fine-tuned on down- stream generation tasks

Polar interrogatives: Interrogatives that in English have the form 'aux NP Pred' (e.g., 'Did Bo leave') whose meaning involves querying the truth of a proposition

Poverty of stimulus arguments: arguments suggesting that the linguistic input a child receives is insufficient for language learning

Presupposition: An implicature that survives embedding under negation. The sentence "The queen of England is not bald". Still presupposes that there is a queen of England.

Quantifier scope ambiguity: A semantic ambiguity where the set referred to by quantifiers such as "every" could be interpreted in multiple ways. For example, "every child climbed a tree" has at least two interpretations of how many trees there are.

Recursive: A procedure that applies to itself

Reinforcement learning: A machine learning learning method that facilitates learning through reward and penalty values assigned to learning outcomes

Representation: Local representation: A representation in which there is a one-to-one correspondence between concepts and components of the representations. A bag-of-words representation is an example of a local representation for language.

Distributed representation: A representation in which concepts are represented by patterns distributed cross the representation. A word embedding is a distributed representation where each word is representation by a vector values, and the full-vector of values is required in order to determine which word is being represented

Distributional representation: A type of distributed representations where vector values are raw counts of word co-occurrences

RNN - recurrent neural network: a neural network which can be used to process sequential data such as text

RSA - rational speech act models: A probabilistic modelling paradigm that predicts the behaviour of a rational speaker

Self-attention: a technique utilised by the Transformer neural architecture for obtaining a contextualised word representation

Semantic (learning) bottleneck: A phenomenon in which agents' linguistic learning data is insufficient to learn the meanings of all the expressions in a language

Semiotic schemas: Structured networks of grounded beliefs. A robot understands the meaning of a cup by verifying its beliefs about its perceived appearance and actions it can perform on this object.

Sensorimotor contingencies: Lawful regularities in the dynamic relations between an agent and its environment

Sigma type: A dependent type. It is a generalization of the cartesian product where the type of the second element of the pair depends on the first element

Sign: A pairing of a situation type (such as an utterance type) with a content

Situated language: Language spoken from a particular point of view within shared physical or simulated context, with other speakers and hence can include references to entities and events in the shared space

Sorites paradox: A form of slippery slope argument originally formulated in terms of heaps of sand. If removing one grain from a heap cannot turn a heap into a non-heap, then, via slippery slope reasoning, one grain of sand is a heap, contrary to fact.

Spatial template: A grid of $a \times b$ cells representing space built for a particular spatial relation. Each cell of the grid contains a degree to which an object in that location satisfies the relation to a landmark placed in the centre cell. Spatial templates are aggregations of experimental subject data where subjects rate for each location of the target surrounding the landmark the applicability of a relation

Synchronic: View of language that focuses on the analysis of the behaviour of speakers in a given time period

Surprisal (information theory): The negative log probability of future events, given a history

Topos: A defeasible principle of reasoning that applies to a certain type of situation. Topoi can be used as a rhetorical resource in dialogue.

Turing machine: A mathematical model of a hypothetical computing machine which uses a predefined set of rules to compute the value of a function for a set of input arguments

TTR - Type theory with records: A mathematical system that represents classificatory judgements made by agents (for example, of entities or situations) as type judgments. Records and record types may be used to represent structured objects and types.

Utility: An abstract numerical unit of value (positive or negative). Rational agents are defined as utility maximising.

Viterbi: a classic dynamic programming algorithm for finding the highest-scoring element in a set of structured objects